Handbook of Research on Contemporary Perspectives on Web-Based Systems

Atilla Elçi
Aksaray University, Turkey

A volume in the Advances in Computer and
Electrical Engineering (ACEE) Book Series

Published in the United States of America by
    IGI Global
    Engineering Science Reference (an imprint of IGI Global)
    701 E. Chocolate Avenue
    Hershey PA, USA 17033
    Tel: 717-533-8845
    Fax: 717-533-8661
    E-mail: cust@igi-global.com
    Web site: http://www.igi-global.com

Library of Congress Cataloging-in-Publication Data

Names: Elci, Atilla, editor.
Title: Handbook of research on contemporary perspectives on Web-based systems
  / Atilla Elci, editor.
Description: Hershey, PA : Engineering Science Reference, [2018] | Includes
  bibliographical references.
Identifiers: LCCN 2017042040| ISBN 9781522553847 (hardcover) | ISBN
  9781522553854 (eISBN)
Subjects: LCSH: Web services. | Web applications.
Classification: LCC TK5105.88813 .H344 2018 | DDC 006.7--dc23 LC record available at https://lccn.loc.gov/2017042040

This book is published in the IGI Global book series Advances in Computer and Electrical Engineering (ACEE) (ISSN: 2327-039X; eISSN: 2327-0403)

British Cataloguing in Publication Data
A Cataloguing in Publication record for this book is available from the British Library.

All work contributed to this book is new, previously-unpublished material. The views expressed in this book are those of the authors, but not necessarily of the publisher.

For electronic access to this publication, please contact: eresources@igi-global.com.

Advances in Computer and Electrical Engineering (ACEE) Book Series

Srikanta Patnaik
SOA University, India

ISSN:2327-039X
EISSN:2327-0403

MISSION

The fields of computer engineering and electrical engineering encompass a broad range of interdisciplinary topics allowing for expansive research developments across multiple fields. Research in these areas continues to develop and become increasingly important as computer and electrical systems have become an integral part of everyday life.

The **Advances in Computer and Electrical Engineering (ACEE) Book Series** aims to publish research on diverse topics pertaining to computer engineering and electrical engineering. **ACEE** encourages scholarly discourse on the latest applications, tools, and methodologies being implemented in the field for the design and development of computer and electrical systems.

COVERAGE

- Electrical Power Conversion
- VLSI Design
- Analog Electronics
- VLSI Fabrication
- Circuit Analysis
- Digital Electronics
- Computer science
- Programming
- Chip Design
- Algorithms

IGI Global is currently accepting manuscripts for publication within this series. To submit a proposal for a volume in this series, please contact our Acquisition Editors at Acquisitions@igi-global.com or visit: http://www.igi-global.com/publish/.

Titles in this Series

For a list of additional titles in this series, please visit: www.igi-global.com/book-series

Soft-Computing-Based Nonlinear Control Systems Design
Uday Pratap Singh (Madhav Institute of Technology and Science, India) Akhilesh Tiwari (Madhav Institute of Technology and Science, India) and Rajeev Kumar Singh (Madhav Institute of Technology and Science, India)
Engineering Science Reference • copyright 2018 • 388pp • H/C (ISBN: 9781522535317) • US $245.00 (our price)

EHT Transmission Performance Evaluation Emerging Research and Opportunities
K. Srinivas (Transmission Corporation of Andhra Pradesh Limited, India) and R.V.S. Satyanarayana (Sri Venkateswara University College of Engineering, India)
Engineering Science Reference • copyright 2018 • 160pp • H/C (ISBN: 9781522549413) • US $145.00 (our price)

Fuzzy Logic Dynamics and Machine Prediction for Failure Analysis
Tawanda Mushiri (University of Johannesburg, South Africa) and Charles Mbowhwa (University of Johannesburg, South Africa)
Engineering Science Reference • copyright 2018 • 301pp • H/C (ISBN: 9781522532446) • US $225.00 (our price)

Creativity in Load-Balance Schemes for Multi/Many-Core Heterogeneous Graph Computing Emerging Research and Opportunities
Alberto Garcia-Robledo (Center for Research and Advanced Studies of the National Polytechnic Institute (Cinvestav-Tamaulipas), Mexico) Arturo Diaz-Perez (Center for Research and Advanced Studies of the National Polytechnic Institute (Cinvestav-Tamaulipas), Mexico) and Guillermo Morales-Luna (Center for Research and Advanced Studies of the National Polytechnic Institute (Cinvestav-IPN), Mexico)
Engineering Science Reference • copyright 2018 • 217pp • H/C (ISBN: 9781522537991) • US $155.00 (our price)

Free and Open Source Software in Modern Data Science and Business Intelligence Emerging Research and Opportunities
K.G. Srinivasa (CBP Government Engineering College, India) Ganesh Chandra Deka (M. S. Ramaiah Institute of Technology, India) and Krishnaraj P.M. (M. S. Ramaiah Institute of Technology, India)
Engineering Science Reference • copyright 2018 • 189pp • H/C (ISBN: 9781522537076) • US $190.00 (our price)

Design Parameters of Electrical Network Grounding Systems
Osama El-Sayed Gouda (Cairo University, Egypt)
Engineering Science Reference • copyright 2018 • 316pp • H/C (ISBN: 9781522538530) • US $235.00 (our price)

701 East Chocolate Avenue, Hershey, PA 17033, USA
Tel: 717-533-8845 x100 • Fax: 717-533-8661
E-Mail: cust@igi-global.com • www.igi-global.com

List of Reviewers

List of Contributors

Table of Contents

Section 1
Engineered Web Now!

Section 2
Web of Things and Semantics Employed

Section 3
Semantic Technology Forward

Section 4
Analytics to the Rescue?

Detailed Table of Contents

Section 1
Engineered Web Now!

Web-based systems are sophisticated software environments accessible via a Web browser over a network connection using HTTP. They contain assorted set of programs, storage, communication and protocol tools providing integrated functionalities. Web-based information systems are ubiquitous over all domains. Sampled in this section are Web-based information system development; tagging and recommendation on content; user interface considerations for servers and mobile terminals; adaptive social networks; and offline use of Web sites.

Chapter 1
A Software Engineering Perspective for Development of Enterprise Applications 1

Anushree Sah, University of Petroleum and Energy Studies, India
Shuchi Juyal Bhadula, Graphic Era University, India
Ankur Dumka, University of Petroleum and Energy Studies, India
Saurabh Rawat, Graphic Era University, India

Enterprise applications are the DNA of any organization, and they hold the business logic, handle large amount of data, support multiprogramming, are easily maintainable, scalable, have high performance and are able to choreograph or orchestrate modules, and are fortified from attacks and vulnerabilities. These enterprise applications are the backbone of any organization and enhance the productivity and efficiency of the organization to a greater extent, thus ensuring the continuity in the business. So, after seeing the need and development of enterprise application, in this chapter, the authors present the idea of developing and discussing enterprise applications.

This chapter presents an overview of service-oriented architecture and web technologies with the objective of presenting challenging issues concerned with various aspects of integrating heterogeneous web applications.

Tag software is included in web applications to facilitate categorization and classification of information. Generally, freely available tag software is adapted or new code written to incorporate tagging. However, there is an absence of requirement and design document for tagging, even academically. It becomes difficult to know the features that can be included in tag software; also, not all features may be required. This chapter presents a framework for integration of tag software in web applications. The framework has four components corresponding to phases of the software development lifecycle. For requirement, a weighted requirement checklist is presented to ease requirement selection. A metric, software estimation, is defined for quantifying selected requirement. A logical design defined for design phase displays interaction of entities with users. For development, best mechanisms are suggested to web applications. Software engineering artefacts are provided to help during testing. A case study is presented where estimation and design is applied to freely available tag software.

The design of web and mobile applications is one of the most challenging fields of the current information technology landscape. Increasingly, companies intend to have a strong presence in the information society, which allows them to advertise their products, services, make online business, interact with customers, among others. However, the development and design of web and mobile solutions have numerous challenges and best practices that should be known and applied. In this chapter, the authors adopt a qualitative methodology based on multiple case studies that allow them to identify a total of six challenges and best practices that are later confronted and compared with the recent findings on the coverage of the topic.

Adaptive social network sites (ASNS) are an innovative approach to a web learning experience delivery. They try to solve the main shortcomings of classical social networks—"one-size-fits-all" approach and "lost-in-hyperspace" phenomena—by adapting the learning content and its presentation to needs, goals, thinking styles, and learning styles of every individual learner. This chapter outlines a new approach to automatically detect learners' thinking and learning styles, and takes into account that thinking and learning styles may change during the learning process in unexpected and unpredictable ways. The approach is based on the Felder learning styles model and Hermann thinking styles model.

Chapter 6

Stuart Dillon, University of Waikato, New Zealand
Karyn Rastrick, University of Waikato, New Zealand
Florian Stahl, University of Muenster, Germany
Gottfried Vossen, University of Muenster, Germany

Whilst access to the internet is becoming increasingly ubiquitous in highly populated, urban areas, for much of the planet web connectively is still largely absent. This is mainly due to geographic remoteness, but bad connectivity or governmental controls might also prevent web users from accessing desired resources. The authors have previously outlined a general approach to cope with such situations, which they termed "Web in your Pocket" (WiPo). WiPo assumes that the user has a smart device to which appropriate data, ideally in curated form, can be pre-loaded so that it remains accessible offline. In this chapter, the authors present the potential usability of WiPo by considering three important use-cases (tourism, health, and search and rescue) demonstrating the vast potential of WiPo. The chapter concludes by considering the practical issues that need to be overcome before it might be implemented in real-world situations.

Section 2
Web of Things and Semantics Employed

As information systems became ubiquitous their influence have reached "everywhere" globally, locally and in to depths generating endless possibilities for connection and connected devices. In turn, 'Web of Things' and eventually 'Internet of Things' evolved to epic dimensions of spread. There came the need to make sense of Big Data flowing in. Sampled in this section are optimized energy management; assisting children with autism; national healthcare delivery; and, making sense in search operations over big data.

Chapter 7

Ali Reza Honarvar, Shiraz University, Iran
Ashkan Sami, Shiraz University, Iran

Many researchers have focused on the reduction of electricity usage in residences because it is a significant contributor of $CO2$ and greenhouse gases emissions. However, electricity conservation is a tedious task for residential users due to the lack of detailed electricity usage. Home energy management systems (HEMS) are schedulers that schedule and shift demands to improve the energy consumption on behalf of a consumer based on demand response. In this chapter, valuable sequence patterns from real appliances' usage datasets are extracted in peak time and off-peak time of weekdays and weekends to get valuable insight that is applicable in the HEMS. Generated data in smart cities and smart homes are placed in the category of big data. Therefore, to extract valuable information from such data an architecture for the home and city data processing system is proposed, which considers the multi-source smart cities and homes' data and big data processing platforms.

Chapter 8

Duygu Çelik Ertuğrul, Eastern Mediterranean University, North Cyprus
Atilla Elçi, Aksaray University, Turkey

Individuals with pervasive developmental disorders should be supported with special education programs that are planned according to the type and degree of the disorder, age, characteristics, and needs of the individual. Search over internet resources may provide suitable educational material and methods (and associated activity/game). However, syntactic search in today's static-based internet is insufficient to offer desired relevant results. An intelligent system able to identify the needed educational methods and material with the help of semantic web-based agents will not only contribute to the development of individuals with disorders, and support education specialists in this process, but also be extremely useful for the families of these individuals in assisting and monitoring their child's developmental progress. In this chapter, an agent-based educational activity suggestion system of children with pervasive developmental disorder for guiding education and training staff activities is proposed.

Chapter 9

Cristina Elena Turcu, University of Suceava, Romania
Corneliu Octavian Turcu, University of Suceava, Romania

This chapter focuses on examining the adoption of the web of things paradigm in healthcare in order to facilitate the development of new web-based systems in more effective and efficient ways. Nowadays, the increasing number of personal health sensors and medical devices present the opportunity for healthcare providers to interact with patients in entirely new ways. In this context, the WoT paradigm could be closely linked to patient care and has the potential to generate changes in healthcare. WoT could also be applied in the social and insurance fields, etc. The social web of things (SWoT) further extends WoT in order to facilitate continued interaction between physical devices and humans, allowing the integration of smart objects with social networks. Although it opens new social possibilities, it was less applied in the delivery of healthcare. Nevertheless, its successful adoption depends on overcoming some open challenges.

Chapter 10

Rahul Pradhan, GLA University, India
Dilip Kumar Sharma, GLA University, India

Information retrieval is a field that is emerging day by day as user needs are growing. Users nowadays are not satisfied with results that merely match the query textual words; they want the query to be understood well and then results to be retrieved. These changing requirements need the query to be processed and its hidden intent uncovered. The authors address this problem by creating a system that understands the hidden temporal intent of the query and classifies it into proposed classes. This chapter works on temporal expressions in the document and classifies the query with respect to the temporal expressions in the document. The work is not limited to just classifying the query but also explores how these classifications will help search engines to make modifications in their user interface, which helps users to reach their desired information faster. Temporal boundaries of queries can be found using this work, which will help to disambiguate certain queries.

Section 3
Semantic Technology Forward

World Wide Web started as a fresh breath to displaying of hitherto local content opening it to sharing. It was great success as a technology. Over time it was realized yet that it was incapable of conveying the "meaning" of data and the intension / understanding of its creator thus needed a human intermediary. So called "Web Science" eventually lead to augmentation by semantic tones through a set of refitted concepts such as ontology and inferencing, and new custom languages, such as RDF and OWL. Sampled in this section are managing ontology change; semantically integrating otherwise heterogeneous structured data; discovering Web services and composing aggregate ones on the go.

Different repositories of ontology are available on the web to share common understandings of the knowledge of different domains with semantic web applications. They store, index, organize, and share ontologies and alignments between them that allow applications to search for and use the appropriate semantics on the fly. The quality of the ontologies and the alignments between them is a great challenge to guarantee the usefulness of ontology repositories. Like ontologies, alignments are subject to changes throughout their life cycle, which can decrease their quality. As a result, alignments must be evolved and maintained in order to keep up with the change in ontology or to meet the demands of applications and users. This chapter reviews and classifies the main ontology alignment change approaches. In addition, the chapter presents a new approach for the alignment change problem. The approach proposes a general framework that consists of a process of change. Various methods, each with a specific purpose, are proposed to automate and support the change process.

Semantic web offers new opportunities to multi-sources integration field, and many approaches like P2P systems are revisited taking into account the new requirements. In this chapter, the authors present their P2P heterogeneous and distributed data integration system. It is a super-peer system, where peers are regrouped by type of data (relational, image, text, etc.) around a super-peer which contains a domain ontology. Peers data sources are exported in a common format in the form of a semantically rich ontology. Schemas reconciliation is done by matching domain and local ontologies by the use of a similarity function whose contribution is based on the direct and indirect semantic neighborhood. Queries are described using ontologies, then routed towards relevant peers thanks to a semantic topology built on top of the existing physical one.

τXSchema is a framework for creating and validating temporal XML documents, while using a temporal schema that consists of three components: a conventional XML schema document annotated with a set of temporal logical and physical annotations. Each one of these components can evolve over time to reflect changes in the real world. In addition, schema versioning has been long advocated to be the most efficient way to keep track of both data and schema evolution. Hence, in this chapter the authors complete τXSchema, which is predisposed from the origin to support schema versioning, by defining the operations that are necessary to exploit such a feature and make schema versioning functionalities available to end users. Precisely, the authors' approach provides a complete and sound set of change primitives and a set of high-level change operations, for the maintenance of each component of a τXSchema schema, and defines their operational semantics. Furthermore, they propose a new technique for schema versioning in τXSchema, allowing a complete, integrated, and safe management of schema changes.

Chapter 14

Web services are meaningful only if potential users may find and execute them. Universal description discovery and integration (UDDI) help businesses, organizations, and other web services providers to discover and reach to the service(s) by providing the URI of the WSDL file. However, it does not offer a mechanism to choose a web service based on its quality. The standard also lacks sufficient semantic description in the content of web services. This lack makes it difficult to find and compose suitable web services during analysis, search, and matching processes. In addition, a central UDDI suffers from one centralized point problem and the high cost of maintenance. To get around these problems, the authors propose in this chapter a novel framework based on mobile agent and metadata catalogue for web services discovery. Their approach is based on user profile in order to discover appropriate web services, meeting customer requirements in less time and taking into account the QoS properties.

Chapter 15

Handling non-functional requirements (NFRs) in web service composition has gained increasing attention in the literature. However, this challenge is still open, despite the efforts of the scientific community, due to its complexity. This complexity starts from the fact that NFRs can represent structural constraints,

QoS attributes, temporal constraints, or behavioral attributes. Therefore, this characterization makes the task of web service composition lifecycle (e.g., specification, verification, integration, etc.) increasingly complicated. Therefore, this chapter investigates this point of view and suggests a complete approach supporting specification, formalization, validation, and code generation of desired composite web service. This approach has the advantage to tackle with quantifiable (i.e., measurable) and behavioral NFRs, and provide a support for composing NFRs with FRs using seamless weaving.

Chapter 16

Khayra Bencherif, Djilali Liabes University, Algeria
Djamel Amar Bensaber, High School of Computer Science of Sidi Bel Abbes, Algeria
Mimoun Malki, High School of Computer Science of Sidi Bel Abbes, Algeria

Semantic mashup applications allow automating the process of services and data integration to create a composite application with a new user interface. Nevertheless, existing mashup applications need to improve the matching methods for discovering semantic services. Moreover, they have to create or modify workflows in mashup applications without the assistance of the original developers. Automating the combination of user interfaces is another challenge in the context of semantic mashups construction. In this chapter, the authors propose an approach that allows automating the combination of data, services, and user interfaces to provide a composite application with an enhanced user interface. The construction of the semantic mashup application is based on the use of domain ontology, a matching tool, and a collection of patterns. In order to demonstrate the effectiveness of this proposal, the authors present a use case to construct a semantic mashup application for a travel agency.

Section 4
Analytics to the Rescue?

Using semantic technology to recover knowledge from semi-/unstructured data sources has always been a trying case. Sheer size of and multiply-sourced data, compounded with lack of pre-specified clear semantics required resorting to approaches statistical in nature, such as machine learning and analytics. Here sampled in this section are approaches to social network analysis; entity recognition in user content; data mining for effective management of telecom users; and, customer reviews rating.

Chapter 17

Soufiana Mekouar, Mohammed V University Rabat, Morocco

The study of social network analysis has grown in popularity in the past decades and has been used in many areas. It is an interesting and useful field that gained an increasing popularity due to the explosion of social media that has emerged with advances in communication systems, which play a critical role in forming human activities and interactions in social systems. The authors present some techniques from a data mining perspective and statistical graph measure that can be used in various applications such as to perform community detection, clustering in a social network, identify spurious and anomalous users, predict links between vertices in a social network, model and improve the information diffusion, design trust models, and improve other applications. Then, the authors provide a recent literature review of such applications and thus outline challenges of social network applications.

The exponential growth of data emerging out of social media is causing challenges in decision-making systems and poses a critical hindrance in searching for the potential information. The major objective of this chapter is to convert the unstructured data in social media into the meaningful structure format, which in return brings the robustness to the information extraction process. Further, it has the inherent capability to prune for named entities from the unstructured data and store the entities into the knowledge base for important facts. In this chapter, the authors explain the methods to identify all the critical interpretations taken over to find the named entities from Twitter streams and the techniques to proportionally link it with appropriate knowledge sources such as DBpedia.

Chapter 19

One of the most important IT sectors that requires big data management is mobile data communication systems (MDCS) of GSM companies. In the charging mechanism of current MDCS, a subscriber "surfs" on the internet that creates data traffic and a counter subtracts the amount of data used by the user from the subscriber's quota. In other words, instant constant quota values are assigned to subscribers without concern for their previous amount of internet usage in current MDCS. Moreover, constant quota values cause constant charge calls in control traffic that are repeated for all new quota requests. Thus, performance degradation occurs because of the repetition of quota request calls and allocations. In this chapter, a dynamic quota calculation system (DQCS) is proposed for dynamic quota allocations and charging in MDCS using data mining approaches as two cascaded blocks. The first block is self-organizing map (SOM) clustering based on a sliding window (SW) methodology followed by the second block, which is the markov chain (MC); the overall system is denoted as "SOM/SW and MC."

Chapter 20

The number of consumers consulting online reviews in order to purchase a product or service, keeps growing. In addition to that, consumers can add an online review in order to express their experience upon the services or products received. This iterative process makes reviews matter regarding consumer's purchase decision. Apart from reviews, consumers are welcomed to provide numerical ratings for the product or services they bought. If a hotel is exposed to an online hotel review site, then it very possible to improve the possibility of a consumer to consider booking a room in this hotel. According to this chapter, regardless of positive or negative reviews, hotel awareness is enhanced. Online reviews significantly improve hotel awareness for lesser-known hotels than for well-known hotels.

Foreword

TECHNOLOGY-MEDIATED INSTRUCTION: MAKING ATIs WORK – FINALLY

Technology-mediated instruction (TMI) has existed for many decades and has evolved dramatically as the dependent hardware, software and learning technologies and theories themselves have evolved. Most people today think of TMI as a variant of eLearning, but in fact, the basic principles of TMI called "programmed learning" were defined more than 100 years ago, later deployed in the mid-1900s in the form of printed programmed instruction (PI) manuals. From a hardware standpoint, programmed learning was first introduced on teaching machines even before the advent of PI manuals. Teaching machines were eventually replaced by a variety of different and evolving computer platforms and support software: first mainframes, then mini-computers followed by personal computers, and more recently, all manner of mobile devices. (For a comprehensive review of this history visit https://en.wikipedia.org/wiki/Programmed_learning#The_two_main_systems_of_programmed_learning)

A question to ask about TMI, and one that has frequently been overlooked, is why use it all? Throughout its multi-decade history the answer should have been, "To provide learners with personalized learning, different than the kind of group instruction they experience in traditional classrooms." Unfortunately, TMI technologists and instructors have often shown more interest in the technology du jour rather than matters that might provide learners with unique and effective individualized learning.

In the world of educational technology, a body of knowledge focusing on individualized instruction and learning has evolved in parallel with the evolution of TMI hardware and software. From time to time, developments in that body of knowledge have intersected with developments in TMI system architectures to suggest best practices for the use of TMI for individualized instruction. One of the more important individualized instructional models, Aptitude by Treatment Interactions (ATI) was developed by Lee J. Cronbach and Richard E. Snow in the 1960s. Cronbach and Snow (1977) defined *aptitude* as "any characteristic of a person that forecasts his probability of success under a given treatment," and *treatment* as "any manipulable variable."

Operationally this means that for a particular instructional task, learners with different *aptitudes* should master the task better if they are presented with instructional material (*treatments*) aligned or suitable or customizable to their own particular aptitude(s). Hence, a learner with high verbal aptitude should perform better on a task with verbally-oriented instructional materials (the "treatment") than from mathematically-oriented instructional materials. Alternatively, for the same learning objective the learner's classmate with a high mathematical aptitude should benefit more from mathematically oriented treatments (instruction). Or, from a different perspective, some people learn better from listening than reading; some learn better from doing rather than watching.

In an attempt to individualize instruction, some early TMI learning systems, notably "branching" PI manuals and teaching machines, attempted to provide information differentially to individual learners based on their responses to questions embedded in the learning material. This kind of construct added a measure of individualized variability to the instructional process, albeit a primitive one, but of course there was no learner aptitude dependency. Eventually, with TMI deployment on computer-based systems it became possible to extend this kind of branching to a larger number of variable paths. And with such systems the nature of student responses could be extended beyond simple multiple choice questions – although in practice, most such systems continued to branch based on only a few keyboard-driven, multiple-choice responses.

Practical Limitations to Deploying ATI in TMI Environments

ATI, practically implemented, means having the TMI system know something about the learner, and in real time, based on the learner's responses to embedded questions, prescribe the next quantum of information (treatment) needed to move the learner towards mastery of a learning objective. This is the same as what a good private tutor would do in a real life, real time, teaching/learning situation.

Unfortunately, two issues that have caused ATI to have limited success in TMI implementations are, i) TMI systems don't know enough about learners' aptitudes, and ii) alternative treatments (or instructional materials) are complex and expensive to develop.

- **Aptitudes:** Historically, a problem with the ATI construct has been that aptitude information about individual learners has been in short supply. As well, in real life situations, aptitudes can change from day to day or even moment to moment, depending on a learner's frame of mind, emotions, etc. So, there is a dynamic aspect to aptitudes that aren't accounted for in the ATI model. A fully formed ATI model should incorporate *aptitude profiles* that would also contain real time, dynamic information about the learner to help prescribe what happens next in an instructional setting.
- **Treatments:** Another challenge for ATI-dependent TMI deployments is the need to develop alternative instructional materials for every possible path in the instructional sequence. The simplest branching construct requires two paths, one for each of a yes/no or right/wrong response. More complex constructs require a sequence for every possible learner response, for example from multiple choice questions. Even more complex is the challenge of providing instructional sequences for expected and unexpected open ended, learner-constructed responses. All of this can become even more burdensome (and expensive) to develop if different treatments suggest the use of multimedia (audio and video). It is for reasons like these that most computer-based TMI deployments, even today, are designed around relatively straightforward multiple-choice constructs. And many of those, especially TMI sequences used for industrial/commercial training purposes simply provide yes/no branches of instruction. Even today's "adaptive learning" systems which attempt to adapt instruction to real time learning situations/conditions are limited for many reasons including the finite number of treatments available to present based on a learner's algorithmically determined learning condition.

However, with today's emerging technologies, many of the heretofore limitations of aptitudes and treatments can be addressed in novel and unique ways.

The Times They Are A-Changing

The twenty-first century is witnessing an explosion of previously unimaginable computing technologies, except perhaps in the minds of science fiction (SF) writers of previous centuries. When they weren't describing end-of-the-earth doomsday scenarios, many in SF were forecasting some of the computing-based phenomena we are witnessing today: limitless processing power, miniaturized communications devices, everything and everybody networked together, electronic social networking, semiconductors embedded in everything and everybody, artificial intelligence, and countless other technologies too numerous to list in this article.

In practice we see these phenomena as laptops, tablets, cell phones, Fit Bits, communicating watches (remember Dick Tracy's 2-Way Wrist Radio?), the Internet, the World Wide Web, Cloud, Fog, and Edge computing, Big Data, the Internet of Everything, AI, Deep Learning, etc. It is these kinds of technologies that can, in one way or another, begin to address some of the historical limitations of TMI to fully realize the benefits of the almost century-old concept of ATIs in TMI.

- **Aptitudes:** Originally, and to only a lesser degree still today, categories of aptitudes have been limited to verbal, mathematical, some personality dimensions, etc. This meant that we have had only a handful of attributes of aptitude available to us to try to devise and select a next best treatment or a next best module of content to present in an instructional session. In an era in which volumes of (big) data about everyone are continuously being collected and stored in the Cloud, it is possible to redefine the original definition of aptitudes to include two categories of data that could drastically extend and improve the utility of a learner's *aptitude profile*. These are 1) static, archived data, and 2) dynamic, real time data.

Today's TMI is "cold-hearted." That is, today's implementations of TMI do not account for learners' emotional states during learning situations, nor do they account for the physiology of a learner. A good instructor, especially a personal tutor adapts his/her instruction based on his/her personal knowledge and perceived real time emotional state of the learner. Is the learner handicapped? Is the learner meeting with psychologists about depression problems /family problems/work problems/etc. Data such as these are more and more being stored somewhere in the Cloud. This means that for good or for bad, such static, archived data could be retrieved to build out a learner's aptitude profile. And of course, there are many other kinds of 'static' data about individuals that are stored in the Cloud. Examples include education, medical, and financial records, insurance information, and even shopping profiles, all of which could be used to build out a learner's aptitude profile.

Then there are the dynamic, real time data that might be useful to complete the dynamic aptitude profile. Is the learner bored? Is the learner tired? Is the learner upset about something personal? Is the learner too cold/hot/thirsty/etc.? Based on a tutor's perception of such matters and conditions, the tutor can alter the content, tone, direction, etc., of a tutorial session. Increasingly, as the Internet-of-Things spreads its sensor-based wings to collect every kind of imaginable real-time data, it will be possible to use biometrics to gather dynamic, real time data about a learner in a learning situation, and to include these as a new dimension of data into a dynamic aptitude profile.

It's not important if there is a causal relationship between all these newly-defined aptitude profiles and the ability to prescribe appropriate "branches" of instruction in TMI sessions. What is important is that AI-driven TMI systems using Big Data analytics be able to make predictive correlations from these attribute profiles to facilitate the instructional process and generate improved learning outcomes.

- **Treatments:** As described previously, developing alternative 'paths' of instruction (treatments) to account for every learner's possible response in a pedagogy session, especially when those responses must be a function of complex learner attributes, is probably impossible using the kinds of tools that we have historically deployed in TMI systems. However, Open Educational Resources (OER), a plethora of freely available online educational materials available on the World Wide Web can begin to address the historical paucity of educational treatments for ATI implementations.

According to Wikipedia, "Open educational resources (OER) are freely accessible, openly licensed text, media, and other digital assets that are useful for teaching, learning, and assessing as well as for research purposes. There is no universal usage of open file formats in OER." (https://en.wikipedia.org/wiki/Open_educational_resources). An almost limitless number of OERs in every subject area, at every level of education, and in every file format can be readily discoverable by TMI systems in order to provide information to a learner based on a learner's response to a stimulus in an interactive learning environment. The challenge now, different than historically when there have been too few OER-equivalents to present to learners, is how to find and present the most appropriate OER based on the aptitude profile of the learner at any point in an instructional session.

So-called "deep learning" tools are beginning to emerge to address this kind of challenge. In fact, there are already developments in which AI systems can be trained to identify and recommend OERs to align with particular learning objectives – at an overall course level and even at a sub-objective (learning module) level within an online course. And as the Web continues to be the world's information database, the number of OERs on the Web will also continue to grow. This means that number of "treatments" available from this growing number of OERs on the World Wide Web will expand to provide limitless "treatments" necessary for use by ATI-based TMI systems of the future. As deep learning becomes even deeper, AI-based recommender systems will become even more proficient at discovering and presenting the next best treatment in individualized instructional sessions.

Conclusion

Where TMI was once mainly characterized by the kinds of hardware that could deliver programmed learning, eventually that focus moved to tools that could provide improved teaching in individualized learning environments. The seminal model of individualized instruction, Aptitude by Treatment Interactions and the tools to effectively deploy it have been limited by technologies that simply were not up to the job.

However, those days are past. Newer technologies and methodologies, emerging almost daily, have the potential to enable ATI-based TMI and in ways that we could only dream about in the past. Internetworking standards, hardware miniaturization, Cloud and related storage technologies, Big Data Analytics, artificial intelligence, deep learning, and biometrics are key to providing the simulated human tutor experience that will one day really deliver on the promised of ATI-based technology mediated individualized instruction.

Sorel Reisman
California State University, USA
October 2017

REFERENCES

Cronbach, L. J., & Snow, R. E. (1977). *Aptitudes and instructional methods*. New York, NY: Irvington.

Foreword

E-LEARNING AND WEB-BASED SYSTEMS

E-learning is my passion and profession - BHK

As communication technologies become more widely available, traditional educational institutions are no longer the only source of information. What is now necessary is to reconsider what makes for meaningful education and apply those practices to digital natives. Prepared along that line of thought, my recent book titled *Revolutionizing Modern Education through Meaningful E-Learning Implementation* (Khan, 2016) evaluates the means by which online education can be improved and systematically integrated more fluidly into traditional learning settings, with special focus on the ethical, pedagogical, design aspects of building, and making available online courses.

With the rapid growth of the Internet and digital technologies, the Web has become a powerful, global, interactive, dynamic, economic, and democratic medium of learning and teaching at a distance (Khan, 1997a; Taylor, 2014). The Internet provides an opportunity to develop learning-on-demand as well as learner-centered instruction and training. There are numerous names for the wide variety of online learning activities, including Web-Based Learning (WBL), Web-Based Instruction (WBI), Web-Based Training (WBT), Internet-Based Training (IBT), Distributed Learning (DL), Advanced Distributed Learning (ADL), Distance Learning, Online Learning (OL), Mobile Learning (or m-Learning) or Nomadic Learning, Remote Learning, Offsite Learning, a-Learning (anytime, anyplace, anywhere learning), Massive Open Online Course (MOOC), etc. The term 'e-learning' is used to represent all open and distributed learning activities.

Recognizing the opportunity that will be provided by Web-based approaches early, I coined the phrase 'Web based instruction' and popularized the concept through my 1997 best-selling book with the same title (Khan, 1997). This book was meant to deal with Web-based instruction in general with a heavy emphasis on experience with the Web in higher education. In succession, my second book titled Web-Based Training (2001) explains how to use the Internet's World Wide Web for e-learning and blended learning in corporations, government agencies and educational institutions.

Importance of Web-based learning have since persisted and created a prominent and versatile base for all wishing to learn. This present book titled *Contemporary Perspectives on Web-Based Systems* follows suit by including chapters on e-learning among other relevant topics. It essentially provides relevant theoretical frameworks, current practice guidelines, industry standards and the latest empirical research findings in broader context of Web-based systems.

Badrul H. Khan
McWeadon Education, USA

REFERENCES

Khan, B. H. (1997). Web-based instruction: What is it and why is it? In B. H. Khan (Ed.), *Web-Based Instruction* (pp. 5–18). Englewood Cliffs, NJ: Educational Technology Publications.

Khan, B. H. (2016). Revolutionizing Modern Education through Meaningful E-Learning Implementation. Hershey, PA: IGI Global. doi:10.4018/978-1-5225-0466-5

Taylor, A. (2014). A look at web-based instruction today: An interview with Badrul Khan, Part 1. *eLearn Magazine*. Retrieved from http://elearnmag.acm.org/archive.cfm?aid=2590180

Foreword

SMART HEALTH AND WEB-BASED SYSTEMS

As we are entering the Internet of Things (IoT) era in the twenty-first century much endeavor of computing professionals has been placed upon the envision, design, development, deployment and evaluation of smart technologies and environments. Meanwhile, as the world is fast ageing, many smart technologies and ambient intelligent systems, riding the wave of emerging IoT technologies, have been employed into our daily living so that older adults may have the luxury to live independently and age in place. Digital health, also termed smart health, denotes the umbrella activities focusing on healthcare and well-being, with stakeholders ranging from researchers, technologists, healthcare professionals, home-based caregivers and alike, as well as insurance industries, government and policy makers.

Since web-based systems emerged in the early 1990s, "living on the web" has become the social norm influencing many aspects of our life. This special collection of "web-based systems" with contemporary perspectives serves to enlighten us on the cutting-edge web development techniques and a variety of web applications. Reading these fine papers can help us understand where we are situated in the IoT era, and stretch our imagination to project where we would be one day. When we become old, we can benefit from Smart Ageing or so-called "Technology Ageing" through many web-based technology platforms such as mobile web, perhaps using whatever new types of devices coming to the scene.

The quality of life of the ageing adults pertains to not only their activities of daily living and functioning in their homes, but also the outdoor living environment where improved mobility and social engagement are of primary concerns. Researchers and developers are facing steep challenges to extend and improve the living space of older adults and people with disability with suitable ICT-centric enabling and monitoring supports such as web-based systems. The winners will be able to innovate products and services including smart transportation, mobility on demand, measured interaction and socialization, among others. It is also of paramount importance to provide well-tested and trustworthy tools to end-users who have special needs.

Today, Artificial Intelligence (AI) or Cognitive Computing as another term for modern AI favored by IBM, has emerged at the center stage. As I explained in my recent article published in *Computer* [January Outlook Issue, Computer, 2016, pp. 24-33], cognitive and behavioral sciences will play an even bigger role in other computing disciplines - notably Human-Computer Interaction and Software Engineering. It is very likely within 15-20 years web-based systems may take cognitive cues directly and continuously from end-users after the system is deployed. That means, we will be able to gain real-time cognitive feedback from end users and understand why and how our products and services are meeting user's expectations, or not. Would it be nice that the system can seek immediate corrective measures to improve services on demand? It will be a very different world by then. Keep your fingers crossed.

Carl K. Chang
Iowa State University, USA

Foreword

We all know the impact of World Wide Web, or the Web, on society. It is well recognized that no other knowledge creation and dissemination medium, including printing press, enabled democratization and distribution of knowledge as effectively as the Web has done. And the impact is exponentially increasing because of the advances in technology that is feeding on itself to make the progress exponential. To keep up with the technology and applications related to the Web is not easy for most people. After the initial progress of the Web based on linked documents, the Web started growing rapidly using media data. Next came Things – things of all types and varieties used in almost any imaginable application. Linking these things meant collecting real time data from multimodal devices to address real time or dynamic problems in society. This meant that the Web of Things will be the basis to address problems ranging from rescue during emergency situations, transportation, manufacturing, education, and the most important health of people. Almost everything is now linked, or connected, to everything and this opens up new opportunities by allowing new perspective to look at previously unsolvable problems.

A major challenge to deal with such exciting opportunities is lack of a cohesive perspective on rapidly emerging technology. People are actively addressing challenges in many countries to address issues and challenges faced in their own societies. In many cases, the knowledge of technology and its applications are growing organically making it very difficult, if not impossible to keep track of contemporary information and knowledge that could be used. Researchers and practitioners have a challenge to find all relevant information using even the best Web tools to find this information.

This book, *Handbook of Research on Contemporary Perspectives on Web-Based Systems*, is exactly what it claims to be. It is a good exhaustive coverage of how the Web is influencing all aspects of human life ranging from health to education to commerce. For example, healthcare is going through a major disruption. Until recently, and even today at most places, the focus has been on diseases and curing diseases. Wearable devices, mobile phones, and now Internet of Medical Things are opening completely new opportunities to bring wellness and health states, rather than diseases, to the focus. As pointed out in a chapter in the book, the volume and variety of data created in this area is transforming our perspective about human health. This is extremely exciting because health is obviously the most important thing for humans. For too long we have considered health in different silos. The Web is linking these silos and opening up new opportunities.

More than applications of the Web it is a strong collection of technologies that are enabling this pervasive presence of information and knowledge in our modern society. This book has chapters on ontologies to user experience. This book is definitely a good place to get an idea of what technology is being used to create novel applications of the Web.

I am delighted to get a chance to get a peek on the book.

Ramesh Jain
University of California – Irvine, USA

Preface

Information systems have long moved to Web with concomitant effect on a flock of associated aspects, some of which are Web technology, semantics, application domain, organization, distribution, storage, access, information assurance and development. The practice on each of those aspects has independently evolved over time more or less equally, yet some, such as, analytics, security and cloud dominance have played more of an important part. So, it is timely to collate a compendium for ready reference displaying the state of art on Web-based systems.

Web-based systems are software application infrastructure suites accessible via a Web browser over a network connection using HTTP. They contain assorted set of well-evolved tools involving programs, storage, communication and protocols molded together to provide integrated functionality (Collis & Moonen, 2009). The most visible side of a Web-based system would be the application. A Web-based application runs inside a Web browser, yet it may as well be a client-based one, that is, a small part of the program is downloaded to a user terminal, be it a PC, pad or smart phone, but processing is done over the Internet on a remote server. Web-based applications are often called as Web apps. Some examples are light applications such as Flash games, online utilities as calculators and calendars; Web services such as WebEx, eBay, and Internet (electronic) banking. The application spectrum further extends from Web-based word processors and spreadsheet applications to Dropbox and likes, and web email services such as GMail, and Yahoo, as well as more intensive enterprise information and management systems. And lately, the cloudized versions of those mentioned where usually the difference is not noticeable by the user.

A simple search on "web-based systems" returned more than 221 million results on Google. Ubiquity of Web-based systems is no surprise given the significant advantages availed, such as, streamlining and improvement of business processes, providing cross platform compatibility, secure live data, reduced costs, being highly accessible, highly deployable, easily managed and updated. Complemented by advances in security and technology, web-based systems have become the information mainstay of businesses, government organizations, and social structure of the society.

As systems moved into the "web-based world," information systems development underwent a radical shift (Harindranath & Zupancic, 2002). At about this time two important concepts were recognized at the outcome of developments that took place. The first is the term 'Web Engineering'; it came to be pronounced "taking inspiration from software engineering" and in "an explicit acknowledgement of the multi-dimensional nature of Web applications" due to the need to manage diversity and complexity of Web application development (Murugesan & Deshpande, 2001). The second is the realization that Web has been for people to read and interpret and not for machines; that is, the Web content used by human beings was not equally understandable by programs and that 'the data' was not available on its own sake as it came attached to its program. "A new form of Web content that is meaningful to computers" would be likely to foster "a revolution of new possibilities," that is called "The Semantic Web" (Berners-Lee, Hendler, & Lassila, 2001). Then on, a new genre of Web technology followed that is structured by specific linguistic expressions based on new standard languages. There came communally recommended specifications of Resource Description Framework (RDF, https://www.w3.org/TR/rdf-primer/) and Web Ontology Language (OWL, https://www.w3.org/TR/owl-features/). Subsequently, many others followed this first step towards redesigning the Web-based World through consensus-built community standards (https://www.w3C.org).

The euphoria created by semantic Web initiative led to proposition of a proper scientific base for 'Web' in particular and Web-based systems in general, that is, a transitioning to a 'Web Science'.

Significant research must still be done to be able to engineer future successful Web applications. We must understand the Web as a dynamic and changing entity, exploring the emergent behaviors that arise from the "macro" interactions of people enabled by the Web's technology base. We must therefore understand the "social machines" that may be the critical difference between the success or failure of Web applications and learn to build them in a way that allows interlinking and sharing. (Hendler, Shadbolt, Hall, Berners-Lee, & Weitzner, 2008)

Web science is taken by many as an enlightening vision and engineering initiative towards building 'the Knowledge Society' (Lytras et al., 2009). By all means, the vision and the drive associated with it are still prevailing today.

Web-based systems were developed using static HTML pages. The technology advanced to respond the need for attractive, changing, interactive, and adaptive presentations through new and evolved tools such as HTML5 and CSS, client-side scripting in JavaScript, XML and Ajax, application development using PHP, ASP.NET in C#, Java Server Faces (JSF), Angular (https://angular.io/) and comparable others. It became possible to address user needs for dynamism through adaptive behavior embedded into the Web pages such as adaptive systems (Wade, Ashman, & Smyth, 2006), user self-service systems (Cooper, Lichtenstein, & Smith, 2009), and e-commerce (Oliver, Livermore, & Sudweeks, 2009) to name a few. The evolution of existing tools and techniques as well as generation of brand new ones used for creating dynamic, responsive, collaborative, adaptive, and semantic oriented Web applications has been continuing ever since.

Web-based systems have been picked up as prime information system by almost all walks of life, study, science, business, government, and enterprises. By and large, education, be it in science or in practice, was one of the early fields of study that picked up information technology, Web, and Web-based systems as early as 1997 (Khan, 1997; http://badrulkhan.com/; Goeller, 1998). The drive is still continuing also incorporating semantic modelling, metasystems and metacognition to name a few topics (Elçi, Elçi, & Çelik, 2016; Elçi, Vural, & Elçi, 2017; Railean, Elçi, Çelik, & Elçi, 2015; Railean, Walker, Elçi, & Liz, 2016), question chain learning mechanism (Zhang & Chu, April 2016), and Massive Open Online Courses (MOOCs, http://mooc.org/; http://moocs.com/about/).

Another important early adaptor of Web-based systems was the e-health and health care related sectors, for example for clinical studies (Veerbeek, Voshaar, & Pot, 2012), disease surveillance (Choi,

Cho, Shim, & Woo, 2016), personal health records (Markle Foundation, 2003; Wang & Dolezel, 2016). Let me also mention Protégé (https://protege.stanford.edu/), the best ontology editor there is offering a suite of tools to construct domain models and knowledge-based applications with ontologies, which was created in a medical school as PhD thesis way back in 1988!

Moving to cloud technology use for Web-based systems and concomitant evolution of Internet of Things, Web of Things, big data and the use of analytics appear to have already created a series of disrupting innovations. It is sure that big data and analytics will carve a big niche in everyone's future (Elçi, 2016, 2017).

OBJECTIVE OF THE BOOK

This book provides a sample of relevant theoretical frameworks, current practice guidelines, industry standards and the latest empirical research findings in web-based systems. Chapters are written by professionals who helped improve understanding of the issues and their strategic role in wherever Web-based application systems have penetrated.

TARGET AUDIENCE

The target audience of this book is professionals and researchers working in the field of Web-based information systems in industry, commerce, education, health, government and research in various disciplines, e.g. enterprise application, social networks, information technology, semantic technology, analytics, and knowledge management. The book as well provides insights and support for executives concerned with the management of Web-based systems in different types of application environments.

ORGANIZATION OF THE BOOK

The book is organized into four sections containing totally 20 chapters.

Section 1: Engineered Web Now!

Section 1 introduces web-based systems as sophisticated software environments accessible via a Web browser over a network connection using HTTP; and, goes ahead covering sample cases of Web engineering. Sampled in this section are the Chapters 1 through 6. A brief description of these chapters follows.

Chapter 1 proposes a logical architectural model of Web-based enterprise application development and evolves a lifecycle addressing many challenges faced, visually, related to system automation, security, harmonizing data, integration of data and application, user demands, selection of technology, internationalization, so on. Also addressed is the skill set required and challenges faced for developing Web-based enterprise applications.

Chapter 2 suggests a life cycle model based on service-oriented architecture and shows steps to integrate web applications using the Web services.

Chapter 3 presents an enhanced framework that eases the process of integrating tag software into web application. The framework addresses issues in requirement elicitation, development, testing, and updating phases.

Chapter 4 identifies challenges and best practices in main approaches and principles adopted by web design and e-business companies in creating immersive user experiences through several structured case study interviews vis-à-vis design of Web and mobile applications.

Chapter 5 outlines a new approach to automatically detect learner's thinking and learning styles, considering they may change over time in an unexpected and unpredictable way. This approach, based on the Felder Learning Styles Model and Hermann thinking styles model, aims at facilitating Adaptive Social Network Site (ASNS) in order to increase the efficiency in Web-based learning.

Chapter 6 presents several use cases of the "Web in your Pocket" (WiPo), offline access to pre-curated Web resources. The important WiPo use cases considered, namely, tourism, health, & search and rescue, demonstrate the potential of WiPo.

Section 2: Web of Things and Semantics Employed

Section 2 introduces the data availed through Internet/Web of Things cases and how to make some sense of it for use in Web-based information systems. Sampled in this section are the Chapters 7 through 10. A brief description of these chapters follows.

Chapter 7 addresses the need to schedule the operation of home appliances in order to reduce the electricity demand, thus cost, of homes by Home Energy Management System (HEMS). This study considers extracting valuable sequence pattern and association rules from large amounts of raw data generated by in-house sensors. Such knowledge mining discovering useful findings on resident behavior helps HEMS managing home appliance electricity demand.

Chapter 8 evolves a semantic approach for monitoring and development of training processes for individuals with Autistic Spectrum Disorder (ASD) along with supporting these processes and extending them. The "Instructive Activity Suggestion System" (IASS) provides an agent-based instructive and educational activity suggestion system for children and their parents.

Chapter 9 examines adoption of ever-growing Web of Things in healthcare delivery, as a modality to change how healthcare can be accessed improving the quality of life. There are good reasons to anticipate that the healthcare sector will overcome obstacles and progress, taking positive steps to embrace IoT/WoT technology, albeit at a slower pace than in other sectors.

Chapter 10 proposes a novel approach contributing to the field of temporal information retrieval area. This approach concerns classifying queries on the basis of query event time, that is, detection of temporal classes on the basis of query temporal profile in order to deduce query intent.

Section 3: Semantic Technology Forward

Section 3 looks into theory and practice of the web beyond World Wide Web and introduces semantics-based operating milieu. Sampled in this section are the chapters 11 through 16. A brief description of these chapters follows.

Chapter 11 presents a new approach for the ontology alignment change problem. It proposes a formal framework consisting of a number of phases in order to facilitate capture of ontology change for maintainers. The framework evolves alignment maintaining consistency with a minimal of change, and permits maintainers validate the new alignment.

Chapter 12 presents a new integration system for heterogeneous data in a P2P environment, called MedPeer. The system employs a method for finding similarities between local concepts in data sources and those of domain ontology through a global similarity measure. The tool allows dealing with concepts contexts where the neighborhood used is not limited to direct links of concepts but goes further by exploiting indirect ones.

Chapter 13 proposes a comprehensive approach for schema versioning in τXSchema-based multitemporal XML repositories. The approach allows designers changing the temporal schema, the conventional schema, and their logical and physical annotations. This then corresponds to supporting transaction-time schema versioning of temporal data.

Chapter 14 provides a general overview of a framework for semantic Web services discovery. It shows different kinds of agents composing the proposed architecture and how they are organized in using communication, services description, semantic matching algorithm, satisfying quality of service requirements, and integration of user profile in services discovery process.

Chapter 15 discusses Web services composition at both design and deployment time considering both Functional Requirements (FRs) and Non-Functional Requirements (NFRs). This work suggests a complete approach consisting of modeling NFRs as scopes and defining their interdependencies, performing a composition with associated FRs, and verifying the conformance of generated result according to user's requirements.

Chapter 16 advances a novel approach in building patterns-based semantic mashups. Recognizing key challenges of semantic composition of Web services, such as creation and/or modification of workflows, computing similarities between data in various services, and automating construction of enhanced composite application, this chapter thus enhances the integration quality of data and services in generating mashup applications.

Section 4: Analytics to the Rescue?

The final section of the book, recognizing the need to deal with knowledge recovery from multiple semi-/un-structured data sources without pre-specified clear semantics, thus, looks into essentially statistical approaches. Sampled in this section are the Chapters 17 through 20. A brief description of these chapters follows.

Chapter 17 provides a brief introduction to social network analysis and outlines advancement as well as limitations on some recent topics high on popularity, such as, influence analysis, community detection, and link prediction.

Chapter 18 presents a working model of named-entity disambiguation techniques and mapping entities to correct matches in, for example, DBpedia. Also considered are the difficulties in the extracted named-entity connecting procedure.

Chapter 19 discusses a Dynamic Quota Calculation System for dynamically allocating and charging usage in Mobile Data Communication Systems. This approach uses two cascaded routines: Self-Organizing Map clustering based on a Sliding Window followed by Markov Chain routine. This way, optimal quota arrangement in the current system and maximum efficiency in signalization are achieved.

Chapter 20 investigates effective and efficient ways to carry out text mining and sentiment analysis on real datasets for a real business issue. The outcome of this work, which is an innovative customer rating framework merging text clustering and sentiment scoring, produces interesting insights that could be used for further research and in other businesses.

Atilla Elci
Aksaray University, Turkey

THANKS

I owe sincere thanks to many fine people who pitched in their effort for this book. Without many authors who offered their best academic studies this book would not have become a reality; I appreciate their contributions. I am hereby expressing my gratitude to the many reviewers who supplied insightful comments on these submissions, thus helping me decide and select the best contributions.

My special thanks go to (Ms) Jan Travers, Director of Intellectual Property and Contracts at IGI Global, for offering me the chance to prepare this summation volume. Support of Colleen Moore and Maria Rohde, also of IGI Global, were greatly appreciated.

REFERENCES

Abubakr, T. (2012). Cloud app vs. web app: Understanding the differences. *Techrepublic Cloud Newsletter*. Retrieved 17 November 2017 from https://www.techrepublic.com/blog/the-enterprise-cloud/cloud-app-vs-web-app-understanding-the-differences/

Berners-Lee, T., Hendler, J., & Lassila, O. (2001, May 17). The Semantic Web. *Scientific American*, *284*(5), 34–43. doi:10.1038cientificamerican0501-34 PMID:11323639

Choi, J., Cho, Y., Shim, E., & Woo, H. (2016). Web-based infectious disease surveillance systems and public health perspectives: A systematic review. *BMC Public Health*, *16*(1), 1238. doi:10.118612889-016-3893-0 PMID:27931204

Collis, B., & Moonen, J. (2009). Collaborative Learning in a Contribution-Oriented Pedagogy. In P. L. Rogers, G. A. Berg, J. Boettcher, C. Howard, L. Justice, & K. D. Schenk (Eds.), *Encyclopedia of Distance Learning* (2nd ed.; pp. 327–333). IGI Global. doi:10.4018/978-1-60566-198-8.ch047

Cooper, V., Lichtenstein, S., & Smith, R. (2009). Web-Based Self-Service Systems for Managed IT Support: Service Provider Perspectives of Stakeholder-Based Issues. In Self-Service in the Internet Age (pp. 231-255). Academic Press.

Elçi, A., Vural, M., & Elçi, A. (2017). Changing Role of Faculty Members in Technology Enhanced Learning Environments: Faculty Members 4.0. In *Proc. International Educational Technology Conference*. Harvard University.

Elçi, A. (2016). *Big Data and Analytics: What's Ahead*. Panel presentation, WEDA Symposium, @ 40th COMPSAC, Atlanta, GA. Available at https://www.linkedin.com/pulse/big-data-analytics-carve-nich-your-future-atilla-el%C3%A7i/

Elçi, A. (2017). *Issues and Innovation in Medical Informatics Panel Presentation* (in Turkish). Akademik Bilisim '17, 10 February, Aksaray, Turkey. Available at https://tinyurl.com/issues-e-health

Elçi, A., Elçi, A., & Çelik, D. (2016). Semantic Modelling for E-Learning Coordination. In B. Khan (Ed.), *Revolutionizing Modern Education through Meaningful Implementation*. IGI Global.

Goeller, K. E. (1998). Web-based collaborative learning: a perspective on the future. In *Proc. Seventh World Wide Web Conference*. Brisbane, Australia: Elsevier Science. 10.1016/S0169-7552(98)00129-9

Harindranath, G., & Zupancic, J. (2002). *New Perspectives on Information Systems Development: Theory, Methods, and Practice*. Springer Science & Business Media. doi:10.1007/978-1-4615-0595-2

Hendler, J., Shadbolt, N., Hall, W., Berners-Lee, T., & Weitzner, D. (2008). Web Science: An Interdisciplinary Approach to Understanding the Web. *Communications of the ACM, 51*(7), 60–69. doi:10.1145/1364782.1364798

Khan, B. H. (1997). Web-based Instruction. *Educational Technology*.

Lytras, M. D., Damiani, E., Carroll, J. M., Tennyson, R. D., Avison, D., Naeve, A., . . . Vossen, G. (Eds.). (2009). *Visioning and Engineering the Knowledge Society - A Web Science Perspective: Second World Summit on the Knowledge Society, WSKS 2009, Chania, Crete, Greece, September 16-18, 2009. Proceedings*. Springer.

Markle Foundation & The Personal Health Working Group. (2013). *Final Report*. Available at http://www.markle.org/sites/default/files/final_phwg_report1.pdf

Murugesan, S., & Deshpande, Y. (2001). *Web Engineering: Managing Diversity and Complexity of Web Application Development*. Springer Science & Business Media. doi:10.1007/3-540-45144-7

Oliver, D., Livermore, C. R., & Sudweeks, F. (2009). *Self-Service in the Internet Age: Expectations and Experiences*. Springer Science & Business Media.

Railean, E., Elçi, A., Çelik, D., & Elçi, A. (2015). Metasystems Learning Design Approach for STEM Teaching and Learning. In STEM Education: An Overview of Contemporary Research, Trends, and Perspectives. Cycloid Publications.

Railean E., Walker, G., Elci, A., Liz, J. (2016). *Handbook of Applied Learning Theory and Design in Modern Education*. IGI Global.

Veerbeek, M. A., Voshaar, R. C. O., & Pot, A. M. (2012). Clinicians' Perspectives on a Web-Based System for Routine Outcome Monitoring in Old-Age Psychiatry in the Netherlands. *Journal of Medical Internet Research, 14*(3), e76. doi:10.2196/jmir.1937 PMID:22647771

Wade, V., Ashman, H., & Smyth, B. (2006). *Adaptive Hypermedia and Adaptive Web-Based Systems: 4th International Conference, Dublin, Ireland, June 21-23, 2006, Proceedings.* Springer.

Wang, T., & Dolezel, D. (2016). *Usability of Web-based Personal Health Records: An Analysis of Consumers* Perspectives. *AHIMA Perspectives in Health Information Management.*

Zhang, Y., & Chu, S. K. W. (2016). New New Ideas on the Design of Web-Based Learning System Oriented to Problem Solving From the Perspective of Question Chain and Learning Community. *International Review of Research in Open and Distributed Learning, 17*(3).

Acknowledgment

I am tremendously grateful of those who offered their best work as chapter manuscript, and withstood through selection process, finalization and suffered preparing the camera-ready final version. Kudos are due to those who touched the finishing line regardless of the order.

One should never underestimate how difficult it could be to get some people do a favor even though it would be in their academic benefit as well. I am indebted to those who pitched in their best review in as short a time as feasible, thus shedding a light to the direction of my decision, without which I would have come to half-blind conclusions. It is great to have partners.

I thank IGI Global for proposing this topic for me to prepare this summation volume.

Then ultimately, I beg excuse of my life friend, my wife, Alev, for I had to shy away from accompanying her in times of joy and need often, especially in the closing months of this book project. I shall make it up to her.

Atilla Elçi
Aksaray University, Turkey

Section 1
Engineered Web Now!

Web-based systems are sophisticated software environments accessible via a Web browser over a network connection using HTTP. They contain assorted set of programs, storage, communication and protocol tools providing integrated functionalities. Web-based information systems are ubiquitous over all domains. Sampled in this section are Web-based information system development; tagging and recommendation on content; user interface considerations for servers and mobile terminals; adaptive social networks; and offline use of Web sites.

Chapter 1
A Software Engineering Perspective for Development of Enterprise Applications

Anushree Sah
University of Petroleum and Energy Studies, India

Shuchi Juyal Bhadula
Graphic Era University, India

Ankur Dumka
University of Petroleum and Energy Studies, India

Saurabh Rawat
Graphic Era University, India

ABSTRACT

Enterprise applications are the DNA of any organization, and they hold the business logic, handle large amount of data, support multiprogramming, are easily maintainable, scalable, have high performance and are able to choreograph or orchestrate modules, and are fortified from attacks and vulnerabilities. These enterprise applications are the backbone of any organization and enhance the productivity and efficiency of the organization to a greater extent, thus ensuring the continuity in the business. So, after seeing the need and development of enterprise application, in this chapter, the authors present the idea of developing and discussing enterprise applications.

INTRODUCTION

The term enterprise refers to a large, for profit organization, which is a group of individuals or entities, apparently working in coordination towards accomplishing some common goals. Intel, General Motors, Wal-Mart, Bank of America, or eBay are some of the examples of large enterprise. Information sharing and dispensation, management of resources and customer relations, handling clients, utilization of knowledge base of business etc. are some of the fundamental requirements which are common to

DOI: 10.4018/978-1-5225-5384-7.ch001

every enterprise. Methods and techniques are required to manage and track the working processes in an enterprise. Collection of software or applications which are developed to assist an organization to solve enterprise problems is referred as Web-based enterprise applications. Organizational systems and procedures are implemented and handled through Management Information System (MIS). Advancement of technologies like IoT (Internet of Things), Cloud and Big Data result into a shift towards new technologies like Web information systems and distributed information systems. At the core, an enterprise still requires an information systems that facilitates management at all levels, hence the term Management Information Systems is still rewarding. To link MIS up with the recent advancements, new components have to be integrated to an existing MIS. In addition, IoT developments should not be considered only as technology driven terms but introduced as a socio-technical viewpoint (Shin, 2014).

A combination of two words, "enterprise" and "application" results into very large and complex software that enables a business enterprise to hold and track their work and information flow. Presently, Web-based enterprise applications are driven by integration of technologies like IoT, distributed systems, big data and cloud computing. These technologies offer a major impact on architecture of an enterprise application. This integration if merged with the existing architecture will significantly change the existing architecture into an interactive architecture. The architecture should be ideal, self-understanding and ubiquitous to observe the current and future needs of the system. The IoT, is a new technology paradigm which globally connects components (machines and devices) through network and facilitate communication and interaction among them. IoT is gaining lots of attention from a wide range of industries as it attempts to provide communication and integration among diverse components of an enterprise. Gartner (2014) predicts that the IoT will reach 26 billion units by 2020, up from 0.9 billion in 2009, and will blow the information available to supply chain partners and the way they operate. IoT when integrated with Web-based enterprise applications will transform business processes into self-updating processes by providing more accurate and real-time visibility. Development of Web-based enterprise applications in integration with the current technologies is a need of hour. These systems are required to be updated and maintained with the emergence of new technologies. Maintenance in Web-based applications should always be a lightweight iterative process. This process may be repeated several times based on user's/ customer's requirements but will not fundamentally modify the Web-based application (Choudhari & Ugrasen, 2015).

Web-based enterprise applications are flexible enough to integrate with other Web-based enterprise applications through interfaces and deployed across a variety of networks. These applications are to be designed in such a way that they are secure and customizable.

Some common and generalized Web-based enterprise applications are listed as follows:

- Automated billing systems
- Payment processing
- Email marketing systems
- Customer Relationship Management (CRM)
- Enterprise Resource Planning (ERP)
- Business Intelligence (BI)
- Business Continuity Planning (BCP)
- Enterprise Application Integration (EAI)
- Enterprise Content Management
- Enterprise search systems

- Enterprise Messaging Systems (EMS)
- Call center and customer support
- Human Resource Management (HRM) systems.

CATEGORIZATION OF WEB-BASED ENTERPRISE APPLICATIONS

Web-based enterprise applications may be categorized based on several particulars as follows:

- **Perceptibility to End User:** This type of Web-based enterprise applications depend upon the visibility to the end users. They can further be classified as 'Front End' and 'Back End' applications depending upon the visibility. Front end applications are visible to the users; they can interact with other applications for capturing order placed by customer. Backend application works behind the scene and helps to fulfill end user requirement; for example, an application for placing order to the third party from the organization or any other application that fulfill organizational needs like payroll system, etc.
- **Industry Domain Specific Application:** These are the applications that are specific to industry or organization. For example, an application of attendance marking for students in a university and the application of attendance marking for employees in an organization.
- **Type of Processing Supported:** This category recognizes the application on the basis of types of processing supported. For example, audit trail or scientific/engineering processing.
- **Custom Built or Readymade Application:** This category covers applications based on their built whether they are custom-built for a particular requirement, customized as per the needs or prebuilt like a billing application that can be used readymade.
- **Host Centric or Distributed Applications:** Depending upon their type whether application depends on one host or the functionalities of application is distributed; they are categorized as host-centric, distributed, or cloud-based applications.

This chapter firstly discusses various types of Web-based enterprise applications in today's scenario. Next section elucidates different methodologies of software engineering approaches including traditional models as well as modern models like Waterfall, Iterative, Rapid Application Development (RAD), Spiral, V, X, Y, W, and Agile models. Further on the chapter discusses software architectures, design principles and methods followed by defining ADL (Architectural Description Language) and its characteristics. Later in the chapter life cycle for developing a Web-based enterprise application is proposed and its various phases are elaborated. After this a case study is discussed using the proposed lifecycle. Next section proposes and defines an architectural model for developing a Web-based enterprise application. The chapter further discusses skills set requirements and challenges for building a Web-based enterprise application.

BACKGROUND OF SOFTWARE ENGINEERING METHODOLOGY

Software engineering is a process of developing quality software within the budget and time. It involves all aspects covering process of software development ranging from the initial phase of system specification, then design, implementation and lastly maintenance of the system once it is used in working environment. This process is called the Software Development Life Cycle (SDLC).

A well-defined strategy is required for development of reliable and quality software application. Following section discusses some of the traditional as well as modern software development process models.

Waterfall Model

A classical model developed by Royce in 1970 named as "Waterfall Model" follows the traditional steps of software engineering process. This model is easy to understand and implement, thus provide a strong foundation for many other lifecycle models. There is no involvement of developer in requirement and planning process. Generally, there are always time delays from coding to testing. This model focuses on defining the complete set of requirements before design and presumes that once a phase is complete, that phase is perfect and in agreement with the prior set plan. The problem with this model is its sequential nature that does not allow going back and making changes in previous phases which are already completed. This model does not provide an early prototype, thus difficult to incorporate risk management.

Iterative Model

Iteration of the development life cycle phases is at the core of the iterative model. A cycle consisting of the steps in software development life cycle is repeated, first with minimum set of requirements. More features and modules are designed, coded and tested in further iterations. Each iteration results into a software with some enhanced features. The most impressive part of this model is that each iteration is followed by an analysis of risk factors. Iterative model is easy to manage as software is designed in small phases but resource consumption is high.

Rapid Application Development (RAD) Model

This model is based upon building prototype of the real product. It was developed by IBM in 80s. A rapid prototype is first designed based on the users set of requirements which is assessed by the user. Refinement of prototypes based upon the feedback is the main key in development of the final system. The problem with this model is continuous participation of user throughout the development process. Also it needs highly reusable components and skilled domain experts.

Spiral Model

This model was proposed and developed by Barry Boehm in 1986. The model can be seen as a blend of two popular models, namely, iterative and an SDLC model. Each path around the spiral is indicative of increased costs. The main focus of this model is a consideration of risk, which is repeatedly left unnoticed in other models. The starting phase involves determining the purpose and limitation of the software, and results into a prototype in second phase which includes risk analysis. The model is developed and tested in third phase and finally next iteration is planned in fourth phase. The radial dimension of the model represents the increasing costs.

V – Model

The major shortcoming of waterfall model is that phases can only start after completion of its predecessor phase. In case if something found wrong during later phases, due to faults in any of the previous phase, we cannot move back to that phase for changes. V-Model overcomes this shortcoming and facilitates way of testing of software at each stage in reverse order. This model verifies and validates each stage after its completion. V-Model, known as 'verification and validation' model makes both these activities run in parallel. In this model, test plans and test cases are predesigned for every stage in accordance with the requirements of that stage. When the product is developed and is ready for testing, it is verified and validated against the designed test cases.

X – Model

Gill and Tomar in their paper (2008) proposed a component based model named X Model. The main focus of X model is on the concept of reusability. Reusability occurs when software is built by reusing the already existing (reusable) components. This model works on development of components for reuse and development of a system through reuse (i.e., reuse existing pre-tested components). Development for reuse, development after alteration, development without alteration and component based software development are the four main concern of X-Model.

Y – Model

Capretz in his work (2005) proposed another life cycle model known as Y-model. The advantage of this model is that it facilitates over lapping and iteration of phases where appropriate. This model consists of following planned phases: domain engineering, frame working, assembly, archiving, system analysis, design, implementation, testing, deployment and maintenance.

The aim of Y-Model is towards software reusability during component based software development. This model set more importance on reusability of available components during software development, progress and structuring of extensively reusable software components which are built on the assumption that they will be reusable for future projects.

W – Model

W-Model separates component development and component-based development as two distinct processes. In this model component-based development process consist of two different life cycles. First is a component life cycle and the second is a system life cycle. Component life cycle is more idealized one, as it accomplished all the necessities and phases of component-based development. System life cycle for development of a component based system is focused toward its domain. To develop a specific component-based system software components are selected, designed and developed in accordance with the offered domain specifications or knowledge. The components which are stored and retrieved from that component repository are grouped on the basis of their specific domains but not in terms system specification.

Agile Model

Agile methodology focuses on promoting constant iteration practices of development and testing. The main aim is to provide early delivery and ongoing improvement based upon regular customer feedback. Successive increments and frequent design changes results in response to the ever-changing customer requirements (Singh, Mishra, Singh, & Upadhyay, 2015). Throughout the process of software development, both the activities development and testing runs in parallel or handled in a concurrent manner. Agile development model proposes a combined effort of incremental and iterative approaches to SDLC. Agile process is divided into individual models for working of designers. An early product is available for the customer which provides him opportunity to work with the product so that if any change is required, can be applied to the software. This model is considered unstructured in comparison to the traditional waterfall model. A quick implementation of small projects can be done by using Agile method. Defects can be found and corrected at any point in time throughout the development process. User acceptance is an important activity which is performed at the end of each run. A continuous and close communication between developer and customer for analyzing the requirements and planning is a key behind this method. Each iteration is associated with its testing activity. With the addition of every new module regression testing is performed.

Advantage of agile method is its adaptability in planning and evolutionary development. Early delivery and continuous enhancement promote quick and flexible response to change.

NEED FOR WEB-BASED ENTERPRISE APPLICATIONS

The demanding and varying needs of an enterprise are often complex and difficult to achieve with the advancement in technologies. IoT, wearable technology, cloud computing, and big data are some of the recent technological developments that increases variety and complexity of data and making every enterprise digital and innovative. These technologies attempt to deliver easy and fast access to information in an enterprise. Firms are investing heavy funds in updating and improving applications to be efficient, winning new customers, and gaining competitive advantage. Varieties of technologies like Enterprise Resource Planning (ERP) systems and Application Service Provider (ASP) Web applications enable an enterprise to meet stated business objectives.

Distributed working environments cause a fundamental shift towards more cost-effective and efficient organizational working structure. Web-based enterprise systems are required that can provide disciplined standards and are often integrated with the existing enterprise applications. The transition to ERP systems involves a series of trade-offs. Although enterprise systems are provided by large and international IT vendors, still a flood of Web-based applications are required to design and integrate to enhance the application flexibility and meeting the local information needs.

SOFTWARE ARCHITECTURE AND DESIGN

High level structure of software system abstraction is based upon the two key concepts of decomposition and composition. All possible functional and non-functional requirements of an application to be developed must conform to the software architecture. Software architecture must explain all the required group of components, the way they connect or interact with each other. It should clearly depict all the knowhow of deployment and configuration of all the components of a software project.

Three basic methods for specifying and defining software architecture are discussed below:

- Unified Modeling Language (UML)
- Architecture View Model (4+1 view model)
- Architecture Description Language (ADL).

Unified Modeling Language (UML)

UML is a pictorial language which provides a standard that assists for analysis of software requirement and also design credentials. UML is presented and described as a language for the purpose of visual modeling. It helps to visualize, identify, build, and document a software system. A complete diagram of UML to implement real life scenario is categorized into structural and behavioral diagrams.

The static aspects of the project are implemented via Structural Diagram. Structural diagram represents the main structure of a program which is fixed and stable. The static parts are represented by classes, interfaces, objects, components and nodes, composite structure, packages and deployment diagrams. The dynamic aspects of the project are captured by Behavioral Diagram. Varying components/parts of the system are represented via these diagrams. UML has different categorization in representing its types of behavioral diagrams. Use case, activity, state machine/state chart, sequence, interaction overview, communication, time sequenced are the diagrams that help in visualizing the project requirements.

Architecture View Model

Multiple views and perspectives of software architecture are an absolute for basic and easy depiction. Representation of different views according to the perspective of different stakeholders can be achieved through Architecture View Model. End users, developers, project managers, and testers have different perceptions and thus need different views of the same project.

4+1 View Model

A software intensive system can be described by 4+1 View Model. It is a multiple view model that simplifies understandability of stakeholders by providing standardized software design document covering all the features of software architecture. It can be visualized in four different views:

- **Logical View:** It depicts the object model of the proposed design.
- **Process View:** Mainly focuses towards describing the activities followed in a system. It controls concurrency and handles synchronization issues in the design.
- **Physical View:** It presents a view by mappings of software onto hardware.
- **Development View:** It depicts structure of the software in its development environment.
- An additional use case view is an important one as it features the high level requirement of a software project.

Architecture Description Languages (ADLs)

Software architecture needs a language that provides syntax and semantics for its definition. ADL provides features for representation of eminent system architecture separate from system's implementation. ADLs must accept the architecture components, their interfacing and the way they interact with other components. It provides a way to decompose and assemble system. ADL is a formal specification language, specifying the software and hardware characteristics of any component. The component may include processes, data, and sub-programs and processors, buses, memory etc. (Wu, Xu, & He, 2009).

Characteristics of Quality Architecture

Quality architecture should preferably supply the following particulars:

- It should simplify the way entities will exist and communicate.
- It should justify the mapping between real world and design.
- It must be adaptable, reusable and scalable to highest level.
- It must be affordable and efficient. It should consume less time and memory.
- It should takes into account the complete domain of the problem.

PROPOSED LIFE CYCLE FOR BUILDING A WEB-BASED ENTERPRISE APPLICATION

Web-based enterprise application development life cycle is the dynamic, iterative process that adapts to the changing requirements of the enterprise over time. It incorporates new business processes, technologies, and new capabilities with the existing components of the enterprise. Formulation of well documented strategies which clearly define the aim, scope, vision and principles of an enterprise is a prerequisite in the development of a quality Web-based enterprise application. A team identifies the requirements and processes which are tailored to enterprise needs. Management, business and engineering life cycles are required to be aligned and integrated to bridge the gap between business enterprise and IT processes. An enterprise life cycle mainly accommodates all the organizational activities making future decisions based upon organizational growth. The enterprise life cycle works upon all the business and technical issues that come along the path towards achieving enterprise business goals.

The enterprise life cycle concentrates on planning of enterprise-level processes and implementing business decisions. On the other hand, a system development life cycle such as SDLC mainly focuses on the practices required in building an independent and personalized system. Figure 1 shows the proposed life cycle for Developing a Web-based enterprise application. Further on, different phases of the life cycle are discussed in detail below.

Requisition Phase

This is the initial phase towards developing Web-based enterprise applications and mainly covers profound analysis of diverse vicinity of an enterprise. Analysis of enterprise and its architecture enables decision makers to locate / provide foundation and background for developing enterprise. Business modeling ac-

Figure 1. Life cycle for developing a Web-based enterprise application

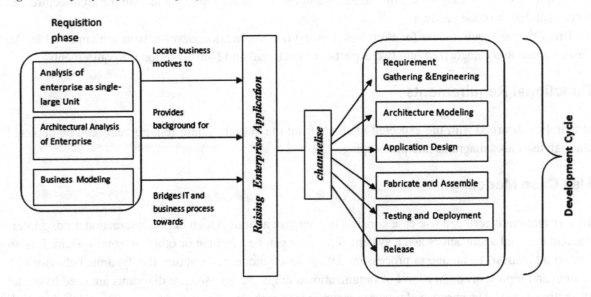

tivities are applied to bridge the gap between IT and business process (Capretz, 2005). The three phases of requisition given in Figure 1 are the most important phases as they craft a basic built-set of user's and business expectation from the application provider. Thoughtful and knowledge driven analysis presented in this phase is the key towards forecasting the final look of the application.

Building an Enterprise Application

With the advancement in technology and on demanding need of enterprise it is required to raise successful Web-based enterprise applications, reaching towards business goals and objectives. An enterprise application is developed in compliance with the established software engineering practices. It must follow all the directions and essential route that enables the design and development team including stakeholders to pilot the Web-based enterprise application from its commencement to rollout (Rawat & Sah, 2013).

Development Cycle

Development of a Web-based enterprise application is subdivided into 6 phases which are discussed below.

Requirement Gathering and Engineering

Requirement gathering and Engineering is a key towards quality development of any project. The main aim of this phase is towards estimating the cost, risk, time, resources and other important factors. Sponsors and customers, process groups, product groups, service groups, IT application groups, IT infrastructure groups, analyst groups are the main stakeholders for project estimation (Kaur & Singh, 2010). This is the first phase of development which provides a specification based upon the built-set collected in requisition phase. Gathering, refining and defining requirements as a specification are the main task of this phase.

The requirement specification document formed in this phase is used for modeling the architecture and future validation of the product.

Broadly, the requirements for Web-based enterprise application development are captured in the design phase and categorized into two aspects as Functional and Non-Functional Requirements.

Functional Requirements

It mainly concerned with the expected methods from the system. These requirements can be depicted through use cases diagrams and prototyping.

Use Case Modeling

In software engineering, a use case consists of stepwise actions which define interaction among internal and external agent/actors and a system. The actor can be a human or other external system. It is an important analysis technique of process modeling which model and capture the dynamic behavior of a system and represents higher level of organizational goals. Set of use case diagrams are used to model the entire system. The purpose of use case diagram is to gather the system requirements and the internal/external factors that influence the system. It depicts the interaction among the requirements and actors (Kayed & Shaalan, 2006). Purposes of a use case diagram include the following:

- Gathering the basic requirements for a system,
- Determining the internal and external factors of the system,
- Identification of actors,
- Depicting the way actors interact.

Use case diagrams can be utilized in different areas such as requirement analysis, as they provide high level design. They also represent the framework of a system and provide a base for reverse engineering as well as forward engineering (Val, Garcia-Valls, & Estevez-Ayres, 2009).

An example depicting the sample use case diagram is given below in Figure 2 which represents an order management system. The diagram shows three use cases namely Order, Special Order, and Normal Order. There is only one actor in the model which is the customer who books the order.

The Order use case is extended further to become a Special Order and Normal Order use cases. Hence, they have extended relationship. One important aspect of use case is that it identifies the boundaries of a system. Figure 2 shows that the only actor, customer, is outside the system boundaries. This means that the customer is an external user that influences the system from outside.

Prototyping

A prototype is an early working module of software with basic functionalities. It gives an idea to the manufacturer about the final look of the software. Software prototyping provides a chance to the manufacturer to understand and visualize final product. It also enables cost & time estimation of final product (Li, Ge, Zhou, & Valerdi, 2012). This process is typically a four-step process for prototyping:

Figure 2. A sample use case diagram

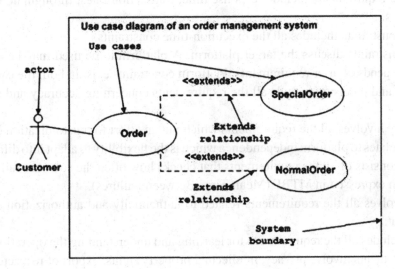

- **Identification of Initial Requirements:** In this step a basic set of requirements are identified for developing the first prototype.
- **Developing Initial Prototype:** In this step an early prototype with minimum requirement set is developed based upon the requirements proposed by the publisher. In its initial phase a prototype may be as simple as a drawing on a whiteboard. For some purpose the prototype may consist of sticky notes on a wall, or an elaborative model which shows basic working and functioning.
- **Reviewing:** In this step prototypes are reviewed to improve the functionality and add quality and functionality of overall system. Review is generally done through beta testing.
- **Revising:** Upgrading the system based upon the feedback of the publisher, tester and target audience.

Prototyping process can be further categorized into two sub models named throwaway and evolutionary models. Throwaway model is used for the purpose of review process and is not used after the process completes. On the other hand evolutionary model is a more complete model for prototyping. This model is used till end of the prototype delivery and is incorporated in the final product. The advantage of using prototype is to get feedback from user/consumer so that the improvements can be made. Customer can determine whether the software application works according to its specifications. Prototype helps in cost and time estimation (Scheer & Habermann, 2000).

Non-Functional Requirements

It is concerned with the way system is expected to behave within the constraints and expected qualities of service. Non-functional requirements are used to judge the operation of a system, rather than specific behaviors. These are the important requirements that describe the attributes proposed by the user for its application (Guo, Xu, Xiao, & Gong, 2012). Various Non-functional requirements are:

- Performance requirements include response time, transaction rates, throughput, benchmark, etc. specifications.
- Operating constraints includes all the execution-time constraints.
- Platform constraints discuss the target platform. A platform to be used may be a custom one or universal, depends on user requirements. Platform constraints exist in both the categories.
- Correctness and precision include all the requirements concerning accuracy and exactness of the result.
- Modifiability involves all the requirements which put an effort for customization of the software.
- Portability relates to platform independence which is the flexibility to adapt into different platforms.
- Reliability consists of all the requirements that checks how often the software fails. The measurement is often expressed in MTBF (Mean Time Between Failures).
- Security involves all the requirements related to authenticity and authorization of the software, system or data.
- Usability includes all the requirements for learning and understanding the operation of the system.
- Legal requirements involve privacy, intellectual property rights, export of restricted technologies, etc.

1. Architectural Modeling

Architects from all the backgrounds such as enterprise, data, integration, solution and enterprise etc. are the key stakeholders for this phase. The architectural model is a kind of scale model. This model represents a physical structure of the final model for the purpose of study, analysis and communication of design ideas. In Web-based enterprise application development and design, a well-defined architectural model is an important success factor. Existing tools and templates can be reused for designing architectural models. A major problem in Web-based enterprise application development is its large, diverse and distributed set of stakeholders and decision makers. Design of a well-defined architecture will provide a proactive decision making ability and identification of reusable components in collaborative aspects.

2. Application Design

Software designers from different domains utilize the architecture defined in the previous phase for design of separate module. In application design phase business requirements are described using different models. Class diagrams, sequence diagrams, object diagrams, activity diagrams, collaboration diagram, state chart diagram, component diagram, deployment diagram, etc. are developed. These diagrams provide a visual view of the system to be developed, and thus makes our work easier to understand by showing the proposed application design in the starting of the life cycle phases. This further reduces the chances of application being rejected due to misunderstanding between end users and developer.

3. Fabricate and Assemble

Components are finally framed and constructed by the programmers in this phase. Components are tested and analyzed as individual units. A systematic review and analysis process is carried out aiming at integration of components as a complete system (Kotonya, Sommerville, & Hall, 2003).

4. Testing and Deployment

A team of domain testers perform integration testing, system testing and user acceptance testing. Testing is a critical phase of any enterprise application, as the application supports as backbones to a number of profitable business organizations. Due to complex processes, cross functional environment and transactional data volume, enterprise testing becomes a complicated and hard process. Entire application is divided into functional units which are tested as a subsystem. Later on, integration testing is performed on pretested integrated components. Finally the entire system is tested by a team of developers, testers and users in working environment.

5. Release

Successful acceptance of the final system will result into release of the product in the actual working environment. Team representatives and presentation experts are the people involved in this phase (Crnkovic, 2005). Documentation manual and other formal documents are provided in this phase that help users to understand the working and use of the application.

Case Scenario

To elucidate the proposed life cycle for developing Web-based enterprise application we are figuring a scenario of XYZ Bank. In Figure 3, all stages and the activities that undergo in the phases are defined. Figure 3is self-explanatory and noticeably separates and identifies different activities that run in different phases.

PROPOSED ARCHITECTURAL MODEL FOR BUILDING A WEB-BASED ENTERPRISE APPLICATION

For managing large scale and increasing complexity of the Web-based enterprise applications, architectural frameworks are designed. They provide methods, approaches and tools to the architects and programmers from the basic level till completion of application. The architectural design aims at providing fine description of documents. It gives the structured guidance to develop Web-based enterprise applications. By using the layered design architecture for building Web-based enterprise applications, we can reduce the impact of modification (if any) to our applications (Tomar & Gill, 2010).

The proposed layered architectural model is shown in Figure 4. Each and every layer has its specialty and specifications. A brief discussion of each layer is given below.

Infrastructure Layer

This layer is the backbone of enterprise architectures. It consist of reusable components like computer hardware, network infrastructure, graphic user interface (GUI), etc. On the service end it may have some general purpose components live blogging facilities, compliance and auditing facilities, etc. For develop-

Figure 3. Developing a Web-based enterprise application for XYZ Bank

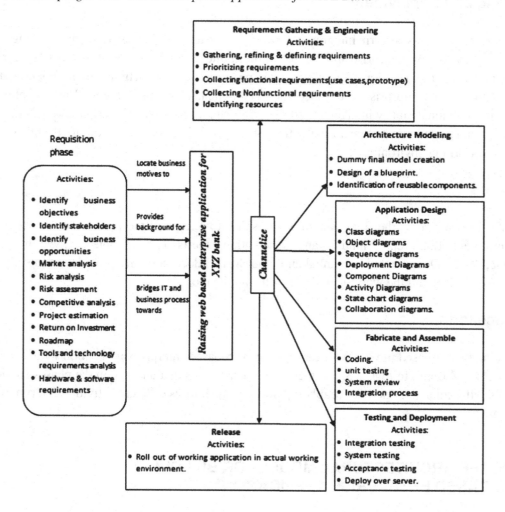

ing an enterprise application, an infrastructure layer is very important. This layer provides support for functioning of each and every layer of the enterprise architecture (Rehan & Akyuz, 2010). In the figure above this is shown as vertical bar at left and right sides.

Data Layer

Data Layer consists of Data Sources and Service Agents. The Data Layer deals with Data Sources as shown in Figure 4 and Services deals with getting information from external or internal services. Almost all Web-based enterprise applications use data stored in databases. Data must be collected, organized, safe guarded, and distributed easily and precisely over the network. Data Layer aids Web-based enterprise applications to communicate or access different external systems. External system can be Database or services. This layer deals with actual enterprise raw data. Most of the time Data Base Administrators (DBA's) maintain it (Smith, O'Brian, Barbacci, & Coallier, 2003).

Figure 4. Architectural model for developing a Web-based enterprise application

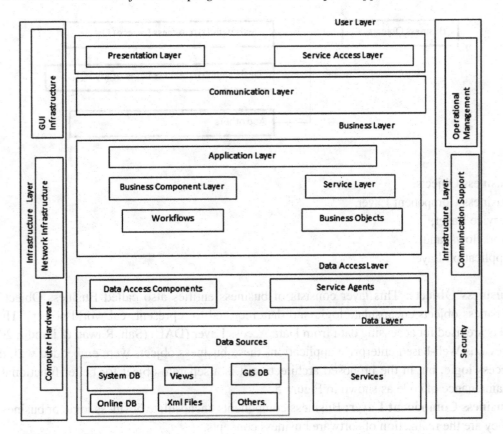

Data Access Layer (DAL)

As it is seen, data layer manages the retrieval and storage of data. So in Data Access Layer the logic is applied to retrieve the data from these databases. Usually in this layer, different code for accessing different databases even for same application is used. For example, suppose in Web-based enterprise application, a demand comes up for changing the database from SQL Server to Oracle database then there is no need to disturb full application, it is sufficient just to change the metod in Data access layer. This helps in reducing the task by not disturbing the whole application (Piette, Caval, Dinont, Seghrouchni, & Taillibert, 2017).

The main aim of this layer is to supply data to business objects without considering database specific codes. Whenever business object or business layer needs data it will call the method in the data access layer rather than directly connecting with the database. It consists of data access component to access databases and service agents to deal with service data (Themistocleous & Irani, 2002).

Service agents are used for interacting and getting information from services of another Web application.

Business Layer

Business Layer encapsulates the business logic and implements the basic functionalities of the system. It interacts with data layer. It consists of several components/layers which are discussed further as follows:

Figure 5. Business object

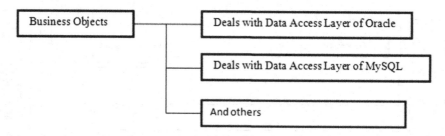

1. Business Objects,
2. Business Component Layer,
3. Service Layer,
4. Workflows, and
5. Application Layer.

- **Business Objects:** This layer consists of business entities also called Business Objects (BO). Business objects encapsulate logic and data required to represent real world objects. These objects are used for accessing data from Data Access Layer (DAL) (Sah, Rawat, & Pundir, 2012). In previous Web-based enterprise applications these business objects were embedded with the data access logic, but in the proposed architecture it is a separate object for better functionality and maintenance of code as shown in Figure 5.
- **Business Component Layer:** Business components encapsulate business logic or business rules. They are the realization of software business concepts.
- **Service Layer:** In this layer application can expose few of its functionalities as services so that they can be used by other applications. These services are implemented using Web services (Kontogiannis, Smith, & O'Brian, 2003).
- **Workflows:** Workflows are the business components working together to perform a business process. These components are orchestrated using middleware languages like BPEL (Business Process Execution Language) or any other business process management tools (Viriyasitavat, Xu, & Martin, 2012).
- **Application Layer:** In Application Layer two or more business processes are combined and provided as single operation so that it becomes easier to use the business logic (Patel & Cassou, 2015).

Communication Layer

For components to interact with each other the communication layer is needed. It helps user layer to communicate with the business layer and with the other components.

User Layer

Web-based enterprise applications are accessed through this layer. It has two sub-layers:

- **Presentation Layer:** This layer provides user interfaces to access the Web-based enterprise applications. It has components like Web forms (UI + Logic behind), User Controls (UI + Logic behind), code to access business tier, etc. (Saxena, Santosh, & Pradhan, 2017).
- **Service Access Layer:** In this layer our application can expose few or more methods as services, so that other applications can access them and make use of their functionalities (Arsanjani, 2004).

SKILL SET REQUIREMENTS FOR BUILDING A WEB-BASED ENTERPRISE APPLICATION

A Web-based enterprise application should be flexible and dynamic enough to handle varied challenges in diverse area. Issues like scalability, delivery, authenticity, integrity are ingrained in enterprise software. A major concern is varying changes in technologies and platforms used by different vendors. Evolutionary architectural approaches and distributed system models are used to meet such challenges.

The Skill Set Requirements for Building an Enterprise Application

The following capacities are deemed necessary for building successful enterprise applications:

- Domain experts in each phase from requirement gathering, analysis, design, implement and testing to give best quality and reliable software.
- Experts with organizational knowledge that understand the internal work flow of the enterprise and collaboration among different vendors.
- Business analysis skill set is very important to analyze each and every step in any phase. A faulty analysis of a process may lead to performance problems at the end.
- Programming skills for writing code, methods in an IDE and platform is required. A skilled programmer can develop, integrate and configure different components using tools and latest technology.
- Testing skills are important for validation and verification of any software. A team of skilled testers will verify each phase with a set of test cases and finally validate the complete system in the presence of user.
- Presentation skills are required to make a product understandable to its target users.
- Knowledge of emerging technologies like IoT, cloud computing and data mining are needed for more interactive application development to meet the market trends.

Challenges for Building Web-Based Enterprise Applications

The never ending demands in business and the changing market trends result into bigger challenges for enterprises. The complexity in development, implementation and maintenance of a Web-based application increases with the growth of an enterprise. Business persons as well as the developers have to face many challenges to rationalized with the latest trends and technologies in order to run a Web-based enterprise application successfully (Soomro & Awan, 2012). A list of challenges are discussed as follows:

- **Handling Changing Demands:** As the market changes, the demands change and grow. In order to maintain a free flow of working, application should be scalable, deployable, and reconfigurable. It should have the ability to load-balance and work-distribution.

- **Efficient Programming:** Programmers must take care in developing and designing application modules. Standards of programming must be followed in such a way that the application caters to the needs of different vendors. Developer must develop Web-based application in line with emerging technologies like IoT and cloud computing.

- **Easy Integration with Other Systems:** The applications should be designed in such a manner so as can be integrated with other existing and emerging technologies like IoT, cloud computing and big data which improve the business environment.

- **Perspective-Based Views:** The system should be flexible enough to generate different views based upon user requirements and feature analysis.

- **Security:** A very important issue to be considered in any application is security. A Web-based enterprise application should be equipped with all the security programs so that can handle existing and future threats. Crucial data stored on central database should not get leaked or hacked (Sharif, Elliman, Love, & Badii, 2004).

- **Integrity Management:** Application should be developed in such a way that it can apply verified integrity check. Data integrity is an important factor that leads to correct and accurate results and analysis. An incorrect or malicious data may result in business failure.

- **User Understanding:** One major challenge for developers is to make the application user friendly. They must provide a rich user experience by giving ease of handle and hiding the complex details.

- **Internationalization:** Developing a Web-based enterprise application which is internationally accepted is one more big challenge. Internationalization is usually done by providing the user interface with different local/national language supports so that any country in the World with any language can understand and use the application. Internationalization is making our system understandable and assessable by everyone.

- **Quality of Service (QoS):** Maintaining quality of service is another challenge. This is the specification or guidelines that must be met to reach the satisfaction of end users. Maintaining the quality of service complying with the rules is a must. Quality of service of an application requires monitoring of different parameters like availability, response time, etc. Quality of service is very important for the success of an application and it also tells the user about the level of quality of service they are using. Maintaining quality of service is a very challenging task (Yan, Peng, Chen, & You, 2015).

- **Technology Selection:** Technology selection is another challenge for Web-based enterprise applications. Quality of application also depends on the selection we made of technologies and platforms. The technology needs to be selected in such a way that in future any changes or modification could be adapted and are easily fitted into the system without reimplementation of whole Web-based enterprise application.

- **Self-understanding:** Web-based applications should be developed in such a way that they can predict the future trends using latest technologies and understand the upgrading required.

- **Governance:** Governance of an enterprise is the process that regulates and controls the performance of an enterprise. Governance can be applied into various domains like infrastructure, processes, projects, portfolios, network, etc. Governance is the process of decision making, forming rules, making norms, and making all the actions accountable among actors of the applications. Most of the time governance is taken care by government or an established governing body.

Enterprise governance constitutes the entire accountability framework of an organization. It has two dimensions:

- Conformance or corporate governance.
- Performance or business governance.

Complying with all the rules of governing body is a challenging task but needs to be followed without failing.

- **Team Productivity:** Team Productivity comes best when whole team is in sync with each other and when proper communication and interlinking of data is there in the team. Increasing the team productivity and making the team work efficiently and effectively is also a challenge for building Web-based enterprise applications.
- **Tools Knowledge:** As more data are available for processing and analysis, the use of data mining tools becomes a necessity. Knowledge of tools helps to address immediate operational issues or inform managers of discoveries regarding competitors' strategic moves and customers' preference (Rawat & Sah, 2012).
- **Security and Privacy:** Large amount of data sharing and information flow throughout the globe will make data vulnerable to attacks. Large amount of data stored in data centers are lacking security and privacy issues. Security issues due to integration of Web-based enterprise applications with emerging technologies need to be handled (Rawat & Sah, 2013).

FUTURE RESEARCH DIRECTIONS

Dynamicity in the market results in varying demands and challenges in substantial amount. Increasing demands and competition in business environment imposed a lot of pressure on Web-based enterprise application providers and developers. Application developers should enhance and extend their offerings with the growing future expectations. Enterprise Web application development trend should results in gearing up the technical and business challenges of an enterprise. From a technical perspective, the biggest challenge is compatibility and upgradability of existing application with future generation of technology. The technical design should justify the number and scope of APIs that are needed in order to adjust existing Web-based enterprise applications with future applications. With the increasing growth of business, sharing and accessing of data and information become cross functional. Data flows across different platforms and used by different vendors in different perspectives; it is the main asset of any enterprise with the three v's (volume, velocity and variety) which becomes very complex to handle and supervise. Handling and securing such voluminous data is the demand of future Web-based enterprise applications.

In the future, Web-based enterprise application should be designed in such a way that it works equally well on mobile applications with an easy to use interface. Also self-adaptable application should be researched which can calculate and predict the future demands by continuous analysis and evaluation of market trends. Voluminous data is generated by IoT devices which results into many challenges for data centers in terms of security and privacy of data (Gartner, 2014). To deal with this massive volume of heterogeneous data upgrading of existing data centers is a must. With the growth of technologies and global information sharing, the attack surface area also grows for hackers and cyber criminals. Still we are lacking in the standards and measures in providing security and privacy of data.

From business perspective, research should be focused on studies of user and market demand for an application. A need of hour is continuous user assessment of application in terms of scope, efficiency and utilization. Focus should be imposed upon proposing generic business models that consist of innovative distribution of workload based on different types of modules and perform trend analysis for upcoming market demands.

CONCLUSION

As the market trends are changing at a very fast pace thus the customer needs and technology are also changing. The Web-based enterprise applications are facing many challenges related to system automation, security of the applications, harmonizing data, integration of data and application, user demands and acceptance, selection of technology, internationalization, etc. In this chapter we proposed and defined a lifecycle for developing Web-based enterprise applications. The chapter also discussed a case study of a Bank information system development. The chapter proposed a logical architectural model of a Web-based enterprise application development. The chapter subsequently focused on defining the skill set required and challenges faced for developing Web-based enterprise applications. In future these Web-based enterprise applications should be developed integrated with advanced technologies and self-adapting to meet market trends and business goals.

REFERENCES

Arsanjani, A. (2004). Service-Oriented Modeling and Architecture. *IBM Developer Works.* Retrieved from www.ibm.com/developerworks/library/ws-soa-design1

Capretz, L. F. (2005). Y: A New Component-based software life cycle model. *Journal of Computer Science, 1*(1), 76-82.

Choudhari, J., & Ugrasen, S. (2015). An Empirical Evaluation of Iterative Maintenance Life Cycle Using XP. *Software Engineering Notes, 40*(2), 1–14. doi:10.1145/2735399.2735406

Crnkovic, I. (2005). Component-based software engineering for embedded systems. *ICSE '05. Proceedings of the 27th international conference on Software engineering.* 10.1145/1062455.1062631

Gartner. (2014). *Gartner says the Internet of Things will transform the data center.* Retrieved March 19, 2014, from http://www.gartner.com/newsroom/id/2684616

Gill, N. S., & Tomar, P. (2008). X Model: A New Component-Based Model. *IACSIT International Journal of Engineering and Technology, 1*(1-2), 1–10.

Guo, J., Xu, L., Xiao, G., & Gong, Z. (2012). Improving multilingual semantic interoperation in cross-organizational enterprise systems through concept disambiguation. *IEEE Transactions on Industrial Informatics, 8*(3), 647–658. doi:10.1109/TII.2012.2188899

Kaur, K., & Singh, H. (2010). Candidate process models for component based software development. *Journal of Software Engineering Academic Journal Inc, India, 4*(1), 16–29.

Kayed, M., & Shaalan, K. F. (2006). A Survey of Web Information Extraction Systems. *IEEE Transactions on Knowledge and Data Engineering, 18*(10), 1411–1428. doi:10.1109/TKDE.2006.152

Kontogiannis, K., Smith, D., & O'Brian, L. (2003). On the Role of Services in Enterprise Application Integration. *Proc. 10th Int'l Workshop Software Technology and Engineering Practice (STEP)*, 103-113. 10.1109/STEP.2002.1267619

Kotonya, G., Sommerville, I., & Hall, S. (2003). Towards A Classification Model for Component-Based Software Engineering. In *Proceedings of, Euro micro Conference, 29th*. Dept. of Computer., Lancaster Univ.

Li, L., Ge, R., Zhou, S. M., & Valerdi, R. (2012). Guest editorial integrated healthcare information systems. *IEEE Transactions on Information Technology in Biomedicine, 16*(4), 515–517. doi:10.1109/TITB.2012.2198317

Patel, P., & Cassou, D. (2015). Enabling High-Level Application Development for the Internet of Things. *Journal of Systems and Software, 103*, 62–84. doi:10.1016/j.jss.2015.01.027

Piette, F., Caval, C., Dinont, C., Seghrouchni, A., & Taillibert, P. (2017). *A Multi-Agent Approach for the Deployment of Distributed Applications in Smart Environments*. Academic Press. .10.1007/978-3-319-48829-5_4

Rawat, S., & Sah, A. (2012). An Approach to Enhance the Software and Services of Health Care Centre. *Computer Eng. and Intelligent Systems. IISTE, 3*(7), 2222–2863.

Rawat, S., & Sah, A. (2013). An Approach to Integrate Heterogeneous Web Applications. *IJCA, 70*(23).

Rehan, M., & Akyuz, G. A. (2010). Enterprise application integration (EAI) service oriented architectures (SOA) and their relevance to e-supply chain formation. *African Journal of Business Management, 4*, 2604–2614.

Sah, A., Rawat, S., & Pundir, S. (2012). Design, Implementation and Integration of Heterogeneous Applications. *IJCA, 54*(5).

Saxena, V., Santosh, H., & Pradhan, C. (2017). *Processing ASP.Net Web Services Using Generic Delegation Approach*. Academic Press. .10.1007/978-981-10-2035-3_16

Scheer, A., & Habermann, F. (2000). Enterprise resource planning: Making ERP a success. *ACM, 43*(4), 57-61.

Sharif, A. M., Elliman, T., Love, P. E., & Badi, A. (2004). Integrating the IS with the enterprise: Key EAI research challenges. *Journal of Enterprise Information Management, 17*(2), 164–170. doi:10.1108/17410390410518790

Shin, D. (2014). A Socio-Technical Framework for Internet of Things Design: A Human-Centered Design for the Internet of Things. *Telematics and Informatics*, *31*(4), 519–531. doi:10.1016/j.tele.2014.02.003

Singh, M. G., Mishra, A., Singh, H., & Upadhyay, P. (2015). Empirical Study of Agile Software Development Methodologies: A Comparative Analysis. *Software Engineering Notes*, *40*(1), 1–6. doi:10.1145/2693208.2693237

Smith, D., O'Brian, L., Barbacci, M., & Coallier, F. (2003). A Roadmap for Enterprise Integration. *Proc 10th Int'l Workshop Software Technology and Engineering Practice (STEP)*, 94-102. 10.1109/STEP.2002.1267618

Soomro, T. R., & Awan, A. H. (2012). Challenges and Future of Enterprise Application Integration. *International Journal of Computers and Applications*, *42*.

Themistocleous, M., & Irani, Z. A. (2002). *Evaluating and Adopting Application Integration: The Case of a Multinational Petroleum Company. In Proc 35th Ann. Hawaii Conf. System Sciences* (pp. 286–294). HICSS.

Tomar, P., & Gill, N. S. (2010). Verification & Validation of Components with New X Component-Based Model. *Proceedings of, Software Technology and Engineering (ICSTE), 2nd International Conference*.

Val, P. B., Garcia-Valls, M., & Estevez-Ayres, I. (2009). Simple asynchronous remote invocations for distributed real-time Java. *IEEE Transactions on Industrial Informatics*, *5*(3), 289–298. doi:10.1109/TII.2009.2026271

Viriyasitavat, W., Xu, L., & Martin, A. (2012). SWSpec: The requirements specification language in service workflow environments. *IEEE Transactions on Industrial Informatics*, *8*(3), 631–638. doi:10.1109/TII.2011.2182519

Wu, S., Xu, L., & He, W. (2009). Industry-oriented enterprise resource planning. *Enterprise Information Systems*, *3*(4), 409–424. doi:10.1080/17517570903100511

Yan, G., Peng, Y., Chen, S., & You, P. (2015). QoS Evaluation of End-to-End Services in Virtualized Computing Environments: A Stochastic Model Approach. *International Journal of Web Services Research*, *12*(1), 27–44. doi:10.4018/IJWSR.2015010103

KEY TERMS AND DEFINITIONS

Architecture Description Languages (ADLs): ADL provides features for representation of eminent system architecture separate from system implementation. ADL must support the architecture components, their interaction, and interfacing.

Functional Requirement: In functional requirement we capture what the system is about to do. These requirements are gathered using use cases and prototypes.

Non-Functional Requirement: It is concerned with the way a system is expected to behave within the constraints and expected quality of service. Non-functional requirements are used to judge the operation of a system, rather than specific behaviors.

Prototyping: A prototype is an early working module of software with basic functionalities. Prototyping is the process of creating prototypes of software applications. It gives an idea to the manufacturer about the final look of the software.

UML: UML stands for unified modeling language. It is a pictorial language that serves as a standard for software requirement analysis and design documents.

Use Cases: A use case is a list of actions or event steps typically defining the interactions between internal and external agent/actors and a system.

Chapter 2
Web Technology Systems Integration Using SOA and Web Services

Anushree Sah
University of Petroleum and Energy Studies, India

Ankur Dumka
University of Petroleum and Energy Studies, India

Saurabh Rawat
Graphic Era University, India

ABSTRACT

This chapter presents an overview of service-oriented architecture and web technologies with the objective of presenting challenging issues concerned with various aspects of integrating heterogeneous web applications.

INTRODUCTION

Service Oriented Architecture (SOA), a flexible, modular approach to delivering IT services, is an essential foundation for emerging technologies like cloud. The cloud will enable real-time delivery of products, services and solutions over the internet. This will also help in dealing with rapid changes in external markets. Therefore, it is essential to consider how these technologies work and what will be the issues and challenges faced by them in the Web environment.

With the adoption of Web technologies, IT users and directors are able to address today's critical challenges of interoperation and at the same time it will provide a solid basis for enterprises to embrace SOA and Web services for the future world. SOA provides significant advantages over current IT architectures.

For this we will consider a case study that will include the application using heterogeneous technologies like Java, Extensible Markup Language (XML), Web service, Extensible Stylesheet Language

DOI: 10.4018/978-1-5225-5384-7.ch002

(XSL), and XSL Transformation tool (XSLT), etc. Communication between different applications is the main concern nowadays in any type of organization and when we talk about software industries it would be the first priority because every other industry is dependent on software directly or indirectly.

With the growing demands of the market and increasing publicity of Web services, today's market aims at providing heterogeneous Web application development. This chapter suggests a life cycle model and also shows steps to integrate Web applications. Using the Web services, software companies are gaining publicity and their work is also reduced, due to increasing reusability. Reusability helps in sharing at low cost Web modules or components that are even expensive and this makes it more economical for each end user to use or consume Web services.

Strategies by which computers speak with each other using markup dialects and mixed media bundles are known as Web innovation. In the previous couple of decades, Web innovation has experienced a sensational change, from a couple of increased site pages to the capacity to do certain work on a system without interference. This chapter will take a gander at few cases of Web technology. Web innovation gets rid of such aspects by giving us approaches to communicate with facilitated data, for example, sites or enterprise applications.

The techniques by which computers communicate with each other using markup dialects and sight and sound bundles are known as Web technology. This chapter discusses about enterprise application integration (EAI), SOA, Web services, Web Service Description Language (WSDL), Simple Object Access Protocol (SOAP) and related Web technology. The chapter also discusses computing with respect to XML and Web services. In this we elaborated the role of XML and Web services in grid computing and then discussed the role of XML and Web services in cloud computing. Different types of techniques are discussed first then an example to integrate the applications is shown. A Java Web service is developed which is then consumed by another Java Web application. This is the way to consume Web services. In other ways Web service can be consumed by a servlet or Java Server Pages (JSP) or by REpresentational State Transfer (REST) Web service or by any other application as per the need in future. If the format of Web service is different from the required or acceptable format then XSLT is used, which will help in converting XML to other formats like HTML or even in different structured XML. Further on, the chapter presents issues and challenges while using SOA and Web services.

The chapter shows an example to communicate two Java application using Web services. This is just an approach to use Web services in real world. The example has not been built for a real client, it only shows a simple integration but if developed further and if more methods are added, it can be used for commercial application and could be used in real world.

BACKGROUND STUDY

The journey of Web service architecture can be traced from the period of Remote Procedure Call (RPC) mechanism in Distributed Computing Environment (DCE) which started in 1990s as a framework for software development. This includes distributed file system for communication purpose among different software applications. DCE originated from UNIX environment while Microsoft came up with its version of implementation termed as MSRPC. RPC was designed for the purpose of distributed computing which allows computing among different physical devices whereas Microsoft version introduces RPC for supporting inter process communication within a single device.

Taking a note on DCE/RPC, it uses client server architecture where procedure is invoked by client which is executed in server. In late 1990's, Dave Winer of UserLand Software developed XML version of RPC termed as XML-RPC. It is light weight RPC system which support elementary data types with few simple commands.

Web service further reaches to new version of architecture termed as Distributed Object Architecture (DOA) such as Java RMI. Java RMI and Dot.Net remoting are second generation distributed objects systems. These transformations towards such types of services resulted in a move towards simplicity, standardization and interoperability. Web services evolved over time and many researchers published different works; description of few recent works done is given next.

Meng and He in the paper "A comparison of approaches to Web service evolution" showed the evolution of Web services. In the paper they analyzed the Web services on the basis of type of evolution, maintainability, granularity of evolution and so on. And later they also discussed few future directions (Meng & He, 2013). The computer systems we are using nowadays are the consequences of the evolution done in the past. Such evolution led to the development of the world in all aspects of life (Ouni, Gaikovina, Kessentini, & Inoue, 2015).

SOA and Web service have been used in the IT market for years. Many old software systems suffer from poor design also called 'antipatterns', so is the case with SOA Web systems. SOA systems also suffer from antipatterns and this is discussed by Ouni, Kessentini, Inoue, & Cinneide in their paper "Search-Based Web Service Antipatterns Detection". They proposed an automated approach for detection of Web service antipatterns using a cooperative parallel evolutionary algorithm (P-EA) (Ouni, et al., 2015). They further compared their approach with the random search, two single population-based approaches and one state-of-the-art detection technique not based on heuristic search. They also showed the statistical result of comparison of different approaches (Ouni, Kessentini, Inoue, & Cinneide, 2017).

WEB BASED APPLICATION DEVELOPMENT TERMINOLOGIES

Enterprise Applications

An enterprise application is the expression used to depict applications that a business would use to help the association in taking care of big business issues. At the point when "enterprise" is joined with "application," it normally alludes to a product stage that is too extensive and excessively complex for individual or private company use. Designing and growing such endeavor applications implies fulfilling hundreds or thousands of discrete necessities. Additionally, every advancement choice you make to fulfil every necessity influences numerous different prerequisites, regularly in ways that are hard to comprehend or foresee — and the inability to meet any of these prerequisites can mean the disappointment of the whole project! They might be sent on an assortment of stages crosswise over corporate systems, intranets, or the Internet. They are information driven, easy to use, and should meet stringent prerequisites for security, organization, and support. To put it plainly, they are profoundly mind boggling frameworks (Rawat & Sah, 2012).

Some examples of common enterprise applications are:

1. Email systems
2. Automated billing system

3.   Business intelligence
4.   Messaging and collaboration systems
5.   Banking Systems, etc.

There can be many more types of enterprise applications prevailing in the market; now let us discuss few advantages and disadvantages of enterprise applications

Few advantages of enterprise applications are:

1.   Information sharing
2.   Streamlined IT processes
3.   Increased efficiency
4.   Reduction of cost of litigation.

Few disadvantages of enterprise applications are:

1.   Systems can be expensive
2.   Systems can be difficult to use
3.   Change in staff or administration can lead to inexperienced handling of the applications.

The World Wide Web is an arrangement of interlinked IT assets that are gotten through the Internet. The two fundamental parts of the Web are the Web program customer and the Web server. Different parts, for example, intermediaries, storing administrations, entryways, and stack balancers, are utilized to enhance Web application qualities, for example, adaptability and security. These extra parts live in a layered design that is situated between the customer and the server (Rawat & Sah, 2012).

Service-Oriented Architecture (SOA)

SOA is an information sharing architecture. It increases abstraction and autonomy. It is an open standard (non-proprietary), shares common services, increases reuse of components, and loosely coupled. To an extent SOA solves the problem OO (Object Oriented) and CO (Component Oriented) could not solve by increasing the level of abstraction. It is an architecture which is efficient for large distributed systems. The developing service oriented architecture (SOA) based strategy utilizes Web services is picking up heaps of enthusiasm for the method for a consistent mix of data frameworks spreading over a few associations. Service oriented architectures include three various types of on-screen characters: service suppliers, service requesters, and disclosure organizations. The service supplier shares some product usefulness as a service to its customers. With a specific end goal to enable customers to get to the service, the supplier additionally needs to distribute a depiction of the service. Since service supplier and service requester, as a rule, do not have any acquaintance with each other ahead of time, the service portrayals are distributed by means of particular revelation organizations. A service is a capacity that is very much characterized, independent and does not rely upon the unique situation or condition of different services. They can arrange the service portrayals and give them in light of a question issued by one of the service requesters. When the service requester finds a reasonable service depiction for its prerequisites, it begins collaborating with the supplier and utilizing the service. Service Oriented architecture comprises of a gathering of services. The correspondence can include either straightforward information passing or it would include at least two services organizing some movement. The main service oriented architecture for some individuals in the past was with the utilization of Distributed Component Object Model (DCOM) or Object Request Brokers (ORBs) in light of the Common Object Request Broker Architecture (CORBA) determination. Web services basically utilize XML to make a hearty association (LISong-hua Li-hong, & Dong, 2009). SOA is a set of principles, policies, standards, guidelines, agreements, and requirements for shared infrastructure.

In Figure 1 we can see that using Web services applications can intercommunicate; although these applications may be built on different platforms and are developed in different environment, still they can intercommunicate. With the help of enterprise bus and an adapter or connector we can make Web services inter communicate with each other (Natchetoi, Kaufman, & Shapiro, 2008).

Web Services

A Web service is any bit of programming that makes itself accessible over the Web and uses an institutionalized XML informing framework. Its main goal is interoperability between enterprises. XML is utilized to encode all interchanges to a Web service. A service is autonomous and has explicit boundaries. Web service is a piece of business logic which is accessible over the Web and which can be reused (Richardson, Ruby, Burgess, & Leey, 2008).

Figure 1. v Interoperability using Web services

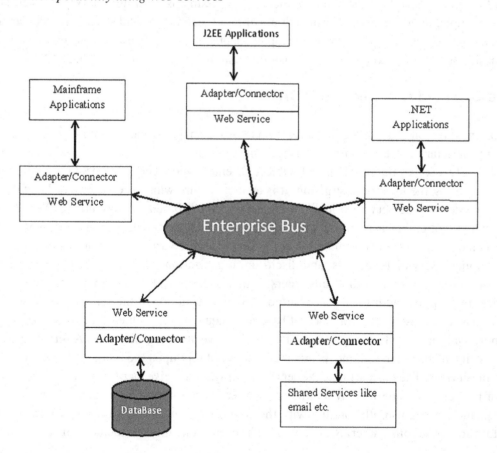

Understanding Services

The idea of services inside an application has been around for some time. Services, much like parts, are planned to be free building binders that on the whole speak to an application domain. Not at all like conventional segments, however, have services had various novel attributes that enable them to take part as a component of an administration arranged design. One of these qualities is finished self-governance from different services (Arroqui, Mateos, Machado, & Zunino, 2012). This implies each administration is in charge of its own space, which normally converts into restricting its degree to a particular business work (or a gathering of related capacities). This planned approach brings about the making of disconnected units of business bound together by a typical consistence to a standard interchangeable structure (Sah, Rawat, & Pundir, 2012).

Present as shown in Figure 2, the basic architectural model for Web services consists of three types of participants:

1. Service provider, who is also called producer of services, creates Web services and advertises them to potential users by registering the Web services with a service broker.
2. Service broker, also called registry of services, maintains a registry of advertised (published) services and might introduce service providers to service requesters.
3. Service requester, also called consumer of services, searches the registries of service brokers for suitable service providers, and then contacts a service provider to use its services (Zhang, et al., 2012).

The framework for Web services is categorized into three areas and the detail specification of all three are already developed as follows:

- **Service Description:** WSDL file is the readable and formal file for Web service description.
- **Service Discovery:** Universal Description, Discovery and Integration (UDDI) is the directory or registry for Web service descriptions.

Figure 2. Basic Web Service Architectural model

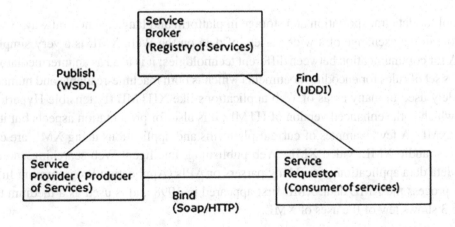

- **Protocols for Communication:** SOAP aids in inter-communication between enterprise Web applications that uses Web service.

XML Web Service

The most generally acknowledged and effective kind of service is the XML Web service. XML Web services give an approach to depict their interfaces in enough detail to enable a client to assemble a customer application to converse with them. This portrayal is typically given in a XML archive called a WSDL record.

Realizing SOA With Web Services

Web services speak to one critical way to deal with understanding a SOA. The World Wide Web Consortium (W3C), which has dealt with the development of SOAP and WSDL particulars, characterizes Web services as: "A product framework intended to help interoperable machine-to-machine association over a network." Interoperability is increased through an arrangement of XML-based open guidelines, for example, WSDL, SOAP, and UDDI. These norms give a typical way to deal with characterizing, distributing, and utilizing Web services (Lin & Chang, 2010).

As an example of one of the few Web services technology platforms, Sun's Java Web Services Developer Pack 1.5 (Java WSDP 1.5) and Java 2 Platform, Enterprise Edition (J2EE) 1.4 can be utilized to create cutting edge Web services to actualize SOA. The J2EE 1.4 stage empowers you to assemble and send Web services in your IT framework on the application server stage. It gives the instruments needed to rapidly manufacture, test, and convey Web services and customers that interoperate with other Web services and customers running on Java-based or non-Java-based stages (Zhang, et al., 2012). What's more, it empowers organizations to uncover their current J2EE applications as Web services. Servlets and Enterprise JavaBeans segments (EJBs) can be exposed as Web services that can be consumed by Java-based or non-Java-based Web service customers. J2EE applications can be considered as Web service customers themselves, and they can speak with other Web services, paying little effort to how they are executed (Lin & Chang, 2010).

Extensible Markup Language (XML)

XML is a tool for data transportation and storage in platform and language neutral way. XML plays an important role in the exchange of a wide variety of data on the Web. XML is a very simple language used in SOA for communication between different technologies; it is used as an intermediator language. XML defines set of rules for encoding documents which is both machine-readable and human-readable. XML is widely used in many areas of Web applications like XHTML (Extensible Hypertext Markup Language) which is the enhanced version of HTML; it is also for presentation aspects but it adheres to the rules of XML. A few examples of current platforms and applications using XML are cell phones, file converters, audio XML, video XML, Web publishing, intelligent Web searching and automating Web task, Meta data applications, etc. Many parsers or APIs (Application Programming Interface) are available to process the XML data. XML first appeared in 1998 and is used as a medium to transport data. Figure 3 shows few of the uses of XML.

Figure 3. Few uses of XML

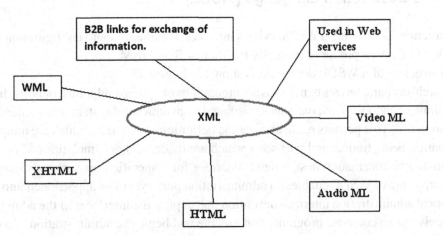

There are thousands of XML based languages in use and most of the software today is XML-enabled to some extent (i.e., it reads, stores, and outputs XML). Information on a website may be represented as XML and converted to a variety of other formats for delivery to different types of client e.g. to HTML or XHTML for ordinary browsers on PCs and to WML for mobile phones or PDAs. The way it is transformed is likely to be using "style sheets" written in XSLT. The same information may also be transformed into completely different formats, e.g. to PDF (Rawat & Sah, 2013).

It is possible that specialist multi-media XML-based languages like SMIL (Synchronized Multimedia Integration Language) may also be used on a Web site. One advantage of XML over HTML is that it makes intelligent searching easier. In the internal enterprise systems of an organization XML (in the form of SOAP messages) may be used to provide the middleware for Web service based distributed systems. Web services can be used as an alternative to distributed object systems such as RMI and CORBA. XML is used to communicate with XML-enabled databases (Wesley & Brebner, 2009).

The enterprise systems may also make use of XML to communicate externally. For instance it may be used to exchange business documents (invoices, etc.) with trading partners. It may also be used to make use of publicly available Web services over the Web, e.g. to get the latest currency exchange rates.

XML is not completely a computer language, it is very much human readable and user defined. It is very easy to code in XML as compared to other languages. XML allows us to implement new languages. It is highly compatible with many languages and we can create our own tags or can use the tags created by others. It is an extendable language. The data of XML files can be displayed on various devices. Any application regardless of the architecture or platform can use the XML data. It is used as a language to communicate between different languages. If the data produced an application is in the form of XML, other applications can directly fetch and use the data. The data can be fetched using XPath (XML Path Language). XPath is the recommendation of W3C. Using XPath an application can traverse and fetch the elements and attributes of an XML file. Furthermore XSLT can be used to convert or transform XML documents to other formats or to the different structured XML as per the need of the application. XSLT helps in manipulating and transforming XML documents (Karande, Karande, & Meshram, 2011).

XML document → XSL Transform →changed XML Document (Output XML)

Web Services Description Language (WSDL)

WSDL is a structure for showing a Web Service's interface. It is the standard configuration for depicting a Web benefit. WSDL was produced mutually by Microsoft and IBM.

The main structure of a WSDL document is shown in Figure 4.

A WSDL archive characterizes benefits as accumulations of system endpoints, or ports. In WSDL, the dynamic meaning of endpoints and messages is isolated from their solid system arrangement or information organization ties. This permits reuse of dynamic definitions: messages, which are unique portrayals of the information being traded, and port sorts which are theoretical accumulations of operations. The solid convention and information design determinations for a specific port sort constitutes a reusable binding. The structure of WSDL enables an administration portrayal to be apportioned into a definition:

"A theoretical administration interface definition that depicts the interfaces of the administration and makes it conceivable to compose programs that execute and begin the administration." In other words, WSDL is much the same as a postcard which has the address of a specific area. The address gives the points of interest of the individual who conveyed the postcard. Subsequently, a WSDL record is the postcard, which has the address of the Web, and thus benefits all the usefulness that the customer needs.

SOAP

SOAP is an acronym for Simple Object Access Protocol, but nowadays it is called just 'SOAP'. It is an XML-based informing convention for trading data among enterprise applications. SOAP is a utilization of the XML particular (Lee, Jie, & Wang, 2015). Various specifics about SOAP are that SOAP:

- Is a correspondence convention intended to impart through Web.
- Can broaden HTTP for XML.

Figure 4.

```
<definitions>

<types>
    data type definitions........
</types>

<message>
    definition of the data being communicated....
</message>

<portType>
    set of operations......
</portType>

<binding>
    protocol and data format specification....
</binding>

</definitions>
```

- Gives information transport to Web administrations.
- Can trade finished reports or call a remote strategy.
- Can be utilized for broadcasting a message.
- Is stage and dialect free.
- Is the XML-based method for characterizing what data is sent and how.
- Empowers customer applications to effectively associate with remote administration, also to summon remote techniques.

Web Services as Computational Computing

Role of XML and Web Services in Grid Computing

Grid computing is a type of computing environment where multiple computers are installed at different geographical locations and they perform specific tasks to achieve a common goal. It tends to be a heterogeneous system without physical coupling. In grid computing, the computers on the network can work on a task together, thus functioning as a supercomputer. When a user opens a Website, at the back-end a request is sent to the Web server and then the response message is returned from the server. All this happens on a Web browser. Web services can be defined as distributed software components which are responsible to provide information to the application using an application oriented interface. (Lee, Lee, Chen, & Hsu, 2013).

XML is a widely used language. It is an open standard used predominantly in Web services. XML and Web services are used in grid computing. Web services provide requested information to the different nodes of the grid computing environment. Information cannot be transferred without having a certain structure. So, XML comes into play. Information is structured using XML so that processing and parsing becomes quicker. The formatting task becomes negligible after the information gets structured and all this happens with the help of XML (Zhou, Yin, Jiang, & Zhang, 2011).

Web services and grid computing were developed separately and have different sets of goals, but when we look deeper both share so many common functionalities. The vulnerabilities that grid computing are facing are also experienced by Web services as the goals of both of these technologies are very much similar. So we suggest that these two share the same result rather than redundantly solving issues for both Web services and grid computing.

Role of XML and Web Services in Cloud Computing

Cloud computing is based on the services provided by XML and Web itself. XML and Web are the components that render cloud computing a success. XML provides a common data format that can be exchanged between a variety of services and languages. It is used to tag the data for cloud storage.

Here are some uses of XML and Web services in cloud computing:

1. Cloud computing uses Web services for connections.
2. Almost every cloud service provider uses the Web for providing their services online.
3. Storage, network, computes all are provided to the user through virtualization.
4. Helps in achieving high availability feature of cloud.
5. Helps in data transaction even in different formats.

6.   XML data is stored in text format. This makes it easier to expand or upgrade to new operating systems, new applications, or new browsers, without losing data.
7.   Different applications can access data.
8.   Cloud providers can design XML API which is useful while working with different libraries and tools.

PROPOSED LIFECYCLE MODEL FOR INTEGRATING WEB APPLICATIONS

The model in Figure 5 is an iterative one which is most suitable for small/medium scale enterprises. The stages of the above model can be defined as

Requirement Elicitation

This is the first stage in the Web application development. In this stage requirement is systematically gathered and then properly documented. Here an accurate and comprehensive understating of project and business needs are gathered. During this phase many stakeholders can participate for well-functioning of the project. For the project, stakeholders include end users, customers, domain specialist, project sponsors, implementation experts, project manager, and analysts. For requirement gathering many techniques are used, often in combinations; few of them are brainstorming, document analysis, focus groups, interviews, observation, prototyping, job shadowing, survey, questionnaire, analysis, etc. (LISong-hua, et al., 2009).

Figure 5. Iterative Web service based application development lifecycle model for medium scale enterprises

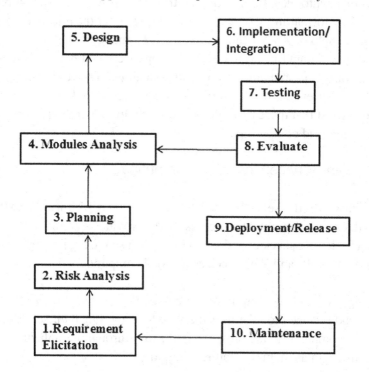

Risk Analysis

In this phase risk associated with the project is evaluated thoroughly. Risk is the likelihood of a specific effect within a specified period or we can say risk analysis is the discussing of vulnerabilities in the applications. For determining component of risk and safety measures, identifying hazards and quantifying risks, risk analysis and risk assessments are an efficient way to get holistic idea of the risks in the enterprise application. Risk analysis is a very important and continuous work which is done as team work. Team is formed from different background people (Bernard, 2007).

- **Processing of Risk Assessment:** Requirement defining → Hazard or vulnerability identification → Analysis of accidents → Estimation of frequency of accidents → Analysis of consequences → Risk Estimation.

There are many methods for risk assessment like index-based method, fault true Analysis, event tree analysis etc., depending upon the need and requirement of the project.

Planning

In the planning phase overall plan of the project is developed with estimated time to delivery. In this phase program management, development, user experience, testing requirements / schedule, release management (deployment plan / schedule) are decided. All planning related activities are done in this phase. Program Evaluation Review Technique (PERT) charts or any other time specific charts are made to set the time deadlines and milestones.

Modules Analysis

In the current market scenario Web applications are not developed from the scratch, in fact we are reusing the components already developed, and Web services promote reusability in Web applications. An enterprise application consists of various modules or we can say that an enterprise application consumes or uses different Web services for making an integrated solution (Harrison, Lee, & West, 2004).

Module analysis is the holistic analysis of the Web service which is usually conducted by business analysts. It comprises of the activities:

- Identifying stakeholders
- Identifying business opportunities
- Identifying business requirements
- Identifying business roadmap
- Identifying business scope
- Identifying business challenges

Design

While building an enterprise application either we will make a new application or we will reuse existing applications as Web services and add more functionalities as per the need thus produce a new application. In the design phase, design model is developed by business analysts.

Business analysts use different tools to develop the model. This model will show a pictorial form of the enterprise application and thus help us to visualize how our completed application will look like. Design phase gives the holistic view of the system to be developed (Ouni, et al., 2017).

Implementation / Integration

During this phase, the developed design is implemented. All the functionality as per the need of the customer is coded and the modules in the form of Web services are bought from the service providers. For already developed modules, service directory is searched and then the required Web service is bought and used by the service requestor. Implementation must use procedures and tools to evolve safe and secure modules.

Following documents are generated after this phase:

- User manual
- Complete business product
- Completion report
- SLA (Service Level Agreement)
- MOU (Memoranda of understanding)
- Disaster recovery plan
- Security plan
- Training material and plan

Testing

This phase is very challenging as it is difficult to say that application is tested for all possible issues. To get the high quality, well-functioning applications it is essential that an enterprise application is well tested using almost all possible configurations that a customer may use. This is an exhausting process and takes time. Unit testing is done at the implementation phase. In Web service-based enterprise application development even integration testing is done at the implementation phase. Every module developed or reused is tested. Then during the testing phase several other testing are performed as per the application needs like product testing, system testing, acceptance testing, regression testing, etc.

Evaluate

During this phase evaluation of the enterprise application is done. Enterprise applications are evaluated for overall requirements. In some enterprises, scores are allotted for each requirement covering and if the score is above the satisfactory limit then Enterprise application is deployed or released. In some other enterprises summary charts are prepared and the group of stakeholder evaluates the application for release.

Usually in the first cycle from step 4 thtough step 8 in the figure a POC (Proof of concept) is produced then when it is passes from the stakeholders then application as a whole is developed in the next round in steps 4 through 8.

Deployment/Release

This is the phase when your application is ready for user consumption or use. When your application passes all the previous phases and thorough testing is also done then it is ready for release, once an application is released it is ready for the use by end users.

Maintenance

After the system become operational maintenance phase starts. In this phase implementation of new requirement or updating in the old requirement is carried out. Even after the testing phase, supervision of the residual errors that may prevail in software is veiled by maintenance phase. System performance, shape up bugs and requested changes are entertained and monitored by this phase (Pautasso & Wilde, 2009).

IMPLEMENTATION DETAILS

Constructing a Simple Web Service and Consuming It by Another Web Service

In our work we are showing how to implement a Java WS and how to consume it by other systems. In this Java is used as the language to develop a Web service and then to consume the developed Web service. Though the developed Web service can be used for consuming by any application and we have consumed the developed Web service by a Java application. JAX-WS uses JAXB for data binding. In our chapter we will use NetBeans as an IDE (Integrated Development Environment) (Potti, Ahuja, Umapathy, & Prodanoff, 2012).

Case Study

Here in this chapter we propose a case study of a calculator. Within calculator we have different methods for basic calculations that will be exposed as Web services for the clients to consume. Next, we use the exposed methods in our Java client application. Step by step process is discussed next.

Step 1: Creating a Web service: For creating a Web service, one can use either a Web container or an EJB container. Here we are using Web container for JavaEE applications. The steps to create a simple Web service are shown next. In NetBeans create a new project by clicking File tab then New Project, then select Web application from the category. Provide a name and select appropriate server as per need. After creating project make a Web service by right clicking the project node and selecting New > Web service. Set all parameters as needed and finish setup. Similar file as shown below will appear. Now add your Web methods to it as shown in Figure 6.

In this code piece, six methods of a Web service are exposed which can be used later by other applications. Once the Web service is developed and deployed over the server, test the Web service by right clicking the name of Web service and clicking Test Web service option you will get a screen as shown in Figure 7.

Figure 6. Web service code

```
package a;
import javax.jws.WebService;
import javax.jws.WebMethod;
import javax.jws.WebParam;
@WebService(serviceName = "HouseWebService")
public class HouseWebService {
    @WebMethod(operationName = "hello")
    public String hello(@WebParam(name = "name") String txt) {
        return "Hello " + txt + " !"; }
    @WebMethod(operationName = "add")
    public int add(@WebParam(name = "a") int a, @WebParam(name = "b") int b) {
        int k=a+b;
        return k;      }
    @WebMethod(operationName = "sub")
    public int sub(@WebParam(name = "a") int a, @WebParam(name = "b") int b) {
        int k=a-b;
        return k;      }
    @WebMethod(operationName = "mul")
    public int mul(@WebParam(name = "a") int a, @WebParam(name = "b") int b) {
        int k=a*b;
        return k;      }
    @WebMethod(operationName = "div")
    public int div(@WebParam(name = "a") int a, @WebParam(name = "b") int b) {
        int k=a/b;
        return k;      }
    @WebMethod(operationName = "mod")
    public int mod(@WebParam(name = "a") int a, @WebParam(name = "b") int b) {
        int k=a%b;
        return k;      }
}
```

In Figure 7 one enters the parameters and tests the methods by clicking the buttons provided. A WSDL file will be generated after deploying the Web service. This WSDL file will be published over the service broker. After that, service requestor will search the broker directory for the service it requires for its application and will bind its application with the Web service provider, thus can use the Web service in its application. The communication between service requestor and service provider will happen in the form of SOAP messages (Mateos, Rodriguez, & Zunino, 2015). A sample soap message is shown next.

Skeleton SOAP Message: Skeleton SOAP Message can be of two types:

1.   SOAP Request
2.   SOAP Response

Now for example, let us click over the Add method in the test window in your browser, you will get SOAP request message and SOAP response message as shown in Figure 8.

Step 2: Consuming a Web Service: For consuming a Web service, we have to make a Standard Web service client, which is as shown in Figure 9.

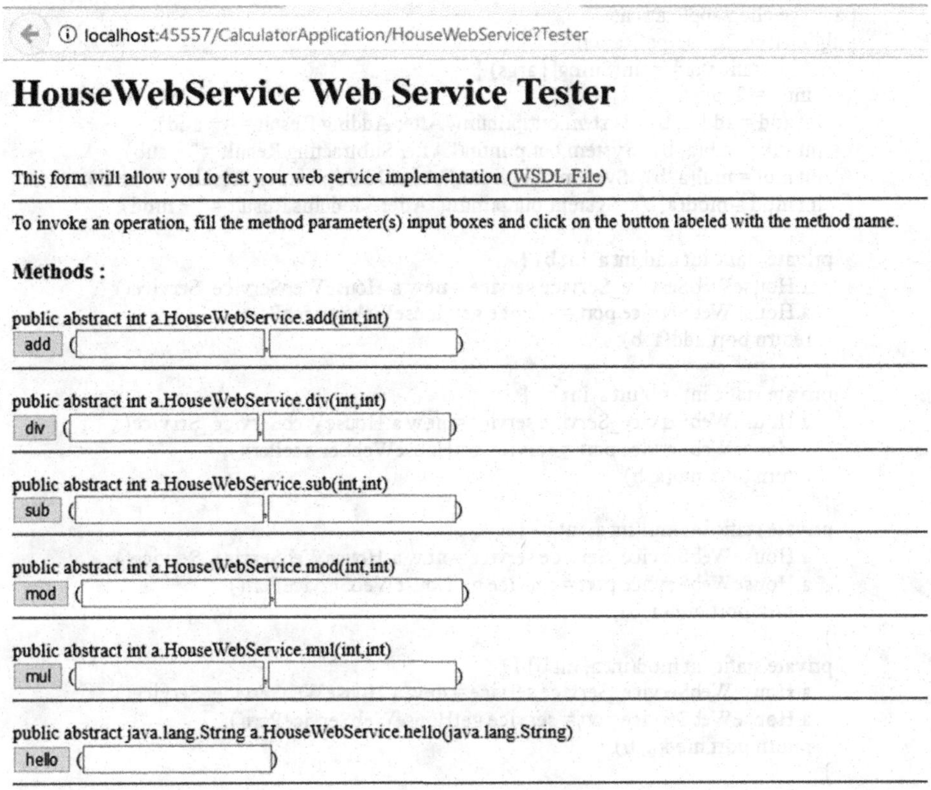

Figure 7. Running of Web service during test phase

← ① localhost:45557/CalculatorApplication/HouseWebService?Tester

HouseWebService Web Service Tester

This form will allow you to test your web service implementation (WSDL File)

To invoke an operation, fill the method parameter(s) input boxes and click on the button labeled with the method name.

Methods :

public abstract int a.HouseWebService.add(int,int)

[add] ([   ] [   ])

public abstract int a.HouseWebService.div(int,int)

[div] ([   ] [   ])

public abstract int a.HouseWebService.sub(int,int)

[sub] ([   ] [   ])

public abstract int a.HouseWebService.mod(int,int)

[mod] ([   ] [   ])

public abstract int a.HouseWebService.mul(int,int)

[mul] ([   ] [   ])

public abstract java.lang.String a.HouseWebService.hello(java.lang.String)

[hello] ([   ])

Figure 8. the code for SOAP request

```
<?xml version="1.0" encoding="UTF-8"?>

<S:Envelope xmlns:S="http://schemas.xmlsoap.org/soap/envelope/"

xmlns:SOAP-ENV="http://schemas.xmlsoap.org/soap/envelope/">

    <SOAP-ENV:Header/>

    <S:Body>

        <ns2:add xmlns:ns2="http://a/">

            <a>5</a>

            <b>5</b>

        </ns2:add>

    </S:Body>

</S:Envelope>
```

Figure 9. Web service client code

```
package clientapplication;
public class ClientApplication {
   public static void main(String[] args) {
      int a = 2, b = 6;
      int add = add(a, b); System.out.println("After Adding Result = " + add);
      int sub = sub(a, b); System.out.println("After Subtracting Result = " + sub);
      int mul = mul(a, b); System.out.println("After Multiplication Result = " + mul);
      int mod = mod(a, b); System.out.println("After Modulus Result = " + mod);
   }
   private static int add(int a, int b) {
      a.HouseWebService_Service service = new a.HouseWebService_Service();
      a.HouseWebService port = service.getHouseWebServicePort();
      return port.add(a, b);
   }
   private static int sub(int a, int b) {
      a.HouseWebService_Service service = new a.HouseWebService_Service();
      a.HouseWebService port = service.getHouseWebServicePort();
      return port.sub(a, b);
   }
   private static int mul(int a, int b) {
      a.HouseWebService_Service service = new a.HouseWebService_Service();
      a.HouseWebService port = service.getHouseWebServicePort();
      return port.mul(a, b);
   }
   private static int mod(int a, int b) {
      a.HouseWebService_Service service = new a.HouseWebService_Service();
      a.HouseWebService port = service.getHouseWebServicePort();
      return port.mod(a, b);
   }
}
```

In the running example developed above we exemplified a Java Web service and its consumption by a Java application. There are a number of ways to produce and consume the Web services, whereas this chapter discusses one of the perspectives.

Issues and Challenges in Using SOA and Web Services

SOA becomes vulnerable to attacks as the technologies XML, WSDL, SOAP, UDDI are open source and they neither have inbuilt security. Thus, because of these technologies SOA becomes vulnerable to attacks. Few issues are discussed next.

- **SOA Lacks Encryption:** Any third person can intercept SOA messages so the confidential data is insecure. Although not related to SOA, the attack called Denial of Service can be put into action by unauthorized users; they can feed the service by making unwanted requests which will lead to the genuine users not getting access to the services.
- **Lack of Logging Feature:** SOA also does not implement an audit trail logging feature. Logs can be recorded to keep track of service uses and request locations but SOA lacks this feature making it less secure.

- **Eavesdropping:** Eavesdropping is another factor that makes SOA insecure. The SOA messages are not transmitted using private networks. The messages are sent over the Internet. "Unwanted listening" can take place in such kind of architecture.

- **Coordination between IT and Security Staffs:** As SOA has many moving portable components so IT staff and security staff have to closely coordinate with each other while starting to develop a SOA project in order to maintain confidentiality, integrity and availability of data in the enterprise.

- **Responsiveness of Web Service:** While Web services are built, the performance environment has to be considered as mentioned in the SOA principles earlier. This is a call for an understanding of the performance requirements so as to build a service that responds promptly to requests, if not we would have a Web service that is non-responsive.

- **Semantic Limitations:** SOA can solve the problems of interoperability across distributed computing environment, but some semantic limitations are present. Every service has a description of its functionalities; a problem arises when the services use different data structures. This is where the semantic layer of SOA comes into action. The semantic layer allows data to be described as concepts, relations and entities representing an abstraction of the real world. This would enable data to be well understood by service consumers and providers. Dealing with semantics in SOA is a very difficult challenge; research is being conducted to investigate more in this area (Pautasso & Wilde, 2009).

- **Poor Requirements:** If requirements are not clearly identified Web services face many issues while they are consumed by other applications. If the requirements are not properly analyzed and identified in the inception of the service then it may affect the finished application a lot; it may sometimes also incur lot of changes even for minor requirement variation and the cost may escalate. Quality of software hugely depends on the correctness and completeness of the requirements. If the requirements are not good, the project will fail.

- **Authentication and Authorization:** Authentication tells us about who the caller is, whether his identity is valid or not, can the caller be trusted. Once the caller is authenticated, the next step is what resources to share with him, this is authorization. Knowing and understanding the caller is a risky task.

- **Integrity and Confidentiality:** Maintaining integrity and confidentiality is another issue. The data received by the service requestor should not have been altered in between while transfer; this is one major issue. WS-Security ensures that the integrity of the data provided by service is maintained for WS- Security adds XML signature specification in the XML file. Signature is kept in <Signature> tag of XML file and is itself encrypted, which is decoded using SOAP message and security token. By confidentiality it is ensured that data is not read in transit. For this XML file is encrypted. Similar keys are shared by sender and receiver.

- **Inadequate Testing:** Proper testing should be done so that the software works properly when needed the most. When more than one service are integrated and used, then chances of error increases in the system.

- **Maintenance:** Maintaining the Web services and updating them with the demands of IT industry is also an issue. Skills and expertise are needed from both functional and technical domain to update the services with the changing market.

FUTURE RESEARCH DIRECTIONS

Enterprise applications are made up of Web services and Web modules. Web services are widely accepted in IT industry. Nothing is flawless in the World so is the case with Web services. There are many issues that can be addressed, added or changed in Web services (Mateos, Rodriguez, & Zunino, 2015). Few research directions to upgrade existing technology are discussed below:

- Security is one major concern for Web services in Web applications, and the basic Web service frameworks lack the basic requirement of security. As we have seen, Web services involve lot of message exchange while using it in real world scenarios. So maintaining confidentiality and integrity can be improved during inter-communication. It is the basic requirement of any Web application that data sent or transferred over the network should be confidential and no unauthorized access be allowed. For this, encryption techniques are used, like the encrypted data is wrapped inside XML tags. In future process of authentication and authorization can be improved and more effective and secure techniques need be developed so that integrated enterprise application generated from these Web services is secured.
- Time complexity and punctuality are also major concerns for integration in heterogeneous Web application. Reducing the time in communication between applications is an open issue.
- Logging feature can be added so that problems or errors can be documented and tracked in the enterprise applications.
- Application level attacks need be taken care of as Web services uses HTTP ports and protocol to both internal and external systems so application servers are more vulnerable to application level attacks.
- In future, work can be done on XML Signatures to make our enterprise application more secure. XML Signatures are added to maintain data integrity and authentication. As XML is vulnerable to security attacks so the case with enterprise applications as they are XML based. XML lacks the well-defined semantics to realize the vision of Web services that are utilized in large enterprise application.
- Though XML, Web services and HPC (High performance computing) are working hand in hand but still requirement for better support of Web services to High Performance Computing architecture is needed.
- Testing is one major concern in using or consuming Web services. Defining a proper set of testing parameters is a very challenging task, so if some major advancement is needed for making a common testing framework.
- As the cloud computing is gaining publicity and most of the companies are moving towards cloud platform, so the enterprise applications are also shifting to cloud. Load balancing of Web services over cloud is one of the important research topics.

CONCLUSION

With the growing demands of the market and increasing publicity of Web services, today's market aims at providing heterogeneous Web applications. This chapter suggests a life cycle model and also shows steps to integrate Web applications. Using the Web services software companies are gaining publicity and their work is also reduced, due to increasing reusability. Reusability helps in sharing at low cost Web modules or components that are even expensive to use during traditional developments. And thus it makes more economic sense for end users to use Web services and service oriented architecture.

This chapter discussed various possible issues during the development and deployment of software applications. It also showed the challenges in using SOA and Web services.

REFERENCES

Arroqui, M., Mateos, C., Machado, C., & Zunino, A. (2012). Restful web services improve the efficiency of data transfer of a whole-farm simulator accessed by android smartphones. *Computers and Electronics in Agriculture, 87,* 14–18. doi:10.1016/j.compag.2012.05.016

Bernard, R. (2007). Information Lifecycle Security Risk Assessment: A tool for closing security gaps. *Computers & Security, 26,* 26-30.

Harrison, R., Lee, S. M., & West, A. A. (2004). Lifecycle engineering of modular automation machines. *Proceedings of the 2nd IEEE International Conference on Industrial Informatics (INDIN '04).*

Karande, A., Karande, M., & Meshram, M. (2011). Choreography and orchestration using business process execution language for SOA with web services. *International Journal of Computer Science Issues IJCSI, 11,* 224–232.

Lee, J., Jie, L. S., & Wang, P. F. (2015). A Framework for Composing SOAP, Non-SOAP and Non-Web Services. IEEE Transactions on Services Computing, 8(2).

Lee, J., Lee, S.-J., Chen, H.-M., & Hsu, K.-H. (2013). Itinerary-Based Mobile Agent as a Basis for Distributed OSGi Services. *IEEE Transactions on Computers, 62*(10), 1988–2000. doi:10.1109/TC.2012.107

Li, S-H., Li-hong, T., & Dong, G. (2009). Research and implementation of related technology for a logistics information system based on SOA. Journal of University of Science and Technology Beijing, 31(1).

Lin, K. J., & Chang, S. H. (2010). A service accountability framework for QoS service management and engineering. Springer.

Mateos, C., Rodriguez, J. M., & Zunino, A. (2015). A tool to improve code-first web services discoverability through text mining techniques. *Software, Practice & Experience, 45*(7), 925–948. doi:10.1002pe.2268

Meng, R., & He, C. (2013). A Comparison of Approaches to Web Service Evolution, International Conference on Computer Sciences and Applications. *Proc. ACM First Int'l Workshop Software Architectures and Mobility.*

Ouni, A., Gaikovina, R. K., Kessentini, M., & Inoue, K. (2015). Web service antipatterns detection using genetic programming. *Proc. Genetic Evol. Comput. Conf.,* 1351–1358. 10.1145/2739480.2754724

Ouni, A., Kessentini, M., Inoue, K., & Cinneide, M. O. (2017). Search-based web service antipatterns detection. IEEE Transactions on Services, 10(4).

Pautasso, C., & Wilde, E. (2009). Why is the web loosely coupled? a multi-faceted metric for service design. In *Proceedings of the 18th international conference on World wide web* (pp. 911–920). ACM. 10.1145/1526709.1526832

Potti, P. K., Ahuja, S., Umapathy, K., & Prodanoff, Z. (2012). Comparing performance of web service interaction styles: Soap vs. rest. *Proceedings of the Conference on Information Systems Applied Research*, 2167, 1508.

Rawat, S., & Sah, A. (2012). An Approach to Enhance the Software and Services of Health Care Centre, Computer Eng. and Intelligent Systems. *IISTE, 3*(7), 2222–2863.

Rawat, S. & Sah, A. (2013). An Approach to Integrate Heterogeneous Web Applications. *IJCA, 70*(23).

Richardson, L., Ruby, S., Burgess, C. J., & Leey, M. (2008). RESTful web services Can genetic programming improve software effort estimation? a comparative evaluation. *Information and Software Technology, 43*(14), 863–873.

Sah, A., Rawat, S., & Pundir, S. (2012). Design, Implementation and Integration of Heterogeneous Applications. *IJCA, 54*(5).

Wesley, A., & Brebner, P. (2009). Service-oriented performance modeling the mule enterprise service bus (esb) loan broker application. In *Software Engineering and Advanced Applications, SEAA'09. 35th Euromicro Conference on* (pp. 404–411). IEEE.

Zhang, J., Zhang, X., Chang, Y., & Lin, K. (2012). The Implementation of a Dependency Matrix-based QoS Diagnosis Support in SOA Middleware. *ICST Transactions on eBusiness, 12*, 7-9.

Zhou, B., Yin, K., Jiang, H., & Zhang, S. (2011). QoS-based Selection of Multi-Granularity Web Services for the Composition. *Journal of Software, VOL., 6*(3), 366–373.

KEY TERMS AND DEFINITIONS

Enterprise Applications: Applications made for enterprises (it includes small, medium, or large-scale enterprises) are called enterprise applications.

SOA: Service-oriented architecture (SOA) is a set of principles, policies, standards, guidelines, agreements, and requirements for shared infrastructure. SOA is an information sharing architecture; it increases abstraction and autonomy.

SOAP: Simple object access protocol (SOAP) is an XML-based informing convention for trading data among enterprise applications. SOAP aids in intercommunication between enterprise web applications that use web services.

Web Services: A web service is any bit of programming that makes it accessible over the web and uses an existing XML informing framework. Its main goal is interoperability between enterprises.

WSDL: Web services description language (WSDL) is a configuration for portraying a web service's interface. The WSDL record is the postcard, which has the address of the web and thus benefits all the usefulness that the customer needs.

XML: XML stands for extensible mark-up language. XML is a tool for data transportation and data storage in platform- and language-neutral way. XML plays an important role in the exchange of a wide variety of data on the web. XML is not completely a computer language; it is very much human readable and user extensible.

Chapter 3
Integrating Tagging Software in Web Application

Karan Gupta
University of Delhi, India

Anita Goel
University of Delhi, India

ABSTRACT

Tag software is included in web applications to facilitate categorization and classification of information. Generally, freely available tag software is adapted or new code written to incorporate tagging. However, there is an absence of requirement and design document for tagging, even academically. It becomes difficult to know the features that can be included in tag software; also, not all features may be required. This chapter presents a framework for integration of tag software in web applications. The framework has four components corresponding to phases of the software development lifecycle. For requirement, a weighted requirement checklist is presented to ease requirement selection. A metric, software estimation, is defined for quantifying selected requirement. A logical design defined for design phase displays interaction of entities with users. For development, best mechanisms are suggested to web applications. Software engineering artefacts are provided to help during testing. A case study is presented where estimation and design is applied to freely available tag software.

INTRODUCTION

The popularity of Web applications has increased tremendously over the last decade. Nowadays, Web applications are available for almost every field, like, medicine, sports, news, and education. With the increasing popularity of Web application, large amount of information is stored in Web in various forms like text, audio and video. To ease burden of users for managing large amount of information, Web applications incorporate tag software.

Tag software incorporated in a Web application improves the search process for a resource. Tag software allows the user to add keywords (also known as tags) to a resource. The resource for tagging may

DOI: 10.4018/978-1-5225-5384-7.ch003

be a video, audio, blog, books etc. Tags added to a resource, generally, describe the resource but can also define its type, its use, pros and cons or something entirely different. Tag software is used in a variety of Web applications, like, products available for sale in an online retail site and albums in a music site.

Several options exist to include tagging functionality in a Web application, like, using free tag software, adapting a freely available tagging code or writing a new code for tagging. The most commonly followed approach is to adapt free tag software to suit the needs of a Web application. The code is modified and customized to match the appearance of Web application. Alternatively, Web applications may write their own new code. Although software exists in form of free tag systems and freely available code, there is no mention of a document stating requirements and design of the tagging functionality. Generally, tagging functionality is integrated on-the-fly depending on the whims and fancy of developer and stated requirements of a Web application.

However, the use of ad-hoc approach increases the burden of Web application owner and developer during the development of tag software. Since, a requirement specification document for tag software is not available, integrating tag software in a Web application becomes difficult. When creating new tag software for integration, the task of requirement elicitation has to be repeated every time, a new. Moreover, the requirement elicited during the requirement specification phase, may not be complete as the Web application has limited or little knowledge about the features of tag software. If existing tag software is to be integrated in a Web application, it becomes a cumbersome task to identify if complete features are provided by the existing tag software or some specific features have been skipped. Also, some features that may be useless for the Web application may remain undetected, which shall affect the size and performance of the tag software.

Due to the absence of availability of design document for tag software, the task of updating the tag software becomes difficult. When using existing tag software, the developer needs to arrive at the architecture of tag software using reverse engineering, i.e. deriving design from the code. This task is required to be performed when in existing tag software, a new feature is required to be added, or an existing one is to be modified or deleted. Also, there is a need to understand the design of tag software in case of error diagnosis. When writing new tag software, the developer needs to start from scratch and repeat the design process every time new code is written.

Here, the authors provide a framework for easing integration of the tag software into a Web application in accordance with various phases of the software development lifecycle. The framework is an enhanced version of our earlier framework, presented in (Gupta & Goel, 2013). The enhanced framework helps the Web application owner and the developer in understanding the tag software. In the enhanced framework, there are four components: (1) Tagging_Requirement, (2) Tagging_Design, (3) Tagging_Development, and (4) Tagging_Test. Each component has a specific task like Tagging_Requirement component performs the task of requirement generation. The four components interact with the Web application owner and the developer to generate and integrate the tagging software into Web application. Each component is divided into sub-components so as to ease the completion of its task.

The enhanced framework is used by both the developer and the owner of Web application during integration of tagging software into a Web application. The developer uses the enhanced framework to understand the structure of the tagging software. The owner of Web application gets to know the different kinds of users accessing the tagging software as well as the different kinds of features provided by the tagging software. The owner of the Web application is able to select these requirements.

The enhanced framework uses various software engineering artefacts developed in (Gupta & Goel, 2014) to ease the task of integration of tag software into Web application. During the requirement elicitation phase, the enhanced framework uses the weighted requirement checklists for elicitation of the requirements. The checklist aids developer and Web application owner in deciding requirements. The weights have been assigned based on a survey conducted on two freely available tag software and six Web applications to determine presence/absence of an operation. Based on this survey, weights have been generated and applied in the checklists, where they depict popularity of associated object. Moreover, an estimation mechanism has been also defined to quantify software selected using weighted requirements checklist. The requirements checklist lists the features available in the tag software.

Also, the estimation mechanism developed in (Gupta & Goel, 2014) is used for quantifying the requirements selected. The estimation mechanism assesses the popularity of tag software based on the weights present in the weighted requirements checklist. The estimation mechanism also acts as a comparison tool when many software applications are present for selection.

During the design phase, the enhanced framework uses the logical view developed in (Gupta & Goel, 2014) to provide the design for tag software in Web application. The design for tag software is in a form of logical view which acts as a design document. The logical view facilitates the Web application owner and the developers in understanding the architecture of tag software. Also, a set of weighted requirements checklist is provided for tag software.

The enhanced framework suggests the best possible mechanism for the development and integration of tagging software in to a Web application during the development phase. The Web application can either choose integrating freely available software or adapt freely available software. The Web application can also choose to develop its own tag software. The decision is based on the features selected by the Web application during the requirement elicitation phase. The enhanced framework also aids in the testing of the integrated tagging software. The framework uses the weighted requirement checklists described above and the estimation mechanism to verify and validate the tagging software.

In this chapter, next section introduces the users of tagging software in Web application. Subsequent sections take up the succession of topics as follows: the enhanced framework for integration of tag software in Web application is illustrated; components of the enhanced framework are explained in succession, namely, Tagging_Requirement which is the requirement elicitation phase; Tagging_Design; Tagging_Development; and, Tagging_Test. A case study demonstrating the usage of the weighted requirement checklist and the logical design is given, followed by Related Works and Future Research Directions. The last section is the conclusion.

USERS OF TAGGING

Users access the tag software present in a Web application to perform different tasks, like, add a resource, add a tag to resource, delete a tag, view a tag cloud, etc. Also, there is a need to perform maintenance task for tag software.

In an earlier paper (Gupta & Goel, 2012), the authors have identified actors of tag software using use case based approach, based on their interaction with the tag software. The three kinds of users have been identified as follows:

- Web Application is the software in which the tag software is integrated.
- Administrator is the person performing task of maintaining the tagging functionality.
- Visitor is a user who uses the tag software.

The interaction between Web application and tag software occurs during incorporation of tagging functionality into the Web application. The settings and features to be included in the tag software in a Web application are identified then and there.

TAGGING FRAMEWORK

The tagging framework helps the user during integration of tagging functionality in a Web application. The framework aids the user during requirement elicitation and specification based on the need of Web application. It also helps the developer in understanding structure of the existing software and adapting or developing software based on the user's requirement. The framework assists by providing software engineering documents and artefacts, as and when required, during the software development lifecycle.

In an earlier work (Gupta & Goel, 2013), the authors have developed a framework for integrating tagging software into Web application. The framework has been developed in accordance with the different phases of the software development lifecycle. An enhanced version of the tagging framework is presented here. Figure 1 shows the tagging framework.

The enhanced framework has four components: (1) Tagging Requirement, (2) Tagging Design, (3) Tagging Development, and (4) Tagging Test. The Tagging Requirement is for use during the requirement elicitation phase as it handles elicitation of requirements for tag software. In the design phase, Tagging Design provides a design outline for tag software to the developer. The Tagging Development component

Figure 1. Tagging Framework

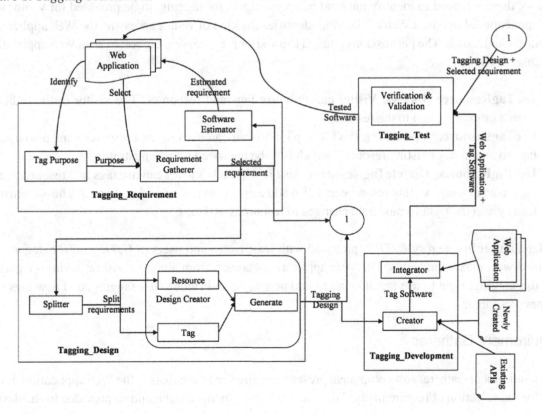

eases implementation of tagging by providing the developer with guidelines and software engineering artefacts required during the implementation of the tagging functionality. The Tagging Test component is for use during testing of integrated tagging functionality in a Web application.

The framework can be used during the various phases of the software development process. Both the Web application and the developer benefit from the framework presented here. During the requirement phase, the framework helps in defining the requirements of tagging. The framework helps in the design phase by providing an outline of design of tagging. The framework is also used during the testing phase for verification and validation of the integrated tagging functionality. The different components of the framework are discussed in the following sections.

Tagging Requirement Component

The Tagging_Requirement is for use during the requirement phase of Web application software development lifecycle. The Tagging_Requirement component performs the task of requirement elicitation. The component consists of three sub-components, namely, Tag Purpose, Requirement Gatherer and Software Estimator. In the following subsections, the authors discuss each of the sub-components.

Tag Purpose

The Tag Purpose sub-component requires the Web application to define the purpose for which tag is incorporated in a Web application. Here, the Web application needs to identify the type of resource on which tagging is to be applied. This is required for defining features of the resource, for tagging.

Also, there is a need to identify the kind of access rights for tagging, to be provided for visitor to a Web application. For this, a Web application identifies the kind of visitor accessing the Web application (Gupta & Goel, 2012). The permissions granted to a visitor for accessing tag software in Web application are categorized as -

- **UseTagResource (UsTR):** Visitor can only use tags and resources. The visitor cannot edit resource or tags applied to the resource.
- **UseTagResource_UpdateTag (UsTR_UpT):** Visitor can use tags and resources and also update tags to an already existing resource, which is to be approved by administrator.
- **UseTagResource_UpdateTagResource (UsTR_UpTR):** Visitor can use tags and resources, add tags to an already existing resource and also add a new resource and add tags to it. The administrator is given the right to moderate changes to resources and tags.

Here, a user in category *UsTR* is provided with least rights and users in *UsTR_UpTR* category are provided with maximum rights. The Web application chooses from among a visitor having - rights to only use tagging; right to use tagging and to add new tags; and right to use tagging, add new tags and add new resource.

Requirement Gatherer

The Requirement Gatherer sub-component presents requirement checklists to the Web application developer for the selection of requirements. The selected requirements are the output provided to the design phase of Web application for tagging. The selected requirements are the functionality and feature of tagging that are provided in a Web application.

The sub-component provides Web application with the weighted requirements checklist for tag software. Also, the output of previous sub-component - tag purpose, is an input to this sub-component. The type of resource defined during tag purpose, is used to include the features of a resource in the checklist. The access rights identified during tag purpose for a visitor, determines the features that are to be made available to a visitor of the tag software. The checklists based on the kind of resource and access rights of a visitor, are provided to a Web application developer for selection of features.

There are three components of the checklist, namely, (1) Tagging home, (2) Tagging dashboard, and (3) Tagging parameter. Three levels of weights are associated to the features defined in the checklist. The requirements from the checklist are selected by a Web application based on its need, and, the weights defined in the checklist on the basis of the popularity of a feature.

Requirement Checklist

The authors have identified and categorized the various requirements of the tagging software based on the three components of tag software – Tagging Home, Tagging Parameters and Tagging Dashboard, in the authors' previous work (Gupta & Goel, 2012).

Tagging Home component is visible to a visitor where the visitor can perform tasks for which permissions have been granted. *Tagging Home checklist* consists of functionality like view resource list, view tags applied to a resource and view tag cloud. During requirement specification, the checklist helps in deciding the functionality to be provided to a visitor of the site.

Tagging Parameters is used by Web application to outline functionality to be provided by the tag software. *Tagging Parameter Checklist* lists the functionality and parameters that are desired in the tag software. It includes functionality like settings for resource sharing, resource subscription and tag description, bundling of tags and display setting of tag cloud. During the requirement phase, the list can be used to identify the parameters and their settings.

Tagging Dashboard is used by administrator for maintaining and updating tag software. Both, resource and tags are to be maintained. *Tagging Dashboard Checklist* includes functionality like add, delete, update a resource, update tags etc. The list helps in determining the functionality to be included in the dashboard and their parameters. Table 1 illustrates a small portion of tagging home checklist. The complete checklist is presented in (Gupta & Goel, 2012).

Weighted Requirement Checklist

The checklists introduced above do not differentiate between the requirements listed, thus treat all the requirements as equal. However, there is a need for assigning weights to the requirements as there are some features in the software which are the basis of its existence. Secondly, in software, there are some additional features which are not necessary in nature but act as value-addition and enhance already existing software. Also, software contains features that are rare in nature and are used seldom in the software. Based on this understanding of features of tag software, the authors have divided the entities, sub-entities and operations of tag software into three different categories, namely, one that is indispensable in nature, as the tag software would not work without them. The second category consists of those features that

Table 1. Tagging Home Checklist

Tagging Home Components	Classification	Parameters
Subscribe	Resource Subscription	Subscribe to a resource
	Tag Subscription	Tag (Tag name)
		Remove
		Edit (Tag name, User-specified name)
Use	Resource Sharing	Same as Table 2 Setting (Resource Sharing)
	Tag Cloud	Search tags
		Resource with same tag
		User's resource with same tag
		System's resource with same tag

are commonly used in tag software and act as value-addition while enhancing the tag software but they are not indispensable by nature. The third category of features of the tag software is those that are rare by nature. These features are used very sporadically in tag software.

For performing this division of features into categories, weights are assigned to each entity, their sub-entities and their operations, based on popularity of features in the tag software. The weighted entities, their weighted sub-entities and weighted operations are then listed into weighted requirement checklists. The generated weighted requirement checklists are used to select operations of the tag software, for inclusion in a Web application. Next, Tag Software Selected (TSS) is calculated to quantify tag software that has been selected using the checklist.

Weights and Categories

The weights have been generated based on a survey performed on various freely available tag software and Web applications which were using tag software. The survey was conducted on two freely available tag software and six Web applications from different walks of life, with integrated tag software. The freely available tag software used here are *FreeTag* (Luk, 2010) and DotTag (2007). The six Web applications used for survey are *delicious.com, flickr.com, citeulike.org, youtube.com, quikr.com* and *jamendo.com*. The software identified for survey were examined for presence/absence of each operation of the tag software. Then, a summation was performed to find the number of times that feature appears in them.

Since the summation value can range from 0 to 8 for each entity, sub-entity and operation, the authors have grouped these into three to stabilize the assignment of category to entities, sub-entities and operations. The three groups represent the set of three categories that have been defined for entities, sub-entities and operations of the tag software. Each of these three categories signifies a different level of popularity and are listed as follows-

- Most-Popular is assigned to those entities, sub-entities and operations with highest level of popularity for tag software. This category is assigned for a summation value between 6 and 8. The weight '3' is associated to the entities, sub-entities and operations falling in this category.

- Intermediate-Popular contains entities, sub-entities and operations that have a summation value between 3 and 5 and are assigned weight 2. These entities are available in limited number of software but not in all the software.
- Least-Popular is assigned to entities, sub-entities and operations with lowest level of popularity for tag software and is assigned weight '1'. The corresponding summation value for the entities, sub-entities and operations is between 0 and 2.

As indicated by their names, 'Most-Popular' depicts highest level of popularity and 'Least-Popular' the lowest. In the next subsection, the weighted requirement checklists are depicted.

Checklists

The requirement checklist for tag software is used as a basis for the weighted requirement checklist presented in this section. The requirement checklist is enhanced to weighted requirement checklist, firstly, by organizing the components entities based on logical view of the tag software. Secondly, weights are assigned to entities, sub-entities and operations in the tag software, based on level of popularity. The weights assigned to each entity, sub-entity and operation is depicted by 'W', in the checklist. The entities, sub-entities and their operations, along with their associated weights are rearranged into three checklists, namely, (1) Tagging Home, (2) Tagging Dashboard, and (3) Tagging Parameters.

Table 2 shows the weighted software requirement checklist for component - Tagging Home. Tagging Home consists of operations that are provided to a visitor of tag software. During requirement specification, this checklist helps in selecting operations that are to be made accessible to visitor. There are nine entities (or part of entities, in case, incomplete entity is included) present in tagging home checklist. These entities allow a visitor to accomplish various tasks which may be popular, like view a resource. Tasks like view a resource are popular, because these tasks are the basic tasks for users without which tag software would not work effectively. On other hand, tasks like subscribe to a tag or share a tag are termed as less popular, since these tasks provide additional capability to the user but do not affect the working of tag software. The detailed checklists can be seen in (Gupta & Goel, 2014).

The three weighted checklists are used for selecting operations of tag software. The selection of entities, sub-entities and operations from checklist is based on the weights assigned to them. For each checklist, firstly, all popular entities (entities with weight '3') are considered for selection. This is followed by consideration of sub-entities in these entities for selection and of operations present in these sub-entities. A similar method is followed for selection of less popular entities, sub-entities and operations.

The output of Requirement Gatherer is for use during the design phase and the testing phase, and, to the software estimator.

Software Estimator

Tag software uses Software Estimator to quantify the number of features selected by a Web application for tag software. The Software Estimator sub-component performs estimation using the weighted requirement checklist estimation formula, discussed in (Gupta & Goel, 2014). The weighted percentage for each checklist is estimated. Also, the value of Tag Software Selected (TSS) is calculated that provides an estimate of the features selected for tag software.

Table 2. Weighted Checklist for Component - Tagging Home

Entity		Sub-Entity		Operation	
Name	**W**	**Name**	**W**	**Name**	**W**
Resource View	3	View	3	View, Title, Resource, Resource Features*, Tags, Date	3
Resource List	2	Type	3	View a list of All resources, View a Tag-Specific list, View a User-Specific list	3
		Details	3	Title, Resource, Resource Features*, Tags, Date	3
		Order	1	Order by Normal/Reverse, Change Timeframe Setting	2
				Order by Date/Alphabetical, Change Entries per page setting, Change Detail level Setting	1
Research Search	2	Search	3	All Resources, User Resources	3
Resource Subscription	3	Subscribe	3	Subscribe, Delete Subscription	3
Resource Use	2	Sharing	3	Share	3
Tag Cloud	1	View	1	(System), (User), (Related)	2
				(Resource), Order(Alphabet/Count), Order(Cloud/List), On(Bundled/Unbundled/All), Usage(1/2/5), Show/Hide Count	1
		Use	2	(System), (User), (Related), Search Tags	2
				(Resource)	1
Tag Search	1	Search	1	Text Box	1
Tag Subscription	1	Subscribe	1	Subscribe Tag, Remove	1
Tag Sharing	1	Sharing	1	Share	1

Estimation

The estimation mechanism estimates the software selected using weighted requirement checklists. It is based on weights assigned to entities, sub-entities and operations of tag software. The estimation mechanism uses a metric - *weighted percentage*, to perform the estimation. Weighted percentage is *sum of weights of some specific selected objects divided by total of weights of all objects present in the set and expressed as a ratio or fraction of 100*. The benefit of using weighted percentage is that (1) Number of features selected is quantified, (2) Weights are integrated into calculation of number of features selected, and (3) Final value is nearest estimation of the total number of features selected.

Here, estimation mechanism consists of a set of three formulas. The estimation is performed at three levels, namely, component, entity and sub-entity. At each level, a formula is used for estimation of weights assigned at that level. As shown below, formula (1), (2) and (3) are used for estimating features in tag software at sub-entity, entity and component level, respectively. The formula at component level provides the weighted percentage for each checklist.

$$SE_j = \frac{\sum_{i=1}^{n_o} po_i \times o_i}{\sum_{i=1}^{n_o} o_i} \tag{1}$$

$$E_k = \frac{\sum_{j=1}^{n_s} ps_j \times s_j \times SE_j}{\sum_{j=1}^{n_s} s_j} \tag{2}$$

$$CL = \frac{\sum_{k=1}^{n_e} pe_k \times e_k \times E_k}{\sum_{k=1}^{n_e} e_k} \times 100 \tag{3}$$

Here,

- po_i, ps_j, pe_k is presence of ith operation, j^{th} sub-entity, k^{th} entity, respectively (1 if selected, 0 otherwise)
- o_i, s_j, e_k is weight assigned to i^{th} operation, j^{th} sub-entity, k^{th} entity, respectively
- n_o is total number of operations in a sub-entity
- SE_j is weighted percentage of jth sub-entity
- n_s denotes total number of sub-entity in entity
- E_k denotes weighted percentage of kth entity
- n_e is total number of entities in the checklist
- CL denotes the weighted percentage for the checklist under consideration

The estimation is performed in the following manner -

- First, formula (1) is used for calculating weighted percentage of a sub-entity. It estimates number of operations selected in a sub-entity and denotes percentage of sub-entity selected.
- Next, weighted percentage of an entity is calculated using formula (2). The weighted percentage of entity estimates the number of sub-entities selected in an entity and denotes percentage of entity selected.
- Finally, weighted percentage of a checklist is calculated using formula (3). The weighted percentage of a checklist estimates the number of entities that have been selected in that checklist and denotes the percentage of checklist selected.

The value, arrived at end of this complete estimation, denotes the weighted percentage of operations selected in an individual checklist. Finally, the calculated value for three checklists is used to estimate the tag software selected using weighted requirement checklists. The software selected is determined by calculating average of the weighted percentage of checklists and is denoted as TSS (Tag Software Selected). TSS indicates quantity of tag software selected using weighted requirement checklists. A higher value denotes that many important features are available in tag software, while, a lower value indicates that important features are left out from tag software. The value of TSS provides an estimate of the features selected for tag software. This value is used by the software estimator sub-component as an output which is provided to the Web application.

Tagging Design Component

The Tagging_Design component facilitates creation of a design document for tag software in Web application. The component can be used during design phase of the software development lifecycle. The component consists of two sub-components, Splitter and Design Creator.

Splitter

The Splitter sub-component performs the task of splitting incoming requirements into the basic buildings blocks of tag software, namely, resource and tag. The sub-component takes input from Requirement Gatherer sub-component of Tagging_Requirement to produce split requirements. The output of Splitter is the split requirements, which, is an input to sub-component Design Creator.

Design Creator

The Design Creator sub-component performs the task of creating a design for tag software in Web application. The sub-component accepts split requirements from its peer sub-component, Splitter. The design consists of two different logical views, namely, Resource and Tag. The Design Creator sub-component develops the Logical view, as discussed in the authors' previous work (Gupta & Goel, 2014).

The logical view is developed by performing a use-case analysis of different Web applications using tag software. The logical view is based on guidelines discussed in Kruchten (1995). The logical view is displayed in form of different interactions that occur between actors and entities of the tag software. The interactions have been divided into main building blocks of that tag software – resource and tag (Smith, 2007). The following subsections discuss entities that form the part of the logical view of tag software followed by displaying of the logical view.

Entities

The entities of tag software are determined using a use-case analysis of various Web applications. The entities represent the principal functionalities that are provided by the tag software. For example, "Resource Update Single" entity contains all the operation concerned with update of a single resource. The entities defined here are further divided into a group of sub-entities. Sub-entities denote the main tasks performed within a particular entity and act as an extension of entity. Each sub-entity contains a group of operations which are provided to actors as a service. For each resource and tag, seven entities have been identified, on basis of their functionality. The entities for the resource and the task they handle are listed as follows:

- Resource Update Single (R_SingleUp) handles updating of a single resource. It allows user to perform tasks like, add a resource and delete a resource.
- Resource Update Multiple (R_MultipleUp) handles updating of multiple resources. It allows a user to perform tasks like, delete a common tag from all the resources.

- Resource Subscription (R_Sub) handles subscription to a resource. A user can perform tasks, like, subscribe to a resource, edit a subscription, etc.
- Resource Use (R_Use) handles sharing of a resource. The user can share information about a resource with other Web sites or select sites for sharing.
- Resource View (R_View) handles viewing a resource and its associated features.
- Resource Search (R_Search) handles searching for a resource. A user can perform tasks, like, search for a resource, search for a user's resource, etc.
- Resource List (R_List) handles viewing a set of resources in form of a list. The resources in a list may be some random resource or specific to a tag (all resources contain that tag). It allows the users to sort the resource list based on different criteria.

The entities identified for the tag and the task they handle are listed as follows:

- Tag Update (T_Up) handles maintenance of tags. A user can create, delete and edit tags.
- Tag Bundle (T_Bundle) handles maintenance of tag bundle. A user can perform tasks, like, create, edit or delete tag bundles.
- Tag Description (T_Descp) handles maintenance of description of tags. It allows user to perform tasks, like, create, edit or delete a description.
- Tag Subscription (T_Sub) handles maintenance of subscriptions of tags. A user can perform tasks like subscribing to a tag.
- Tag Search (T_Search) handles searching of tags. A user can perform tasks, like, search for tags.
- Tag Sharing (T_Share) handles sharing of tags. A user can share information about a tag with other Web sites or select sites for sharing.
- Tag Cloud (T_Cloud) handles tag cloud. A tag cloud can be generated at four different levels, system, user, related and resource. This entity allows user to use tag cloud for finding a tag, finding resources associated with a tag, etc.

The entities identified provide different functionalities to actors of the tag software. The entities can be extended for any new feature or functionality.

Logical View of Tag software

The logical view of tag software is based on the two main building blocks of tag software - resource and tag. Here, the authors present logical view for tag component of the software. The complete logical design is available in an earlier work (Gupta & Goel, 2014). In this view, the interaction of Web application, one of the actors, with the tag software is not shown as that occurs only once during creation. Moreover, only the entities and sub-entities are depicted but the operations are not depicted.

The logical view for resource consists of seven entities - Resource Update Single, Resource Update Multiple, Resource Subscription, Resource Use, Resource View, Resource Search, Resource List View and Resource List Use. Figure 1 shows entities and sub-entities and the interactions that occur between the actors of tag software, the entities and their sub-parts. It can be seen that two kinds of actors – Administrator and Visitor interact with the entities. The administrator can access all entities present in *Resource* except *Resource View and Resource Subscription*. The visitor can also access all entities available in *Resource* using two access permission levels, 'UsTR' and 'UsTR_UpTR'.

Figure 2 shows logical view for tag. The view shows entities, sub-entities and their interaction with users – visitor and administrator. The logical view for tag consists of seven entities, namely, Tag Update, Tag Bundle, Tag Description, Tag Subscription, Tag Search, Tag Sharing and Tag Cloud. A visitor having access permissions *UsTR* and *UsTR_UpT* interact with entities present in this view. The administrator can access all entities in tag except *T_Search* and *T_Subscription*.

For the actor *visitor*, there are three levels of permissions that can be granted while accessing the tag software. Some interactions with tag software are common to a visitor having any type of permission. To avoid repetition, the authors show the interaction of each entity with respect to the lowest level of visitor that has access to it. In other words, for visitor (UsTR_UpTR), only those interactions are shown that are not common with visitor (UsTR) and visitor (UsTR_UpT). Similarly, for visitor (UsTR_UpT), interactions not common with visitor (UsTR) are shown.

The logical view is used for integrating tag software into a Web application. In next section, the authors describe the weighted requirement checklists that categorize requirements of tag software based on their popularity and help the Web application in selecting entity, sub-entity and operations of tag software.

Tagging Development Component

Tagging_Development is used during the implementation phase of software development cycle to create and integrate tag software in a Web application. The component is further divided into two sub-components, namely, Creator and Integrator.

Figure 2. Logical View for Tag

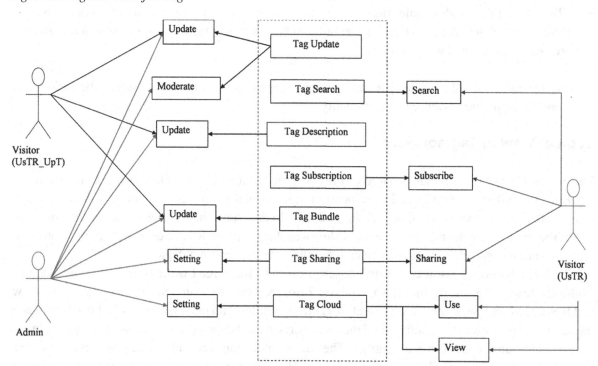

The *Creator* sub-component is active during the integration of tag software in a Web application. This sub-component helps the developer in performing the task of creating the tag software. For creating the software, three options are available as follows:

- Use freely available existing software,
- Use freely available code,
- Write new code.

Any of the three methods can be used for creation of the tag software. The sub-component helps the developer in selection of the method for creation by providing an estimate as to which option is best among available ones.

Integrator sub-component provides guidelines for integrating tag software in a Web application. These guidelines are used by the developer to easily integrate the tag software. Table 3 shows the guidelines for integration of tag software in a Web application. It can be seen that in the resource part, the entities accessible to visitor (UsTR) are to be placed in public domain and is accessible to any visitor of the site. On the other hand, entities available to visitor (UsTR_UpTR) are login-based. Similar premise is followed for the tag part of the structural design.

Tagging Test Component

Tagging_Test is used during testing of the integrated tag software. There is only one sub-component in this component, namely, Verification & Validation. The requirements output of Tagging_Requirement component, design output of Tagging_Design and Web application integrated with tag software developed during Tagging_Development is input to this component. The component verifies and validates the developed software based on selected requirements and design.

The *Verification* sub-component checks and concludes whether tagging software is built right. The *Validation* sub-component validates the integrated tagging software with the help of Web application owner so that it can be verified that tagging software "is built right."

The framework explained here expedites integration of tagging software into Web application. It uses the logical view, weighted requirement checklists and the associated estimation mechanism that have been developed here to aid the integration of tag software into Web application.

Table 3. Guidelines for integration of Tag Software

Part of Structural Design	User Type	Specific Instruction
	Visitor (UsTR)	Public Domain
Resource	Visitor (UsTR_UpTR)	Login-based
	Administrator	Private Domain
	Visitor (UsTR)	Public Domain
Tag	Visitor (UsTR_UpT)	Login-based
	Administrator	Private Domain

CASE STUDY

This section presents illustration of application of Weighted Requirement Checklist and estimation mechanism to free available tagging software. Table 4 and 5 show the weighted requirement checklist for the two components Tagging Home and Tagging Dashboard, respectively, when applied to FreeTag and DotTag. In the tables, features present in software are listed in their respective columns. 'F/D' denotes weighted percentage at entity and sub-entity level. For example, in entity "Resource List" and sub-entity "View", the weighted percentage value at sub-entity level for FreeTag is '0.77', and for DotTag is '0.77'. A value '0' denotes that the feature is not present in the tag software under study.

Also, as seen from the table, entity Resource Subscription, Resource Use, Tag Subscription and Tag Sharing are not provided in Tagging Home, neither by FreeTag nor by DotTag, therefore, not present in table. Also, Table 4 depicts the difference between the operations provided by FreeTag and DotTag in case of Resource View entity. DotTag provides only two operations while FreeTag provides five operations for the Resource View entity. Also, Table 5 depicts that Tag bundle and Tag Description entities are not defined by both FreeTag and DotTag software. After estimating the weighted percentage at entity and sub-entity level, weighted percentage for component level is estimated. The result of estimation is depicted in Figure 3.

Table 4. Result of Applying Weighted Requirement Checklist for Tagging Home

Entities		Sub -Entities		Operations – FreeTag	Operations – DotTag
Name	**F/D**	**Name**	**F/D**	**Name-FreeTag**	**Name-DotTag**
Resource View	0.83/0.33	View	0.83/0.33	View,Tags,Title,Resource,Date	View,Tags
Resource List	0.77/0.77	Type	1/1	View a list of All resources, View a Tag-Specific list, View a User-Specific list	View a list of All resources, View a Tag-Specific list, View a User-Specific list
		Detail	0.79/0.79	Title, Resource, Tags, Date	Title, Resource, Tags, Date
Tag Cloud	0.41/0.41	View	0.33/0.33	On(System), On(Related)	On(System), On(Related)
		Use	0.44/0.44	On(System), On(Related)	On(System), On(Related)

Table 5. Result of Applying Weighted Requirement Checklist for Tagging Dashboard

Entities		Sub -Entities		Operations – FreeTag	Operations – DotTag
Name	**W**	**Name**	**W**	**Name**	**Name**
Resource List	0.77/0.77	Type	1/1	View a list of All resources, View a Tag-Specific list, View a User-Specific list	View a list of All resources, View a Tag-Specific list, View a User-Specific list
		Details	0.79/0.79	Title, Resource, Tags, Date	Title, Resource, Tags, Date
Resource Update Single	0.19/0.19	Update	0.25/0.25	Delete all Tags from a resource	Delete all Tags from a resource
Tag Update	0.75/0.75	Update - Resource	1/1	Add Tag, Delete Tag, Edit Tag	Add Tag, Delete Tag, Edit Tag

Figure 3. Estimation of functionalities provided by FreeTag and DotTag

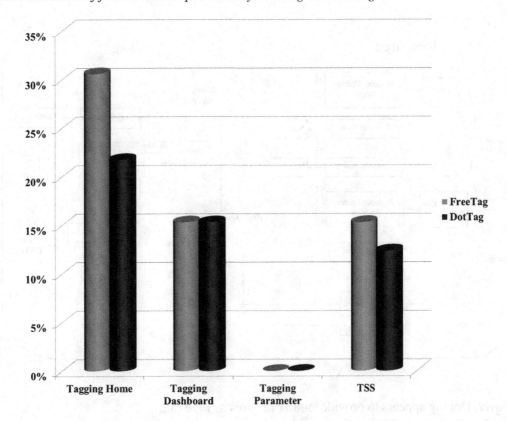

Based on these tables, the value of TSS is calculated for both software. Here, TSS for FreeTag is 15.31% and TSS for DotTag is 12.37% as illustrated in Figure 3.

It is evident from these different statistics that requirement specification covers all the features provided by the free available software. In fact, they provide more than double the number of features. In case of requirement specification, one can see that out of the three checklists, both the software provide limited features in only two checklists, due to their existence in form of APIs. The benefit of having requirement specification is evident, since the two freely available software have a limited number of available features; a Web application integrating any of these would be severely handicapped.

Moreover, the Web application is benefited as it selects the requirement based on the popularity of a feature. Also, as illustrated, using estimation mechanism, Web application can then calculate tag software being selected. In case of different existing software being available for selection, Web application can use our estimation mechanisms as a tool to compare them.

Applying the Logical View

Similar to the illustration performed of the weighted requirement checklist, the authors here present an illustration of application of the logical view to freely available tagging software. After the study, it was found that features defined in tag software FreeTag and DotTag, are all present in logical view. However, the number of features in FreeTag and DotTag are far less than the possible features that tag software can provide, as depicted in Figure 4.

Figure 4. Logical view for FreeTag and DotTag

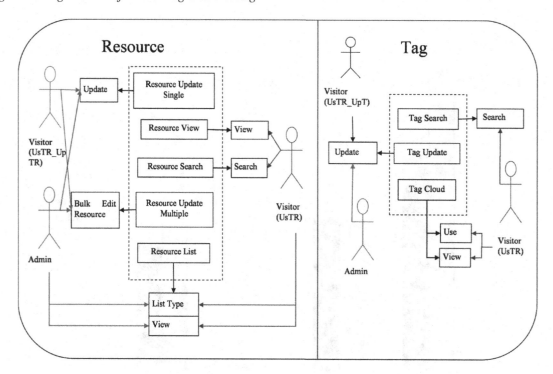

Moreover, DotTag appears to provide similar features as FreeTag.

It is evident from these different statistics that all the features provided by the free available software are present in our design. Moreover, being in the form of APIs, the effect of their existence shows in the design part. The benefit of having design document is evident, since the two freely available software have a limited number of available features; a Web application integrating any of these would be severely handicapped. Also, developer can use logical view to understand architecture of required tag software.

RELATED WORK

Academically, research work has been carried out in relation to identification of tags present in the tag software. Golder and Huberman (2009) presented information dynamics in "collaborative tagging systems". They standardized the form a tag takes in tag software by categorizing them into seven classes. Robu, Halpin & Shepherd (2009) focused on categorization of tags. Here, Delicious.com is used to find a categorization scheme that emerges from unsupervised tagging by individual users.

The users of the tag software have been studied as well with researchers defining their behaviors and categories. Santos-Neto, Condon, Andrade, Iamnitchi & Ripeanu (2009) characterized interest sharing in the system using pair wise similarity between users' activity. Körner, Kern, Grahsl & Strohmaier (2010) distinguished users of tag software into two parts - categorizers, who categorize resources, and, describers, who describe resources using tags. Schöfegger, Körner, Singer, & Granitzer (2012) used supervised learning mechanisms to analyze online tagged academic literature and extracted user characteristics from tagging behavior.

Also, several research publications exist for the effect of poorly managed tags in the tag software. Helic, Strohmaier, Trattner, Muhr & Lerman (2011) apply a pragmatic framework to folksonomies to provide improved navigability of social tagging systems and to evaluate different folksonomy algorithms from a pragmatic perspective. Tournéa & Godoy (2012) performed an empirical study on value of tags in resource classification to increase the quality of resource classification. Zhang, Tang & Zhang (2012) examined temporal factor in users' tagging behaviors for ranking tags. Bracamonte & Poblete (2011) presented an algorithm which propagates tags automatically in a graph structure, called visual-semantic graph. Manimaran & Duraiswamy (2012) proposed an algorithm to detect overlapping communities in folksonomies using complete hypergraph structure.

Tags have also been used in requirement elicitation phase. Connolly, Keenan & Ryder (2008) developed a prototype tool which is used during the requirement phase for storing and tagging the elicited requirements. Ossher et al. (2009) used tagging during pre-requirement phase for easing process of filtering important business concerns. Tags are also used in fields such as recommender system (Milicevic, Nanopoulos, & Ivanovic, 2010) and RFID systems (Juels, Rivest, & Szydlo, 2003; Carbunar, Ramanathan, Koyutürk, Jagannathan, & Grama, 2009).

Tags have also been used to develop an insight into the emotions of the users (Shalin Hai-Jew, 2017). The author used Robert Plutchik's Wheel of Emotion to achieve this task. Li et. al, (2016) on the other hand, conducted a survey to understand what people tag about an image. A comprehensive treatise of three closely linked problems (i.e., image tag assignment, refinement, and tag-based image retrieval) was presented. Gruetze, Yao, & Krestel (2015) focused on time-dependent hashtag usage of the Twitter community to annotate shared Web-text documents. They introduced a framework for time-dependent hashtag recommendation models and introduced two content-based models. Wu, Yao, Xu, Tong, & Lu (2016) put their focus on the content based tag recommendation and proposed a generative model (Tag2Word), where they generated the words based on the tag-word distribution as well as the tag itself.

An extensive search for research papers related to requirement and design document for tag software in Web application was carried out but did not yield any results. Generally, a freely available tagging functionality like FreeTag, DotTag is adapted and incorporated into a Web application. However, Web application owner has little or limited knowledge about possible features that tag software can provide, and their need in a tag software. For developer, absence of any kind of design document hardens task of updating tag software. Thus, a design and specification of features are required for easing integration of tag software into Web application.

FUTURE RESEARCH DIRECTIONS

The concepts described in this chapter can be extended in the following manner: (1) development of tools for tag software, (2) tag software in cloud, and (3) standalone tag software.

Developing a Tool

The framework for integration of tagging software into Web application can be developed into a tool which eases this process. The tool would help the Web application owner and the developer during the various stages of the software development lifecycle. In addition to this, the software engineering artefacts can also be used as a basis for creating standalone tools for the tag software.

A tool can be developed that allows the Web application to select the requirements of tag software. The tool allows the selection of requirements based on proposed weighted requirement checklists for tag software. After the selection of features of tag software, the tool would provide an estimate of the software selected to the Web application. The estimate depicts the popularity of the tag software selected using the estimation mechanism. The tool would provide four values to the Web application, one for each of three component checklist and the fourth representing TSS for the whole software.

A second tool can be developed for the design phase of tag software. The tool would provide the architecture of the tag software to its users. The developer could use this architecture to easily construct outline of the tag software. The developer only needs to provide the selected operations as input. Based on input provided by the developer, the tool would generate the design and display it to the developer.

The third tool, that could be developed, would allow the users to compare their requirement specification and their design with freely available existing software. The tool could take its input from the earlier described tools and then display the result of comparison based on the presence/absence of the selected features in freely available existing software.

Tag Software in Cloud

The tag software can also be incorporated into a cloud, where, it could be used to categorize and classify the data stored on the cloud. In such a case, the requirements and design of the tag software have to be adapted based on the features of the cloud. This adaptation would need a detailed study of cloud features and infrastructure. Moreover, the mechanism to be used for making tag software available on the cloud would have to be studied.

Standalone Tag Software

In case of the tag software being developed as standalone software, there will be a need to adapt requirement and design accordingly. A study would have to be performed in this regard. The study would also have to consider whether the standalone tag software, being developed, is in the form of a Web application or a desktop software, as this would affect the requirements and design tremendously.

CONCLUSION

In this chapter, an enhanced framework is presented that eases the process of integrating tag software into Web application. The framework helps during requirement elicitation phase by providing weight requirement checklists to the Web application. The checklist acts as a selection tool for the Web application where all features of tag software can be viewed and selected based on their need and importance in software. During design phase, the framework provides a logical view for tag software. The logical view provides a structure to tag software which aids developer in understanding internal working of the software. It also helps during updating and analysis of the tag software by developer. Also, during development phase, the framework advises the best available option for development. The framework helps in testing phase by using the software engineering artefacts like weighted requirement checklists to verify and validate the developed tagging software.

REFERENCES

Bracamonte, T., & Poblete, B. (2011). Automatic image tagging through information propagation in a query log based graph structure. In K. S. Candan, S. Panchanathan, B. Prabhakaran, H. Sundaram, W.-c. Feng, & N. Sebe (Eds.), *Proceedings of the 19th ACM international conference on Multimedia* (pp. 1201-1204). Scottsdale, AZ: ACM. 10.1145/2072298.2071974

Cameron, R. (2004). *CiteULike*. Retrieved August 15, 2017, from http://www.citeulike.org/

Carbunar, B., Ramanathan, M. K., Koyutürk, M., Jagannathan, S., & Gram, A. (2009). Efficient tag detection in RFID systems. *Journal of Parallel and Distributed Computing, 69*(2), 180–196. doi:10.1016/j.jpdc.2008.06.013

Connolly, D., Keenan, F., & Ryder, B. (2008). Tag Oriented Agile Requirements Identification. In *Proceedings of the 15th Annual IEEE International Conference and Workshop on the Engineering of Computer Based Systems* (pp. 497-498). Belfast, UK: IEEE Computer Society.

DotTag. (2007). *DotTag*. Retrieved August 12, 2017, from http://dottag.codeplex.com/

Flickr. (2004). *Flickr*. Retrieved August 10, 2017, from http://www.flickr.com/

Golder, S. A., & Huberman, B. A. (2005). *The Structure of Collaborative Tagging Systems*. Computing Research Repository.

Gruetze, T., Yao, G., & Krestel, R. (2015). Learning Temporal Tagging Behaviour. In *Proceedings of the 24th International Conference on World Wide Web (WWW '15 Companion)*. ACM. 10.1145/2740908.2741701

Gupta, K., & Goel, A. (2012). Tagging requirements for web application. In S. K. Aggarwal, T. V. Prabhakar, V. Varma, & S. Padmanabhuni (Eds.), *Proceedings of the 5th India Software Engineering Conference* (pp. 81-90). Kanpur, India: ACM. 10.1145/2134254.2134269

Gupta, K., & Goel, A. (2013). Software Engineering for Tagging Software. *International Journal of Software Engineering and its Application, 4*(4), 65-76. doi: 10.5121/ijsea.2013.4406

Gupta, K., & Goel, A. (2014). Requirement Estimation and Design of Tag software in Web Application. *International Journal of Information Technology and Web Engineering, 9*(2), 1–19. doi:10.4018/ijitwe.2014040101

Hai-Jew, S. (2017). Flickering Emotions: Feeling-Based Associations from Related Tags Networks on Flickr. In S. Hai-Jew (Ed.), *Social Media Data Extraction and Content Analysis* (pp. 296–341). Hershey, PA: IGI Global; doi:10.4018/978-1-5225-0648-5.ch010

Helic, D., Strohmaier, M., Trattner, C., Muhr, M., & Lerman, K. (2011).Pragmatic evaluation of folksonomies. In S. Srinivasan, K. Ramamritham, A. Kumar, M. P. Ravindra, E. Bertino, & R. Kumar (Eds.), *Proceedings of the 20th international conference on World wide web*, (pp. 417-426). Hyderabad, India: ACM.

Hurley, C., & Chen, S. (2003). *Delicious*. Retrieved August 30, 2012, from https://del.icio.us/ http://www.delicious.com/

Jamendo. (2005). *Jamendo - The #1 platform for free music*. Retrieved August 28, 2017, from http://www.jamendo.com/en

Juels, A., Rivest, R. L., & Szydlo, M. (2003). The blocker tag: selective blocking of RFID tags for consumer privacy. In S. Jajodia, V. Atluri, & T. Jaeger (Eds.), *Proceedings of the 10th ACM conference on Computer and communications security* (pp. 103-111). Washington, DC: ACM. 10.1145/948109.948126

Körner, C., Kern, R., Grahsl, H.-P., & Strohmaier, M. (2010). Of categorizers and describers: an evaluation of quantitative measures for tagging motivation. In M. H. Chignell, & E. Toms (Eds.), *Proceedings of the 21st ACM conference on Hypertext and hypermedia* (pp. 157-166). Toronto, Canada: ACM. 10.1145/1810617.1810645

Kruchten, P. (1995). The 4+1 View Model of Architecture. *IEEE Software*, *12*(6), 42–50. doi:10.1109/52.469759

Li, X., Uricchio, T., Ballan, L., Bertini, M., Snoek, G. M., & Bimbo, A. (2016). Socializing the Semantic Gap: A Comparative Survey on Image Tag Assignment, Refinement, and Retrieval. *ACM Computing Survey, 49*(1). DOI: 10.1145/2906152

Luk, G. (2010). *GitHub*. Retrieved August 25, 2017, from https://github.com/freetag

Manimaran, P., & Duraiswamy, K. (2012). Identifying Overlying Group of People through Clustering. *International Journal of Information Technology and Web Engineering*, *7*(4), 50–60. doi:10.4018/jitwe.2012100104

Milicevic, A. K., Nanopoulos, A., & Ivanovic, M. (2010). Social tagging in recommender systems: A survey of the state-of-the-art and possible extensions. *Artificial Intelligence Review*, *33*(3), 187–209. doi:10.100710462-009-9153-2

Ossher, H., Amid, D., Anaby-Tavor, A., Bellamy, R., Callery, M., Desmond, M., & ... . (2009).Using tagging to identify and organize concerns during pre-requirements analysis. In *Proceedings of the 2009 ICSE Workshop on Aspect-Oriented Requirements Engineering and Architecture Design* (pp. 25-30). IEEE Computer Society. 10.1109/EA.2009.5071580

Quikr. (2008). *Quikr Classifieds: Post Free Classifieds Ads, Search Free Classified Ads online*. Retrieved July 31, 2017, from http://www.quikr.com/

Robu, V., Halpin, H., & Shepherd, H. (2009). Emergence of consensus and shared vocabularies in collaborative tagging systems. *ACM Transactions on the Web*, *3*(4), 1–34. doi:10.1145/1594173.1594176

Santos-Neto, E., Condon, D., Andrade, N., Iamnitchi, A., & Ripeanu, M. (2009).Individual and social behavior in tagging systems. In C. Cattuto, G. Ruffo, & F. Menczer (Eds.), *Proceedings of the 20th ACM conference on Hypertext and hypermedia* (pp. 183-192). Torino, Italy: ACM. 10.1145/1557914.1557947

Schöfegger, K., Körner, C., Singer, P., & Granitzer, M. (2012).Learning user characteristics from social tagging behavior.In E. V. Munson, & M. Strohmaier (Eds.), *Proceedings of the 23rd ACM conference on Hypertext and social media* (pp. 207-212). Milwaukee, WI: ACM. 10.1145/2309996.2310031

Smith, G. (2007). *Tagging: people-powered metadata for the social web*. New Riders Publishing.

Tournéa, N., & Godoy, D. (2012). Evaluating tag filtering techniques for web resource classification in folksonomies. *Expert Systems with Applications*, *39*(10), 9723–9729. doi:10.1016/j.eswa.2012.02.088

Wu, Y., Yao, Y., Xu, F., Tong, H., & Lu, J. (2016). Tag2Word: Using Tags to Generate Words for Content Based Tag Recommendation. In *Proceedings of the 25th ACM International on Conference on Information and Knowledge Management (CIKM '16)*. ACM. 10.1145/2983323.2983682

YouTube. (2005). *YouTube*. Retrieved August 21, 2017, from http://www.youtube.com/

Zhang, L., Tang, J., & Zhang, M. (2012).Integrating temporal usage pattern into personalized tag prediction. In Q. Z. Sheng, G. Wang, C. S. Jensen, & G. Xu (Eds.), *Proceedings of the 14th Asia-Pacific international conference on Web Technologies and Applications* (pp. 354-365). Kunming, China: Springer-Verlag. 10.1007/978-3-642-29253-8_30

KEY TERMS AND DEFINITIONS

Developer: The entity who has the responsibility of developing and integrating the tagging software into a web application. The entity can be a single person or a group of people or an organization.

Framework: A mechanism that has been developed to ease the completion of a task. It can be a set of guidelines or it may provide various artefacts during its lifecycle.

Resource: The main entity/object which is displayed/maintained in the web application. It can be a research paper or a video file or an audio file or a bookmark. Basically, it is the object that is showcased in the web application.

Tag: A keyword that is associated to the resource. The tag can be related or unrelated to the resource. It may or may not describe any personal information about the resource. It could also be used to classify or categorize the resource.

Tag Software: The software that allows the classification and categorization of the data among other benefits.

Web Application: The software/application into which the tagging software has to be integrated.

Web Application Owner: The entity who owns the web application. This entity can be a single person or a group of people or a company.

Chapter 4
UX Challenges and Best Practices in Designing Web and Mobile Solutions

Fernando Almeida
University of Porto, Portugal

José Augusto Monteiro
Higher Polytechnic Institute of Gaya, Portugal

ABSTRACT

The design of web and mobile applications is one of the most challenging fields of the current informa-tion technology landscape. Increasingly, companies intend to have a strong presence in the information society, which allows them to advertise their products, services, make online business, interact with customers, among others. However, the development and design of web and mobile solutions have numerous challenges and best practices that should be known and applied. In this chapter, the authors adopt a qualitative methodology based on multiple case studies that allow them to identify a total of six challenges and best practices that are later confronted and compared with the recent findings on the coverage of the topic.

INTRODUCTION

Information technologies (IT) have become fundamental in professional and personal daily life. Through the Internet, people access to a wide range of services from their workplace, home or on the go. At the same time, the growth and constant evolution of the Internet have also increased the number of devices capable of accessing information. This popularization of the Internet, coupled with the idea of using mobile devices while performing daily tasks, contributed to the increased number of ubiquitous and heterogeneous devices.

Design of interfaces is a relevant field of study in the context of Human-Computer Interaction (HCI). This area is notoriously challenging and requires multidisciplinary competences from the teams respon-sible for the design and conception of Web and mobile interfaces. One of the great challenges is to create

DOI: 10.4018/978-1-5225-5384-7.ch004

"clean" and intuitive interfaces, and the success of a design task depends to a large extent on the use of elements with which user identifies himself. User Experience (UX) emerges as a highly debated and subjective topic. It is difficult to objectively and directly tell how to create good user experiences, but it is possible to learn how to design an interface to provide a satisfying experience for someone who uses it, and identify all aspects of user interaction with that product, service, or environment.

The challenge of making Web application accessible to all devices is extremely demanding. In the Web context, we can already find a significant number of challenges and best practices, but that significantly increases in the mobile paradigm. While on desktops there is more space for a variety of ways to trigger actions and provide a greater volume of information to a user that is only focused on the computer, mobile devices need to prioritize the information that needs to be accessible, which divides his/her attention between the smartphone, tablet or other devices with other routine activities. In addition, care must be taken regarding the size and memory of the mobile devices. It is to overcome these challenges that the UX has become increasingly important and more present in mobile app projects.

This paper intends to identify and synthesize the main challenges and suggested best practices in designing Web and mobile solutions. For that, we adopt a multiple case study approach and we compare the results obtained from those interviews with the recent findings identified in the literature. The paper is organized as follows: we initially perform a review of literature in the field of Web design process, development frameworks and UX experience. After that initial phase, we present the adopted methodology, highlighting the structure of the multiple case study approach. Then, we analyze and discuss the findings obtained from the case studies and we compare it with the recent advancements of the literature in the field. Finally, future research directions are hinted and the conclusions of this work are drawn.

BACKGROUND

The Evolution of Web Design Process

The evolution of Web design process can be characterized by a set of notable events in terms of technology advances and social paradigms. Its evolution can be grouped in eight phases (Work, 2011): (i) the early 1990s; (ii) the mid-1990s; (iii) the late 1990s; (iv) the year 2000; (v) the early to mid-2000s; (vi) the mid-2000s; (vii) the late 2000s; and (viii) the mobile Web.

Tim Berners-Lee invented the World Wide Web (WWW) in 1989. The Web was originally conceived and developed to meet the demand for automatic information-sharing among scientists in universities and institutes around the world (CERN, 2013). The first websites of the early 1990s were text-based sites in a single column format. Websites looked like a series of text documents strung together by inline links.

In the mid-1990s the design process evolved to table-based sites and online page builders. The use of tables made it possible to create multiple column websites, allowing a better content organization and navigation layout. Websites have gained color and images. Animated text, scrolling text and gif images started to become popular across many sites. Frame pages have also become a popular way to clearly distinguish the body of the website from the sidebar navigation. Furthermore, websites started to be built online in a very simple and intuitive way. Free page builders, such as Angelfire or Geocities, allowed anyone with an Internet connection to build their own website.

The late 1990s were characterized by the rise of Flash. Flash was introduced in 1996 and turned possible to design any shapes, layouts, animations, interactions, use any font and all this in just one tool

(Ruluks, 2014). Therefore, many websites became a combination of table-based design and Flash elements for spice.

The year 2000 was marked by the Internet bubble that resulted from the excessive valuation of Internet-based businesses. At the technical level, we were assisted by the emergence of Cascade Style Sheets (CSS). The CSS allowed designers to separate website content from Web design. The design elements of a webpage, such as background, color, text size, etc. could be defined in the style sheet rather than in the HTML of the page itself. This development made it easier to maintain and update a website, improved the consistency of design, turned possible presenting different styles to different viewers, and brought search engine optimization benefits (Bradley, 2006).

The early to mid-2000s assisted to the rise of JavaScript. Web designers began ditching tables and using JavaScript for page layouts. JavaScript was used to extend functionality in websites. It is a relatively easy language and it is executed on the client side. Additionally, JavaScript executed relatively fast at the user side. As the code is executed on the user's computer, results and processing are completed almost instantly depending on the task, avoiding the need to be processed on the site's Web server and sent back to the user consuming local as well as server bandwidth (Jscripters, 2017).

In the mid-2000s appeared the semantic Web (later called, Web 3.0). It is characterized as a Web design movement aimed at allowing machines to understand Web pages as well as human viewers do. The information becomes knowledge on analyzing the semantics and the network information or knowledge is the semantic Web. The concept integrates different data sources, such as semantic rules, ontologies, Web services and Web processes (Vanitha, Yasudha, Venkatesh, Ravindra, & Lakshmi, 2011).

In the late 2000s we had the advent of Web 2.0. The Web design began to take a turn towards interactive content and Web applications. Asynchronous JavaScript and XML (AJAX) were used for smoothing content transitions and application development. Web 2.0 introduced the idea of Web as a platform. The concept was such that instead of thinking of the Web as a place where browsers viewed data through small windows on the readers' screens, the Web was actually the platform that allowed people to get things done (Darwish & Lakhtaria, 2011).

Finally, the mobile Web emerged as a new paradigm. Currently, more and more websites have alternative mobile version(s) or they have a responsive design that dynamically adapts to the dimensions of the mobile device. Mobile sites contain the bare essentials of the regular websites and offer a different experience of use. Webpages are formatted tall and skinny rather than short and wide. Navigation is minimal and reduced to the most important areas of the site. Furthermore, mobile sites often communicate with the device's hardware to determine location, movement, etc. The challenges of building mobile solutions started to appear in terms of performance, deal with different size and resolutions, battery consumption, and portability (Wasserman, 2010; Inukollu, Keshamoni, Kang, & Inukollu, 2014).

The Role of Frameworks

HTML / CSS frameworks have contributed to automate the process of website creation, namely when a fast result is demanded to develop multi-device solutions (Almeida & Monteiro, 2017). Another concern that is automated by some of these frameworks is the accessibility needs (Power, Freire, & Petrie, 2009). Most of the frameworks provide accessibility features with low development efforts. Despite the disadvantage of carrying more code lines than necessary, when the framework does not have a significant impact on website loading, its adoption can be beneficial to productivity.

The motivation that leads us to an update of the comparative analysis was to perceive how frameworks adoption is evolving and to compare how accessibility phenomena are dealt by "CSS framework industry" (Almeida & Monteiro, 2017). Accessibility feature was introduced as a new dimension to the analysis table, but we decided to keep the same framework products, used in the last analysis: Bootstrap, Foundation, Skeleton, YAML, Gumby, Kube, and ResponsiveAeon. A resume of what the role of each dimension is in the analysis is provided below. To avoid discrepancies in the analysis and make a clear understanding, a small number of dimensions were selected: License, Version, Documentation, Pre-processor, Browser Support, Accessibility, Popularity, and Size. These dimensions are briefly taken up below.

- **License:** Identifies what license applies to each framework. The matter of this dimension is to help the reader to choose the framework according to the legal implications regarding the use of this tool.
- **Version:** Versioning is a practice common in informatics products. This dimension indicates the evolution of the framework and could be helpful to analyze its maturity. For a given framework, the period of time between versions and the modifications included in each version may act as an indicator of how the framework evolves.
- **Documentation:** This contains the main information about the use and the examples of the framework. In the context of the software, documentation is very relevant to developers. The volume and quality of the documentation of software products may influence decisively the choice of the developers. This dimension was classified in three levels: (i) Good – meaning information is well documented and well organized; (ii) Relevant – meaning the documentation is minimalist and useful; (iii) Poor – meaning the documentation is weak or non-existent.
- **Pre-Processor:** In this dimension the pre-processors of each framework were identified. However, some frameworks do not resort to it. The pre-processor is relevant for the gain of productivity in the creation of the style sheets, allowing more organized styles without redundant code. The benefits of the pre-processor are not consensual among all Web developers. There are developers who consider them a waste of time because of the slow learning curve.
- **Browser Support:** This dimension is responsible for identification of browsers where the framework works according to the industry standards. Considering the purpose of the frameworks of this study, compatibility with the existing browsers is relevant for the success of the product. The more different browsers and the framework are compatible, the more useful it becomes for the developers. This implies the importance of keeping up with the most popular browsers. So, in the plan of browsers, stay updated is very relevant.
- **Accessibility:** The accessibility dimension identifies if the framework has accessibility features and if it follows accessibility standards. In this dimension information was provided about if the framework uses accessibility features or not and if they are standard compatible.
- **Popularity:** The preferences of the developers for one product or another, most of the times, are influenced by the reputation of the product in the community. This dimension evaluates the popularity of the frameworks by using GitHub as reference. The option for GitHub takes into consideration three factors: (i) the need to obtain the software to "take a look"; (ii) the wide use of GitHub by developers' community; (iii) the fact that GitHub may act as a common reference to all the selected frameworks on this study. The importance of this dimension is to present to the reader a view of the users' interest in a certain framework.

- **Size:** The size dimension was considered to inform the reader about the length of the package of each framework. The reference used is based on the size of the pack at the moment of download. When considering that the frameworks add a set of the components to the projects, it is necessary to enlighten developers on which is the "amount of software" they will add to each new project. Table 1 (in the Appendix) presents the selected frameworks for the study and the dimensions necessary to analyze each one.

Comparing the present analysis (Table 1) with the analysis referred by Almeida and Monteiro (2017), the following can be observed: (i) Most of the frameworks have updated versions, except Skeleton and Responsive Aeon. (ii) Most of the packages have slightly increased its size, probably caused by the introduction of new features. Kube is the exception; there are no perceived changes; (iii) Bootstrap continues to increase substantially its popularity. Foundation is growing up too and the other frameworks have no significant changes on popularity; (iv) Other dimensions have no perceived changes.

The recent adopted dimension, Accessibility, is assumed by Bootstrap, Foundation and YAML, as a native feature. The other frameworks do not mention its adoption or how to deal with it.

The Concept of User Experience

Kujala, Roto, Vainio-Mattila, Karapanos, & Sinnelä (2011) stated that user experience (UX) is a multi-dimensional concept. In fact, it doesn't apply only to the design area, but also to other disciplines such as business, philosophy, anthropology, cognitive science, social science, amongst others (Sun & May, 2014). According to Stokes (2013), UX can be defined as "all the experiences (physical, sensory, emotional and mental) that a person has when interacting with a digital tool". Associated with the notion of UX certain other concepts appear that are relevant (Stokes, 2013):

- User experience design (UXD or UED) is defined as "the process of applying proven principles, techniques and features to a digital tool to create and optimize the user experience";
- User-centered design (UCD) is defined as "the design philosophy that prioritizes the user's needs and wants above all else, and places the user at the center of the entire experience. This often entails research and testing with real users of the site or product";
- User interface (UI) is defined as "the user-facing part of the tool or platform - the part of the actual website, application or tool that the user interacts with";
- Usability is defined as "how user friendly, efficient and slick the digital product is".

The advancement of the UX followed the evolution of the Web design paradigm. According to Buley (2015) there are four key points:

- **Usable Experiences (1980s - 1990s):** The goal of interface design was focused on efficiency, reduced errors, and the ability to execute expert functions;
- **Transactional Experiences (1990s - 2000s):** UX evolved to support non-experts engaging with transactional systems. Success is measured in conversions and increased revenue;
- **Ubiquitous Experiences (2000s - 2010s):** Connected devices and increased competition turned UX goals toward omni-channel adoption and repeat use;

- **Transformative Experiences (2010s - Current):** Software enabled new UX enhanced business models, powered by the user data and network effects.

UX is increasingly focused on understanding user behavior. Hassenzahl, Eckoldt, Diefenbach, Laschke, Lenz, & Kim (2013) advocate that psychological needs to understand and categorizes experience. The idea is to design "experience patterns", which will help to capture the essence of an experience and inscribe it into artifacts. The concept of emotional user experience has been debated in the literature and Jokinen (2015) stated that this concept is dependent on the user's technological problem-solving tendency, frustration tendency, pre-task self-confidence, and task performance.

Robert and Lesage (2010) considered that the measurement of UX should satisfy several criteria, such as: (i) validy, (ii) reliability, (iii) sensitivity, (iv) diagnosticity, (v) selectivity, (vi) obstruction, and (vii) span. Beyond these elements, Robert and Lesage (2010) advocated that measures of UX need to be acceptable for the users, standardized, easy and rapid to use, and has a low cognitive complexity. In order to be acceptable by the user, Stokes (2013 introduced the concept of desirability and usefulness. The former intends to quantify the pleasant experience and the latter the added value to the user.

The emergence of new responsive frameworks and the growth of mobile devices have made UX even more attractive. Yadav and Barwal (2014) demonstrated that responsive designing have reduced the effort of organizations in developing and maintaining the websites for different devices. Lestari, Hardianto, and Hidayanto (2014) conducted a study to assess the user experience quality of responsive Web design for mobile devices. The findings demonstrated that responsive Web design was able to maintain a good level of user experience quality of the website, content readability and enjoyment. On the other side, responsive Web design required more scroll and click than nonresponsive one when exploring its information architecture. UX is also taking into account when designing mobile solutions for specific purposes. Stanton and Ophoff (2013) proposed a method for mobile learning that does not prescribe the content and structure, but rather facilitates the process of planning and creating a course while ensuring that the various aspects such as technology, context, usability, and pedagogy are considered along with the objectives of the course. Sun and May (2014) stated the importance of user centered and co-design methods to maximize the user experience for personalized services delivered over a mobile device. Finally, Grubert, Kranz, & Quigley (2016) suggested that design, technical, social and perceptual challenges can appear when dealing with mobile multi-device ecosystems.

METHODOLOGY

Based on the study developed by Almeida and Monteiro (2017), a qualitative methodology was employed and the emerging contributions in the field of Web and mobile development were identified and analyzed, in order to discuss their relation and pertinence to the findings obtained from the multiple case studies.

Case study research allows the exploration and understanding of complex issues. According to Zainal (2007), it can be considered a robust research method particularly when a holistic, in-depth investigation is required. Additionally, the case study research approach allows us to combine the existing theoretical knowledge with new empirical insights (Meyer, 2001; Vissak, 2010; Queirós, Faria, & Almeida, 2017). Njie and Asimiran (2014) too stated that case studies are particularly suitable to unravel a complex phenomenon or one with little information about. In the context of our work it would be relevant to identify

UX challenges and best practices that can be adopted when designing Web and mobile solutions, which is still an unexplored topic that lacks empirical validation.

As shown in Figure 1, the first stage of the methodology is conducting an extensive literature review on the subject in order to formulate a theory about approaches and challenges faced by companies when designing Web and mobile solutions. Then, we started by designing the questionnaire and defined two entity types that will let us understand the differences between two different approaches followed by companies in the field. Then, we are ready to select the cases and start the fieldwork stage. After that, each case study was written and a data analysis approach was adopted for each question of our questionnaire. Finally, in the conclusion stage we made a cross-case analysis in order to understand the common aspects and differences among each company, we compared the findings with the up-to-date literature in the field and we draw the conclusions.

For the purpose of this research, we used data collected from in-depth interviews in six case studies. Within these six case studies, we found two types of entities: in group I, we have Web Design specialized companies with core business being mainly Web / Mobile design / development and Search Engine Optimization (SEO), and in group II, we have companies in which Web Design is a fundamental point for creating information systems and e-business solutions. According to the suggestion of Yin (2009), case studies were chosen by means of theoretical rather than statistical sampling, and were carried out in close interaction with practitioners.

We divided our interview in four sequential parts: (i) contextual, (ii) diagnostic, (iii) evaluative, and (iv) strategic. The contextual dimension tries to identify the form and nature of what exists, searching for attitudes, perceptions and experiences. The full list of questions is provided below.

Figure 1. Phases of the adopted methodology

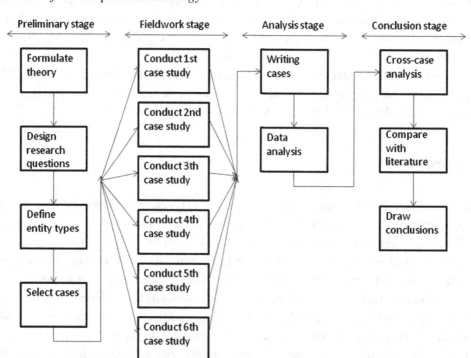

- **Q1:** What is the main business field of your company? Is it only dedicated to Web design or has it a wider IT scope?
- **Q2:** What were the main challenges faced by Web designer companies during the past years?
- **Q3:** What are the most common mistakes Web designers make?

The diagnostic dimension intends to examine the reasons or causes of what exists. It mainly tries to identify the factors that underlie particular attitudes or perceptions and why some decisions or actions are taken, or not taken. The full list of questions is provided below:

- **Q4:** What is the software development methodology adopted by your company? How important is the customer participation in this process?
- **Q5:** Did the company already adopt specific-device design? (If yes, which platforms?)
- **Q6:** Did the company already adopt any technique of adaptive or responsive design?
- **Q7:** Does your company implement Web design frameworks during the development process? (If yes, which frameworks?)

The evaluative dimension appraises the effectiveness of what exists and how objectives are achieved. The full list of questions is provided below:

- **Q8:** How are the user experiences (UX) of a Website measured?
- **Q9:** What is the perception of your company regarding the mean time of development of a Website? This time has been increased or decreased during the last years?
- **Q10:** What are the three main aspects that you consider most valuable when you use a framework for Web design?
- **Q11:** Do you consider easier to reach high levels of User Experience Design (UX) or high levels of User Interface Design (UI)?

Finally, the strategic dimension tries to identify new theories, policies, plans or actions in order to mitigate previously identified issues or propose new and improved solutions.

- **Q12:** What challenges is your business currently struggling to address?
- **Q13:** What makes your company different from your competitors?

ANALYSIS AND DISCUSSION OF RESULTS

Contextual Dimension

- **Q1:** What is the main business field of your company? Is it only dedicated to Web design or has it a wider IT scope?

Significant differences were found in the business fields adopted by the companies according to their group. Companies in the group I started their business as Web designers, but they are progressively expanding their core business to other associated areas, such as marketing, Web hosting and accounting service. This happens because their main customers are micro companies or small and medium-sized enterprises (SMEs) that typically need to have more than one specific service. The findings indicate that their human resources are more versatile and it is common to find short-term outsourcing contracts to solve specific tasks, such as accounting service, hardware repair, among others. Key competitive advantages for these companies are their contacts' network, high versatility and low response time. On the other side, companies of group II tend to be more specialized and offer higher IT intensive knowledge services. Key competitive advantages include well-established software engineering processes, high quality of services and a strong ability to do business in the international marketplace. In fact, and particularly in small companies where the internal market is reduced, it is essential to look to their business as an international business since the beginning.

The existence of low entry barriers and the abundance of Web frameworks that let clients to design and develop their own Web presence, leaded to a cannibalization of the Web design paradigm. Emberton (2011) considers Web design a decent sustenance, but a poor investment. He points out two difficulties: (i) it is differentiated on the market for starters; and (ii) projects revenue is based on fixed rates. For instance, typically the reward of a Web design company is the same if the project is a storming success or not. Based on our companies it was possible to confirm the first issue, but not the second. This can happen as new business models emerge based on access and usage rates, which are now possible by the emergence of new analytical technologies such as Google Analytics.

The companies in group II have a greater diversity of services. Some of them, particularly those most innovative, are more receptive to embrace self-cannibalization. According to Yu and Malnight (2016) self-cannibalization occurs when a company chooses to proactively replace one product or process with another that is potentially worthless. It was not possible to find evidences that company in group I also adopt a self-cannibalization strategy. Instead, they tend to move progressively for a business model strategy adopted by companies of Group II;

- **Q2:** What were the main challenges faced by Web designer companies during the past years?

During the interviews it was possible to identify four categories of challenges: (i) technology life-cycle, (ii) heterogeneity of technologies and devices, (iii) UX experience, and (iv) customer needs.

Technology life-cycle (TLC) represents the commercial gain of a product through the financial returns during its life-cycle and considering its expenses on research and development phases. The shape of the technology life cycle is often characterized as an S-curve (Park, Sung, and Kim, 2015). Evidences collected by Shahmarichatghieh, Härkönen, and Tolonen (2016) demonstrated that there is a strong bond between product life-cycle and technology life-cycle. Therefore, when a company is developing a new platform based on new technologies, it is important that they recognize if the technology is growing or disappearing. The problem in the field of Web development is even greater, because there is not only a single Web technology, but several of them. Therefore, the appearance of new frontend technologies and new devices bring new challenges to the development process. Additionally, and due to short TLC in Web platforms, there is a regular need to convert old fixed-width websites.

The high heterogeneity of technologies and devices were systematically identified as being the most difficult challenges to overcome. Increasingly, customers are asking for innovative solutions on the market that offer new services and a better user experience, which takes advantage of the natural evolution of the technology. However, a relevant question emerges: How can we ensure that the new application version keeps working on older devices?

The answer to this question is not easy. Software testing, such as portability and regression testing, helps to detect and correct this problem. However, sometimes these issues will only be identified later when the software is already in operation on the market. This causes significant financial costs, long hours of work on the bug correction and loss of image in the market.

UX experience was considered a very challenging element during the interviews. Many companies find it difficult to define the scope and limits of UX definition and this is often the main obstacle, because it isn't possible to measure and quantify UX experience, without being able to define it. In literature, Bachl, Tomitsch, Wimmer, and Grechening (2010) identified a total of eight multi-touch challenges divided into three categories, such as screen-based challenges, user-based challenges and input-based challenges. The eight elements identified by Bach et al. (2010) included: (i) affordance of screens; (ii) accessibility; (iii) multi-user support; (iv) tactile user feedback; (v) ergonomics; (vi) individual differences;; (vii) gestures and patterns; and (viii) supporting data input. Only the first three challenges previously identified were also stated as relevant in our interviews.

Vermeeren, Law, Roto, Obrist, Hoonhout, and Mattila (2010) looked into user experience evaluation methods and identified five properties that an evaluation method should have, respectively: (i) scoping; (ii) practicability; (iii) utility; (iv) specificity; and (v) scientific quality. Only the last element was not considered as fundamental during the interviews, since the companies gave more importance to its practical applicability for each client. Vermeeren et al. (2010) also identified that the main method of collecting UX experience is based on the use of surveys. In addition to this method, companies also mentioned other two relevant approaches: observation of usage behavior and customer service feedback.

Many of the previous UX challenges are common between Web and mobile platforms. However, there are other that stand out in the mobile environment. Budiu (2015) divides these challenges in terms of limitations and strengths. The limitations identified were: (i) small screen; (ii) portable equal to interruptible; (iii) single window; (iv) touchscreen; and (v) variable connectivity. On the other side, mobile devices offer unique features, such as GPS, camera, accelerometer, and voice, which potentiate the appearance of new services.

Associated with UX experience appears also the customer needs. Listening to the customer is about permanently opening the channels of communication between company and client. It's also known that identification of the customer needs is much easier than identify the customer wishes. The sales department plays a key role at this stage. The idea is to establish a close relationship with the customer and use a mix of open and closed-ended questions. The former stimulates the customer talk about their problems, needs and desires; the latter is very useful in directing choices and decisions. The adoption of agile approaches in software development has also contributed to a better identification of the customers' needs. Agile software approaches encourage the participation of the customer in the development process (Majava, Nuottila, Haapasalo, Kris, & Law, 2014). Additionally, Petersen and Wohlin (2009) revealed that customers appreciate active participation in projects as it allows them to control the project and development process and they are kept up to date. Besides that, customers are perceived by programmers as very valuable, allowing developers to have discussions and get early feedback.

In literature, it was possible to identify five additional groups of challenges (Barret, 2015; Brown, 2016):

- **Integration:** To allow seamless synchronization with third-party applications;
- **Security:** To safeguard a website against malware, hackers and delusion. As stated also by Betts (2016), security is a not only a design challenge, but also a product challenge.

- **Page Loads Speed:** To avoid hiccups and slow processing of Web pages. Two approaches emerge: (i) using caching; and (ii) adoption of content delivery networks;
- **Retention:** To keep visitors coming back to the website;
- **Balancing Mobile and Desktop:** To keep both versions functional and attractive. Two approaches emerge: (i) designing for mobile-first and gradually building up for device sizes; and (ii) content-first, where you start with content and add features bit-by-bit to accommodate devices as well as browsers.

- **Q3:** What are the most common mistakes Web designers make?

A common issue among all companies and also pointed in the previous question is the importance of listening to the customers. The customer-centric paradigm emerges in the literature as a strategy to be adopted by IT companies (Hauk & Padberg, 2016). The use of prototyping emerges as good practice in order to boost productivity and efficiency. Adiseshiah (2016) considers that prototyping can be an excellent way to achieve effective collaboration across multiple teams because it stems from a process of bringing people together, discussing a problem and moving towards solutions.

Other pointed issue stated out by companies is the support maintenance process. Often companies do not define a business model that adequately includes the maintenance phase. The costs of this phase are often ignored or not totally included, which originates a significant increase in the total cost of the project. This situation is particularly critical for companies in group I, whose profit margins are quite low.

Finally, some issues emerge in the operational phase of the application in terms of performance, expandability, accessibility and usability. These problems arise due to poor project planning at the design phase and due to a poor project risk assessment.

Diagnostic Dimension

- **Q4:** What is the software development methodology adopted by your company? How important is the customer participation in this process?

Agile methodologies have attracted increasing interest in the software development community. There is currently a very significant increase in the use of agile methodologies in the software industry, particularly in startups. The interviewed companies were very receptive to the use of agile methodologies and pointed out that there are making efforts to improve the software development process. At this level, there are concerns about ensuring a correct division of labor and guarantee high motivation of the team. There is also interest in ensuring that agile methodologies can be used on a larger scale. For this, it is necessary to look for the projects in terms of scalability, integration with traditional software development methodologies, and adoption of quality management standards (Alhazmi, Bajunaid, & Aziz, 2017; Turetken, Stojanov, & Trienekens, 2017).

All interviewed companies stated that the participation of the client is important in the Agile software development approach. However, some companies have indicated that in more complex projects or projects in traditional sectors of activity, it is sometimes difficult for the client to systematically monitor the development of the project. At this level, the role of the product owner assumes significant importance. Sverrisdottir, Ingason, and Jonasson (2014) reported that there are projects that have two product owners on the same product, where one is responsible for the business aspect and the other is responsible for technical aspects of the product.

- **Q5:** Did the company already adopt specific-device design? (if yes, which platforms?)

The majority of the companies (75%) stated that they already adopted specific-device design for Android and iOS devices. The main reported differences in terms of design between both languages are specific language elements, integration with other technologies and navigation style. Besides those elements, the study conducted by Müller (2016) identified other differences in terms of app icons, app bars, grid, typography, assets, and screen densities.

During the interviews it was possible to identify that larger companies choose to have different technological teams for development in Android and iOS. None of the companies reported significant technical development issues for these devices, but it was mentioned that it is common to launch in the market two versions of the application (Android and iOS) at different times. This situation causes difficulties in the version control system, and implies a longer development process time and a more complex maintenance process.

- **Q6:** Did the company already adopt any technique of adaptive or responsive design?

Both techniques are adopted by companies. However, some differences were found in their approach by companies from group I and group II. The companies from group I are readier to use a responsive design approach instead of an adaptive approach. This happens because the projects are typically less complex, which facilitates the adoption of responsive design frameworks that significantly help and decrease the time of application development process. On the other hand, adaptive design is more commonly used by Group II companies. The use of the JavaScript language assumes particular relevance in adaptive development paradigm.

In the literature, there are several studies that analyze and look for the differences between responsive and adaptive design paradigms. Soegaard (2017) stated that responsive design is easier and takes less work to implement. However, it affords less control over the application design on each screen size. Then, a question arises: Why is it the most popular method for creating new sites at this moment? Soegaard (2017) responded to this question by stating that there are a large number of cheap templates available for the majority of Content Management Systems (CMS), which decreases the time of development and reduce costs. Schwarz (2016) looks to the adaptive design as a more accurate, because adaptive design responds itself to the entire device environment.

Both studies of the literature review confirm the interpretation and assessments resulting from the case studies.

- **Q7:** Does your company implement Web design frameworks during the development process? (If yes, which frameworks?)

There are significant differences between the adoption of Web design frameworks for companies of group I and group II.

Group I companies use intensive responsive design frameworks, with emphasis on the adoption of Bootstrap and Skeleton. Based on the interviews, three reasons emerge for the adoption of these frameworks: (i) reduction of development time; (ii) help in the design process; and (iii) adaptation to various devices. In the literature, we can also point out other advantages such as: browser compatibility and accessibility (Kramer, 2014).

Group II companies use only sporadically responsive design frameworks. Given the complexity of some projects, the source code obtained with the use of these frameworks would have to be edited significantly. Alternatively, some of these companies have built their own development frameworks, which are more tailored to the specificities of their projects. This approach brings unequivocal benefits, but implies greater difficulties for junior programmers that typically don't have knowledge of these frameworks. Therefore, the learning curve is superior because these frameworks are not explored in an academic context.

Evaluative Dimension

- **Q8:** How are the user experiences (UX) of a Website measured?

The basic requirement for a good UX design is to meet the specific needs of the user. For that, the website needs to use visuals, layout, and architecture that truly reflect what the user expects. A/B testing was pointed by two of our interviews as a testing technique that can be used to understand the behavior of the users and to deliver more relevant information. Additionally, all companies stated that UX design goes beyond the experience with the user, but it is a process that involves all the team. Programmers, digital marketing specialists, project managers and sales team must be involved in the process of setting and optimizing the company's design. Hellweger, Wang, and Abrahamsson (2015) confirmed this vision and considered that UX design is a work that goes far beyond giving users what they say they want. It is a constant cycle that involves interactivity tests, navigation technologies, behavioral studies, origin analyzes and conversions effectiveness.

For the majority of the companies considered that it is important to implement internal and external UX metrics. However, only one company defined specific use key performance indicators (KPIs) according to each project. Instead, they typically use the Google Analytics, which is not always a good option because the KPIs that a company should monitor are solely dependent on the goal of the website. In any case, it is possible to find studies that analyze the importance of the various types of KPIs offered by Google Analytics. Hey (2016) advocates that as a first step the company should define and distinguish between macro and micro objectives. Then, Hey (2016) suggested the ten most relevant KPIs, which are: (i) number of visitors; (ii) ratio of new/returning visitors; (iii) session duration; (iv) bounce rate; (v) number of users from organic SERPs; (vi) number of newsletter opened; (vii) average page load time; (viii) average time on page; (ix) AdSense revenue; and (x) conversion rate.

- **Q9:** What is the perception of your company regarding the mean time of development of a Website? This time has been increased or decreased during the last years?

There is no consensus on this issue, but it was possible to find that all companies reported difficulties in estimating the development time of a website. In literature, we can also find several studies that look into the process of software estimation. One of the most interesting studies in the field was made by Castrounis (2015) and pointed out seven reasons: (i) the productivity and experience level of the engineer; (ii) oscillations in the schedules and possibility of illness of the collaborators; (iii) difficulties in identifying completely the functional requirements; (iv) underestimation of the work; (v) unforeseen issues with maintainability, architectural flaws/imperfections, scalability, performance, testability, etc.; (vi) time associated with R&D, architecture, mockups and prototypes; and (vii) administrative work and non-engineering related requests. There are also studies that look to the consequences of a bad estimation. Clayton (2014) pointed out five consequences: (i) loss of credibility; (ii) internal team friction; (iii) poor morale; (iv) low quality software; and (v) project failure.

Another point that doesn't reach a consensus answer is if the time of development a website has been increased or decreased during the last days. The main reason for such divergent opinions is related to the intrinsic notion of a website project. This task can be so simple as creating a Web presence using a responsive framework, but also it can include an application of much greater complexity that involves the knowledge of the business logic. In addition, the need to test a website on multiple platforms leads to an increase in the project development time.

- **Q10:** What are the three main aspects that you consider most valuable when you use a framework for Web design?

Two companies do not adopt frameworks. Therefore, the results only include data collected from four case studies. These companies identified two important criteria: (i) framework should be easy to use; and (ii) code generation quality. When the framework is easy to be used, it enables new collaborators to quickly start producing. Having a low learning curve is particularly important in the IT industry, where there is a high employee turnover (Purohit, 2016; Rhatigan, 2016). For its part, having a high quality of the produced code will allow a later ease of adaptation of the code to specific needs. All the companies, with more predominance in Group II companies, stated that the need to edit the code produced by responsive design frameworks is common in order to correct any anomalies and also to contemplate the integration with other applications.

- **Q11:** Do you consider easier to reach high levels of User Experience Design (UX) or high levels of User Interface Design (UI)?

There is consensus that UX is more difficult to define and measure than UI. This view is also broadly confirmed in the literature. Law, Van Schaik, and Roto (2014) indicate that UX is a recently established area and, therefore, it is still difficult defining the scope of UX. They also state that the adoption of UX measurements by IT companies is commonly ambivalent and skeptical. Tan, Rönkkö, and Gencel (2013) report also difficulties faced by the mobile industry to use UX measurement instruments. They found that those difficulties arise from the use of diverse definitions and terminology for usability and UX aspects and attributes, and the lack of a taxonomy for these attributes with links to well-defined measures in the literature. Finally, Sauro (2016) looks at the main challenges that organizations feel when they try to measure the UX. According to Sauro (2016), the difficulties begin immediately by defining the first steps of the process, knowing what should be measured, where to find qualified professionals, what methods to adopt, and who should lead this initiative.

Strategic Dimension

- **Q12:** What challenges is your business currently struggling to address?

Two types of challenges were mentioned in the interviews. The former related to the evolution of technology; the latter about the adaptability of the business model. In the first group, companies predict that Web programming languages will be widely used. The new paradigm is to adopt hybrid approaches that could adapt content in real time. In the second group, companies stated the importance to think globally and act punctually. The ability of innovation, and the existence of an innovation strategy, is pointed out by companies and also in literature as an important differential between market leaders and other companies. Companies that fail to innovate have the risk of losing ground competition, thereby losing key employees or simply operating inefficiently (Pisano, 2015).

Some authors in literature also make some predictions about the evolution of Web design for 2017 and beyond. Jensen (2016) predicts the following tendencies: (i) white spaces and clean designs; (ii) embracement of motion and movement; (iii) return of the gradient; (iv) shortened messaging; (v) usability over SEO; (vi) personalization of photos and videos; and (vii) accommodation of cross-device traffic. Williams (2016) state the following trends: (i) layouts that let content shine; (ii) better collaboration between designers, and between designers and developers; (iii) improved design-to-development workflows; (iv) big, bold type; (v) complex layouts rooted in graphic design principles; (vi) scalable vector graphics (SVGs); (vii) constraint-based design tools; (viii) more and brighter color; (ix) more focus on animation; (x) unique layouts; (xi) flexbox; (xii) complex CSS grid layouts; (xiii) focus on designing for content delivery, personalization, and conversion; (xiv) more focus on conversation; (xv) the fight against fake news; (xvi) more peeks inside design and content; (xvii) new designer deliverable (code created in new ways); and (xviii) virtual reality on the Web.

- **Q13:** What makes your company different from your competitors?

The differentiation between the companies is not only based on a single and isolated domain. The technological and social dimensions are both important. Companies are looking for ever more challenging projects where multidisciplinary teamwork is needed. In fact, most current competitors can become future partners. When looking to project management levels, it is expected that agile methodologies can grow even more (Kelkar, 2017).

At the technological level, there is a greater need for integrated applications built on different technologies. At this level, the role of big data emerges as the future key basis of competition for existing companies (Almeida & Calistru, 2013). Big data doesn't only represent the information inside the company. In fact, big data come from everywhere: sensors data, social media sites, digital pictures and videos, purchase transaction records, cell phone GPS signals, etc. (Mukherjee & Shaw, 2016).

Another technology that is expected to have a radical impact on the industry is the Internet of Things (IoT). Curiously, in the interviews this topic was not mentioned, much because its impact is still quite uncertain. Sánchez (2017) considers that the appearance of IoT will cause changes in the way projects are designed. The developer will have to design not just the software to a specific device, but also the entire ecosystem to predict how the application will best serve the user.

FUTURE RESEARCH DIRECTIONS

One of the main challenges in building UX for Web and Mobile platforms is the need to guarantee differentiated user experiences. In addition, the technological device used to access information should be taken into consideration. It is expected to have more and more content adapted to the device and there is increased research in the field of dynamic adaptation. For example, the content to be shown to the user should be customized according to the characteristics of the access network.

Finally, it is important to mention the growing importance of engaging customers and users in the process of building UX for Web and mobile environments. Agile methodologies adopt this principle, but there are still difficulties in integrating these external agents into the development cycle of a product, especially when we have to deal with tight deadlines and budget constraints. In an approach to deal with this issue, several companies only consider the involvement of these external agents in the validation phase. It would be relevant to investigate the impact of this approach on the final quality of the product and define a framework that could facilitate the integration of clients and final users in the research and design phases. It would also be interesting to test the impact of this suggested approach in terms of UX.

CONCLUSION

Currently, companies need to have multiple contact channels to interact with their current and potential customers. Increasingly, Web-enabled mobile development solutions are being sought. This situation originates changes in the process of modeling and application development, with the growing need to adopt new techniques and frameworks. Numerous challenges are placed to Web design companies in order to create immersive user experiences, personalized for each user and distinct according to the characteristics and features of the access device.

The challenges in terms of UX are most common in the Web and mobile environment. At this level, six types of challenges were identified, respectively: (i) short technology life-cycle; (ii) heterogeneity of technologies and devices; (iii) measurement of UX experience; (iv) identification of customer needs; (v) choosing a Web/mobile design framework; and (vi) emergence of new technologies and business models. It is also important to conclude that it is not possible to place these challenges in two distinct groups (e.g., Web and mobile), since the same user can access the application from a Web or mobile interface. However, in the mobile platform these challenges become even more demanding, particularly in an environment where we have a high heterogeneity of technologies and devices.

Finally, in terms of best practices, it was also possible to identify six groups: (i) importance of listening to the customers; adoption of prototyping techniques; use of the A/B testing approach; have a good project planning that is sufficiently flexible to be reactive; include the maintenance phase in the business plan and implement internal and external UX metrics.

REFERENCES

Adiseshiah, E. (2016). *UX and prototyping - identifying problems and prototyping solutions for better UX design*. Retrieved July 14, 2017, from https://www.justinmind.com/blog/identifying-problems-and-prototyping-solutions-for-better-ux-design/

Alhazmi, E., Bajunaid, W., & Aziz, A. (2017). Important success aspects for total quality management in software development. *International Journal of Computers and Applications, 157*(8), 8–11. doi:10.5120/ijca2017912783

Almeida, F., & Calistru, C. (2013). The main challenges and issues of big data management. *International Journal of Research Studies in Computing, 2*(1), 11–20. doi:10.5861/ijrsc.2012.209

Almeida, F., & Monteiro, J. (2017). Approaches and Principles for UX Web Experiences. *International Journal of Information Technology and Web Engineering, 12*(2), 49–65. doi:10.4018/IJITWE.2017040103

Bachl, S., Tomitsch, M., Wimmer, C., & Grechening, T. (2010). Challenges for designing the user experience of multi-touch interfaces. *Proceedings of the ACM Symposium on Engineering Interactive Computing Systems*, 1-6.

Barret, L. (2015). *Web design and development in 2016: common challenges.* Retrieved July 7, 2017, from http://blog.debugme.eu/common-challenges-development/

Betts, G. (2016). *Security vs. UX: how to reconcile one of the biggest challenges in interface design.* Retrieved July 14, 2017, from https://www.fastcodesign.com/3059293/security-vs-ux-how-to-reconcile-one-of-the-biggest-challenges-in-interface-design

Bradley, S. (2006). *The Benefits Of Cascading Style Sheets.* Vanseo Design. Retrieved July 4, 2017, from http://vanseodesign.com/css/benefits-of-cascading-style-sheets/

Brown, E. (2016). *7 biggest challenges of Web design.* Retrieved July 7, 2017, from https://www.designmantic.com/blog/infographics/7-biggest-web-design-challenges/

Budiu, R. (2015). *Mobile user experience: limitations and strengths.* Nielsen Norman Group. Retrieved July 17, 2017, from https://www.nngroup.com/articles/mobile-ux/

Buley, L. (2015). *How to modernize user experience?* Forrester Research. Retrieved July 6, 2017, from http://www.tandemseven.com/wp-content/uploads/2015/03/How_To_Modernize_User_Exp.pdf

Castrounis, A. (2015). *Why software development time estimation doesn't work and alternative approaches.* Retrieved July 12, 2017, from https://www.innoarchitech.com/why-software-development-time-estimation-does-not-work-alternative-approaches/

CERN. (2013). *The birth of the Web.* Retrieved July 4, 2017, from https://home.cern/topics/birth-web

Clayton, R. (2014). *Software estimation is a losing game.* Retrieved July 12, 2017, from https://rclayton.silvrback.com/software-estimation-is-a-losing-game

Darwish, A., & Lakhtaria, K. (2011). The impact of the new Web 2.0 technologies in communication, development, and revolutions of societies. *Journal of Advances in Information Technology, 2*(4), 204–216. doi:10.4304/jait.2.4.204-216

Emberton, O. (2011). *Why we gave up Web design after 10 successful years.* Retrieved July 7, 2017, from https://silktide.com/why-we-gave-up-web-design-after-10-successful-years/

Grubert, J., Kranz, M., & Quigley, A. (2016). Challenges in mobile multi-device ecosystem. *The Journal of Mobile User Experience, 5*(5), 1–22.

Hassenzahl, M., Eckoldt, K., Diefenbach, S., Laschke, M., Lenz, E., & Kim, J. (2013). Designing moments of meaning and pleasure, experience design and happiness. *International Journal of Design*, 7(3), 21–31.

Hauk, J., & Padberg, J. (2016). *The Customer in the Center of Digital Transformation*. Detecon Management Report. Retrieved July 10, 2017, from https://www.detecon.com/sites/default/files/dmr_crm_special_heft_e_01_2016_1.pdf

Hellweger, S., Wang, X., & Abrahamsson, P. (2015). *The contemporary understanding of user experience in practice*. Retrieved July 12, 2017, from https://arxiv.org/ftp/arxiv/papers/1503/1503.01732.pdf

Hey, I. (2016). *Google Analytics: these are the 10 most important KPIs for your website*. Retrieved July 12, 2017, from https://en.onpage.org/blog/google-analytics-these-are-the-10-most-important-kpis-for-your-website

Inukollu, V., Keshamoni, D., Kang, T., & Inukollu, M. (2014). Factors influencing quality of mobile apps: Role of mobile app development life cycle. *International Journal of Software Engineering and Its Applications*, 5(5), 15–34. doi:10.5121/ijsea.2014.5502

Jensen, K. (2016). *How Web design evolved in 2016: simplify or perish*. Retrieved July 13, 2017, from https://www.bopdesign.com/bop-blog/2016/10/web-design-evolved-2016-simplify-perish/

Jokinen, J. (2015). Emotional user experience: Traits, events, and states. *International Journal of Human-Computer Studies*, 76, 67–77. doi:10.1016/j.ijhcs.2014.12.006

Jscripters. (2017). *Developing a JavaScript based website with AJAX/JQUERY*. Retrieved July 4, 2017, from http://www.jscripters.com/javascript-advantages-and-disadvantages/

Kelkar, K. (2017). *Predictions and trends for 2017*. Retrieved July 14, 2017, from https://www.userzoom.com/user-experience-research/predictions-ux-design-research-2017/

Kramer, J. (2014). *Responsive design frameworks: just because you can, should you?* Retrieved July 11, 2017, from https://www.smashingmagazine.com/2014/02/responsive-design-frameworks-just-because-you-can-should-you/

Kujala, S., Roto, V., Vainio-Mattila, K., Karapanos, E., & Sinnelä, A. (2011). UX curve: A method for evaluating long-term user experience. *Interacting with Computers*, 23(5), 473–483. doi:10.1016/j.intcom.2011.06.005

Law, E., Van Schaik, L., & Roto, V. (2014). Attitudes towards user experience (UX) measurement. *International Journal of Human-Computer Studies*, 72(6), 526–541. doi:10.1016/j.ijhcs.2013.09.006

Lestari, D., Hardianto, D., & Hidayanto, A. (2014). Analysis of user experience quality on responsive web design from its informative perspective. *International Journal of Software Engineering and Its Applications*, 8(5), 53–62.

Majava, J., Nuottila, J., Haapasalo, H., Kris, M., & Law, Y. (2014). Customer needs in market-driven product development: Product management and R&D standpoints. *Technology and Investment*, 5(01), 16–25. doi:10.4236/ti.2014.51003

Meyer, C. (2001). A Case in Case Study Methodology. *Field Methods*, *13*(4), 329–352. doi:10.1177/1525822X0101300402

Mukherjee, S., & Shaw, R. (2016). Big data - concepts, applications, challenges and future scope. *International Journal of Advanced Research in Computer and Communication Engineering*, *5*(2), 66–74.

Müller, B. (2016). *Designing native apps for Android and iOS: key differences and similarities*. Cheesecake Labs. Retrieved July 11, 2017, from https://cheesecakelabs.com/br/blog/designing-native-apps-for-android-and-ios-key-differences-and-similarities/

Njie, B., & Asimiran, S. (2014). Case study as a choice in qualitative methodology. *IOSR Journal of Research & Method in Education*, *4*(3), 35–40.

Park, H., Sung, T., & Kim, S. (2015). Strategic implications of technology life cycle on technology commercialization. *Proceedings of the International Association for Management of Technology (IAMOT 2015)*, 2736-2748.

Petersen, K., & Wohlin, C. (2009). A comparison of issues and advantages in agile and incremental development between state of the art and an industrial case. *Journal of Systems and Software*, *82*(9), 1479–1490. doi:10.1016/j.jss.2009.03.036

Pisano, G. (2015). You need an innovation strategy. *Harvard Business Review*. Retrieved July 13, 2017, from https://hbr.org/2015/06/you-need-an-innovation-strategy

Power, C., Freire, A., & Petrie, H. (2009). Integrating accessibility evaluation into web engineering processes. *International Journal of Information Technology and Web Engineering*, *4*(4), 54–77. doi:10.4018/jitwe.2009100104

Purohit, M. (2016). A study on employee turnover in IT sector with special emphasis on Wipro and Infosys. *IOSR Journal of Business and Management*, *18*(4), 47-51.

Queirós, A., Faria, D., & Almeida, F. (2017). Strengths and Limitations of Qualitative and Quantitative Research Methods. *European Journal of Education Studies*, *3*(9), 369–387.

Rhatigan, C. (2016). *The 4 industries with the worst retention rates*. Retrieved July 12, 2017, from https://www.tinypulse.com/blog/industries-with-the-worst-retention-rates

Robert, J., & Lesage, A. (2011). Designing and evaluating user experience. In G. A. Boy (Ed.), *Handbook of Human-Computer Interaction: A Human-centered Design Approach* (pp. 321–338). Ashgate.

Ruluks, S. (2014). *A brief history of Web design for designers*. FROONT. Retrieved July 4, 2017, from http://blog.froont.com/brief-history-of-web-design-for-designers/

Sánchez, D. (2017). *UX best practices: home automation ecosystem design*. Retrieved July 14, 2017, from https://uiux.blog/ux-best-practices-home-automation-ecosystem-design-55b752b64bf5

Sauro, J. (2016). The challenges and opportunities of measuring the user experience. *Journal of Usability Studies*, *12*(1), 1–7.

Schwarz, D. (2016). *What is adaptive design? (and is it different from responsive design?)*. Retrieved July 11, 2017, from https://www.sitepoint.com/adaptive-design-different-responsive-design/

Shahmarichatghieh, M., Härkönen, J., & Tolonen, A. (2016). Product development activities over technology life-cycles in different generations. *International Journal of Product Lifecycle Management, 9*(1), 19–44. doi:10.1504/IJPLM.2016.078861

Soegaard, M. (2017). *Adaptive vs. responsive design.* Retrieved July 11, 2017, from https://www.interaction-design.org/literature/article/adaptive-vs-responsive-design

Stanton, G., & Ophoff, J. (2013). Towards a method for mobile learning design. *Issues in Informing Science and Information Technology, 10,* 501–523. doi:10.28945/1825

Stokes, R. (2013). eMarketing: The essential guide to marketing in a digital world. Durham: Quirk Education Pty.

Sun, X., & May, A. (2014). Design of the user experience for personalized mobile services. *International Journal of Human-Computer Interaction, 5*(2), 21–39.

Sverrisdottir, H., Ingason, H., & Jonasson, H. (2014). The role of the product owner in scrum-comparison between theory and practices. *Procedia: Social and Behavioral Sciences, 119,* 257–267. doi:10.1016/j.sbspro.2014.03.030

Tan, J., Rönkkö, K., & Gencel, C. (2013). A framework for software usability and user experience measurement in mobile industry. *Proceedings of Joint Conference of the 23rd International Workshop on Software Measurement and the 8th International Conference on Software Process and Product Measurement,* 156-164. 10.1109/IWSM-Mensura.2013.31

Turetken, O., Stojanov, I., & Trienekens, J. (2017). Assessing the adoption level of scaled agile development: A maturity model for scaled agile framework. *Journal of Software: Evolution and Process, 29,* 1–18.

Vanitha, K., Yasudha, K., Venkatesh, M., Ravindra, K., & Lakshmi, S. (2011). The development process of the semantic Web and Web ontology. *International Journal of Advanced Computer Science and Applications, 2*(7), 122–125. doi:10.14569/IJACSA.2011.020718

Vermeeren, A., Law, E., Roto, V., Obrist, M., Hoonhout, J., & Mattila, K. (2010). User experience evaluation methods: current state and development needs. *Proceedings of the 6th Nordic Conference on Human-Computer Interaction: Extending Boundaries,* 521-530. 10.1145/1868914.1868973

Vissak, T. (2010). Recommendations for Using the Case Study Method in International Business Research. *Qualitative Report, 15*(2), 370–388.

Wasserman, A. (2010). Software engineering issues for mobile application development. *Proceedings of the FSE/SDP Workshop on Future Software Engineering Research,* 397-400. 10.1145/1882362.1882443

Williams, J. (2016). *18 Web design trends for 2017.* Retrieved July 13, 2017, from https://webflow.com/blog/18-web-design-trends-for-2017

Work, S. (2011). *The Evolution of Web Design.* Kissmetrics. Retrieved July 4, 2017, from https://blog.kissmetrics.com/evolution-of-web-design/

Yadav, P., & Barwal, P. (2014). Designing responsive websites using HTML and CSS. *International Journal of Scientific & Technology Research, 3*(11), 152–155.

Yin, R. K. (2009). *Case study research: Design and methods* (4th ed.). Sage Publications.

Yu, H., & Malnight, T. (2016). *The best companies aren't afraid to replace their most profitable products.* Retrieved July 7, 2017, from https://hbr.org/2016/07/the-best-companies-arent-afraid-to-replace-their-most-profitable-products

Zainal, Z. (2007). Case study as a research method. *Journal Kemanusiaan, 9,* 1–6.

KEY TERMS AND DEFINITIONS

Asynchronous JavaScript and XML (AJAX): Set of techniques for programming and web development that uses technologies such as JavaScript and XML to load information asynchronously.

Big Data: Very large sets of data that can only be stored, used, and analyzed with the help of technological tools and methods.

Cascade Style Sheets (CSS): Language used to define the presentation of web pages built with markup language, such as hypertext markup language (HTML).

Flash: Technology used in a web environment that allows the creation of vector animations.

Human-Computer Interaction (HCI): Discipline related to the design, evaluation, and implementation of interactive computing systems for human use in a social context.

Prototyping: The process of design, execution, and creation of a prototype.

User Experience: The quality of experience a person has when interacting with a specific design.

User Interface: Represents the user interaction layer, that is, everything that is visually perceptible on some platform and leads the user to a positive interaction.

APPENDIX

Table 1. Comparison of frameworks

	Bootstrap	Foundation	Skeleton	YAML	Gumby	Kube	ResponsiveAeon
Web	http://getbootstrap.com/	http://foundation.zurb.com/	http://getskeleton.com/	http://www.yaml.de/	http://www.gumbyframework.com/	https://imperavi.com/kube/	http://newaeonweb.com.br/responsiveaeon/
License	MIT License	MIT License	MIT License	Creative Commons	MIT Licence	MIT Licence	MIT Licence
Last Version	3.3.7	6.4.1	2.04	4.1.2	2.0	6.5.2	1.0.0
Documentation	Good	Good	Good	Relevant	Good	Relevant	Poor
Pre-processor	LESS, SASS	SASS	LESS; SASS	-	SASS	LESS	LESS; SASS
Browser support	Desktop: Chrome; Firefox; Internet Explorer (only Windows; Opera Safari (only Mac). Mobile: Chrome; Firefox; Opera; Safari (iOS only).	Chrome, Firefox, Safari, Opera, Mobile Safari, and IE Mobile (last two versions); Internet Explorer 9+ Android Browser 2.3+	Chrome latest; Firefox latest; Opera latest; Safari latest; IE latest	Latest Google Chrome; Mozilla Firefox 3.6+; Opera 10+ Apple Safari 4+; Internet Explorer 6+	Chrome; Firefox; Opera; Internet Explorer 8 - 10	all modern browsers, both desktop and mobile, including latest Chrome, Firefox, Safari, Opera, IE and Edge	Only specify "updated browser"
Accessibility	Follows common Web standards (with minimal extra effort, can be used to create sites that are accessible)	Fully-accessible for visual impaired, motor disabilities and auditory disabilities (provide captions on videos).	Not mentioned	Includes accessibility features	Not mentioned	Not mentioned	Not mentioned
Popularity (stars on GitHub)	> 112.8K	> 25.9K	> 14.3K	> 260	>3K	> 1.1K	> 115
Size (on GitHub)	4,5M	9,8M	11K	450K	815K	89K	119K

Chapter 5
Development of Adaptive Social Network Based on Learners' Thinking and Learning Styles

Mahnane Lamia
LRS Laboratory, University of Badji Mokhtar, Algeria

Hafidi Mohamed
LRS Laboratory, University Badji Mokhtar, Algeria

ABSTRACT

Adaptive social network sites (ASNS) are an innovative approach to a web learning experience delivery. They try to solve the main shortcomings of classical social networks—"one-size-fits-all" approach and "lost-in-hyperspace" phenomena—by adapting the learning content and its presentation to needs, goals, thinking styles, and learning styles of every individual learner. This chapter outlines a new approach to automatically detect learners' thinking and learning styles, and takes into account that thinking and learning styles may change during the learning process in unexpected and unpredictable ways. The approach is based on the Felder learning styles model and Hermann thinking styles model.

INTRODUCTION

A distinct feature of an Adaptive Social Network Site (ASNS) is the learner model it employs, that is, a representation of information about an individual learner (De Bra, Aroyo, & Cristea, 2004; Henze & Nejdl, 2004). Learner modeling and adaptation are strongly correlated, in the sense that the amount and nature of the information represented in the learner model depend largely on the kind of adaptation effect that the system has to deliver. In fact, we see a problem arising when group formation assumes similar learning styles, thinking styles, levels of knowledge and abilities for learners (Ruiz, Díaz, Soler, & Pérez, 2008). This is because learners that are less able will feel that it is too difficult for them to follow and those that are more capable will feel as though the learning method is too easy. Thinking style, learning style, level of knowledge, preferences and ability of learner are part of learner's characteristics, which have significant influence on the learning activity in the group formation. In this chapter we focused

DOI: 10.4018/978-1-5225-5384-7.ch005

our attention on the learner model, which allows for the discovery of thinking and learning styles of learners that have access to an ASNS.

The chapter has been structured as follows: The background knowledge on the research subject is given in the next section. The proposed approach is explained subsequently, and some experimental results related to the subject area are analyzed in the succession of sections. Finally, future research directions and conclusion are given at the end.

BACKGROUND AND RELATED SCIENTIFIC WORK

This section is organized in three subsections; firstly, the general context of the educational social networks is briefly introduced. Secondly, we focus on the thinking style. We conclude with learning styles models.

Social Networks for Education

Social networking is widespread in today's society. In Web-based education systems context, social networking sites have been used for establishing relationships with peers, providing social support, creating information, and maintaining contact (Yu, Tian, Vogel, & Kwok, 2010; Pimmer, Linxen, & Grohbiel, 2012; Rambe, 2013). Hwang, Kessler, & Francesco (2004) demonstrated that college students' social networking with professors and peers boosts their knowledge acquisition and improves their academic performance. Social networks have been investigated to be a better learning environment in higher education than other commonly used learning management systems in facilitating interaction, communication, collaboration, and learning motivation (Chen, 2014) (Gabarre, Gabarre, Din, Shah, & Karim, 2013, Pimmer et al., 2012). Social networks provide a learning environment more suitable than other Web-based education systems that educators are already familiar with especially in facilitating opportunities for interaction, dissemination of learner-created content, student engagement, and immediateness (Gabarre et al., 2013).

Here are some examples of the social networks that are used in education:

- In Jernej, Matevž, Andrej, Félix, & José (2012), the authors proposed an integration of e-learning systems with social networks and display its supporting software. The authors solved the low level of interaction between users through direct relationship between learning content and communication between users and teachers in e-learning systems. Suggested use of social networks increases the interaction between users in e-learning environments. The approach depends on the virtual classroom, integrating e-learning system COOME (an internet-based system for production) with Facebook.
- In Du, Fu, Zhao, Liu, & Liu (2013), the authors proposed an interactive and collaborative e-learning platform which integrates social software with a Learning Management System (LMS). This platform provides personalized space for users where they can interact and collaborate with others. The personalized space of users contains their course network, social network and knowledge network. This platform connects course network of users with his/her social network and knowledge network. Furthermore, users are able to build their personalized social network and knowledge network during the process of learning.

- In Meishar-Tal, Kurtz, & Pieterse (2012), the authors used a Facebook group as an alternative to LMS. Their approach reviews the current research on the use of Facebook in academia and analyzed the differences between a Facebook group and a regular LMS. The authors used a Facebook group as a course website, serving as a platform for delivering content and maintaining interactions among the students and between the students and the lecturer.
- In Kurtz (2014), the author studied the effect of integrating Facebook group and course website on participation and perceptions on learning; so that used two virtual platforms for learning, and showed that Facebook can be used for discussion and exchange of knowledge. Students reported that Facebook helps enhance the interaction and social learning processes with emphasis on the involvement of the learner, and contributes effectively to frequent interaction with peers and the instructor.

Thinking Styles Models

Each person thinks and behaves in preferred ways that are unique to the individual. These dominant thinking styles are the results of the native personality interacting with family, education, work, and social environments (Danielson & DeLisi, 2002; Cano-Garcia & Hughes, 2000). People's approaches to problem solving, creativity, and communicating with others are characterized by their thinking preferences (Harrison & Bramson, 1984; Jabolokow & Kathryn, 2000). For example, one person may carefully analyze a situation before making a rational, logical decision based on the available data. Another may see the same situation in a broader context and look for several alternatives. One person will use a very detailed, cautious, step-by-step procedure. Another has a need to talk the problem over with people and will try solve it intuitively.

Thought processes have been studied since ancient history; several models have been proposed on how the human brain works. One of the well known models is the Herrmann model (HBDI) (Bono, 1998; Haik & Moustafa, 2007; Bawaneh, Abdullah, Saleh, & Yin, 2011a ; Bawaneh, Zain, & Saleh, 2010; Bawaneh, Abdullah, Saleh, & Yin, 2011b; Salmiza, 2010), which divides the brain into a four quadrant brain dominance model (see Table 1).

Learning Styles Models

The concept of learning style has a broad-meaning. In this research, it is proposed and defined as an individual's preferential focus on different types of information, ways of perceiving the information and understanding it (Li, Chen, Tsai, 2008). "Learning Styles" are categorized and developed by educational researchers to classify learners based on their customary approach to perceiving and processing information (Kolb, 1984). Educational research and practice have demonstrated that learning can be enhanced when the instructional process accommodates the various learning styles of a student. (e.g. Buch & Sena, 2001; Calver, Howard, & Lane, 1999). The research argued that a student can learn efficiently, retain the information longer, and apply the knowledge more effectively when their learning styles are consistent with teaching styles (Calver et al., 1999; Felder, 1993). A number of Web based education systems have been developed applying different learning style theories as well as Felder-Silverman's Model (Lui, 2007). Those systems offer personalized content depending on the students' learning styles, known as adaptive presentation. Felder Silverman's theory classifies learners into four different groups according to their preference in Sensing/Intuitive, Verbal/Visual, Active/Reflective, and Sequential/Global (Table 2).

Table 1. Adaptive teaching for HBDI model

Quadrant	Description	Teaching Strategies
Theorist (Blue)	• Are innovative and hate repetitive work, rather discover possibilities and relationships, assimilate new concepts easily, don´t like courses that require much memory and tedious calculation. • Think about quietly before going ahead. • Stop periodically to review what have been learning. • Stop periodically to think possible questions. • Stop periodically to think possible applications.	• Discussion panel • Case study • Presentation • Question and answer method
Organizer (Green)	• Learn through small orderly steps when these are logically associated and follow small orderly steps logically associated when solving problems	• Presentation • Question and answer method
Innovator (Yellow)	• Rather receive information spoken or verbally and remember what they read or hear. • Specific, facts and procedure oriented, enjoy problem solving by following well established procedures, patient when dealing with details, enjoy practical work, lab class and can memorize things easily. • Tend to comprehend and assimilate new information when they practice using it (discussion, implementation, group presentations) and rather learn working with others	• Learning based on problem solving • Games and simulations • Role playing • Project design method
Humanitarian (Red)	• Rather work with visual representations when receiving information and remember what they see. • Are innovative and hate repetitive work, rather discover possibilities and relationships, assimilate new concepts easily, don´t like courses that require much memory and tedious calculation. • Tend to comprehend and assimilate new information when they practice using it (discussion, implementation, group presentations) and rather learn working with others. • Learn through big leaps, suddenly and almost randomly, can solve complex problems quickly and put things together in an innovative way but may have difficulties to explain how they did it.	• Games and simulations • Presentation • Discussion panel • Role playing • Case study • Project design method • Learning based on problem solving • Brainstorming

Table 2. Felder-Silverman's learning theory

Dimensions	Description	Electronic Media
Sensing	• Prefer to learn facts, procedures and real cases.	• Forums, Wikis, Animations, graphics, pictures,
Intuitive	• Prefer to learn concept, theories, and symbols.	• Internet research, Tutorial systems, Web Quest
Visual	• Learn via visual images (pictures, charts or graphs, etc).	• Forums, Wikis, Animations, Graphics, Pictures, Simulations, Hypertext, eBooks, Slideshows, Videoconference, Videos
Verbal	• Learn via verbal sources (written and spoken words, i.e. lectures or reading etc.).	• Audio Recording, Audio conference, Videoconference, Videos, Web seminars.
Active	• Learning by doing (trying things out).	• Wikis, Chat, e-mail, Internet research.
Reflective	• Learning by reflecting (thinking thing through before doing).	• Digital magazines, Digital newspapers, eBooks, Hypertext, Slideshows, Internet research, Student Response System, Tutorial systems.
Sequential	• Learn in a certain sequence, assimilate and understand information in a linier and incremental step, but lack a grasp of big picture.	• Audio Recording, Audio conference, Digital magazines, eBooks, Hypertext, Slideshows.
Global	• Learn globally, absorb information in unconnected chunks and achieve understanding in large holistic jumps without knowing the details.	• Forums, Online learning communities, Wikis, Chat, e-mail, Internet research.

DISCUSSION

- The majority of the traditional educational social networks do not consider the adaptation according to the user's profile in their approaches (Troussas, Junshean, & Virvou, 2016; Gomes, Ricardo Prudêncio, Meira, Azevedo Filho, André, Nascimento, & Oliveira, 2013; Gamila, Pavla, Jan, Katerina, & Václav, 2010; Railean, Elçi, & Elçi, 2017; Elçi, Elçi, Celik, 2016).
- Less attention was intended to study the application of machine learning techniques for generation of group profiling in educational social networks (Gomes et al; 2013).
- Several researches are made in the group formation where all of them are vocalized on grouping learners using different criteria. These researches present some limitations where the grouping of learners is static while the characteristics of learners are dynamic.

ARCHITECTURE OF PROPOSED SYSTEM

The main characteristic of proposed system is that it can be adapted to the thinking style and to the learning style acquired by the student. The system was organized in the form of three basic components: The learner model, the domain model, and the adaptation model. These three components interact to adapt to different aspects of the instructional process. Figure 1 illustrates the system architecture.

Learner Model

In our approach, learner's thinking and learning styles are stored in the learner model as values in the interval [0,1] representing a student's probability of preference. If self assessment questionnaires are

Figure 1. Architecture of proposed system

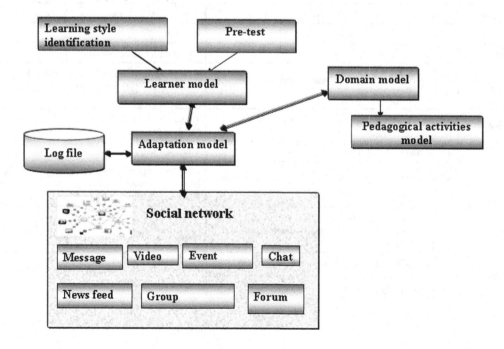

used for initialization of probabilistic, as ILS and HBDI, the learner model can be booted from the data obtained by the questionnaires, considering the proportion of responses scored for each thinking and learning styles inside a dimension. Using this approach, a learner's thinking and learning styles are represented by:

TSLS= {(Pth, Po, Pin, Ph), (Pa, Pr), (Ps, Pi), (Pvi, Pve), (Pseq, Pg)} | Pth+ Po+ Pin+ Ph=1, Pa+Pr=1, Ps+Pi=1, Pvi+Pve=1, Pseq+Pg=1}

where:

- Pth is the probability of the student's preference for the Theoretician TS;
- Po is the probability of the student's preference for the Organiser TS;
- Pin is the probability of the student's preference for the Innovator TS;
- Ph is the probability of the student's preference for the Humanitarian TS;
- Pa is the probability of student's preference for the active LS;
- Pi is the probability of student's preference for the intuitive LS;
- Pr is the probability of student's preference for the reflective LS;
- Ps is the probability of student's preference for the sensitive LS;
- Pvi is the probability of student's preference for the visual LS;
- Pve is the probability of student's preference for the verbal LS;
- Pseq is the probability of student's preference for the sequential LS;
- Pg is the probability of student's preference for the global LS.

Therefore, there are 64 possible thinking and learning styles combinations.

We propose that during each different learning session the learner should interact with a set of learning objects which satisfies a specific thinking and learning styles. For example, considering a student's probable thinking and learning styles, as stated by Table 3, we can deduce that this learner is probably (Th)eoritecal, (Ve)rbal, (G)lobal, (R)eflective and (S)ensitive.

The selection of thinking and learning styles combinations is done by a stochastic selection method. There are a variety of stochastic selection methods, for example Roulette Wheel Selection, Stochastic Universal Sampling, Simple Tournament and Stochastic Tournament. In this approach we use the Roulette Wheel Selection, due to it's adequacy to our approach. In this method, individual candidates have a fitness that measures how adapted they are to the environment, which gives them a proportional slice in the roulette. The individual's probability of selection is given by the proportion between its fitness and the entire population's fitness, as shown in Equation 1. The sum of probabilities of all the individuals must equal 1.

Table 3. Student's probable thinking and learning styles

Th	In	o	h	Ve	Vi	Seq	G	A	R	S	I
71.10	12.35	10.15	6.40	88.97	11.03	10.85	89.15	14.60	85.40	84.84	13.16

$$\mathrm{Pr}_i = \frac{fitness}{\sum_{x=1}^{n} fitness_x} \tag{1}$$

So, we calculate the accumulated probability for each individual, as shown in Equation 2.

$$q_0 0; q_1 = q_0 + \mathrm{Pr}_1; ...; q_{n-1} + \mathrm{Pr}_n = 1 \tag{2}$$

Finally, we generate a random number in the interval [0,1] representing the roulette spin. If the generated number is in the interval [q0, q1], the individual 1 is selected. If the number is in the interval [q1, q2], the individual 2 is selected, and so on, as shown in Equation 3.

$$q_{i-1} < \mathrm{Pr}_i \leq q_i \tag{3}$$

Once each Thinking and Learning Styles Combinations (TLSC) has been assigned a fitness value, they can be chosen with probability given by their relative fitness. A binary representation of thinking and learning styles combinations is used.

After each learning session, we apply recombination and mutation operators, based on genetic algorithms. The recombination operator recombines thinking and learning styles combinations in order to (probably) produce more fitted individuals. During recombination, the parents are stochastically selected through Roulette Wheel Selection method. The role of parent selection is to distinguish among individuals based on their quality, in order to allow the better individuals to become parents of the next generation. We are using here the single-point crossover. This crossover operation is not necessarily performed on all strings in population. Instead, it is applied with a probability when the pairs are chosen for breeding.

The mutation operator is then applied to the new thinking and learning styles combinations with a probability (mutation rate). Mutation causes the individual genetic representation to be changed according to some probabilistic rule. In the binary string representation, mutation will cause a single bit to flip, 0 to 1 or 1 to 0. The bit to be flipped is randomly chosen.

It's important to consider that thinking and learning styles stored in learner model are constantly updated. In order to decide how thinking and learning styles must be updated, it is taken into account the thinking and learning styles combinations selected during a learning session. When the student shows a learning problem during a learning session, the student's preferences in learner model that accords to the selected thinking and learning styles combinations are decremented, considering a probable inconsistency in these preferences.

The learner's preferences in learner model that discords to the selected thinking and learning styles combinations are incremented, making them stronger, considering that the learning difficulties appeared because they were not present in the selected thinking and learning styles combinations.

Domain Model

The domain model is used for storage, organization and description of the learning content. This learning content is divided into three chapters, each of which consists of several lessons. Every lesson contains:

presentation, games and simulations, learning based on problem solving, discussion, case study, qustion/answer method, project and practical work, as shown in Figure 2.

Adaptation Model

When an adaptation model shows a learning problem during a learning session (unsatisfactory performance), the Thinking and Learning Styles (TLS) stored in the learner model, which appear in current TLSC, are decremented, considering a probable inconsistency in these preferences. Students' preferences, which do not appear in current TLSC, are incremented (reinforced), making them stronger, considering that the learning difficulties appeared because they were not present in the selected TLSC. These updates are executed by the following rules:

Rule 1
α ← 1/ (learner's performance value * (|learner [di]$_A$ - learner[di]$_B$|))
Rule 2
IF (learner [di]$_A$ ≥ learner[di]$_B$) and (TLSC[di] = "A") THEN
. . .learner[di]$_A$ ← learner[di]$_A$ - α
. . .learner[di]$_B$ ← learner[di]$_B$ + α
Rule 3
IF (learner [di]$_B$ ≥ learner[di]$_A$) and (TLSC[di] = "B") THEN
. . .learner[di]$_A$ ← learner[di]$_A$ + α
. . .learner[di]$_B$ ← learner[di]$_B$ - α

Figure 2. Domain model

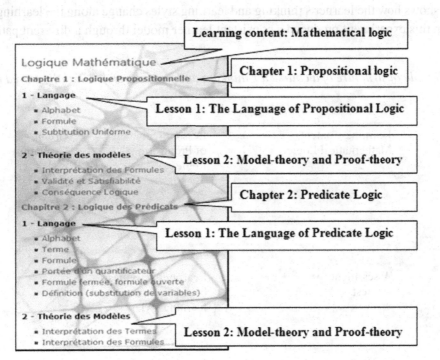

```
Rule 4
IF (learner [di]_A ≥ learner[di]_B) and (TLSC[di] = "B") THEN
. . learner[di]_A ← learner[di]_A +α
. . .learner[di]_B ← learner[di]_B - α
Rule 5
IF (learner[di]_B ≥ learner[di]_A) and (TLSC[di] = "A") THEN
. . .learner[di]_A ← learner[di]_A - α
. . .learner[di]_B ←learner[di]_B + α
```

SYSTEM'S FUNCTIONS

When the first time learners enter in the system, they sign up by using a registration form. Once a learner registers, a learner profile will be created to store all his information and will be saved in the database; a unique identification (ID) is generated for the learner for further reference and tracking of his progress.

After successful registration, our system shows an introduction page to the learner, explaining the thinking and learning styles categories and their general characteristics. Then it offers to answer the thinking and learning styles questionnaires. Our system computes the answers given by the user and deduces thinking and learning styles based on the HBDI and ILS models.

As an example let's consider a student with the following learning and thinking styles: TSLS= {(Pth, Po, Pin, Ph), (Pa, Pr), (Ps, Pi), (Pvi, Pve), (Pseq, Pg)} .The student's learning and thinking styles in learner model are initially defined as: TSLS={(5.0, 10.0, 60.0,25.0), (70.0,30.0), (35.0,65.0), (40.0,60.0), (45.0,55.0)}. Figure 3 shows a snapshot corresponding to the course.

As can be seen, TSLS are initially inconsistent and doesn't express all the student's preferences correctly. Table 4 presents the results obtained from an execution of genetic algorithm.

Figure 4 shows how the learner's thinking and learning styles change along the learning process. All repetitions in this experiment produced a consistent learner model through a different path.

Figure 3. Example of structure of a course for thinking and learning styles initially stored in the learner model

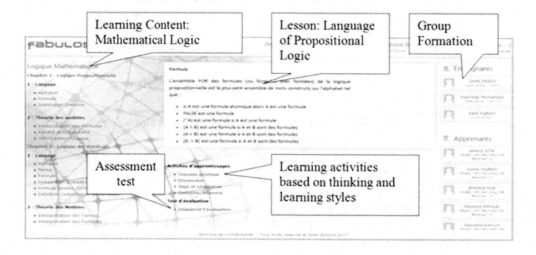

Table 4. Thinking and learning styles stored in the learner model

Pth	Po	Pin	Ph	Pa	Pr	Ps	Pi	Pvi	Pve	Pseq	Pg
15	5	30	50	69.83	30.17	65.48	34.52	75.29	24.71	19.01	80.99

Figure 4. Possible evolution of thinking and learning styles stored in the student model

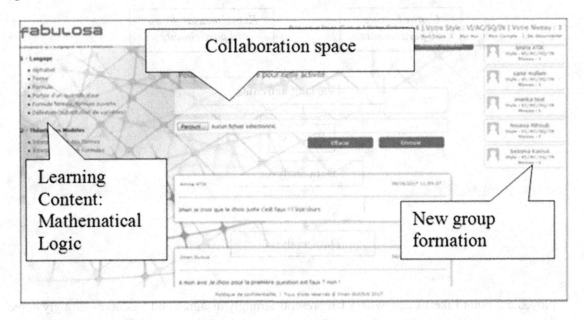

EXPERIMENTAL DESIGN AND PROCEDURES

Figure 5 shows the procedure of the experiment. In the first stage, the students were instructed in the basic knowledge of mathematical logic course. After receiving this fundamental knowledge, the students were asked to take a pre-test, which aimed to evaluate their basic knowledge before participating in the course.

In the second stage, the students in the experimental group were arranged to learn with the ASNS; that is, they were provided with an adaptive interface and learning content by taking both their learners' thinking and learning styles and learners' skill level into account. On the other hand, the students in the control group learned with traditional social network. After conducting the course, the students took a post-test and answered a questionnaire.

DATA COLLECTION AND RESEARCH INSTRUMENT

The research instruments used in this study were as follows:

- System Usability Scale (SUS) is a reliable, efficient, and inexpensive instrument used for measuring users' subjective perception of a system (Brooke, 1996). To effectively assess the participants' perception of system usability, we modified our questionnaire items based on the SUS and em-

Figure 5. The procedure of the experiment

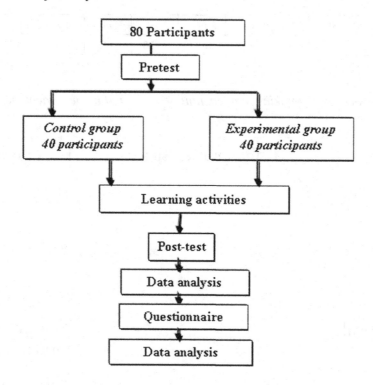

ployed a 5-point Likert scale, where 1 represents strongly disagree and 5 denotes strongly agree. The questionnaire items were then modified and confirmed by experts, forming a scale that is applicable for this study.

- Learning effectiveness test, which comprises a pre-test and post-test. The pre-test aimed to confirm that the two groups of students had the equivalent basic knowledge required for taking this particular subject unit. The post-test focused on evaluating the students' skill level about mathematical logic course. Both the pre-test and post-test were designed by the teacher who taught the mathematical logic course to the two groups of students.

Table 5 presents the parameters of the present study.

EVALUATION OF SYSTEM USABILITY

Usability testing was conducted in this study, in which usability scale was distributed to the 40 students in the experimental group after they had used the system. After the students completed the questionnaire, we analyzed the reliability of the scale. The results showed that the value of the usability scale completed by the 40 students in the experimental group was 0.787, which exceeded the optimal reliability standard of 0.7, indicating that the questionnaire results were satisfactorily reliable.

We then performed frequency distribution by analyzing the percentage sum of the two scores for the anchor of scale in the 5-point scale (strongly agree and agree).

Table 5. Parameters of study using ASNS

Variables	Description
Domain	Mathematical logic
ID	Identify sample (N = 80)
thinking style	Four thinking styles were assessed: (1–4).
Learning style	Eight learning styles were assessed: (1-8).
Group	1. experimental group (N=40) 2. control group (N=40)
Learning performance	The score was evaluated on a 5-points
Learning activities	Games and simulations, learning based on problem solving, discussion, case study, question/answer method, and project.

Table 6 shows that users' subjective perception of overall usability was 51.7%, with Q3, Q7, and Q8 yielding the highest score. For Q3, 62.2% of the users perceived the system to be easy to use; for Q7, 57.8% of the users believed that most people can learn to use the system quickly; and for Q8, 68.9% of the users thought using the system were not difficult to use and operate.

Subsequently, by using the calculation formula of the usability test, we obtained the final SUS score. Table 7 summarizes the statistical results of the scores. The learners' SUS mean score of the system is 63.56, with a median of 65, minimum of 35, maximum of 90, and standard deviation of 14.76. The results indicated that the learners' mean SUS score a little bit less than the median, implying that users were moderately satisfied.

Thus, unfamiliarity with the system and insufficient time are potential reasons engendering a moderate level of usability.

Table 6. Statistical analysis for SUS

			Mean Standard Percentages of Items in Scale Deviation (%)				
			1	2	3	4	5
Q1	3.36	1.004	4.4	11.1	42.2	28.9	13.3
Q2	3.80	0.919	6.7	6.7	37.8	26.7	22.2
Q3	3.80	0.919	2.2	2.2	33.3	37.8	24.4
Q4	3.44	1.056	4.4	13.3	31.1	35.6	15.6
Q5	3.62	0.984	2.2	8.9	33.3	35.6	20.0
Q6	3.47	0.815	2.2.8	2.2	53.3	31.1	11.1
Q7	3.60	1.009	4.4	6.7	31.1	40.0	17.8
Q8	3.89	1.027	4.4	2.2	24.4	37.8	31.1
Q9	3.60	1.009	2.2	8.9	37.8	28.9	22.2
Q10	3.13	1.057	11.1	8.9	42.2	31.1	6.7
Total	3.54	1.014	4.4	7.1	36.7	33.3	18.4

Table 7. Results of calculation with SUS scale equations

	Samples	Mean	Median	Minimum	Maximum	Standard Deviation
Total	40	63.56	65	35	90	14.76

EVALUATION RESULTS OF LEARNING EFFECTIVENESS

The students in the control group underwent a post-test after they had received learning activities through traditional social network, whereas the experimental group underwent a post-test after they had experimented with the ASNS. The goal was to investigate and compare the learning effectiveness of learners after they had used the ASNS of this study.

Table 8 presents the statistical results of the learning effectiveness exhibited among the students in the control group. The mean post-test score (M = 61.14) is higher than the mean pre-test score (M = 55.51), showing an increase of 5.63. However, the p-value was 0.116 (p > 0.005), indicating no significance. Moreover, the effect size was d = 0.35 (0.2 < d < 0.5), suggesting a small effect; therefore, traditional social network exerted no significant effect on the improvement of learning effectiveness.

The statistical results of learning effectiveness among students who received ASNS-based learning activity recommendation are shown in Table 9.

The results show that the mean post-test score (M = 78.78) is higher than the mean pre-test score (M = 59.36), presenting an increase of 19.42, with a p-value of 0.000 (p < 0.001). Thus, using the ASNS significantly enhances students' learning effectiveness. Furthermore, the effect size was d = 0.93, which is greater than 0.8, further showing that a learning method involving ASNS strongly and significantly influenced the improvement of learners' learning effectiveness during learning activity recommendation.

Overall, although the learning outcome of the control group improved, the improvement was non-significant. By comparison, the performance of the experimental group improved substantially, suggest-

Table 8. Statistical analysis results for the control group

	Samples	Mean	Standard Deviation	t	P-value	d
Pre-test score	40	55.51	18.08	-1.612	0.116	0.35
Post-test score	40	61.14	13.94			

Table 9. Statistical analysis results for the experimental group

	Samples	Mean	Standard Deviation	t	p-value	d
Pre-test score	40	59.36	28.67	-7.006	0.000	0.93
Post-test score	40	78.78	12.93			

ing that using the system exerted a highly significant influence on learners' performance. This shows that compared with traditional social network, using the ASNS in learning activity recommendation significantly influenced students' learning effectiveness.

FUTURE RESEARCH DIRECTIONS

The results of the experiment conducted in this research have shown that our approach is promising and encourages further research in this direction. It will be useful to automatically detect learning styles and to optimize knowledge sharing in mining social network.

Predicting Users' Learning Style by Interactions in Social Networks

Identifying a user's learning style can contribute to know, for example, his/her potential needs in different contexts. The most commonly used procedure to obtain this information consists of asking the user to fill in questionnaires. However, users can find this task too time-consuming, since most of the learning style questionnaires include many questions to answer in order to obtain an accurate user profile.

On one hand, we think that user learning style should be obtained as unobtrusively as possible, yet without compromising the reliability of the model built. Some research has already been done related to automatic or semi-automatic user modeling acquisition. Several works have tried to infer some learning style characteristics.

On the other hand, we think that learning style can be inferred by analyzing how users interact in social networks. In this context, the user interactions on social networks are a good measure of user behavior in real life.

Optimizing Knowledge Sharing in Social Networks

Learners have to engage in social network for sharing knowledge to achieve their personalized learning goals. However, without intelligent Web-based systems, learners have to self-organize knowledge sharing by finding a relevant knowledge sharer, structuring the interaction and maintaining the communication process. According to cognitive load theory, these activities could induce extraneous load because they are not directly relevant to learning itself but to the learning environment. For this, it is considered imperative to reduce extraneous load and we used an intelligent Web-based system to support knowledge sharing by matching learners together, providing role specifications.

Mining Social Networks

Data from social network can provide valuable knowledge to inform student learning. Analyzing such data, however, can be challenging. The complexity of students' behaviors reflected from social network content requires human interpretation. However, the growing scale of data demands automatic data analysis techniques.

CONCLUSION

Adaptive Social Network Site (ASNS) has been considered a promising approach to increase the efficiency in Web-based learning. A necessary characteristic in this approach is the precise, dynamic and continuous identification of learners' thinking and learning styles in order to provide well-adapted learning experiences.

In this context, a major challenge is the development of systems able to efficiently acquire learners' preferences. The information about learners' thinking and learning styles, acquired by psychometric instruments, encloses some degree of uncertainty (Price, 2004; Roberts & Erdos, 1993). Furthermore, in most of the existing approaches, the assumptions about learners' preference, once acquired, are no longer updated.

In this context, this work presents a new approach to automatically detect and precisely adjust learners' thinking and learning styles. Our approach gradually and constantly modifies the learner model using a set of rules that detect which thinking and learning styles should be adjusted at a specific point of the learning process, considering the learner's performance.

REFERENCES

Bawaneh, A. K. A., Abdullah, A. G. K., Saleh, S., & Yin, K. Y. (2011a). The effect of Herrmann Whole Brain Teaching Method on Students' Understanding of Simple Electric Circuits. *European Journal of Physics Education*, 2(2), 1–23.

Bawaneh, A. K. A., Abdullah, A. G. K., Saleh, S., & Yin, K. Y. (2011b). Jordanian student's thinking styles based on Hermann whole brain model. *International Journal of Humanities and Social Science*, 1(9), 89–97.

Bawaneh, A. K. A., Zain, A. N. M., & Saleh, S. (2010). The Relationship between Tenth Grade Jordanian Students' Thinking Styles based on the Herrmann Whole Brain Model and Their Track Choice for the Secondary School Level. *European Journal of Soil Science*, 14(4), 567–580.

Bono, Y. (1998). *The Cort Program for Teaching Thinking*. Publishing and Distribution Amman.

Brooke, J. (1996). SUS: A quick and dirty usability scale. In P. W. Jordan, B. Weerdmeester, A. Thomas, & I. L. McLelland (Eds.), *Usability evaluation in industry* (pp. 189–194). London: Taylor and Francis.

Buch, K., & Sena, C. (2001). Accommodating diverse learning styles in the design and delivery of online learning experiences. *International Journal of Engineering Education*, 17(1), 93–98.

Calver, C. A., Howard, R. A., & Lane, W. D. (1999). Enhacing Student Learning Through Hypermedia Courseware and Incorporation of Student Learning Style. *IEEE Transactions on Education*, 42(1), 33–38. doi:10.1109/13.746332

Cano-Garcia, F., & Hughes, E. H. (2000). Learning and Thinking Styles: An Analysis of their interrelationship and influence on academic achievement. *Educational Psychology*, 20(4), 413–430. doi:10.1080/713663755

Chen, Y. (2014). The effect of using a Facebook group as a learning management system. *Computers in Education Journal, 5*(4), 42–53.

Danielson, R. L., & DeLisi, P. S. (2002). Thinking Styles of North American IT Executives. *Proceedings of the Third Annual Global Information Technology Management World Conference.*

De Bra, P., Aroyo, L., & Cristea, A. (2004). Adaptive web-based educational hypermedia. In Web dynamics, adaptive to change in content, size, topology and use. Springer. doi:10.1007/978-3-662-10874-1_16

Du, Z., Fu, X., Zhao, C., Liu, Q., & Liu, T. (2012). Interactive and collaborative e-learning platform with integrated social software and learning management system. In *Proceedings of the 2012 International Conference on Information Technology and Software Engineering* (pp. 11-18). Springer Berlin Heidelberg.

Elçi, A., Elçi, A., & Celik, D. (2016). Semantic Modelling for E-Learning Coordination. In B. Khan (Ed.), *Revolutionizing Modern Education through Meaningful Implementation*. IGI Global. Retrieved from http://www.igi-global.com/book/revolutionizing-modern-education-through-meaningful/146987

Felder, R. M. (1993). Reaching the Second Tier: Learning and Teaching Styles in Engineering Education. *Engineering Education, 78*(7), 674–681.

Gabarre, S., Gabarre, C., Din, R., Shah, P. M., & Karim, A. A. (2013). Using mobile Facebook as an LMS: Exploring impeding factors. *GEMA Online Journal of Language Studies, 13*(3), 99–115.

Gamila, O., Pavla, D., Jan, M., Katerina, S., & Václav, S. (2010). Using Spectral Clustering for Finding Students' Patterns of Behavior in Social Networks. DATESO 2010, 118-130.

Gomes, J., Ricardo, B., Prudêncio, C., Meira, L., Azevedo Filho, A., ... Nascimento, O. H. (2013). Group Profiling for Understanding Educational Social Networking. *The 25th International Conference on Software Engineering and Knowledge Engineering*, 101-106.

Haik, Y., & Moustafa, K. A. F. (2007). Thinking and learning preferences for a sample of engineering students at the United Arab Emirates university. *Emirates Journal for Engineering Research, 12*(1), 65–71.

Harrison, A. F., & Bramson, R. M. (1984). *The Art of Thinking*. New York: Berkley Books.

Henze, N., & Nejdl, W. (2004). A logical characterization of adaptive educational hypermedia. *New Review of Hypermedia and Multimedia, 10*(1), 77-113.

Hwang, A., Kessler, E. H., & Francesco, A. M. (2004). Student networking behaviour, culture, and grade performance: An empirical study and pedagogical recommendations. *Academy of Management Learning & Education, 3*(2), 139–150. doi:10.5465/AMLE.2004.13500532

Jabolokow, K. W. (2000). Thinking about Thinking: Problem Solving Style in the Engineering Classroom. *ASEE Annual Conference and Exposition: Engineering Education Beyond the Millennium.*

Jernej, R., Matevž, P., Andrej, K., Félix, B., & José, V. B. (2012). Integration of Learning Management Systems with Social Networking. *Platforms E-learning in a Facebook supported environment*, 100-105.

Kolb, D. A. (1984). *Experiential Learning*. Englewood Cliffs, NJ: Prentice-Hall.

Kurtz, G. (2014). Integrating a Facebook group and a Course Website: The effect on Participation and Perceptions on Learning. *American Journal of Distance Education, 28*(4), 253–263. doi:10.1080/089 23647.2014.957952

Li, Y. S., Chen, P. S., & Tsai, S. J. (2008). A comparison of the Learning Styles among Differenct Nursing Programs in Taiwan: Implications for Nursing Education. *Nurse Education Today, 28*(1), 70–76. doi:10.1016/j.nedt.2007.02.007 PMID:17391813

Lui, F. (2007). Personalized Learning Using Adapted Content Design for Science Students. *Proceedings of the ECCE 2007 Conference*, 293-296.

Meishar-Tal, H., Kurtz, G., & Pieterse, E. (2012). Facebook groups as LMS: A case study. *The International Review of Research in Open and Distributed Learning, 13*(4), 33–48. doi:10.19173/irrodl.v13i4.1294

Pimmer, C., Linxen, S., & Grohbiel, U. (2012). Facebook as a learning tool? A case study on the appropriation of social network sites from mobile phones in developing countries. *British Journal of Educational Technology, 43*(5), 726–738. doi:10.1111/j.1467-8535.2012.01351.x

Price, L. (2004). Cognitive control, cognitive style and learning style. *Educational Psychology, 24*(5), 681–698. doi:10.1080/0144341042000262971

Railean, E., Elçi, A., & Elçi, A. (2017). *Metacognition and Successful Learning Strategies in Higher Education*. Hershey, PA: IGI Global; doi:10.4018/978-1-5225-2218-8

Rambe, P. (2013). Converged social media: Identity management and engagement on Facebook Mobile and blogs. *Australasian Journal of Educational Technology, 29*(3), 315–336. doi:10.14742/ajet.117

Roberts, M. J., & Erdos, G. (1993). Strategy selection and metacognition. *Educational Psychology, 13*(3), 259–266. doi:10.1080/0144341930130304

Ruiz, M. P. P., Díaz, M. J. F., Soler, F. O., & Pérez, J. R. P. (2008). Adaptation in current e-learning systems. *Computer Standards & Interfaces, 30*(1-2), 62–70. doi:10.1016/j.csi.2007.07.006

Salmiza, S. (2010). The effectiveness of brain based teaching approach in dealing with the problems of student's conceptual understanding and learning motivation towards physics. *Proceedings 2nd Paris International Conference on Education, Economy and Society*, 174–185

Troussas, C., Espnosa, J. K., & Virvou, M. (2016). Affect Recognition through Facebook for Effective Group Profiling Towards Personalized Instruction. *Informatics in Education, 15*(1), 147–161. doi:10.15388/infedu.2016.08

Yu, A. Y., Tian, S. W., Vogel, D., & Kwok, R. C. (2010). Can learning be virtually boosted? An investigation of online social networking impacts. *Computers & Education, 55*(4), 1494–1. doi:10.1016/j. compedu.2010.06.015

KEY TERMS AND DEFINITIONS

Adaptive Hypermedia Systems: Adaptive hypermedia systems (AHS) build a model of goals, preferences, and knowledge of the individual user and use this throughout the interaction for adaptation to the needs of user, making it possible to deliver "personalised" views or versions of a hypermedia document without requiring programming by the author(s).

Adaptive Social Network: Adaptive learning system is a process where learning contents are delivered to learners adaptively, namely, the appropriate contents are delivered to the learners in an appropriate way at an appropriate time based on the learners' needs, knowledge, preferences, and other characteristics. Adaptive social network is a process where connections are made among like-minded learners, so they can achieve learning goals via communication and interaction with each other by sharing knowledge, skills, abilities, and materials.

Learner Model: A distinct feature of a social network is the learner model it employs, that is, a representation of information about an individual learner. Learner modeling and adaptation are strongly correlated, in the sense that the amount and nature of the information represented in the learner model depend largely on the kind of adaptation effect that the system has to deliver.

Learning Style: Learning style discusses learners' personal differences in preferences to receive and process information during instruction. It influences students' motivation and technology use. Individual learning styles should be considered by teachers and other education practitioners when designing and implementing classroom activities utilizing social networking sites. Preparing a learning environment that reflects students' needs is essential in improving their academic performance.

Thinking Style: Thinking style refers to the way a person's natural predisposition in processing information embodying the qualities of thinking processes as well as types of thinking. Understanding of a person's thinking style is important in all areas of social dealings. Models of thinking styles are varied, some of which are concerned with thinker's personality traits, and others were interested in answering the question of how a thinker receives, processes, and align experiences, whereas others were focused on the sensory perceptual medium most preferable to a thinker when receiving, processing and aligning experiences. These models are: Carl Jung, Kolb, Dunn and Dunn thinking style model, Myers Briggs type indicator (MBTI) model, McCarthy, Honey and Mumford, Felder Silverman, Sternberg model, and Herrmann model.

Chapter 6
Using the Web While Offline:
A Case Comparison

Stuart Dillon
University of Waikato, New Zealand

Karyn Rastrick
University of Waikato, New Zealand

Florian Stahl
University of Muenster, Germany

Gottfried Vossen
University of Muenster, Germany

ABSTRACT

Whilst access to the internet is becoming increasingly ubiquitous in highly populated, urban areas, for much of the planet web connectively is still largely absent. This is mainly due to geographic remoteness, but bad connectivity or governmental controls might also prevent web users from accessing desired resources. The authors have previously outlined a general approach to cope with such situations, which they termed "Web in your Pocket" (WiPo). WiPo assumes that the user has a smart device to which appropriate data, ideally in curated form, can be pre-loaded so that it remains accessible offline. In this chapter, the authors present the potential usability of WiPo by considering three important use-cases (tourism, health, and search and rescue) demonstrating the vast potential of WiPo. The chapter concludes by considering the practical issues that need to be overcome before it might be implemented in real-world situations.

INTRODUCTION

Online data is both superabundant and growing at an unprecedented rate. It is also being used for an increasing number and variety of contexts and use cases, which can easily be verified in many applications in both the private and business domains. In less than 10 years we have become almost completely reliant on cloud-based services for entertainment, information, education, and communication and increasingly

DOI: 10.4018/978-1-5225-5384-7.ch006

businesses are favoring cloud applications and platforms over local installations. Accessing "The Cloud" however is only possible with the availability of a reliable and efficient Internet connection. While this is indeed the case most of the time in western, urban contexts, situations remain where a user or an application cannot access the Web, due to server unavailability, bad connectivity, or access restrictions. In this chapter, we consider the case where Web access is (temporarily or permanently) unavailable due to various reasons, yet a user desires the most relevant and up-to-date Web data appropriate to their needs. To achieve this, we build upon the Web-in-your-Pocket (WiPo) architecture presented in Dillon, Stahl, & Vossen (2013a) and present a detailed proof of concept for its future application by studying how the WiPo concept can be applied to three distinct use cases.

WiPo is based on the concept of having access to a specialized data service that has been configured precisely to a user's needs that automatically sources, curates, and delivers data in a subject-centric way. This user-tailored data service is available online, but is unique in that it can also be made available offline on mobile devices. This latter "application" we name as "Web in your Pocket" or WiPo for short, shares some of the characteristics of digital newsstands such as Zinio or digital notebooks such as Evernote. A key feature of WiPo is the ability to obtain automatic updates of highly dynamic data as and when internet access is available. Unlike search engines, which "pull" information from the Web following a manual, user-initiated ad-hoc query, WiPo takes the form of a service from which information can be obtained from various public (open) and private (closed) sources that follows a (more or less detailed) specification of what is desired and which has undergone some form of curation.

As we have outlined in Dillon et al., (2013a) use cases can be distinguished by various dimensions, most notably by (1) the type of application, i.e., profit or not-for-profit, (2) data provision frequency, i.e., one-off data access or continuously refreshing/updating or something in between, and (3) data broadness, i.e., the number of data sources consulted (singular or multiple). The use-cases we present in this chapter have been selected as they provide a diverse range of applications that demonstrate these dimensions and are not solely business-profit-focused. The first case address the tourist scenario utilizing a private WiPo application where the user is interested in up to date data coming from a variety of relevant sources, before travelling with intermittent Web access. Next is a health application which is both for-profit and not-for-profit (potentially used by both medical practitioners and patients), requires regular data updates, and relies on a number of public and (importantly) private data sources. Finally, the very specific case of Search and Rescue is considered. In this application, data needs to be continually updated as Web access allows, where multiple, predominantly private, sources are employed.

The objective of this chapter is to clearly articulate practical real-world applications of the WiPo concept. This will be achieved by firstly summarizing relevant related work giving particular attention to well-established and relevant technologies on which WiPo is founded. The chapter then presents brief overview of WiPo. These two sections are intentionally brief as a more detailed description is provided in Dillon et al., (2013a) and the reader is encouraged to read this. We then demonstrate the potential of WiPo through the consideration of the three carefully selected use cases. The general characteristics of these cases are highlighted to demonstrate the flexibility and application breadth of WiPo. Following that we collect several considerations regarding an implementation of WiPo. Finally, directions for further research and development of the WiPo concept are outlined, in particular in the direction of coping with today's information overload. For more specific discussion of the WiPo concept, as well as some basic consideration of issues pertaining to security and pricing, the reader is directed to Dillon et al., (2013a).

BACKGROUND

The Web in the Pocket (WiPo) concept is in a broad sense comparable to the notion of a (materialized) data warehouse (Inmon, 2005; Vossen, Schönthaler, & Dillon, 2017) that is made portable and only intermittently connected to the primary data sources. Also related is research on search engines, e.g. Cafarella, Halevy, & Madhavan (2011) who examine how search engines can index Web pages, also referred to as deep Web sites, that to date cannot be indexed by traditional search algorithms. Building data marts or services on these deep Web sources is described by Baumgartner, Campi, Georg, & Herzog (2010). Generally speaking, however, retrieval and indexing of documents from such sources is no longer the problem it used to be, though far from being solved in its entirety (Baeza-Yates & Raghavan, 2010).

There are several issues to address in order to fully satisfy current and likely future information needs. Dopichaj (2009) found that it was technically impossible using traditional search to meaningfully answer queries such as "return all pages that contain product evaluations of fridges by European users". A similar conclusion was reached by Ceri (2010). To solve this, Dopichaj advocates the Semantic Web, the idea of which is to enhance text on the Web by semantic information to make it machine understandable. Ceri (2010), on the other hand, proposed the so called Search Computing (SeCo) framework of which a detailed description of the architecture is provided by Bozzon, Brambilla, Ceri, Corcoglioniti, Gatti & Milano (2010a). In brief, a query to a SeCo search engine is processed by a query optimizer that determines suitable search services to which it sends sub-queries. Campi, Ceri, Gottlob, Maesani, & Ronchi (2010) describe how service marts (e.g., as suggested by Baumgartner et al., 2010) can be built and registered with the framework. Search service results are then joined and displayed to users. In a subsequent step, users have the opportunity to modify their queries. This is referred to as liquid query processing (Bozzon, Brambilla, Ceri, & Fraternali, 2010b). In order to realize this framework, two new user groups need to be created: providers of data offering data as a services and developers building search services based on data services. Another significant limitation of search, and one that is yet to be addressed by artificial intelligence, and able to cope with the vast quantities of information available on the web, humans are more adept at processing unstructured information and at recognizing unusual circumstances and their consequences (Nagar & Malone, 2011).

We have previously outlined (Dillon et al., 2013a) our vision for digital curation as a powerful, process-based tool for dealing with multiple, often contradictory data sources. One of the few previous approaches combining curation and Web Information Retrieval (IR) has been proposed by Sanderson, Harrison & Llewellyn (2006) who suggest (focusing on a single domain) a process similar to life science data consolidation as described by Kulikova, Aldebert, & Althorpe (2004). In life science, for instance, different institutions contribute to a nucleotide sequence databases; to ensure consistency data are exchanged on a nightly bases (Kulikova et al., 2004). Sanderson et al., (2006) apply this procedure to content retrieval by sending predefined queries to preregistered services on a nightly basis. Relevant information is harvested and temporarily stored. The retrieved information is then audited by (human) data curators who decide upon its relevance and discard what is unwanted. Moreover, care is taken to prevent harvesting the same data more than once. A similar harvest and curation approach was suggested by Lee, Marciano, Hou, & Shah (2009) who outline ideas to enhance their ContextMiner (see contextminer.org, as an example of a tool offering contextual information to data) by making it scalable. However, apart from the research cited here there is seemingly no in-depth research on combining data curation and IR and even the approaches of those cited appear to limited potential to serve information needs on a large scale in a sophisticated way. In any data curation process humans are probably needed at some point, which is why the education and qualification of data curators is also discussed in the literature (Heidorn, Tobbo, Choudhury, Greer, & Marciano, 2007; Smith, 2008; Palmer, Allard, & Marlino, 2011).

We next propose a significant advancement to the field of data curation and information retrieval with a concept that also takes into account data access inconsistency and mobile data visualization.

WiPo Overview

The overall process view of the WiPo approach is generic and applicable to many use cases. The concrete application design, however, is use-case dependent, i.e., the individual steps of the process has to be implemented considering the purpose of the application and the specific needs of the respective user. Figure 1 shows the overall WiPo architecture, where thin arrows indicate a relationship between two items and block arrows represent the flow of data within the process.

At the highest level the overall WiPo process consists of five steps: Input Preparation, resulting in a list of potential sources and pre-filters; Source Selection, resulting in a list of sources; Data Mining, resulting in raw data; Past Filters, reducing the raw data to "relevant" raw data; and finally Curation. Using a suitable interface, a user will upload documents, supply a list of relevant links, and potentially also keywords. Input Preparation will then convert the given documents to a standard file format (e. g., XML) so that generic classifier can be applied. Any given URLs will be crawled and also fed into the classifier. In that way from both Figure 1 data curation and the WiPo process the given documents and URLs, the essence is extracted in the form of topics or additional keywords. These mined keywords as well as the user-supplied keywords are then used to choose appropriate sources from a list of all available sources (which might also be extended based on user supplied URLs). Furthermore, relevant additional

Figure 1. WiPo Data Process

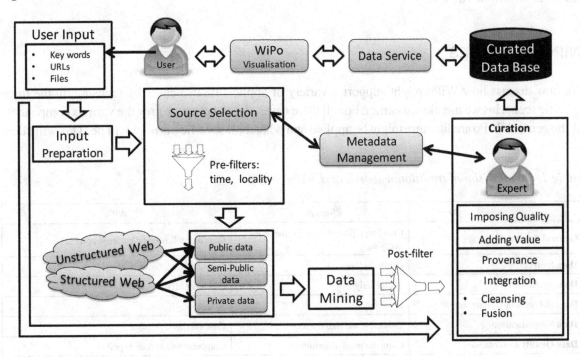

dimensions such as time or location are determined to generate a list of data sources. Pre-filters might also be applied such as when the user specifies the exclusion of certain data or the services purchased excludes private sources. A future consideration will be the inclusion of language conversion or translation, depending on where or by whom it is used.

A major aspect of WiPo is the curation component, which is intended to assure high data quality of the output. As outlined in Dillon et al. (2013a), the original idea of "digital" curation was first discussed in the library sciences, where it is focused on large sets of physical, biological, or astronomical data with the aim of preserving data gained through scientific experiments for later usage (Choudhury, 2008; Palmer et al., 2011). What is done to given data has also proved useful in other contexts such as data warehousing, namely data extraction, data cleansing, data fusion, data integration, and data provenance or lineage. However, we assume here that additionally an "expert" will verify and eventually even modify the results of these operations prior to their delivery to the user. This expert can in some cases be an algorithm, i.e., software, in others it may be an externally provisioned service, perhaps with human or even crowd involvement. WiPo has also been proposed as a possible solution to modern-day information overload. Dillon, Stahl, Vossen & Rastrick (2013b) describe how contemporary information overload is caused, in part, by issues of poor or inadequate information management and, as a result, it impacts the quality of decision making. Information management and decision making can both be addressed by condensing the amount of information available. This means that an adequate process of information management can provide information that is ready to be consumed because it is reduced to a size that can be handled by an individual. The curation result will be documented in an index, repository, or a catalogue that also comprises meta-data for future updates and enhancements. A more technical summary of the WiPo architecture is provided later where we outline a prototypical implementation.

WiPo offers a unique and innovative approach to data provisioning that differs in a number of ways from traditional approaches. The uniqueness of it is best outlined through a comparison with traditional search as shown in Table 1.

WIPO USE CASES

We now discuss how WiPo might support a variety of application use-cases by focusing on the three specific scenarios we mentioned earlier. For all three cases, we elaborate on how the various components of the general WiPo architecture might be applied and what their specific purpose will be. This will allow

Table 1. Comparison of traditional search and WiPo

	Search	**WiPo**
General Approach	Crawling followed by one-time index querying	Crawling followed by curation process
Data Sources	Public, online	Public/private, online/offline
Data Availability	Online only	Online or offline
Data Refreshing/Update	Upon request	Automatic
Data Sophistication	Limited – one size fits all	Customizable, flexible
Data Quality Determinant	Computational algorithms	Computer and human expert

us to (1) conduct a comparison between the various cases as a means of identifying their commonalities (and differences), and (2) to draw general conclusions on the requirements that individualization and personalization impose on a data service whose goal is to help individuals or organizations to cope with the information overload such a data service is likely to impose.

Tourism

Tourism is an information-intensive industry, yet information portability is traditionally not easily achieved. Consider a hypothetical example of a tourist, wishing to travel through a mountainous region without internet coverage, but wishes to access information about the location he or she is looking in. WiPo would permit the user, who we assume to have a mobile device, to access appropriate data, preferably in curated form, that has been loaded in advance, so that it remains accessible offline. Traditionally, the user would utilize one of several travel-related websites. Alternatively, s/he could install dedicated apps such as itravelnz.com or tuhura.com on his smartphone and go from there. The problem s/he faces is that when they are without Web access they are only partially covered by these services and is heavily reliant on information s/he has previous downloaded. It is exactly here where WiPo comes in. To be more precise, the user might state as input that s/he plans to do a hiking trip along the Central Plateau of New Zealand's North Island, and that it needs to be completed within eight days at a reasonable budget and that s/he is particularly interested in paleo-botany, i.e., the identification of plant remains from geological contexts. To this end, s/he is familiar with the PaleoNet pages, which support the communication among paleontologists, as well as sources such as the Paleo-botanical Section of the Botanical Society of America or the International Organization of Palaeobotany. So her/his input to WiPo will consist of a list of keywords describing (a) her/his field of interest and (b) her/his intended route. Based on this input, WiPo will be able to execute a dedicated crawl and search of the Web regarding accommodation, transportation, weather, health tips, emergency precautions, history, and stone formations, extracted from multiple sites, and will then try to arrange these findings in a list of prioritized items, starting from paleo-related topics and ending in weather and general travel conditions. We imagine that these items will take the forms of textual abstracts of information found on the Web (the section on implementation considerations below will indicate how we intend to realize this), which are either classified according to the users original keywords or clustered according to WiPo's findings. During the curation step, the results will be composed into a plan that is ordered along a timeline indicating a sequence of steps along a recommended path. The composition will integrate data that is overlapping as well as eliminate redundant findings; it will also record the data sources especially for scientific data. Ultimately, WiPo will return a document comprising all the information resulting from the curation step, which will contain a map as well as a schedule and relevant roadside information. Given that users tend to be very sensitive with regard to the speed of service delivery, WiPo should in this case return immediate results where ever possible (e.g., transportation timetables). In cases where results need to be compiled according to specific user's needs this should be done within (a few) hours. Thus, this service can be considered a medium-term service in this case.

Health

There exists a vast array of technology-related opportunities within the health sector and as such, rich grounds for research. The health use case allows us to consider a multi-user application of WiPo. The primary user is likely to be the patient, perhaps a sufferer of a particular, probably chronic, condition. The user will require access to their medical records, provided by a private source such as a national health database. Primary users may also have an interest in relevant medical support groups, research centers etc. which will be accessed from a range of sites, both public and private. Users may even be willing to pay for higher-quality information, such as what would come from member-only sources. Secondary users, such as caregivers, friends, or family may also find value in this application of WiPo. Medical personnel, in particular paramedics, are another key user group and would use WiPo, should they need to rapidly obtain patient information when "out in the field". Careful consideration will need to be given to access rights and permissions to ensure that confidentiality breaches do not occur. We anticipate that for medical personnel, WiPo will only be used when traditional database access is not possible and WiPo will only provide key emergency information such as significant patient medical conditions, allergies etc. For now we focus on the primary user of this possible WiPo service. Unlike in the previous tourist case, this application will benefit from the involvement of many primary users (patients) in order to unfold its full potential; maybe even a dedicated social network could be installed to enable collaborative filtering. Given that this service is intended for continued usage, users might tolerate a longer search period (e.g., a couple of days) as long as the resulting data quality is sufficiently high. Further, medical conditions do not go away, in particular if they are chronic, even though sufferers will come and go; thus this service can be considered a long term service. Long term services usually provide functionality that informs users of new developments and novel information; consequently, this is something that should be added to WiPo for this particular use case.

Search and Rescue

In our final and most detailed case, we consider the very specialized application of search and rescue services. Search and rescue is typically context specific and can involve one of many complex scenarios. For example, in New Zealand, Search and Rescue support is sought in a wide array of situations. One such situation is a missing child in an urban area, such as a school aged child wandering from school grounds. Another very common situation where search and rescue services might be utilized to locate a tramper is overdue or lost in mountainous terrain. Each situation requires an array of specific information needs. While specific situations vary greatly within one region, additional variances are introduced by policies and governance structures in specific countries or even states/regions within a country. Such variance in situations and process makes for an ideal WiPo case.

More specifically, in the situation where a search team is searching for a lost party – perhaps lost in dense forest or bushland – WiPo would aid the rapid data collection and compilation required. Traditionally "search managers" in an incident management center would gather information from a range of sources such as search theory texts, historical search databases, maps, as well as online sources such as weather forecast providers. Specific information on the lost party is also gathered, such as health information about the lost party. Additional complications are added to this case such as challenging terrain and extremely limited Web connectivity. Information gathered is then utilized by multiple members of a search management team as well as field members of the search team. Historically this information would be in a variety of formats both online and offline. Search teams who will go into the field – in this case the dense forest – would also need an array of information. Such team members would often be given maps, copies of photos and any other relevant information. In addition, individuals would take their own notes at team briefings. Dealing with such an array of online and offline information over multiple users presents many challenges especially when dealing with more informal information sources such as handwritten notes taken in haste. A search and rescue WiPo based application would allow users to input specific information requirements such as the profile of the lost party, mapping requirements, and regional information requirements such as weather information. WiPo would then extract specific profile information, URL selections, and keywords to match relevant search specific information requirements. The relevant data from an array of sources would be compiled and manipulated by using tools such as data mining. A specific example of how data might be mined is searching for specific problem spots in the specific type of terrain in the region in prior searches. Data would then be matched and integrated to provide end users with an array of search specific graphical and text based information in the WiPo application. The development of a search and rescue WiPo would likely involve a major sponsor as well as contributions from government and non-government organizations. It is inherent to search and rescue that it is time-critical, therefore this service must be a (very) short-term service. Moreover, this service also needs to be refreshed as fast as possible whenever the situation at hand changes in order to be able to handle the situation optimally. Rastrick, Stahl, Vossen & Dillon (2015) tested the WiPo concept with a number of New Zealand Search and Rescue personnel. These included search managers, technical experts, and field volunteers. Upon learning of the core functionality of WiPo, and the alignment of that will the typical search and rescue situation, study participants were unanimously positive about its potential for improving search and rescue management and outcomes. In particular, it was the ability to access "pre-sourced", stored data whilst out of internet "range" that appealed most to the study participants. We see search and rescue being a perfect future application for WiPo, or indeed similar technologies.

Case Comparison

Comparing the representative cases outlined above, WiPo is obviously applicable to all of them and potentially many more. As stated earlier, however, WiPo always has to be tailored towards its specific use case. Thus, we have mapped how we envisage the usage of the different applications introduced in the previous subsections against the primary components of the WiPo architecture. A summary can be found in the Appendix. Notice that all cases can be characterized by the same set of attributes, and we expect the same to hold for other use cases not considered here. Next, we present the relevance of the components as well as general characteristics derived from the study of these cases:

- **Target User:** The target user can be an individual, a group of individuals, an organization, or even a governmental organization. Thus, WiPo can be exploited by a variety of customers for their purposes, and it can help these customers to have access to proper information in their individual use cases;
- **User Input:** Input can range from a few keywords and URLs to comprehensive user profiles containing information about, e.g., their medical history, and to documents from which tags or keywords need to be extracted by WiPo;
- **Additional Input:** Input may in many cases be processed completely automatically and thus, additional input will also be determined automatically. In other cases an interactive mode must be available to get all necessary information from the user;
- **Source Selection / Service Composition:** Although highly topic- and case-dependent, original sources are in all cases predefined sources and user-added Web resources. Depending on the case,

WiPo may not be able to provide all the information requested from its own database, but may have to refer to other data services. These aspects may even lead into the related area of data marketplaces, discussed, for example, by Schomm, Stahl, & Vossen (2013) or Vossen et al. (2017), where negotiations might become necessary with external data providers in order to stay within a user-specified budget;

- **Type of Information:** As can be seen from the search & rescue case, where a lost person's behavior might affect that type of information, in some cases static as well as dynamic data would be needed;
- **Data Mining and Curation:** Again, though use-case dependent the actual steps are fairly similar. Examples illustrating that can be found in the Appendix;
- **Service Response Time:** The time the WiPo service takes to respond can also vary from one application the next, and may range from long to medium to short and even very short. As the use cases discussed above indicate, some may need an instantaneous response, while others may tolerate an overnight computation;
- **Service Refreshing Requirements:** Like a data warehouse that is being used for decision-making purposes, a data service provisioned by WiPo will need none, or user-specified (i.e., periodic or on-demand) or user-independent refreshing and maintenance. A typical example is the health care case discussed above, where new research results may become known over time which should be incorporated into what a user already knows about a particular condition. On the other hand, our traveler Tom will most likely not revisit the Central Plateau in the near future again, so that an update to the data he has received will not be needed;
- **Visualization & Output:** This will have to be adapted to the specific use case as much as possible and can take any form such as tables of additional references, sophisticated charts, probabilistic analyses, or maps indicating recommended routes or dangerous areas;
- **Business Model:** In order to describe suitable business models for WiPo in general and for the use cases in particular, we build on previous research such as Rappa (2010) as well as on our own research regarding applied pricing models on data markets (Schomm et al., 2013; Muschalle, Stahl, Löser, & Vossen, 2012; Vossen et al., 2017). Data market pricing is considered as WiPo can be seen as a service (re)selling data. Readers interested in a more technical view of electronic business are referred to Papazoglou and Ribbers (2006).

Rappa (2010) distinguishes nine basic business models, each with several sub-forms. Most of the cases in this chapter, represented first and foremost by the tourism case, provide information to end-users and thus can be considered a content provider. In Rappa's classification, this is a sub-form of the subscription models, but explicitly includes free and freemium pricing, which are widely adopted by the market (Schomm et al., 2013; Muschalle et al., 2012; Vossen et al., 2017). Although not explicitly included by Rappa, it would be worth considering package or tiered pricing (Muschalle et al., 2012). The tiers could be realized as follows:

- **Basic:** This version of the service will be free, e.g., in case where the data accumulated is free (such as open governmental data) or there is so much competition (as in the travel and tourism industry) that users are highly price sensitive;

- **Intermediate:** The data service will in many cases need to go beyond a registration requirement in order to access the desired data; to this end, the service will use a generic registration independent of the particular user, but the user must be registered with WiPo for that, as illustrated in Figure 2. Given that it is likely that cost will incur to access protected content, there may be a charge for this tier;
- **Premium:** In this version the service would also include enhanced functionality besides access to the data of the lower tier. For instance this could be a more sophisticated recommender than in the basic version. Consequently, this would be charged at a premium price.

Arguably, this way of pricing is just a form of bundled pay-per-use or usage-based pricing (Schomm et al., 2013; Muschalle et al., 2012) which again is widely adopted. Rappa puts this metered subscription in the category of utility models. In particular when plenty of computation and curation is necessary, for instance in the medical case, it would also be comprehendible to apply pure usage-based pricing, where it is charged based on the amount of data processed/ provided and/or on the amount of computation necessary.

Applicable in particular to the health case would be the community model or more precisely the social network model of Rappa's classification, while a distinct business model in terms of pricing it typically follows the free (usually supported by advertising) or freemium model described above. Probably applicable to only a few cases (e.g., the search and rescue case) but nevertheless a valid model for WiPo is Rappa's manufacturer purchase or lease model. In this case the entire WiPo software would be sold or licensed to a customer so that they can run it according to their needs. This model is already successfully applied by some data markets (Muschalle et al., 2012).

Figure 2. WiPo registration handling

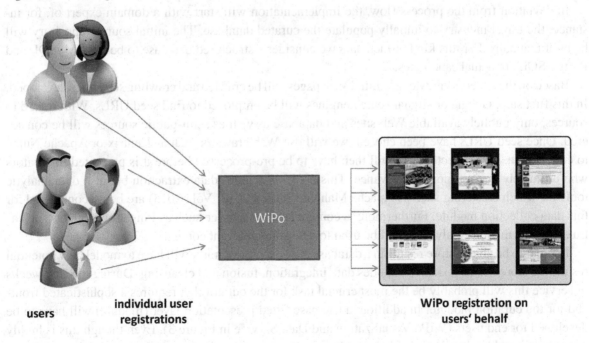

| users | individual user registrations | | WiPo registration on users' behalf |

IMPLEMENTATION CONSIDERATIONS

We next briefly elaborate on implementation considerations for WiPo, primarily indicating that building a service such as WiPo is not an insurmountable task. In particular, we look at how to build a version of WiPo from a host of existing services, as many functional components referred to in WiPo already exist in isolation. Therefore, it is likely that an initial version of WiPo can be built by selecting relevant existing services and integrating them appropriately. Clearly, an alternative would be to build WiPo from scratch, which is not considered further here because of the extraordinary efforts that would go along with this "reinvention of the wheel". Thus, only an orchestrator will be implemented in the first place.

In terms of organization we intend to develop the prototype using Feature Driven Development (FDD) as well as Test Driven Development (TDD). FDD refers to the fact that we want to use the architecture and use cases as requirement specification and develop the actual prototype in an agile fashion feature by feature. This implies that we do not have any concrete data model in mind at the outset. Nevertheless, we plan to build a modular architecture in order to be able to exchange one module for another if it turns out that a better technology becomes available. Due to TDD (where tests are coded before any implementation is done), we notice immediately if such an exchange can lead to problems with the already existing software (Martin, 2008; Puri, 2009).

In Figure 3 we present a simplified version of the architecture shown in Figure 1 which will serve as a blueprint (set of modules) for the first implementation. The main part of the prototype will be the orchestrator which can be seen as the "glue" between all other parts. At this point, we plan to implement it in Java. Its main task will be feeding data into services or other components and storing the results in a database (which could be a relational database, a more recent NoSQL system, or even incorporated as service, e.g., Amazon RDS or Amazon DynamoDB). In favor of being in full control of the data ourselves, we currently consider NoSQL systems such as MongoDB the most useful because of their flexibility. All this comprises the curated database module.

In deviation from the process flow, the implementation will start with a domain expert of, for instance, the travel industry to initially populate the curated database. The initial source repository will be built manually. For this kind of metadata we consider a structured database to be best. MySQL and PostgreSQL are actual candidates.

Based on the expert's knowledge, initial Web pages will be crawled and crawling schedules developed. In this first step, Google or similar search engines will be employed to find seed URLs. With regard to sources, only publicly available Web sites and database as well as semi-public sources will be considered. Once seed URLs have been chosen, we will use Web crawlers such as Hentrix or Apache Nutch to collect data. The collected data will then have to be pre-processed before it is presented to curators who ultimately decide upon its relevance. This process includes data extraction but also data analytic tools for which clustering such as Apache Mahout (Steffen 2013; Volz 2013) are being considered for this data collection module. Furthermore, a content analysis service such as Pingar or products such as Luxid® Information Analytics could be used to determine relevant content.

In order to be able to store results in a database, however, the curator will have to model how potential results are stored. This task also includes data integration, fusion and cleansing. During the first weeks of service this will probably be the most crucial task for the curator that requires a sophisticated front-end for the curation module. In addition, a use-case fitted presentation layer (module) will have to be developed for end users (WiPo Visualization and Data Service in Figure 3). Even though this is highly use-case-dependent, it will probably be built making heavy use of external sources such as JavaScript

Figure 3. Basic WiPo service implementation

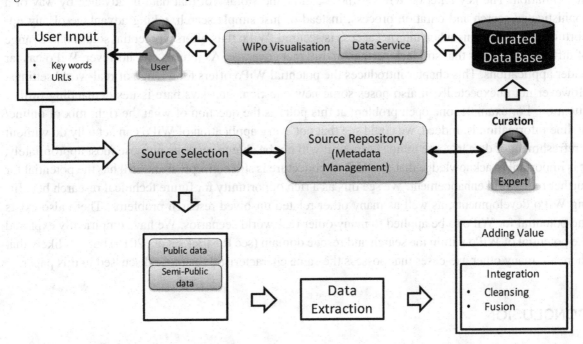

and Ajax libraries (e.g., jQuery and jQuery UI with their many plug-ins), charting libraries, and third-party map services such as Google Maps. Additionally, frameworks such as Bootstrap are currently under consideration to simplify front-end development.

In the initial implementation users will only be asked to provide keywords and URLs. The orchestrator matches these keywords against an index build on the curated database, for instance using Apache Solr. New URLs will be added to the source repository and crawled instantly. Simultaneously, the keywords will also be fed into a search engine such as Google to determine new, possibly valuable, sources. These will then also be set up for dedicated crawling.

Eventually the data flow will be as follows: Data will be autonomously collected from the Internet, reviewed by curators, and stored in the curated database. However, users can also trigger data collection by providing additional URLs which can be crawled. In order to exchange data easily between different components it is likely that either JSON or XML will be used as a format. The former has the advantage that many NoSQL databases store data in JSON. At this point, it is hard to tell how much data we will actually be collected because of the numerous unknowns such as the specificity of the data being searched for, and the amount of data returned and subsequently curated in response to the sought data.

FUTURE RESEARCH DIRECTIONS

In this chapter, we have introduced three particular use cases for our general WiPo architecture: tourism, health, and search & rescue. We have described how WiPo might be exploited in each case, identifying commonalities and differences as we do. WiPo is intended as a tool for individualized information management that handles situations in which users are offline, yet demand up to date data relevant to that situation. The key tenet of WiPo is the location and storage of that data in advance by way of a sophisticated search and curation process, instead of just simple search, taking advantage of any opportunity to update this when internet access is secured. WiPo thus offers a potential solution to a range of different scenarios that still lack permanent internet coverage. As it turns out, however, WiPo has far wider applications. This chapter introduces the potential WiPo offers for a range of real-world settings. However not unexpectedly, it also poses some new questions and lays bare issues demanding further attention. For example, one open problem at this point is the question of what the right mix of online/offline information is. Indeed, we could see that not every application of WiPo can actually do without a refreshment of data in some minor form, or it will not be able to serve its purpose most appropriately. It is important to acknowledge that the WiPo architecture is still conceptual and still has the potential for further real-world enhancement. We see this as a rich opportunity for future technical research benefiting WiPo developments, as well as many other related unsolved research problems. There also exists the potential for WiPo to be applied to many other real-world scenarios. We have empirically explored the potential of WiPo within the search and rescue domain (see Rastrick, et al., 2015) but it is likely that there are many other use-cases that possess the same characteristics as those discussed in this paper.

CONCLUSION

By looking at the example cases of tourism, healthcare, and search & rescue, we present a novel perspective on a somewhat larger context and problem, that of the information overload, that people have been struggling with and complaining about since the inception of the Web. The phrase "we are drowning in data, but starving for information" is a well-known characterization of this situation, yet WiPo is able to point to a solution. This solution is based on the recognition that, even in the presence of an abundance of data, it is often not of interest to find all that exists, but only some of what is relevant for a particular purpose or to a particular situation.

REFERENCES

Baeza-Yates, R., & Raghavan, P. (2010). Next Generation Web Search. In *Challenges and Directions*. Springer-Verlag Berlin.

Baumgartner, R., Campi, A., Georg, G., & Herzog, M. (2010). Web Data Extraction for Service Creation. In *Challenges and Directions*. Springer-Verlag Berlin.

Bozzon, A., Brambilla, M., Ceri, S., Corcoglioniti, F., Gatti, N., & Milano, P. (2010a). Building Search Computing Applications. In *Challenges and Directions*. Springer-Verlag Berlin.

Bozzon, A., Brambilla, M., Ceri, S., & Fraternali, P. (2010b). Liquid query: Multi-domain exploratory search on the web. In S. Ceri & M. Brambilla (Eds.), *Search Computing. Challenges and Directions. Springer-Verlag*. doi:10.1145/1772690.1772708

Cafarella, M. J., Halevy, A., & Madhavan, J. (2011). Structured data on the Web. *Communications*, *54*(2), 72–79.

Campi, A., Ceri, S., Gottlob, G., Maesani, A., & Ronchi, S. (2010). Service Marts. In *Challenges and Directions*. Springer-Verlag Berlin.

Ceri, S. (2010). Search Computing. In *Challenges and Directions*. Springer-Verlag Berlin.

Choudhury, G. S. (2008). Case Study in Data Curation at Johns Hopkins University. *Library Trends*, *57*(2), 211–220. doi:10.1353/lib.0.0028

Dillon, S., Stahl, F., & Vossen, G. (2013a). Towards the Web in Your Pocket: Curated Data as a Service. In *Advanced Methods for Computational Intelligence*. Springer.

Dillon, S., Stahl, F., Vossen, G., & Rastrick, K. (2013b). A Contemporary Approach to Coping with Modern Information Overload. *Communications of the ICISA*, *14*(1), 1–24.

Dopichaj, P. (2009). RankingVerfahren für Web-Suchmaschinen. In D. Lewandowski (Ed.), *Handbuch Internet-Suchmaschinen*. Heidelberg, Germany: Nutzerorientierung in Wissenschaft und Praxis. AKA, Akad. Verl.-Ges.

Heidorn, P., Tobbo, H., Choudhury, G., Greer, C., & Marciano, R. (2007). Identifying best practices and skills for workforce development in data curation. *Proceedings of the American Society for Information Science and Technology*, *44*(1), 1–3. doi:10.1002/meet.1450440141

Inmon, W. H. (2005). *Building the Data Warehouse* (4th ed.). New York: John Wiley & Sons.

Kulikova, T., Aldebert, P., & Althorpe, N. (2004). The EMBL Nucleotide Sequence Database. *Nucleic Acids Research*, *32*(90001), 27–30. doi:/gkh120 PMID:1468135110.1093/nar

Lee, C. A., Marciano, R., Hou, C.-y., & Shah, C. (2009). From harvesting to cultivating. In *Proceedings of the 9th ACM/ IEEE-CS joint Conference on Digital Libraries*. Austin, TX: ACM Press.

Martin, R. C. (2008). *Clean Code: A Handbook of Agile Software Craftsmanship*. Hoboken, NJ: Prentice-Hall.

Muschalle, A., Stahl, F., Löser, A., & Vossen, G. (2012). Pricing Approaches for Data Markets. *6th International VLDB Workshop on Business Intelligence for the Real Time Enterprise (BIRTE)*, 129-144.

Nagar, Y., & Malone, T. W. (2011). Making Business Predictions by Combining Human and Machine Intelligence in Prediction Markets. *Proc. 32nd International Conference on Information Systems*.

Palmer, C. L., Allard, S., & Marlino, M. (2011). Data curation education in research centers. In *Proceedings of the 2011 iConference* (pp. 738–740). New York: ACM. 10.1145/1940761.1940891

Papazoglou, M., & Ribbers, P. (2006). *E-Business: Organizational and Technical Foundations*. New York: John Wiley & Sons.

Puri, C. P. (2009). *Agile Management: Feature Driven Development*. Global India Publications Pvt Ltd.

Rappa, M. (2010). *Business Models on the Web*. Available online at http://digitalenterprise.org/models/models.html

Rastrick, K., Stahl, F., Vossen, G., & Dillon, S. (2015). WiPo for SAR: Taking the Web in Your Pocket when Doing Search and Rescue in New Zealand. *International Journal of Information Systems for Crisis Response and Management, 7*(4), 46–66. doi:10.4018/IJISCRAM.2015100103

Sanderson, R., Harrison, J., & Llewellyn, C. (2006). A curated harvesting approach to establishing a multiprotocol online subject portal: Opening information horizons. In *6th ACM/IEEE-CS Joint Conference on Digital Libraries 2006*. ACM.

Schomm, F., Stahl, F., & Vossen, G. (2013). Marketplaces for Data: An Initial Survey. *SIGMOD Record, 42*(1), 15–26. doi:10.1145/2481528.2481532

Smith, P. L. II. (2008). Where IR you? Using "open access" to extend the reach and richness of faculty research within a university. *OCLC Systems & Services, 24*(3), 174–184. doi:10.1108/10650750810898219

Steffen, D. (2013). *Parallelized Analysis of Opinions and their Diffusion in Online Sources* (Master thesis). University of Münster, Germany.

Volz, V. (2013). *Searching for Crowdfunding Projects using Mahout* (Bachelor Thesis). University of Münster, Germany.

Vossen, G., Schönthaler, F., & Dillon, S. (2017). *The Web at Graduation and Beyond – Business*. Springer Nature, Switzerland: Impacts and Developments. doi:10.1007/978-3-319-60161-8

KEY TERMS AND DEFINITIONS

Curation: The involvement of a human to review and tend to data.

Data as a Service: An extension of the established cloud computing models (e.g., software as a service) that characterizes a service orientation of data.

Offline Information Access: The ability to collect and locally store web data for later access.

Search and Rescue: The activity undertaken to locate and recover missing persons.

Semantic Web: The idea of which is to enhance text on the web by semantic information to make it machine understandable.

URL: Uniform resource locator.

Web in Your Pocket: The name given by the authors to a concept of being able to access web data without an internet connection.

APPENDIX

Use Case Comparison

Table 2 provides a summary of the three described use cases against a number of relevant attributes. It shows that a 'one size fits all' approach is unlikely to serve the needs of different cases. We believe that the use of standardized attributes and an associated modular design provides a good balance between having all uses cases adopt a single architecture versus establishing use case-specific architectures.

Table 2. Summary of the three described use cases against relevant attributes

Use Case → Attribute ↓	Tourism	Health Care	Search and Rescue
Target user The main user group. Recognizing this is important as user needs and capabilities often vary.	Individual	Group of individuals	Governmental or not for profit organizations
User Input Incorporates both the type of data input (e.g., text, URLs, calendar information etc.) as well as particular content (e.g., budget information, medical details etc.)	• Destination/Location • Calendar limitations • Intended Route • Nature of the trip • Budget • Personal notes • Particular interests • Other restrictions, e.g., disabilities • Previously collected URLs	• Personal medical history • Summary of current medical condition • Keywords on specific concerns • Relevant personal notes, maybe a diary • Budget, or how much he/she is willing or able to spend • Previously collected URLs User profile, e.g., allergies, current medication (if any), incompatibilities	• Profile of lost party, e.g., health, physical condition • Key information on the lost party • Last known location • Type of rescue, e.g., air, ambulance, dog search • Type of transportation
Additional Input Any non-standard input that needs to be considered. It is often these types of input that prevent the adoption of standardized architectures.	• URL selection for Web crawling • Keywords extracted from the user input as well as from the Web pages crawled	• URL selection for Web crawling • Keywords extracted from the user input as well as from the Web pages crawled	• Location orientation • Weather conditions • Here and for finding out about the lost person's behavior, a Q&A option must be provided to interactively determine the situation and how it changes
Source Selection / Service composition This characterizes the primary non-human data input sources.	• Web sites about • Accommodation • Events • Transportation • Deals • Weather • Insurance • Health tips • Currency • Emergency • Reviews, advice, recommendations	• Web sites such as • Free medical blogs • Clinical decision support resources (e.g. uptodate.com) • Medical journals • Support groups • Closed communities	• Weather data • Manuals • Databases • Health characterization, what-if instructions
Type of Information Static or dynamic	Mainly Static	Mainly Static	Mainly dynamic situation-specific

continued on following page

Table 2. Continued

Use Case → Attribute ↓	Tourism	Health Care	Search and Rescue
Data Mining The manner by which required data is extracted from the data sources listed above.	• Specialized index construction • Clustering based on keywords determined • Classification based on user input • Association-rule mining for creating suggestions	• Content-based filtering • Collaborative filtering	• Search for similar previous cases • In this case data mining will also occur after the fact, as the service provider will want to determine what lessons were learnt and what can be improved or done differently in the future.
Curation The key process of taking the mined data, as well as that directly provided by the user(s), and then applying a set of context-specific rules to produce the required high-quality data.	• Trust analysis • Reduce data mining results (e.g., cut down the amount of associations rules) • Preparation of a trip plan • Data integration • Data provenance to keep track, • e.g., of the origins of price information	• Trust analysis • Data integration • Data provenance to keep track, • e.g., of the original sources in order to allow users to follow up on them • All of this oriented on the user profile	• Matching of predefined instructions with current situation • Integration as well as fusion of data
Service response time Classifies the likely curation duration, in-part determined by user needs	• Fast (seconds) for trivial information • Medium (minutes / hours) for computational intensive information specifically tailored	• Fast / medium (seconds) for trivial information • Long (hours / day) for highly curated patient-specific information	Fast (seconds / minutes) to enable task forces to work as efficient as possible
Service refresh requirements How often the curation process is applied	Medium (hours) as most of the information is static only recent events need to be updated	Long (days) as most of the information is static and it is potentially hard to mine new information for a specific user	Fast (seconds / minutes) as this is applied in a highly time-critical setting
Visualization & Output The required user output format	• Maps • Schedule • Instructions • Responses to user inquiry • Extension of the existing personal notes	• Prediction • Recommendations of o Text abstracts o Links o Statistics o Ranked based of the user profile	• Maps and other graphics • Images • Siri-type search team tasks and mission instructions • Scenario analysis
Business model The anticipated manner by which revenue might be generated from the WiPo application	• Freemium: • Basic service is free • Advanced service will likely include a nominal charge either subscription or pay-per-use based	• Tiered Pricing (increasing price per levels) o Basic service o Intermediate service o Professional service o Pay-per-Use o Social network	• Software selling, licensing • Applying a "bill me later" policy based on o Pay-per-use o Tiered pricing

Section 2
Web of Things and Semantics Employed

As information systems became ubiquitous their influence have reached "everywhere" globally, locally and in to depths generating endless possibilities for connection and connected devices. In turn, 'Web of Things' and eventually 'Internet of Things' evolved to epic dimensions of spread. There came the need to make sense of Big Data flowing in. Sampled in this section are optimized energy management; assisting children with autism; national healthcare delivery; and, making sense in search operations over big data.

Chapter 7
Improve Home Energy Management System by Extracting Usage Patterns From Power Usage Big Data of Homes' Appliances

Ali Reza Honarvar
Shiraz University, Iran

Ashkan Sami
Shiraz University, Iran

ABSTRACT

Many researchers have focused on the reduction of electricity usage in residences because it is a significant contributor of CO2 and greenhouse gases emissions. However, electricity conservation is a tedious task for residential users due to the lack of detailed electricity usage. Home energy management systems (HEMS) are schedulers that schedule and shift demands to improve the energy consumption on behalf of a consumer based on demand response. In this chapter, valuable sequence patterns from real appliances' usage datasets are extracted in peak time and off-peak time of weekdays and weekends to get valuable insight that is applicable in the HEMS. Generated data in smart cities and smart homes are placed in the category of big data. Therefore, to extract valuable information from such data an architecture for the home and city data processing system is proposed, which considers the multi-source smart cities and homes' data and big data processing platforms.

INTRODUCTION

Incorrect utilization of appliances alongside absence of a smart energy infrastructure leads to unnecessary energy consumption and waste in most places. Many researchers have focused on the reduction of electricity usage in residences because of its role in CO_2 and greenhouse gases emissions. However, electricity conservation is a tedious task for residential users due to lack of detailed electricity usage data.

DOI: 10.4018/978-1-5225-5384-7.ch007

Today, thanks to development of sensors, the power use information of apparatuses can be gathered effortlessly. Specifically, an expanding number of smart power meters, which helps data collection of appliance usage, have been deployed. If representative patterns of appliance electricity usage existed, inhabitants can adjust their apparatus utilization to conserve energy effectively (Chen, Deng, Wan, Zhang, Vasilakos, & Rong, 2015). Appliance usage patterns offer clients better assistance with understanding how they utilize the apparatuses at home and distinguish irregular uses. Additionally, appliance manufacturers may be encouraged to design clever control of smart appliances (Chen, Yi-Cheng, Chen, Peng, & Lee, 2014).

Data analysis system of smart environments is an instance of the context-aware applications, which help to make decisions in such a way to benefit the users of the system by analyzing and reasoning about the environmental situation. Home energy management systems (HEMS) are a kind of such systems in the smart home. HEMS schedule and shift demands to improve the energy consumption on behalf of a consumer based on demand response. Considering multiple objectives such as energy costs, environmental concerns, load profiles, and consumer comfort, HEMS usually create optimal consumption and production schedules.

In this research, valuable sequence patterns from real appliances' usage dataset of SGSC (Motlagh, Foliente, & Grozev, 2015) are extracted using PrefixSpan (Han et al., 2001) in peak time and off-peak time of weekdays and weekends to get valuable insights that is applicable in HEMS. Data generated in smart city and at smart home is placed in the category of big data as it has similar challenges as described in (Russom, 2011) (Honarvar, & Sami, 2016), and that can best be attributed along the so-called 3 V's: Volume, Velocity, and Variety. Therefore, to extract valuable information from such kind of data architecture for the home and city data processing system is proposed which considers the multi-source smart cities and homes' data and big data processing platforms.

The experiments in this research were implemented on the proposed system in which Spark is used as the main big data processing engine. The contributions of this research are as follows: 1) Extracting usage sequences from the power usage data of each appliance in four cases (off-peak time of weekdays and weekends, peak time of weekdays and weekends) which can be used as valuable information for HEMS to schedule the devices using multiple objectives such as energy costs, environmental concerns, load profiles, and consumer comfort; 2) Proposing a big data architecture for the home and city data processing system which considers the multi-source smart cities and homes' big data; 3) Some findings show that the dataset and the imbalanced distribution for computations can impact the efficiency of PrefixSpan when implemented on a distributed environment such as Apache Spark.

Background is surveyed in the following. Then on the proposed system architecture and datasets are introduced. After experiments and results are given, future research directions and conclusions are listed.

BACKGROUND

Big Data

Big Data is the unavoidable result of our ability to create, collect and store digital data at a never-before-seen scale. This generation and collection of large datasets has further encouraged analysis and knowledge extraction process with the belief that with more data available, the information that could be obtained from it will be more exact. In any case, the standard calculations that are utilized as part of data mining are not generally ready to manage these enormous datasets. Most definitions of big data focus on the size of data in storage. Size matters, but there are other important attributes of big data, namely data variety and data velocity. The three Vs of big data make up a complete and thorough definition. Also, each of the three Vs has its own consequences for analytics. One of the things that makes big data really big is that it is coming from a greater variety of sources than ever before. Many of the newer ones are Web sources, including logs, clickstreams, social media, smart cities, and smart homes.

Traditional data analysis methods focusing on small/large data and running on single processor are unable to deal with today's data storage of huge size. So, new ways and technologies are demanded for carefully studying and handling big data. Developing efficient methods to carefully study and understand big data to extract useful knowledge is nevertheless still important. Strategies for analyzing and processing big data may include (Wang & Huang, 2015): parallel and distributed computation, instance selection and dimensionality reduction, and incremental learning.

Internet of Things (IoT) and Big Data

IoT is an important happening that permits everything to convey data, process information, and analyze context. In the process of doing so, a large amount of data with different content and formats has to be processed efficiently and quickly through data mining algorithms. IoT is empowered by utilizing a few unique advances, including the Web, wireless communication, huge information examination or big data analytics, distributed computing, sensors, and data mining calculations.

IoT idea emerged from the need to computerize, manage, and investigate all sensors, gadgets, and instruments around. With a specific end goal to settle on insightful choices both for individuals and for the things in IoT, data mining innovations are coordinated with IoT advances for decision making support and system optimization (Chen, Feng, Deng, Wan, Zhang, Vasilakos, & Rong, 2015).

The massive data generated by IoT are considered having highly valuable and useful information. Technically, all things on the IoT may create data that contains various kinds of valuable information. Difficulties and specialized issues on the best way to process and handle such data and how to extract useful information have emerged recently. We realize that numerous potential applications can be developed by analyzing big data. Data mining will most likely assume a critical part in making this sort of system smart enough to provide more smart services and convenient environments (Tsai, Lai, Chiang, & Yang, 2014).

Creating data is much easier than to analyze it. The explosion of data will certainly become a serious problem of IoT. Various researches have attempted to solve the emerging problem of big data in IoT. The data from IoT are generally too big and too complex to be processed by the tools developed previously, thus we should use the new platforms evolved specifically for big data processing based on distributed and parallel systems such as Hadoop and Spark.

Frequent Sequential Pattern Mining

With the emergence of computing in all aspects of environments, the amount of accessible data has exploded. A great deal of data is produced in cities, homes, etc., which are all stored in computers and ready for access in mass. Data mining is an important tool for the people who wish to analyze all these data in order to determine the associated patterns. In this way, machine learning can attempt to tell how to automatically discover a good predictor based on the past experiences.

It is obvious that the time-stamp is an important attribute of each dataset, which is important in the data mining process and can give us more accurate and useful information. In recent years, sequential pattern mining (Mabroukeh & Christie, 2010) has become an essential data mining technique and been employed in many applications, such as intrusion detection system, gene analysis in bioinformatics, and customer behavior prediction in ecommerce website. In general, the main objective of the sequential pattern mining is to discover the frequent sequences within a transactional database. Through numerous approaches, including the projection-based (Guralnik & Karypis, 2004; Zaki, 1998; Han, et al., 2000), apriori-based (Agrawal & Srikant, 1995; Ayres, Flannick, Gehrke, & Yiu, 2002), and pattern-growth-based algorithms (Han, Pei, & Yan, 2005), efficient enumeration of frequent sequences have been proposed to mine the sequential patterns. The problem was first proposed in (Agrawal & Srikant, 1995), and the formal definition can be described as follows:

Definition 1: Let D be a sequence database, and $I = \{x_1, ..., x_m\}$ be a set of m different items. $S = \{s_1, ..., s_t\}$ is a sequence, consisting of an ordered list of the itemsets. An itemset s_i is a subset of items $\subseteq I$. A sequence $S_a = \{a_1, ..., a_n\}$ is a subsequence of sequence $S_b = \{b_1, ..., b_m\}$, where $1 \leq i_1 < ... < i_n \leq m$ such that $a_1 \subseteq b_{i1}, a_2 \subseteq b_{i2}, ..., a_n \subseteq b_{in}$. The sequential pattern mining aims to find the complete set of sequential patterns whose occurrence frequencies $\geq$ min sup * |D|, where min sup is the minimum support threshold.

PrefixSpan: Prefix-Projected Sequential Pattern Growth

Pattern growth is a method of frequent-pattern mining that does not require candidate generation. The technique originated in the FP-growth algorithm for transaction databases (Han, 2004). The general thought behind this method is as follows: it discovers the frequent single items, then compresses this information into a frequent-pattern tree, or FP-tree. The FP-tree is used to generate a set of projected databases, each associated with one frequent item. Each of these databases is mined separately. The algorithm builds prefix patterns, which it concatenates with suffix patterns to find frequent patterns, avoiding candidate generation (Han, et al., 2001).

Here, we look at PrefixSpan, which extends the pattern-growth approach to instead mine sequential patterns. In (Han, 2001) a novel, scalable, and efficient sequential mining method is proposed, called PrefixSpan. Its general idea is to examine only the prefix subsequences and project only their corresponding postfix subsequences into projected databases. In each projected database, sequential patterns are grown by exploring only local frequent patterns.

Home Energy Management System (HEMS)

Under the smart grid paradigm, a two-way communication is activated by Automatic Meter Reading (AMR) devices between power utilities and home consumers, which is highly reliable and it is an opportunity for economic incentives of smart home for controlling the demand-side resources. As a response to hiking electricity prices, some adjustments are made in home electricity usage during peak-load. The economic incentives are as follows: saving in electricity bill, enhancement in utilization of efficiency of household appliances and conservation of home energy.

Smart HEMS can be defined as follows: the optimal system that provides energy management services for an efficient monitoring and managing generation, storage, and consumption in smart houses

(Han, Jinsoo, Choi, Park, & Lee, 2011). Communication and sensing techniques in Home Area Networks (HANs) provides the possibility to gather information regarding the energy consumption of all household appliances, in addition it is possible to have a remote real-time monitoring and control for different operational modes of smart home appliances using a personal computer or a smart phone (Han, et al., 2011). Furthermore, HEMS provides the optimum utilization status of home appliances, the energy storage as well as management services for distributed energy resources (DERs) and HESS (Lee, Choi, Park, Han, & Lee, 2011).

With the aim of participating in electricity storage and demand response, it is necessary for HEMS to be more flexible in management and control of smart home appliances, and renewable energy resources (Al-Ali, El-Hag, Bahadiri, Harbaji, & Haj, 2011). In addition, the active control services such as real time data regarding the energy consumption and the pricing of energy in smart homes are available for the consumers based on HEMS. The household consumers can select through the human-machine interface and they can set the service time of various appliances for more efficient energy consumption (Son, Pulkkinen, Moon, & Kim, 2010).

In real-life, the house gateways such as a smart meter are used as an interactive communication interface between power utilities and the smart house. In fact, demand response signal is collected by the smart meter from power utilities that are considered as the input for the smart HEMS; therefore, it can optimize the home appliance scheduling in response to the residential demand. Electric vehicle (EV) as a special type of schedulable load which consumes energy of grids to provide the transportation needs of consumers and it can also be considered as a power supply for other household loads within the smart community environment in emergencies. Currently, solar photovoltaic (PV) is involved in distributed renewable generations in residential areas. Residential on-site energy sources, fully integrated in the interactive generation management and operations of HEMS, let smart houses not to be dependent on the power from the transmission systems.

Related Works

The breakdown of entire house power utilization among the significant end-uses is gainful to expand the homeowners' awareness about the real energy performance of houses. Because of the physical placement of sensors on individual appliances to gather end-use load data, conventional load checking systems can be depicted as intrusive techniques. This poses as a long-term intrusion onto the private life and property. In (Farinaccio & Zmeureanu, 1999) researchers presents the development of a new rule-based pattern recognition approach, used to disaggregate the total power utilization of a house into the real end-uses. The target of the work presented in that examination is to show that end-use load information can be acquired by utilizing just the entire house load data, and applying a pattern recognition approach, to detect individual appliance loads from rapid sampling of electric current at the main entry point into the house.

(Gajowniczek, & Ząbkowski, 2017) presented an extensive analysis aimed at forecasting electricity loads on the individual household level using neural network. The impacts of residents' daily activities and appliance usages on the power consumption of the entire household are incorporated to improve the accuracy of the forecasting model. Short-term electricity load forecasting for 24 hours ahead, not on the aggregate but on the individual household level, which fits into the Residential Power Load Forecasting (RPLF) methods addressed in the proposed approach.

Authors in (Silipo, & Winters, 2013) analyzed smart energy data from the Irish Smart Energy Trials, where the power use of 6000 family units and organizations was observed over time via meter IDs. The objective of this work is to recognize groups with common electricity behaviour to make the creation of customized contract offers worth it. Indeed, the energy usage of 6000 meter IDs, sampled every half an hour for longer than a year, produced a considerable amount of data, whose processing takes quite a long time even on a dedicated and powerful machine, especially during the data transformation steps before clustering. Therefore this research offered a "big data" opportunity as a side effect, but no implementation or approach to tackle this kind of dataset was experimented in their works.

(Shailendra, &Yassine, 2017) extracted complex interdependencies among multiple appliances operating concurrently, and identify appliances responsible for major energy consumption using an unsupervised progressive incremental data mining mechanism applied to smart meters energy consumption data through frequent pattern mining. In this paper, the results demonstrated that the appliance associations are a direct reflection of the consumer energy usage behaviour while revealing personal preferences depicting expected comfort. This information can be applied to energy saving programs and related decision making processes while buying in the much-required consumer confidence to achieve successful persistent results.

(Chen, et al., 2015) presented an idea (correlation pattern) to capture the usage patterns and correlations among appliances probabilistically. They also introduced several pruning techniques to improve the performance of the proposed algorithm. The proposed method was applied on a real-world dataset to show the practicability of correlation pattern mining.

There have been lots of efforts made in both industry and academia to turn cities into smart cities, for example, in the European project of SmartSantander (Sanchez, Luis, Muñoz, Galache, Sotres, Santana, Gutierrez, & Ramdhany, 2014), more than 15,000 sensors have been installed around an area of approximately 13.4 square miles in the Spanish city of Santander. In (Cheng, Longo, Cirillo, Bauer, & Kovacs, 2015), the system architecture and the major design issues of a live City Data and Analytics Platform, namely CiDAP was introduced. This platform is able to deal with historical data, near-time data, and also real-time data. The CiDAP platform is also architecturally scalable, flexible, and extendable to be integrated with different scales of smart city infrastructures. It was deployed and integrated with a running IoT experimental testbed SmartSantander, one of the largest smart city testbeds in the world.

(Zhou, Yang, & Shao, 2017) developed an improved fuzzy clustering model for the monthly electricity consumption pattern mining of households. The results revealed the different electricity consumption patterns of different households and demonstrated the effectiveness of the clustering-based model. The customer segmentation based on consumption pattern mining in electric power industry is of great significance to support the development of personalized and targeted marketing strategies and the improvement of energy efficiency.

In (Strohbach, Ziekow, Gazis, & Akiva, 2015) a case study from the smart grid domain, that illustrates the application of big data on smart home sensor data, was discussed. The case was taken from PeerEnergyCloud (PEC) project (PeerEnergyCloud, 2015) that ran a smart grid pilot in a German city. The pilot incorporates establishments of smart home sensors in private homes that measure energy utilization and power quality such as power voltage and frequency at a few electrical plugs in every home. Every sensor takes estimations at regular intervals and streams the outcomes into a cloud-based infrastructure that runs analytics for several different use cases. They implemented three scenarios in their labs using data from deployed sensors, including: Power quality analytics that shows the benefits of big data batch processing technologies, Real-time grid monitoring that shows the benefits of in-stream analytics, and Forecasting energy demand that shows the need to combine both batch and stream processing.

Researches in (Zhuhadar, Thrasher, Marklin, & Pablos, 2017) proposed a real time optimal schedule controller for HEMS that applies a new binary backtracking search algorithm (BBSA) for energy consumption management. The BBSA provides optimal scheduling of home appliances and controls the total load demand; so home appliances can be scheduled to be used at specific times. Prototype of smart sockets hardware and graphical user interface software were designed to illustrate the HEMS proposed in the paper and to offer the interface for loads and scheduler. Common home appliances such as air conditioner, water heater, refrigerator, and washing machine were considered to be controlled. Scheduling algorithm was used under two cases as follows: A: operation at weekday (4 to 11 pm), B: weekend at different time of the day. To examine the accuracy of the developed controller in the HEMS, experimental results achieved from the proposed BBSA schedule controller were compared to results of the binary particle swarm optimization (BPSO) schedule controller. It was shown that BBSA schedule controller performs better compared to the BPSO schedule controller in term of the reduction of the energy usage as well as total electricity bill and saving the energy at peak hours of certain loads.

Authors in (Ahmed, Mohamed, Shareef, Homod, & Abd Ali, 2016) developed modeling for four load types as follows: air conditioner, electric water heater, washing machine, and refrigerator and they were based on customer lifestyle and priority using MATLAB/ SIMULINK. Furthermore, using artificial neural network (ANN) a home energy management controller was proposed for optimal prediction in terms of ON/OFF status of the home appliances. The feedforward neural network type and Levenberg-Marquardt (LM) training algorithm were considered to train the ANN in MATLAB toolbox. Results indicated that ANN-based controller proposed in the paper led to decrease energy consumption for home appliances at specific times.

Researchers in (Ahmad et al., 2017) proposed an optimized home energy management system (OHEMS) that facilitated the integration of renewable energy source (RES) and energy storage system (ESS) and led to incorporation of the residential sector into DSM activities. The proposed OHEMS reduces the electricity cost through household appliance scheduling as well as ESS compared to the dynamic pricing of electricity market. In the first stage, using multiple knapsack problems the constrained optimization problem was mathematically formulated and it was solved through heuristic algorithms; genetic algorithm (GA), binary particle swarm optimization (BPSO), wind driven optimization (WDO), bacterial foraging optimization (BFO) and hybrid GA-PSO (HGPO) algorithms. Next, MATLAB simulations were applied to evaluate the performance of the proposed scheme and heuristic. Results indicated that the integration of RES and ESS leads to the electricity bill reduction as well as reduction of peak-to-average ratio (PAR) by 19.94% and 21.55% respectively. In addition, the HGPO algorithm-based home energy management system was more efficient than the other heuristic algorithms, and it could decrease the bill by 25.12% and PAR by 24.88%.

Authors in (Javaid, Naseem, Rasheed, Khan, Alrajeh, & Iqbal, 2017) designed a HEM controller based on four heuristic algorithms as follows: Bacterial Foraging Optimization Algorithm (BFOA), Genetic Algorithm (GA), Binary Particle Swarm Optimization (BPSO), and Wind Driven Optimization (WDO). In addition, a hybrid algorithm which is Genetic BPSO (GBPSO) was presented in this research. Then, considering the essential home appliances in Real Time Pricing (RTP) environment all abovementioned algorithms were tested. Simulation results indicated that each algorithm in the HEM controller decreased the electricity cost and curtailed the PAR. GA based HEM controller had relatively better performance in term of PAR reduction; it curtailed about 34% PAR.

SYSTEM ARCHITECTURE

The growing urban population has brought major challenges in smart cities, such as minimizing the air pollution level, managing the traffic, controlling the power usage, and using the scare energy resources efficiently. In order to overcome such problems, the citizens as well as the city decision-makers will need a system to provide the capacity of making a right assessment of the urban situations based on the data generated in cities. The abundance of data sources in the context of smart cities can provide a foundation to apply the data analysis techniques in order to offer the novel services that can increase the citizens' quality of life. The data in smart cities can be produced by all stakeholders, including citizens, companies, and governments (Correia, 2005). The data sources include the public data (such as cartography, traffic status, land use, etc.) as well as the data generated by citizens using their smartphones, or the digital traces related to their activities in cities and power usage data of home appliances that have the potential of extracting the hidden insights for urban planners.

With the advent of the ICT and the sensor systems in the field of smart meters for metering the utility service usage, parking lots, intelligent transportation system, and the other domains in smart cities, a huge volume of data is being continually generated. A big-data analytics system for a smart city is necessary to address the huge volume of data, the multiple heterogeneous data sources, and the requirements for data analytics for real-time and offline decision-making and urban planning, respectively.

In this section, architecture of a system is proposed to address the concerns, associated with big data, multiple data sources, heterogeneity, and independent data silos in smart cities. The proposed architecture includes some subsystems for sensing and collecting the data generated in smart cities or homes, and combining and integrating the data from various sources, including heterogeneous sources and big data analytics in real-time and batch. This architecture is depicted in Figure 1.

The first layer of this architecture is a distributed system that allocates the sensors over a city in order to monitor/record events in the city. In this layer, the sensors and actuators are located. These sensors capture the data produced in a city by citizens and infrastructures. In addition, the actuators are responsible for performing the actions issued by the application layer. The municipal organizations, citizens, city infrastructures, etc. can produce or capture various data for different purposes and problems at hand. This causes to create independent data silos, related to a single urban system. These datasets are diverse in data models and schemas. Therefore, interoperability makes some challenges that should be addressed and tackled by use of semantic Web and ontology. The annotation of the data by semantic Web can be fulfilled in layer 2 in the pre-processing subsystem. The layer C1 is responsible for communication between subsystems of data collection and data combination. The layer C2 is responsible for communication between subsystems of data combination and big-data analytics. These layers use various communication technologies, such as Wi-Fi, WiMAX, LTE, etc. to fulfil their mission. Layer 3 is responsible for the data combination process. The output of this layer is the full image of a city, which represents the events, status, features, and actions occurring in the city. Such data can be exploited to extract valuable knowledge that could not be revealed in separated data silos.

Heterogeneity, generation rate, and volume of data present some challenges for data analytics. The amount of data in smart cities is being expanded exponentially. Therefore, an efficient analysis of a large dataset in real-time and offline has become an important basis for managing the city dynamics. Layer 4 manages the big-data analytics by exploiting the big-data platforms (e.g., Spark and Hadoop), which

Figure 1. An architecture for multi-source big data analytics for smart city

Apply the knowledge (Applications) and sends alert to actuators	5
Real-time and Batch Big Data Analytics using Spark and Hadoop	4
Communication infrastructure	C2
Situation + Event + Activity (SEA) / Data Fusion & Integration (Spatial, Temporal and Semantic) — Raw Data	3
Collect & Pre-process & Convert Data to Common Representation	2
Communication infrastructure	C1
Sensors + Extra Data Sources (Domain knowledge or Ontologies) + Actuators	1

are capable of big-data processing in real time and offline. Finally, in layer 5, the extracted information from the analytical layer is applied and taken into action through the actuators in layer 1 in order to make the city smarter and help the citizens to have a better life.

DATASET

For our experiments, electricity usage data from HAN plugs of the Smart Grid Smart City (SGSC) project (Motlagh, Foliente, & Grozev, 2015) was used. This dataset is from the customer trial conducted as part of SGSC project (2010-2014). It provides one of the few linked data sets of customer time of use (half hour increments) and detailed information on appliance use. The project was jointly funded by the Australian Government and an industry consortia, led by Ausgrid.

Part of this dataset contains electricity usage data from HAN plugs employed to measure the usage of various home appliances and/or rooms in individual households that participated in the SGSC customer trials. Electricity usage is recorded in half hour increments (kWh). The HAN Dataset contains 10,828,122 records for electricity usage of 110 appliances and 808 customers between 02-Mar-2013 and 28-Feb-2014. Customers having irrelevant logs (less than 1000 records) for power usage were omitted from the dataset. The number of customers is 301 and the number of records for these customers is 10,639,969. Fields of each record contains CUSTOMER_ID, READING_TIME, PLUG_NAME, READING_VALUE, CALENDAR_KEY and RECORD_COUNT. Samples of this dataset depicted in the Figure 2.

For the purpose of experiments, READING_TIME, PLUG_NAME and READING_VAL are extracted from each record and if a record contains an appliance with electricity usage below one kWh, it would be deleted from the dataset. Four categories of sub datasets are created from the initial dataset which are related to the weekdays, and weekends. Each of these two datasets then are split to off-peak times, and peak times. The specified range of these times is demonstrated in Table 1. The number of records for these datasets is illustrated in Table 2.

As we want to explore usage sequences of appliances, multiple records of the initial dataset were merged as a single record and a usage sequence of appliances for a day are created. If an appliance

Figure 2. Samples of the Home Area Network dataset from SGSC project

14:48:40 19-08-10014678.2013.Microwave.0.281420.1
14:48:40 19-08-10014678.2013.Microwave.0.281420.1
14:48:40 19-08-10014678.2013.TV.0.281420.1
14:48:41 19-08-10014678.2013.DishWasher.0.281420.1
14:48:41 19-08-10014678.2013.Kettle.0.281420.1
14:48:41 19-08-10014678.2013.WashingMachine.002.281420.1
14:48:42 19-08-10014678.2013.AirCon.003.281423.1
15:18:42 19-08-10014678.2013.Microwave.041.281423.1
15:18:43 19-08-10014678.2013.TV.0.281423.1

Table 1. times of peak times and off-peak times in Australia

Days	Peak Time	Off-Peak Times
Weekdays	02 PM – 08 PM	00AM – 02 PM 8 PM – 12 PM
Weekends	07 AM – 02 PM 8 PM – 10 PM	00 AM – 07 AM 02 PM – 08 PM 10 PM – 12 PM

Table 2. The numbers of records in the sub-dataset

Dataset Name	# of Records
Weekdays_Peak_times	2,226,641
Weekdays_off_peak_times	5,303,290
Weekend_peak_times	1,432,793
Weekend_off_peak_times	1,677,245

electricity usage is below one kWh in a record, it was deleted. If multiple logs for each appliance are captured in the same hour, we produced one record for that device and considered it in the ON state if at least one device with usage measure above one kWh is captured. The electricity usage measures are converted to on/off state for each device and usage sequences for appliances are created based on the order of captured time.

EXPERIMENTS AND RESULTS

PrefixSpan as a sequence-pattern mining algorithm, with various thresholds has been experimented with in Apache Spark as the big data processing engine of the proposed architecture for extraction of frequent sequence patterns and association rules. The algorithm was implemented in Java language with Apache Spark framework and tested on a cluster in which Hadoop YARN and HDFS are also deployed.

In the experimented cluster, six nodes are considered and each node has Intel core i3-4160 CPU 3.60 GHz*4 with 6 GB main memory. Nodes in the clusters are connected through 802.11 WiFi (WLP3s0) interface with 72 Mb/s.

In this section, the useful extracted appliance usage patterns in sub datasets related to weekdays and weekends with some findings are discussed. To show the practicability of mined sequence patterns and association rules, we conducted our experiments in four states. In the first case, usage data for the peek time of weekdays was experimented. Off-peak time of weekdays, pick time of weekends, and off-peak time of weekends were experimented in the other cases of the experiments.

Some useful extracted association rules with the confidence higher than other extracted rules are depicted in Tables 3-6. The results show that most patterns in all sub-datasets are similar, and some differences only exist in peak time of weekdays. In this case the *Hot Water System* is frequently used with other appliances which are not seen in the other cases. This device is a schedulable device, therefore the HEMS can apply this fact to schedule the operation of it to the off peak time or an appropriate time in order to reduce the electricity cost and electricity usage of homes according to the requirements.

Table 3. Useful extracted patterns

Off-Peak Time Weekdays			
Antecedent	**Consequent**	**Support**	**Confidence**
Dryer and Washing and AirCon	Oven	13.757	76.923
Kitchen and AirCon	Oven	14.286	77.778
Computer and TV and AirCon	Oven	16.402	61.29
AirCon and Dishwasher	Oven	21.693	60.976
Washing and TV and AirCon	Oven	23.28	61.364
AirCon and Microwave	Oven	24.339	58.696
Dryer and AirCon	Oven	28.571	66.667
Computer and AirCon	Oven	30.688	62.069
Washing and AirCon	Oven	42.857	60.494

Table 4. Useful extracted patterns

Peak Time Weekdays			
Antecedent	**Consequent**	**Support**	**Confidence**
Washing and TV and AirCon	Oven	23.81	44.444
AirCon and Microwave	Oven	24.339	58.696
AirCon and Microwave	Hot Water System	24.339	45.652
Dryer and AirCon	Oven	26.984	64.706
Dryer and AirCon	Hot Water System	26.984	43.137
Computer and AirCon	Oven	29.101	61.818
Washing and AirCon	Oven	42.328	61.25
TV and AirCon	Oven	47.09	57.303

Table 5. Useful extracted patterns

Off-Peak Time Weekends			
Antecedent	Consequent	Support	Confidence
Kitchen and AirCon	Oven	14.286	74.074
Washing and TV and AirCon	Oven	17.46	60.606
AirCon and Dishwasher	Oven	18.519	62.857
AirCon and Microwave	Oven	22.222	64.286
Dryer and AirCon	Oven	26.984	62.745
Computer and AirCon	Oven	28.042	58.491
Washing and AirCon	Oven	39.683	62.667
TV and AirCon	Oven	46.032	60.92

Table 6. Useful extracted patterns

Peak Time Weekends			
Antecedent	Consequent	Support	Confidence
AirCon	Oven	59.788	32.743
Washing and TV	AirCon	77.249	30.822
Washing and TV	Oven	77.249	27.397
Washing	TV	88.36	29.94

If a HEMS is used in the homes, operational cost of electricity could be reduced by 23.1% or residential peak demand would be reduced by 29.6% (Beaudin & Zareipour, 2015). The HEMS finds the optimal schedule for operation of appliances considering scheduling algorithms, and dispatches signals to devices to operate appropriately. Understanding the usage patterns of appliances during a typical day can be beneficial for energy saving, sustainability, suspend the scheduled tasks to off-peak hours, and automatic control the home apparatus, for instance switching on/off, suspension/resumption of the operation timetable and additionally the change of degree in view of the dynamics of environment.

Appliance utilization patterns not just offer clients to better understand how they utilize the apparatuses at home; they likewise distinguish anomalous uses of them. Besides, it encourages apparatus makers' design of intelligent control for smart appliances.

FUTURE RESEARCH DIRECTIONS

One of the evaluation metrics for a HEMS is the comfort of users or inhabitants of homes. To reach such a goal the personal schedule for operations of appliances is needed for each home. In the future works employing sequence of frequent patterns of appliances' power usage big data, preferences of customers will be extracted. These preferences can be applied to create personal schedule for clients. To find the preferences of each customer a huge processing of power usage big data of users need to be affected in a long period. The volume of power usage data for each home is so big and the processing for knowledge mining is not a frequent process, therefore the challenges of integration of smart grid, HEMS, big data, and cloud computing will be considered in the future works.

CONCLUSION

Many researchers have focused on the reduction of electricity usage in residences because it is a significant contributor of CO_2 and greenhouse gases emissions. However, electricity conservation is a tedious task for residential users due to the lack of detailed electricity usage data. If representative patterns of appliance electricity usage were available, residents can adapt their appliance usage behaviours to conserve energy effectively.

Knowledge mining plays a vital role in the process of searching of information that provide useful findings on resident behaviour and the state of the home. The rapid increase of sensors in the home results in large amounts of raw data that must be analyzed to extract relevant information. Unavoidably, the improper uses of household appliances alongside the absence of a smart energy infrastructure gives to unnecessary energy use or waste in most residences.

As the appliances' usage data is so large which is called big data, extracting valuable information needs big data processing tools such as Spark and Hadoop. In this chapter, by experimenting with PrefixSpan algorithm on the proposed system, valuable sequence pattern and association rules were extracted from real appliances' usage dataset of SGSC.

The findings show that most patterns in all sub-datasets prepared for four cases (peak time of weekends, off-peak time of weekends, peak time of weekdays, and off-peak time of weekdays) are similar, and some differences only exists in peak time of weekdays. In this case the *Hot Water System* is frequently used with other appliances which are not seen in the other cases. This device is schedulable; therefore the HEMS can apply this fact to schedule its operation to off peak time or another appropriate time in order to reduce the electricity cost and electricity usage of homes according to the requirements.

REFERENCES

Agrawal, R., & Srikant, R. (1995, March). Mining sequential patterns. In *Data Engineering, 1995. Proceedings of the Eleventh International Conference on* (pp. 3-14). IEEE. 10.1109/ICDE.1995.380415

Ahmad, A., Khan, A., Javaid, N., Hussain, H. M., Abdul, W., Almogren, A., & Azim Niaz, I. (2017). An Optimized Home Energy Management System with Integrated Renewable Energy and Storage Resources. *Energies*, *10*(4), 549. doi:10.3390/en10040549

Ahmed, M. S., Mohamed, A., Shareef, H., Homod, R. Z., & Ali, J. A. (2016, November). Artificial neural network based controller for home energy management considering demand response events. In *Advances in Electrical, Electronic and Systems Engineering (ICAEES), International Conference on* (pp. 506-509). IEEE. 10.1109/ICAEES.2016.7888097

Al-Ali, A. R., El-Hag, A., Bahadiri, M., Harbaji, M., & El Haj, Y. A. (2011). Smart home renewable energy management system. *Energy Procedia, 12,* 120–126. doi:10.1016/j.egypro.2011.10.017

Ayres, J., Flannick, J., Gehrke, J., & Yiu, T. (2002, July). Sequential pattern mining using a bitmap representation. In *Proceedings of the eighth ACM SIGKDD international conference on Knowledge discovery and data mining* (pp. 429-435). ACM. 10.1145/775047.775109

Beaudin, M., & Zareipour, H. (2015). Home energy management systems: A review of modelling and complexity. *Renewable & Sustainable Energy Reviews, 45,* 318–335. doi:10.1016/j.rser.2015.01.046

Chen, F., Deng, P., Wan, J., Zhang, D., Vasilakos, A. V., & Rong, X. (2015). Data mining for the internet of things: Literature review and challenges. *International Journal of Distributed Sensor Networks, 11*(8), 431047. doi:10.1155/2015/431047

Chen, Y.-C., Chen, C.-C., Peng, W.-C., & Lee, W.-C. (2014). *Mining Correlation Patterns among Appliances in Smart Home Environment*. Advances in Knowledge Discovery and Data Mining.

Cheng, B., Longo, S., Cirillo, F., Bauer, M., & Kovacs, E. (2015, June). Building a big data platform for smart cities: Experience and lessons from santander. In *Big Data (BigData Congress), 2015 IEEE International Congress on* (pp. 592-599). IEEE.

Correia, Z. P. (2005). Towards a stakeholder model for the co-production of the public-sector information system. *Information Research: An International Electronic Journal, 10*(3), n3.

Farinaccio, L., & Zmeureanu, R. (1999). Using a pattern recognition approach to disaggregate the total electricity consumption in a house into the major end-uses. *Energy and Building, 30*(3), 245–259. doi:10.1016/S0378-7788(99)00007-9

Gajowniczek, K., & Ząbkowski, T. (2017). Electricity forecasting on the individual household level enhanced based on activity patterns. *PLoS One, 12*(4), e0174098. doi:10.1371/journal.pone.0174098 PMID:28423039

Guralnik, V., & Karypis, G. (2004). Parallel tree-projection-based sequence mining algorithms. *Parallel Computing, 30*(4), 443–472. doi:10.1016/j.parco.2004.03.003

Han, J., Choi, C. S., & Lee, I. (2011). More efficient home energy management system based on ZigBee communication and infrared remote controls. *IEEE Transactions on Consumer Electronics, 57*(1).

Han, J., Choi, C. S., Park, W. K., & Lee, I. (2011, June). Green home energy management system through comparison of energy usage between the same kinds of home appliances. In *Consumer Electronics (ISCE), 2011 IEEE 15th International Symposium on* (pp. 1-4). IEEE. 10.1109/ISCE.2011.5973168

Han, J., Pei, J., Mortazavi-Asl, B., Pinto, H., Chen, Q., Dayal, U., & Hsu, M. C. (2001, April). Prefixspan: Mining sequential patterns efficiently by prefix-projected pattern growth. *Proceedings of the 17th international conference on data engineering,* 215-224.

Han, J., Pei, J., & Yan, X. (2005). Sequential pattern mining by pattern-growth: Principles and extensions. *Foundations and Advances in Data Mining,* 183-220.

Han, J., Pei, J., & Yin, Y. (2000, May). Mining frequent patterns without candidate generation. [). ACM.]. *SIGMOD Record*, *29*(2), 1–12. doi:10.1145/335191.335372

Honarvar, A. R., & Sami, A. (2016). Extracting Usage Patterns from Power Usage Data of Homes' Appliances in Smart Home using Big Data Platform. *International Journal of Information Technology and Web Engineering*, *11*(2), 39–50. doi:10.4018/IJITWE.2016040103

Javaid, N., Naseem, M., Rasheed, M. B., Mahmood, D., Khan, S. A., Alrajeh, N., & Iqbal, Z. (2017). A new heuristically optimized Home Energy Management controller for smart grid. *Sustainable Cities and Society*, *34*, 211–227. doi:10.1016/j.scs.2017.06.009

Lee, J. I., Choi, C. S., Park, W. K., Han, J. S., & Lee, I. W. (2011, September). A study on the use cases of the smart grid home energy management system. In *ICT Convergence (ICTC), 2011 International Conference on* (pp. 746-750). IEEE. 10.1109/ICTC.2011.6082716

Mabroukeh, N. R., & Ezeife, C. I. (2010). A taxonomy of sequential pattern mining algorithms. *ACM Computing Surveys*, *43*(1), 3. doi:10.1145/1824795.1824798

Motlagh, O., Foliente, G., & Grozev, G. (2015). Knowledge-mining the Australian smart grid smart city data: A statistical-neural approach to demand-response analysis. In *Planning Support Systems and Smart Cities* (pp. 189–207). Springer International Publishing. doi:10.1007/978-3-319-18368-8_10

PeerEnergyCloud (PEC) Project. (2015). Retrieved 2016, from https://data.gov.au/dataset/smart-grid-smart-city-customer-trial-data

Son, Y.-S., Pulkkinen, T., Moon, K.-D., & Kim, C. (2010). Home energy management system based on power line communication. *IEEE Transactions on Consumer Electronics*, *56*(3), 1380–1386. doi:10.1109/TCE.2010.5606273

Strohbach, M., Ziekow, H., Gazis, V., & Akiva, N. (2015). Towards a big data analytics framework for IoT and smart city applications. In *Modeling and processing for next-generation big-data technologies* (pp. 257–282). Springer International Publishing. doi:10.1007/978-3-319-09177-8_11

Tsai, C. W., Lai, C. F., Chiang, M. C., & Yang, L. T. (2014). Data mining for Internet of Things: A survey. *IEEE Communications Surveys and Tutorials*, *16*(1), 77–97. doi:10.1109/SURV.2013.103013.00206

Wang, X., & Huang, J. Z. (2015). *Uncertainty in learning from big data*. Academic Press.

Zaki, M. J. (1998, November). Efficient enumeration of frequent sequences. In *Proceedings of the seventh international conference on Information and knowledge management* (pp. 68-75). ACM.

Zhou, K., Yang, S., & Shao, Z. (2017). Household monthly electricity consumption pattern mining: A fuzzy clustering-based model and a case study. *Journal of Cleaner Production*, *141*, 900–908. doi:10.1016/j.jclepro.2016.09.165

Zhuhadar, L., Thrasher, E., Marklin, S., & de Pablos, P. O. (2017). The next wave of innovation—Review of smart cities intelligent operation systems. *Computers in Human Behavior*, *66*, 273–281. doi:10.1016/j.chb.2016.09.030

KEY TERMS AND DEFINITIONS

Big Data: Big data is a term for data sets that are so large or complex that traditional data processing application software is inadequate to deal with them. The main characteristics of these datasets are volume, variety, and velocity.

Electricity Usage Sequence Pattern: A frequent sequence pattern of appliances' usage in homes. This pattern shows which appliances are used together frequently.

Home Energy Management System: HEMS is an instance of the context-aware applications that schedules and shifts demands to improve the energy consumption on behalf of a consumer based on demand response.

Internet of Things: The internet of things (IoT) is the inter-networking of physical devices, with electronics, software, sensors, actuators, and network connectivity that enables these objects to collect and exchange data.

Smart City: A smart city is an integration of information and communication technology and internet of things technology to manage the city's assets.

Smart Home: A residence that has appliances that are capable of communicating with one another and can be controlled remotely.

Chapter 8
Educational Activity Suggestion System of Children With Pervasive Developmental Disorder for Guiding Education and Training Staff Activities

Duygu Çelik Ertuğrul
Eastern Mediterranean University, North Cyprus

Atilla Elçi
Aksaray University, Turkey

ABSTRACT

Individuals with pervasive developmental disorders should be supported with special education programs that are planned according to the type and degree of the disorder, age, characteristics, and needs of the individual. Search over internet resources may provide suitable educational material and methods (and associated activity/game). However, syntactic search in today's static-based internet is insufficient to offer desired relevant results. An intelligent system able to identify the needed educational methods and material with the help of semantic web-based agents will not only contribute to the development of individuals with disorders, and support education specialists in this process, but also be extremely useful for the families of these individuals in assisting and monitoring their child's developmental progress. In this chapter, an agent-based educational activity suggestion system of children with pervasive developmental disorder for guiding education and training staff activities is proposed.

INTRODUCTION

Pervasive developmental disorders (PDD) are spectrum disorders of children which include delays in the development of multiple basic functions such as socialization and communication. These disorders are known by various names such as Autistic Spectrum Disorder (ASD), Rett Syndrome, Disintegrative Disorder of Childhood, Asperger's Syndrome, and "not otherwise specified" (Atypical Autism) (McPart-

DOI: 10.4018/978-1-5225-5384-7.ch008

land & Volkmar, 2012). Early childhood education and adulthood business and professional training of the individuals with PDD should be supported with special education programs that are planned according to the type and degree of the disorder, and age, characteristics and needs of the individual. Once these education programs are executed properly, significant progress is gained in terms of acquisition in individual skills and social integration.

PDD is a general diagnostic group containing multiple disorders; it is a state of insufficiency in social interaction, language development, and behavior problems starting at early childhood. Behavior issues include repetitive limited interest and interaction. Such conditions affect several aspects of childhood development, and lead to permanent and chronic dysfunctions (Nordenhof & Gammeltoft, 2007).

The momentum in the rise of such cases reached very high levels especially in the previous decade. This situation led governments to develop educational activities. Awareness of parents, increase in social awareness, and developments in fields such as medicine and psychology, and additional financial resources devoted to the solution of related problems have contributed to achieving better statistics. In order to develop social, physical and cognitive skills of the individuals with PDD, and to integrate them into the society, both parents and institutions are under financial and moral obligations. In addition, insufficient number of qualified staff and high price of services isolate individuals with PDD and their parents from society. Furthermore, people with PDD may also have physical or psychological problems just like others. Special educational methods are needed for the individual to learn how to act according to the cultural norms in his/her society (Jordan, 2003; Aydın, 2008). Special educational solutions can be developed by employing recent contemporary technologies on the current acknowledged and applied educational activities that are crucial in shaping the personality, imagination, and social development of the children suffering PDD.

It is admitted today that applying scientific methods starting from the pre-school education is vital in identifying individuals with PDD and helping them adapt to society. In other words, preventing a child from playing games limits his/her healthy development (Sevinç, 2003). Choosing the right methods is important at this point because people with PDD have their own way of communicating and often they cannot understand other people's attitudes. That's why they might have problems in adapting to the society, and have difficulty to participate in educational games which are the first steps to become a member of the society (Koçak, 2002). For example, individuals with ASD generally prefer sensory-motor activities (Sucuoğlu, 2005). In the next section, a literature review is given about recent contemporary Web technologies and current smart device systems and solutions such as mobile apps for the children suffered from ASD. In third section, the proposed Instructive Activity Suggestion System (IASS) is being dealt with and then fourth section elaborates on the system architecture. A case study of using the designed system and the obtained results are mentioned in the fifth section. This chapter concludes with a summary and findings.

LITERATURE BACKGROUND

Internet and domain-related software are the most important means of deciding on the choice of educational activity for the individuals with PDD to help them adapt to society. Yet, often wrong or imperfect educational methods or activities are offered to parents and specialists because the current Web system and its search engines are designed for human understanding instead of machine understanding. Therefore, they are not conducive to semantic search of the data (Holmes & Willoughby, 2005).

The Semantic Web (SW) technology (Berners-Lee, Hendler, & Lassila, 2001) can find and suggest proper activities for developing individuals' skills and their social integration. The SW technology was first proposed in (Berners-Lee et al., 2001) as an extension of the current web and as a subset of artificial intelligence technology in which information has a well-defined meaning. The semantic approach enables better cooperation between computers and people, and is used to create "intelligent agents" that can allow users to find the answers to their queries more precisely via ontologies. Gruber (2008) described 'ontology' as a conceptual language of the semantic web that is a specification of a conceptualization of a knowledge domain. Precisely, ontology is a controlled vocabulary and formally describes concepts and their relationships. Recently, many ontological languages have been proposed and standardized such as Resource Description Framework Schema (RDFS) (Lassila & Swick, 1999) and Web Ontology Language (OWL) (McGuinness & Van Harmelen, 2004). According to the World Wide Web Consortium (W3C), OWL is a family of knowledge representation languages for reasoning/inferencing on ontologies. The latest version of OWL is OWL 2.0 (W3C Recommendation, 2012). OWL expresses concepts in ontological form with specific spatial terms and properties. Additionally, each concept described in the ontology encapsulates a subset of instance data from the domain of discourse. Thus, the SW provides to share and integrate information not only in natural language but also by using the associated software so it can be understood, interpreted, and expressed in a way that makes it easier to find the required data using the software.

Depending on the recent contemporary technologies and widespread use of mobile devices, it is observed that mobile devices have an important role in easily accessing and gathering data for any domain. Moreover, with the high demand for use of tablets, smart phones, and other smart digital devices, it is not amazing that there has been a movement in the development of mobile applications and mobile learning for education sector. Numerous applications for digital devices are being created for educational purposes (Jeng, Wu, Huang, Tan, & Yang, 2010). This depicts the route for developers to design mobile applications for special education and children according to their special needs. Hence, the special education area needs smarter mobile systems with strong knowledgebase management that provides better educational services for PDD. Though the offer of these applications is still quite limited, it is a growing market (Withagen, 2014).

Recently, the special education mobile market has become extremely popular and provides to support education of the individuals suffering from PDD or ASD. This market also supports the parents and professionals for PDD field. In investigating parenting stress in parents of children with ASD, the parents of children with other developmental delay, and the parents of typically developing children, the researchers (Silva & Schalock, 2012) found mean parenting stress in the ASD group to be four times that of the typical group and double that of the other developmental delay groups. Other researchers (Allen & Shane, 2014) reviewed the literature on stress in parents of children with ASD, as well as the literature on caregiver involvement in, and attitudes toward, augmentative/alternative communication strategies. The researchers clarified the potential impact of mobile technologies on parental stress level, helped to define appropriate future research directions, and contributed to development of appropriate caregiver training.

Another approach (Al Mamun et all., 2016) is for diagnosis and early detection of ASD children that is vital to start their special education program as soon as possible. The researchers suggested a cloud based framework titled as Smart Autism. Smart Autism can diagnose and provide early detection of autism in early stages of childhood. The detection process consists of screening and confirmation phases. Smart Autism is considered suitable by researchers for different age group of people in one platform.

Another study on ASD (Bonnot, Bonneau, Doudard, & Duverger, 2016) discusses the psychological status of parents. The researchers investigate observed symptoms of the child with ASD and their effect on the quality of life, psychological status and anxiety of the child's parents over a 6-month period using the Smart Autism application. Their aim was to find the evolution of a child's behavior over 6 months and the (psychological and social) effects of these changes on their parents. The application provides some feedback to enhance parents' motivation in the filling process. Smart Autism mobile app provides ecological momentary assessment of behavioral symptoms of children with ASD and quality of life of parents.

Another research (Aresti-Bartolome & Garcia-Zapirain, 2014) analyzes current technologies for individuals suffering from ASD, their parents and professionals treating them. The technologies of virtual reality applications, telehealth systems, social robots and dedicated applications are considered and classified by the areas they center on: communication, social learning, imitation skills and other ASD-associated conditions. The researchers obtained and showed that the technologies can help to work on skills of ASD sufferers.

In summary, in the majority of the above-mentioned studies, there has been a common conviction about both use of the smart mobile devices and the fact that steadily increasing use of mobile apps has significant implications for the daily life of individuals suffered from ASD. This chapter discusses an *Instructive Activity Suggestion System (IASS)* inclusive of the Semantic Web technology for supporting the training activities of individuals suffered from ASD, and also their parents, professionals and training staff. The aim of the system is to suggest suitable training and educational activities in both home and class in order to improve social life quality of the individuals. The system is an ontology-based Web application designed to use semantic search and inference techniques. The ontological knowledge base of the system is developed first using OWL. User interface as well is being reworked for ease of use, catering to user needs and for anywhere / anytime availability. This study is interdisciplinary in nature. Next section describes the aim of the proposed system and used methods in developing.

THE PROPOSED INSTRUCTIVE ACTIVITY SUGGESTION SYSTEM

The Aim of the IASS

IASS aims to help parents and professionals in the field to deal with and follow the domain of widespread ASD in today's scientific world, making judicial use of computers, networks, and SW technology. It provides suitable educational methods (i.e., activities or games) and materials for use by the children with ASD in order to develop required skills and eliminate insufficiencies in their social interaction, language capacity and behavior development. The ontology knowledge base of IASS includes educational methods, activities and their steps of the activities using the OWL language. All related concepts, properties, and relations between these concepts and features about ASD are defined in the system ontology. IASS provides sorting out of symptoms and anomalies, suggesting activities, compiling performance scores, and deciding on new activity based on user preferences by utilizing semantic descriptions of its available methods and activities. IASS can be used by parents, pre-school educators, primary schools, special educational institutions and experts working for these institutions, university students studying in related fields, and individuals interested in ASD.

The IASS consists of the following three mainline services:

1. **Searching for and Proposing an Educational Activity:** Recognizing the problem/need, accessing the database and proposing an educational activity in accordance with the perceived needs of the individual concerned, i.e. those with disorder, members of family, teacher, health assistants, etc.
2. **Application of the Educational Activity:** This is the process followed when the chosen educational activity is applied. In the case of a complicated activity, IASS supplies a guide on how to carry it out by following the appropriate steps interactively, with the help of a family member or a professional. The system can guide along the cycle of the chosen activity and give feedbacks about it.
3. **Assessment:** After the application of the chosen educational activity, in order to monitor the development of individual's skills, success percentages of applied educational activity are calculated. Scientific tests are used for calculations at this stage. If the tests are based on performance, IASS can help the professional or the family member on administering them and calculating the results. Suggestions about the child's overall development and his/her particular skills are made at this stage.

The rest of this section highlights IASS's technical advantages and its contribution to users.

Technical Advantages of the IASS

A foundation named "Tohum Otizm Vakfı" runs a project titled "Project to increase participation of children with autism to pre-school education through an e-learning portal targeted to parents" in accordance with the EU's program. Software by Rethink Autism (P. Trisha) is also being offered to help parents and teachers through easy-to-follow, Web-based curriculum and proven teaching tools. They both serve for the same purpose: guiding parents and teachers of children with autism or otherwise PDD. Yet the most apparent problem with both is that they are designed for the general case, not to the specificity of an individual. The SW technology of IASS aims to overcome such difficulties of current Web. Ontology knowledge base of IASS serves both in Turkish and in English in order to make it available internationally. It appears that there is no other similar application like IASS yet.

Defined User Roles of the System

IASS complements and to some extend provides the expertise of a special education professional embodied in a computerized application readily usable by any person with access to Internet. The contributions of the system may be summarized by defining the roles of the IASS as follows:

Contribution to an education expert:

- An educational expert can hold in mind only some of the educational activities. IASS can maintain a much larger database of activities pertaining to numerous educational approaches in the field, and it can be fitted to search Web sources for new ones. So, the most appropriate method and activities for a certain children's requirement can be chosen in a more sophisticated and healthy way.
- IASS can be used judiciously in training special education experts. Educational experts can search concepts, properties or relationships of educational activities for a specific problem on its knowledgebase ontology, evaluate its suggestions, and take advantage of being supported by an expert educational system.

- Educational experts can get leads support from the IASS in resolving difficult cases.
- Expert educationists can be aware of the latest trends, developments, and activities in the field through IASS.
- Educational experts can reach all the background information of the children through history records kept in IASS.
- Educational experts can have a chance to monitor the development of the groups and individuals they are responsible for as a whole or individually.

Contribution to the national special education authority:

- It will be possible to decide on, follow up with, and revise the curriculum for special education by the Ministry of National Education of the country through study of extensively documented case stories made possible by IASS.

Contribution to parents:

- Parents can learn about educational activities/games to help their children's education at home.
- Such a system will be motivating the parents who are desperate about the children's anomalies, consequently help regain such children to school and to the society.
- Parents can easily reach to the information about their children's education, current development status and progress over time.

Contribution to the children with PDD:

- Individuals with PDD can gain lots of important skills with the help of such an educational system, thus integrate to the society faster.
- Individuals with pervasive developmental disorder will gain self-confidence thanks to plausible activities chosen by the system.

Next section introduces the methods used.

Methods Used

As the knowledgebase of IASS is semantic-based with OWL used in creating domain ontologies of the field, it eases semantic search and inference. In developing each ontology in the Ontology Knowledgebase (OKB), Protégé OWL editor (2014) with OWL 2.0 support is the preferred tool. As Java programing language is used in the functional architecture of IASS, inference over the OKB is through Jena API (2011). Important algorithms of the methodology base of IASS are as follows:

- Jaro-Winkler distance (Winkler, 1999),
- 'Semantic Matchmaking' algorithm (Paolucci, Kawamura, Payne, & Sycara, 2002; Çelik & Elçi, 2013; Çelik, Elçi, & Elverici, 2011; Çelik & Elçi, 2011),
- Natural Language Processing (NLP) approaches (Chowdhury, 2003), and
- Regular-expressions (Kaznacheev, 1969).

Based on these methods, the text of the user input is matched with the concepts in the ontology (semantic matching) and then these are served as clues to define symptoms, identify the ailment, approaches to follow and educational methods to use. The semantic matching approach is similar to that of some recent studies of semantic search of services in accordance with the users' needs (Çelik & Elçi, 2013; Çelik, Elçi, & Elverici, 2011; Çelik & Elçi, 2011).

ONTOLOGY KNOWLEDGEBASE (OKB) OF THE PROPOSED SYSTEM

IASS involves several specialized domain ontologies in its knowledgebase. They are introduced in this section.

Methods Ontology (MO)

The MO defines the concepts (lower/upper/hierarchical structure), properties and relations of methods used in the ASD domain. While creating this ontology, basic objectives of the special education are taken into consideration as specified by the Ministry of National Education of Turkey (MEB) for the individuals with ASD. Basic objectives intended for the development of the individual's skills are classified as follows that are discussed in Special Education and Rehabilitation Centre Support Training Programme for Pervasive Developmental Disorders program document (ORGM, 2008)

- Matching and imitation skills which are prerequisites for gaining functional skills,
- Skills in starting and sustaining social interaction,
- Receptive and expressive language skills,
- Communication skills,
- Gaining independent study and organization skills along with functioning skills,
- Self-care and daily skills,
- Academic skills,
- Social life participation and social adaptation skills.

The above-mentioned objectives are sorted into bundles of skills and educational methods thus forming a taxonomy to start with. Thus, the activities that are performed in each method type and its scope are grouped under different classes as qualities and skills.

This taxonomy is then turned into an ontology which is ultimately used in identifying the appropriate activity to propose. For example: let's say that the method definitions included in the "expressive language skills" concept (lower-class) under the concept (class) "language skills", and what these methods bring to the individual are already defined within the ontology, it will shed light into choosing an appropriate activity for the individual's nature (Table 1, Lines 20-22). According to the example, if the educational activities suggested by the system are applied and achieved, the individual will have gained the following skills:

- Specific speaking (i.e. to talk about a specific subject),
- Sequencing/sorting (to explain the events in an order of occurrence),
- Expressing the past (to talk about the past events).

Let's say that the first step ('Specific Speaking' skill methods and activities) can be applied or if these skills already exists in the individual, then the study can be done on "does the child have the second step?" or "should it be implemented?".

For Example: If a parent enters a query stating 'the child talks about a subject we specified but cannot explain the events in their order of occurrence', the system can draw out and infer from ontology that these two specifications are discussed under the context of language skills; furthermore, it is clear that child already possesses 'Specific Speaking' skills, thus the second level 'explaining the events in an order of occurrence' is recommended.

The 'has Specific_Speaking_Skills' given in Table 1 in the lines 26-30 is an acquisition that belongs to 'Expressive_Language_Skills' and points to a 'Method'. In addition, the activity that will provide this skill points to a 'Description_Card_Game' concept under the Activities Ontology that has the features of 'hasSpecific_Speaking_Skill' and is a method of 'Teaching_With_Tips' in Table 1 within the lines 31-34 (rdf:resource = "&Activities; Description_Card_Game).

Table 1. A portion of MO (right column) for the ASD domain (left column)

Skills		
– Skills	1	`<owl:Class rdf:ID="Skill"/>`
– Matching Skills	2	`<owl:Class rdf:ID="Method"/>`
▪ Co-objects matching	3	`<owl:Class rdf:ID="Matching-Skills">`
▪ Co-picture matching	4	`<rdfs:subClassOf rdf:resource="#Skill"/>`
▪ Object-picture matching	5	`</owl:Class>`
▪ Colour matching	6	`<owl:Class rdf:ID="Co-objects_Matching">`
▪ Shape matching	7	`<rdfs:subClassOf rdf:resource="#Matching_Skills"/>`
– Imitation Skills	8	`</owl:Class>`
▪ Motor imitation studies	9	`<owl:Class rdf:ID="Co-picture_Matching">`
○ Gross motor	10	`<rdfs:subClassOf rdf:resource="#Matching_Skills "/>`
○ Fine motor	11	`</owl:Class>`
○ Facial expressions	12	`<owl:ObjectProperty rdf:about="#hasMethod">`
▪ Group movement imitation studies	13	`<rdfs:range rdf:resource="#Skill"/>`
	15	`<rdfs:domain rdf:resource="#Method"/>`
▪ Verbal imitation studies	16	`<owl:inverseOf>`
○ Sound	17	`<owl:ObjectProperty rdf:about="#hasSkill"/>`
○ Words	18	`</owl:inverseOf>`
○ Sentences	19	`</owl:ObjectProperty>`
– Follow-up Instructions Skills	20	`<owl:Class rdf:ID="Expressive_Language_Skills">`
– Use of visual support	21	`<rdfs:subClassOf rdf:resource="#Language_Skills"/>`
– Receptive Language Skills	22	`</owl:Class>`
▪ Listening and Attention Orientation	23	`<owl:Class rdf:ID="Receptive_Language_Skills">`
▪ Differentiation	24	`<rdfs:subClassOf rdf:resource="# Language_Skills "/>`
○ Objects	25	`</owl:Class>`
○ Events	26	`<owl:ObjectProperty rdf:about="#hasSpecific_Speaking_Skill">`
○ People	27	`<rdfs:label rdf:resource="talking about a specific subject"/>`
○ Sounds	28	`<rdfs:range rdf:resource="#Expressive_Language_Skills"/>`
▪ Sequencing/Sorting Events	29	`<rdfs:domain rdf:resource="#Method"/>`
– Expressive Language Skills	30	`</owl:ObjectProperty>`
– Game and Music Skills	31	`<Method rdf:ID="Teaching_With_Tips">`
– Self-care Skills	32	`<hasSpecific_Speaking_Skill`
– Daily Skills	33	`rdf:resource="&Activities;Description_Card_Game"/>`
– Using Various Tools and Equipments	34	`</Method>`
– Motor Skills	35	`</rdf:RDF>`
– Social Skills		
– Reading and Writing		
– Mathematics		

At this point, let us examine the importance of the semantic base of the system through an example: if 'Co-objects matching' is mentioned, it can be verified by IASS that it is a 'Matching Skill' and that the individual has gained the qualification. Behind all this functional work, the system implements the semantic search/criticism with such reasoning at necessary steps, such as problem identification, specifying findings, identifying a target and educational method to reach there.

Concepts Ontology (CO)

The CO consists of metadata about the concepts that correspond to commonly used terms in this domain, hierarchical structures within the concepts, features of concepts, if any, and their relationship with each other. In Table 2, class definitions under the *Ontology of Concepts*, only a limited portion is shown that contains various general concepts: *'Date'*, *'Year'*, *'Month'*, *'Day'*, *'Age'*, *'Game'*, or *'Gender'*, etc.. This ontology includes many features and associations aside from the concept definitions. Concepts will be needed in order to identify an individual's problem, indication, and findings.

For instance, in a problem query, if the *'F.84.2'* concept is mentioned instead of the term *'Rett's Syndrome'*, it should be determined that both in fact point to the same concept and that they have synonym property (Table 2, lines 13-19). The ontology concepts will be linked to the other ontologies in the knowledgebase, via URIs, thus enabling the application to identify all relevant information about classes of the other similar / same concepts within the other ontologies.

Table 2. A portion of CO for the ASD domain

<!— Concepts Ontology in English Language -->	
	`<owl:importsrdf:resource=".../ OntologyKBs/Concepts.owl"/>`
1	`<owl:importsrdf:resource=".../ OntologyKBs/Concepts.owl"/>`
2	`<owl:Ontology rdf:about=""/>`
3	`<owl:Class rdf:ID="Month">`
4	`<rdfs:subClassOf>`
5	`<owl:Class rdf:ID="Date"/>`
6	`</rdfs:subClassOf>`
7	`</owl:Class>`
8	`<owl:Class rdf:ID="Year">`
9	`<rdfs:subClassOf>`
10	`<owl:Class rdf:ID="Date"/>`
11	`</rdfs:subClassOf>`
12	`</owl:Class>`
13	`<owl:Class rdf:ID="Autism">`
14	`<rdfs:subClassOf>`
15	`<owl:Class rdf:ID="Pervasive_Developmental_Disorder"/>`
16	`</rdfs:subClassOf>`
17	`<Autism rdf:ID="Retts_Syndrome">`
18	`<Synonym rdf:datatype="&Concepts;Autism">F.84.2</Synonym>`
19	`</Autism>`
20	`<owl:Class rdf:ID="Game">`
21	`<rdfs:subClassOf>`
22	`<owl:Class rdf:ID="Pedagogical_Activity"/>`
23	`</rdfs:subClassOf>`
24	`</owl:Class>`

In addition, not every activity is appropriate for every age group or gender; in this case, applicability features must be defined for activities/games. Inter-activity association, according to many similar feature definitions and skill types, are also included in this ontology. A section from the activities ontology is shown in Table 3.

Activities Ontology (AO)

The AO includes the semantic structure and definitions of the educational activities/games that are implemented by the qualified teachers and parents of the individuals with PDD. This ontology contains

Table 3. A portion of AO showing declarations for the ASD domain

1	<!— Some class definition examples for activities ontology-->
2	<Declaration><Class IRI="#Game"/></Declaration>
3	<Declaration><Class IRI="#Game_Tools"/></Declaration>
4	<Declaration><Class IRI="#Game_Features"/></Declaration>
5	<Declaration><Class IRI="# Types_Of_Games "/></Declaration>
6	<Declaration><Class IRI="#Game _Place "/></Declaration>
7	<Declaration><Class IRI="#Name_Of_Game"/></Declaration>
8	<Declaration><Class IRI="#Game _URL"/></Declaration>
9	<Declaration><Class IRI="#Number_Of_Players"/></Declaration>
10	<Declaration><Class IRI="#Game _materials"/></Declaration>
11	<Declaration><Class IRI="#Game _Environment"/></Declaration>
12	<Declaration><Class IRI="#Concepts_Of_Games"/></Declaration>
13	<Declaration><Class IRI="#Finger_Games"/></Declaration>
15	<Declaration><Class IRI="#Theatratical_Games"/></Declaration>
16	<Declaration>Class IRI="#Class"/></Declaration>
17	<Declaration><Class IRI="#Sport_Games"/></Declaration>
18	<Declaration><Class IRI="#Creativity_Development"/></Declaration>
19	<Declaration><Class IRI="#Age_Groups"/></Declaration>
20	<Declaration><Class IRI="#Ability_Talent_Games"/></Declaration>
21	<Declaration><Class IRI="#Brain_Memory_Games"/></Declaration>
22	<!— Some Object Property examples for activities ontology-->
23	<Declaration><ObjectProperty IRI="#hasAgeGroup"/></Declaration>
24	<Declaration><ObjectProperty IRI="#hasGamePlace"/></Declaration>
25	<Declaration><ObjectProperty IRI="#hasGameTools"/></Declaration>
26	<Declaration><ObjectProperty IRI="#Development"/></Declaration>
27	<Declaration><ObjectProperty IRI="#hasGender"/></Declaration>
28	<Declaration><ObjectProperty IRI="#hasGroupGame"/></Declaration>
29	<!— Some activity/game definition examples for activities ontology-->
30	<Declaration><NamedIndividual IRI="#Tug_Game"/></Declaration>
31	<Declaration><NamedIndividual IRI="#Blind_Man's _Buff "/></Declaration>
32	<Declaration><NamedIndividual IRI="#Jumping_Rope"/></Declaration>
33	<Declaration><NamedIndividual IRI="#Stop_Ball_Game"/></Declaration>
34	<Declaration><NamedIndividual IRI="#Brothers_Game"/></Declaration>
35	<Declaration><NamedIndividual IRI="#Whispering_Game"/></Declaration>
36	<Declaration><NamedIndividual IRI="#Find_The_Opposite"/></Declaration>

the definitions of all the classes under the educational activities (sub-super class/hierarchical structure), their features and relationships between them. Activities are classified as one-step or multi-step, meaning complex activities; and, most of them are game-based. Activities vary according to the targeted skills and method types. Any activity that develops the language skills can also develop an individual's social skills. A portion of AO is shown in Table 3.

The *metod* definition (i.e. *Teaching_With_Tips*) in the MO and an *activity* definition (i.e. *Description_Card_Game*) in the AO are linked through *owl:ObjectProperty* (i.e. *hasSpecific_Speaking_Skills*), thus, enabling access to the activities in that method's group that is appropriate for the feature. Additionally, the *'hasAgeRange* given above in Figure 1 is an indication that belongs to *'AgeRanges'* concept in the *Concept Ontology (as a Range concept)* and its domain points to the concept *'Game'* in the AO. The *'Description_Card_Game'* concept has *owl:ObjectProperty* (i.e. *hasAgeRange*) in AO that indicates another concept *'5-9 Ages'* in AO.

QUERYING THE OKB OF THE PROPOSED SYSTEM

Ontologies are scrutinized using an (ontology) query language in order to verify integrity, accuracy, and entailments for the semantic conclusions that may be needed. In programming to use ontologies in Java environment, programmers need to create a knowledge model, query, and generate inference results by using ontology parsers.

A knowledge model based on the activities ontology is prepared and only the game section of it is shown expanded in Figure 2. The ontology is expressed in OWL 2.0 in this case study; the query language of Protégé tool is used. The importance of educational games for the individuals with PDD was already noted above. The games, which are applied in order to alleviate the social communication problems in

Figure 1. The schematic relationship example between Method and Activity Ontologies. Defined properties indicate the lines 26-34 of Table 1

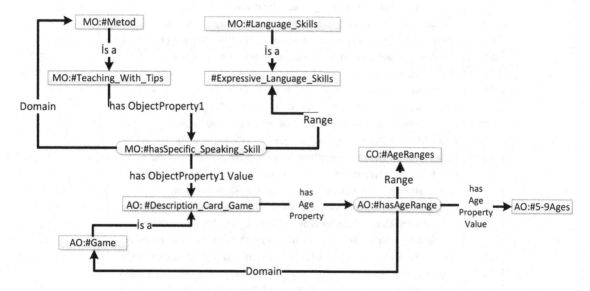

Figure 2. Parent/education specialist is seeking a type of intelligence-memory game

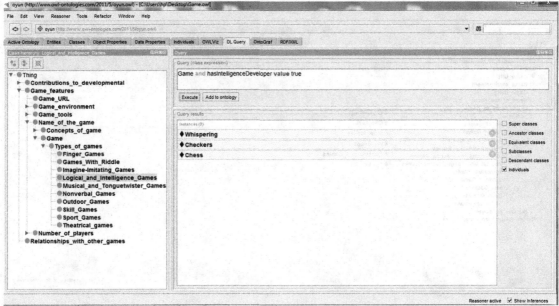

particular, meaning limited/repetitive interest, and behavior problems, are used by the highly qualified teachers starting from an early age of a child.

For example: if we want to develop a child's social behavior and intelligence through one of the alternative activities/games, then it is easier to locate it using IASS and its ontologies. In the following case study, in response to the query *'searching for a game and this game should have mind-developing features'*, the knowledgebase returns *'Whispering, Checkers, Chess'* results (Figure 2).

Query: Game and hasIntelligenceDeveloper value true
Result: Whispering, Checkers, Chess

As another example, again if we want to develop a child's social side and intelligence and we want an appropriate game for all gender types this time; querying as shown below, *'searching for a game for all the female-male children, for a unisex group'*, then the knowledge base returns *'Whispering, Checkers, NineStones, Playdough, ConstructionGames, Chess'* results (Figure 3).

Query: Game and hasGender value Unisex
Result: Whispering, Checkers, Nine_Stones, Playdough, Construction_Games,Chess

A combination of the above two queries are shown below; a game is being sought for both mind-developing and of mixed group. Only Whispering, Checkers and Chess results are being returned (Figure 4).

Query: Game and (hasIntelligenceDeveloper value true and hasGender value Unisex)
Result: Whispering, Checkers, Chess.

Figure 3. Parent/education specialist is seeking intelligence-memory games

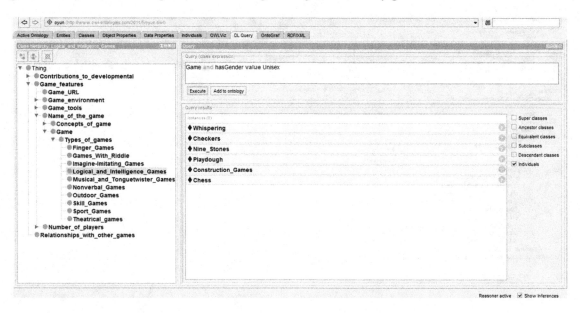

Figure 4. Parent/education specialist is questioning for a group of intelligence-memory game

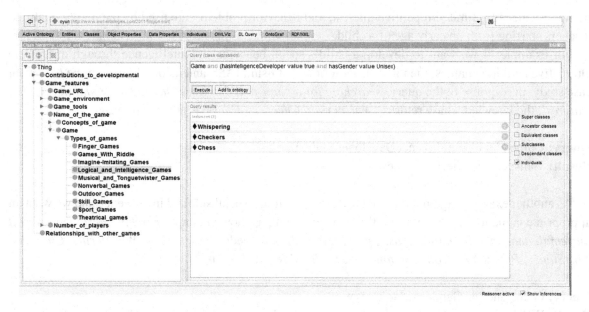

As shown in the Figure 5, ontologies inside the OKB are linked to each other via URIs, with their concept specifications and association definitions. A *feature* definition in the methods ontology and a *method* definition in the activities ontology are linked, thus, enabling access to the activities in that method's group that is appropriate for the feature. It is possible to choose the activities included in a method group as per an individual's age, gender, educational performance, game area, game type, and number of people, etc.

Figure 5. The flow of educational activity queries among the ontologies of OKB

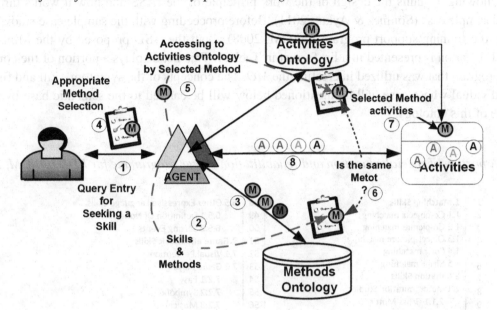

This goes as follows: symptoms/findings that the user entered are first compared against the appropriate symptoms/findings concepts defined in the methods ontology with the help of an agent (Figure 5, Step 1). Then, using NLP and semantic matching algorithms, in line with symptoms and findings queried, pre-defined skills/achievements in the ontology are obtained (Figure 5, Step 2). The skills/achievements found are brought to the user in order for the requested achievement skills to be verified. The user selects the required achievement(s) and forwards it to the agent. The agent finds the necessary methods, again in the methods ontology, for the scanned skill (Figure 5, Step 2 & 3). Appropriate methods are determined by the expert trainer (Figure 5, Step 4). Then the agent queries the same method in the activities ontology in order to access the pre-defined activities that are appropriate for the chosen method (Figure 5, Step 5). The agent reaches, at this point, to all the activities that belong to the chosen method group and appropriate for the individual (Figure 5, Step 6&7). A list of the activities is presented to the user (Figure 5, Step 8). How to select the most appropriate activity for the individual is presented in the next section.

CASE STUDY AND WORKING PRINCIPLE OF THE PROPOSED SYSTEM

An account is created in the system for each individual with ASD by his/her parents or a domain professional. More than one user type may access and follow an individual's account. User types of the system are parent, teacher, psychologist, and trainer who can monitor the instant development of a child suffered from ASD through the system. Even though the functions allowed to be carried out by each user type show differences, the semantic-based work principle of the IASS is set on the same technical approach and knowledge base. However, there may be restrictions on functions in the interface depending on user type. For example, the trainer can update the changes in an individual's development, but parents of same individual can only read that information.

The following explains the design of the work principle of the IASS and how it works through a published sample case (Sönmez & Aykut, 2011). Before proceeding with the sample case study, a section from the training support program (ORGM, 2008) about the ASD proposed by the Ministry of National Education is presented in a list format in Table 4. This list displays a portion of the complete training program that was utilized in creating the *MO*. The concepts of the symptom, skill and findings of the individual whose case will be mentioned below will be carried to the semantic base by taking advantage of this ontology.

Table 4. A portion of special education and rehabilitation center programme for PDD (ORGM, 2008)

1	**1.Matching Skills**	48	6.5 Other Expressive Language Skills
2	1.1 Co-objects matching	49	6.5.1 Definition Of Nonexistence
3	1.2 Co-picture matching	50	6.5.2 Sorting Events
4	1.3 Object-picture matching	51	**7.Game and Music Skills**
5	1.4 Color matching	52	7.1 Visual Perception
6	1.5 Shape matching	53	7.2 Game Playing
7	**2.Imitation Skills**	54	7.2.1 Easy
8	2.1 Motor Imitation Studies	55	7.2.2 Symbolic
9	2.1.1 Gross Motor	56	7.2.3 Musical
10	2.1.2 Fine Motor	57	7.3 Music
11	2.1.3 Facial Expressions	58	7.3.1 Rhythm
12	2.2 Group Movement Imitation Studies	59	7.3.2 Singing
13	2.3 Verbal Imitation Studies	60	7.3.3 Musical Instruments
15	2.3.1 Sound	61	**8.Self-Care Skills**
16	2.3.2 Words	62	8.1 Personal Care And Cleaning
17	2.3.3 Sentences	63	8.1.1 Taking Care of Bathroom Needs
18	**3.Follow-up Instruction Skills**	64	8.2 Dressing and Undressing
19	3.1 Basic Instructions	65	8.3 Eating
20	3.1.1 Single Action	66	**9.Daily Life Skills**
21	3.1.2 Dual Actions	67	9.1 Kitchen Works
22	3.1.3 Triple or More Actions	68	9.2 House Works
23	3.2 Group Instructions	69	9.3 Using a Variety of Tools and Materials
24	3.2.1 Single Actions	70	**10.Motor Skills**
25	3.2.2 Dual or More Actions	71	10.1 Development of Gross Motor Skills
26	**4.Use of Visual Support**	72	10.2 Development of Fine Motor Skills
27	**5.Receptive Language Skills**	73	**11.Social Skills**
28	5.1 Listening and Attention Orientation	74	11.1 Social Communication
29	5.2 Differentiation	75	11.2 Peer Communication
30	5.2.1 Objects	76	**12.Reading and Writing Skills**
31	5.2.2 Events	77	12.1 Perception Studies
32	5.2.3 People	78	12.2 Reading and Writing Preparation
33	5.2.4 Sounds	79	12.3 First Reading and Writing
34	5.3 Sorting Events	80	12.4 Reading and Writing
35	**6.Expressive Language Skills**	81	12.5 Grammar Rules
36	6.1 Asking and Answering Questions	82	**13.Mathematic Skills**
37	6.2 Definitions	83	13.1 Relations Between Objects
38	6.2.1 Actions	84	13.2 Rhythmic Counting
39	6.2.2 Objects	85	13.3 Natural Numbers
40	6.2.3 People	86	13.4 Addition
41	6.3 Information Transfer	87	13.5 Subtraction
42	6.3.1 Providing Information About Events	88	13.5 Multiplication
43	6.4 Grammar Rules	89	13.6 Division
44	6.4.1 Pronoun	90	13.7 Problem Solving
45	6.4.2 Sentence	91	13.8 Clusters
46	6.4.3 Phrase	92	13.9 Fractions
47	6.4.4 Opposite Words	93	13.10 Dimensions
		94	13.11 Geometric Shapes

A Case Study on Instructive Activities

Expected skill is "Being able to take care of bathroom needs alone!" The subject mentioned in this case attends a private special education and rehabilitation center; his current symptoms and findings are as follows:

- Is able to carry out basic instructions and able to imitate gross motor and fine motor movements (has the 2.1. and 3.1. group skills).
- However, on the actions that require the usage of hand and finger muscles (holding a pen, bead threading, etc.), the individual requires adult assistance (has the 10.1 group skills but is limited on the 10.2 group skills).
- Expressive linguistic skills are limited to the words of mother, father and food (group 6 skills are limited).
- Related to the dressing skills, the individual is able to remove his/her socks independently (the "dressing and undressing" skills of the 2nd sub-group of the group 8 are limited).
- Has bathroom control but does not have the skill to begin taking care of bathroom activity.

'Carries out bathroom skills as dependent on the mother' (one of the *"personal care and cleaning"* skills, the *"taking care of bathroom needs"* skills under the 1st sub-group of group 8 skills is limited).

In line with the symptoms and findings of the mentioned skills, when the system-suggested training activity is questioned by the consultant trainer or a parent, the functional audit trail mechanism of the system will be as given below.

Let's say that at this point, a sentence such as 'be able to take care of bathroom needs alone' is entered. The IASS agent does not have any information yet on the meaning of this sentence and under which category it belongs. The system investigates the familiar sentence patterns and previously entered queries of class and association definitions in the *Methods Ontology* in the OKB; and, then it determines the similar skill classes and relationships. The algorithms utilized for searching and identifying symptoms during this process are already mentioned in the Methods Used section above.

The IASS agent searches for the appropriate skill concepts in the ontology, downloads the results to the user interface, and asks the user to identify the desired skill class. Thus, the system identifies the skill class, i.e. the training program that the agent needs to focus on. In the next steps, the system suggests the appropriate training method(s) and chooses the most appropriate method for the individual in line with such information as the individual's previous achievements, current symptoms and findings, learning capacity and target level. All related methods of *'taking care of bathroom needs'* skills are available in the OKB, however, not every method is appropriate for every individual; so the choice varies depending on the individual's particulars as noted. The expert trainer decides on which of the recommended training method should be chosen.

In contrast to the training expert user, the IASS limits the choices of the parent to those strictly recommended by itself at the present. If the features of the individual are matching a group, then the system can easily suggest an appropriate method; otherwise, the system directs the parent to an educational specialist.

Continuing with our sample case, the process proceeds as follows:

- The query 'Be able to take care of bathroom needs alone!' is input for the problem analysis and method determination phase (Figure 6, Step 1).

Figure 6. Analysis of determination of perceived problem on the educational activity

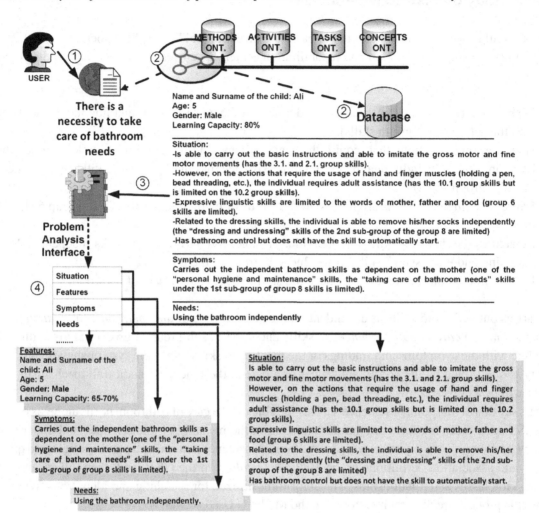

- In order to determine the most appropriate method for the individual, the system accesses all the relevant information of the individual from the knowledgebase (Figure 6, Step 2).
- In the methods ontology, the 'Taking Care of Bathroom Needs' will be specified (Figure 6, Step 2) at the same time as a sub-group under the 'Personal Care and Cleaning' (8.1 in Table 4) and as an upper-group under the 'Self-Care Skills' (Clause 8 in Table 4).
- The system completes the problem analysis process and accesses the concepts in Table 4 in order to determine the most appropriate method for the individual and does the necessary inference and then presents the appropriate method(s) to the user (Problem analysis input: Figure 6, Step 3)
- At this stage, let us assume that the method suggested to the trainer / parent as a result of the system's own recommendation algorithm be a 'Real-Time Hint' (Figure 7, Step 4). Thus, the problem analysis and method determination phase is completed.
- Let us accept that the 'Real-Time Hint' method is chosen for implementation: at this point, the system searches the activities ontology and begins to identify the activities that can help achieve the 'Taking Care of Bathroom Needs' skill.

Figure 7. Presenting the skill-appropriate method to the user

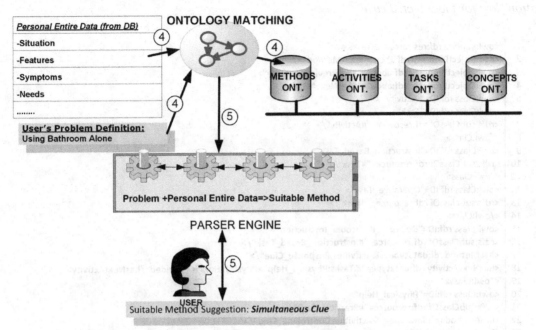

- The activities for the 'Real-Time Hint' are found via the activities ontology and suggested to the trainer/parent for selection and approval. For example: let's say that the 'Education Steps' is suggested and accepted as an activity for the independent bathroom skill.
- While this activity was being considered, existing information about the child's previous and current condition are also used. According to the child's current condition, it can be observed that the child, partially achieving motor skills and with limited gross motor skills, is not self-sufficient in the fine motor skills. Thus, the step 'Physical Assistance' in this activity is selected for it is appropriate for the current condition of the child.
- As it can be deduced from this sample case, while some activities are atomic-structured, others consist of a stream of continuous sub-activities. An atomic activity is single-stepped; with a single implementation, it can be completed and concluded in one step. But, workflow ontology is needed for the complex-structured activities that contain several sub-activities for which precedes/follows attributes ('hasNextActivity', 'hasPreviousActivity', etc.) should figure in the ontology knowledge base (Table 5, Lines 3 & 4).
- The listed activity flow below refers to the sub-activities of a complex-activity which was given as an example in the sample case. In order to achieve *Independent Bathroom Skills* and the *Flow in the Education Steps Activity* take place in the following sequence:
  - "Do your bathroom" instruction is given (response hint) that is shown in Table 5 lines 15-19.
  - Physical assistance is given (Controlling hint) that is indicated in Table 5 lines 20-25.
  - Trial sessions are done (1 per hour) that is indicated in Table 5 lines 26-32.
  - Roll calling is done (on the first bathroom visit of the day).
  - Answer given to the response is evaluated (rewarding for correct responses, ignoring incorrect responses, giving a "continue" directive for the unresponsive situations or going back to the controlling hint.

Table 5. The ontological definition and association of the first three atomic functions of the phased education flow for the selected case

```
1    <owl:imports rdf:resource="../Tasks.owl"/>
2    <owl:ObjectProperty rdf:about="#hasMethod">
3    <owl:ObjectProperty rdf:about="#hasPreviousActivity">
4    <owl:ObjectProperty rdf:about="#hasNextActivity">
5    <owl:Class rdf:ID=" Activity" />
6    <owl:Class rdf:ID="Task">
7    <rdfs:subClassOf rdf:resource="#Activity"/>
8    </owl:Class>
9    <owl:Class rdf:ID="Instruction_Based_Task">
10   <rdfs:subClassOf rdf:resource="#Task"/>
11   </owl:Class>
12   <owl:Class rdf:ID="Operative_Task">
13   <rdfs:subClassOf rdf:resource="#Task"/>
14   </owl:Class>
15   <owl:Class rdf:ID="Do_Your_Bathroom_Instruction">
16   <rdfs:subClassOf rdf:resource="#Instruction_Based_Task"/>
17   <hasMethod rdf:datatype="&Activities;Response_Clue"/>
18   <hasNextActivity rdf:datatype="&Tasks;Physical_Help">Physical Help is Provided</hasNextActivity>
19   </owl:Class>
20   <owl:Class rdf:ID="Physical_Help">
21   <rdfs:subClassOf rdf:resource="#Practical_Task"/>
22   <hasMethod rdf:datatype="&Activities;Controlling_Clue"/>
23   <hasPreviousActivity rdf:datatype="&Tasks;Do_Your_Bathroom_Instruction">
     Do Your Bathroom Instruction is Given </hasPreviousActivity>
24   <hasNextActivity rdf:datatype="&Tasks; Trial_Session"> Trial Session is Done</hasNextActivity>
25   </owl:Class>
26   <owl:Class rdf:ID="Trial_Session">
27   <rdfs:subClassOf rdf:resource="#Practical_Task"/>
28   <hasMethod rdf:datatype="&Activities; Hourly_Control"/>
29   <hasPreviousActivity rdf:datatype="&Tasks; Physical_Help"> Do Your Bathroom Instruction is Given
30   </hasPreviousActivity>
31   <hasNextActivity rdf:datatype="&Tasks; Examination_Session">Examination Sessions are
     Done</hasNextActivity>
32   </owl:Class>
```

Sequencing the steps of a complex activity to be proposed by IASS is generated by the Planning Engine of the IASS. Overall function of the Planning Engine is shown in Figure 8. In this case, *'Physical Assistance'* function is being suggested, which is the second flow of the education step activities that are used in order for the individual to achieve independent bathroom skills (Figure 8 Step 9).

When it is time to determine the next step, the planning engine decides on the future atomic activity by looking at the last implemented one and at the sequencing information of the atomic activities (tasks) that are described in the chosen complex activity group within the *Tasks Ontology*. This takes place in line with the personal information (*occurrence of single-step assumption and not ignoring the results of that assumption*) and in relation to the chosen complex activity. Currently implemented in Figure 8, the *'Do_Your_Bathroom_Directive'* and the future activity information *'Physical Assistance'* are extracted through the ontological sequencing order (Table 5, lines 15-25) and suggested to the user as the next activity (Figure 8 Step 8).

With the start of each new activity, the IASS requests from the user to enter the positive and negative results upon completion. The observed result values are then entered into the database and under the

Figure 8. Presenting the user with the steps of a complex activity chosen by the system planner

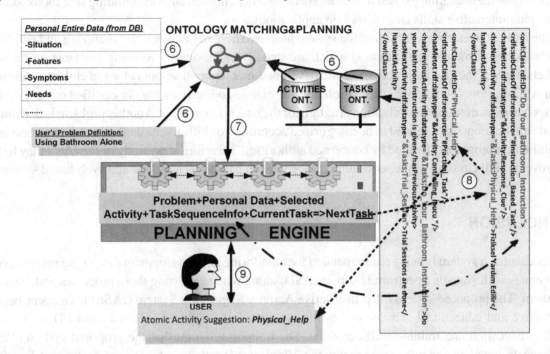

ontology as values such as *'Successful'* or *'Unsuccessful'*. Then, the process can be continued with the next atomic activity or, if needed, a new atomic activity can be created.

Result of the Training Activity: While Ali was only able to fulfill the first objective at the initial level, it was seen that he carried out the first 4 objectives of the skill, independently, during the first roll call session following his mother's assistance. During the second roll call session, he independently carried out the first 6 steps, and during the 3rd roll call session, all of the steps. 3 days after the training, he was visited upon the telephone call of the mother. Ali's skills at the end of the training level were recorded for three successive sessions. As a result of the evaluation, it was seen that Ali carried out, independently, all the steps of his skills in all three sessions.

FUTURE RESEARCH DIRECTIONS

Today, specialists and governments dealing with PDD are trying to minimize the problems experienced by individuals through educational methods chosen carefully after extensive research. However, because of various reasons, the parents of the children who cannot access health care organizations are trying to give appropriate education at home. During these trainings while selecting the educational methods, the parents prefer internet and related software. The future direction of the proposed system will be about developing its mobile application which will be again a recommendation system in order to suggest most appropriate mobile application(s) and games for PDD/ASD children to help their education.

Recently, many mobile applications are available in the market (for example OTSIMO, https://otsimo.com/tr/). However, as we discussed in literature background section, they have different functionalities and purposes for educating pervasive development disorder children such as; building fine motor skills, developing interactive skills etc. via mobile applications.

The aim of the extended version of the system proposed here in future will be analyzing and defining the categories of mobile application(s) which are steadily increasingly becoming available on mobile markets. One of the crucial problems of the developed mobile application(s) for the children suffered from ASD on stores is the certification problem. All mobile applications are not certified or verified by any special education and rehabilitation program for the education of PDD. Another problem is that those mobile application(s) are needed to be categorized according to skills focused in a special education and rehabilitation program officiated by concerned authorities. Therefore, next study of the IASS may be to improve its skills to suggest proper training procedures to parents as a mobile and Web-based system.

CONCLUSION

In this chapter, a system is being recommended for monitoring and development of training processes of individuals with Autistic Spectrum Disorder (ASD) along with supporting these processes and extending them. The proposed system titled Instructive Activity Suggestion System (IASS) is an agent-based instructive and educational activity suggestion system for the children suffered from PDD/ASD for guiding education and training staff activities. The training program that the proposed system offers has been designed, taking into consideration the *"Pervasive Developmental Disorders Support Training Program"* prepared by the Ministry of National Education, Turkey.

Within the semantic infrastructure and overall architecture of the system, there are totally four domain ontologies as follows: a general Concepts Ontology covering concepts pertaining to ASD; a Methods Ontology consisting of special education and training methods; an Activities Ontology of special education activities-cum-games; and a Tasks Ontology of sorting information between activities and methods.

The IASS discovers and judges the suitability of the most appropriate method(s) and relevant activities for an individual taking into consideration personal data such as existing skill set and the qualifications that are expected to be enhanced. Semantic binding such as sort order among activities are also considered in ultimately recommending the needed activity and its tasks for execution. The ontologies developed in the system are such that researchers may employ them in other studies in this country and abroad; they are carefully structured and annotated for subsequent upgrades. With the expanding use and popularity of the system over time, it may be possible to support individuals with ASD through their parent's proxy in their homes without requiring showing up at a special educational institution or health care center. Furthermore, special education experts can continuously follow-up and monitor progress of such patients remotely.

REFERENCES

Al Mamun, K. A., Bardhan, S., Ullah, M. A., Anagnostou, E., Brian, J., Akhter, S., & Rabbani, M. G. (2016, August). Smart autism—A mobile, interactive and integrated framework for screening and confirmation of autism. In *Engineering in Medicine and Biology Society (EMBC), 2016 IEEE 38th Annual International Conference of the* (pp. 5989-5992). IEEE.

Allen, A. A., & Shane, H. C. (2014). Autism spectrum disorders in the era of mobile technologies: Impact on caregivers. *Developmental Neurorehabilitation, 17*(2), 110–114. doi:10.3109/17518423.20 14.882425 PMID:24694311

Aresti-Bartolome, N., & Garcia-Zapirain, B. (2014). Technologies as support tools for persons with autistic spectrum disorder: A systematic review. *International Journal of Environmental Research and Public Health, 11*(8), 7767–7802. doi:10.3390/ijerph110807767 PMID:25093654

Aydın, A. (2008). *Adaptation of symbolic play test to Turkish and comparison of symbolic play behavior of children with normal, autistic, and mental disorder at pre-school period* (PhD thesis). Marmara University.

Berners-Lee, T., Hendler, J., & Lassila, O. (2001). The semantic web. *Scientific American, 284*(5), 28–37. doi:10.1038cientificamerican0501-34 PMID:11341160

Bonnot, O., Bonneau, D., Doudard, A., & Duverger, P. (2016). Rationale and protocol for using a smart-phone application to study autism spectrum disorders: SMARTAUTISM. *BMJ Open, 6*(11), e012135. doi:10.1136/bmjopen-2016-012135 PMID:27881525

Çelik, D., & Elçi, A. (2011). Ontology-based matchmaking and composition of business processes. In *Semantic Agent Systems* (pp. 133–157). Springer Berlin Heidelberg. doi:10.1007/978-3-642-18308-9_7

Çelik, D., & Elçi, A. (2013). A broker-based semantic agent for discovering Semantic Web services through process similarity matching and equivalence considering quality of service. *Science China. Information Sciences, 56*(1), 1–24. doi:10.100711432-012-4697-1

Çelik, D., Elci, A., & Elverici, E. (2011, July). Finding suitable course material through a semantic search agent for Learning Management Systems of distance education. In Computer Software and Applications Conference Workshops (COMPSACW), 2011 IEEE 35th Annual (pp. 386-391). IEEE.

Chowdhury, G. G. (2003). Natural language processing. *Annual Review of Information Science & Technology, 37*(1), 51–89. doi:10.1002/aris.1440370103

Gruber, T. (2008). Ontology. *Encyclopedia of Database Systems (Springer-Verlag)*. Retrieved from http://tomgruber.org/writing/ontology-definition-2007.htm

Holmes, E., & Willoughby, T. (2005). Play behaviour of children with autism spectrum disorders. *Journal of Intellectual & Developmental Disability, 30*(3), 156–164. doi:10.1080/13668250500204034

Jena, R. D. F. API. The Apache Software Foundation (2011). Last accessed on January 30, 2015 from http://jena.apache.org/

Jeng, Y. L., Wu, T. T., Huang, Y. M., Tan, Q., & Yang, S. J. (2010). The add-on impact of mobile applications in learning strategies: A review study. *Journal of Educational Technology & Society, 13*(3), 3–11.

Jordan, R. (2003). Social play and autistic spectrum disorders: A perspective on theory, implications and educational approaches. *Autism, 7*(4), 347–360. doi:10.1177/1362361303007004002 PMID:14678675

Kaznacheev, V. I. (1969). Language of Regular Expressions. In *Synthesis of Digital Automata* (pp. 135–140). Springer.

Koçak, N. (2002). The importance of play and toys in the education of children with disorders. In *Proc. XI. National Special Education Congress*. Konya: Eğitim Kitapevi Yayınları.

Lassila, O., & Swick, R. R. (1999). Resource Description Framework (RDF). *Model and Syntax. W3C Recommendation*. Retrieved from https://www.w3.org/TR/WD-rdf-syntax-971002/

McGuinness, D. L., & Van Harmelen, F. (2004). OWL web ontology language overview. *W3C recommendation, 10*(10), Retrieved from https://www.w3.org/TR/owl-features/

McPartland, J., & Volkmar, F. R. (2012). Autism and Related Disorders. Handbook of Clinical Neurology, 106. doi:10.1016/B978-0-444-52002-9.00023-1

MEB. (n.d.). *Ministry of National Education of Turkey, Ankara*. Retrieved from http://www.meb.gov.tr/english/indexeng.htm

Nordenhof, M. S., & Gammeltoft, L. (2007). *Autism, play and social interaction*. Jessica Kingsley Publishers.

ORGM. (2008). *Special Education and Rehabilitation Centre Support Training Programme for Pervasive Developmental Disorders*. General Directorate of Special Education Institutions of Ministry of National Education. Retrieved from http://orgm.meb.gov.tr/meb_iys_dosyalar/2013_09/04010347_yaygngeliimselbozukluklardestekeitimprogram.pdf

OWL 2.0. (n.d.). *OWL 2 Web Ontology Language Document Overview*. W3C Recommendation. Retrieved from http://www.w3.org/TR/owl2-overview/

Paolucci, M., Kawamura, T., Payne, T. R., & Sycara, K. (2002, June). Semantic matching of web services capabilities. In *International Semantic Web Conference* (pp. 333-347). Springer Berlin Heidelberg.

Protégé, O. W. L. (2014). *Ontology Editor, Protégé 4. 1 tool website, Stanford University*. Retrieved from http://protege.stanford.edu/

Sevinç, M. (2003). *Development in early childhood and new approaches in education*. İstanbul: Morpa Kultur Publicaitons.

Silva, L. M., & Schalock, M. (2012). Autism parenting stress index: Initial psychometric evidence. *Journal of Autism and Developmental Disorders, 42*(4), 566–574. doi:10.100710803-011-1274-1 PMID:21556967

Sönmez, N., & Aykut, C. (2011). Teaching a child with pervasive developmental disorder how to use the bathroom independently by the mother via simultaneous clues. *International Journal of Human Science, 8*(2).

Speaks, A. (2009). *ASD video glossary*. Retrieved from https://www.autismspeaks.org/what-autism/video-glossary/glossary-terms

Sucuoğlu, B. (2005). Autism and children with autistic disorders. In *Children with Special Needs and Introduction to Special Training* (pp. 359–34). Ankara: Gündüz Eğitim ve Yayıncılık.

Trisha, P. (n.d.). *Rethink*. Available: http://www.rethinkwords.com/

Winkler, W. E. (1999). *The state of record linkage and current research problems.* Statistical Research Division, US Census Bureau. Available from http://www.census.gov/srd/www/byname.html

Withagen, Y. (2014). *Determining Usability Factors of Tablet Applications for High Functioning Children with Autism Compared to Children Without Autism.* Academic Press.

KEY TERMS AND DEFINITIONS

Ontology: It is a formal naming and definition of the types, properties, and interrelationships of the entities that really or fundamentally exist for a particular domain of discourse. It is thus a practical application of philosophical ontology, with a taxonomy.

Semantic Web: The semantic web is an extension of the world wide web through standards by the world wide web consortium (W3C).

Chapter 9
New Perspectives on Sustainable Healthcare Delivery Through Web of Things

Cristina Elena Turcu
University of Suceava, Romania

Corneliu Octavian Turcu
University of Suceava, Romania

ABSTRACT

This chapter focuses on examining the adoption of the web of things paradigm in healthcare in order to facilitate the development of new web-based systems in more effective and efficient ways. Nowadays, the increasing number of personal health sensors and medical devices present the opportunity for healthcare providers to interact with patients in entirely new ways. In this context, the WoT paradigm could be closely linked to patient care and has the potential to generate changes in healthcare. WoT could also be applied in the social and insurance fields, etc. The social web of things (SWoT) further extends WoT in order to facilitate continued interaction between physical devices and humans, allowing the integration of smart objects with social networks. Although it opens new social possibilities, it was less applied in the delivery of healthcare. Nevertheless, its successful adoption depends on overcoming some open challenges.

INTRODUCTION

In order to increase the overall quality of patient care, and also to reduce costs, the healthcare industry is constantly bound to adapt to the many occurring changes, from advances in diagnostic and therapeutic procedures to state of the art information technology.

Various worldwide surveys conducted in relation to this field reveal that one of the biggest technological initiatives in the healthcare industry is the Internet of Things (IoT) (Anon-a, 2015; Anon-b, 2015). And, inspired by the IoT concept, a new application development paradigm emerged in recent years, the so-called Web of Things (WoT). WoT enables connections and interactions with various physical

DOI: 10.4018/978-1-5225-5384-7.ch009

things (such as medical devices, sensors, etc.) the same way as any other Web resource (Anon-c, 2017; Guinard & Trifa, 2009; Guinard & Trifa, 2016; Raggett, 2015a; Raggett, 2015b; Zeng, Guo & Cheng, 2011; Bovet & Hennebert, 2013; Guinard, Trifa, & Wilde, 2010; Guinard, Trifa, Mattern & Wilde, 2011; Trifa, Wieland, Guinard, & Bohnert, 2009), so the physical things become an integral part of the Web (Guinard et al., 2010).

Several papers and studies have focused on this new paradigm and the ways in which it can be applied in various fields. This chapter focuses on examining the challenges of adopting WoT in healthcare field in order to facilitate the development of new Web-based systems in more effective and efficient ways. We also present some WoT platforms and various enabling technologies that could be exploited in order to extend the current applications in the healthcare area and align them to the perspective of the new WoT paradigm. The movement of healthcare out of healthcare facilities (hospitals, laboratories, etc.) and into people's homes will be greatly facilitated by the latest remote sensing devices of all kinds connected to physicians and care givers. The examples are numerous and the potential for cost savings and improved care is overwhelming. Social Web of Things (SWoT) further extends WoT in order to facilitate continued interaction between physical devices and humans, opening up new social possibilities. Thus, social networks can be used for storing and sharing information of interest for WoT interactions. In order for things in WoT to understand each other, sharing a common understanding of the structure of information is required. We highlight the lessons to be learnt from the past, open challenges and some possible directions for future research.

The aim of this chapter, completely aligned with the purpose of the volume, is examining the adoption of WoT in healthcare. The authors provide an overview of the impact WoT can have in healthcare and the inherent challenges to be addressed in order to make its adoption a reality in the field.

BACKGROUND

Nowadays, advent of digital technology, fast growing number of available low-cost consumer grade smart devices and pervasive use of heterogeneous sensors (such as temperature, pressure, humidity, accelerometers, gyroscopes, altimeters, etc.), facilitate continuous development of IoT and WoT in various fields (Bi, Da Xu, & Wang, 2014; Cai et al., 2014; Po Yang & Wenyan Wu, 2014; Wang, Bi & Da Xu, 2014), particularly in healthcare (Amendola, Lodato, Manzari, Occhiuzzi, & Marrocco, 2014; Daniel, Casati, Silveira, Verga & Nalin, 2011; Fan, Yin, Xu, Zeng & Wu, 2014; He & Zeadally, 2015; Li et al., 2011; Li, Li & Zhao, 2014; Zheng, Martin, Brohman & Xu, 2014; Xu et al., 2014; Yang et al., 2014). Advances in IoT/WoT technologies enable the development of new systems, that could deliver various medical services (e.g., patient monitoring or even medical care providing) to anyone at any time and in any place (even at any distance). According to a survey conducted by Forrester Consulting on behalf of Zebra Technologies (Anon-a, 2015), 97% of the surveyed healthcare industry professionals agree that IoT is the most strategic solution their organization will undertake this decade. Nine of ten healthcare IT departments are ready to make the necessary changes in order to implement IoT solutions. Over half of the healthcare organizations surveyed have already begun implementing IoT solutions in their practice, and another 30 percent of all respondents are planning to do so within the next year. Around the world, there are some success cases and best practices that have been used as examples for the adoption of WoT in healthcare. Thus, in recent years, a wide range of healthcare IoT/WoT applications have been developed and deployed, providing various solutions to support and enhance prevention, early diagnosis, treatment, monitoring and management in terms of health and lifestyle.

This shift from traditional healthcare to the use of new technology and engineering innovations is justified by current trends in world demographics, as reflected by a growing number of studies (Anon-k, 2010): an alarming rise in chronic diseases, the prevalence rate of suboptimal health status (SHS), and increased longevity, etc. Just to give an example, the prevalence rate of SHS (which is also called "the third state" - between health and disease) accounts for 75% of the world population, as reported by a World Health Organization report (He, Fan & Li, 2013). Only in China, there are an estimated 900 million people in this status.

Tackling the problem of chronic diseases in Europe alone, more than a third of the population (that means over 100 million individuals) is affected by a chronic disease (e.g., heart, respiratory or liver diseases). The high costs of the long-term treatment and care of patients suffering from these diseases could generate an enormous financial burden. Moreover, there is an increasing worldwide demand to derive greater value from the resources allocated to healthcare systems (Anon-d, 2016). The focus on disease prevention could reduce these costs, for example, actively dealing with various risk factors associated with most chronic illnesses (e.g., insufficient physical activity, unhealthy diet, etc.). However, speaking in budgetary terms, only about 3% of the current health expenditure is allocated to prevention, although investing in prevention could help cut off future costs related to the treatment and care of preventable diseases.

There is increasing widespread recognition that the patient is "the single most underused person in health care", as Harvard Professor David Cutler wrote in an article in MIT Technology Review (Anon-a, 2015).

Involving patients in the decision making process related to their own care and treatment contributes to the patient empowerment and improves the outcomes. In fact, by involving people in the healthcare and decision making processes facilitates self-management, which has been proved by many studies to be highly effective (Couturier, Sola, Borioli, & Raiciu, 2012; De Iongh, Fagan, Fenner, & Kidd, 2015; De Silva, 2011; Hibbard & Greene, 2013; Norris, Lau, Smith, Schmid & Engelgau, 2002; St. John, Davis, Price, & Davis, 2010; Wheeler, 2003; Anon-e, 2015; Anon-f, 2015; Anon-g, 2014; Anon-h, 2010; Anon-i, 2011) in that it improves health outcomes (increases life expectancy, reduces costs, etc.). Therefore, a study performed by Nesta (Anon-j, 2013) estimates that £4.4bn could be saved in the National Health Service (NHS) in England through "greater participation and self-management of long term conditions". Also, one US study reveals that self-management could amount to a 21% reduction in costs (Hibbard & Greene, 2013).

Reviews of evidence around self-management indicate that supporting self-management might be a solution to some of the issues faced by healthcare. Supporting self-management means providing encouragement and integrated information about patients in order to help people develop the necessary knowledge, skills and confidence to manage their own health conditions. However, self-management can have a practical and emotional impact on people's lives and on the way they think, feel and act. The challenge is to identify the best ways to support self-management and to help health professionals, patients, and care givers make this a reality.

The WoT paradigm could be closely linked to patient care, having the potential to change the healthcare and social fields. The adoption of WoT in healthcare is being driven by various technologies, some of which are presented in the following sections of this chapter.

WEB OF THINGS IN HEALTHCARE AND RELATED RESEARCH FIELDS

The purpose of this chapter is to draw researchers' attention to the emerging adoption of WoT in healthcare. In this field, the WoT makes use of synergies that are generated by different transformative technologies. Aiming to understand how the combination of various technologies can be successfully used in providing solutions in healthcare scenarios, this section describes some popular technologies and related works that have used them.

Web of Things

According to (Anon-c, n.d.), "the Web of Things aims to build the Internet of Things in a truly open, flexible, and scalable way, using the Web as its application layer."

WoT is viewed as an evolution of the IoT paradigm, "which aims at interconnecting devices into the Internet as Web resources, using traditional Web standards (such as HTTP, REST, URI, etc.) to facilitate accessing the objects' capabilities. The inclusion of services from smart things makes WoT different from the traditional Web" (Minerva, Biru & Rotondi, 2015; Zeng et al., 2011).

WoT can be defined as the application layer of IoT, enabling interoperability across platforms, as some researchers proposed in (Guinard & Trifa, 2009; Guinard & Trifa, 2016).

Thus, WoT was designed to be easily integrated in the existing Web so it can make full use of its infrastructure and standards to minimize the effort of integrations across applications and systems. Although WoT is built on the existing Web standards, such as REST, HTTP, JSON, WebSockets and TLS, it will also require new ones. Also, we have to mention that there are ongoing efforts to standardize WoT (Anon-l, n.d.).

But the connection of things to the Web must be safe, secured and interoperable.

According to researchers, in order to describe things in WoT, a Web Thing Description format is needed. Also, in order to allow the interaction with various things, a REST style Web Thing API can be used. According to (Raggett, 2015a), "thing descriptions can be used to create proxies for a thing, allowing scripts to interact with a local proxy for a remote entity". A model for Web Things used to "describe the virtual counterpart of physical objects in the Web of Things" was proposed in (Anon-m, 2017). The Web API for Things has also been defined "to be followed by anyone wanting to create a product, device, service, or application for the Web of Things". These proposed model and protocols "aim at making the interaction between Things in the IoT accessible through Web standards to facilitate the implementation of Web applications making use or retrieving data from real-world objects" (Anon-m, 2017).

WoT/IoT platforms provide a solution to the increasing demand of WoT/IoT applications in various domains. Thus, these platforms enable developers and implementers to focus on the specific, differentiated and unique value the application provides and "outsource common, industry-wide features and functionality" (Lucero, 2016).

WoT Platforms

Currently, there already are many IoT platforms, and simply choosing one to solve a problem can be a challenge in itself. The challenge increases for those who create an application that needs to bridge many IoT platforms. According to (Raggett, 2015b), a solution is to "enable worldwide discovery and interoperability by exposing these platforms through the Web with a new class of webservers that support an open framework for the Web of Things (WoT)".

Next we present various WoT platforms suitable for the healthcare field which can be used for enabling the development of WoT-based solutions in the context of real-world use cases (Table 1).

Social Web of Things Paradigm

WoT and IoT neglect an important part of human behavior: socialising, and might partly explain their slow adoption by individuals.

Social networking has seen a meteoric success in bringing people together online (Dasgupta, 2010), creating or reconfiguring social conventions and social contexts by means of technology.

The concept of Social Web of Things (SWoT), proposed by User Experience Lab at Ericsson Research, is described as the relationship between Social Networks and IoT, being used to render the interconnected nature of IoT understandable and acceptable (Formo, Laaksolahti, & Gårdman, 2011). Therefore, in SWoT, devices are viewed as "beings" in social networks, while the interconnections and communication between these devices can be represented through social relations, respectively social interactions.

To this end, the SWoT consists of the social Web and WoT, which means that "people can connect with devices and services in a social network service, where they can say what they do, what they want, follow others, discuss with each other, complete tasks together, or even just "like" or "re-tweet" each other" (Formo, 2012; Rau et al., 2015).

According to the authors of (Rau et al., 2015), "SWoT could activate users' intuitive understanding of social network services, and make the interaction with SWoT natural in their own ways". This conclusion was formulated after analyzing the results obtained in a four-phase study conducted among users

Table 1. WoT Platforms for healthcare field

WoT Platform	Features (Addressed, Devices, etc.)	Ref
Web-of-Things Inspired e-Health Platform for Integrated Diabetes Care Management	Diabetes	(Al-Taee, Sungoor, Abood, & Philip, 2013)
Semantic Web of Things (SWoT) Generator	N/A	("SWoT: Semantic Web of Things," n.d.)
µWoTOP (micro Web of Things Open Platform)	Wireless biometric sensors (e.g., heart monitors, accelerometers, body thermometers, etc.)	(Corredor, Metola, Bernardos, Tarrío, & Casar, 2014)
WoTKit	Pulse oximeters (unknown), Phidget sensors and actuators	(Blackstock & Lea, 2012), (Anon-q, n.d.)
GaaS	Home appliances and sensors, medical and wellbeing, wearable devices	(Wu et. al., 2012)
EcoHealth	Attached body sensors, monitoring heartbeat rate and blood pressure	(Maia et al., 2014)
CardioNet	Patients with cardiovascular diseases, measure parameters such as ECG, blood pressure, temperature, oxygen level, and heartbeat rate, Cooking Hacks e-Health Sensor shield in conjunction with the Arduino Uno platform	(Sebestyen, Hangan, Oniga, & Gal, 2014)
Paraimpu	Ambient Assisted Living (AAL) sensors	(Anon-n, n.d.)
Weio	N/A	("WeIO," n.d.)

living in Beijing. The study designed "an interactive Internet of Things service on mobile devices based upon the concept of SWoT, with which users can interact with IoT in the same way they use the social network services" (Rau et al., 2015).

It should be noted that although some research trends in the literature were not originally presented under the SWoT umbrella, they align with this paradigm by combining the social role with WoT. However, due to the relative novelty of this paradigm, it has not been fully exploited not only in healthcare, but also in other domains.

Nowadays, social networking worldwide has become an essential part of computing. WoT is seen as a key component for future systems in various domains, including healthcare. Combining these two different paradigms, social networking and WoT in one paradigm already known as SWoT, might offer users the advantages of each paradigm with the addition of the advantages gained from mixing them.

Medical Devices as Things

The healthcare field already uses various devices for assisting or monitoring patients' health and many types of medical devices and sensors are already embedded in clinical and administrative settings. Also, currently, there is an increasing number of personal health sensors and other consumer-owned devices, that can be used to monitor various parameters, such as sleep, blood pressure or glucose. These devices are more or less affordable, wearable, implantable, or ingestible, and consumers are becoming comfortable using them, for example, for various health and activity monitoring services. Moreover, the adoption level shows that there is an increasing trend in using these devices in the future. According to (Anon-p, 2016), the exponentially growing demand might reach 20 billion medical connected devices by 2020. Other studies, like the one performed by the IBM Institute for Business Value, report that the estimated number of medical devices connected to the Internet is expected to increase from 10 billion in 2014 to 50 billion over the next decade.

All these wearables and other consumer-owned devices generate so called own patient-generated health data (PGHD), which are currently used only partially or not at all to derive actionable insights from it.

In order to improve clinical outcomes and patient care quality, healthcare organizations (hospitals, small practices, etc.) are looking for "medical device data to be more interoperable, complete, standardized, detailed, and accurate". Currently, there is a high level of adopting medical devices connected to each other, some of which being also connected to the Internet. Various standards related to medical devices were already developed or represent a work in progress. Thus, for example, IEEE proposed a standard for medical devices communication profile for Web services. "The scope of this standard is a communication protocol specification for a distributed system of point-of-care (PoC) medical devices and medical IT systems that need to exchange data or safely control networked PoC medical devices by defining a profile for Web service specifications and defining additional Web service specifications as part of this standard" (IEEE SA - 11073, 2016).

WoT enables medical devices and not only, to "speak" the same language, so as to communicate and interoperate freely on the Web (Formo, 2012; Mayer, Guinard, & Trifa 2012). Thus, WoT allows interacting with a smart thing through Web protocols. Along with physical devices, it might use traditional Web services (Anon-f, 2015; Anon-w, 2016; Al-Taee, Sungoor, Abood, & Philip, 2013; "SWoT: Semantic Web of Things," n.d.) or tiny Web servers already embedded, even in resource-constrained devices (Corredor, Metola, Bernardos, Tarrío, & Casar, 2014; Anon-q, n.d.; Blackstock & Lea, 2012; Wu et. al., 2012). Moreover, the so-called smart gateways enable the extent of WoT to devices that are not IP-enabled (Maia et al., 2014; Sebestyen, Hangan, Oniga, & Gal, 2014; Anon-n, n.d.). Therefore, various medical devices already on the market could be integrated in WoT. For example, once a medical device provides a Web API to access it, it could be integrated into WoT and other things (humans and machine clients alike) can invoke its services with the help of ordinary Web requests.

The future of healthcare is expected to focus more on interconnected devices and the data generated by these devices as a great source of data analysis.

Big, Fast and Smart Data

Nowadays, data becomes a "torrent flowing into every area of the global economy" (Anon-v, 2010), regardless whether the information comes from private or public sources. And healthcare is probably one of the most data-intensive industries around.

According to various researchers, big data can generate significant value across various sectors of the global economy, "enhancing the productivity and competitiveness of companies and the public sector and creating substantial economic surplus for consumers. For instance, if US health care could use big data creatively and effectively to drive efficiency and quality, we estimate that the potential value from data in the sector could be more than $300 billion in value every year, two-thirds of which would be in the form of reducing national health care expenditures by about 8 percent" (McKinsey, 2011). According to the Centre for Economics and Business Research (Anon-o, 2016), big data in the UK has the potential to generate healthcare benefits of £14.4 billion for 2012-2017, equivalent to nearly 10 percent of the nation's 2012 healthcare expenditure. From 2015 to 2020, the report estimates the total benefit to the UK healthcare of big data analytics to amount to 10,906 £m. The researchers consider that big data capabilities are a need, not only in healthcare.

All medical devices and sensors, smartphones, and other consumer-owned devices, including PCs and laptops, social media sites, etc. have allowed billions of individuals around the world to contribute to an avalanche of rich data, that could offer benefits in terms of reducing costs and improving patient care, but for which there are no standards or protocols to facilitate the aggregating information from them.

According to (Groves, Kayyali, Knott, & Kuiken, 2016), "this information is a form of 'big data', so called not only for its sheer volume but for its complexity, diversity, and timeliness". But, according to various research teams (McKinsey, 2011), healthcare providers, for instance, discard 90 percent of the data they generate. Instead, they should convert the terabytes and zettabytes of big data that is not currently used (classified as dark data) into useful data in order to improve patient experience. And, both patients and physicians must be willing and able to use insights from it.

Worldwide, various healthcare stakeholders are now beginning to analyze big data to obtain insights that could and should help to find solutions to problems related to the variability in the quality of healthcare and the increasing healthcare costs. For example, using specific applications and analytical tools, researchers can mine the data in order to identify most effective treatments for certain conditions or to develop patterns related to the side effects of drugs, thus obtaining important information that can help improving patient care and substantially decreasing healthcare spending.

Although these efforts are still in their early stages, as technological capabilities and understanding advance, it is expected that new ideas will be developed for the applicability of big data analysis. It is also necessary that this data be quickly understood. The current trend is represented by the transition from big data, where analytics are processed after-the-fact in batch mode, to fast data, where data analysis is done in real-time to provide immediate insights. In healthcare, time is the essence. A few seconds of delay in understanding the information could cost not only money, but also lives. In order to provide insights in real time, the use of fast data, which is processed as it is collected, is needed.

Smart data refers to information that actually makes sense. Intelligent algorithms could be applied on data in order to add intelligence. Thus, meaningless numbers could be turned into valuable insights, from which, for example, patterns could be extracted and processed. And different machine learning methods could deal with the challenges in IoT/WoT in order to extract higher level information. In fact, intelligent processing and analysis of big data is the key to developing smart IoT/WoT applications. Various studies discussed the potential and challenges of machine learning for IoT/WoT data analytics (Mahdavinejad et al., 2017).

There are some risks associated with big data in healthcare, such as the danger of exposing confidential patient information. In order to capture big data's full potential, stakeholders across healthcare need to protect patient privacy as more information becomes public, and ensure that safeguards are in place to protect healthcare organizations that release information.

In the following section, we will be addressing some security considerations.

Security Considerations

Information management in healthcare might prove difficult, especially when dealing with healthcare records consisting of disparate data (e.g., family medical histories, billing information, etc.). These records are stored and shared across many different locations, such as hospital archives, clinical laboratories, insurance providers, and even the mobile devices of individuals (patients or caregivers).

In this context, the challenge in healthcare is to secure from attacks a significant amount of sensitive information, whilst maintaining it immediately accessible and uncompromised. Despite the fact that the U.S. regulatory requirements, such as those under the Health Insurance Portability and Accountability Act (HIPAA), provide guidance for safeguarding healthcare data, the Cisco Security Capabilities Benchmark Study (Anon-w, 2016) claims that "healthcare organizations are still not implementing as full an array of strong security defenses as organizations in other industries". The consequences are significant, as shown in a study performed by Ponemon Institute, proving that between 2012 and 2013, 90% of the surveyed healthcare organizations reported at least one data breach, with an average economic impact of $2 million per incident (Anon-g, 2014). Moreover, according to the Identity Theft Resource Center, in 2013, the healthcare industry accounted for more than 44% of all breaches, more than it had ever experienced before. Since then, the percentage decreased to a little more than 35% in 2015.

And "the potential cost of breaches for the U.S. healthcare industry could be as much as $5.6 billion annually" (Anon-g, 2014). According to the 2015 Cost of Data Breach analysis by Ponemon Institute (Anon-f, 2015), in 2014, worldwide, the average cost of a healthcare breach was estimated at $363 per exposed personally identifiable record.

The adoption of the (Social) WoT will bring a large number of changes, especially in healthcare delivery. Thus, the WoT will support the provision of new healthcare services to patients, most of which are very eager to use them; nevertheless without the implementation of effective security controls, the use will significantly increase the number of security risks and introduce new WoT-related risks that healthcare organizations will inevitably face. For example, potentially sharing of medical or even personal information, without the consent or knowledge of the owner, gives rise to serious security problems.

The European Network Information and Security Directive (NIS) ("Directive (EU) 2016/1148, 2016), (Anon-x, 2016), imposes the obligation to maintain adequate security in network and information systems and includes a data breach notification requirement, such as the General Data Protection Regulation (GDPR); nevertheless, these obligations could affect certain (S)WoT services.

In order to assure a comprehensive defense mechanism against all types and sizes of cyber threats, most security practitioners recommend a multiple defenses in place approach, such as a combination of cyber protection technologies to assure a multiple layered defense, each focusing on different aspects of a potential cyberattack. Nevertheless, securing the healthcare systems from attacks must allow the constant easy access to these systems and data.

Moreover, the adoption of (S)WoT in healthcare will require the change of the user-centric security approach toward a thing-oriented model. Thus, for example, the authentication of things, not just people, is required. As yet, there are no common mechanisms to handle the devices' identity management or to protect the authentication credentials attached to things.

Therefore, as healthcare professionals cannot afford to take risks, in order to make the (S)WoT widely usable and drive its successful adoption in healthcare, significant research for providing true, intelligent, even holistic security is needed.

But, besides the filtering through massive amounts of data and quickly establishing what is and what is not useful, another problem regards the presentation of the resulting information in a secure and meaningful way, to the right person, at the right time. According to (Cumming, Fowlie, & McKendrick, 2010), "there is the question of context and relevance, a question that technology developers haven't yet succeeded in solving, but which artificial intelligence (AI) and machine learning will probably play a role in".

The development of (S)WoT and all of the above related fields, and not only, has an impact in many areas, including the medical sector.

The next section briefly summarizes an evolution of medicine models, considering the P's of healthcare and the impact that the SWoT might have on these models.

Medicine Models and SWoT

Throughout the evolution of medicine, several models have been considered. In this section we refer to the Pi medicine models, where *i* ranges from 0-6.

The P0 medicine model was strongly centered on the physician and it is considered the dawn of medicine (Bragazzi, 2013). Over time this medicine model evolved, becoming P3 model, characterized by three capabilities: personalization, predictability and prevention. A change in paradigm occurred when a new capability was taken into consideration: participatory. According to the editors of the Journal of Participatory Medicine, Jessie Gruman and Charles W. Smith participatory medicine is defined as "a cooperative model of health care that encourages, supports and expects active involvement by all parties (clinicians, patients, caregivers, administrators, payers and communities) in the prevention, management and treatment of disease and disability and the promotion of health" (Gruman & Smith, 2009). There were several variants for the names of this new model, such as personalized medicine, precision medicine and P4 medicine. Due to the fact that the first two terms do not take into consideration the four features of this paradigm, we use the term "P4 medicine" which we consider more adequate than the other ones. Although the P4 medicine model was considered a visionary one in comparison to traditional medicine, there were scientists that objected to it. Thus, Gorini and Pravettoni consider that this new model "lacks a consideration of the psychological needs and values that make each individual unique" (Gorini & Pravettoni, 2011). At their suggestion, a fifth P was added, with the attention focusing on the psycho-cognitive aspects. Once *i* was incremented, the P4 medicine model advanced to the P5 medicine model. The addition of the public feature led to the next medicine model: P6. In other words, the P6 medicine model is a personalized, predictive, preventive, participatory, psycho-cognitive and public model. G. Cumming and others defined this model as a "P4 + C^n Hippocratic revolution" (Cumming et al., 2010), where C^n stands for "community, collaboration, self-caring, co-creation, co-production, and co-development using technologies delivered via the Internet". According to (Bragazzi, 2013), "patients do not limit themselves to browse health-related information on the Web, but they actively exploit all of the Web's potential", including the social networks. Moreover, Topol stated that "our go-to source for health and medical information is moving away from our doctor—it is increasingly by crowdsourcing and friend sourcing our entrusted social network" (Topol, 2013).

As can be seen in Figure 1, the evolution of medicine models can be compared to the development of a grapevine. We chose this model because it is a complex system of interactions between the various factors determining the development of a grapevine, such as temperature, solar radiation, soil water deficit, etc. Similarly, the medicine models developed in time have resulted from interactions between a number of factors briefly presented below. We chose leaves to represent the new features of the models and a bunch of grapes to represent C^n from P6 medicine model. We can also consider that as a trellis supports the growth of a grapevine, so emerging technology also supports the development of medicine models.

After an extensive review of research publications and projects related to (Social) WoT, along with various platforms and applications in the healthcare field (some of them being presented in the first sections of our chapter), we attempted to give an overview of the already proven implications of adopting (S)WoT in healthcare at a worldwide level. Our conclusion is that the results already obtained by researchers, and also the proposed goals, imply updating the current medicine model.

In this sense, we propose the extension of this medicine model. Hence, through the adoption of the Social Web of Thing in healthcare, a new form of medicine could be taken into consideration. This form ensures the fulfillment of the healthcare delivery criteria presented in (Srini, 2011): Content, Context, Communication, Convenience, Customization, which can be referred to as P6 + C^5. We must emphasize

Figure 1. Medicine models

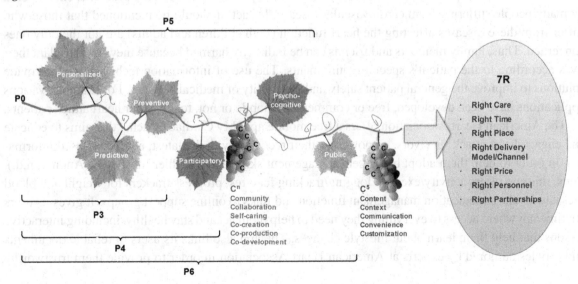

that, in this context, the meaning of the word "community" taken into account in the definition of the P6 medicine ($P4 + C^n$) should be extended, referring not only to humans, but to a community of things (living and non-living entities). Consequently, in order to represent $P6 + C^5$, we add another bunch of grapes to model C^5.

This medicine model, supported by the adoption of SWoT in healthcare, is in accordance with the right principles of healthcare delivery defined by (Srini, 2011): Right Care (right to access and right to waive), Right Time, Right Place, Right Delivery Model/Channel, Right Price, Right Personnel, Right Partnerships. Considering all these, we propose to formulate this concept as in: $P6 + C^5 => 7R$.

Next section deals with the application of the Social WoT paradigm to healthcare context, evaluating the potential and implications of SWoT approach for people with complex medical conditions, such as cardiovascular diseases.

SWoT-BASED BENEFITS FOR PEOPLE WITH CARDIOVASCULAR DISEASES

Context

Cardiovascular diseases (CVD), covers a range of diseases related to the circulatory system, including heart diseases and cerebrovascular disease (stroke) (Anon-z, n.d.); according to a scientific study that examined every country over the past 25 years (Roth & al., 2017), CVD account for one-third of deaths throughout the world and the United States Institute of Medicine statistics reveal that cardiac arrest is the third leading cause of death in the United States. Statistics show that about 450,000 Americans die each year from cardiac arrest and about 25 percent of people survive cardiac arrests in the hospital, while just over 10 percent survive outside the hospital (Anon-s, n.d.). According to (Anon-r, 2014), mortality from CVD will rise from 1,118,457 in 2014 to 1,215,088 in 2020. Also, costs related to cardiovascular diseases hit €122.6 billion by 2020 in six major European economies (France, Germany, Spain, Italy, Sweden and the United Kingdom) (Anon-r, 2014). The authors of this report warn that unless actions are taken to address this challenge, the economic burden will become ever more substantial.

Next, we focus on presenting a Social WoT (SWoT) approach to solve some problems encountered by many people suffering from cardiovascular disease. In fact, it should be mentioned that those who suffer from these diseases affecting the heart function (both children and adults) are not the only ones concerned. Thus, family members and friends can be indirectly harmed because they have to adapt their lives according to the patient's special requirements. The use of information technology can provide solutions to improve the general patient safety and the quality of medical services. For example, various applications have been developed, free or commercial, mobile or not, to empower heart attack patients.

The American Heart Association offers a free mobile app, My Cardiac Coach, "that aims to educate and engage heart attack survivors, empowering their recovery with the latest, evidence-based information in order to help them adopt better self-management skills and healthier lifestyles" (Anon-y, n.d.). Thus, this app offers activity/exercise logging/tracking features, progress trackers for weight and blood pressure levels, a medication management function and links to online support groups. It gives its users anytime/anywhere access to everything they need to help them get and stay healthy, including interactive lessons that help them learn about lifestyle changes. The app also links its users to reliable documents and articles authored by experts at American Heart Association in order to provide them trustworthy information about heart attack warning signs, risk factors, diagnosis, treatment, and life as a survivor or caregiver (Anon-y, n.d.).

Researchers have also paid attention to cardiac arrests outside the hospital, when it is difficult to give first aid. Shortening the time bystanders recognize out-of-hospital cardiac arrest to when they deliver shocks with automated external defibrillators (AEDs) could save lives as each earned minute increases the chances of survival by 10%. According to research showed at the American Heart Association's Scientific Sessions 2015 ("Sudden cardiac arrest?", n.d.), Japanese researchers from Kyoto University developed an app, called AED-SOS, which signals co-rescuers in communities when an out-of-hospital cardiac arrest has occurred and where. Co-rescuers then deliver the needed lifesaving AEDs to the out-of-hospital cardiac arrest scene.

In order to reduce the time between out-of-hospital cardiac arrest and resuscitation, by directing nearby trained responders to cardiac arrest victim more than three minutes before the emergency services arrive, the European Heart Rhythm Association (EHRA), a registered branch of the European Society of Cardiology, developed the EHRA First Responder App (Anon-u, 2017), currently being rolled out in several cities in Germany. "Based on GPS tracking technology, the app is used by the existing emergency services (reached in many countries by dialing 112) to locate trained 'app rescuers' and then automatically direct them to the scene of cardiac arrest" (Anon-u, 2017). The target is for an app rescuer to arrive three to four minutes after the cardiac arrest, thus decreasing the death risk with about 10% per minute. The application has also a location database for publicly accessible AED (Anon-aa, n.d.). The applications described above, and not just these, are not integrated, and sometimes are difficult to access.

Next we try to present WoT potential in improving the lives of patients with heart disease.

A SWoT-Based Solution

Nowadays there are many systems designed and implemented over time in the field of healthcare in order to fulfill the needs of a wide range of scenarios. Although many of these systems provide good ad-hoc solutions satisfying the specified requirements, most of them cannot be easily reused and/or adapted to build new applications and services.

This section focuses on presenting a platform proposal that was designed to improve the connectivity and reusability of data in order to provide different types of healthcare (Figure 2). This system could communicate with various medical devices and healthcare IT systems. For example, a high-risk patient could have a device similar to the "personal data tracker" ("a portable electrocardiogram built into a smartphone case"), presented in (Hernandez, 2014), that could send the doctor notifications regarding the patient's state of health. Other sensors could be used to track the weight of patient. Capturing, combining and analyzing various data across multiple disparate data sources could provide a more complex view of the patient.

There are several factors that put people at increased risk for heart attack. People with cardiovascular disease should take extra precautions to protect themselves during extreme temperatures, be it high or low. Extreme weather conditions can put excessive stress on the heart, triggering, for example, a heart attack and/ or may also lead to other diseases, such as stroke.

Changes in atmospheric pressure may also cause changes in the cardiovascular system. Thus, lowering of pressure can cause increased blood pressure, tachycardia, headache, palpitations, chest tightness; sometimes angina attacks and even the onset of myocardial infarction, and thrombotic accidents are precipitated. By monitoring the mobile phone and included sensors, the system records, for example, the

Figure 2. A SWoT-based Solution

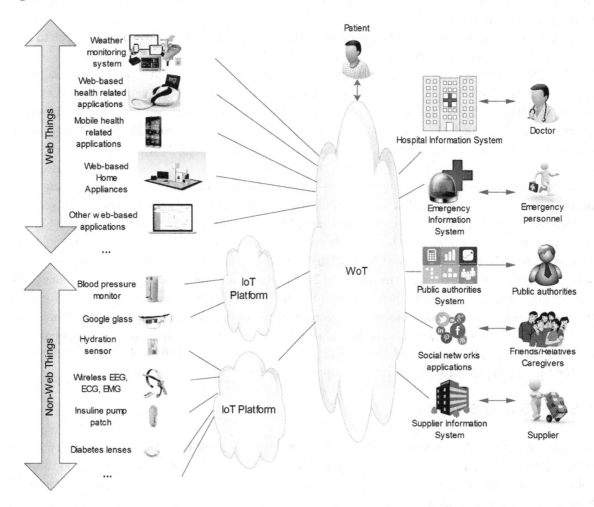

information related to the location and the movement/activity of the patient. By monitoring the forecast, the system will alert the patient when changes occurring in the weather might affect his/her condition. Therefore, the system plays an active role in disease prevention. It can also monitor the patient program, encourage him/her to make regular exercises according to the program established with the doctor, and give suggestions related to proper diet, etc.

The system will enable real-time recommendations and alerts using prescriptive analytics. Data is processed as it is collected, in order to provide real-time insights. For example, a lack of movement or other activity could indicate that the patient is not feeling well or even that he/she is having an attack. If the system detects that something is wrong with the user, it can automatically notify a third party, such as the user's family or a physician. Also, it can connect to the EHRA First Responder App in order to ask for help from trained 'app rescuers', as those presented in a previous section. In addition, it could offer information about nearby publicly accessible AEDs.

Identifying patients in need and ensuring that the right care reaches the right patient at the right time is one of the features of SWoT adoption in healthcare, as outlined in the above section on medicine models.

The system allows a continuous and more comprehensive understanding of personal health trends. Thus, for example, the outcomes obtained by analyzing the patient's behavior and integrating them with other behavioral health data sources could lead to early identification of the risks of cardiovascular disease. It is a difficult task, because the cardiovascular diseases can appear suddenly and unexpectedly or take the form of a long-term condition.

Taking into consideration the potential of technological innovations, we expect that the adoption of SWoT in healthcare meets the features of the last medicine model presented in a previous section and that it leads to more and more interesting uses, some of which could help substantially reduce the soaring costs of healthcare.

FUTURE RESEARCH DIRECTIONS

The healthcare system should deliver higher quality, more cost-effective care. Unfortunately, current electronic health data still cannot be shared across organizational, vendor and geographic boundaries. Nevertheless, this information must be securely available to those who need it. Patients will increasingly demand more information and knowledge, better healthcare processes, but with more security and privacy protections. The outcome should be a healthcare system that delivers higher quality, more cost-effective care.

There are good reasons, some of which presented in this chapter, to estimate that the healthcare sector will overcome obstacles and progress, taking positive steps to embrace IoT/WoT technology, albeit at a slower pace than in other sectors.

In order to successfully adopt WoT/ IoT in healthcare, an interoperable health IT infrastructure is needed. And, in order to enable interoperability in healthcare, Office of the National Coordinator for Health IT (ONC) released the final version of the Connecting Health and Care for the Nation: A Shared Nationwide Interoperability Roadmap Version 1.0 (Anon-t, 2015). ONC defines interoperability in the Roadmap as, "the ability of a system to exchange electronic health information with and use electronic health information from other systems without special effort on the part of the user." The Roadmap also continues in stating that "all individuals, their families, and health care providers should be able to send, receive, find and use electronic health information in a manner that is appropriate, secure, timely and reliable to support the health and wellness of individuals through informed, shared decision-making" (Anon-t, 2015).

In order to achieve interoperability, the Roadmap sets out a number of period goals which are as follows:

- **2015-2017:** Send, receive, find and use priority data domains to improve health care quality and outcomes.
- **2018-2020:** Expand data sources and users in the interoperable health IT ecosystem to improve health and lower costs.
- **2021-2024:** Achieve nationwide interoperability to enable a learning health system, with the person at the center of the system that can continuously improve care, public health, and science through real-time data access.

It is important that governments support initiatives such as the ONC roadmap.

CONCLUSION

This chapter aims to examine the adoption of the ever-growing WoT in healthcare, as a modality to change how we access healthcare, with strong effects on improving the quality of life. The authors provide an overview of the impact of WoT in healthcare and the inherent challenges to be addressed in order to make WoT a reality in the field. We considered the medicine models and, based on new features, we depicted their evolution. Based on the various results presented in worldwide research publications, we proposed an update of the current medicine model.

We have tried to examine the evolving technologies that have the capabilities to transform the ways healthcare is accessed, thus improving patient experience and, ultimately, quality of life. The healthcare system will have to change significantly for healthcare stakeholders to take advantage of WoT.

WoT could help improving the collection, organization, and exchange of the wealth of patient data in order to create new insights. For instance, WoT could help physicians detect early-warning signals for the development and exacerbation of various conditions, including heart disease.

REFERENCES

Al-Taee, M. A., Sungoor, A. H., Abood, S. N., & Philip, N. Y. (2013). Web-of-Things inspired e-Health platform for integrated diabetes care management. *2013 IEEE Jordan Conference on Applied Electrical Engineering and Computing Technologies (AEECT)*. 10.1109/AEECT.2013.6716427

Amendola, S., Lodato, R., Manzari, S., Occhiuzzi, C., & Marrocco, G. (2014). RFID technology for IoT-based personal healthcare in smart spaces. *IEEE Internet of Things Journal*, *1*(2), 144–152. doi:10.1109/JIOT.2014.2313981

American Heart Association - Building healthier lives, free of cardiovascular diseases and stroke. (n.d.). Retrieved from https://www.heart.org

Bhatt, Y., & Bhatt, C. (2017). Internet of Things in HealthCare. In *Internet of Things and Big Data Technologies for Next Generation Healthcare* (pp. 13–33). Springer International Publishing. doi:10.1007/978-3-319-49736-5_2

Bi, Z., Da Xu, L., & Wang, C. (2014). Internet of things for enterprise systems of modern manufacturing. *IEEE Transactions on Industrial Informatics*, *10*(2), 1537–1546. doi:10.1109/TII.2014.2300338

Blackstock, M., & Lea, R. (2012, June). WoTKit: a lightweight toolkit for the web of things. In *Proceedings of the Third International Workshop on the Web of Things* (p. 3). ACM. 10.1145/2379756.2379759

Bovet, G., & Hennebert, J. (2013). Offering web-of-things connectivity to building networks. *Proceedings of the 2013 ACM conference on Pervasive and ubiquitous computing adjunct publication - UbiComp '13 Adjunct*. 10.1145/2494091.2497590

Bragazzi, N. L. (2013). From P0 to P6 medicine, a model of highly participatory, narrative, interactive, and "augmented" medicine: Some considerations on Salvatore Iaconesi's clinical story. *Patient Preference and Adherence*, *7*, 353. doi:10.2147/PPA.S38578 PMID:23650443

Cai, H., Da Xu, L., Xu, B., Xie, C., Qin, S., & Jiang, L. (2014). IoT-based configurable information service platform for product lifecycle management. *IEEE Transactions on Industrial Informatics*, *10*(2), 1558–1567. doi:10.1109/TII.2014.2306391

Ciortea, A., Boissier, O., Zimmermann, A., & Florea, A. M. (2013). Reconsidering the social web of things. *Proceedings of the 2013 ACM conference on Pervasive and ubiquitous computing adjunct publication - UbiComp '13 Adjunct*. 10.1145/2494091.2497587

Connecting Health and Care for the Nation, A Shared Nationwide Interoperability Roadmap. (2015). Retrieved from The Office of the National Coordinator for Health Information Technology website: https://www.healthit.gov/sites/default/files/hie-interoperability/nationwide-interoperability-roadmap-final-version-1.0.pdf

Corredor, I., Metola, E., Bernardos, A. M., Tarrío, P., & Casar, J. R. (2014). A Lightweight Web of Things Open Platform to Facilitate Context Data Management and Personalized Healthcare Services Creation. *International Journal of Environmental Research and Public Health*, *11*(5), 4676–4713. doi:10.3390/ijerph110504676 PMID:24785542

2015. Cost of Data Breach Study: Global Analysis. (2015). Ponemon.

Couturier, J., Sola, D., Borioli, G. S., & Raiciu, C. (2012). *How can the internet of things help to overcome current healthcare challenges*. Retrieved from https://papers.ssrn.com/sol3/papers.cfm?abstract_id=2304133

Cumming, G., Fowlie, A., & McKendrick, D. (2010). H= P4+ C and Health Web Science: "A Hippocratic Revolution in Medicine." *Proceedings of the ACM WebSci, 11*, 14-17. Retrieved from http://www.websci11.org/fileadmin/websci/Papers/Health_WS_Workshop-A_Hippocratic_Revolution.pdf

Cutler, D. (2013). *Why Medicine Will Be More Like Walmart*. Retrieved from http://www.technology-review.com/news/518906/why-medicine-will-be-more-like-walmart

Daniel, F., Casati, F., Silveira, P., Verga, M., & Nalin, M. (2011). Beyond Health Tracking: A Personal Health and Lifestyle Platform. *IEEE Internet Computing*, *15*(4), 14–22. doi:10.1109/MIC.2011.53

Dasgupta, S. (2010). *Social computing: concepts, methodologies, tools and applications*. IGI Global. doi:10.4018/978-1-60566-984-7

De Iongh, A., Fagan, P., Fenner, J., & Kidd, L. (2015). *A practical guide to self-management support. Key components for successful implementation*. Academic Press.

De Silva, D. (2011). *Evidence: helping people help themselves*. The Health Foundation.

Directive (EU) 2016/1148 of the European Parliament and of the Council of 6 July 2016 concerning measures for a high common level of security of network and information systems across the Union. (2016). Retrieved from http://eur-lex.europa.eu/eli/dir/2016/1148/oj

Dunkels, A. (2003). Full TCP/IP for 8-bit architectures. *Proceedings of the 1st international conference on Mobile systems, applications and services - MobiSys '03*, 85-98. 10.1145/1066116.1066118

Engineering the Internet of Things: Wearables and Medical Devices. (2016). Retrieved from ANSYS website: http://www.ansys.com/-/media/Ansys/corporate/resourcelibrary/brochure/ib-wearables-and-medical-devices.pdf

Erola, A., Castellà-Roca, J., Viejo, A., & Mateo-Sanz, J. M. (2011). Exploiting social networks to provide privacy in personalized web search. *Journal of Systems and Software, 84*(10), 1734–1745. doi:10.1016/j.jss.2011.05.009

European Chronic Disease Alliance Policy. (2010). Retrieved from http://www.alliancechronicdiseases.org/fileadmin/user_upload/policy_papers/ECDA_White_Paper_on_Chronic_Disease.pdf

Fan, Y., Yin, Y., Da Xu, L., Zeng, Y., & Wu, F. (2014). IoT-Based Smart Rehabilitation System. *IEEE Transactions on Industrial Informatics, 10*(2), 1568–1577. doi:10.1109/TII.2014.2302583

Fast, A., Jensen, D., & Levine, B. N. (2005, August). Creating social networks to improve peer-to-peer networking. In *Proceedings of the eleventh ACM SIGKDD international conference on Knowledge discovery in data mining* (p. 568-573). ACM. 10.1145/1081870.1081938

Formo, J. (2012). *A Social Web of Things | Strategic Design Blog*. Retrieved from http://www.ericsson.com/uxblog/2012/04/a-social-web-of-things/

Formo, J., Laaksolahti, J., & Gårdman, M. (2011, August). Internet of things marries social media. In *Proceedings of the 13th International Conference on Human Computer Interaction with Mobile Devices and Services* (p. 753-755). ACM.

Fourth Annual Benchmark Study on Patient Privacy & Data Security. (2014). Retrieved from Ponemon Institute website: http://www2.idexpertscorp.com/ponemon-report-on-patient-privacy-data-security-incidents/

Gorini, A., & Pravettoni, G. (2011). P5 medicine: A plus for a personalized approach to oncology. *Nature Reviews. Clinical Oncology, 8*(7), 444. doi:10.1038/nrclinonc.2010.227-c1 PMID:21629214

Groves, P., Kayyali, B., Knott, D., & Kuiken, S. V. (2016). *The 'big data' revolution in healthcare: Accelerating value and innovation.* Retrieved from http://repositorio.colciencias.gov.co:8081/jspui/bitstream/11146/465/1/1661-The_big_data_revolution_in_healthcare.pdf

Gruman, J., & Smith, C. W. (2009). Why the Journal of Participatory Medicine? *Journal of Participatory Medicine*. Retrieved from http://www.jopm.org/opinion/editorials/2009/10/21/why-the-journal-of-participatory-medicine/

Guinard, D., Fischer, M., & Trifa, V. (2010, March). Sharing using social networks in a composable web of things. In *Pervasive Computing and Communications Workshops (PERCOM Workshops), 2010 8th IEEE International Conference on* (pp. 702-707). IEEE. 10.1109/PERCOMW.2010.5470524

Guinard, D., & Trifa, V. (2009, April). Towards the web of things: Web mashups for embedded devices. In *Workshop on Mashups, Enterprise Mashups and Lightweight Composition on the Web (MEM 2009), in proceedings of WWW (International World Wide Web Conferences), Madrid, Spain* (Vol. 15). Academic Press.

Guinard, D., & Trifa, V. (2016). *Building the web of things: with examples in node. js and raspberry pi.* Manning Publications Co.

Guinard, D., Trifa, V., Mattern, F., & Wilde, E. (2011). From the Internet of Things to the Web of Things: Resource Oriented Architecture and Best Practices. In D. Uckelmann, M. Harrison & F. Michahelles (Eds.), Architecting the Internet of Things (pp. 97-129). Springer.

Guinard, D., Trifa, V., & Wilde, E. (2010, November). A resource oriented architecture for the web of things. In Internet of Things (IOT), 2010 (p. 1-8). IEEE. doi:10.1109/IOT.2010.5678452

He, C., Fan, X., & Li, Y. (2013). Toward Ubiquitous Healthcare Services With a Novel Efficient Cloud Platform. *IEEE Transactions on Biomedical Engineering, 60*(1), 230–234. doi:10.1109/TBME.2012.2222404 PMID:23060318

He, D., & Zeadally, S. (2015). An Analysis of RFID Authentication Schemes for Internet of Things in Healthcare Environment Using Elliptic Curve Cryptography. *IEEE Internet Of Things Journal, 2*(1), 72–83. doi:10.1109/JIOT.2014.2360121

Healthcare Financial Management Association (HFMA). (2017). Retrieved from http://www.hfma.org/DownloadAsset.aspx?id=46524

Healthcare Security: Improving Network Defenses While Serving Patients. (2016). CISCO.

Hernandez, D. (2014, March 10). *Big data healthcare: The pros and cons of remote patient monitoring.* Retrieved from http://medcitynews.com/2014/03/big-data-healthcare-pros-cons-remote-patient-monitoring/

Hibbard, J., & Greene, J. (2013). What The Evidence Shows About Patient Activation: Better Health Outcomes And Care Experiences; Fewer Data On Costs. *Health Affairs, 32*(2), 207–214. doi:10.1377/hlthaff.2012.1061 PMID:23381511

Identity Theft Resource Center Breach Statistics. 2005-2015. (n.d.). Retrieved from http://www.idtheftcenter.org/images/breach/2005to2015multiyear.pdf

IEEE SA - 11073-20702-2016 - Standard for Medical Devices Communication Profile for Web Services. Health informatics--Point-of-care medical device communication Part 20702: Medical Devices Communication Profile for Web Services. (n.d.). Retrieved July 30, 2017, from http://standards.ieee.org/findstds/standard/11073-20702-2016.html

Improving cyber security across the EU - Consilium. (2016). Retrieved from http://www.consilium.europa.eu/en/policies/cyber-security/

Introducing My Cardiac Coach. (n.d.). Retrieved from https://www.heart.org/HEARTORG/Conditions/HeartAttack/My-Cardiac-Coach_UCM_489280_SubHomePage.jsp

IoT to Revolutionize Healthcare Industry: Survey. (2015). Retrieved from http://www.machinetomachinemagazine.com/2015/04/14/iot-to-revolutionize-healthcare-industry-zebra-survey/

Kleinberg, J. (2008). The convergence of social and technological networks. *Communications of the ACM, 51*(11), 66–72. doi:10.1145/1400214.1400232

Kramer, S. (2017, January 16). *Overcoming Obstacles for IoT in the Healthcare Industry*. Retrieved from https://www.futurum.xyz/overcoming-obstacles-iot-healthcare-industry/

Li, L., Li, S., & Zhao, S. (2014). QoS-Aware Scheduling of Services-Oriented Internet of Things. *IEEE Transactions on Industrial Informatics*, *10*(2), 1497–1505. doi:10.1109/TII.2014.2306782

Li, X., Lu, R., Liang, X., Shen, X., Chen, J., & Lin, X. (2011). Smart community: An internet of things application. *IEEE Communications Magazine*, *49*(11), 68–75. doi:10.1109/MCOM.2011.6069711

Lucero, S. (2016). *IoT platforms: Enabling the Internet of Things*. HIS Technology. Retrieved from https://cdn. ihs. com/www/pdf/enabling-IOT. pdf

Mahdavinejad, M. S., Rezvan, M., Barekatain, M., Adibi, P., Barnaghi, P., & Sheth, A. P. (2017). Machine learning for Internet of Things data analysis: A survey. *Digital Communications and Networks*.

Maia, P., Batista, T., Cavalcante, E., Baffa, A., Delicato, F. C., Pires, P. F., & Zomaya, A. (2014). A web platform for interconnecting body sensors and improving health care. *Procedia Computer Science*, *40*, 135–142. doi:10.1016/j.procs.2014.10.041

Mayer, S., Guinard, D., & Trifa, V. (2012, October). Searching in a web-based infrastructure for smart things. In *Internet of Things (IOT), 2012 3rd International Conference on the* (p. 119-126). IEEE. 10.1109/IOT.2012.6402313

McKinsey, B. D. (2011). *Big data: The next frontier for innovation, competition, and productivity*. Retrieved from McKinsey Global Institute Report website: http://www.mckinsey.com/business-functions/digital-mckinsey/our-insights/big-data-the-next-frontier-for-innovation

Minerva, R., Biru, A., & Rotondi, D. (2015). Towards a definition of the Internet of Things (IoT). *IEEE Internet Initiative*, (1).

Mislove, A., Gummadi, K. P., & Druschel, P. (2006, August). Exploiting social networks for internet search. In *5th Workshop on Hot Topics in Networks (HotNets06). Citeseer* (p. 79). Academic Press.

Norris, S., Lau, J., Smith, S., Schmid, C., & Engelgau, M. (2002). Self-Management Education for Adults with Type 2 Diabetes: A meta-analysis of the effect on glycemic control. *Diabetes Care*, *25*(7), 1159–1171. doi:10.2337/diacare.25.7.1159 PMID:12087014

Paraimpu - You are Web. (n.d.). Retrieved from http://www.paraimpu.com/

Raggett, D. (2015a). Building the Web of Things. *Proceedings of the Conference on Open Web, Privacy, Security, Technology, Web of Devices, Web of Things*. Retrieved from https://www. w3. org/blog/2015/05/building-the-web-of-things

Raggett, D. (2015b). The Web of Things: Challenges and Opportunities. *Computer*, *48*(5), 26–32. doi:10.1109/MC.2015.149

Rau, P. L. P., Huang, E., Mao, M., Gao, Q., Feng, C., & Zhang, Y. (2015). Exploring interactive style and user experience design for social web of things of Chinese users: A case study in Beijing. *International Journal of Human-Computer Studies*, *80*, 24–35. doi:10.1016/j.ijhcs.2015.02.007

Rising Stars, H. B. A. Healthcare Vision 2020 - PharmaVOICE: PharmaVOICE. (2016, May). Retrieved from http://www.pharmavoice.com/editors-choice-pdf/hba-rising-stars-healthcare-vision-2020/

Romer, K., Ostermaier, B., Mattern, F., Fahrmair, M., & Kellerer, W. (2010). Real-Time Search for Real-World Entities: A Survey. *Proceedings of the IEEE, 98*(11), 1887–1902. doi:10.1109/JPROC.2010.2062470

Roth, G. A., Johnson, C., Abajobir, A., Abd-Allah, F., Abera, S. F., Abyu, G., ... Alla, F. (2017). Global, Regional, and National Burden of Cardiovascular Diseases for 10 Causes, 1990 to 2015. *Journal of the American College of Cardiology*.

Sebestyen, G., Hangan, A., Oniga, S., & Gal, Z. (2014, May). eHealth solutions in the context of Internet of Things. In *Automation, Quality and Testing, Robotics, 2014 IEEE International Conference on* (p. 1-6). IEEE.

Self Care Reduces Costs And Improves Health: The Evidence. (2010). Expert Patients Programme.

Smartphone app directs first responders to cardiac arrest three minutes before ambulance. (2017, June). Retrieved from https://www.escardio.org/The-ESC/Press-Office/Press-releases/smartphone-app-directs-first-responders-to-cardiac-arrest-three-minutes-before-ambulance

Special report on managing information: Data, data everywhere. (2010). Retrieved from http://www.economist.com/node/15557443

Srini, J. (2011). *The Future of mHealth*. Retrieved from http://www.slideshare.net/HowardRosen129/the-future-of-mhealth-jay-srini-march-201.1

Srivastava, S., Pant, M., Abraham, A., & Agrawal, N. (2015). The technological growth in eHealth services. *Computational and Mathematical Methods in Medicine*. PMID:26146515

St. John, A., Davis, W. A., Price, C. P., & Davis, T. M. (2010). The value of self-monitoring of blood glucose: A review of recent evidence. *Journal of Diabetes and Its Complications, 24*(2), 129–141. doi:10.1016/j.jdiacomp.2009.01.002 PMID:19230717

State of the Market: The Internet of Things (IoT) 2015: Discover How IoT is Transforming Business Results. (2015). Retrieved from http://www.verizonenterprise.com/state-of-the-market-internet-of-things/

SWoT: Semantic Web of Things. (n.d.). Retrieved from http://sensormeasurement.appspot.com/?p=m3api

The Business Case for People Powered Health. (2013). Retrieved from NESTA website: http://www.nesta.org.uk/sites/default/files/the_business_case_for_people_powered_health.pdf

The economic cost of cardiovascular disease from 2014-2020 in six European economies. (2014). Retrieved from Centre for Economics and Business Research website: https://www.cebr.com/wp-content/uploads/2015/08/Short-Report-18.08.14.pdf

The First Responder App Concept - firstresponderapps Webseite! (n.d.). Retrieved from https://www.firstresponderapp.com/

The International Statistical Classification of Diseases and Related Health Problems 10th Revision (ICF X). (n.d.). Retrieved from World Health Organization website: www.who.int/whosis/icd10/

The Value of Big Data and the Internet of Things to the UK Economy. (2016). Retrieved from Centre for Economics and Business Research website: https://www.sas.com/content/dam/SAS/en_gb/doc/analystreport/cebr-value-of-big-data.pdf

Topol, E. (2013). *The creative destruction of medicine: How the digital revolution will create better health care*. Basic Books.

Trifa, V., Wieland, S., Guinard, D., & Bohnert, T. M. (2009). *Design and implementation of a gateway for web-based interaction and management of embedded devices*. DCOSS.

Vermesan, O., & Friess, P. (Eds.). (2014). *Internet of things-from research and innovation to market deployment* (Vol. 29). Aalborg: River Publishers.

Wang, C., Bi, Z., & Da Xu, L. (2014). IoT and Cloud Computing in Automation of Assembly Modeling Systems. *IEEE Transactions on Industrial Informatics*, *10*(2), 1426–1434. doi:10.1109/TII.2014.2300346

Web of Things – Architecting the Web of Things, for techies and thinkers! (n.d.). Retrieved from https://webofthings.org

Web of Things (WoT) Architecture. (n.d.). Retrieved October 25, 2017, from https://www.w3.org/TR/wot-architecture/

Web Thing Model. (2017, April 25). Retrieved from http://model.webofthings.io/

WeIO. (n.d.). Retrieved from http://we-io.net/

Weiser, P., & Ellis, A. (2015). *The Information Revolution Meets Health: The Transformative Power and Implementation Challenges of Health Analytics*. SSRN Electronic Journal. doi:10.2139srn.2593879

Wheeler, J. R. (2003). Can a disease self-management program reduce health care costs? The case of older women with heart disease. *Medical Care*, *41*(6), 706–715. doi:10.1097/01.MLR.0000065128.72148. D7 PMID:12773836

WoTKit – a fully featured IoT platform. (n.d.). Retrieved from http://sensetecnic.com/products-and-services/wotkit-a-fully-featured-iot-platform/

Wu, Z., Itälä, T., Tang, T., Zhang, C., Ji, Y., Hämäläinen, M., & Liu, Y. (2012, April). Gateway as a service: A cloud computing framework for web of things. In *Telecommunications (ICT), 2012 19th International Conference on* (p. 1-6). IEEE.

Xu, B., Da Xu, L., Cai, H., Xie, C., Hu, J., & Bu, F. (2014). Ubiquitous Data Accessing Method in IoT-Based Information System for Emergency Medical Services. *IEEE Transactions on Industrial Informatics*, *10*(2), 1578–1586. doi:10.1109/TII.2014.2306382

Yang, G., Xie, L., Mantysalo, M., Zhou, X., Pang, Z., Xu, L., ... Zheng, L.-R. (2014). A Health-IoT Platform Based on the Integration of Intelligent Packaging, Unobtrusive Bio-Sensor, and Intelligent Medicine Box. *IEEE Transactions on Industrial Informatics*, *10*(4), 2180–2191. doi:10.1109/TII.2014.2307795

Yang, P., & Wu, W. (2014). Efficient Particle Filter Localization Algorithm in Dense Passive RFID Tag Environment. *IEEE Transactions on Industrial Electronics*, *61*(10), 5641–5651. doi:10.1109/TIE.2014.2301737

Yazar, D., & Dunkels, A. (2009). Efficient application integration in IP-based sensor networks. *Proceedings of the First ACM Workshop on Embedded Sensing Systems for Energy-Efficiency in Buildings - BuildSys '09*, 43-48. 10.1145/1810279.1810289

Zeng, D., Guo, S., & Cheng, Z. (2011). The Web of Things: A Survey (Invited Paper). *Journal of Communication*, 6(6). doi:10.4304/jcm.6.6.424-438

Zheng, X., Martin, P., & Brohman, K. (2014). CLOUDQUAL: A Quality Model for Cloud Services. *IEEE Transactions on Industrial Informatics*, 10(2), 1527–1536. doi:10.1109/TII.2014.2306329

KEY TERMS AND DEFINITIONS

Big Data: The term is used for large and/or complex sets of structured or unstructured data that cannot be processed in traditional ways. As a concept, big data is defined around the four V's: volume (scale of data), velocity (analysis of streaming data), variety (different forms of data), and veracity (uncertainty of data).

Fast Data: This concept, occurring soon after "big data," enables fast and efficient data usage in order to provide instant results and responses. This type of data is used when speed is important.

Internet of Things (IOT): The concept depicts a world where different things, living and non-living entities, are connected to a single common network.

Medicine Models: Over time, various medicine models have been developed in order to describe which factors and in what ways affect and facilitate the success of patient care.

Smart Data: This term refers to data, often from big data and the IoT, that has value. Currently, big data is turned into smart data and there is an increasing focus on smart data instead of big data.

Social Web of Things (SWoT): Considered as a valuable resource in several areas, this concept reflects the shift of the WoT toward a Social WoT that involves the use of social networks.

Web of Things (WoT): This term refers to a paradigm related to things (various real-world living or non-living entities) that can become a part of the world wide web. This concept describes approaches, software architectural styles, and programming patterns.

Chapter 10
TempClass:
Implicit Temporal Queries Classifier

Rahul Pradhan
GLA University, India

Dilip Kumar Sharma
GLA University, India

ABSTRACT

Information retrieval is a field that is emerging day by day as user needs are growing. Users nowadays are not satisfied with results that merely match the query textual words; they want the query to be understood well and then results to be retrieved. These changing requirements need the query to be processed and its hidden intent uncovered. The authors address this problem by creating a system that understands the hidden temporal intent of the query and classifies it into proposed classes. This chapter works on temporal expressions in the document and classifies the query with respect to the temporal expressions in the document. The work is not limited to just classifying the query but also explores how these classifications will help search engines to make modifications in their user interface, which helps users to reach their desired information faster. Temporal boundaries of queries can be found using this work, which will help to disambiguate certain queries.

INTRODUCTION

We are in the big pool of data and it is accumulating day by day. This data needs to be processed and requires to be understood through its attributes and features. These attributes are actually the signals that help us in process of judging whether data is relevant with respect to user needs and query (Sharma & Sharma, 2012). On the same path, most of the search engines look for features, signals and prioritize their results in the form of ranked list which goes through most relevant to least relevant. Many conventional search engines use only the Web structure information and pattern matching, rather than query intention; therefore, prioritizing or ranking results based on query intention is still an area of research which needs to be explored. In the aim of improving the ranking of search results, temporal information hidden in Web pages and documents can be exploited to give more meaningful ranking functions.

DOI: 10.4018/978-1-5225-5384-7.ch010

This chapter will discuss an approach that will consider 'Query Understanding' which is a widely used approach in most of the popular search engines; this technology plays an important role in judging the document relevance. While using the search engines or any other information retrieval system the user demands to get more improved results. Such as, the user does not just want the results that match the document which contains query terms, but requests search engine to first understand the query, its intention and then provide results. In the same way, we can observe that the user does not care or bother to write or spell query terms correctly; s/he depends upon spell correction facility provided by search engines. Query understanding technology will help search engines to understand the intention of the query, so that by the help of this understanding the ranking function can be modified or improved, aiming to meet the user's changing demands. This technology does not just limit itself to ranking function but also helps search engines in presenting the information and results in more lucid and interesting way. For instance, when a user fires the query "India Gate", then the user's intention may be either information about India Gate or its history or its location, so search engine can also show map snippet in the result list to help user to find the route to India Gate. This task of improving visualization of results relies on different parameters such as language, context, and location (Sharma & Sharma, 2017; Singh & Sharma, 2013).

There are many queries that will be temporally ambiguous, such as "Milan Fashion Week", that will not be a single event in time since it reoccurs. Another such queries is "Battle of Panipat" which is not reoccurring at same time interval. It is hard to predict which battle or which fashion week information the user is seeking. Such queries require analysis of returned documents based on temporal dimension (Pustejovsky, Knippen, Littman, & Saurí, 2005).

Conventional search engines cannot harness the temporal dimension in documents. If we are able to understand the query intent and integrate the knowledge gained through temporal analysis of documents we can return much better results, because now we can quantify the relevance on the basis of query intent and temporal aspect of the document. To collect the temporal information of the document and its content, we can use dates and time mentioned in the document, timestamp attached to blogs, Facebook posts, and microblog as tweets and emails (Salah Eldeen & Nelson, 2013). One can also perform carbon dating of the Web using the timestamp of server available in the metadata of Web page or document on the Web usually found in a form ofcreation date, the current timestamp of the server, or modification date. The major point of concern is about the response time of the system, as some methods taking time are actually futile in the field of information retrieval. For if ranking and results are not available in a timely manner then we will start losing users, which will impact on the economic feasibility of the system. Time itself poses a major issue in front of us concerning on how to manage and normalize the temporal information. Pin-pointing a timestamp to a timeline is tough if we get timestamps from different locations all having different time zones and therefore their meaning differs from one place to other (Alonso, Gertz, & Baeza-Yates, 2007; Alonso, Strötgen, Baeza-Yates, & Gertz, 2011).

Some of the issues that our research confronts are firstly seeking temporal information or features in the document, then understanding and processing it. The first issue our research faces regarding the identification of temporal information in a document is the form of "tomorrow", "six months" or "today". Alonso et al. (2007) categorized the temporal information present in the document content into three major classes as proposed by Schilder & Habel (2001). These categories will be discussed below.

- **Explicit Temporal Expression:** This is the category of temporal expressions that contains temporal information that is in the form of years, dates and timestamps. These expressions are easy to timeline as they refer to a specific point in time. For example, "August 2017" is an explicit temporal expression. This category of temporal expression does not require much computation and they are easy to normalize to a point in time. Still we have some of the issues such as 12/08/2017 can be 12th August 2017 or 8th December 2017; to resolve such issue we require metadata of the document.

Figure 1 contains two explicit temporal expressions i.e. *2017* and *2020* and two implicit temporal expression *Diwali* and *Today*. Explicit Temporal Expression 2017 and 2020 require no normalization but Diwali and Today needs to normalization using the document's date of creation therefore today normalizes to 15-Oct-2017 and Diwali a Hindu festival reoccur every year so normalize to date of year 2017 as 19-Oct-2017.

- **Implicit Temporal Expression:** This category of temporal expressions is the name of festivals, events, national holidays, etc., for example, "Holi 2017", "Easter 2018" or "Indian Republic Day 2017". Some preprocessing is required to pin temporal expressions to timeline information. There is the requirement of taggers, to identify and find out these temporal expressions in the content of the document, we also normalize them after extracting using prior available information. For example, "Gandhi Jayanti 2017" normalizes to "2017/02/10" in the format "yyyy/dd/mm" since "Gandhi Jayanti" always fall on 02nd October. There is another example of query "Mother's Day 2017" which normalizes to "2017/14/05" as we use the prior knowledge that Mother's Day always fall on second Sunday of May. So, if we normalize Mother's Day in 2017 that will be normalized to second Sunday of May of 2017 (See Figure 1).
- **Relative:** This category of temporal expression is similar to implicit expressions but differ in many ways. Such temporal expressions cannot be pinpointed to timeline without using some information about the expression and the context in which it is stated. For instance "Christmas" expression has some temporal information but one needs more knowledge in order to normalize this expression to a year, without which it is difficult to place it on the timeline. Expressions like "today", "tomorrow" can be pined to timeline only when we know when it is spoken or written and in which context. Consider the text "I have visited my aunt Annie's house yesterday" where the word "yesterday" is a relative temporal expression but to normalize it to a point in time we need to know the date on which this text is written; for instance, if it is written on 24th August then this 'yesterday' will be normalized to 23rd August. But, to do so we need to have date of creation of the document. All this information can be found in metadata of the document from where we

Figure 1. Temporal Expression Example

```
Date of Creation: 10/15/2017

Sensex to hit 38000 and Nifty could
hit Mount 11k by next Diwali as it
shows the trend so far this year 2017,
Analysts today reports that Sensex
climbing near 50,000 or 45,000 by
2020
```

can infer. There are cases where we need to refer to the point in time that is present in a content of the document. Expressions like "on Sunday" and "after two months" requires extensive natural language processing as we need to refer to a specific point in time. To resolve this, we have to perform tense-based analysis of the text.

We will classify queries into classes on the basis of their temporal intent. We will first check whether the submitted query has any temporal intent, and then test whether the temporal intent has temporal ambiguity. User queries that have no temporal intent will be classified as *Atemporal* (see Figure 2). Queries that have some temporal intent will then be classified for ambiguity. If they are not ambiguous, then they will be classified to class *Temporal Unambiguous* within the queries that have clear temporal intent. Queries having temporal intent, i.e. classified as temporal query, but their temporal intent is vague, that is not limited to a specific point in time, might be of reoccurring nature classified as *Temporal Ambiguous* (Jones & Diaz, 2007). The system we are trying to build will take care of both cases of relevance, temporal as well as contextual.

The users, who are usually reluctant or lazy to specify their query needs explicitly, often use the least number of words to express it, so a lot of times these short queries pose a challenging task to understand their intention. Conventional search engines focus mostly on content and avoid including temporal aspect of the query to their ranking function. To include temporal aspect to ranking function and add more relevance we will propose a new framework and then evaluate the relevancy of the results (Sharma & Sharma, 2011).

Queries that fall in *Temporal Ambiguous* class need be disambiguated. Researchers came up with various methods for disambiguation, varying from disambiguation on the basis of the user profile, past searches, query log to catch the overall trend, click through rate and many other ways (Metzler, Jones, Peng, & Zhang, 2009).

We are considering queries that have some temporal intent but since this intent change with time there is a peculiar problem that comes with the intention of the user. For example, a user query about "which is the tallest building in the World?" may result in the answers of this query change through time. Other cases are the queries like "Presidential Election Results" and "Friendship Day" for they occur on different days and time at different locations. Queries like these need to be disambiguated so that we will find user intention clearly and know about which event the user is seeking information. Search engines conventionally post results using the approach of 'recent event on top' for they don't have any better algorithm for this task (Sharma & Sharma, 2010).

In this chapter, our proposed approach will firstly classify the query into their appropriate temporal classes and then will try disambiguating them. We will as well propose some changes in ranking function and user interfaces of search engines.

Figure 2 shows the frequency of each year appears in a set of relevant documents found with respect to given query. Figure 2 makes it quite evident that not every query is temporal by chart of "fish" which has almost no temporal information, while query "cricket world cup" has lot of temporal information for years like 2007, 2011, 2015, this makes query evident to be temporal; and, an example of ambiguous query with respect to temporal dimension. Query "Las Vegas Shooting" is an example of temporal unambigous query that has crystal clear temporal positioning in year 2017.

Figure 2. Frequency charts for query "fish" (top), "Cricket World Cup" (middle) and "Las Vegas Shooting" (bottom)

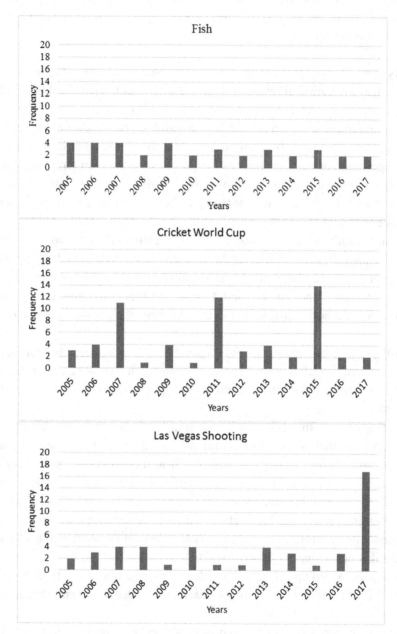

This chapter will introduce readers to the state of art in temporal query analysis problem area through related work and literature survey in the next section. This section will showcase researchers milestones in the field of temporal aware Retrieval systems. Problem and proposed approach are discussed in the next section. Descriptions of the dataset and result analysis of proposed system are given then on. This chapter ends after offering Future Research Directions and Conclusion.

RELATED WORK

Tagging and named-entity recognition have been the major area of research. Named-Entity Recognition and Classification (NERC) has been the sub tasks of Information Extraction (IE) field. Nowadays, crowdsourcing for document annotation is used by many researchers. Alonso, Gertz, and Baeza-Yates (2009) explored news articles using crowdsourcing for annotation. Researchers nowadays use Human Intelligence Task (HIT) to get a document annotated as may be provided by Amazon Mechanical Turk (AMT) which helps to find and collect temporal expressions from documents. Documents get annotated by HIT having temporal expression in dates, years, duration, etc. HIT also annotates names of an entity into domains as currency, industry, company, location, event, celebrity, etc. These domains are predefined and can be increased upto some extent. This process will help us to obtain richer temporal tagging of documents which is semantically correct as human readers are annotating them and helps us to order results into some chronological fashion on the timeline.

Kalczynskiet & Chou (2005) explained the importance of time and how it can affect the search result relevancy. Their paper discusses the role of vector space model and how to extend it to Temporal Aware Retrieval System. Challenges come while normalizing the temporal to some dates in time; for example "Last Monday", "day before yesterday", "in the beginning of next year". As a solution they proposed to present membership of expression to dates using fuzzy logics.

Nunes, Ribeiro, and David (2008) discovered that users are less likely to pose any temporal queries, and that they try to frame their information needs in least number of words which might be because of their lazyness. Queries which contain temporal expressions are likely to be discussing some event or happening of current timeframe. Queries seeking information about sports scores, news articles, product launch, and holidays mostly contain temporal expression and have temporal intent.

Jeong and Moon (2017) proposed an interesting study of human behavior through interval patterns between their online activities on social media platforms Twitter, Wikipedia, Me2DAY and Enron email. They focused on the diversity among the patterns of different users. They experimentally observed that interval pattern or signature is different from one person to other, and more importantly they are persistent. These patterns are resilient under changing environment. They are helpful in differentiating one person from others.

In their paper Alonso et al. (2011) tried to bring the focus of research fraternity toward the importance of time and show that this research gap can be exploited to help conventional search engines to gain more relevancy. Our work is inspired from this paper; we took an issue from this paper of query intent understanding which is not been taken care or exploited by conventional search engines.

Chavoshi, Hamooni, and Mueen (2017) performed temporal pattern mining on bot activities in Twitter. Their approach claims to differentiate between bots and human with 81% precision. The bot detection platform they developed is DeBot, they evaluated their result on four features such as number of activity per user in two hours as they observe bots are overactive; second feature is number of deletions a user perform in two hours; third feature is the percentage of tweets that contain URLs which will give an estimate of how much data is from outside of Twitter; and, fourth feature is the percentage of retweets indicating the fraction of tweets generated automatically. The mentioned authors take high value of above features as an indication of some abnormal behavior.

Alonso et al. (2007) explained in their paper what temporal information retrieval is and how we can formally define it. This paper showcases the work done in the field of temporal information retrieval. They show the challenges and issues a research can face while working in the field of information retrieval.

Evaluation challenges, temporal tagging, normalization of temporal tags are the major issues discussed in this paper. Through examples of different applications, the paper discusses many areas that can take advantage of temporal information from documents.

Arıkan, Bedathur, and Berberich (2009) proposed a language model that uses a probabilistic approach to find relevancy among query and documents, and then provided a ranking of them. The analysis of results claims to improve the ranking for the query having some temporal intent. The existing system does not provide relevant result in top five result but after catching temporal dimension top five results are also relevant.

Mani and Wilson (2000) worked on English news articles to find and normalize the temporal tags among content of the document. Their proposed system uses annotation from both hand-crafted by human and by using some machine learning approach.

Oshino, Asano, and Yoshikawa (2010) proposed an approach based on document creation date, modification date, deletion date using a time graph mode. To represent temporal information in time graph, authors label the nodes of graph with creation or modification date. The basic key idea on which authors work is that there will be few pages on topic if it was discussed first or in its initial days, then in second phase gradually more pages will come up as people start talking about it, in third phase there will be an explosion as lot of people will be discussing it. So numerous pages will be created, then creation of new pages will go down and if there was again a high rise in number of pages created this will point to that a new development might have taken place about the topic. The paper showed a very efficient way that how one can use the temporal information in metadata to find the Web pages that starts, discuss and summarizes a topic.

Sato, Uehara, and Sakai (2003) considered Web as a WWW archive and used temporal attributes of documents such as creation time, modification time and accessed time. They developed a temporal database that has document and temporal information stored in its meta-data. In this paper, authors constructed a system to determine whether a particular document exists at a point of time or in a time interval.

Campos, Dias, Jorge, and Nunes (2012) dealt with implicit query and tried to find the temporal intent of such queries that do not have any date. The proposed method will help "on-the-fly" identification and understanding of implicit query. They defined a rule-based model that detects the temporal expression such as mm ddyyyy or yyyy. Authors perform Query Execution on the data from which results having any explicit temporal information are filtered by help of their rule-based model to mark dates expressed in numerical patterns.

Agarwal and Strotgen (2017) discussed the novel approach named TɪWɪKɪ searching Wikipedia with Temporal Constraint. It uses the explicit temporal expressions of user query and then produced ranking based on aggregated values of temporal and textual relevance. It explains the framework that is required to build a search engine on top of document collection that has some temporal expressions. They used queries with temporal constraints and queries that have only temporal constraint (no text).

Schockaert, De Cock, and Kerre (2008) used temporal expression in Web documents and tried finding temporal boundary to events that have vague boundaries such as "Cold War" and "World War I". The approach followed by them uses fuzzy logic to find membership of each year to query lifetime and use this prediction or membership value to calculate boundary of query.

Jatowt, Antoine, Kawai, and Akiyama (2015) studied the dynamics of remembering and expecting process to social media users. This paper puts focus on microblogging users who share information about their life and daily events. The study suggests the scope of temporal attention of users with specific time frames (e.g. near, distant past or near, distant future).

Pradhan & Sharma (2014) and Yadav, Sharma, and Pradhan (2015) investigated the problem in Temporal Queries and how to disambiguate them.

Basile, Caputo, Semeraro, and Siciliani (2016) proposed a temporal retrieval system that harnesses the temporal information. They actually allow the user to enter query with temporal constraint. They can now easily disambiguate because user can provide more information regarding information needs.

Our approach uses implicit temporal expression while approaches proposed in the past majorly concentrate on explicit expressions. We use a novel approach to identify the boundaries of temporal expressions, so far, the classes we identify as anticipated and unanticipated have not been much explored by researchers. Our system concentrates on improving response time, as we try to keep it as minimum as possible because long response time will affect the economic feasibility of system, therefore we keep the preprocessing as minimum as we can, we only used it to normalize temporal expressions.

PROPOSED FRAMEWORK

Information retrieval systems often find queries that have some temporal intent but to properly process such queries requires better understanding and pre-processing. Since such queries entails results from a time period, there is great need to understand user intention and information needs as well as a better user interface that helps educate the user to add more parameters to their queries. There is also a need to change and upgrade user interface to accommodate the information needs of temporal aware queries.

It has been proved alreadt by researchers and psychologists that humans are reluctant to changes. This is the prime reason that User Interface (UI) of search engines do not get upgraded or modified, despite the recommendations of Human Computer Interaction scientists. Search engines fear that they may lose users by modification in UI. Gradual incorporation of changes that had been observed by researchers can easily be digested by users while performing some beta testing. Suppose a high school student completing his CS assignment on "Android OS" requires a timeline that shows chronological ordering of different versions; or, a journalist will be glad if timeline of an event can be seen; a person querying about location of a building might require results in the form of a map or as a street address but as a list of at the most 10-20 documents.

We will classify the query on the basis of topic, i.e. content and also on its temporal profile, i.e. such as the duration of time or the point in time which the query event actually points to. We have certain challenges in this: finding whether the topic we have in query is of past, future, or present. Classification of temporal query into these classes of past, present, and future will act as a query detection technique. By detection of classes we can create or modify the visualization of results as depicted in Figure 3. For example, if the query fired is "Lincoln Assassination", our classifier will classify the query as of past, i.e. since the event query concerns happened in the past. Our system will create visualization of results in a form of timeline of events related to the query.

We propose in this chapter following temporal classes:

1.   Past Query

A query that refers to an event that took place in the past or a historical event, for example the query "Operation Desert Shield". This query is related to an event that happened during 1990-1991, these dates

Figure 3. List of prominent year about query "Battle of Panipat". This year list shows that query has some temporal intent but that is ambiguous, for system to determine the particular battle which user intents to view the result, a list of years help user and system to know query intent clearly.

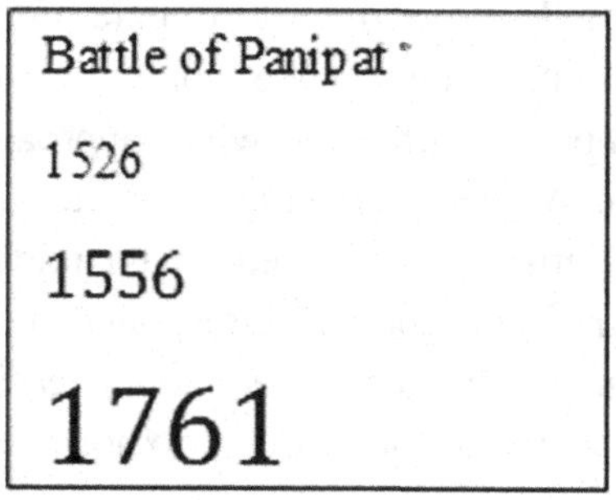

Battle of Panipat
1526
1556
1761

are of past and therefore this query has some temporal dimension. We will observe that the documents that will come up must be relevant with respect to this query, containing dates, year or timestamp of years around 1990-1991. This time period or range of year will suggest that query is temporally unambiguous and have fixed temporal meaning. Since these range of year will lie in far left of histogram when we take the current year as the center of histogram, we can easily classify the query to be of past (Pradhan & Sharma, 2015; See Figure 4).

2.   Present Query

Present query is a query that concerns an event belonging to current year or an ongoing year or a continuous event such as "ICC Cricket World Cup" or "Harvard Convocation". While finding relevant documents from document collection, it is found that most of the documents found relevant to query either belong to current year or in range of close by years. If we create a set of years then we see current year fall to it with proximity with spike in histogram (See Figure 4).

3.   Future Query

Queries such as "next general election", "FIFA 2018" or "Annabelle 2" concern an event that is going to be held either next year or in future. In other words, we can say queries concerned with events that are not yet happened or took place. Profiles of queries shown in the form of histogram in Figure 3c clearly depicts the years in which query event going to be held will be at some distance. Such queries can be of a kind "when will be the next general election" (See Figure 4).

4.   Anticipated Query

These are the kind of queries that are about some most talked about events. For instance people start talking about a movie long before it is released; such queries are of an anticipated event when it is just announced. Another example "Harvard Application for summer 2018" will be discussed in student forums for quite long before even Harvard opens up for fresh applications (See Figure 5).

Figure 4. Query "Occupy Wall Street" histogram has the year 2011 which is current year for our dataset hence query is present, whereas query about a movie "Batman Begins" which was released in the year 2005 has histogram skewed towards past years, therefore, this query is of past; and, the third query about a sports event that is going to be held in 2016 is a future query with respect to dataset current year 2015.

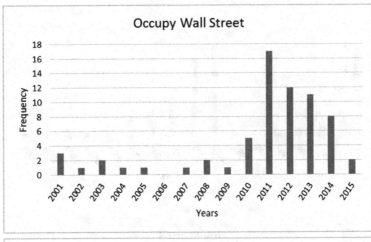

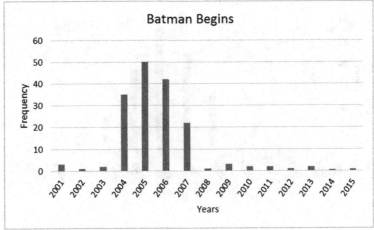

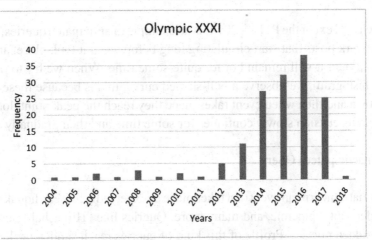

Figure 5. The frequency of years appearing in relevant documents for two queries "Deepwater Horizon" and "Toy Story 3"

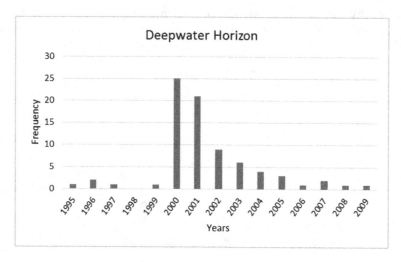

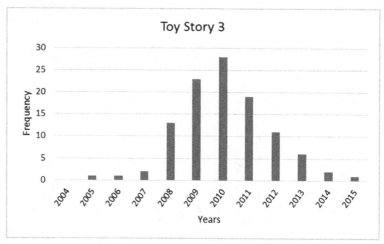

"UN Modi speech" ("Text of the PM's", 2014) is an example of anticipated queries, many news article, blogs and social network posts that start circulating long before even it took place, and when things are so much talked about then it will remain hot for quite some time. When we try to project a profile for such queries using histogram, we observe a bell-shaped curve, this is because these queries are slowly becoming talk-of-town and then when event takes place they reach the peak point, lots of articles, blogs come up on Web and discussion slowly continues for some time and then gradually wear out.

5.   Sudden (or Unacticipated) Query

Sudden query is that concerns an event that takes place unexpectedly like earthquake, tornado, political assassination, murder, riot, epidemic, and many more. Queries like "Himachal Landslides", "Kashmir stone pelting" are sudden queries. Profile of this kind of queries reach sudden peak and then gradually die down. This peak reach is because they are not expected such as "Nirbhaya Delhi rape case"; this event becomes appearing all over the Web and social network, many blogs, posts, tweets, news articles come up discussing and after some time people slowly forget things and they move on and stop discussing it (See Figure 5).

Figure 5 shows the frequency of years appearing in relevant documents for two queries "Deepwater Horizon" and "Toy Story 3". We can notice from the histogram on top that there is sudden spike in year 2000 for query "Deepwater Horizon" as this query might be concerned with event that happened suddenly in year 2000 when no one was expecting it. Histogram below is depicting a query whose event was anticipated i.e. "Toy Story 3" this query is discussed before its actual release in year 2010, these discussion may be about its production on social media or blogs and if we notice it continues after release too as it will be discussed for awards and recognitions.

6.   Reoccuring Query

Reoccurring query discusses an event that happens again and again in certain time interval. For example, some sports event such as "French Open" or "Cricket World Cup", "Miss Universe Pageant", some festivity such as "Christmas" or "Diwali", etc.

Our proposed approach tries to classify the temporal queries to the first three tense-based classes and then to get better understanding about the query's temporal intent we will test it for sudden, anticipated and reoccurring classes of temporal queries. User search results are collected in the form of triplets as <title, url, snippet>, where title is Web page title, url is link of Web document, and snippet is part of Web document containing some relevant text with respect to query. It might contain some of the keywords from the query, meta tags of Web page, or document which are also shown in snippet as they are designed to provide information about Website to search engine's crawlers (see Figure 6).

Queries are processed in several steps in our proposed framework. The steps are highlighted below.

Identification of Temporal Expressions

Traditional information retrieval systems provide us with good enough results on conceptual aspect. For each query to decide if it should redirect to Temporal Information Retrieval (T-IR) system we need to figure out whether this query has any temporal intent or not.

To test this, we will first extract the query result from underlying search engine then from each of these results we will find temporal expressions such as year, date, or timestamp. We will use taggers to identify implicit temporal expressions as *today, tomorrow, last week, September* and many more.

Figure 6. The query 'Sino China Border Dispute' when fired returns results in form of Title, Web Snippet and URL

Title:	2017 Doklam: How India refused to play Chinese checkers
Web Snippet:	India and China have a long history of mistrust and went to war in 1962...
URL:	http://shanghaiist.com/2017/india-china-border-clash-ends.php

We use some rule-based taggers to tag temporal SMS lingo such as 2nite, nxt s@rda, 2moro, nxt week, 2day. We use, to encounter such slangs or lingo in social network domain. We need to convert these expressions into dates for this purpose we require a reference time. Creation date or modification dates can be used for this purpose.

Temporal or Atemporal?

Classifying or creating temporal profile we need to first check out if the query is of temporal intent or not. Atemporal queries should not be redirected to T-IR system. So, in order to solve this classification problem we follow the technique proposed in (Campos, Dias, & Jorge, 2011).

Campos et al. use the three parameters tSnippets(q), tTitle(q), tUrl(q) with respect to the query q. tSnippets(q) will calculate the ratio between number of snippets having dates in form of years (implicit temporal expression is also being resolved to numerical years in form of yyyy) to total number of snippets retrieved. Other parameters tTitle(q) and tUrl(q) will be calculated in same manner as with dates (or normalized dates) in title and URL respectively.

Now, after computation of the three parameters tSnippets(q), tTitle(q), tUrl(q), we will compute another parameter Temporal Average TA(q) using these three parameters. TA(q) is the weighted average of these three parameters.

$$TA\Big(q\Big) = \frac{w_1 * tSnippet\Big(q\Big) + w_2 * tTitle\Big(q\Big) + w_3 * tUrl\Big(q\Big)}{3}$$

These weights are to be chosen in such a way that they sum up to 1 ($w_1 + w_2 + w_3 = 1$) and our purpose to compute weighted average is because observing that information in title of Web snippet is more informative and correct, therefore w_2 has more value than others. We can use this weighted scheme to give more weight to results having high rank, such as Top 5 results will be given more weight than others. If TA (q) < 10% then we classify that query as Atemporal i.e. having no temporal intent, otherwise that query is classified as "temporal query" i.e. query having some temporal intent (Jones & Diaz, 2007).

Plotting Temporal Information

For classification of queries into tense classes, we create histograms for those queries classified as temporal. Plotting temporal information about query will create horizontal axis with years that are occurring in query results (both explicit and implicit) and vertical axis represents the frequency of occurrence at each year. One can also see years occurring in results <title, url, snippet> as bins and frequency as count of their occurrence (See Figure 7).

To identify the time periods or dates in form of years that focuses on query topic or period of interest, we need to identify the surge in histogram; this surge will define the period of time that is of our interest. We will be using algorithm to figure out the maximum subarray from this array of frequency to identify temporal positioning of query.

Figure 7. Query histogram for query "Killing bin Laden". Vertical axis represent frequency i.e. number of times a year occurs in search result snippets and horizontal axis represents the years or range of years that are occurring in search results.

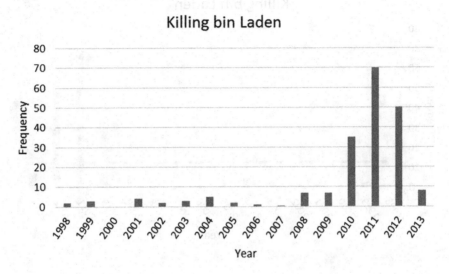

Smoothing and Slicing

For employing maximum subarray algorithm, we need some data preprocessing for smoothing the histogram. This can be achieved by taking the average of frequency array then we need to discard all the frequency that are below this average, so that we replace all these frequencies that are below average as $-\infty$. Actually, this process will slice the histogram below average, as in Figure 8 horizontal line denotes the average line, below which is chopped off. This will throw away those small spikes that occur otherwise they act as noise for our algorithm for finding maximum subarray.

Finding Temporal Position

Temporal positioning of query is to identify the time period for which query topic is of interest or active. This positioning can be identified by peak of interest in query histogram. This behavior of having high frequency for few years compared to others is because as an event being announced (remember announced not happened) news article and blogs start coming up, this number goes up until that event took place, then it slowly starts diminishing. Plotting a histogram for one-time event; we observe that a set of consecutive years appear to be having relatively high frequency, this is temporal positioning of query. These years also denote query timespan or lifetime of query. For example, [2010-2012] is timespan of query "Killing bin Laden" (See Figure 8).

Now, to automate the process of identifying this surge we will be using a popular algorithm for finding maximum subarray named as Kadane's Algorithm (Bentley, 1984) after its contributor. This will identify the surge in array of frequency which is sorted chronologically, this will provide us with starting and ending years of query life span (starting and ending index of subarray), from which we can classify this query into our proposed classes (See Figure 9).

Figure 8. Query histogram for query "Killing bin Laden" after smoothing. Orange line represents the average bar i.e. it acts as horizontal axis

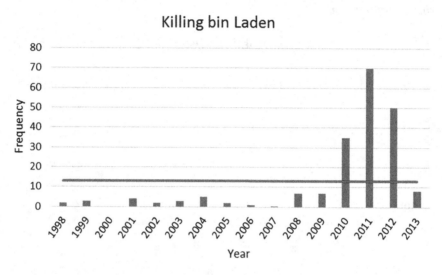

Figure 9. Algorithm to determine if array is increasing function or not

Let $f[y_s \cdots y_e]$ be maximum subarray and $y_{max} \in [y_s \cdots y_e]$ be the year having maximum frequency i.e. number of documents among all years in max subarray.

$i = y_s$

$flag = 0$

$while\ i < y_{max}\ and\ -\alpha \leq f[i+1] - f[i]$

$\quad i = i + 1$

$if\ i == y_{max}$

$\quad print\ "increasing\ function"$

Classification Into Tense Classes

After identifying starting and ending years, we can follow rule-based approach for classification of query into tense classes. Temporal Positioning of query can be defined by y_s and y_e (See Figure 10).

A query fall in class PAST if years in query temporal positioning are lesser than y_c the current year. If y_c belongs to the years in query temporal positioning $\left[y_s \cdots y_e\right]$ then query is an ongoing event and it will be classified into class PRESENT. A query falls in class FUTURE if years in query temporal positioning are greater than y_c.

$$TenseClassifier(q) = \begin{cases} past & if\, y_s < y_c \, and\, y_e < y_c \\ present & if\, y_s \leq y_c \, and\, y_c \leq y_e \\ future & if\, y_s > y_c \, and\, y_e > y_c \end{cases}$$

Finding Temporal Profiles

We use subarray and find the maximum spike in the query histogram and store that year in y_{max}. Now from starting year we will apply the following method:

We use the above algorithm to check whether the subarray is increasing function up to y_{max} or not. We took $\propto$ margin in this, because frequency in array may vary by some difference (two years can have some difference in their frequencies, for increasing $f[y_{i+1}] - f[y_i]$ should always be positive. But this is not always true. We need to give some margin in it i.e. $\propto$). How much of this difference is permissible would be based on the number of results one considers.

If a query has increasing profile, then we classify it as Anticipated because it can't be sudden, as sudden queries don't have an increasing profile.

In a similar way, we test for decreasing function. Only if it fails the previous test and if it appears decreasing between $y_{max} \cdots y_e$ then we classify it as a sudden query (See Figure 11).

RESULTS AND EVALUATION

This section will discuss results and evaluation.

Dataset

The dataset used for evaluation purposes is GISQC_DS (Campos, 2011). This dataset was contributed by (Campus, 2011) which consists of 540 queries that were picked from Google Insight since it shows the hottest and top trending most searched queries during January 2010 to October 2010.

Figure 10. Steps for query classification into anticipated and into sudden classes

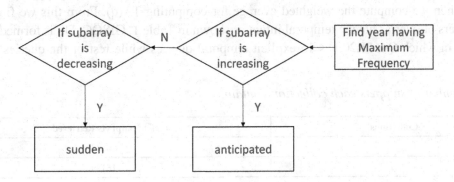

Figure 11. TempClassifier Framework

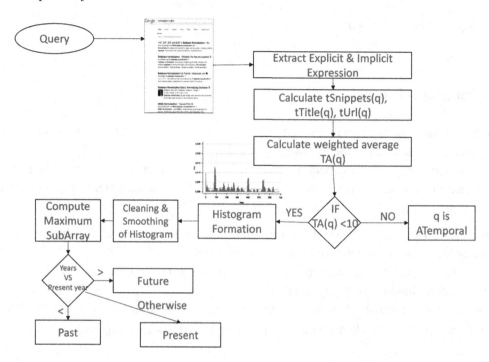

This dataset contains 20 queries in different categories as computer and electronics, entertainment, food, games, education, internet, personal care, etc. There are 27 pre-defined categories from which queries are picked and added to this dataset. This dataset is divided into three collections Q465R20, Q450R20 and Q450R100, where Q stands for number of queries that dataset contains and R stands for the number of results per query. Results of the queries are extracted by searching them in search engines as Bing (http://www.bing.com) and Yahoo! (www.yahoo.com) in December 2010.These collections has no duplicate search results; any such results were eliminated.

Evaluation

We perform our algorithm by finding whether the particular query is temporal in intent or not. For this, we compute three measures for each query q that we discussed earlier such as TSnippet(q), TUrl(q) and TTitle(q), then we compute the weighted average for computing TA(q). From this we find there are large numbers of queries having temporal intent as shown in Table 1. GISQC_DS is formed from three collections in which Q465R20 has 15 explicit temporal queries while rest of the queries is implicit.

Table 1. Number of snippets each collection contain

Collections	# of Snippets Retrieved
Q465R20	16648
Q450R20	16129
Q450R100	62842

Therefore, it has the maximum number of temporal intent queries as compared to other two collections. Collection Q450R100 has more queries of temporal intent than Q450R20 while both collections have same number of queries, the only difference between them is that one collection contains only first 20 results retrieved for a particular query while other contains first 100 results. Table 2 clearly shows that top Web snippets retrieved by search engines do not contain dates or years.

We compare our results with (Campos, Dias, & Jorge, 2011) and find that ours are better. Since they gave more weight to numbers of snippets not years while we assign more weight to titles, as they describes the whole document better, more dates appear in titles than URL snippet and anything written in that has more weight.

Most of the retrieved results have dates in titles then in snippet, and least number of dates appears in URL. We can conclude that overall 87% of URLs contain dates or temporal expression in URL, 95.3% of titles contain dates while 93.1% of snippets contain date. Most of the numeric data in URL is of no temporal use, it is either some dimension of image or some page number value.

To evaluate the classification algorithm, we need to form the ground truth for each of these collections. For ground truth we find that number of queries fall in the category of past queries, but most of the queries belong to present category and there are few queries that were discussing a future event. Summary of this data is presented in Table 3.

Figure 12. Chart shows the ground truth for tense classes on dataset three document collections

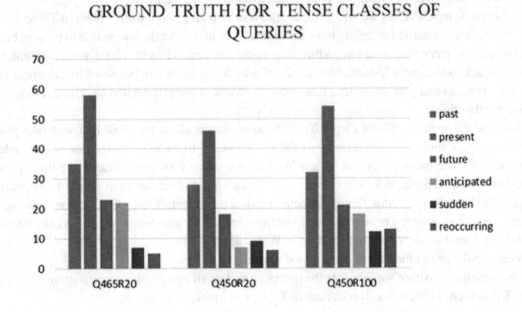

Table 2. Classification of Queries into Temporal

Collections	# of Queries Having Temporal Intent
Q465R20	118
Q450R20	91
Q450R100	112

Table 3. Ground Truth for the three data collections

Collections	# of Queries					
	Past	Present	Future	Anticipated	Sudden	Reoccurring
Q465R20	35	58	23	22	7	5
Q450R20	28	46	18	7	9	6
Q450R100	32	54	21	18	12	13

Table 3 shows the ground truth about temporal classes. Here, we can observe that the number of queries falling into the present class is much higher than that of the other two classes. This is because user intent to search for queries about ongoing events such as "General Election India" is among hot topics in May 2014. Similarly, ratio of past queries with present is also higher because people quite often look or search for things or event that have already took place such as wars, sports event, politics, social and cultural topics. We also find queries having temporal intent more related to events in sports, politics, and history.

On acquisition of ground truth, we need to employ our classification algorithm to classify the queries. We find out the histogram for queries that have temporal intent. Then we subject it to Kadane's Algorithm (Bentley, 1984) for finding maximum subarray. Upon the result of this algorithm we have starting year and ending year of this subarray. This will provide us with the temporal positioning of the query. E.g. query "Killing bin laden" has temporal positioning around 2011 (see Figure 7).

To evaluate TempClassifier we will compare the results with ground truth shown in Table 3.

Queries that are classified correctly have the highest rate in past while lowest rate in present because any of the year in query time span has ending year as current year. Than we classify it as present, but in some cases such as the query "Arushi Murder Case" which is a past event but since its judgment comes after a long time its end year cause true false positive. Most of queries related to criminal cases cause this misclassification.

Future queries such as "World Cup T20 2018" seek results about an event that will take place in future. Sometimes some user fire a query as "Scary Movie 6" to look for movie that will be released next week, but since many blogs and review Web sites contain Web pages discussing this upcoming movie, this will cause problem for our classifier. These two reasons are the main cause of low precision.

Figure 13 shows that our classifier works better on data set collection Q450R100 because the number of snippets is more compared to other collections; these results are also better because traditional search engines do not tend to show results with time in Web snippets.

Similar are the charts for classes present and future.

To evaluate the classifier, we calculate the precision and recall using following equations as discussed in (Van Rijsbergen, 1986) this will take data in Table 4 as input.

$$A = \sum \# of\, queries\, are\, correctly\, classified\, to\, class\, c_i$$

$$B = \sum \# of\, queries\, are\, tagged\, as\, c_i$$

Table 4. Result of Query Classification using TemporalClassifier showing values for True Positive

Collections	# of Queries Correctly Classified					
	Past	Present	Future	Anticipated	Sudden	Reoccurring
Q465R20	28	17	21	6	5	4
Q450R20	22	14	16	4	7	6
Q450R100	26	16	19	12	8	10

Figure 13. Query histogram for "Olympic XXXI". We can observe that temporal positioning of this query is [2013-2017] which is going to come hence we can classify this query as futuristic

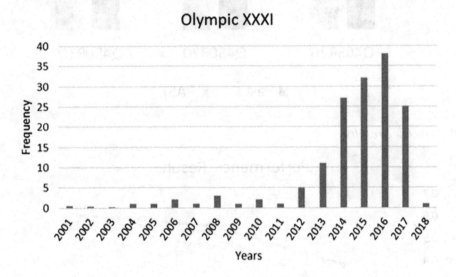

$$C = \sum \# \, of \, queries \, whose \, category \, is \, c_i$$

$$Precision\left(P\right) = \frac{A}{B}$$

$$Recall\left(R\right) = \frac{A}{C}$$

$$F1 = \frac{2 \times Precision \times Recall}{Precision + Recall}$$

For computing F1-measure we will be having three classes therefore we will be taking average of the F1 for each class against ground truth (Shen et al., 2005).

Our performance results are shown in Figure 14 and Figure 15. We have an average precision and recall, but they can be improved if some other heuristics are used to classify present queries as they cause most of the false positive and false negative.

Figure 14. Comparison between query classified as "past" and their ground truth, we can observe that classifier performance improves with number of results considered.

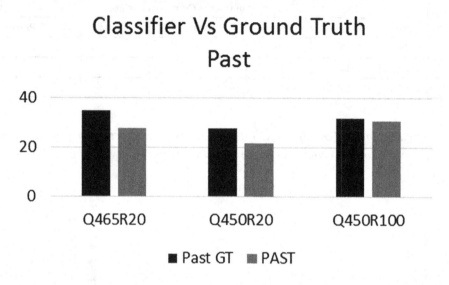

Figure 15. Performance results

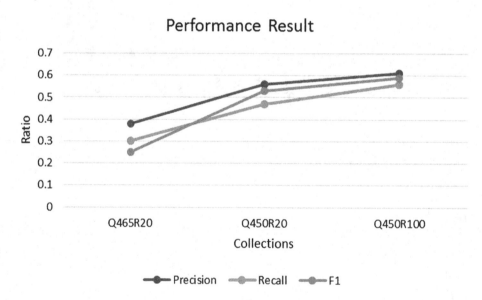

FUTURE RESEARCH DIRECTIONS

Our proposed approach profiles queries temporally based on the temporal expressions contained in the set of relevant documents. Proposed work has some limitations, but these limitations open scope for some future work. Our work is limited to Shakespearean English, as on advent of social network, we need to include more words in the class of temporal expressions which earlier was not qualifies as valid expressions. Our approach uses underlying conventional search engine to find set of relevant documents. We need to create our own dataset that catches the current updates in underlying search engine technology and we may find better results and more issues to work on.

CONCLUSION

Our work in this chapter concerns classifying queries on the basis of query event time. Introduction to research area of temporal information retrieval and literature survey is discussed. Proposed work and methodology are given; then, result analysis of each stage of our proposed framework was covered.

Classification of queries on their temporal profile is a complex task, and far from being mature. There are many issues to be addressed, such as temporal tagging, their length, normalization of these tags, tradeoff between accuracy and processing time demands. To address these problems various ways are proposed in literature.

This chapter proposed a novel approach to address the issue of query intent in field of Temporal Information Retrieval, i.e., "detection of temporal classes on the basis of query temporal profile". In our proposed approach traditional search engines are the underlying layer. Their results for a particular query provide us with relevant documents and then we perform temporal tagging on these documents to understand the query temporal intent. There are two phases in the proposed approach for query detection, first building query temporal profile and then classifying the query into proposed classes. On the basis of collected temporal tags we firstly judge whether query has some temporal intent or not, if query is found to be of temporal intent, then temporal profile is investigated. Based on the profile we find temporal boundary of the query using famous Kandane Algorithm (Bentley, 1984) that solves the popular maximum subarray problem.

The approach proposed contributes to temporal information retrieval area. As far as we surveyed the literature related to field of information retrieval we find that this is the first attempt to classify queries on the basis of their implicit temporal intent. We kept the preprocessing of documents or query to be at minimum as possible. The prime reason to avoid preprocessing is to make system fast and perform classification on the other techniques as ChronoSeeker (Kawai, Jatowt, Tanaka, Kunieda & Yamada, 2010) involves considerable amount of preprocessing. Our approach detects and classifies temporal queries into temporal classes.

On analyzing the results, we can affirm that our approach is fast and reliable. When we perform analysis of our work, we find that our approach is at par with Campos et al. (2012) in both quality wise and statistically. This conclusion is drawn on the basis of results and differences in approach. Campos et al. did not consider or give more importance to top results; in their work each result is same irrespective of its ranking. Time complexity of our approach is in linear time, i.e. $O(n)$.

ACKNOWLEDGMENT

Authors would like thank Dr. Ricardo Campos for his support and encouragement. He provided us with dataset and other resources, which this article would not be possible without. Thanks go to Dr. Alev Elçi for editing this manuscript.

REFERENCES

Agarwal, P., & Strötgen, J. (2017, April). Tiwiki: Searching Wikipedia with Temporal Constraints. In *Proceedings of the 26th International Conference on World Wide Web Companion* (pp. 1595-1600). International World Wide Web Conferences Steering Committee.

Alonso, O., Gertz, M., & Baeza-Yates, R. (2007). On the value of temporal information in information retrieval. In *ACM SIGIR Forum* (Vol. 41, No. 2, pp. 35-41). ACM. 10.1145/1328964.1328968

Alonso, O., Gertz, M., & Baeza-Yates, R. (2009). Clustering and exploring search results using timeline constructions. In *Proceedings of the 18th ACM conference on Information and knowledge management* (pp. 97-106). ACM. 10.1145/1645953.1645968

Alonso, O., Strötgen, J., Baeza-Yates, R. A., & Gertz, M. (2011). Temporal Information Retrieval: Challenges and Opportunities. *TWAW, 11*, 1–8.

Arıkan, I., Bedathur, S., & Berberich, K. (2009). Time will tell: Leveraging temporal expressions in ir. WSDM.

Basile, P., Caputo, A., Semeraro, G., & Siciliani, L. (2016). Time Event Extraction to Boost an Information Retrieval System. In *Information Filtering and Retrieval* (pp. 1–12). Springer International Publishing.

Bentley, J. (1984). Programming pearls: Algorithm design techniques. *Communications of the ACM, 27*(9), 865–873. doi:10.1145/358234.381162

Campos, R. (2011). *Google Insights for Search Query Classification dataset (GISQC_DS)*. Available from: http://www.ccc.ipt.pt/~ricardo/datasets/GISQC_DS.html

Campos, R., Dias, G., & Jorge, A. M. (2011). *What is the Temporal Value of Web Snippets?* TWAW.

Campos, R., Dias, G., Jorge, A. M., & Nunes, C. (2012). Enriching temporal query understanding through date identification: how to tag implicit temporal queries? In *Proceedings of the 2nd Temporal Web Analytics Workshop* (pp. 41-48). ACM. 10.1145/2169095.2169103

Chavoshi, N., Hamooni, H., & Mueen, A. (2017, April). Temporal Patterns in Bot Activities. In *Proceedings of the 26th International Conference on World Wide Web Companion* (pp. 1601-1606). International World Wide Web Conferences Steering Committee.

Jatowt, A., Antoine, É., Kawai, Y., & Akiyama, T. (2015, May). Mapping Temporal Horizons: Analysis of Collective Future and Past related Attention in Twitter. In *Proceedings of the 24th International Conference on World Wide Web* (pp. 484-494). International World Wide Web Conferences Steering Committee. 10.1145/2736277.2741632

Jeong, J., & Moon, S. (2017, April). Interval Signature: Persistence and Distinctiveness of Inter-event Time Distributions in Online Human Behavior. In *Proceedings of the 26th International Conference on World Wide Web Companion* (pp. 1585-1593). International World Wide Web Conferences Steering Committee.

Jones, R., & Diaz, F. (2007). Temporal profiles of queries. *ACM Transactions on Information Systems, 25*(3), 14, es. doi:10.1145/1247715.1247720

Kalczynski, P. J., & Chou, A. (2005). Temporal document retrieval model for business news archives. *Information Processing & Management, 41*(3), 635–650. doi:10.1016/j.ipm.2004.01.002

Kawai, H., Jatowt, A., Tanaka, K., Kunieda, K., & Yamada, K. (2010). ChronoSeeker: Search engine for future and past events. In *Proceedings of the 4th International Conference on Uniquitous Information Management and Communication* (p. 25). ACM. 10.1145/2108616.2108647

Mani, I., & Wilson, G. (2000). Robust temporal processing of news. In *Proceedings of the 38th Annual Meeting on Association for Computational Linguistics* (pp. 69-76). Association for Computational Linguistics.

Metzler, D., Jones, R., Peng, F., & Zhang, R. (2009). Improving search relevance for implicitly temporal queries. In *Proceedings of the 32nd international ACM SIGIR conference on Research and development in information retrieval* (pp. 700-701). ACM. 10.1145/1571941.1572085

Nunes, S., Ribeiro, C., & David, G. (2008). Use of temporal expressions in Web search. In *Advances in Information Retrieval* (pp. 580–584). Springer Berlin Heidelberg. doi:10.1007/978-3-540-78646-7_59

Oshino, T., Asano, Y., & Yoshikawa, M. (2010). Time graph pattern mining for Web analysis and information retrieval. In *Web-Age Information Management* (pp. 40–46). Springer Berlin Heidelberg. doi:10.1007/978-3-642-14246-8_7

Pradhan, R., & Sharma, D. K. (2014, August). Explicit Tense Classifier. In *Contemporary Computing (IC3), 2014 Seventh International Conference on* (pp. 443-448). IEEE. 10.1109/IC3.2014.6897214

Pradhan, R., & Sharma, D. K. (2015). TemporalClassifier: Classification of Implicit Query on Temporal Profiles. *International Journal of Information Technology and Web Engineering, 10*(4), 44–66. doi:10.4018/IJITWE.2015100103

Pustejovsky, J., Knippen, R., Littman, J., & Saurí, R. (2005). Temporal and event information in natural language text. *Language Resources and Evaluation, 39*(2-3), 123–164. doi:10.100710579-005-7882-7

Salah Eldeen, H. M., & Nelson, M. L. (2013). Carbon dating the Web: estimating the age of Web resources. In *Proceedings of the 22nd international conference on World Wide Web companion* (pp. 1075-1082). International World Wide Web Conferences Steering Committee. 10.1145/2487788.2488121

Sato, N., Uehara, M., & Sakai, Y. (2003). Temporal ranking for fresh information retrieval. In *Proceedings of the sixth international workshop on Information retrieval with Asian languages-Volume 11* (pp. 116-123). Association for Computational Linguistics. 10.3115/1118935.1118950

Schilder, F., & Habel, C. (2001). From temporal expressions to temporal information: Semantic tagging of news messages. In *Proceedings of the workshop on Temporal and spatial information processing-Volume 13* (p. 9). Association for Computational Linguistics. 10.3115/1118238.1118247

Schockaert, S., De Cock, M., & Kerre, E. E. (2008). Acquiring vague temporal information from the Web. In *Proceedings of the 2008 IEEE/WIC/ACM International Conference on Web Intelligence and Intelligent Agent Technology-Volume 03* (pp. 265-268). IEEE Computer Society. 10.1109/WIIAT.2008.82

Sharma, D. K., & Sharma, A. K. (2010). Deep Web Information Retrieval Process: A Technical Survey. *International Journal of Information Technology and Web Engineering, 5*(1), 1–22. doi:10.4018/jitwe.2010010101

Sharma, D. K., & Sharma, A. K. (2011). A Novel architecture for deep Web crawler. *International Journal of Information Technology and Web Engineering, 6*(1), 25–48. doi:10.4018/jitwe.2011010103

Sharma, D. K., & Sharma, A. K. (2012). Search Engine: A Backbone for Information. *ICT Influences on Human Development, Interaction, and Collaboration, 117.*

Sharma, D. K., & Sharma, A. K. (2017). Deep Web Information Retrieval Process. *The Dark Web: Breakthroughs in Research and Practice: Breakthroughs in Research and Practice*, 114.

Shen, D., Pan, R., Sun, J. T., Pan, J. J., Wu, K., Yin, J., & Yang, Q. (2005). Q 2 C@ UST: Our winning solution to query classification in KDDCUP 2005. *ACM SIGKDD Explorations Newsletter*, 7(2), 100–110. doi:10.1145/1117454.1117467

Singh, R., & Sharma, D. K. (2013, April). Enhanced-RatioRank: Enhancing impact of inlinks and outlinks. In *Information & Communication Technologies (ICT), 2013 IEEE Conference on* (pp. 287-291). IEEE.

Text of the PM's Statement at the United Nations General Assembly. (2014, September 27). Retrieved from http://www.narendramodi.in/text-of-the-pms-statement-at-the-united-nations-general-assembly-2

Van Rijsbergen, C. J. (1986). A non-classical logic for information retrieval. *The Computer Journal*, 29(6), 481–485. doi:10.1093/comjnl/29.6.481

Yadav, A., Sharma, D. K., & Pradhan, R. (2015, September). Implicit queries based Temporal Information Retrieval using temporal taggers. In *Reliability, Infocom Technologies and Optimization (ICRITO) (Trends and Future Directions), 2015 4th International Conference on* (pp. 1-6). IEEE. 10.1109/ICRITO.2015.7359271

KEY TERMS AND DEFINITIONS

Confusion Matrix: Is a table with two rows and two columns that reports the number of false positives, false negatives, true positives, and true negatives. It shows for each pair of classes $<c_1, c_2>$, how many documents from c_1 were incorrectly assigned to c_2.

Information Retrieval: Information retrieval (IR) is finding material (usually documents) of an unstructured nature (usually text) that satisfies an information need from within large collections (usually stored on computers).

Precision: The fraction of the returned results that are relevant to the information need.

Query: It is a natural language expression that helps the information retrieval systems or search engine to identify the information need of user.

Recall: The fraction of the relevant documents in the collection of returned results.

Tagging: It is a process of adding some more meta data to document or piece of text that will help computer in understanding it.

Web Crawlers: They are the bots or spiders that gather the pages from web by downloading them, and use them for indexing purposes for search engines.

Section 3
Semantic Technology Forward

World Wide Web started as a fresh breath to displaying of hitherto local content opening it to sharing. It was great success as a technology. Over time it was realized yet that it was incapable of conveying the "meaning" of data and the intension / understanding of its creator thus needed a human intermediary. So called "Web Science" eventually lead to augmentation by semantic tones through a set of refitted concepts such as ontology and inferencing, and new custom languages, such as RDF and OWL. Sampled in this section are managing ontology change; semantically integrating otherwise heterogeneous structured data; discovering Web services and composing aggregate ones on the go.

Chapter 11
Methods for Ontology Alignment Change

Ahmed Zahaf
Laboratoire Technologies De Communications (LTC), University Dr. Moulay Tahar, Algeria

Mimoun Malki
LabRI-SBA Laboratory, Ecole Supérieure en Informatique, Algeria

ABSTRACT

Different repositories of ontology are available on the web to share common understandings of the knowledge of different domains with semantic web applications. They store, index, organize, and share ontologies and alignments between them that allow applications to search for and use the appropriate semantics on the fly. The quality of the ontologies and the alignments between them is a great challenge to guarantee the usefulness of ontology repositories. Like ontologies, alignments are subject to changes throughout their life cycle, which can decrease their quality. As a result, alignments must be evolved and maintained in order to keep up with the change in ontology or to meet the demands of applications and users. This chapter reviews and classifies the main ontology alignment change approaches. In addition, the chapter presents a new approach for the alignment change problem. The approach proposes a general framework that consists of a process of change. Various methods, each with a specific purpose, are proposed to automate and support the change process.

INTRODUCTION

Ontologies and alignments between them enhance semantic interoperability for many Web applications such as Web services interoperability and query answering on the Web to name a few (Euzenat & Shvaiko, 2013). While ontologies provide specifications of the semantics of vocabularies in order to share a common understanding of domain knowledges, alignments overcome heterogeneity and diversity in these specifications.

With the emergence of the semantic Web, ontology repositories such as Swoogle (Ding et al, 2004), Watson (D'Aquin,, Gridinoc,, Angeletou,, Sabou,, & Motta, 2007), OntoSelect (Buitelaar, Eigner,, & Declerck, 2004), the DAML ontology library (http://www.daml.org/) and Schema.org (http://schema.

DOI: 10.4018/978-1-5225-5384-7.ch011

org/) have proliferated and are accessible to a wide audience. They store, index, organize and share ontologies. Early semantic Web applications such as AquaLog (Lopez, Pasin, & Motta, 2005) and Magpie (Dzbor, Domingue, & Motta, 2003) integrate ontologies starting with the design phase. This hampers their dynamism to diversify their fields of application. Thanks to ontology repositories, a new generation of applications (Motta & Sabou, 2006) can find and use dynamically appropriate ontologies in the run-time. For instance, PowerAqua (Lopez, Motta, & Uren, 2006), the successor of AquaLog, is a cross-domain question answering system. It locates thanks to Watson (http://watson.kmi.open.ac.uk/WatsonWUI/), online semantics documents that match user's queries. Besides ontologies, some repositories such as Bioportal (http://bioportal.bioontology.org), AgroPortal (http://agroportal.lirmm.fr/), and Alignment server (http://alignapi.gforge.inria.fr/aserv.html) consider alignments as first class objects, enhancing the dynamic interoperability of ontologies. They, store, index, organize and share alignments. These infrastructures allow applications to seek and use on the fly the appropriate alignments.

The quality of ontologies and alignments between them is a great challenge to guarantee the usefulness of these repositories. Like ontologies, alignments are subject to changes throughout their life cycle, which can decrease their quality. Many reasons can trigger this change. Alignments cannot keep their consistency in time because of the dynamicity of ontologies. For instance, adding new knowledge in ontologies can make alignments inconsistent (Euzenat, 2015). Retracting knowledge from ontologies in response to some needs forces also alignments to follow this change. Another reason that can trigger the alignment change is alignment debugging and repair. Indeed, ontology matching tools may produce redundant, missed, or erroneous correspondences that can lead to an alignment inconsistency (Wang & Xu, 2008; Jean-Mary, Shironoshita, & Kabuka, 2009; Meilicke & Stuckenschmisdt, 2009; Meilicke & Stuckenschmisdt, 2007; Qi, Ji, & Haase, 2009).

As a result, alignments must be evolved and maintained in order to keep up with the change in ontology or to meet the demands of applications and users. However, methods for the alignment change should cover the following underlying issues:

- **Change Capture:** Alignments maintainers may request to express the alignment change in terms of predefined changes, to parse a journal of an ontology change, or to identify and make explicit the ontology change when only versions of the evolved ontologies are available.
- **Alignment Consistency:** Alignment change methods need to produce consistent alignments. The alignment consistency is expressed as a set of constraints qualified as hard since their violation makes the alignment obsolete and useless.
- **Minimality of Change:** Different ways may exist for resolving same inconsistency. One criterion that can guide the resolution is the principle of minimal change. Unlike consistency, the minimal change expresses a soft constraint since it doesn't affect the usefulness of the alignment. Which means; consistency constraints take precedence over minimal change during resolution of inconsistency. Sometimes, it is inevitable to sacrifice the minimal change against the consistency satisfaction. The challenge question is how to ensure the compromise between the consistency and the minimal of change constraints.
- **User Involvement:** The alignment change is a knowledge intensive task which can't be fulfilled without the involvement of users. Maintainers may want to review the change before its implementation. They may seek justifications for consistency violations, validate the change, recover the unnecessary changes, adapt, track, or cancel the change. Hence, they need a friendly easily interaction with the alignment change methods.

Guiding by these underlying issues of the alignment change problem, this chapter reviews and classifies the main ontology alignment change approaches. Besides, the chapter presents a new approach for the alignment change problem. The approach proposes a general framework that consists of a change process with four phases: a phase for change capture, a phase for semantics of change, a phase for change validation, and a phase for change implementation. Various methods, each having a specific purpose, are proposed for concretizing the change process. Inspired by base revision theory (Hansson, 1999), the chapter designs two new operations for the alignment contraction and the alignment consolidation change. The alignment contraction can be applied following a deleted axiom from one of the aligned ontologies or a deleted correspondence from the alignment itself. The alignment consolidation is applied to establish consistency of an inconsistent alignment whatever the origin of the inconsistency may be. Both operations are general that can be applied during the alignment evolution as well as the alignment debugging. Methods to compute justifications for the alignment consistency violation that are useful during the alignment validation phase were proposed as well.

The remainder of this chapter is organized as follows. Next is the background of the chapter. Its content is two-folds: a theoretical foundation and the state of the art of alignment change. First, the notions of ontologies and the alignment between them are presented. Then, the chapter explores the state of the art of works done to resolve the problem of alignment change. The analysis of these works is undertaken in accordance with the aforementioned issues of the alignment change problem. Then the proposed change process as well as the proposed methods for each phase of the process is outlined. Future and emerging trends of the alignment change problem and conclusions complete the chapter.

BACKGROUND

Ontologies

Ontology (with a big O) is a branch of philosophy for studying the nature and identities of things. In this discipline, philosophers try to answer questions concerning what things exist, which attributes characterize them and how such things can be grouped. Transferred to Artificial Intelligence, ontologies (with a little o) are computational artifacts that symbolize a special kind of knowledge. According to Gruber (1993), "for AI system, what exist is that which can be represented". So, ontology specifies explicitly the objects, concepts, and other entities that are assumed to exist in some area of interest and the relationships that hold among them. This was behind the Gruber definition of an ontology "explicit specification of a conceptualization" (Gruber, 1993). An explicit specification of a conceptualization can be done extensionally or intentionally (Guarino, Oberle, & Staab, 2009). The extensional specification is listing all possible interpretations of the vocabulary elements used by the conceptualization to name its elements. This is not always possible if the universe of discourse or the set of possible interpretations is infinite. However, the intentional specification constrains the intended meaning of the vocabulary elements by using a set of suitable axioms. The set of such axioms capture the intended interpretations corresponding to the specified conceptualization and exclude the unintended ones.

In summary, ontology is an axiomatization of the intended meaning of a vocabulary used by a conceptualization of some area of interest. The manner of the axiomatization had led Uschold and Gruninger (2004) to give a continuum of kinds of ontologies (Figure 1). The spectrum expresses the meaning expressiveness as well as the formality of ontologies that increase from left to right. We qualify the two

Figure 1. Ontologies spectrum

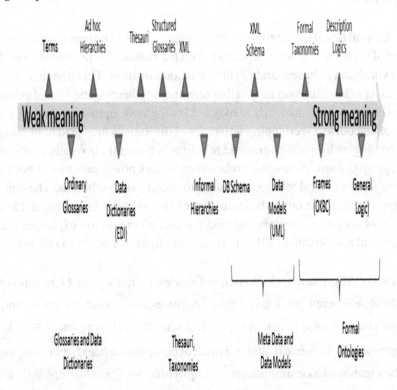

poles of the spectrum by "weak meaning" and "strong meaning" respectively. On the weak side, we can express a very simple meaning; on the strong side, we can express an arbitrary and complex meaning. Hence, an ontology ranges from a simple set of terms with less or no explicit meaning to a simple notion of a taxonomy (knowledge with minimal hierarchy or structure), to a thesaurus (words and synonyms), to a conceptual model (with much complex knowledge), to a logical theory (which is very rich, complex, consistent, and a very significant knowledge).

For an ontology as a logical theory, axioms act as constraints for interpretations of the vocabulary. An interpretation which satisfies all axioms of an ontology constitutes a model of that ontology. The model notion establishes a consequence relation between axioms of ontology languages and ontologies.

Definition 1 (Ontology Consequence): An axiom δ is a logical consequence of an ontology o (noted $o \vDash \delta$) if and only if every model of o satisfies δ.

We consider in this chapter only monotone logics.

Definition 2 (Monotone Ontology): An ontology is monotone if and only if $o \subseteq o'$ then for all δ, such that $o \vDash \delta$ then $o' \vDash \delta$.

Definition 3 (Inconsistent Ontology): An ontology o is inconsistent if and only if o has no model. Otherwise, it is consistent.

Ontology Alignment

According to Guarino et al (2009), an ontology can only approximate the specification of a conceptualization and the degree of such specification depends (1) on the richness of the universe of discourse, (2) on the richness of the vocabulary chosen, and (3) on the axiomatization. This divergence in the vocabulary chosen as well as in its axiomatization also called terminology heterogeneity and conceptual heterogeneity respectively (Euzenat & shvaiko, 2013) may lead to the development of heterogenic ontologies of the same universe of discourse. Overlapping universes of discourses may lead to overlapping ontologies as well. Relating ontologies by stating semantic relations between their vocabularies constitutes which is called an ontology alignment. A semantic relation expresses how meanings of both vocabularies are related. Usually, the set-theoretical relations are used to specify such relations. The equivalence relation expresses related meanings are the same, the inclusion relation expresses meanings inclusion, the overlapping relation expresses meanings overlapping, and the exclusion relation expresses meanings disjointness. We follow Euzenat and Shvaiko (2013) to define an alignment between two ontologies as follows.

Definition 4 (Ontology Alignment): Given two ontologies o_1 and o_2, let Q be a function that defines sets of matchable elements $Q(o_1)$ and $Q(o_2)$. A correspondence between o_1 and o_2 is a 4-tuple (e, e', r, n) such that $e \in Q(o_1)$, $e' \in Q(o_2)$, r is a semantic relation, and $n \in [0,1]$ is a confidence value. An alignment M between o_1 and o_2 is a set of correspondences between o_1 and o_2. We restrict r to be one of the semantic relations from the set $\{\equiv (equivalence), \subseteq (subsomption), \perp (disjonction)\}$.

Even, a mapping should be a mathematical function whereas an alignment is a general semantic relation between ontologies; some authors (Kalfoglou & Schorlemmer, 2003; Noy, 2009) use the term mapping instead of alignment.

Alignment Semantics

Since alignments relate ontologies, interpretations of semantic relations should show how interpretations of ontologies are related. We distinguish two approaches to relate interpretations of ontologies relatively to the domains of interpretations. When ontologies describe the same domain of interpretation, an alignment interpretation becomes a part of the global interpretation formed by the union of the different interpretations of the aligned ontologies. This is informally presented in Figure 2. In this approach, the aligned ontologies together with the alignment form a global ontology.

For contextual interpretations which reflect different points of view on the same real world entities, semantic relations of an ontology alignment are interpreted as bridge rules relating these interpretations (Bouquet, Giunchiglia, Van Harmelen, Serafini, & Stuckenschmidt, 2003). These rules express how to translate instances from a source to target ontology. Figure 3 shows intuitive interpretations of some bridge rules.

The above-cited approaches rely on model theoretic semantics to give an extensional interpretation for alignments. The model theoretic semantics expresses extensionally how meanings of two different vocabularies are related. An alternative approach intentionally constrains relations between meanings. Reductionist semantics (Meilicke & Stuckenschmidt, 2009) gives an axiomatization to constraint the alignment between entities in different ontologies. Within this semantics, an alignment interpreted as a set

Figure 2. Model theoretic based alignment global semantics

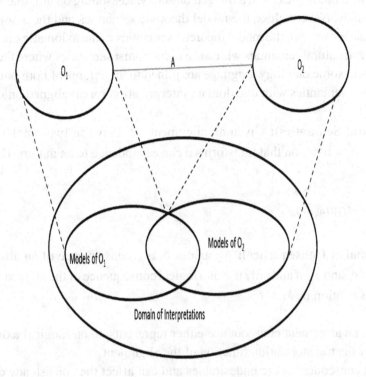

Figure 3. Model theoretic based alignment contextual semantics

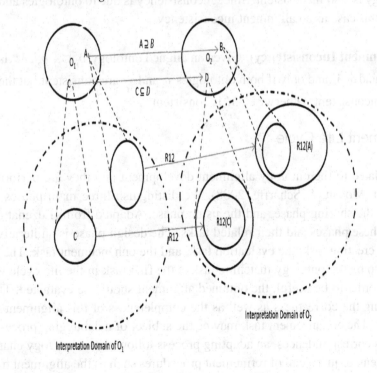

of axioms together with ontologies form a merged ontology. Reasoning on alignment turns to reasoning on this merged ontology. Nevertheless, the model theoretic semantics and the axiomatic semantics are not disjoint but we can move from the model theoretic semantics to the axiomatic one and vice versa. For instance, the alignment natural semantics which is a reductionist semantics where the semantic relations translated to axioms in some ontology language are joined to all axioms of both ontologies correspond to the model-theoretic semantics with one domain interpretation for all aligned ontologies.

Definition 5 (Natural Semantics): Given an alignment M between two ontologies o_1 and o_2 and trans : $M \rightarrow A$, a function that transforms a correspondence to an axiom. The aligned ontology is defined by

$$o_1 \cup_M o_2 = o_1 \cup o_2 \cup trans(M)$$

Definition 6 (Alignment Consequence): An axiom δ is a consequence of an alignment M between two ontologies o_1 and o_2 if and only if δ is a logical consequence of the aligned ontology $o_1 \cup_M o_2$. We denote this relation by $M \vDash \delta$.

An axiom that is an alignment consequence either represents an ontological axiom or the image of a correspondence by the transformation function of the alignment.

Some alignment consequences are undesirables and can affect the consistency of ontologies or the whole aligned ontology. In this case, the alignment is inconsistent. When an ontology is inconsistent, the aligned ontology is also inconsistent. Since inconsistency is due to ontologies and not to alignment, we can't consider this case as an alignment inconsistency.

Definition 7 (Alignment Inconsistency): Given an aligned ontology $o_1 \cup_M o_2$, M is inconsistent with respect to o_1 and o_2 if and only if both ontologies o_1 and o_2 are consistent but the aligned ontology $o_1 \cup_M o_2$ is inconsistent. Otherwise, M is consistent.

Ontology Alignment Life Cycle

Many tasks are related to the ontology alignment development and they are performed as long as its life cycle (Euzenat, Mocan, & Scharffe, 2008). We distinguish three main phases of this life cycle: The design phase, the sharing phase, and the using phase. Adapted from (Euzenat & shvaiko, 2013), Figure 4 outlines these phases and their related tasks. The design phase is an iterative process formed by three tasks: the creation task, the evaluation task, and the enhancement task. The task of alignment creation known also by the ontology matching task is the first task in the life cycle which aims to create alignments. In order to be useful, the obtained alignment should be evaluated. The evaluation task consists of assessing the correctness as well as the completeness of this alignment which might lead to an enhancement. The enhancement task may be the subject of a debugging process if the alignment contains erroneous correspondences, an adapting process following an ontology change, enhancing an incomplete alignment, or just a call of refinement procedures such as the alignment trimming relatively to a fixed threshold. The tasks of creation, evaluation, and enhancement might then go through an itera-

Figure 4. Ontology alignment life cycle

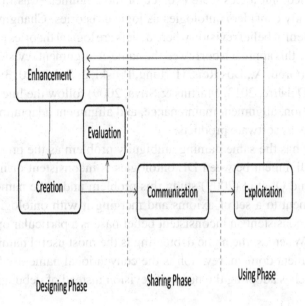

tive process until an alignment is deemed worth publishing. During the sharing phase, the alignment can be stored and communicated to other parties interested in such an alignment. Open servers are now available to store, index, organize and share alignments. For instance, Bioportal is an open community-based repository of biomedical ontologies. Users can browse alignments, upload new alignments, and download alignments that the repository has (Noy, Griffith, & Musen, 2008). In the final phase, the alignment can be exploited. Servers can deliver the alignment in different formats in order to ensure its large usefulness. Then, applications interpret it according to their needs and using it to perform actions, like mediation and merging.

THE STATE OF THE ART

Naming Disambiguation

Ontology alignment can be the subject of change during two phases of its life cycle. The change may be needed during the design phase before alignment delivery to diagnose and repair alignment produced by ontology matching tools. Created alignments might contain errors such as redundancy, inconsistency, imprecision, or an abnormal behavior. This process of change is called alignment debugging and repair (Wang & Xu, 2008). While alignment evolution is the process of alignment change after delivery during the using phase. The change may be needed following an ontology change or enhancing an incomplete alignment.

In the literature, approaches studied the alignment evolution problem under various names: alignment adaptation, alignment maintenance, alignment evolution, and alignment revision (Dos Reis, Pruski, & Reynaud-Delaître, 2015). Under the name alignment revision, Euzenat (2015) study the problem of restoring consistency of a network of ontologies formed by a set of ontologies connected by a set of alignments when concerned ontologies were evolved or the alignment was improved by adding some correspondences. This study considers ontologies as logical theories. Changing logical theories is the classical philosophy problem of belief revision where beliefs are logical theories (Alchourrón, Gärdenfors, & Makinson, 1985). While this approach borrowed the name of alignment revision from philosophy community other approaches (Groß, A., Dos Reis, Hartung, Pruski, & Rahm, 2013; Dos Reis, Dinh, Pruski, Da Silveira, & Reynaud-Delaître, 2013; Martins & Silva, 2009) follow the line of software engineering to adopt alignment evolution, alignment maintenance, and alignment adaptation names by considering ontologies and alignments as software products.

Alignment debugging has the same naming ambiguity problem as the process of alignment evolution. When a produced alignment between DL ontologies is inconsistent or incoherent, Meilicke and Stuckenschmidt (2009) and Qi et al (2009) study this problem under the name of alignment revision. By converting the alignment to a set of axioms and merging it with ontologies, they obtain a global knowledge base. Making consistent an inconsistent belief base is a particular operation in base revision theory (Hansson, 1999). Whereas, the name debugging is the most useful naming for programs debugging in software development domain, revision is the conventional name used for base change theory which leads these approaches adopting the name of revision instead of debugging name.

Classification

The alignment evolution task is of great importance as it aims to keep the alignment useful and ready in time during its life cycle. Alignment evolution approaches follow different ways to maintain and evolve alignments. Some approaches view the problem of alignment evolution as an adaptive process. The main challenge for these approaches is how to modify alignments according to the detected changes in ontologies. Sometimes, an ontology change such as adding concepts has no impact on the alignment but designers prefer to extend it out of the need with new correspondences in order to enhance its usefulness. For some scenarios, this extension can be classified as a perfective evolution. However, the same extension might become more than necessary for an application that requests a full interoperability and integration. In this scenario, the extension should be classified as an adaptive evolution since it was born following a change in application's needs. Hence, we qualify this type of approaches as an adaptive and perfective evolution. When an alignment extension or an ontology change hamper the usefulness of the alignment by introducing errors, other kind of approaches try to identify and correct these errors. We qualify this kind of approaches as a corrective evolution. Similar techniques used by different approaches that aim to correct errors during alignment debugging can also be applicable for the alignment evolution problem. Following this classification, we present and discuss the outcomes of these approaches. The issues of the alignment change problem fixed a priori in the introduction of this chapter are the main guide of this discussion. Table 1 summarizes this discussion.

Alignment Adaptive and Perfective Evolution

The main objective of adaptive evolution approaches is adapting alignments according to changes in the implied ontologies. Approaches of this category (Groß et al, 2013; Dos Reis et al, 2013; Khattak, Pervez, Khan, Khan, Latif, & Lee, 2015) consider an ontology as a directed acyclic graph (DAG). They support the detection of several basic as well as complex changes including concepts addition, deletion, split, merge, and move. Then, they use an ontology change handler to guide the alignment evolution process that converts the change either to an alignment between the versions of the evolved ontology (Groß et al, 2013) or to a set of actions that adapt the affected correspondences according to the type of change (Dos Reis et al, 2013; Khattak et al, 2015).

Groß et al. (2013) present two approaches for adapting the ontology alignment: the composition-based and diff-based adaptation approaches. Both approaches adapt the old alignment by composing it with some generated alignment between versions of the evolved ontology. Besides, they seek a new match for an added concept with concepts of the target ontology to enhance the alignment with new correspondences.

Dos Reis et al. (2013) present an automatic adaptation approach relying on a change handler which converts the change to mapping adaptation actions for adapting the affected correspondences according to the type of change. They proposed five distinct mapping adaptation actions that represent different possibilities for adapting alignment: correspondences addition, correspondences remove, correspondences move, correspondences derivation, and modification of semantic relations. Before every mapping adaptation action, an operation of matching is performed to determine the position (e.g, the concept) where the new correspondence should be re-allocated or from which is derived.

Regardless of the change type, Khattak et al (2015) act by deleting all correspondences concerned by the change and then add new correspondences by partially re-computing the alignment. The approach reuses completely the unaffected part of the alignment and the changed elements in the source or the target ontology of the alignment are automatically matched with the complete current version of the other ontology.

According to authors of these approaches, the outcome of the adaptation process is a valid alignment. However, alignment validity is not explicitly defined but they let it to expert's appreciation.

Alignment Corrective Evolution

Unlike adaptive evolution approaches, approaches of corrective evolution detect and correct erroneous correspondences. Qualified as erroneous, all correspondence contributes to the violation of certain constraints defined following an evolution of the ontology or an evolution of the alignment.

In (Martins & Silva, 2009), an alignment is an instance of Semantic Bridge Ontology (SBO). The evolution of alignment in this approach is a process that aims to preserve the semantics of this ontology when the deletion of concepts in the source or the target ontology is observed. Deletion of concepts leads to invalid entities of the ontology SBO. Inspired by strategies applied in Stojanovic's ontology evolution framework (Stojanovic, 2004), they propose a list of strategies to correct invalid entities of SBO. In order to preserve as much as possible the old alignment, they sort the list of invalid entities. According to authors, ensuring SBO validity implies alignments validity. This is true at the structural level since valid entities in SBO always give valid correspondences in alignment. Moreover, this validity is given with a minimality of change by sorting invalid entities. These approaches study only the impact of deleted concepts on alignments. It is not clear how they can ensure alignments validity for other types of change.

Euzenat (2015) study the problem of restoring consistency of a network of ontologies formed by a set of ontologies connected by a set of alignments when concerned ontologies were evolved or the alignment was improved by adding some correspondences. The author considers an ontology as a logical theory formed by a set of axioms. Mirroring the framework of AGM model of belief revision (Alchourrón et al., 1985), the approach introduces a set of postulates which constitute constraints to be fulfilled by any operator of local change on alignments as well as on ontologies. Then it provides postulates for revising the network of ontologies when an ontology of the network is revised by an axiom or an alignment is revised by a new correspondence. The approach provides alternatives strategies in order to minimize the network change. For instance, one can only change the concerned ontology while others can change only alignments since ontologies are the pillars of knowledge and its worth not to modify them only if there is no other way. As it is mentioned by the author, this work can be considered as a first step to understand revision in networks of ontologies that may help to consider the problem of base revision. Belief sets in the AGM framework are closed sets under the logical consequence relation. While the framework presents nice results it lacks practicability since closed sets are infinite or at least very large sets that cannot be incorporated easily into a computational framework (Peppas, 2008).

The practical encoding of ontologies and alignments in knowledge bases managed by knowledge systems to have access to and to reason about domain knowledge (Grimm & al., 2011) was the main motivation for Zahaf and Malli (2016b) to inspire from belief base revision theory for the alignment evolution under ontology change. They draw a set of constraints that an alignment evolution under ontology change should satisfy in order to be correctly evolved. Then, they propose an automatic method to reach this objective. In another work (Zahaf & Malli, 2016a), the same authors adapt the kernel contraction framework of belief revision theory (Hansson, 1994) to design rational operators and to formulate the set of postulates that characterize each class of these operators. Later, Zahaf, Fellah, Bouchiha, & Malki (2016) extend this framework by two new operations for the contraction and the consolidation of alignment evolution under ontology change by adapting the partial meet contraction framework of belief revision theory (Hansson, 1999). This chapter extends their works by proposing a new approach for the alignment change problem whatever the origin of change would be. The approach proposes a general framework that consists of a process of change. Various methods, each with a specific purpose, are proposed to automate and support the change process.

Alignment Debugging

Alignment debugging is the process of diagnosis and repair of invalid correspondences. Techniques used in alignment debugging can also be applicable in the alignment evolution task, precisely, for the alignment corrective evolution.

For some ontology matching tools, the diagnosis of invalid correspondences is based on patterns of reasoning which are correct but incomplete reasoning methods. Lily (Wang & Xu, 2008) uses four types of patterns: redundant mapping, imprecise mapping, inconsistent mapping, and abnormal mapping. ASMOV (Jean-Mary et al., 2009) uses five types of patterns to check semantics: multiple-entity correspondences, crisscross correspondences, disjoint-subsumption contradiction, subsumption and equivalence incompleteness, domain and range incompleteness. The pattern disjoint-subsumption contradiction used by ASMOV corresponds to the inconsistent mapping pattern used by Lily. YAM++ (Ngo & Bellahsene, 2012) relies on ALCOMO (http://web.informatik.uni-mannheim.de/alcomo/) system to debug alignments. ALCOMO (Meilicke & Stuckenschmidt, 2007) uses disjoint-subsumption contradiction pattern to check the satisfiability preservation of entities by alignments.

Independent approaches (Meilicke & Stuckenschmidt, 2009; Qi et al, 2009) use the notion of minimal conflict set (Reiter, 1987) to establish the coherency of alignments between description logics based ontologies. The alignment coherency is a sort of logical consistency such that satisfiable ontological entities should preserve their satisfiability even when ontologies are connected by alignments. This set presents the advantage to repair the problem of alignment incoherency by fixing one element in the set.

METHODS

Alignment Evolution Process

As already mentioned in the introduction of this chapter, the process of the alignment change needs methods to (1) facilitate the change capture for maintainers, (2) evolve alignment from a consistent state to another consistent state, (3) conduct the alignment to a new consistent state with a minimal of change, and (4) validate the alignment by maintainers. To fulfill the above requirements, we propose the following alignment change process: a phase for the change capture, a phase for the change semantics, a phase for the change validation, and a phase for the change implementation. Figure 5 outlines this process.

- **Change Capture:** The alignment change can occur at the request of changing the alignment itself or following the evolution of the ontologies connected. This phase lets maintainers to express their request for alignment change in terms of predefined changes, to parse a journal of ontology change, or to identify and make explicit the ontology change when only versions of evolved ontologies are available.
- **Semantics of Change:** The objective of this phase is resolving alignment inconsistency due to change. Although the change can be done in different ways, the principle of minimal change is the main guide in order to keep the old alignment as much as possible.
- **Change Validation:** During the phase of semantics change, the system resolves the different types of inconsistencies by proposing changes on alignment. Proposed changes should be reviewed by users before implementation. Alignments maintainers may validate the change, recover the unnecessary changes, adapt, track, or cancel the change. Hence, the objective of this phase is to rationalize and to facilitate the interaction with users. To rationalize the interaction, methods for inconsistency explanation are needed. Even though the objective of the previous phase is resolving inconsistencies with a minimal change; the proposed change may still be containing unnecessary changes. Hence, the user can request the recovering of these changes. Detecting such changes is not an easy task. Thanks to inconsistency checking and explanation, the user will adapt the change, reject it partially or reject it completely.
- **Change Implementation:** The change in previous phases is done on a copy of the original old alignment. After the change is validated by users, the change is confirmed and to be ready for delivery. The final change is the difference between the old and the new delivered alignment. The format of both alignment and associated change should be machine readable. This allows the parsing and exploitation of changes by maintenance tools of depending applications.

Figure 5. The ontology alignment change process

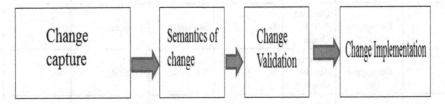

This change process is general and can be implemented in different ways. In what follows, we propose different methods to support and automatize the process.

Change Capture Methods

Methods for change capture let maintainers to express their request for alignment change in terms of predefined changes, to parse a journal of an ontology change, or to identify and make explicit the ontology change when only versions of the evolved ontologies are available.

According to definition 4, the following types of changes can be identified and considered as predefined.

An alignment can be changed by adding, deleting, or modifying its correspondences; a correspondence can be modified by changing the type of its semantic relation, renaming its entities, rated by attaching new confidence values, or annotated. Alignment visualization methods (Maedche, Motik, Silva, & Volz, 2002; Tang, Yao, Sun, & Qian, 2009) can help to change the alignment. They allow maintainers to visualize the ontologies being aligned together with the alignment between them. Hence, maintainers can change the existing correspondences that require maintenance.

Ontology change is the result of any significant ontology modification. The modification can touch the meaning axiomatization of the vocabulary or the vocabulary itself. The vocabulary change is the set of added or deleted vocabulary elements. The axiomatic change is the set of added or deleted axioms.

Table 1. Classification of alignment change approaches

	Category	Ontology Model	Ontology Change	Alignment Model	Alignment Consistency	Change Minimality	User Involvement
Groß et al, 2013	Adaptive and Perfective Evolution	Directed Acyclic Graph	Basic and Complex	Syntactic	Not defined	No	Adapting semantic relations
Dos Reis et al, 2013	Adaptive and Perfective Evolution	Directed Acyclic Graph	Basic and Complex	Syntactic	Not defined	No	Automatic
Khattak et al, 2015	Adaptive and Perfective Evolution	Directed Acyclic Graph	Basic and Complex	Syntactic	Not defined	No	Automatic
Martins & Silva, 2009	Corrective Evolution	Directed Acyclic Graph	Basic	Syntactic	Structural	Yes	Choose strategies
Euzenat, 2015	Corrective Evolution	Logical Theory	Basic	Semantic	Logical	Yes	Automatic
Zahaf & Malki, 2016a, Zahaf & Malki, 2016b Zahaf et al., 2016	Corrective Evolution	Logical Theory	Basic	Semantic	Logical	Yes	Automatic
Lily	Debugging	Directed Acyclic Graph	No	Semantic	Logical	No	Automatic
ASMOV	Debugging	Directed Acyclic Graph	No	Semantic	Logical	No	Automatic
ALCOMO	Debugging	Logical Theory	No	Semantic	Logical	No	Automatic

Usually, ontology evolution approaches (Stojanovic, 2004; Plessers, 2006; Klein, 2004; Palma, Haase, Corcho, & Gómez-Pérez, 2009) deliver evolution logs that store the implemented change as an instance of an ontology of change. Methods for ontology parsing and visualization (Katifori, Halatsis, Lepouras, Vassilakis, & Giannopoulou, 2007) are also welcome to parse and visualize the ontology change. However, in open and distributed environments such as the semantic Web where ontologies and alignments are submitted to different authorities, the journal of change is often available in an unreadable machine format. Maintainers want to identify and make explicit the ontology change in order to understand what happened and correctly update their alignments. Methods for comparing versions of the same ontology (Redmond & Noy, 2011; Kremen, Smid, & Kouba, 2011; Zahaf, 2012) may help to detect what has been changed in a version relatively to another and to make explicit the change in a machine readable format.

Semantics of Change Methods

Methods for the change semantics aim at resolving the inconsistency of the alignment while retaining the principle of minimal change. There is not a single miracle method for all types of alignment changes, but each method is tailor-made for one type of change. An alignment change is a set of operations that can be performed on the alignment itself or on one of its connected ontologies. The alignment change consists of deleting, adding, and modifying correspondences. Deleting and adding correspondences are two basic operations. The modification operation is a complex operation. It consists in modifying the aligned entities, the semantic relation, or the confidence value. The change of connected ontologies consists of deleting and adding vocabulary elements on the one hand, and deleting and adding axioms on the other hand.

Inspired by base revision theory (Hansson, 1999), different operations of change can be envisaged for the alignment change: alignment expansion, alignment contraction, and alignment revision. The alignment expansion is the set-theoretically adding of correspondences to an alignment without affecting the alignment consistency. The alignment contraction can be applied following a deleted axiom from one of the aligned ontologies or a deleted correspondence from the alignment. The alignment revision restores the alignment consistency following the addition of new correspondences or new axioms in ontologies. A particular operation of the alignment revision is alignment consolidation. The alignment consolidation is applied to establish consistency of an inconsistent alignment.

In what follows, this section presents two operations for the alignment contraction and the alignment consolidation. They are called confidence-based partial meet alignment contraction and confidence-based partial meet alignment consolidation respectively. Please note that these operations are general that can be applied during alignment evolution as well as alignment debugging.

Confidence-Based Partial Meet Alignment Contraction

Given an alignment M and an axiom α (e.g., The axiom α may be an axiom belonging to an ontology or an image of some correspondence.), an alignment contraction noted $M - \alpha$ is the minimal contraction of correspondences to ensure the success of axioms and correspondences deletion. Success means that a successfully removed axiom from an ontology or a deleted correspondence from an alignment should not be regenerated again by this alignment after the change unless they are tautologies. The constraint of success is also called the ontology change preservation constraint (Zahaf and Malki, 2016b) which can be formulated as follows.

[Success] if $\nvDash \alpha$ then $M - \alpha \nvDash \alpha$

The change strategy of the alignment contraction to ensure success is only correspondences deletion. Which means neither modification nor addition of new correspondences are authorized to fulfill the change. This is also called the inclusion postulate in the jargon of base revision theory (Hansson, 1999) and it is formulated as follows.

[Inclusion] $M - \alpha \subseteq M$

Of course the change should be minimal as much as possible. The principle of minimal change for the contraction change is formulated by two postulates in base revision theory (Hansson, 1999). The former is called the relevance postulate which can be reformulated as follows.

[Relevance] if $c \in M$ and $c \notin M - \alpha$, then there is a subset M' such that $M - \alpha \subseteq M' \subseteq M$ and that, $M' \nvDash \alpha$ but $M' \cup \{c\} \vDash \alpha$.

Satisfying the relevance postulate means a correspondence is discarded only if it is responsible somehow for implying the contracted axiom. The latter is called the core-retainment postulate. It is a weak form of the former that can be reformulated as follows.

[Core-Retainment] if $c \in M$ and $c \notin M \div \alpha$, then there is a subset M' of M such that, $M' \nvDash \alpha$ but $M' \cup \{c\} \vDash \alpha$.

The objective of any contraction operation is to compute a maximal subset of M that fails to imply α. However, there is more than one subset that satisfies this condition. The set of these maximal subsets is called the alignment reminder set. Formally,

Definition 8 (Alignment Remainder Set): The alignment remainder set $M \perp \alpha$ of M by α is the set of subset M' such that:

$$\left[\begin{array}{l} M' \subseteq M \ \left(subset\, of\, M \right) \\ M' \nvDash \alpha \left(don't\, imply\, \alpha \right) \\ for\, all\, M'', M' \subseteq M''\, M'' \vDash \alpha \left(is\, \max imal \right) \end{array} \right.$$

Then, the contraction uses a function which is called alignment selection function to select from $M \perp \alpha$ some elements which supposed to be the most entrenched subsets of the alignment.

Definition 9 (Alignment Selection Function): An alignment selection function γ for M is a function that for all α:

$$\begin{cases} \gamma(M \perp \alpha) \subseteq M \perp \alpha & \text{if } M \perp \alpha \neq \phi \\ \gamma(M \perp \alpha) = \{M\} & \text{otherwise} \end{cases}$$

The alignment selection function is a general function that allows selecting cautiously the most entrenched subsets. A particular function that we call the confidence-based alignment selection function uses the confidence value noted $n(c)$ attached to a correspondence c to select the most trusted subsets. A subset is more trusted than another if and only if it has the highest total of the confidence values attached to its correspondences. Hence, the confidence-based alignment function can be defined as follows.

Definition 10 (Confidence-Based Alignment Selection Function): A confidence-based alignment selection function γ_n for M is a selection function that for all α:

if $x \in \gamma_n(M \perp \alpha)$, for all $z \in M \perp \alpha$, such that $z \neq x$
then $\sum\limits_{c \in z} n(c) \leq \sum\limits_{c \in x} n(c)$

There may be more than one trusted subset. The confidence-based partial meet contraction operation computes the intersection of them.

Definition 11 (Confidence-Based Partial Meet Alignment Contraction): Let M an alignment, α is an axiom and γ_n a confidence-based alignment selection function, the confidence-based partial meet contraction of M by α is the mathematical application which associates a given alignment M to the new alignment:

$$M - \alpha = \cap \gamma_n(M \perp \alpha)$$

Proposition 1: The confidence-based partial meet alignment contraction operation satisfies the success, inclusion, and the relevance postulates.

Proof:

Let $-_{\gamma_n}$ be a confidence-based alignment contraction operation for some confidence-based selection function γ_n such that $M -_{\gamma_n} \alpha = \cap \gamma_n(M \perp \alpha)$ and demonstrates that it satisfies the success, inclusion, and the relevance postulates.

To show $-_{\gamma_n}$ satisfies the success, we need to show for $\nvdash \alpha$ that $M -_{\gamma_n} \alpha \nvdash \alpha$.

Since $\nvdash \alpha$, $M \perp \alpha \neq \phi$. Hence, by the definition of a selection function (See definition 9), $\phi \neq \gamma_n(M \perp \alpha) \subseteq (M \perp \alpha)$. Let $x \in \gamma_n(M \perp \alpha)$. It follows from $x \in (M \perp \alpha)$ that $x \nvdash \alpha$. Or, from

$x \in \gamma_n(M \perp \alpha)$, we have $\cap \gamma_n(M \perp \alpha) \subseteq x$. By monotony, from $x \nvDash \alpha$ and $\cap \gamma_n(M \perp \alpha) \subseteq x$, we conclude that $\cap \gamma_n(M \perp \alpha) \subseteq x \nvDash \alpha$.

To show $-_{\gamma_n}$ satisfies the inclusion, we need to show for all α, that $M -_{\gamma_n} \alpha \subseteq M$. There are two cases, according to whether or not α is a tautology:

Case 1: $\vDash \alpha$. Then $M \perp \alpha = \phi$. It follows from the definition of a selection function that $\gamma_n(M \perp \alpha) = \{M\}$. Hence, $\cap \gamma_n(M \perp \alpha) = \{M\} \subseteq M$.

Case 2: $\nvDash \alpha$. Then $\phi \neq \gamma_n(M \perp \alpha) \subseteq M \perp \alpha$. Since every element of $M \perp \alpha$ is a subset of M, so every element of $\gamma_n(M \perp \alpha)$, and so is $\cap \gamma_n(M \perp \alpha)$.

To show $-_{\gamma_n}$ satisfies the relevance, we need to show for all α, if $c \in M$ and $c \notin M -_{\gamma_n} \alpha$, then there is a subset M' such that $c \notin M -_{\gamma_n} \alpha \subseteq M' \subseteq M$ and that, $M' \nvDash \alpha$ but $M' \cup \{c\} \vDash \alpha$. Again there are two cases:

Case 1: $\vDash \alpha$. Then $M \perp \alpha = \phi$. It follows from the definition of a selection function that $\gamma_n(M \perp \alpha) = \{M\}$. Hence, $\cap \gamma_n(M \perp \alpha) = \{M\}$. It follows there is no c such that $c \in M$ and $c \notin \gamma_n(M \perp \alpha)$. Hence, the relevance is satisfied because its initial conditions are not satisfiable.

Case 2: $\nvDash \alpha$. Then $\phi \neq \gamma_n(M \perp \alpha) \subseteq M \perp \alpha$. It follows from $c \notin \cap \gamma_n(M \perp \alpha)$ that there is some element $M' \in \gamma_n(M \perp \alpha)$ such that $c \notin M'$. It follows from $M' \in (M \perp \alpha)$ that $M' \nvDash \alpha$. Furthermore, since $M' \in (M \perp \alpha)$ it follows from $M' \subseteq M' \cup \{c\} \subseteq M$ that $M' \cup \{c\} \vDash \alpha$, i.e. because M' should be maximal. We can also see from $M' \in \gamma_n(M \perp \alpha)$ that $\cap \gamma_n(M \perp \alpha) \subseteq M' \subseteq M$. Hence, the relevance is satisfied in this case as well.

Confidence-Based Partial Meet Alignment Consolidation

An alignment consolidation operation is applied to establish consistency of an inconsistent alignment whatever the origin of the inconsistency may be. Therefore, the alignment revision operation following the addition of new axioms into ontologies can be replaced by a consolidation operation. This is true since ontology artefacts maintenance can be performed after the ontology maintenance has been done. This practice is the most frequent in the Web based ontology engineering discipline (Klein, 2004; Plessers, 2006). This means maintainers are only authorized to modify alignments.

In this section, we define a new operation of consolidation that operates with a minimal contraction to establish consistency of an inconsistent alignment. In other words, this operation satisfies the consistency, inclusion and the relevance postulates.

We adapt definition 8 of the alignment remainder set notion to define a particular remainder set that we call alignment consistent remainder set and we denote it by $M \perp^{\perp}$. Formally,

Definition 12 (Alignment Consistent Remainder Set): The alignment consistent remainder set $M \perp^{\perp}$ of M is the set of M' such that:

$$\begin{cases} M' \subseteq M \ \left(subset \, of \, M\right) \\ M' \ is \ consistent \\ for \ all \ M", M' \subseteq M", M" \ is \ inconsistent \ \left(is \ \max imal\right) \end{cases}$$

Since the alignment is initially inconsistent we should prevent the selection function to choose the alignment itself i.e., the second condition of definition 8 where the consistent remainder set is empty. Furthermore, we should force the selection function to select only consistent sets. To satisfy these conditions, we define a new selection function that we call consistent alignment selection function.

Definition 13 (Consistent Alignment Selection Function): A consistent alignment selection function γ for M is a function such that: $\gamma(M \perp^{\perp}) \subseteq M \perp^{\perp}$.

Therefore, we introduce a new function that we call confidence-based consistent alignment selection function as follows.

Definition 14 (Confidence-Based Consistent Alignment Selection Function): A confidence-based consistent alignment selection function γ_n for M is a consistent alignment selection function such that:

$$if \ x \in \gamma_n(M \perp^{\perp}), \ for \ all \ z \in M \perp^{\perp}, \ such \ that \ z \neq x$$
$$then \ \sum_{c \in z} n(c) \leq \sum_{c \in x} n(c)$$

Hence, we define the confidence-based alignment partial meet consolidation as follows.

Definition 15 (Confidence-Based Partial Meet Alignment Consolidation): Let M an alignment and γ_n a confidence-based consistent alignment selection function from the alignment consistent remainder set $M \perp^{\perp}$, the partial meet consolidation of M denoted by M_{c,γ_n} is the operation defined as:

$$M_{c,\gamma_n} = \cap \gamma_n(M \perp^{\perp}).$$

Proposition 2: The confidence-based partial meet alignment consolidation satisfies the consistency, the inclusion, and the relevance postulates.

Proof:

Let M_{c,γ_n} be a confidence-based alignment consolidation operation on an alignment M for some confidence-based selection function γ_n such that $M_{c,\gamma_n} = \cap \gamma_n(M \perp^{\perp})$ and demonstrates that it satisfies the consistency, inclusion, and the relevance postulates.

To show M_{c,γ_n} is consistent, let $x \in \cap\gamma_n(M \perp^\perp)$. It follows from $x \in M \perp^\perp$ that x is consistent. Or, from $x \in \gamma_n(M \perp^\perp)$, we have $\cap\gamma_n(M \perp^\perp) \subseteq x$. By monotony, from x consistent and $\cap\gamma_n(M \perp^\perp) \subseteq x$ we conclude that $\cap\gamma_n(M \perp^\perp)$ is consistent.

The inclusion follows directly from the definition. Since $\cap\gamma_n(M \perp^\perp) \subseteq M \perp^\perp \subseteq M$ we have $M_{c,\gamma_n} \subseteq M$.

If $c \in M$ and $c \notin M_{c,\gamma_n}$, then there is $x \in \gamma_n(M \perp^\perp)$ such that $c \notin x$. Of course $M_{c,\gamma_n} = \cap\gamma_n(M \perp^\perp) \subseteq x \subseteq M$. x is consistent but $x \cup \{c\}$ is inconsistent. This satisfies the relevance postulate.

These operations of contraction and consolidation are general so they can be applied during alignment evolution as well as alignment debugging. They use the confidence values attached to correspondences to select the most trusted subsets. However, in alignment evolution following the ontology change confidence values represent trust degrees in correspondences before the ontology change. Therefore, before applying these operations an update of these trust degrees is needed in order to reflect the new change. Trust updating can be performed manually by an expert's new rating or computed again by methods of partial ontology matching (Fellah, Malki, & Elci, 2016) to cover only the changed entities of the aligned ontologies.

Change Validation Methods

Even though the proposed methods for changing the alignment are fully automatic, users may still need to review the change and validate it by themselves. An important issue that can hamper their work is the absence of inconsistency checking and justification. Users may request an adaptation of the proposed change but they can't guarantee the consequences of this adaptation on alignment consistency. This section introduces the notion of alignment inconsistency justification and methods to compute all justifications.

Definition 16 (Alignment Justification): Given an alignment M and an Ω a set of undesirable logical consequences of M; J_M is a justification of Ω if and only if:

$$\begin{cases} \qquad J_M \subseteq M \quad \left(subset\,of\,M\right) \\ J_M \vDash \Omega \quad \left(\Omega \; is\,an \; alignment\,consequence\,of\,J_M\right) \\ for\,all\;J_M{'}, J_M{'} \subseteq J_M, J_M{'} \nvDash \Omega \; \left(J_M \; is \; \min imal\right) \end{cases}$$

The algorithm to find an alignment justification is an adaptation of the algorithm presented in (Baader, Penaloza, & Suntisrivaraporn, 2007) to compute a minimal subset of an ontology that is responsible for an entailment of Ω, a given set of undesirable logical consequences. Similar to the algorithm presented in (Baader et al., 2007), algorithm 1 can compute an alignment justification in polynomial time in the size of the aligned ontology.

To compute all justifications, we adapt the Hitting Set Algorithm proposed by Reiter (1987) to diagnose systems. Reiter's algorithm finds all minimal hitting sets given a collection of conflicts sets. The algorithm traces a tree such that its each node is labeled by a conflict set and edges are labeled by the

Algorithm 1. Alignment Justification algorithm

```
Alignment Justification  ( M,o₁,o₂,Ω )
Input: o₁,o₂ // two ontologies
        M // M is an alignment between o₁ and o₂
        Ω // Ω is a set of undesirable logical consequences
Output Jₘ:Jₘ // an  alignment Justification
```

1. $J_M \leftarrow M$
2. for $c \in J_M$
3.   do
4.   if $J_M \setminus \{c\} \vDash \Omega$
5.   then $J_M \leftarrow J_M \setminus \{c\}$
6. return J_M

elements of these conflicts sets. A minimal hitting set is the minimal set that intersects each conflict set which correspond to a minimal branch of the tree. We consider the set of justifications as the collection of conflicts set that we find them dynamically. At the beginning, we use algorithm1 to compute a justification of the alignment M which we take it as the label of the root. At each node n, a justification of the remainder of M by H_n, the set of elements of the constructed branch is computed if such an alignment justification exists. Unfortunately, the Hitting set algorithm has an exponential time (Rymon, 1991). Algorithm 2 outlines the process.

FUTURE RESEARCH DIRECTIONS

A major observation that can be drawn from this chapter is that the problem of ontology alignment change has not received a lot of importance and many investigations must be carried out to solve the related issues. Investigations should touch the fundamental as well as the methodology aspects of this problem.

Results of this chapter are within the alignment natural semantics framework. We need further investigations within the alignment contextual semantics (Bouquet et al, 2003). We have assumed that ontology languages verify some logical properties such as monotony. What about non-monotonous languages?

The problem of the conservativity principle for ontology alignment has been identified as an important problem by semantic Web community (Atig, Zahaf, & Bouchiha, 2015). We think that the study of this problem is not investigated yet in its right framework. Base revision theory may constitute a good inspiration for methods resolving the related issues.

At the methodology side, the proposed framework can be extended in many ways. The framework models the alignment change as a process of four phases. Methods have been proposed to automate and support the different phases. Methods for the semantics of change phase cover the contraction and the consolidation types of change. Adding correspondences to alignments can lead to an inconsistency that

Algorithm 2. All Alignment Justifications algorithm

```
AllAlignmentJustification ( M,o₁,o₂,Ω )
```
$\text{Input: } o_1, o_2$ // two ontologies

       M // M is an alignment between o_1 and o_2

       Ω // Ω is a set of undesirable logical consequences

Output: AJ // a set of Alignment Justifications

1. Stack $\leftarrow$ Empty
2. $C \leftarrow$ Alignment Justification (M,o_1,o_2,Ω)
3. $AJ \leftarrow \{C\}$
4. for $c \in C$
5.   do insert $\{c\}$ in the top of the stack
6. While Stack not Empty
7.   do $H_n \leftarrow$ last element of the stack
8.   remove last element of the stack
9.   If $M \setminus H_n \vDash \Omega$
10.   Then $C \leftarrow$ Alignment Justification ($M \setminus H_n, o_1, o_2, \Omega$)
11. $AJ \leftarrow AJ \cup \{C\}$
12.   for $c \in C$
13.   do insert $H_n \cup \{c\}$ in the top of the stack
14.   EndIf
15. return AJ
16. End.

may lead us to think of a consolidation change to resolve inconsistency issues. However, the consolidation may violate the postulate of success of change by taking off the added correspondences as well in order to restore the consistency. We continue on the light of base revision to investigate how to deal with this problem.

Furthermore, we hope to extend this study to deal with the problem of restoring the consistency of a network of ontologies formed by a set of ontologies connected by a set of alignments when concerned ontologies were evolved or the alignment was improved by adding some correspondences. The work of Euzenat (2015) is a first step to understand the revision of the network of ontologies that may help to consider the problem within the framework of base revision theory.

Another related problem is the maintenance of semantic annotations. Annotations express semantic links between documents contents and domain ontologies. Ontology change might decrease the quality of annotations and make them obsolete and useless. In spite of the recent advances in annotation systems, maintenance of existing annotations remains under studied (Cardoso et al., 2016).

CONCLUSION

This chapter reviews and classifies the main approaches of alignment change problem. Besides, the chapter presents a new approach for the ontology alignment change problem. This approach proposes a formal framework that consists of a number of phases, each having a specific purpose. The framework facilitates the ontology change capture for maintainers, evolves alignment from a consistent state to another consistent state, conducts to a new consistent state with a minimal of change, and permits maintainers validate the new alignment. The framework identifies a set of predefined changes for the alignment change and recommends various methods from the literature for the change capture. On the light of belief base revision theory, the framework offers two new operations for the alignment contraction and consolidation respectively as well as a list of constraints to characterize the alignment change requirements. The alignment contraction can be applied following a deleted axiom from one of the aligned ontologies or a deleted correspondence from the alignment itself. The alignment consolidation is applied to establish consistency of an inconsistent alignment whatever the origin of the inconsistency. Both operations are general that can be applied during alignment evolution as well as alignment debugging. Furthermore, the framework offers methods to explain inconsistencies and to compute these explanations that are useful during the alignment validation phase. Finally, the chapter discusses future and emerging trends of the problem of alignment change.

REFERENCES

Alchourrón, C. E., Gärdenfors, P., & Makinson, D. (1985). On the logic of theory change: Partial meet contraction and revision functions. *The Journal of Symbolic Logic, 50*(02), 510–530. doi:10.2307/2274239

Atig, Y., Zahaf, A., & Bouchiha, D. (2016). Conservativity Principle Violations for Ontology Alignment: Survey and Trends. *International Journal of Information Technology and Computer Science, 8*(7), 61–71. doi:10.5815/ijitcs.2016.07.09

Baader, F., Penaloza, R., & Suntisrivaraporn, B. (2007). Pinpointing in the Description Logic EL+. In *Annual Conference on Artificial Intelligence* (pp. 52-67). Springer Berlin Heidelberg.

Bouquet, P., Giunchiglia, F., Van Harmelen, F., Serafini, L., & Stuckenschmidt, H. (2003, October). C-owl: Contextualizing ontologies. In *International Semantic Web Conference* (pp. 164-179). Springer Berlin Heidelberg.

Buitelaar, P., Eigner, T., & Declerck, T. (2004). OntoSelect: A dynamic ontology library with support for ontology selection. *Proceedings of the Demo Session at the International Semantic Web Conference.*

Cardoso, S. D., Pruski, C., Da Silveira, M., Lin, Y. C., Groß, A., Rahm, E., & Reynaud-Delaître, C. (2016). Leveraging the Impact of Ontology Evolution on Semantic Annotations. In *Knowledge Engineering and Knowledge Management: 20th International Conference, EKAW 2016, Bologna, Italy, November 19-23, 2016 Proceedings, 20,* 68–82.

D'Aquin, M., Gridinoc, L., Angeletou, S., Sabou, M., & Motta, E. (2007). *Watson: A gateway for next generation semantic Web applications.* Poster session at the International Semantic Web Conference (ISWC 2007), Busan, Korea.

Ding, L., Finin, T., Joshi, A., Pan, R., Cost, R. S., Peng, Y., & Sachs, J. (2004). Swoogle: a search and metadata engine for the semantic Web. In *Proceedings of the thirteenth ACM international conference on Information and knowledge management* (pp. 652-659). ACM. 10.1145/1031171.1031289

Dos Reis, J. C., Dinh, D., Pruski, C., Da Silveira, M., & Reynaud-Delaître, C. (2013). Mapping adaptation actions for the automatic reconciliation of dynamic ontologies. In *Proceedings of the 22nd ACM international conference on Information & Knowledge Management* (pp. 599-608). ACM. 10.1145/2505515.2505564

Dos Reis, J. C., Pruski, C., & Reynaud-Delaître, C. (2015). State-of-the-art on mapping maintenance and challenges towards a fully automatic approach. *Expert Systems with Applications, 42*(3), 1465–1478. doi:10.1016/j.eswa.2014.08.047

Dzbor, M., Domingue, J., & Motta, E. (2003). Magpie–towards a semantic Web browser. In *International Semantic Web Conference* (pp. 690-705). Springer Berlin Heidelberg.

Euzenat, J. (2015). Revision in networks of ontologies. *Artificial Intelligence, 228,* 195–216.

Euzenat, J., Mocan, A., & Scharffe, F. (2008). Ontology alignment: an ontology management perspective. In M. Hepp, P. D. Leenheer, A. D. Moor, & Y. Sure (Eds.), Ontology management: semantic Web, semantic Web services, and business applications (pp. 177–206). New-York: Springer.

Euzenat, J., & Shvaiko, P. (2013). *Ontology matching* (Vol. 18). Heidelberg, Germany: Springer. doi:10.1007/978-3-642-38721-0

Fellah, A., Malki, M., & Elci, A. (2016). A similarity measure across ontologies for Web services discovery. *International Journal of Information Technology and Web Engineering, 11*(1), 22–43. doi:10.4018/IJITWE.2016010102

Grimm, S., Abecker, A., Völker, J., & Studer, R. (2011). Ontologies and the semantic Web. In *Handbook of Semantic Web Technologies* (pp. 507–579). Springer Berlin Heidelberg. doi:10.1007/978-3-540-92913-0_13

Groß, A., Dos Reis, J. C., Hartung, M., Pruski, C., & Rahm, E. (2013). Semi-automatic adaptation of mappings between life science ontologies. In *International Conference on Data Integration in the Life Sciences* (pp. 90-104). Springer Berlin Heidelberg. 10.1007/978-3-642-39437-9_8

Gruber, T. R. (1993). A translation approach to portable ontology specifications. *Knowledge Acquisition, 5*(2), 199–220. doi:10.1006/knac.1993.1008

Guarino, N., Oberle, D., & Staab, S. (2009). What is an Ontology? In *Handbook on ontologies* (pp. 1–17). Springer Berlin Heidelberg. doi:10.1007/978-3-540-92673-3_0

Hansson, S. O. (1994). Kernel contraction. *The Journal of Symbolic Logic, 59*(03), 845–859. doi:10.2307/2275912

Hansson, S. O. (1999). *A Textbook of Belief Dynamics. Theory Change and Database Updating*. Dordrecht: Kluwer. doi:10.1007/978-94-007-0814-3

Jean-Mary, Y. R., Shironoshita, E. P., & Kabuka, M. R. (2009). Ontology matching with semantic verification. *Journal of Web Semantics, 7*(3), 235–251. doi:10.1016/j.websem.2009.04.001 PMID:20186256

Kalfoglou, Y., & Schorlemmer, M. (2003). Ontology mapping: The state of the art. *The Knowledge Engineering Review, 18*(01), 1–31. doi:10.1017/S0269888903000651

Katifori, A., Halatsis, C., Lepouras, G., Vassilakis, C., & Giannopoulou, E. (2007). Ontology visualization methods—a survey. *ACM Computing Surveys, 39*(4), 10, es. doi:10.1145/1287620.1287621

Khattak, A. M., Pervez, Z., Khan, W. A., Khan, A. M., Latif, K., & Lee, S. Y. (2015). Mapping evolution of dynamic Web ontologies. *Information Sciences, 303*, 101–119. doi:10.1016/j.ins.2014.12.040

Klein, M. (2004). *Change management for distributed ontologies* (PhD thesis). University of Vrije, Netherlands.

Kremen, P., Smid, M., & Kouba, Z. (2011). OWLDiff: A practical tool for comparison and merge of OWL ontologies. In *Database and Expert Systems Applications (DEXA), 2011 22nd International Workshop on* (pp. 229-233). IEEE. 10.1109/DEXA.2011.62

Lopez, V., Motta, E., & Uren, V. (2006). Poweraqua: Fishing the semantic Web. In *European Semantic Web Conference* (pp. 393-410). Springer Berlin Heidelberg.

Lopez, V., Pasin, M., & Motta, E. (2005). Aqualog: An ontology-portable question answering system for the semantic Web. In *European Semantic Web Conference* (pp. 546-562). Springer Berlin Heidelberg. 10.1007/11431053_37

Maedche, A., Motik, B., Silva, N., & Volz, R. (2002, October). MAFRA—a mapping framework for distributed ontologies. In *International Conference on Knowledge Engineering and Knowledge Management* (pp. 235-250). Springer.

Martins, H., & Silva, N. (2009). A User-driven and a Semantic-based Ontology Mapping Evolution Approach. ICEIS, (1), 214-221.

Meilicke, C., & Stuckenschmidt, H. (2007). Applying logical constraints to ontology matching. In *Annual Conference on Artificial Intelligence* (pp. 99-113). Springer Berlin Heidelberg.

Meilicke, C., & Stuckenschmidt, H. (2009). An efficient method for computing alignment diagnoses. In *International Conference on Web Reasoning and Rule Systems* (pp. 182-196). Springer Berlin Heidelberg. 10.1007/978-3-642-05082-4_13

Motta, E., & Sabou, M. (2006). Next generation semantic Web applications. In *Asian Semantic Web Conference* (pp. 24-29). Springer Berlin Heidelberg.

Ngo, D. H., & Bellahsene, Z. (2012). YAM++:(not) Yet Another Matcher for Ontology Matching Task. BDA: Bases de Données Avancées.

Noy, N. F. (2009). Ontology mapping. In *Handbook on ontologies* (pp. 573–590). Springer Berlin Heidelberg. doi:10.1007/978-3-540-92673-3_26

Noy, N. F., Griffith, N., & Musen, M. A. (2008). Collecting community-based mappings in an ontology repository. In *International Semantic Web Conference* (pp. 371-386). Springer Berlin Heidelberg. 10.1007/978-3-540-88564-1_24

Palma, R., Haase, P., Corcho, O., & Gómez-Pérez, A. (2009). Change representation for OWL 2 ontologies. In *Proceedings of the 6th International Conference on OWL: Experiences and Directions* (vol. 529, pp. 142-151). CEUR-WS.org.

Peppas, P. (2008). Belief revision. In Handbook of knowledge representation (pp. 317–359). Elsevier.

Plessers, P. (2006). *An Approach to Web-based Ontology Evolution* (PhD thesis). University of Brussels, Belgium.

Qi, G., Ji, Q., & Haase, P. (2009). A conflict-based operator for mapping revision. In *International Semantic Web Conference* (pp. 521-536). Springer Berlin Heidelberg.

Redmond, T., & Noy, N. (2011). Computing the changes between ontologies. *Joint Workshop on Knowledge Evolution and Ontology Dynamics*, 1-14.

Reiter, R. (1987). A theory of diagnosis from first principles. *Artificial Intelligence, 32*(1), 57–95. doi:10.1016/0004-3702(87)90062-2

Rymon, R. (1991). *A Final Determination of the Complexity of Current Formulations of Model-Based Diagnosis (Or Maybe Not Final?)*. Technical Report No. MS-CIS-91-13. University of Pennsylvania.

Stojanovic, L. (2004). *Methods and tools for ontology evolution* (PhD thesis). University of Karlsruhe.

Tang, F., Yao, L., Sun, Y., & Qian, M. (2009, November). Visualizing semantic mapping based on view graph. In *Knowledge Acquisition and Modeling, 2009. KAM'09. Second International Symposium on* (Vol. 3, pp. 124-127). IEEE. 10.1109/KAM.2009.318

Uschold, M., & Gruninger, M. (2004). Ontologies and semantics for seamless connectivity. *SIGMOD Record, 33*(4), 58–64. doi:10.1145/1041410.1041420

Wang, P., & Xu, B. (2008). Debugging ontology mappings: A static approach. *Computer Information, 27*(1), 21–36.

Zahaf, A. (2012). Alignment Between Versions of the Same Ontology. In ICWIT (pp. 318-323). Academic Press.

Zahaf, A., Fellah, A., Bouchiha, D., & Malki, M. (2016, July). Partial meet contraction and consolidation of ontology alignment. In *2016 7th International Conference on Computer Science and Information Technology (CSIT)* (pp. 1-6). IEEE.

Zahaf, A., & Malki, M. (2016a). Kernel Contraction and Consolidation of Alignment under Ontology Change. *Journal of Information Technology and Computer Science, 8*(8), 31–42. doi:10.5815/ijitcs.2016.08.04

Zahaf, A., & Malki, M. (2016b). Alignment Evolution under Ontology Change. *International Journal of Information Technology and Web Engineering, 11*(2), 14–38. doi:10.4018/IJITWE.2016040102

KEY TERMS AND DEFINITIONS

Alignment Change: Any modification on the alignment correspondences.

Alignment Debugging: Is the task of alignment change before alignment delivery to diagnose and repair ontology alignments produced by matching tools.

Alignment Evolution: Is the task of alignment change after delivery in order to keep up with the change in ontology or to meet the demands of applications and users.

Alignment Revision: Is the task of change of an alignment between ontologies as logical theories.

Belief Base Revision: Is the process of changing a finite set of beliefs to take into account a new belief.

Ontology Alignment: A set of correspondences stating how entities of different ontologies semantically are related.

Chapter 12

Proposition of a New Ontology–Based P2P System for Semantic Integration of Heterogeneous Data Sources

Naïma Souâd Ougouti
Université des Sciences et de la Technologie d'Oran Mohamed Boudiaf, Algeria

Hafida Belbachir
Université des Sciences et de la Technologie d'Oran Mohamed Boudiaf, Algeria

Youssef Amghar
INSA Lyon, France

ABSTRACT

Semantic web offers new opportunities to multi-sources integration field, and many approaches like P2P systems are revisited taking into account the new requirements. In this chapter, the authors present their P2P heterogeneous and distributed data integration system. It is a super-peer system, where peers are regrouped by type of data (relational, image, text, etc.) around a super-peer which contains a domain ontology. Peers data sources are exported in a common format in the form of a semantically rich ontology. Schemas reconciliation is done by matching domain and local ontologies by the use of a similarity function whose contribution is based on the direct and indirect semantic neighborhood. Queries are described using ontologies, then routed towards relevant peers thanks to a semantic topology built on top of the existing physical one.

INTRODUCTION

Exponential development of information exchange through Web has increased the difficulties to find relevant information which is represented and stored in a multitude of heterogeneous data sources. Several solutions were proposed and are rather old. We have seen the emergence of data warehouses, mediators and P2P systems.

DOI: 10.4018/978-1-5225-5384-7.ch012

The data warehouse approach consists in carrying out integration by building real databases gathering relevant information of considered applications. The user will work directly on the data stored in the warehouse.

The mediator approach is a method where the data is accessible only from the information sources, the user in this case will work on abstract views built with the aim of describing the various data sources. Searching information from such sources requires the construction of execution plans to obtain the whole results from information sources.

The Peer-to-peer (P2P) solution is a recent approach; it can be seen like a generalization of mediators/ data warehouses architectures. These integration systems follow a decentralized approach for integration of autonomous and distributed peers containing data which can be shared. The principal objective of such systems is to provide a semantic interoperability between several sources with the absence of global schema (Ougouti, Belbachir, Amghar, Benharkat, 2010).

With the advent of semantic Web, new possibilities are offered and many traditional approaches are revisited giving by these interesting results. We can say today that semantic Web and P2P systems have opened up several research possibilities in data integration field that includes a variety of knowledge-based techniques, like semantic data modeling, ontology definition, query translation, query optimization, and terminology mapping. The main objective of semantic Web is to add semantics to Web data sources and allow data from diverse sources (possibly stored using different schemas) to be accessed seamlessly. This is possible by the use of multiple tools such as Ontologies which provide a vocabulary that describes a domain of interest and a specification of the meaning of terms used in the vocabulary (Euzenat & Shvaiko, 2016).

We have noted that the majority of integration systems treat a maximum one data model or two at the same time and do not allow complex and multimodal queries whose results can be various types of data like texts, videos and images. The goal of authors is to propose solutions to these problems by presenting in this article, the new version of their data integration system in a P2P environment called MedPeer. In the first version of this work (Ougouti, Belbachir, Amghar, Benharkat, 2011), they presented a very basic architecture that does not reflect the actual one. There is a great difference between the content of the peer and super-peer of the two versions. They will give more details on new functionalities, present mediation process that relies on a new similarity function, Query description with an ontology, semantic topology construction and semantic routing solution.

This paper is organized as follows:

In the next section, the authors present a state of the art of the most representative approaches of integrating data in a P2P environment. The new version of MedPeer Architecture is introduced by presenting in detail the peer and Super-Peer structure and their different functionalities. Then, the source description module which is an important component of a peer is taken up. The authors describe the solution proposed for calculating similarity between domain ontology concepts and local ontologies ones in the main function of the matching manager module. Subsequently, they explain how the semantic topology is built and present modules related to the query management: query description with an ontology, Relevant Peers search module and Query reformulation module. The main results of experiments for evaluating the similarity function and query semantic routing are explained. Finally, the authors complete this chapter by future research directions and conclusion sections.

STATE OF THE ART

The vertiginous growth of Web information sources leads to revise the way of building information retrieval systems. A new idea consists on using P2P architecture that allows a very great number of connected sources and network dynamicity. Many P2P systems maintain as their principal objective to provide a semantic interoperability between several sources in the absence of a global schema. In what follows, the authors present the most important research on the topic.

Edutella (Nejdl et al., 2002) provides an access to distributed collections of numerical resources described by metadata and RDF through a P2P network. The common data model is described thanks to Datalog in the form of Java classes and the queries transmitted between peers are represented by RDF. PEPSINT (Cruz, Xiao, Hsu, 2004) permits semantically integrating heterogeneous XML and RDF data sources in a P2P infrastructure, by using hybrid P2P architecture and Global-as-View mediation approach. It uses a global RDF ontology located on the super-peer node. Hyperion (Arenas, et al., 2003) is a peer data management system for relational databases without a global schema. Information exchange among peers is possible through the definition of correspondences tables and correspondences expressions that store semantic similarities between peers' schemas elements. A query manager uses tables and correspondences expressions to rewrite a query expressed on source peer schema to a target one. However, the correspondence tables are created manually by specialists. PeerDB (Ng, Ooi, Tan, Zhou, 2003) is a P2P distributed data sharing system for distributed relational databases. It combines multi-agent systems properties with those of P2P systems. Each peer provides a relational database described by metadata (keywords). To find the relevant peer for its query, a peer distributes it to all its neighbors. Each node receiving the query compares the set of keywords describing query relations with those describing the relations it holds. The relevant relations will then be sent to peer initiator that will rewrite the query and send it to the relevant peers. Query reformulation is made by agents. There is no conventional mappings discovery process between peers' schemas. Piazza (Halevy, et al., 2004) offers a language for mediation between data sources on the Semantic Web, and maps both the domain structure and document structure. Piazza also enables interoperation of XML data with RDF data that is accompanied by rich OWL ontologies. Mappings in Piazza are provided at a local scale between small sets of nodes, and query answering algorithm is able to chain sets mappings together to obtain relevant data from across the Piazza network. SEWASIE (Bergamashi et al., 2003) is the only system that allows all the exchange of structured, semi-structured and unstructured data but without giving too many details. It offers a globally integrated ontology to represent everything. SenPeer (Faye, 2007) is a P2P system for data sharing. It has a super-peer architecture, where peers are regrouped by semantic fields. The difference with our method is that we use OWL2 ontologies and we consider both structured and unstructured data regrouped by their data type. Cerqueus, Cazalens, Lamarre (2012) propose two independent and complementary solutions for the problem of semantic heterogeneity: the GoOD-TA protocol aims at reducing heterogeneity through ontology-driven topology adaptation and DiQuESh, a top-k algorithm for distributed information retrieval that is intended to ensure interoperability. Results obtained show that GoOD-TA nicely reduces the semantic heterogeneity related to the system topology, handle the evolution of peers' descriptors, and are suitable for dynamic systems.

Compared with other works presented above, MedPeer is designed to deal with complex queries that have texts, images and videos as results. Such queries are frequently used especially in the medical field. For example, one may want to answer to this type of query: "Find all medical reports, audio recordings, videos of open-heart surgeries of patients whose age is above 60 years." Moreover, MedPeer is a completely ontology-based homogeneous system which is built on top of the real heterogeneous sources. Homogeneity is provided by semantic mediation assured by the proposed similarity function which is applicable on all ontologies defined within the system.

MEDPEER ARCHITECTURE

MedPeer Topology

This section presents the new architecture version of MedPeer system. New modules and new features have been introduced into latest peer and super-peer structures (Ougouti et al., 2011).

MedPeer has a super-peer architecture based on regrouping of peers according to data type (Texts, Images, Relational Databases, Semi-structured Databases). It consists of three levels as follows:

1. Super-peers level, where each Super-Peer manages the peers containing the same data type it is meant to represent. It contains a domain ontology specific to the field it manages;
2. Peers level, where each peer contains one or more local ontologies which describe local sources; and
3. Data sources level, where each data source can belong to a different model.

Peer Structure

Each peer has the following components as also depicted shown in Figure 2.

Figure 1. MedPeer Architecture

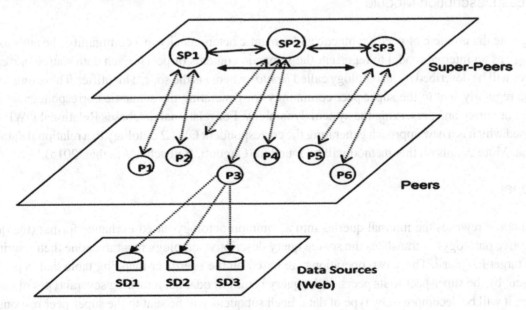

Figure 2. Peer Structure
Data Source (DS)

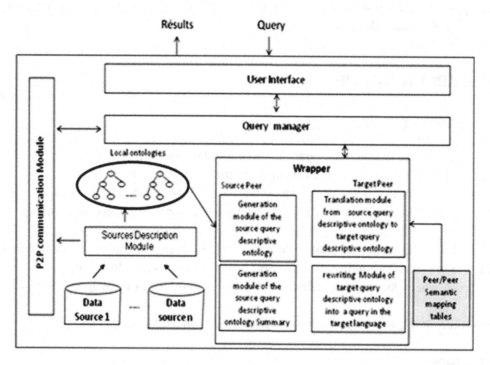

Each peer is independent from the others; it contains one or more data sources which can be relational databases, XML documents or an image database. The peer contains its own indexing and research system by using a suitable interrogation language (SQL, XQuery, visual, etc).

Sources Description Module

To regulate the problem of peer's syntactic and semantic heterogeneity in a community, the authors use ontology as an internal model to represent the semantic contents of peers. Each data source present in the peer will be described by an ontology called *lsonto $_i$*, where i is the source identifier. These ontologies will be regularly sent to the super-peer community for generating the semantic correspondences with domain ontology and preserving the system dynamicity. For relational databases Relational.OWL2E is proposed which is a new approach generating the correspondent OWL2 ontology to a relational database schema. More details on this method will be found in (Ougouti, Belbachir, Amghar, 2015).

Wrapper

This module rewrites the internal queries into a common ontology-based exchange format (the query descriptive ontology). It translates the source query descriptive ontology to a target one then rewrites it in the target language. These two operations are based on the peer/peer mapping table that is periodically sent by the super-peer to its peers. If the query is multimodal i.e. returning several types of data in answer, it will be decomposed by type of data. Each subquery will be sent to the super-peer responsible for treating it.

Query Manager

This module allows the execution of local queries on local peer and the routing of global queries expressed in a common format (Query Descriptive Ontologies) to the super-peer in charge of the community.

User Interface

This module allows the user to formulate a local query on its data, or a global one on the network. The queries may refer just to one type of data and thus carried out within the same community or to many types of data and thus carried out through different communities.

Communication Module

JXTA Open Source platform of Sun is used to enable the communication between peers.

Super-Peer Structure

Each super-peer has the following components as also depicted in Figure 3.

Local Ontologies

Each super-peer stores local ontologies of peer's sources for which it is responsible. It receives regularly and after each update a copy of these ontologies to ensure dynamicity of the system.

Figure 3. Super-Peer Structure

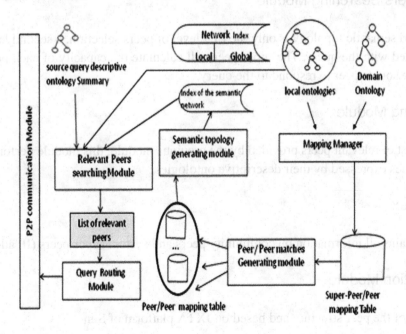

Domain Ontology

Each super-peer stores a domain ontology that will be used as a shared vocabulary for explicit and coherent description of domain knowledge.

Mapping Manager

The purpose of this module is to find all the mappings between data sources' local concepts and those of domain ontology thanks to the similarity function introduced in this work. This function presents the advantage of taking into account linguistic and semantic aspects of concepts and the different characteristics of the semantic area. These matches will then be stored in tables and used for query rewriting and routing.

Peer/Peer Matches Generating Module

The goal of this module is to extract correspondences between pairs of peers and to store them in tables that will be sent to all peers. These tables will help query rewriting and construction of the semantic topology.

Semantic Topology Generating Module

Based on peer/peer mapping tables previously generated, this module performs calculations of semantic affinity between pairs of peers to decide whether or not the semantic link between them will be added to semantic topology. An index of all the semantic links is generated at the end of this step.

Relevant Peers Searching Module

The constructed semantic topology is only the first level of peers selection, a second level of screening is strongly linked with the query. The super-peer will calculate the capacity of each peer semantically related with the source peer to respond to the query.

Query Routing Module

Based on the list of relevant peers provided by the previous module, this module performs the effective routing of queries expressed by their descriptive ontologies.

Network Index

The index contains all information on community peers and system super-peers (IP address, speed..).

Communication Module

Similar to that of the peer structure and based on JXTA platform of Sun.

Community Creation and Peer Adhesion

When a new super-peer *SPj* joins the system, it must present its Domain ontology. It announces its arrival to peers and waits until those among them that are interested propose their adhesion. This Asp_j advertisement is in the form of an XML document, containing the following information: $Aspj = (IDSP_j, URIOsj, TDj, \epsilon_{acc}, TTL)$, in which *IDSPj* is the identifier of the super-peer *SPj* and thus of the community which it represents, *IRIOsj* represents the international resource identifier of the community domain ontology, *TDj* the community data type (BDR, XML, Texts, Images....), ϵ_{acc} the minimum value similarity to accept a mapping between a local concept and a domain ontology one. The *TTL* (time to live) represents a given delay that stops the advertisement from buckling.

When a peer *Pi* is interested in the super-peer advertisement, it formulates an adhesion request *PiAdh* = (*IDP*, *IRIOli*), where *IDP* is the identifier of the peer and *IRIOli* the international resource identifier of its local ontology. For each adhesion, the super-peer index adds this information to its structure. The peer must manifest itself periodically to its super-peer.

Fault Tolerance

In this architecture, the super-peer is the access point for its peers to the network. With this consideration, when the super-peer becomes unavailable or leaves the network, all peers attached to it will be isolated. To increase the robustness, we introduce a self-organization to deal with such situation. Peers and super-peers send messages to each other to show they are still online. Super-peer sends to its peers a list of alternates if it is no longer available. Each peer can then contact one of these super-peers in hope to be indexed. The contacted sponsor can accept or refuse the connection according to current load, which is determined by its computing capacity, storage, but also its bandwidth. If a peer becomes unavailable or suddenly leaves the network, its super-peer removes it from its index. If the peer fails because of an unexpected fault, this is detected by the super-peer when it doesn't get the registration message after the expiry of *TTL* (Time To Live).

SOURCE DESCRIPTION MODULE

Each peer data source will be described by an ontology using our new approach Relational.OWL2E (Ougouti et al., 2015). These ontologies will be regularly sent to the super-peer community, to enable it to generate semantic correspondences with domain ontology. This permits to deal with possible data sources modifications and with system dynamicity. The database content information is obtained from its data dictionary (catalogue), and then the corresponding ontology is generated by translating tables, attributes (columns), datatypes (possibly with length restrictions), primary keys, unique keys and foreign keys into ontology concepts.

MAPPING MANAGER MODULE

Ontology matching is the operation that finds correspondences between semantically related entities of ontologies. Giunchiglia, Yatskevich and Shvaiko (2007) consider semantic matching as a fundamental technique which applies in many areas such as resource discovery, data integration, data migration, query translation, peer to peer networks, agent communication, and schema and ontology merging. Semantic matching is a type of ontology matching technique that relies on semantic information encoded in light-weight ontologies to identify nodes that are semantically related. It operates on graph-like structures and has been proposed as a valid solution to the semantic heterogeneity problem, namely managing the diversity in knowledge.

Relevant Work in This Field

In this field, diverse solutions have been proposed in the last decades and several studies on the state of the art have been presented as in (Shvaiko & Euzenat, 2013; Bernstein, Madhavan, Rahm, 2011; Rahm, 2011). In what follows, the authors will introduce some methods that are based on a global similarity measure which is a weighted sum of several properties.

PROMPT (Noy & Musen, 2001) proposes an alignment module called Anchor-Prompt, which provides the reconciliation of ontologies as follows: First, language matchers determine an initial set of similar concepts, then, from that list, an algorithm analyzes the ways in subgraphs defined by these concepts and determines which classes frequently appear in the same positions on similar paths.

OLA (OWL Lite Alignment) (Euzenat, Loup, Touzani, Valtchev, 2004) uses characteristics of entities to align, like their types: classes, properties, or individuals and their relationships with other entities to measure their similarity. The final measure value is the weighted sum of the partial similarity values for each characteristic.

COMA++ (Aumueller, Do, Massmann, Rahm,, 2005) is an extension of the previous COMA proto-type (Do & Rahm, 2002). It is a customizable and generic tool for matching both schemas and ontologies specified in languages such as SQL, XML Schema or OWL.

AROMA (David, Guillet, Briand, 2006) is divided into three successive main stages: the pre-pro-cessing phase helps prepare ontologies through the acquisition of terms contained in the descriptions and instances of entities by using Natural Language Processing (NLP) tools. The mining Phase consists of the discovery of association rules between entities relying on the following assumption: An entity "A" will be more specific than or equivalent to an entity "B" if the vocabulary (i.e. terms and also data) used to describe "A", its descendants, and its instances tends to be included in that of "B". The last post-processing phase produces consistent and minimal alignments, eliminates inconsistencies and removes redundant relations.

SAMBO (Lambrix & Tan, 2006) is a system for matching and merging OWL biomedical ontologies. It uses various similarity based matchers, including terminological, structural and background knowledge based, using UMLS (Unified Medical Language System) as corpus of knowledge.

ASMOV (Automated Semantic Mapping of Ontologies with Validation) (Jean-Mary & Kabuka, 2007) is an approach that can be summarized in two steps: (i) similarity calculation, and (ii) semantic verification. The implemented algorithm of similarity calculation is automatic; it calculates the final similarity from the weighted sum of four measures: lexical elements, structural relationships, internal structure and extensions (instances of classes and property values).

SenPeer (Faye, 2007) is a P2P Data Management system having various data models (relational, object or XML). It is organized under a super-peer type with a regrouping of peers by semantic fields. The knowledge of a peer is represented through a semantic network called sGraph which can represent schema components of the different data models used. The similarity between two nodes belonging to two different sGraphs is a function of their semantic descriptions with keywords, their types and their semantic relationships with other concepts (only direct neighbourhood).

RiMOM (Li, Tang, Li, Luo, 2009) is a dynamic multi-strategy ontology matching framework. It uses two basic matching methods: linguistic similarity and structural similarity. The strategy selection dynamically regulates the concrete feature selection for linguistic matching, the combination of weights for similarity combination, and the choice of the concrete similarity propagation strategy. Finally, an alignment refinement is done for extracting the final results.

LogMap (Jimenez-Ruiz & Cuenca Grau, 2011) is a highly scalable ontology matching system with 'built-in' reasoning and diagnosis capabilities. The first step after parsing the input ontologies is their lexical indexation. LogMap indexes the labels of the classes in each ontology as well as their lexical variations, and allows enriching these indices by using external sources (e.g., WordNet or UMLS-lexicon). The second step is the structural indexation: LogMap classifies the input ontologies using either incomplete structural heuristics, or an off-the-shelf complete DL reasoner. The core of LogMap is an iterative process that alternates mapping repair and mapping discovery steps until no context is expanded. The output of this process is a set of mappings that is likely to be 'clean', in the sense that it will not lead to unsatisfiable classes when merged with the input ontologies.

Hertuda (Hertling, 2012) is a string based matcher. It generates only homogeneous matchings that are compatible with OWL Lite/DL. For each concept all labels, comments and URI fragments are extracted. Then these terms form a set. To compare two concepts, respectively sets of terms, each element of the first set is compared with each element of the second set. The best value is the similarity measure for these concepts.

S-Match (Giunchiglia, Autayeu, Pane, 2012) is an open source semantic matching framework that provides several semantic matching algorithms and facilities for the development of new ones. It includes components for transforming treelike structures into lightweight ontologies, where each node label in the tree is translated into propositional description logic (DL) formula, which univocally codifies the meaning of the node. S-Match contains the implementation of the basic semantic matching, the minimal semantic matching, and the structure preserving semantic matching (SPSM) algorithms. The basic semantic matching algorithm is a general purpose matching algorithm, very customizable and suitable for many applications. Minimal semantic matching algorithm exploits additional knowledge encoded in the structure of the input and is capable of producing minimal mapping and maximal mapping. SPSM is a type of semantic matching producing a similarity score and a mapping preserving structural properties: (i) one-to-one correspondences between semantically related nodes; (ii) functions are matched to functions and variables to variables.

LYAM++ (Yet Another Matcher - Light) (Tigrine, Bellahsene, Todorov, 2015) is a fully automatic cross-lingual ontology matching system that uses the openly available general-purpose multilingual semantic network BabelNet in order to recreate the missing semantic context in the matching process. The overall processes consist of three main components: a terminological multilingual matcher, a mapping selection module and, finally, a structural matcher.

Finally, for more information, there is an annual evaluation campaign for alignment tools, called The OAEI (The Ontology Alignment Evaluation Initiative) which compares the results obtained by the participating alignment methods on different ontologies. The latest report of this campaign is available in (Cheatham et al, 2015).

Recent ontology alignment works emerged in the development process of service oriented architectures. They attempt to match semantic Web services which use different ontologies by proposing a novel semantic similarity measure like in (Fellah, Malki, Elçi, March 2016), (Fellah, Malki, & Elçi, June 2016), (Çelik & Elçi A., 2008), (Çelik & Elçi A., 2013), (Çelik & Elçi A., 2014).

Similarity Measure

The alignment of local ontologies with domain ontology aims to find the set of semantic correspondences established through similarity measures between concepts. The authors choose to use a method that combines several matching techniques like in (Euzenat et al., 2004; David et al., 2006; Faye, 2007). The global similarity score belongs to the interval [0,1] and is a weighted sum of the partial matching scores; it is thus based on linguistic, structural and semantic techniques.

This choice is justified by the use of ontologies that describe relational database schemas. Attributes and table names have been annotated previously by adding synonyms. These ontologies contain also data types and relationship information between concepts, hence the need to include partial similarities in the global similarity function. Semantic neighborhood similarity used is of order "n", it does not only care for direct neighbours (father/son) of the concept, but indirect ones also. This represents a contribution with regard to other methods. All these partial similarities are weighted according to the importance of each one.

Given two ontologies O_d (domain ontology) and O_l (local ontology), aligning these two ontologies is to find $|O_d| \times |O_l|$ correspondences $<IDij, ci(o_d), cj(o_l), \gamma_{ij}>$ between elements, where ID_{ij} a unique identifier of the correspondence, the concept $ci(o_d) \in O_d$, the concept $cj(o_l) \in O_l$ and γ_{ij} the degree of similarity between the two concepts evaluated in the interval [0,1].

The mediation process between two concepts includes the following steps:

1. Calculate the linguistic similarity of the two concepts, this step comprises itself three sub-phases:
   a. Calculate partial similarity of concepts data types.
   b. Calculate partial similarity of concepts synonyms.
   c. Calculate partial similarity of concepts comments.
   d. The linguistic similarity is the weighted sum of the three partial similarities cited above.
2. Calculate semantic similarity by comparing concepts neighbors.
3. Calculate the global similarity which is a weighted sum of linguistic similarity and semantic similarity.
4. Finally, the semantic affinity between the two concepts is established if the degree of global similarity is greater than a minimum threshold.

The global similarity between two concepts $ci(o_d)$ and $cj(o_l)$ is thus calculated as follows:

$$Sim_g(ci(o_d),cj(o_l)) = \lambda.Sim_l(ci(o_d),cj(o_l)) + (1-\lambda)Sim_v(ci(o_d),cj(o_l)) \quad (1)$$

With Sim_l: concept's linguistic similarity, Sim_v: their semantic neighborhoods similarity and $\lambda \in [0,1]$. Both last measures are based in their calculation on the lexical similarity between two concepts that will be introduced in the next section.

Lexical Similarity

Lexical similarity between two words A and B is based on lexical similarity measure (SL) proposed by (Maedche & Staab, 2002), itself based on the distance of Levenshtein (dl) (Levenshtein, 1966).

$$SL(A,B) = max(0, \frac{min(|A|,|B|) - dl(A,B)}{min(|A|,|B|)})Î[0,1] \tag{2}$$

This function calculates the similarity of terms A and B by taking into account the number of atomic actions (add, delete character) needed to transform one string into another one. It is the ratio between the number of these editing actions and the length of the shorter of the two words. For example, given the two words A="Date-of-birth" and B="Dateofbirth" dl(A,B)=2 and $SL(A,B) = \dfrac{9}{11}$.

Linguistic Similarity

Linguistic similarity of two concepts is a weighted sum of the similarity of their two sets of synonyms Simsyn (ci(od),cj(ol)), the similarity of their data types Simt (ci(od),cj(ol)) and the similarity of their comments Simcom (ci(od),cj(ol))

$$Sim_l\left(ci\left(o_d\right), cj\left(o_l\right)\right) = w.\, Sim_{syn}\left(ci\left(o_d\right), cj\left(o_l\right)\right) + a.Sim_{type}\left(ci\left(o_d\right), cj\left(o_l\right)\right) + \mu.Sim_{com}\left(ci\left(o_d\right), cj\left(o_l\right)\right)$$

with ω, α, μ ≥0 and ω+α + μ =1

Similarity of Types

We consider that data type similarity values are in the range [0,1] and are already known and defined in a table given by The Cupid System (Madhavan, Bernstein, Rahm, 2001).

Similarity of Synonyms

The similarity between two sets of synonyms is based on the measurement proposed by Tversky (1977), who calculates the similarity between two objects by comparing their common and distinctive characteristics: the more they share characteristics, and the less they have distinctive ones, the more they are similar.

This similarity is given by the following formula:

$$Sim_{syn}(c_i\left(o_d\right), c_j\left(o_l\right)) =$$

$$\frac{\left|syn\left(c_i\left(o_d\right)\right) \cap syn\left(cj\left(o_l\right)\right)\right|}{\left|syn\left(c_i\left(o_d\right)\right) \cap syn\left(cj\left(o_l\right)\right)\right| + \alpha\left|syn\left(c_i\left(o_d\right)\right) \setminus syn\left(cj\left(o_l\right)\right)\right| + (1-\alpha)\left|syn\left(cj\left(o_l\right)\right) \setminus syn\left(c_i\left(o_d\right)\right)\right|} \tag{4}$$

with:

syn $(c_{i(Od)})$: The set of domain ontology concept$_i$ synonyms.
syn $(c_{j(Ol)})$: The set of local ontology concept$_j$ synonyms.
$0 \leq \alpha \leq 1$

Similarity of Comments and Labels

The annotation properties bridge the gap between the ontological modeling of a domain and its lexical features. These properties include first rdfs:label which associates to a resource terms to annotate it. These labels, when recovered are added to the set of synonyms. A second interesting property is rdfs:comment which provides a textual description of the resource. To calculate the similarity of the text contained in comments, we use the cosines function which quantifies the similarity between two vectors containing the term weights as the cosines of the angle between them. When the comments are the same, the angle between the vectors is equal to 0 and the cosines is equal to 1 and when the comments are different we should have orthogonal vectors, so their similarity equal to 0.

$$Similarity\,(A, B) = \cos(\theta) = \frac{A.B}{AB} = \frac{\sum_{i=1}^{n} A_i \, x \, B_i}{\sqrt{\sum_{i=1}^{n} A_i^2} \, x \sqrt{\sum_{i=1}^{n} B_i^2}} \tag{5}$$

Since weight can't be negative, then there will be $0 \leq$ similarity $(A, B) \leq 1$.

Semantic Neighborhood Similarity

Considering context in calculating the semantic similarity is very important because two concepts related to similar entities have a high probability to be similar, too.

We consider the semantic neighborhood of a concept I noted V(ci) as the set of concepts that have either a direct or indirect semantic link with the concept.

We consider also that G is the graph corresponding to the ontology O, G = {N, R} where N is the set of nodes (concepts) of this graph and R the set of arcs (semantic links) between these concepts. We introduce the following concepts:

- **Node (Ci):** The node corresponding to concept (Ci).
- **Father (n):** The father node of n
- **Son (n):** The son node of n

Let n1 = node (c1), n2 = node (c2) and r = the link between n_1 and n_2, and let us introduce the following operations:

- **Coming-To:** $N_2 \in$ coming-to $(n_1; r)$ iff $n_2 =$ Father (n_1) and $l\,[(n_2, n_1)] = r$
- **Outgoing-From:** $N_2 \in$ outgoing-from $(n_1; r)$ iff $n_2 =$ son (n_1) and $l\,[(n_1, n_2)] = r$

We define the order 1 neighbourhood (direct links) of node n_i as follows:

$V1 (n_i) = \{nj \,/\, nj \in$ Coming-to $(n_i; r1)$ or $n_j \in$ Outgoing-from $(n_i; r2)\}$

In our work we consider the indirect neighborhood of order n, defined as:

$V (n_i) = V1 (n_i) \cup V2 (n_i) \cup V3 (n_i) \cup ... .. \cup Vn (n_i)$

$V_k(ni)$ contains direct neighbours of all concepts present in $V_{k-1} (ni)$

$$\forall ci \in V_{k-1}\left(ni\right) / \; V_k\left(ni\right) = \cup V1\left(Ci\right)$$

This neighbourhood can be seen as a set of concepts which are in a radius n of the concept ni in the graph. This radius depends on size of the graph ontologies and will be defined by experimentation. For a fairly large radius, neighbourhoods can differ significantly and the neighbourhood's similarity will be low; in contrast, a small radius increases the probability of having a neighbourhood containing more common elements.

The semantic neighbourhood similarity is based on linguistic similarity of the two nodes to be compared; it is given by the following formula:

$$Sim_v\left(c_i\left(o_d\right), c_j\left(o_l\right)\right) = \frac{\left|\; \{x \in V\left(c_i\left(o_d\right)\right) / \; \exists y \in V\left(c_j\left(o_l\right)\right) \wedge Sim_l\left(x, y\right) > \varepsilon_{acc} \;\}\;\right|}{\left|V\left(c_i\left(o_d\right)\right) \cup V\left(c_j\left(o_l\right)\right)\right|} \tag{6}$$

Example

Let us consider the alignment of the BDmed1 local ontology (Figure 4) with the domain Ontology (only concepts needed for the example in Figure 5).

We will unroll our similarity algorithm on the correspondence found between

«Social-sec-num » of domain ontology and "NSS" of local ontology. We assume for this example that the comments were not informed, all the weights fixed to 0,5 and the ε_{acc} similarity threshold is fixed to 0,6.

The global similarity is given by the following formula:

Sim_g(Social-sec-num, NSS)= 0,5xSim_l(Social-sec-num, NSS)+ 0,5xSim_v(Social-sec-num, NSS)

Linguistic similarity is given by the following formula:

Sim_l(Social-sec-num, NSS)= 0.5xSim_{syn}(Social-sec-num, NSS)+0.5xSim_t(Social-sec-num, NSS).

"Social-sec-num" and "NSS" are both string data type so the Similarity of data type is:

Figure 4. BDmed1 local ontology

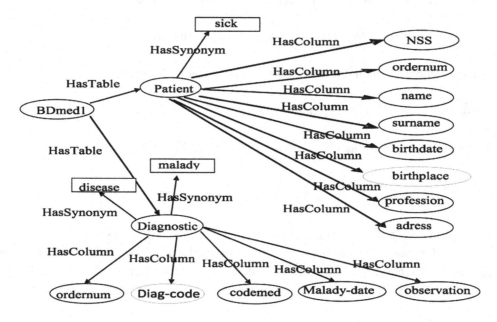

Figure 5. An extract of the Domain Ontology

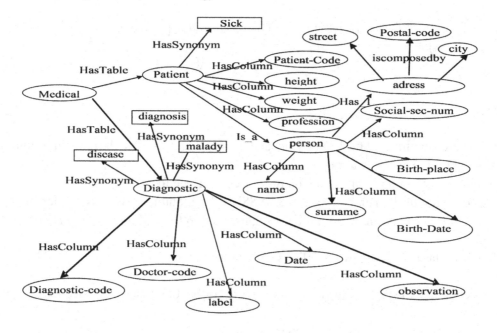

Sim_t (Social-sec-num, NSS) =1.

The set of "Social-sec-num" synonyms is: {NSS, soc-sec-num }
The set of "NSS" synonyms is: {Numss, social-sec-num, NSS }

Synonyms "soc-sec-num" and "social-sec-num" are considered lexically identical as their lexical similarity Siml = 0.63 is greater than the threshold (0.6).

$$Sim_{syn}\left(Social - sec - num, NSS\right) =$$

$$\frac{\left|\{NSS, \; soc - sec - num\}\right|}{\left|\{NSS, \; soc - sec - num\}\right| + 0,5\left|\{ \; \}\right| + 0,5\left|\{Numss\}\right|} = \frac{2}{2,5} = 0,8$$

Thus:

Sim_l(Social-sec-num, NSS)= 0.5× 0.8 + 0.5 × 1= 0,9

The neighborhood similarity Sim_v (Social-sec-num, NSS) is given by the following formula:

$$Sim_v\left(Social - sec - num, NSS\right) = \frac{\left|\{x \in V\left(Social - sec - num\right) / \exists y \in V\left(NSS\right) \wedge Sim_l\left(x, y\right) > \varepsilon_{acc} \; \}\right|}{\left|V\left(Social - sec - num\right) \cup V\left(NSS\right)\right|}$$

We must define now V (Social-sec-num) and V (NSS).
"Social-sec-num" neighborhood:

V1 (Social-sec-num) = {person}

V2 (Social-sec-num) = V1 (person) = {patient, adress, Birth-place, Birth-Date, surname, name}

V3 (Social-sec-num) = V1 (adress) ∪ V1 (patient) = {street, postal-code, city} ∪ {sick, patient-code, height, weight, profession} = {street, postal-code, city, sick, patient-code, height, weight, profession}

Thus:

V (Social-sec-num) = V1 (Social-sec-num) ∪ V2 (Social-sec-num) ∪ V3 (Social-sec-num)

V (Social-sec-num) = {person, patient, adress, Birth-place, Birth-Date, surname, name, street, postal-code, city, sick, patient-code, height, weight, profession}

"NSS" neighborhood:

V1 (NSS) = {patient}

V2 (NSS) = V1 (patient) = {sick, order-num, name, surname, Birthdate, Birthplace, profession, adress}

V (NSS) = V1 (NSS) ∪ V2 (NSS) = {patient, sick, order-num, name, surname, Birthdate, Birthplace, profession, address}

Linguistic similarity between the following concepts has been established:

Patient → Patient
Sick → Patient
Sick → Sick
Order-name → patient-code
name → name
surname → surname
Birthdate → Birth-date
Birthplace → Birth-place
Profession → Profession
Address → Adress
Thus we have 10 matches.

Sim_v (Social-sec-num, NSS) = 10/24 = 0,41

The global similarity will be equal to

Sim_g (Social-sec-num, NSS) = 0.5x0.9+ 0.5x 0,41 = 0.65 > ε_{acc} =0.6

The similarity is then established between the two concepts «Social-sec-num» and «NSS». Let us consider now only the neighborhood of order 1 (Direct links), then:

V (NSS) = {patient}

V (Social-sec-num) = {person}

Sim_l (person, patient) = 0.5 ×1= 0.5 < ε_{acc},

thus there is no match between person and patient.

Sim_v (Social-sec-num, NSS) = 0

We have already found that:

Sim_l (Social-sec-num, NSS) = 0,9

Thus:

Sim_g (Social-sec-num, NSS) = 0.5 x 0.9+ 0.5 x 0= 0.45 < ε_{acc} =0.6

The authors note here that if they had considered only direct links, neighbourhood similarity would have been 0 because "patient" and "person" are not similar and the global similarity would have been 0.45, therefore the correspondence between "NSS" and "social-sec-num" would not have been established.

This last section shows the importance of considering indirect links that explore multiple depth levels of the neighborhood in calculation of neighborhood similarity. This is the principal contribution of The MedPeer system comparing to other methods like SenPeer System (Faye, 2007) which stops the neighborhood to direct links only.

SEMANTIC TOPOLOGY

Nowadays, it has been clearly demonstrated that the inundation principle in query routing in P2P systems slows down the scale passage. It is thus imperative, to proceed through a semantic and intelligent routing.

Semantic topology in MedPeer is built on top of the physical network, to allow routing queries towards the relevant peers only. It is built by the super-peer on the basis of semantic mappings already established. If P is the set of peers related to the same super-peer, semantic topology is expressed through a graph Γ = (P, A) with P a set of nodes and A $\in$ (P) x (P) a set of arcs such that for every arc (P1, P2) $\in$ A, a matching function has established their semantic similarity. This last function has as input the mapping table between the two pairs derived from the SP/P mapping table. Its role is to measure the affinity degree between peers that will be greater than a certain threshold to validate this correspondence. This function is given by the following formula:

$$Sim_{P_i/P_j} = \frac{|\{x \in c(o_{li}) \, / \, \exists y \in c(o_{lj}) \wedge sim_g(x,y) > \varepsilon_{acc}\}|}{Min(|c(o_{li})|, |c(o_{lj})|)} \qquad (6)$$

with:

O_{li}, O_{lj}: P_i and P_j Local Ontologies.
$C(O_{Li})$, $C(O_{Lj})$: The sets of concepts of the two local ontologies of P_i and P_j.

QUERY MANAGEMENT

Query Description Module

Query is first expressed by a source peer on its schema to be treated locally. If the results are not sufficient or the user wishes to obtain more, this query is then dedicated to be performed on the rest of the network. It will be then reformulated into an exchange format on the form of an ontology named the query descriptive ontology. This latter will be sent to the super-peer that will calculate the capacity of each semantic neighbors to support this query. Then, the source query descriptive ontology is sent to peers able to run it and is translated to target query descriptive ontology.

The SQL query is seen as a tree that consists of two sub-trees: The condition sub-tree (WHERE clause) and Result sub-tree (SELECT clause).

To represent this information in the ontology, we have defined 6 classes and 6 relationships (properties) between them; they are summarized in the following two tables:

Example

We illustrate this algorithm by an example. Suppose we have 'BDmed1' Database located in Peer P1 that defines two relations:

BDmed1
Patient (ordernum, name, surname, birthdate, birthplace, profession, address, NSS)
Diagnostic (ordernum, diag_code, codemed, malady_date, observation)

Suppose the user at peer P1 issues the following query to search information about patients that have a visit on "21/09/2014":

Select ordernum, birthplace, NSS
From patient, Diagnostic

Table 1. Classes in the query descriptive ontology

Classes	Observations
Root	Class representing the root of the query
Attribute	Class of the attributes present in the query
Relational-Operator	Class of relational operators
Logical-operator	Class of logic operators
Function	Class of functions
Subquery	Class of subqueries

Table 2. Properties in the query descriptive ontology

Propriétés	rdfs:domain	rdfs:range	Observations
Return	Root Subquery	Attribute	A query or subquery returns an attribute as result
Hasconstraint-Where	Root	Relational-Operator	Specify the content of the Where clause.
Hasconstraint-log	Subquery	logical-Operator	Specify the content of a constraint.
hasoperand	Rel. Operator	Attribute Subquery	Specify the operands (classes) of a relational operator .
Hasoperand1	Rel. Operator	Data type	Specify the operands (class and datatype) of a relational operator .
Constraint-line	logical-Operator	Relational-Operator	Specify the content of logical operator constraint.

Where patient.ordernum=Diagnostic.ordernum
And Diagnostic.malady_date='21/09/2014'

The descriptive ontology for this query has the following tree structure as depicted in Figure 6.

RELEVANT PEERS SEARCH MODULE

As already mentioned above, when the super-peer receives the source query ontology, it will evaluate the semantic neighbor's ability to execute it. To perform and facilitate this, source query descriptive ontology will be summarized into another minimal ontology called Ores(Q) written on the same model as local ontologies, it will contain only the attributes and tables present in the query. This permits us to have two ontologies on the same model in order to execute the mapping algorithm for evaluating the capacity of the target peer to execute the query.

Once Ores (Q) generated, the capacity of each semantic neighbor peer to support the query will be calculated as follows:

$$Cap\left(P_i, Q\right) = \frac{\mid \{x \in C\left(OL_i\right) / \exists y \in C(O\,\mathrm{Re}\,s\left(Q\right) \wedge Sim_g\left(x,y\right) > \varepsilon_{acc} \mid}{\left| C\left(O\,\mathrm{Re}\,s\left(Q\right)\right)\right|} \in [0,1] \quad (7)$$

with:

OL_i: The Target Peer P_i local Ontology
ORes (Q): Source query descriptive ontology summary ORes (Q)

Figure 6. The tree structure for query descriptive ontology

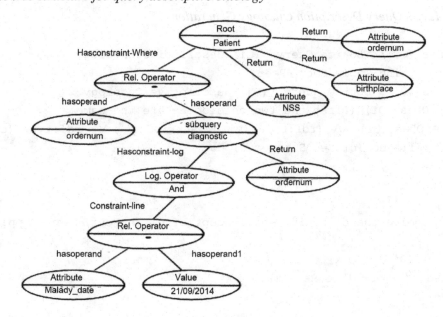

259

Algorithm 1. Source query descriptive ontology summary generation

```
Input   :  Local Ontology Ol_i, Source query descriptive ontology ODes (Qi)
Output:   Source query descriptive ontology summary ORes (Qi)
For all  c_i ∈ ODes (Qi) do
        If rdf:type (ci) = "Root" or rdf:type (ci) = "Subquery" then
                x ←Findclassdef (ci,Ol_i)
                Add (x, Ores (Q_i))
                For all pj ∈ HasColumnProperty (Ci) do
                        y← Range (Pj)
                        z← Findclassdef (y,Ol_i)
                        Add (z, Ores (Qi))
                Endfor
Endif
Endfor
```

C (OL_i), C (ORes (Q)): The two concept sets of the above ontologies.
|C (ORes (Q)) |: Number of concepts of ORes (Q)

QUERY REFORMULATION MODULE

The query reformulation consists of rewriting a source peer query on an equivalent target peer query. In MedPeer system, it consists of translating the source query description ontology into equivalent target query description ontology by replacing the source ontology entities by their associated semantic equivalents target entities.

Algorithm 2: Target Query Description Ontology Generation

```
Input:    ODes (Qi): Source Query (Qi) descriptive Ontology
  TabPi-Pj: Mapping Table Peer_i/Peer_j
Output:  ODes (Qj): Source query (Qj) descriptive Ontology
ODes (Qj) ← ODes (Oi) (First the two ontologies are the same)
For all c_i ∈ ODes (Qi)  ∧ (rdf:type (ci)= 'Attribute'  ∨  rdf:type (ci) =
'Root'  ∨  rdf:type (ci) = 'Subquery') do
Find (TabPi-Pj, ci, cj)
If Exists then
x ← cj
// (x will receive the cj equivalent concept of ci in Peer_i/Peer_j mapping ta-
ble)
Replace (ODes (Oj), ci, x)
        Else  " Impossible Reformulation "
        End if
EndFor
```

The wrapper of the target peer will after this step, convert this query descriptive ontology to a real query in the target language.

We illustrate this process by an example. Suppose we have two peers that share medical data: peer P1 defines 'Bdmed1' database and peer P2 defines 'BDmed2' database.

BDmed1:

Patient (ordernum, name, surname, birthdate, birthplace, profession, address, NSS)
Diagnostic (ordernum, diag_code, codemed, malady_date, observation)

BDmed2:

Sick-person (code, patient-name, patient-surname, birthdate, birth-city, N_street, street, postal-code, city, NSS)
Medical-File (code, id_file, creation-date)
Malady (code, id_file, diag-code, diag-date, observation)
Let us consider this query on Database Bdmed1 on Peer P1:
Select ordernum, birthplace, NSS
From patient, Diagnostic
Where patient.ordernum = Diagnostic.ordernum
And Diagnostic.malady_date = '21/09/2014'
The mapping table Peer$_1$/Peer$_2$ gives the following matches:
Ordernum → code, birthplace → birth-city, NSS → NSS, patient → sick-person, Diagnostic → Malady, Malady-dat → diag-date.

This last query will be reformulated on BDmed2 as follows:

Select code, birth-city, NSS
From sick-person, Malady
Where sick-person.code = Malady.code
And Malady.diag-date = '21/09/2014'

And here some extracts of the target query descriptive ontology

```
<?xml version="1.0"?>
<!DOCTYPE rdf:RDF
[
<!ENTITY owl "http://www.w3.org/2002/07/owl#" > <!ENTITY xsd "http://www.
w3.org/2001/XMLSchema#" >
<!ENTITY rdfs "http://www.w3.org/2000/01/rdf-schema#" >
<!ENTITY rdf "http://www.w3.org/1999/02/22-rdf-syntax-ns#" >
 <!ENTITY reqsql "http://www.semanticweb.org/k/ontologies/2014/9/targetqsql#">
]>
<rdf:RDF
        ........
```

```
<owl:NamedIndividual rdf:about="&targetqsql;sick-person">
        <rdf:type rdf:resource="&targetqsql;root"/>
        <reqsql:hasconstraint-where rdf:resource="&targetqsql;egal_1"/>
        <reqsql:return rdf:resource="&targetqsql;sick-person.NSS"/>
        <reqsql:return rdf:resource="&targetqsql;sick-person.birth-city"/>
        <reqsql:return rdf:resource="&targetqsql;sick-person.code"/>
</owl:NamedIndividual>
<owl:NamedIndividual rdf:about="&targetqsql;Malady.diag-date">
        <rdf:type rdf:resource="&reqsql;attribute"/>
</owl:NamedIndividual>
<owl:NamedIndividual rdf:about="&targetqsql;Malady.code">
         <rdf:type rdf:resource="&reqsql;attribute"/>
</owl:NamedIndividual>
 …..
<owl:NamedIndividual rdf:about="&targetqsql;sick-person.NSS">
        <rdf:type rdf:resource="&targetqsql;attribute"/>
</owl:NamedIndividual>
<owl:NamedIndividual rdf:about="&targetqsql;sick-person.birth-city">
        <rdf:type rdf:resource="&targetqsql;attribute"/>
</owl:NamedIndividual>
<owl:NamedIndividual rdf:about="&targetqsql;sick-person.code">
        <rdf:type rdf:resource="&targetqsql;attribute"/>
 </owl:NamedIndividual>
……..
</rdf:RDF>
```

RESULTS OF THE EXPERIMENTS AND DISCUSSION

In this section, the authors introduce the results obtained after testing the similarity function they proposed then they present the simulation results of query semantic routing.

Similarity Function Evaluation

To evaluate and measure the quality of the similarity function, the authors use metrics of precision, recall, f-measure and overall that are used in information retrieval. For this purpose, the following definitions must be presented:

- The number of correspondences found by the system and believed to be correct by an expert (True Positives: TP).
- The number of correspondences found by the system and believed to be incorrect by the expert (False Positive: FP).
- The number of correspondences not found by the system and believed to be correct by the expert (False Negative: FN).

$$Precision = \frac{|Relevant \cap Retrieved|}{|Retreived|} = \frac{|TP|}{|TP + FP|} \qquad (8)$$

$$Recall = \frac{|Relevant \cap Retrieved|}{|Relevant|} = \frac{|TP|}{|TP + FN|} \qquad (9)$$

$$F - measure = \frac{2 \times Recall \times Precision}{Precision + Recall} \qquad (10)$$

$$Overall = Recall * \left(2 - \frac{1}{Precision}\right) \qquad (11)$$

All values of the metrics cited above obtained from several executions are listed in Table 3.

Compared to other methods, the MedPeer approach behaves well as it is seen in Figure 7 and Figure 8.

We notice a slight inferiority of MedPeer method recall compared to other approaches. We know that recall is a metric that indicates the fraction of relevant matches that have been found, it is directly influenced by the number of extracted False Negative results. However, the authors noticed that the majority of False Negative responses are justified by a low score in the similarity of synonyms, this is due to a different annotation of the same concept by different persons and to the threshold value (0.6), several matches could be established if the similarity threshold was for example set to 0.55.

Evaluation of Query Semantic Routing

The authors presented in last section, the query semantic routing algorithm which aims to direct queries directly to relevant peers. In what follows, they will try to show interest to reduce the number of peers to be queried in large-scale systems. For this task and like several other systems, they chose to use simulation of discrete events to test and evaluate the performance of their system. Several discrete event simulators exist; they chose to use SimJava (Howell & McNab, 1998) which consists of a set of tools allowing simulation of static networks of active entities that communicate by sending objects through ports.

Table 3. Results of the metrics obtained on the alignment of ontologies

Metric	Value
Precision	0.97
Recall	0.81
F-measure	0.87
Overall	0.78

Figure 7. Comparison of MedPeer with other systems

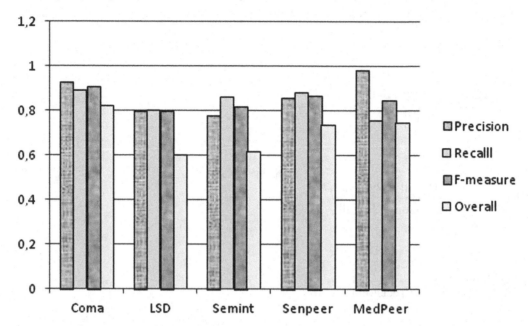

Figure 8. Comparison between MedPeer and other systems by metric

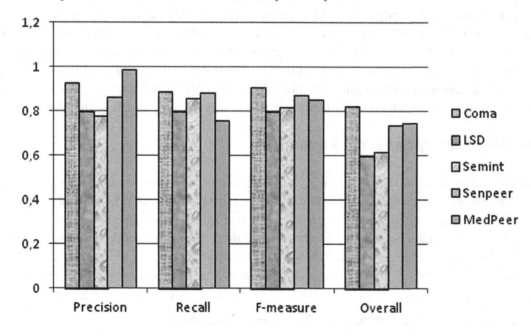

The authors conducted the simulation for the three cases as given below. Figures 9 and 10 illustrate the results achieved in terms of number of exchanged messages and response time.

- **Configuration 1 (CONF1):** The query generated by a peer is sent to all peers of its community without distinction.

Figure 9. Number of messages for the tree configurations

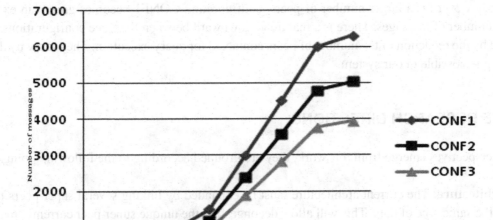

Figure 10. Response time for the tree configurations

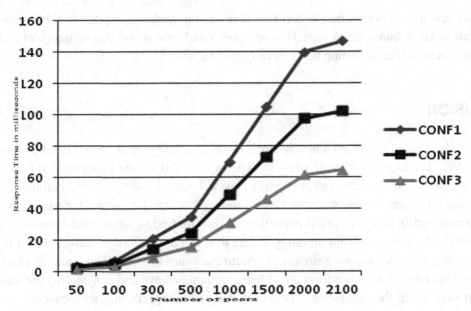

- **Configuration 2 (CONF2):** The query is only sent to a peer's originator of the query neighbors in the underlying semantic topology.
- **Configuration 3 (CONF3):** The query is only sent to the subset of peers able to treat it.

For these three configurations, they calculated the average number of messages and response times obtained from several executions.

These figures show that for a number of peers less than 500, number of messages and response times are close; however for a larger number of peers, configuration CONF1 becomes greedy in execution time and number of messages. There is a real trend downward between the three configurations; this is explained by the reduction of the number of peers contacted for query execution. They show by this that the scaling is possible in our system.

FUTURE RESEARCH DIRECTIONS

Several perspectives emerge from this work; they are grouped according to the following points:

- **Architecture:** The current architecture must be expanded by linking several super-peers managing the same type of data. This will allow decongesting the unique super-peer currently managing all peers having the same data model and will improve the fault tolerance of the system.
- **Similarity Measure:** Weights used in the similarity measure have been defined by experimentation. It would be better to conduct a more detailed study based on a scientific approach to determine these weights and then show the impact of these parameters on the performance of the proposed method by conducting several experiments. This measure has been tested on small ontologies, more tests need to be done on larger ontologies to consolidate the obtained results.

As future research opportunities within this domain, the authors propose to think about how to integrate unstructured data sources such as images, texts and videos into this architecture and allow to formulate complex queries returning these three types of answers.

CONCLUSION

In this paper, the authors presented a new heterogeneous data integration system in a P2P environment called MedPeer. The idea of grouping peers by type of data and managing structured data as well as unstructured one in a unique P2P system is rather new and has not been proposed before.

To overcome the semantic and syntactic heterogeneity, schemas are exported in a common ontology format. The authors also presented in this paper their method for finding similarities between data sources local concepts and those of domain ontology thanks to a global similarity measure which is based on several characteristics. The ontology alignment system combines linguistic and semantic characteristics of concepts. This method has the advantage of being comprehensive and considering the maximum of information encoded in the ontologies. The tool developed allows dealing with concepts contexts by calculating similarity between the two sets of their neighbors. The neighbourhood used is not limited to direct links of concepts but goes further by exploiting indirect ones.

The generated mapping tables permit to build a semantic topology on top of the physical one. This permits super-peers to root queries only to relevant peers avoiding by this to overload the network by flooding which represents a serious obstacle to scalability. Another contribution consists of describing queries with ontologies, this facilitates the query reformulation. The authors believe they are the first to have proposed this solution.

The architecture presented in this paper can be extended for multimedia data sources. For future work, the authors hope to continue by proposing a solution for managing image, text and video data.

REFERENCES

Arenas, M., Kantere, V., Kementsietsidis, A., Kiringa, I., Miller, R. J., & Mylopoulos, J. (2003). The Hyperion Project: From Data Integration to Data Coordination. *SIGMOD Record, 32*(3), 38–53. doi:10.1145/945721.945733

Aumueller, D., Do, H., Massmann, S., & Rahm, E. (2005). Schema and Ontology Matching with COMA++. *Proc. SIGMOD Conf.*, 906–908.

Bernstein, P. A., Madhavan, J., & Rahm, E. (2011). Generic schema matching, ten years later. PVLDB, 4(11), 695-701.

Çelik, D., & Elçi, A. (2008). Ontology-based QoS Model for Appropriate Selection and Composition of Web Services. *International Review on Computers and Software, Praise Worthy Prize S.r.l., 3*(2), 176-184. Retrieved from http://www.praiseworthyprize.com/IRECOS-latest/IRECOS_vol_3_n_2.html#Ontology-based

Çelik, D., & Elçi, A. (2013). A broker-based semantic agent for discovering Semantic Web services through process similarity matching and equivalence considering quality of service. *Science China Information Sciences, 56*(1), 1–24. Retrieved from http://link.springer.com/article/10.1007/s11432-012-4697-1

Çelik, D., & Elçi, A. (2014). Semantic composition of business processes using Armstrong's Axioms. *The Knowledge Engineering Review, 29*(2), 248–264. Retrieved from http://journals.cambridge.org/repo_A92IA4Dd

Cerqueus, T., Cazalens, S., & Lamarre, C. (2012). An Approach to Manage Semantic Heterogeneity in Unstructured *P2P Information Retrieval Systems. IEEE International Conference on Peer-to-Peer Computing*, Tarragona, Spain.

Cheatham, M., Dragisic, Z., Euzenat, J., Faria, D., Ferrara, A., Flouris, G., ... Zamazal, O. (2015). Results of the Ontology Alignment Evaluation Initiative 2015. *Proc. 20th ISWC ontology matching workshop (OM)*, 60–115.

Cruz, I., Xiao, H., & Hsu, F. (2004). *Peer-to-Peer Semantic Integration of XML and RDF Data Sources. Internal report*. Department of Computer Science, University of Illinois at Chicago.

David, J., Guillet, F., & Briand, H. (2006). Matching directories and OWL ontologies with AROMA. *Proceedings of the 15th ACM international conference on Information and knowledge management*, 830– 831. 10.1145/1183614.1183752

Do, H., & Rahm, E. (2002). COMA - a system for flexible combination of schema matching approaches. *28th International Conference on Very Large Data Bases*, 610–621.

Euzenat, J., Loup, D., Touzani, M., & Valtchev, P. (2004). Ontology alignment with OLA. *Proceedings of the 3rd EON Workshop at 3rd International Semantic Web Conference*, 59–68.

Euzenat, J., & Shvaiko, P. (2016). *Ontology matching tutorial (v17)*. The 13th International Conference on Concept Lattices and Their Applications (CLA-2016), Moscow, Russia.

Faye, D. C. (2007). *Médiation de données sémantique dans SenPeer, un système pair-à-pair de gestion de données* (PhD thesis). Nantes University.

Fellah, A., Malki, M., & Elçi, A. (2016). A Similarity Measure across Ontologies for Web Services Discovery. *International Journal of Information Technology and Web Engineering, 11*(1), 22-43. DOI: 10.4018/IJITWE.2016010102

Fellah, A., Malki, M., & Elçi, A. (2016). Web Services Matchmaking Based on a Partial Ontology Alignment. *International Journal of Information Technology and Computer Science (IJITCS), 8*(6), 9-20. Retrieved from http://www.mecs-press.org/ijitcs/ijitcs-v8-n6/IJITCS-V8-N6-2.pdf

Giunchiglia, F., Autayeu, A., & Pane, J. (2012). S-Match: An Open Source Framework for Matching Lightweight Ontologies. Semantic Web Journal, 3(3), 307-317.

Giunchiglia, F., Yatskevich, M., & Shvaiko, P. (2007). Semantic matching: Algorithms and implementation. *Journal on Data Semantics, 9,* 1–38.

Halevy, A., Ives, Z., Madhavan, J., Mork, P., Suciu, D., & Tatarinov, I. (2004). The piazza peer data management system. *IEEE Transactions on Knowledge and Data Engineering, 16*(7), 787–798. doi:10.1109/TKDE.2004.1318562

Hertling, S. (2012). *Hertuda Results for OEAI 2012. Seventh International Workshop on Ontology Matching*, Boston, MA.

Howell, F., & McNab, R. (1998). Simjava: a discrete event simulation library for java. In *First International Conference on Web-based Modelling and Simulation*. San Diego CA: Society for Computer Simulation.

Jean-Mary, Y., & Kabuka, M. R. (2007). *ASMOV: Ontology Alignment with Semantic Validation*. Vienna, Austria: SWDB-ODBIS Workshop.

Jimenez-Ruiz, E., & Cuenca Grau, B. (2011). Logmap: Logic-based and scalable on-ontology matching. The Semantic Web–ISWC 2011, 273–288.

Lambrix, P., & Tan, H. (2006). SAMBO – a system for aligning and merging biomedical ontologies. *Journal of Web Semantics, 4*(1), 196–206. doi:10.1016/j.websem.2006.05.003

Levenshtein, V. (1966). Binary codes capable of correcting deletions, insertions, and reversals. *Soviet Physics, Doklady, 10*(8), 707–710.

Li, J., Tang, J., Li, Y., & Luo, Q. (2009). Rimom: A dynamic multistrategy ontology alignment framework. *IEEE Transactions on Knowledge and Data Engineering, 21*(8), 1218–1232. doi:10.1109/TKDE.2008.202

Madhavan, J., Bernstein, P. A., & Rahm, E. (2001). Generic schema matching with cupid. *VLDB '01: Proceedings of the 27th International Conference on Very Large Data Bases*, 49–58.

Maedche, A., & Staab, S. (2002). Measuring similarity between ontologies. *EKAW '02: Proceedings of the 13th International Conference on Knowledge Engineering and Knowledge Management: Ontologies and the Semantic Web*, 251–263. 10.1007/3-540-45810-7_24

Nejdl, W., Wolf, B., Qu, C., Decker, S., Sintek, M., Naeve, A., . . . Risch, T. (2002). EDUTELLA: A P2P Networking Infrastructure Based on RDF. *Proceedings of the 11th International World Wide Web Conference*.

Ng, W. S., Ooi, B. C., Tan, K., & Zhou, A. (2003). PeerDB: A P2P-based System for Distributed Data Sharing. *Proceedings of the 19th International Conference on Data Engineering (ICDE 2003)*, 633–644.

Noy, N., & Musen, M. (2001). Anchor- PROMPT: Using non-local context for semantic matching. Proceedings workshop on ontology and information sharing. *IJCAI*, 63–70.

Ougouti, N. S., Belbachir, H., & Amghar, Y. (2015). A New OWL2 Based Approach for Relational Database Description. *International Journal of Information Technology and Computer Science*, 7(1), 48–53. doi:10.5815/ijitcs.2015.01.06

Ougouti, N. S., Belbachir, H., Amghar, Y., & Benharkat, N. (2010). Integration of Heterogeneous Data Sources. *Journal of Applied Sciences (Faisalabad)*, 10(22), 2923–2928. doi:10.3923/jas.2010.2923.2928

Ougouti, N. S., Belbachir, H., Amghar, Y., & Benharkat, N. (2011). Architecture Of MedPeer: A New P2P-based System for Integration of Heterogeneous Data Sources. *Proceedings of the International Conference on Knowledge Management and Information Sharing (KMIS)*, 351-354.

Rahm, E. (2011). Towards large-scale schema and ontology matching. In *Schema Matching and Mapping* (pp. 3–27). New York: Springer Heidelberg. doi:10.1007/978-3-642-16518-4_1

Shvaiko, P., & Euzenat, J. (2013). Ontology matching: State of the art and future challenges. *IEEE Transactions on Knowledge and Data Engineering*, 25(1), 158–176. doi:10.1109/TKDE.2011.253

Tigrine, A., Bellahsene, Z., & Todorov, K. (2015). LYAM++ Results for OAEI 2015. *Proc. 20th ISWC ontology matching workshop (OM)*, 176-180.

Tversky, A. (1977). Features of similarity. *Psychological Review*, 84(4), 327–352. doi:10.1037/0033-295X.84.4.327

KEY TERMS AND DEFINITIONS

Data Integration: Is the process that provides a unified view of different data sources in order to share them and give a common response to a posed query.

Heterogeneous Data Sources: Data sources having different ways for representing and storing the same data.

Ontologies: A set of concepts and relations between them representing a domain.

Ontology Alignment: Is the process of determining correspondences between concepts in different ontologies.

Peer-to-Peer (P2P) System: Is a system modeled as a set of interconnected nodes ("peers") that share resources and exchange information without the use of a centralized peer.

Query Management: In data integration domain, the query management is the process that permits writing a query in a common model in order to rewrite it easily in target peer vocabulary and peer local language, then return the results to the source peer.

Semantic Routing: This process consists of routing queries only to relevant peers. The selection of peers is performed using semantics that are extracted from peers' content and their behavior.

Semantic Web: The semantic web is an extension of the current web in which semantic is added to information in order to give a well-defined meaning to each resource and to enable computers and people to work in cooperation.

Chapter 13
Supporting Structural Evolution of Data in Web-Based Systems via Schema Versioning in the tXSchema Framework

Zouhaier Brahmia
University of Sfax, Tunisia

Fabio Grandi
University of Bologna, Italy

Barbara Oliboni
University of Verona, Italy

Rafik Bouaziz
University of Sfax, Tunisia

ABSTRACT

τXSchema is a framework for creating and validating temporal XML documents, while using a temporal schema that consists of three components: a conventional XML schema document annotated with a set of temporal logical and physical annotations. Each one of these components can evolve over time to reflect changes in the real world. In addition, schema versioning has been long advocated to be the most efficient way to keep track of both data and schema evolution. Hence, in this chapter the authors complete τXSchema, which is predisposed from the origin to support schema versioning, by defining the operations that are necessary to exploit such a feature and make schema versioning functionalities available to end users. Precisely, the authors' approach provides a complete and sound set of change primitives and a set of high-level change operations, for the maintenance of each component of a τXSchema schema, and defines their operational semantics. Furthermore, they propose a new technique for schema versioning in τXSchema, allowing a complete, integrated, and safe management of schema changes.

DOI: 10.4018/978-1-5225-5384-7.ch013

INTRODUCTION

Nowadays several Web-based applications using XML (W3C, 2008) repositories (e.g., banking, accounting, personnel management, airline reservations, weather monitoring and forecasting, e-government and e-commerce) are temporal in nature (Grandi, 2015) and require a full history of data and schema changes, which must be managed efficiently, consistently, and in a transparent way with regard to the end user. Notice that for generic temporal databases (Dyreson & Grandi, 2009), XML provides an excellent support for temporally grouped data models (Wang & Zaniolo, 2008), which have long been considered as the most natural and effective representations of temporal information (Clifford, Croker, Grandi, & Tuzhilin, 1995). Besides, schema versioning has long been advocated to be the more appropriate solution to support a complete data and schema history in databases (De Castro, Grandi, & Scalas, 1997; Grandi, 2002).

In a temporal setting, XML data can evolve along transaction-time and/or valid-time; thus, they can have a transaction-time, a valid-time or a bitemporal format. When XML data of different temporal formats can coexist in the same XML repository, we talk about a multitemporal XML repository.

Whereas schema versioning is required by several applications using multitemporal XML repositories, both existing XML DBMS and XML tools do not provide support for that feature until now (Colazzo, Guerrini, Mesiti, Oliboni, & Waller, 2010; Brahmia, Grandi, Oliboni, & Bouaziz, 2015; Brahmia, Grandi, Oliboni, & Bouaziz, 2017b). Therefore, XML Schema designers and developers have to employ ad hoc methods to manage schema versioning.

In order to propose a general approach for schema versioning in multitemporal XML repositories, the possible choices were as follows: (i) having different levels of schema specifications, that is a level for the data structure and one or more levels for temporal dimensions, and (ii) pushing the possible multitemporality one level higher. In this context, "Which is the right way to consider XML documents sharing the same data structure and having different time dimensions?" could be a good question. Hence, we dealt with the problem to define the different levels we need, and to define the mappings between such levels.

After surveying the state of the art of (multi-)temporal XML data models supporting schema versioning, we concluded that the resulting overall framework could be not very dissimilar from the one introduced by Snodgrass and colleagues in (Currim, Currim, Dyreson, & Snodgrass, 2004; Dyreson, Snodgrass, Currim, Currim, & Joshi, 2006; Snodgrass, Dyreson, Currim, Currim, & Joshi, 2008), named τXSchema. This latter is an infrastructure, composed of an XML schema language and a suite of tools, for constructing and validating temporal XML documents under schema versioning. The τXSchema language extends the XML Schema language (W3C, 2004) to explicitly support time-varying XML documents. τXSchema has a three-level architecture for specifying a schema for time-varying data. The first level is for the *conventional schema* which is a standard XML Schema document that describes the structure of a standard XML document, without any temporal aspect. The second level is for the *logical annotations* of the conventional schema, which identify which elements can vary over time. The third level is for the *physical annotations* of the conventional schema, which describe where timestamps should be placed and how the time-varying aspects should be represented.

Finally, we were in front of two options: either extending the τXSchema approach or proposing a completely different approach. We have chosen the first one, for the reasons which follow:

1. We came up with a similar requirement for having different levels for schema specification, so any alternative approach we could propose would not be so far from the τXSchema principles.

2.   In case we decide to move away from τXSchema, we must then be very convincing in justifying our choice (e.g., by highlighting strong limitations of the τXSchema approach which we need to overcome).

3.   The τXSchema approach is well known in the research community and thus it could be better to use it as a starting point, instead of putting forward a brand new proposal.

4.   In the τXSchema approach, there is room enough for extensions and, thus, we could define a set of schema changes and solve the semantics of change and change propagation problems for such operations on top of it.

In (Currim et al., 2004), the authors introduce τXSchema but did not discuss schema versioning. In (Dyreson et al., 2006) and in (Snodgrass et al., 2008) the authors deal with schema versioning in τXSchema: in (Dyreson et al., 2006) the authors focus on cross-schema change validation and in (Snodgrass et al., 2008) the authors extend it by discussing how to accommodate gaps in the existence time of an item, transaction semantics, and non-sequenced integrity constraints. All previous works on τXSchema focus on capturing a time-varying schema and validating documents against such a schema. Since the focus of these works was to validate time-varying documents against time-varying schemata, they suppose that any kind of change can be made on the schema and, thus, they do not deal with what kinds of meaningful schema change operations can be supported, or how the schema changes would be actually effected in an operational environment.

In this chapter, we investigate these issues by proposing a general approach for schema versioning in τXSchema-based multitemporal XML repositories. We study versioning of conventional schema and versioning of logical and physical annotations, in a broader perspective and in an integrated environment. Since new schema versions are usually created after changing the current ones, schema change operations are the core of any schema versioning process. Therefore, we propose two sets of low-level schema change operations, that we will call primitives, one set for changing conventional schema and the other set for changing logical and physical annotations. To help τXSchema designers and to make our approach more useful, we propose also two sets of high-level operations for changing the same components; a high-level schema change operation is a valid sequence of change primitives, that correspond to frequent schema evolution needs and allows to express complex changes in a more compact way (Guerrini, Mesiti, & Rossi, 2005). XML repository designers could use these high-level operations or these primitives to make any change on τXSchema schema, by composing them into valid sequences and collectively executing them on the considered component (the conventional schema, the logical annotations or the physical annotations) within the same transaction. Here, a transaction consists of a sequence of valid schema change operations (i.e., high-level or primitives) that would be carried out on the τXSchema framework and that would be either all successfully completed or all cancelled.

Furthermore, in the τXSchema framework, the *temporal schema* must be updated after changing the conventional schema and/or the corresponding annotations, since it ties these two components together (see subsection "Architecture"). In order to complete the picture, we have also defined a set of primitives which can be used for managing the temporal schema necessary updates. Moreover, for the same reasons mentioned above, we propose a set of high-level operations that provides an interface to designers for consistently updating temporal schema.

Notice that each one of the three proposed sets of primitives is complete, that is each component of a τXSchema schema (i.e., a conventional schema, an annotation document, or a temporal schema) can be generated starting from an empty component (i.e., from an empty conventional schema, annotation document, or temporal schema) by applying a sequence of primitives, and for each component a sequence of primitives exists for transforming it in the empty component. Moreover, this set is sound: i.e., each primitive applied to a consistent component produces a consistent component.

With respect to our previous work, the current one takes into account the temporal schema and deals with managing all τXSchema schema changes (i.e., those acting on conventional schema, on annotation documents, and on temporal schema) in an integrated manner. It also introduces high-level schema change operations that are more helpful for designers to perform their tasks of defining and changing schema.

The remainder of this chapter is organized as follows. The next section briefly describes the τXSchema framework. The "Completing the Framework: A Proposed Technique for Schema Versioning in τXSchema" section presents how τXSchema schema are versioned in our approach. The "Schema Changes in the τXSchema Framework" section introduces the operations that we propose for updating the temporal schema, and for changing the conventional schema and the logical and physical annotations; we distinguish here between low-level operations and high-level ones. The "Related Work Discussion" section discusses related work and emphasizes the novel contributions of our approach. The last section summarizes the proposed approach and gives some remarks on our future work.

THE τXSCHEMA FRAMEWORK

In this section, first we briefly present the τXSchema architecture (more details can be found in (Currim et al., 2009)), and then we provide a motivating example that illustrates the usage of τXSchema.

Architecture

The τXSchema framework (Currim et al., 2009) allows a designer to create a temporal XML schema for temporal XML documents from a conventional schema (written in standard XML Schema language), logical annotations, and physical annotations. Figure 1 illustrates the architecture of τXSchema. We note that only the components which are shaded in the figure (i.e., boxes 3, 5, 6, and 7) are specific to an individual time-varying document and need to be supplied by a designer.

The designer starts with the conventional schema (box 3) which is a standard XML Schema document that describes the structure of the conventional document(s). A conventional document is a standard XML document that has no temporal aspects.

Then, the designer augments the conventional schema with logical annotations (box 5), specifying (i) whether an element or attribute varies over valid time or transaction time, (ii) whether its lifetime is described as a continuous state or a single event, whether the item itself may appear at certain times (and not at others), and (iii) whether its content changes. If no logical annotations are provided, the default logical annotation is that anything can change. However, once the designer has annotated the conventional schema, elements that are not described as time-varying are static and, thus, they must have the same content across every XML document in box 7.

After that, the designer augments the conventional schema with physical annotations (box 6), which specify the timestamp representation options chosen by the designer, such as where the timestamps are placed and their kind (e.g., valid time or transaction time) and the kind of representation adopted. The location of timestamps is largely independent of which components vary over time. Timestamps can be located either on time-varying components (as specified by the logical annotations) or somewhere

Figure 1. Architecture of τXSchema

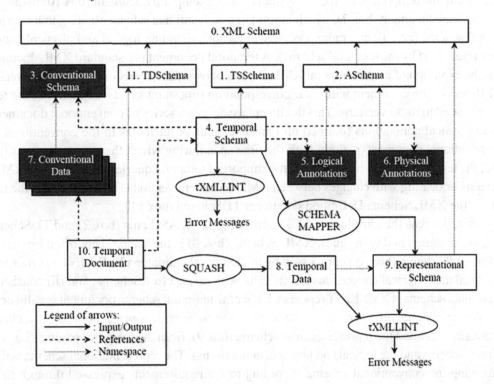

above such components. Two documents with the same logical information will look very different if we change the location of their physical timestamps. Changing an aspect of even one timestamp can make a big difference in the representation. τXSchema supplies a default set of physical annotations, which is used to timestamp the root element with valid and transaction times. However, explicitly managing them can lead to more compact representations.

Logical and physical annotations are orthogonal and are independently maintained, although they are stored together in a single document related to the conventional schema, which is a standard XML document named the annotation document. The schema for the logical and physical annotations is given by ASchema (box 2).

By separating the conventional schema, logical annotations, and physical annotations, the three-level architecture of τXSchema guarantees data independence and allows each component to be changed independently.

Finally, when the designer finishes annotating the conventional schema, he/she asks the system to save his/her work. As a result, the system creates the temporal schema (box 4) in order to provide the linking information between the conventional schema and its associated logical and physical annotations. The temporal schema is a standard XML document that ties the conventional schema, logical annotations, and physical annotations together. The temporal schema in the τXSchema environment is the logical equivalent of the conventional XML Schema in the non-temporal XML environment. This document contains sub-elements that associate a series of conventional schema definitions with logical and physical annotations, along with the time span during which the association were in effect. The schema for the temporal schema document is TSSchema (box 1).

After creating the temporal schema, the system creates a temporal document (box 10) in order to link each conventional document (box 7), which is valid to a conventional schema (box 3), to its corresponding temporal schema (box 4), and more precisely to its corresponding logical and physical annotations (which are referenced by the temporal schema). A temporal document is a standard XML document that maintains the evolution of a non-temporal XML document over time, by recording of all the versions (or temporal slices) of the document with their corresponding timestamps and by specifying the temporal schema associated to these versions. This document associates a series of conventional documents with logical and physical annotations (defined on (sub-)elements or attributes in the conventional schema of that conventional documents), along with the time span during which the association was in effect. Therefore, the temporal document facilitates the support of temporal queries involving past XML document versions or dealing with changes between XML document versions. The schema for the temporal document is the XML Schema Definition document TDSchema (box 11).

Notice that, whereas the introduction of TSSchema (box 1), ASchema (box 2) and TDSchema (box 11) is due to Snodgrass and colleagues, XML Schema (box 0) is the standard endorsed by the W3C.

The temporal schema (box 4) is processed by the temporal validator τXMLLINT in order to ensure that the logical and physical annotations are (i) valid with respect to ASchema, and (ii) consistent with the conventional schema. τXMLLINT reports whether the temporal schema document is valid or invalid.

Once the annotations are found to be consistent, the Schema mapper generates a standard XML Schema document, called the representational schema (box 9), from the temporal schema (i.e., from the conventional schema and the logical and physical annotations). The representational schema is the result of transforming the conventional schema according to the requirements expressed through the different annotations. It becomes the schema for temporal data (box 8). Temporal data can be created in four ways: (i) automatically from the temporal document (box 10) (i.e., from non-temporal data (box 7) and the temporal schema (box 4)), using the Squash tool; (ii) automatically from data stored in a (temporal) database, i.e., as the result of a "temporal query" (Dyreson, 2001; Gao & Snodgrass, 2003; Noh & Gadia, 2006; Rizzolo & Vaisman, 2008) or a "temporal view" (Snodgrass, Böhlen, Jensen, & Steiner, 1998); (iii) automatically from a third-party tool; (iv) manually (i.e., temporal data are directly inserted by the user into the τXSchema repository). Moreover, temporal data are validated against the representational schema through τXMLLINT which reports whether these data are valid or invalid.

Motivating Example

Assume that a new bank requires an XML repository for storing data and schema of customer accounts. On February 1, 2017, the designer creates the first version of the conventional schema shown in Figure 2. Each account in this bank is described by its number, the name of its owner, its opening date, and its balance. Then, the designer annotates this first version of the conventional schema with some logical and physical annotations. As to logical annotations, suppose that he/she decides to make the content of the <Balance> element varying in transaction-time (in order to keep the history along transaction time of the changes the balance of each account undergoes). As to physical annotations, suppose that he/she chooses to add a transaction-time physical timestamp to the element <Account> (i.e., whenever any element below <Account> changes, the entire <Account> element is repeated to represent a new temporal version). The first version of the annotation document related to the conventional schema of the bank is shown in Figure 3. Finally, the designer creates the temporal schema to define the links between the conventional schema and the annotation document, as shown in Figure 4. Without loss of generality, we

Figure 2. First version of the conventional schema (Bank_V1.xsd), on February 1, 2017

```xml
<?xml version="1.0" encoding="UTF-8"?>
<xsd:schema xmlns:xsd="http://www.w3.org/2001/XMLSchema">
 <xsd:element name="Bank">
  <xsd:complexType>
   <xsd:sequence>
    <xsd:element ref="Account"/>
   </xsd:sequence>
  </xsd:complexType>
 </xsd:element>
 <xsd:element name="Account">
  <xsd:complexType>
   <xsd:sequence>
    <xsd:element name="OwnerName" type="string"/>
    <xsd:element name="OpeningDate" type="date"/>
    <xsd:element name="Balance" type="float"/>
   </xsd:sequence>
   <xsd:attribute name="Number" type="nonNegativeInteger" use="required"/>
  </xsd:complexType>
 </xsd:element>
</xsd:schema>
```

Figure 3. First version of the annotation document (BankAnnotations_V1.xml), on February 1, 2017

```xml
<?xml version="1.0" encoding="UTF-8"?>
<annotationSet xmlns="http://www.cs.arizona.edu/tau/tauXSchema/ASchema">
 <logical>
  <item target="Bank/Account/Balance">
   <transactionTime kind="state" content="varying" existence="constant"/>
   <itemIdentifier name="balanceID" timeDimension="transactionTime">
    <field path="."/>
   </itemIdentifier>
  </item>
 </logical>
 <physical>
  <stamp target="Bank/Account" dataInclusion="expandedVersion">
   <stampKind timeDimension="transactionTime" stampBounds="extent"/>
  </stamp>
 </physical>
</annotationSet>
```

assume a temporal granularity of one day (i.e., this corresponds to consider at most one schema change transaction executed per day).

COMPLETING THE FRAMEWORK: A PROPOSED TECHNIQUE FOR SCHEMA VERSIONING IN τXSCHEMA

In this section, we describe how τXSchema conventional schema and τXSchema logical and physical annotations are versioned in our approach. Detailed studies were presented in (Brahmia, Bouaziz, Grandi,

Figure 4. Temporal schema (BankTemporalSchema.xml) on February 1, 2017

```
<?xml version="1.0" encoding="UTF-8"?>
<temporalSchema xmlns="http://www.cs.arizona.edu/tau/tauXSchema/TSSchema">
 <conventionalSchema>
  <sliceSequence>
   <slice location="Bank_V1.xsd" begin="2017-02-01" />
  </sliceSequence>
 </conventionalSchema>
 <annotationSet>
  <sliceSequence>
   <slice location="BankAnnotations_V1.xml" begin="2017-02-01" />
  </sliceSequence>
 </annotationSet>
</temporalSchema>
```

& Oliboni, 2012a; Brahmia, Grandi, Oliboni, & Bouaziz, 2012b) and (Brahmia, Bouaziz, Grandi, & Oliboni, 2010; Brahmia, Bouaziz, Grandi, & Oliboni, 2011).

The first step of a schema versioning sequence is the creation of the first schema version: the designer creates a conventional schema (i.e., an XSD file) annotated with some logical and physical annotations in an independent document (which is stored as an XML file), through, for instance, a graphical interface. Moreover, he/she creates the temporal schema (also stored as an XML file) that ties together the conventional schema and the annotations.

In further steps of the versioning sequence, when necessary, the designer can independently change the conventional schema, the logical or the physical annotations.

Changing the conventional schema leads to a new version of it. Similarly, changing a logical or a physical annotation leads to a new version of the whole annotation document. Therefore, the temporal schema is updated after each change of the conventional schema or of the annotation document.

Schema change operations performed by the designer are high-level, since they are usually conceived having in mind high-level real-world object properties. Each of these high-level schema change operations is then mapped onto a sequence of low-level schema change operations (or schema change primitives). The mapping is performed by the schema change processor and allows the implementation of the operations themselves.

In this paper, we investigate primitive changes and high-level changes. Each high-level change can be expressed as a sequence of primitive changes. Thus, the consistency of the resulting conventional schema (the resulting annotation document or the resulting temporal schema, respectively) is always guaranteed, if primitive changes preserve the conventional schema (the annotation document or the temporal schema, respectively) consistency.

Notice that in our approach, like in (Snodgrass et al., 2008), the temporal schema, which ties the conventional schema and the annotations together, is not "explicitly" versioned; for each conventional schema (i.e., all the versions of this schema) and its associated annotation document (i.e., all the versions of this document), there is always one XML document that represents the temporal schema, which is updated when the conventional schema and/or the annotation document are changed. In fact, in the τXSchema framework, the temporal schema is instrumental to support versioning of anything can change in the managed XML document repository. As a consequence, by its nature, the temporal schema comes out "implicitly" versioned (i.e., all versions of a temporal schema document are stored within this document; the version of a temporal schema, valid at any given time Tx, could be extracted from that schema by removing all the <slice ... begin=Ty/> elements where Ty>Tx). Thus, we think that other kinds of versioning of the temporal schema are neither necessary nor could be meaningfully put at user's disposal (without getting out of the τXSchema framework).

Notice also that neither conventional schema versioning nor annotation versioning lead automatically to proliferation of schema versions. The creation of a new conventional schema version (a new annotation document version, respectively) is anyway a seldom task during the XML repository lifetime, which can only be performed by a designer of this repository. This task may consist of dozens of (low-level or high-level) schema change operations which are grouped together in the same single transaction.

SCHEMA CHANGES IN THE τXSCHEMA FRAMEWORK

In this section, we introduce a principled approach to the definition of schema change operations. We first present our design principles, then we describe operations for updating temporal schema, next we introduce operations for changing conventional schema, and last we present operations for changing logical and physical annotations. For each component of the schema in the τXSchema framework (i.e., conventional schema, annotations and temporal schema), we propose a set of low-level operations, that we will call primitives, as well as a set of high-level operations, for changing that component. For each operation, we describe its arguments and define its operational semantics. We introduce also mapping of high-level operations onto the proposed primitives.

As far as the proposed set of primitives is concerned, they are non-further decomposable in terms of the other ones and make up a complete set of changes, that is, any possible complex change can be defined via a combination/sequence of them.

Design Principles

The definition of the operations will obey the following principles and conventions:

1. All operations acting on the *Conventional Schema* (CS) (on the *Annotation Document* (AD), or on the *Temporal Schema* (TS), respectively) must work on a valid CS (AD, or TS), i.e., operations must have a valid CS (AD, or TS) as input and produce a valid CS (AD, or TS) as output.
2. All CS (AD, or TS) change operations need to work on an XSD (XML) file storing the CS (AD, or TS), whose name must be supplied as argument.
3. For all operations, arguments which are used to identify the object on which the operation works are in the first place of the argument list.
4. Operations adding elements with possibly optional attributes have the values for all the attributes as arguments; empty places in the argument list stand for unspecified optional attributes.
5. For operations changing elements (i.e., set operations), values are specified only for attributes that are changed; the value "unchanged" means that the corresponding attribute is not updated; an empty place in the argument list means that the corresponding attribute receives a nil value.
6. Elements without attributes which are just containers for sets of sub-elements (e.g., <conventionalSchema/>, <sliceSequence/>, and <annotationSet/> in the temporal schema document; <logi-

cal/>, <physical/>, and <orderBy/> in the annotation document) can be managed by the operations concerning the sub-elements, without specific operations acting on them (i.e., the container is created when the first sub-element is created and is deleted when the last sub-element is deleted).

7.   As far as the logical and physical annotations are concerned:
   a.   Item and Stamp elements are identified by their "target" attribute; an "item path" ("stamp path") argument does not seem to be necessary; also because the order of item (stamp) elements within the logical (physical) container is irrelevant.
   b.   The definition of include/defaultTimeFormat are exactly the same both for <physical/> and for <logical/>. In case, the same operations acting on include/defaultTimeFormat can be used either for <physical/> or <logical/> elements (with an argument toWhat to choose between them).

The lists of operations in the following subsections are the applications of the design principles presented above.

Operations for Changing the Temporal Schema

Updating the temporal schema is a task that must be done within the same transaction that changes the corresponding conventional schema and/or the annotation document. In the following subsections, first we will present the proposed operations (primitives and high-level operations) acting on the temporal schema and then we will give an example that shows their use.

Change Primitives

We define four change primitives that act on the temporal schema, and list them in Table 1. For the sake of space, we choose to present only the effects of the following operations: CreateTemporalSchema and AddSlice.

The effect of the CreateTemporalSchema("TS.xml") primitive, that is the contents of the TS.xml file after its application, is as follows:

```
<?xml version="1.0" encoding="UTF-8"?>
<temporalSchema xmlns="http://www.cs.arizona.edu/tau/tauXSchema/TSSchema"/>
```

The effects of the AddSlice("TS.xml", conventionalSchema, empty, "CS_V1.xsd") primitive are described in the following:

1.   The contents of the TS.xml file is updated as follows (the transaction time associated to the execution of the transaction that includes this primitive is 2009-03-01, which is used as value of begin in the <slice/> element):

```
<?xml version="1.0" encoding="UTF-8"?>
<temporalSchema xmlns="http://www.cs.arizona.edu/tau/tauXSchema/TSSchema">
    <conventionalSchema>
     <sliceSequence>
```

Table 1. Change primitives acting on the temporal schema

Change Primitive	Description
CreateTemporalSchema(TS.xml)	It produces valid empty TS. According to the design principle (2), the argument is the name of the XML file where the new TS is stored.
RemoveTemporalSchema(TS.xml)	It removes the TS.xml file from disk, with the constraint that the argument represents an empty TS (i.e., like the one above initially created by CreateTemporalSchema). Any other contents must have been removed before.

AddSlice(TS.xml, toWhat, sourceSlice, targetSlice)	Adds the <slice/> element with specified sourceSlice and targetSlice to the toWhat (i.e., <conventionalSchema/> or <annotationSet/>) container.
	- The sourceSlice parameter could be:
	  1) The keyword empty; in this case the resource pointed by targetSlice is initialized to an empty conventionalSchema or annotationSet according to the toWhat value.
	  2) The keyword current; in this case the resource pointed by targetSlice is initialized with a copy of the current conventionalSchema/annotationSet resource (according to toWhat), whose location is found in the TS.xml temporal schema file by choosing the slice with the maximum value of begin in the corresponding sliceSequence (note: after the creation of the *first* schema version, this is the normal case).
	  3) A specified file name (URL): in this case, a copy of the specified resource is renamed as targetSlice and used as the new location (e.g., this case is used to create a new conventional schema version from an already existing XML schema file, which could be quite common when creating the first schema version but can be used also later for reuse purpose and/or integrating independently developed schemata into a τXSchema framework).
	  - The targetSlice parameter is the value assigned to the location attribute of <slice/> and must not correspond to the URL of any already existing XML file/resource.

RemoveSlice(TS.xml, fromWhat, targetSlice)	It removes the <slice/> element with specified targetSlice from the fromWhat (i.e., <conventionalSchema/> or <annotationSet/>) container.

```
    <slice location="CS_V1.xsd" begin="2009-03-01" />
   </sliceSequence>
  </conventionalSchema>
</temporalSchema>
```

2.   A new empty conventional schema, titled "CS_V1.xsd", is created as follows:

```
<?xml version="1.0" encoding="UTF-8"?>
<xsd:schema xmlns:xsd="http://www.w3.org/2001/XMLSchema" />
```

Once the TS.xml file has been created, further executions of the AddSlice primitive will simply add new <slice/> subelements to the <sliceSequence> element.

As far as the AddSlice primitive is concerned, we give the two following notices:

- We need the two parameters source/target (and must distinguish between the source and target involved in the schema change) because when we apply the primitive changes to conventional schema or annotation set, we cannot spoil the "old version" by applying the changes on it to incrementally produce the "new version": the old version must be retained as it is (as part of the "old" slice) despite the creation of the new version (which becomes part of the "new" slice). The initial copy from source to target is a simple proposed solution to this problem.

Table 2. High-level change operations acting on the temporal schema

Change Operation	Description

DefineTemporalSchema(
    TS.xml,
    sourceFirstVersionCS, targetFirstVersionCS,
    sourceFirstVersionAD,
    targetFirstVersionAD)
	It creates a new temporal schema document (TS.xml) that includes a first version of a conventional schema (sourceFirstVersionCS) and a first version of the corresponding annotation document (sourceFirstVersionAD).
	This operation is mapped onto the following list of primitives:
	(1) CreateTemporalSchema(TS.xml)
	(2) AddSlice(TS.xml, conventionalSchema, sourceFirstVersionCS, targetFirstVersionCS)
	(3) AddSlice(TS.xml, annotationSet,sourceFirstVersionAD, targetFirstVersionAD)

UpdateTemporalSchema(
    TS.xml,
    sourceNewVersionCS, targetNewVersionCS,
    sourceNewVersionAD, targetNewVersionAD)
	It updates a temporal schema by including a new conventional schema version, sourceNewVersionCS, or a new annotation document version, sourceNewVersionAD (only one of these two parameters can be omitted).
	This operation is mapped onto the following list of primitives:
	(1) If (sourceNewVersionCS is not null) then
	    AddSlice(TS.xml, conventionalSchema, sourceNewVersionCS, targetNewVersionCS)
	(2) If (sourceNewVersionAD is not null) then
	    AddSlice(TS.xml, annotationSet, sourceNewVersionAD, targetNewVersionAD)

- The third option for the sourceSlice parameter (i.e., the URL) is not strictly necessary in our approach (as everything could be created from scratch via a suitable sequence of primitive operations); we only considered it because it would be useful to reuse, for example, an available XML Schema file as conventional schema version in our framework (e.g., see the example below).

High-Level Change Operations

We define five high-level operations that act on the temporal schema, and list some of them in Table 2. For the sake of space, we choose to present only the effects of the DefineTemporalSchema operation. More detailed description of the operations' operational semantics and their effects on the TS can be found in (Brahmia, Grandi, Oliboni, & Bouaziz, 2014a).

Running Example

Let us resume the illustrative example presented in the subsection "Motivating Example" above, dealing with the management of customer accounts in a bank. We focus here on the temporal schema and assume that the two other components have been designed as independent XML files with an XML editor, or reused from another project. In particular, we assume to start from a conventional schema "Bank.xsd" (with the same contents as the XSD file in Figure 2) and an annotation document "BankAnnotation.xml" (with the same contents as the XML file in Figure 3), and want to integrate them in our initial τXSchema framework with the use of primitives acting on the temporal schema. To this purpose, we consider the following schema change transaction, which is executed on February 1, 2017.

   Begin Transaction

1. CreateTemporalSchema("BankTemporalSchema.xml")
2. AddSlice("BankTemporalSchema.xml", conventionalSchema, "Bank.xsd", "Bank_V1.xsd")

3. AddSlice("BankTemporalSchema.xml",annotationSet, "BankAnnotations.xml", "BankAnnotations_V1.xml")

Commit

The primitive (i) initializes an empty temporal schema file "BankTemporalSchema.xml"; the primitive (ii) creates the first conventional schema version "Bank_V1.xsd" as a copy of "Bank.xsd" and adds the corresponding slice to the temporal schema file; the primitive (iii) creates the first annotation document version "BankAnnotation_V1.xml" as a copy of "BankAnnotation.xml" and adds the corresponding slice to the temporal schema file. The resulting initial τXSchema framework is the one we considered in the subsection "Motivating Example". In particular, the resulting temporal schema file is as in Figure 4. The transaction time associated to the execution of this transaction, 2017-02-01, has been used as value of begin in the temporal schema file.

Notice that the "Bank_V1.xsd" and "BankAnnotation_V1.xml" could also have been designed from scratch by using the keyword empty corresponding to option 1) in the AddSlice primitive and then applying, in the same transaction, a suitable sequence primitives acting on the conventional schema and on the annotation document; these primitives will be introduced in the next subsections "Operations for Changing the Conventional Schema" and "Operations for Changing Logical and Physical Annotations", respectively.

Alternatively, the same results could be obtained if the designer uses one high-level operation (i.e., DefineTemporalSchema), through the following schema change transaction, which is executed on February 1, 2017.

Begin Transaction

1. DefineTemporalSchema("BankTemporalSchema.xml",

```
"Bank.xsd", "Bank_V1.xsd",
"BankAnnotations.xml", "BankAnnotations_V1.xml")
```

Commit

Operations for Changing the Conventional Schema

Since the conventional schema is defined using the XML Schema language (W3C, 2004) which is a standard language to define schema for XML documents, it is worth mentioning that we do not address here the full XML Schema definition (e.g., involving the latest W3C Part 1: Structures and Part 2: Datatypes recommendations) which is quite complex, but we focus indeed on a subset of it which we consider very significant for applications, that is the latest W3C Part 0 recommendation (W3C, 2004).

An XML Schema consists of several components. After studying the XML Schema Definition (Part 0), we have listed forty-two XML Schema components (e.g. complexType, element, attribute, and sequence) in (Brahmia et al., 2012a, sec. 4). For each component, we presented its attributes and its containers (i.e., where the component can be included).

Since the change of a conventional schema leads automatically to a change of the corresponding temporal schema, they should be performed always within the same transaction.

In the following subsections, first we present the proposed change primitives, then we describe high-level change operations, acting on the conventional schema, and last we give an example of their use.

Change Primitives

In this subsection, we propose the set of primitives for changing a conventional schema (their total number is one hundred and twenty-four). The idea is that each primitive deals with an XML Schema component and adds, deletes or modifies attributes of such a component. For this reason, some arguments of the primitives are the attributes of the corresponding XML Schema components. Due to space limitations, we list only some of these primitives in Table 3. Furthermore, we choose to present only the effects of AddSequence change primitive. More detailed description of the primitives' operational semantics and their effects on the CS can be found in (Brahmia et al., 2012a).

The effect of the AddSequence(CS.xsd, toWhat, parentComponentPath, precedingComponentPath, id, minOccurs, maxOccurs) primitive, that is the contents of the CS.xsd file after its application, is as follows:

```
If (toWhat=complexType and parentComponentPath="/element1" and
precedingComponentPath=.)
<xsd:schema    xmlns:xsd="http://www.w3.org/2001/XMLSchema">
  ...
  <xsd:element name="element1">
   <xsd:complexType>
    <xsd:sequence    id="id" minOccurs="minOccurs"
                     maxOccurs="maxOccurs">
    </xsd:sequence>
   </xsd:complexType>
  </xsd:element>
...
</xsd:schema>
```

Table 3. Change primitives acting on the conventional schema

Change Primitive	Description
AddElement(CS.xsd, toWhat, parentComponentPath, precedingComponentPath, id, name, type, default, fixed, abstract, final, ref, minOccurs, maxOccurs, block, form, nillable, substitutionGroup)	Adds the <element/> component with specified id, name, type, default, fixed, abstract, final, ref, minOccurs, maxOccurs, block, form, nillable, and substitutionGroup to the toWhat (i.e., <all/>, <choice/>, <sequence/>, or <schema/>) container, at the position defined by the path of its parent XML Schema component (parentComponentPath) and the path of its preceding XML Schema component (precedingComponentPath). If this latter is not specified by the designer, it means that the <element/> component is the first element in the toWhat container (or the parent XML Schema component).
AddSequence(CS.xsd, toWhat, parentComponentPath, precedingComponentPath, id, minOccurs, maxOccurs)	Adds the <sequence/> component with specified id, minOccurs, and maxOccurs to the toWhat (i.e., <complexType/>, <choice/>, <sequence/> or <group/>) container, at the position defined by the path of its parent XML Schema component (parentComponentPath) and the path of its preceding XML Schema component (precedingComponentPath). If this latter is not specified by the designer, it means that the <sequence/> component is the first element in the toWhat container (or the parent XML Schema component).

High-Level Change Operations

We define a set of high-level operations that act on the conventional schema, and list some of them in Table 4. More detailed description of the operations' operational semantics and their effects on the CS can be found in (Brahmia et al., 2014a).

As far as the AddSubElement operation is concerned, notice that if this latter is applied to a simple element like:

```
<xsd:element name="model-name" type="xsd:string"/>
```

It must transform this element, for instance, into:

```
<xsd:element name="model-name">
    <xsd:complexType mixed="true">
        <xsd:sequence/>
    </xsd:complexType>
</xsd:element>
```

Before the AddElement primitive can be used to add the new subelement to the "sequence".

Table 4. High-level change operations acting on the conventional schema

Change Operation	Description

AddSubElement(CS.xsd, parentElementPath, precedingElementPath, (id, name, type, default, fixed, abstract, final, ref, minOccurs, maxOccurs, block, form, nillable, substitutionGroup))	It adds a sub-element (that could be the first one or a new one) to an existing element (parentElementPath).
	This operation can be effected by means of an AddElement primitive only if the target element has already a "sequence", "choice", or "all" structure.
	This operation is mapped onto the following list of primitives:
	If (parentElementPath refers to an element having a "sequence", "choice", or "all" structure) then
	(1) AddElement(CS.xsd, structure, parentComponentPath, precedingComponentPath, id, name, type, default, fixed, abstract, final, ref, minOccurs, maxOccurs, block, form, nillable, substitutionGroup)
	Else
	(1) DeleteAttribute(CS.xsd, element, '//@type')
	(2) AddComplexType(CS.xsd, element, parentComponentPath, precedingComponentPath,,,,,, "true",)
	(3) AddSequence(CS.xsd, complexType, parentComponentPath, precedingComponentPath,,,)
	(4) AddElement(CS.xsd, sequence, parentElementPath, precedingElementPath, id, name, type, default, fixed, abstract, final, ref, minOccurs, maxOccurs, block, form, nillable, substitutionGroup)

ReplaceAttributeWithNewAttribute(CS.xsd, parentComponentPath, precedingComponentPath, attributeName, (id, name, type, default, fixed, use, form, ref))	It replaces an existing attribute of an <element/> component with a new attribute, in "CS.xsd". This operation must update: - all other components of "CS.xsd" that are using (or referring to) the replaced attribute (e.g. <key>, <unique>, and <keyref> components); - all <stamp> components, in the current version of the AD corresponding to "CS.xsd", that are referring to the replaced attribute. This operation is mapped onto the following list of primitives: (1) DeleteAttribute(CS.xsd, element, parentComponentPath, precedingComponentPath, attributeName) (2) AddAttribute(CS.xsd, element, parentComponentPath, precedingComponentPath, id, name, type, default, fixed, use, form, ref)

Running Example

Let us resume the illustrative example presented in the subsection "Motivating Example" above. Suppose that on March 1, 2017, the designer realizes that he/she also needs information about all financial transactions done on each bank account. Then, he/she changes the first version of the conventional schema by adding a complex element <FinancialTransactions> to the Account element. This new element contains a sequence of another complex element <FinancialTransaction> which is composed of three simple elements: <FinancialTransactionDate>, <FinancialTransactionType>, and <FinancialTransactionAmount>.

The second version of the conventional schema is shown in Figure 5. Thus, the temporal schema is also updated by adding a new slice related to this new version of the conventional schema, as shown in Figure 6. Changes are presented in purple bold type.

The sequence of primitives that have been performed on the temporal schema (BankTemporalSchema. xml) and on the first version of the conventional schema (Bank_V1.xsd) to produce the second one (Bank_V2.xsd) is listed in the transaction which follows:

Figure 5. Second version of the conventional schema (Bank_V2.xsd), on March 1, 2017

```
<?xml version="1.0" encoding="UTF-8"?>
<xsd:schema xmlns:xsd="http://www.w3.org/2001/XMLSchema">
 <xsd:element name="Bank">
  <xsd:complexType>
   <xsd:sequence>
    <xsd:element ref="Account"/>
   </xsd:sequence>
  </xsd:complexType>
 </xsd:element>
 <xsd:element name="Account">
  <xsd:complexType>
   <xsd:sequence>
    <xsd:element name="OwnerName" type="string"/>
    <xsd:element name="OpeningDate" type="date"/>
    <xsd:element name="Balance" type="float"/>
    <xsd:element name="FinancialTransactions">
     <xsd:complexType>
      <xsd:sequence>
       <xsd:element name="FinancialTransaction" maxOccurs="unbounded">
        <xsd:complexType>
         <xsd:sequence>
          <xsd:element name="FinancialTransactionDate" type="date"/>
          <xsd:element name="FinancialTransactionType" type="string"/>
          <xsd:element name="FinancialTransactionAmount" type="float"/>
         </xsd:sequence>
        </xsd:complexType>
       </xsd:element>
      </xsd:sequence>
     </xsd:complexType>
    </xsd:element>
   </xsd:sequence>
   <xsd:attribute name="Number" type="nonNegativeInteger" use="required"/>
  </xsd:complexType>
 </xsd:element>
</xsd:schema>
```

Figure 6. Temporal schema (BankTemporalSchema.xml) on March 1, 2017

```xml
<?xml version="1.0" encoding="UTF-8"?>
<temporalSchema xmlns="http://www.cs.arizona.edu/tau/tauXSchema/TSSchema">
 <conventionalSchema>
  <sliceSequence>
   <slice location="Bank_V1.xsd" begin="2017-02-01" />
   <slice location="Bank_V2.xsd" begin="2017-03-01" />
  </sliceSequence>
 </conventionalSchema>
 <annotationSet>
  <sliceSequence>
   <slice location="BankAnnotations_V1.xml" begin="2017-02-01" />
  </sliceSequence>
 </annotationSet>
</temporalSchema>
```

Begin Transaction

1. AddSlice("BankTemporalSchema.xml", conventionalSchema, current, "Bank_V2.xsd")
2. AddElement("Bank_V2.xsd", sequence, "Account", "Account/Balance",, "FinancialTransactions",,,,,,,,,,,,)
3. AddComplexType("Bank_V2.xsd", element, "Account/FinancialTransactions",,,,,,,,)
4. AddSequence("Bank_V2.xsd", complexType, "Account/FinancialTransactions",,,,)
5. AddElement("Bank_V2.xsd", sequence, "Account/FinancialTransactions",,, "FinancialTransaction",,,,,,,, unbounded,,,,)
6. AddComplexType("Bank_V2.xsd", element, "Account/FinancialTransactions/ FinancialTransaction",,,,,,,,)
7. AddSequence("Bank_V2.xsd", complexType, "Account/FinancialTransactions/ FinancialTransaction",,,,)
8. AddElement("Bank_V2.xsd", sequence, "Account/FinancialTransactions/FinancialTransaction",,, "FinancialTransactionDate", date,,,,,,,,,,)
9. AddElement("Bank_V2.xsd", sequence, "Account/FinancialTransactions/FinancialTransaction", "Account/FinancialTransactions/FinancialTransaction/FinancialTransactionDate",, "FinancialTransactionType", string,,,,,,,,,,)
10. AddElement("Bank_V2.xsd", sequence, "Account/FinancialTransactions/FinancialTransaction", "Account/FinancialTransactions/FinancialTransaction/FinancialTransactionType",, "FinancialTransactionAmount", float,,,,,,,,,,)

Commit

The transaction time associated to the execution of the transaction above is 2017-03-01, which is used as value of begin in the temporal schema file.

Alternatively, the same results could be obtained if the designer uses six high-level change operations (instead of ten change primitives), through the following schema change transaction, which is executed on March 1, 2017.

Begin Transaction

1. UpdateTemporalSchema("BankTemporalSchema.xml", current, "Bank_V2.xsd",,)
2. AddSubElement("Bank_V2.xsd", "Account", after, "Account/Balance", (,"FinancialTransactions",,,,,,,,,,,))
3. AddSubElement("Bank_V2.xsd", "Account/FinancialTransactions", first,, (,"FinancialTransactio n",,,,,,,,unbounded,,,,))
4. AddSubElement("Bank_V2.xsd", "Account/FinancialTransactions/FinancialTransaction", first,, (,"FinancialTransactionDate",date,,,,,,,,,,))
5. AddSubElement("Bank_V2.xsd", "Account/FinancialTransactions/FinancialTransaction", after, "Account/FinancialTransactions/FinancialTransaction/FinancialTransactionDate", (,"FinancialTr ansactionType",string,,,,,,,,,,))
6. AddSubElement("Bank_V2.xsd", "Account/FinancialTransactions/FinancialTransaction", after, "Account/FinancialTransactions/FinancialTransaction/FinancialTransactionType", (,"FinancialT ransactionAmount",float,,,,,,,,,,))

Commit

Operations for Changing Logical and Physical Annotations

Since the change of an annotation document leads automatically to a change of the corresponding temporal schema, they should be performed always within the same transaction.

In the following subsections, first we present the proposed change primitives, then we describe high-level change operations, acting on the annotation document, and last we give an example which shows their use.

Change Primitives

We organize the proposed primitives into three categories: (i) primitives that are common to the logical and to the physical annotations, (ii) primitives that are specific to the physical annotations, and (iii) primitives that are specific to the logical annotations. More detailed description of the primitives' operational semantics and their effects on the AD can be found in (Brahmia et al., 2010).

Primitives Common to Logical and Physical Annotations

These primitives can be applied either to the <logical/> or to the <physical/> container. We define six primitive and list some of them in Table 5. Here, we choose to present only the effect of the AddDefaultTimeFormat primitive.

The effect of the AddDefaultTimeFormat(AD.xml, toWhat, plugin, granularity, calendar, properties, valueSchema) primitive, that is the contents of the AD.xml file after its application, is as follows:

```
If (toWhat = physical)
<?xml version="1.0" encoding="UTF-8"?>
<annotationSet  xmlns="http://www.cs.arizona.edu/tau/tauXSchema/ASchema">
```

Table 5. Change primitives common to logical and physical annotations

Change Primitive	Description
AddInclude(AD.xml, toWhat, annotationLocation)	Adds the \<include/> element with specified annotationLocation to the toWhat (i.e., \<physical/> or \<logical/>) container. Notice that any number of \<include/> elements can be added, hence the annotationLocation is generally needed to distinguish between them.
AddDefaultTimeFormat(AD.xml, toWhat, plugin, granularity, calendar, properties, valueSchema)	Adds the \<defaultTimeFormat/> element with specified plugin, granularity, calendar, properties, and valueSchema to the toWhat (i.e., \<physical/> or \<logical/>) container.

```
<physical>
  <defaultTimeFormat>
    <format plugin="plugin" granularity ="granularity"
            calendar="calendar" properties="properties"
            valueSchema="valueSchema"/>
  </defaultTimeFormat>
</physical>
</annotationSet>
```

Primitives Specific to the Logical Annotations

These change primitives can be applied only to the \<logical/> container. We identify forty one change primitives, and list some of them in Table 6. Here, we choose to present only the effects of the AddValidTimeToItem primitive.

For example, the effect of the AddValidTimeToItem(AD.xml, itemTarget, validTimeKind, validTimeContent, validTimeExistence) primitive, that is the contents of the AD.xml file after its application, is as follows:

```
<?xml version="1.0" encoding="UTF-8"?>
<annotationSet  xmlns="http://www.cs.arizona.edu/tau/tauXSchema/ASchema">
  <physical>
    ...
  </physical>
```

Table 6. Change primitives related to the logical annotations

Change Primitive	Description
AddItem(AD.xml, itemTarget)	Adds the \<item/> element with specified itemTarget to the \<logical/> container.
AddValidTimeToItem(AD.xml, itemTarget, validTimeKind, validTimeContent, validTimeExistence)	Adds the \<validTime/> element with specified validTimeKind, validTimeContent, and validTimeExistence to the \<item/> element with specified itemTarget in the \<logical/> container, where the three last arguments are optional. Possible values of some arguments: - validTimeKind: either state or event. - validTimeContent: either constant or varying. - validTimeExistence: one of constant, varyingWithGaps, varyingWithoutGaps.

```
<logical>
  <item target="itemTarget">
   <validTime kind="validTimeKind" content="validTimeContent"
              existence="validTimeExistence"/>
  </item>
</logical>
</annotationSet>
```

Primitives Specific to the Physical Annotations

These change primitives can be applied only to the <physical/> container. We define nine change primitives and list some of them in Table 7. Here, we choose to present only the effect of the AddOrderByFieldToStamp primitive.

The effect of the AddOrderByFieldToStamp(AD.xml, stampTarget, newOrderByField) primitive, that is the contents of the AD.xml file after its application, is as follows:

```
If (newOrderByField in {validTime, transactionTime})
<?xml version="1.0" encoding="UTF-8"?>
<annotationSet  xmlns="http://www.cs.arizona.edu/tau/tauXSchema/ASchema">
  <physical>
   <stamp target="stampTarget" dataInclusion="stampDataInclusion">
    <stampKind timeDimension="stampKindTimeDimension"
               stampBounds="stampKindStampBounds"/>
    <format plugin="stampPlugin" granularity="stampGranularity"
            calendar="stampCalendar" properties="stampProperties"
            valueSchema="stampValueSchema" />
    <orderBy>
     <field>
      <time dimension="newOrderByField" />
     </field>
    </orderBy>
```

Table 7. Change primitives related to the physical annotations

Change Primitive	Description
AddStamp(AD.xml, stampTarget, stampDataInclusion, stampKindTimeDimension, stampKindStampBounds)	Adds the <stamp/> element with specified stampTarget, stampDataInclusion, stampKindTimeDimension, and stampKindStampBounds to the <physical/> container, where the three last arguments are optional. Possible values of some arguments: - stampDataInclusion: one of expandedEntity, referencedEntity, expandedVersion, or referencedVersion. - stampKindTimeDimension: one of validTime, transactionTime, or bitemporal. - stampKindStampBounds: either step or extent.
AddOrderByFieldToStamp(AD.xml, stampTarget, newOrderByField)	Adds a <field/> element having the value newOrderByField to the <orderBy/> element of the <stamp/> element with specified stampTarget in the <physical/> container.

```
    </stamp>
  </physical>
</annotationSet>
```

High-Level Change Operations

We define a set of high-level operations that act on the annotation document. We organize the proposed operations into three categories: (i) operations that are common to the logical and to the physical annotations, (ii) operations that are specific to the logical annotations, and (iii) operations that are specific to the physical annotations. More detailed description of the operations' operational semantics and their effects on the AD can be found in (Brahmia et al., 2014a).

Operations Common to Logical and Physical Annotations

These change operations can be applied either to the <logical/> or to the <physical/> container. We list some of them in Table 8.

Operations Specific to the Logical Annotations

These change operations can be applied only to the <logical/> container. We list some of them in Table 9.

Table 8. Change operations common to logical and physical annotations

Change Operation	Description
IncludeAnnotationFiles(AD.xml, logicalAnnotationFileLocation, physicalAnnotationFileLocation)	It allows the designer to include, in the annotation document "AD. xml", an XML document that contains logical annotations, located at logicalAnnotationFileLocation, or an XML document that contains physical annotations, located at physicalAnnotationFileLocation (only one of these two parameters can be omitted). This operation is mapped onto the following list of primitives: (1) If (logicalAnnotationFileLocation is not null) then AddInclude(AD.xml, logical, logicalAnnotationFileLocation) (2) If (physicalAnnotationFileLocation is not null) then AddInclude(AD.xml, physical, physicalAnnotationFileLocation)
SpecifyDefaultTimeFormatUsedInAnnotationDocument(AD.xml, annotationType, pluginUsed, granularityOfTimeFormat, calendricSystemUsed, dateFormatProperties, valueSchemaUsedForDate)	It allows the designer to specify the default time format used in the annotation document "AD.xml" for logical or for physical annotations (according to the annotationType parameter that should have the value logical or physical). This operation is mapped onto the following list of primitives: If (annotationType = logical) then AddDefaultTimeFormat(AD.xml, logical, pluginUsed, granularityOfTimeFormat, calendricSystemUsed, dateFormatProperties, valueSchemaUsedForDate) Else AddDefaultTimeFormat(AD.xml, physical, pluginUsed, granularityOfTimeFormat, calendricSystemUsed, dateFormatProperties, valueSchemaUsedForDate)

Table 9. Change operations related to the logical annotations

Change Operation	Description
DefineTimeVaryingItem(AD.xml, elementLocation, (validTimeKind, validTimeContent, validTimeExistence), transactionTime, frequency, (itemIdentifierName, itemIdentifierTimeDimension))	It allows the designer to define a new time-varying item (as a logical annotation) in the annotation document "AD.xml". This operation inserts a non-empty new <item/> element in the <logical/> container. This operation is mapped onto the following list of primitives: AddItem(AD.xml, elementLocation). AddValidTimeToItem(AD.xml, elementLocation, validTimeKind, validTimeContent, validTimeExistence) AddTransactionTimeToItem(AD.xml, elementLocation) AddFrequencyToItem(AD.xml, elementLocation, frequency) AddItemIdentifierToItem(AD.xml, elementLocation, itemIdentifierName, itemIdentifierTimeDimension)
DropTimeVaryingItem(AD.xml, elementLocation)	It allows the designer to drop an existing time-varying item from "AD.xml". This operation deletes the corresponding <item/> element and all its sub-elements from the <logical/> container. This operation is mapped onto the following list of primitives: DeleteItemIdentifierFromItem(AD.xml, elementLocation) DeleteFrequencyFromItem(AD.xml, elementLocation) DeleteTransactionTimeFromItem(AD.xml, elementLocation) DeleteValidTimeFromItem(AD.xml, elementLocation) DeleteItem(AD.xml, elementLocation)

Operations Specific to the Physical Annotations

These change operations can be applied only to the <physical/> container. We list some of them in Table 10.

Running Example

Let us resume the illustrative example of the subsection "Motivating Example". Suppose that on June 1, 2017, the designer decides to keep the history of the balance of each account along both transaction and valid times. Then, he/she changes the first version of the annotation document by modifying the item related to the Balance element: he/she adds an empty <validTime> element. Suppose that he/she also decides to add another physical timestamp (having a bitemporal kind) to the element <Balance>. The second version of the annotation document is shown in Figure 7. Thus, the temporal schema is also updated by adding a new slice related to this new version of the annotation document, as shown in Figure 8. Changes are presented in purple bold type.

The sequence of primitives, that have been performed on the temporal schema (BankTemporalSchema. xml) and on the first version of the annotation document (BankAnnotations_V1.xml) to produce the second one (BankAnnotations_V2.xml), could make up the following transaction (the transaction time associated to the execution of this transaction is 2017-06-01, which is used as value of begin in the temporal schema file):

Begin Transaction

1. AddSlice("BankTemporalSchema.xml",annotationSet,current, "BankAnnotations_V2.xml")
2. AddValidTimeToItem("BankAnnotations_V2.xml", "Bank/Account/Balance", state, varying, constant)

Table 10. Change operations related to the physical annotations

Change Operation	Description
SpecifyPhysicalTimeStamp(AD.xml, physicalTimeStampTarget, subElementRepresentation, (stampKindTimeDimension, stampKindStampBounds), (plugin, granularity, calendar, properties, valueSchema), orderingField, pathOfElementOrAttribute, timeDimensionOrderBy)	It allows the designer to define a new physical timestamp (as a physical annotation) in the annotation document "AD.xml". This operation inserts a non-empty new <stamp/> element in the <physical/> container. This operation uses at least the following primitive: AddStamp(AD.xml, stampTarget, stampDataInclusion, stampKindTimeDimension, stampKindStampBounds) and in most the following ones: AddStamp(AD.xml, stampTarget, stampDataInclusion, stampKindTimeDimension, stampKindStampBounds) SetFormatInStampKind(AD.xml, stampTarget, stampPlugin, stampGranularity, stampCalendar, stampProperties, stampValueSchema) AddOrderByFieldToStamp(AD.xml, stampTarget, newOrderByField)
ChangePhysicalTimeStamp(AD.xml, physicalTimeStampTarget, subElementRepresentation, (stampKindTimeDimension, stampKindStampBounds), (plugin, granularity, calendar, properties, valueSchema), orderingField, pathOfElementOrAttribute, timeDimensionOrderBy)	It allows the designer to change an existing physical timestamp in the annotation document "AD.xml". This operation changes attributes (i.e., target and dataInclusion) and/or sub-elements (i.e., <stampKind/> and <orderBy/>) of the <stamp/> element. This operation uses the following primitives: SetDataInclusionInStamp(AD.xml, stampTarget, stampDataInclusion) SetStampKindInStamp(AD.xml, stampTarget, stampKindTimeDimension, stampKindStampBounds) SetFormatInStampKind(AD.xml, stampTarget, stampPlugin, stampGranularity, stampCalendar, stampProperties, stampValueSchema) DeleteFormatFromStampKind(AD.xml, stampTarget) AddOrderByFieldToStamp(AD.xml, stampTarget, newOrderByField) DeleteOrderByFieldFromStamp(AD.xml, stampTarget, OrderByField) ChangeOrderByFieldInStamp(AD.xml, stampTarget, oldOrderByField, newOrderByField)

Figure 7. Second version of the annotation document (BankAnnotations_V2.xml), on June 1, 2017

```xml
<?xml version="1.0" encoding="UTF-8"?>
<annotationSet xmlns="http://www.cs.arizona.edu/tau/tauXSchema/ASchema">
 <logical>
  <item target="Bank/Account/Balance">
   <transactionTime kind="state" content="varying" existence="constant"/>
   <validTime kind="state" content="varying" existence="constant"/>
   <itemIdentifier name="balanceID" timeDimension="transactionTime">
    <field path="."/>
   </itemIdentifier>
  </item>
 </logical>
 <physical>
  <stamp target="Bank/Account" dataInclusion="expandedVersion">
   <stampKind timeDimension="transactionTime" stampBounds="extent"/>
  </stamp>
  <stamp target="Bank/Account/Balance" dataInclusion="expandedVersion">
   <stampKind timeDimension="bitemporal" stampBounds="extent"/>
  </stamp>
 </physical>
</annotationSet>
```

Figure 8. Temporal schema (BankTemporalSchema.xml) on June 1, 2017

```
<?xml version="1.0" encoding="UTF-8"?>
<temporalSchema xmlns="http://www.cs.arizona.edu/tau/tauXSchema/TSSchema">
 <conventionalSchema>
  <sliceSequence>
   <slice location="Bank_V1.xsd" begin="2017-02-01" />
   <slice location="Bank_V2.xsd" begin="2017-03-01" />
  </sliceSequence>
 </conventionalSchema>
 <annotationSet>
  <sliceSequence>
   <slice location="BankAnnotations_V1.xml" begin="2017-02-01" />
   <slice location="BankAnnotations_V2.xml" begin="2017-06-01" />
  </sliceSequence>
 </annotationSet>
</temporalSchema>
```

3.   AddStamp("BankAnnotations_V2.xml", "Bank/Account/Balance", expandedVersion, bitemporal, extent)

Commit

Alternatively, the same results could be obtained if the designer uses three high-level change operations (instead of four change primitives), through the following schema change transaction, which is executed on June 1, 2017.

Begin Transaction

1.   UpdateTemporalSchema("BankTemporalSchema.xml",,, current, "BankAnnotations_V2.xml")
2.   ChangeFormatOfTimeVaryingItem("BankAnnotations_V2.xml", "Bank/Account/Balance", bitemporal, (state, varying, constant))
3.   SpecifyPhysicalTimeStamp("BankAnnotations_V2.xml", "Bank/Account/Balance", expandedVersion, (bitemporal, extent), (,,,,),,,,)

Commit

RELATED WORK DISCUSSION

Schema versioning has been widely and deeply studied in the context of temporal relational databases (e.g., (De Castro et al., 1997), (Wei & Elmasri, 2000) and (Brahmia, Mkaouar, Chakhar, & Bouaziz, 2012c)) and temporal object-oriented databases (e.g., (Grandi & Mandreoli, 2003), (Galante, Dos Santos, Edelweiss, & Moreira, 2005), and (Cordeiro, Galante, Edelweiss, & dos Santos, 2007)). In the XML setting, a bibliography of work about temporal representation and evolution of documents and data on the web has been presented in (Grandi, 2004). In (Guerrini & Mesiti, 2009), a comparative study of the XML schema evolution support in mainstream commercial DBMSs (MS SQL Server, Oracle, IBM

DB2, and Tamino) had also been provided. Both the state of the art and the state of the practice, as of August 2013, of managing temporal and multiversion XML documents, have been studied by Faisal and Sarwar (2014).

In (Brahmia & Bouaziz, 2008), the authors proposed six generic operations for XML schema change; three operations act on an XML Schema "element" (i.e., addition, deletion and modification of an XML Schema element) and three operations act on an "attribute" of an XML schema "element" (i.e., addition, deletion and modification of an attribute). In the present work, a completion of the work started by Brahmia and Bouaziz (2008) is done in the context of the τXSchema approach, at a deeper and more detailed level: in the end, we introduced one hundred and twenty primitives to change all components that belong to the definition of the XML Schema language (W3C, 2004), and not only to change "elements" or "attributes".

In (Guerrini et al., 2005), a set of primitives for updating XML Schema has been defined. But these primitives deal only with "simple types", "complex types" and "elements". Our work is both more detailed and more global since it proposes primitives for changing all components of an XML Schema Definition (W3C, 2004), and not only for changing "simple types", "complex types" and "elements".

In (Guerrini & Mesiti, 2008), the authors presented X-Evolution, which is a web-based tool making the primitives defined by Guerrini et al. (2005) available to the user both through a graphical interface and through a specifically tailored schema update language named XSchemaUpdate. In (Cavalieri, Guerrini, & Mesiti, 2011a), the authors present EXup which is an engine for specifying XSchemaUpdate statements, translating them in XQuery Update Facility (W3C, 2011) expressions and evaluating them against XML Schema and associated documents. After studying these two tools, we noticed that they support only XML Schema evolution and they do not provide all primitives for changing XML Schema. However, our present work gives all necessary primitives for changing XML Schema in a context that supports schema versioning (which is more general and more powerful than schema evolution). Notice that Cavalieri, Guerrini, Mesiti, and Oliboni (2011b) have proposed an algorithm that applies a set of rules for optimizing sequences of XML schema change or XML document change operations.

Based on the principles of the model driven development paradigm, Nečaský, Klímek, Malý, and Mlýnková (2012) defined an approach for evolving XML schemata: schema changes performed at conceptual level are semi-automatically propagated to all related conceptual and logical XML schemata. Besides, Malý, Mlýnková, and Nečaský (2011) and Klímek, Malý, Mlýnková, and Nečaský (2012) dealt with XML schema versioning and XML schema evolution respectively, in an environment that is based on the model driven architecture approach. Indeed, in (Malý et al., 2011), the authors proposed to revalidate existing XML instance documents, which are valid to the changed XML schema version, with respect to the new XML schema version, through the execution of an XSLT (W3C, 2007) script, which result from the comparison of the new schema version to the last one, on all these instance documents. In (Klímek et al., 2012), the authors presented a tool, named eXolutio, for automatically changing PIM (PSM, respectively) schemata and propagating such a change to all involved PSM (PIM, respectively) schemata. Notice that an experimental assessment, in a real e-health system, of both the approach of Nečaský et al. (2012) and eXolutio presented in (Klímek, Malý, Nečaský, & Holubová, 2015). Before all these contributions, in 2011, the GEA framework was proposed in (Domínguez et al., 2011) and is based on managing schema evolution at abstract/conceptual level, by working on an UML class diagram, generating the corresponding XML Schema file, and propagating changes to all related UML models and involved XML/XSD documents.

When XML schemata evolve, already defined XSLT stylesheets and XPath (W3C, 2014) expressions could be affected. For this reason, some authors have focused on revising/correcting XSLT stylesheets, when changed XML schema are defined as XSD files, like in (Kwietniewski, Gryz, Hazlewood, & Van Run, 2010) or DTD files, like in (Wu & Suzuki, 2016). Some other authors, like Genevès, Layaïda, and Quint (2011) and Hasegawa, Ikeda, and Suzuki (2013), dealt with adapting old XPath expressions, which were specified while taking into account the previous XML schema version, according to the new XML schema version. Besides, XML namespaces could also evolve over time and have effects at both schema and instance levels; this issue was studied by Brahmia, Grandi, and Bouaziz (2016b, 2016c) in an environment that supports XML schema versioning, by proposing a systematic approach that allows an XML DBA expressing changes to XML namespaces defined in XML schemata and transparently updating all related XML schemata/documents, through the generation of new versions of these XML schemata and XML documents.

The works of Bouchou and Duarte (2007) and Amavi, Chabin, Ferrari, and Réty (2014) aimed at proposing conservative XML schema evolution approaches, i.e., approaches that preserve the validity of underlying XML documents when their XML schemata evolve. The difference between the two contributions consists in the fact that in (Bouchou & Duarte, 2007), the authors define an XML schema as a sequence of regular expression-based rules and work on these regular expressions to make their approach safe and correct, whereas in (Amavi et al., 2014) the authors used conversion and inversion techniques to define mappings between two successive conservative XML schema versions.

Several algorithms were proposed for detecting differences between XML schema versions, like Xy-Diff (Cobena, Abiteboul, & Marian, 2002), X-Diff (Wang, DeWitt, & Cai, 2003), DTD-Diff (Leonardi, Hoai, Bhowmick, & Madria, 2007), and XS-Diff (Baqasah, Pardede, Rahayu, & Holubová, 2015a). Notice that Leonardi et al. (2007) compared their algorithm to both XyDiff and X-Diff, and showed that it is significantly faster than them. Moreover, Baqasah et al. (2015a) compared their algorithm to XyDiff and X-Diff and showed that it is much faster than XyDiff but has a speed which is almost equal to that of X-Diff.

To merge XML schema versions, Baqasah, Pardede, and Rahayu (2014a) introduced an approach that is based on a set of rules to resolve conflicts when merging XML schemata, a set of transformations functions to fix paths of merged XSD components, and a tool which is an enhanced version of another tool for monitoring XML schema versions, named XSM and previously proposed by the same authors in (Baqasah, Pardede, & Rahayu, 2014b). After that, in (Baqasah, Pardede, & Rahayu, 2015b), the authors dealt with XML schema versioning and showed how to maintain compatibility of schema versions in a collaborative cloud computing context, based on an extended version of the XSM tool. Notice that the Zaniolo's team dealt with temporal XML versioning in a relational-XML environment. For instance, Wang, Zaniolo, and Zhou (2008) proposed a unified XML-based approach that allows (i) representing in XML the content of a transaction-time relational database that supports schema versioning, (ii) expressing temporal complex queries (Wang & Zaniolo, 2008) on such content via XQuery (W3C, 2010), and (iii) executing these queries after transparently converting them to SQL/XML (Eisenberg & Melton, 2004) queries.

The works, that are more strictly related with our approach, are (Currim et al., 2004), (Dyreson et al., 2006), (Snodgrass et al., 2008) and (Currim et al., 2009). All these works focus on validating time-varying XML documents against time-varying schemata in the τXSchema framework. They suppose that any change could be made on the schema, and thus, they do not study how the schema changes are performed, or what schema change operations should be provided. Schema versioning in the τXSchema framework (Snodgrass et al., 2008) means versioning of conventional schema and versioning of annotations. In (Brahmia et al., 2010; Brahmia et al., 2011), we studied versioning of annotations. We proposed a complete and sound set of change primitives for physical and logical annotations and defined their operational semantics. In (Brahmia et al., 2012a; Brahmia et al., 2012b), we completed the picture by studying versioning of the conventional schema: we proposed another complete and sound set of change primitives for supporting the evolution of this schema. In (Brahmia, Grandi, Oliboni, & Bouaziz, 2014b), we defined two sets of high-level operations for the creation and maintenance of temporal and conventional schemata in τXSchema. The operations of each one these sets have been categorized into basic operations, i.e., atomic operations, and complex ones, i.e., operations that can be defined via basic operations. All details on these operations, plus another set of high level operations for creating and changing annotations, were provided in (Brahmia et al., 2014a). After that, the paper (Brahmia, Grandi, Oliboni, & Bouaziz, 2014c) extended our previous works about τXSchema by proposing a general approach for schema versioning in that framework. Our approach allows a complete management of schema changes in τXSchema-based multitemporal XML repositories and guarantees the maintenance of a full history of evolving data and schemata.

As far as high-level schema change operations are concerned, there are three works that are more strictly related with our current work: (Guerrini et al., 2005), (Prashant & Kumar, 2006), and (Nečaský et al., 2012). In (Guerrini et al., 2005), the authors introduced a set of high-level evolution primitives that could be used by an XML Schema designer to express complex schema changes; each high-level primitive is expressed as a sequence of atomic primitives which are also proposed in (Guerrini et al., 2005). But due to space limitations, they do not give enough details on these high-level primitives (e.g. their complete set, what atomic primitives that compose each high-level primitive and in what way?, and their operational semantics). Furthermore, the authors do not refer the reader to any technical report or any other work. They present an example in which they use only two high-level primitives: insert_substruct and collapse_substruct. They note that these high-level primitives mainly include primitives for inserting, moving, and changing whole substructures rather than single elements.

In (Prashant & Kumar, 2006), the authors proposed a set of three high-level DTD change operations (i.e., SubtreeMoveUp, SubtreeMoveDown, and RelationshipInverse) and studied their effect on XML documents whose DTD is being evolved. The authors noted that this set of high-level operations is based on the set of primitive DTD change operations that was proposed in (Su, Kramer, Chen, Claypool, & Rundensteiner, 2001).

In (Nečaský et al., 2012), the authors proposed a set of composite operations for changing XML schema at conceptual levels (i.e., PIM and PSM levels), within an approach based on the principles of Model-Driven Development. Obviously, each composite operation is a sequence of two or more atomic operations. But the authors give only three composite operations and do not refer the reader to a work in which he/she find more details or the full list of possible composite operations. In fact, the authors suppose that the particular set of composite operations depends on the choice of the vendor of a particular system and the requirements of users. Their aim in (Nečaský et al., 2012) was to demonstrate that the proposed mechanism can be used in real-world situations.

Similar to these related works (i.e., (Guerrini et al., 2005), (Prashant & Kumar, 2006), and (Nečaský et al., 2012)), our current work proposes also high-level schema change operations that are validity preserving (i.e., each operation applied to a consistent conventional schema produces a consistent conventional schema). Moreover, our further contributions are as follows:

1.   We have proposed a large set of high-level operations in order to provide more various user-friendly operations that could be directly implemented by creators of tools or systems for XML Schema evolution/versioning. Notice here that our proposed set of high-level operations is not complete: we do not claim to provide all possible high-level operations, since we could not list all requirements of all XML Schema designers; but, if required, an XML Schema designer could build a new customized high-level operation by composing some primitives and/or some high-level operations.

2.   We have classified the proposed high-level operations in basic operations (i.e., high-level operations that cannot be defined by using other basic high-level operations) and complex operations.

3.   We have not proposed only operations for manipulating portions of schema (i.e., sub-schema or sub-tree), but also operations dealing with whole conventional schema, XML Schema elements, XML Schema attributes, and XML Schema constraints (datatype restrictions, and key, unique, cardinality, and referential integrity constraints).

Moreover, with regard to previous works on τXSchema, the novel contributions of our approach are as follows:

1.   We are the first ones to fully address the XML Schema definition as presented in the W3C Part 0 recommendation (W3C, 2004);

2.   We deal with versioning of logical and physical annotations;

3.   We define all schema change primitives that must be supported;

4.   We propose user-friendly high-level operations that allow designers changing conventional schema, logical and physical annotations, and temporal schema;

5.   We specify how the schema changes are made;

6.   We capture the implied modifications on the conventional schema and on the annotation document to the temporal schema.

FUTURE RESEARCH DIRECTIONS

Future work can follow two main paths: (i) extending the approach proposed in this paper, by focusing on other aspects related to schema versioning in τXSchema, and (ii) dealing with schema versioning in a more broader sense, by studying it in other interesting related fields (e.g., emerging databases, modern applications).

Extension of Our Approach

Currently, a tool that allows designers to define and change τXSchema schemata, while supporting schema versioning, is being developed at the University of Sfax (Tunisia). It implements our schema versioning approach and all proposed low-level and high-level schema change operations. A graphical designer interface similar to that proposed in (Dixon, 2013) is planned to equip the tool.

As a part of our future work, we plan to extend our approach by studying complex temporal queries under schema versioning in the τXSchema framework. To do this, we will start from the τXQuery language (Gao & Snodgrass, 2003), which allows users to perform temporal queries in that framework under a single schema version, and extend it with multi-schema query features (Grandi, 2002).

Last but not least, as currently τXSchema supports schema versioning along transaction-time only, we aim in our future work at extending τXSchema to also support valid-time schema versioning and bitemporal schema versioning, so that it could be useful for several temporal XML applications that require performing retroactive and/or proactive schema changes. To this aim, we will start from specifications provided in (De Castro et al., 1997) dealing with these two schema versioning approaches in the relational setting, possibly with some other related design options, mentioned by the same authors, like the multi-pool solution, for storage and manipulation of instances in the presence of multiple schema versions, and the asynchronous management policy, for managing the interaction between instance versioning and schema versioning.

Schema Versioning Research in Other Related Fields

In a broader context, we propose the following open research issues for schema versioning:

1. Explicit schema versioning support is absent in all commercial systems (i.e., DBMSs and schema management tools), as shown in (Colazzo et al., 2010; Faisal & Sarwar, 2014). Thus, this aspect needs further efforts in order to provide more efficient practical solutions for database designers and administrators.
2. Schema versioning support is also absent in the standard SQL language, though its last version SQL:2011 supports some temporal features (Kulkarni & Michels, 2012). Hence, SQL cannot be used to exploit the potentialities of a relational database supporting schema versioning. Assuming the proliferation of different versions of schema and associated data, an interesting research topic would be to suggest suitable extensions to SQL, beyond the proposed TSQL2 extensions (De Castro et al., 1997) and MSQL (Grandi, 2002), in order to allow applications to access data defined under multiple schemas.
3. Since several modern applications (e.g., cloud computing, internet of things, social networks, big data analysis, biological and biomedical applications) use new types of databases called emerging databases (e.g., NoSQL and NewSQL databases, mobile databases, sensor databases, multi-model databases, stream databases), future research work in the database community should also be devoted to schema versioning in these domains. Although a lot of work has been done on schema evolution in NoSQL databases (e.g., (Klettke, Störl, Shenavai, & Scherzinger, 2016), (Saur, Dumitras, & Hicks, 2016), (Scherzinger, Sombach, Wiech, Klettke, & Störl, 2016), (Haubold, Schildgren, Scherzinger, & Deßloch, 2017), and (Meurice & Cleve, 2017)), to the best of our knowledge, currently there is only one contribution, proposed by Brahmia, Brahmia, Grandi, and Bouaziz (2017a), which deals with schema versioning in a NoSQL setting. In this work, the authors have provided a systematic approach for managing transaction-time schema versioning in a temporal JSON-based NoSQL framework, named τJSchema, previously introduced by the same authors in (Brahmia, Brahmia, Grandi, & Bouaziz, 2016a).
4. Nowadays, many enterprises use Web and distributed databases and, thus, schema changes have to be effected more frequently, since user requirements, laws and technologies change rapidly. Therefore, it will be very interesting and useful to study schema versioning in Web and distributed environments. Among the first works in this area, we find (Rae, Rollins, Shute, Sodhi, & Vingralek, 2013), which describes techniques used by Google's F1 DBMS (Shute et al., 2013) to support schema evolution in a globally distributed environment.

5. The database provenance is very useful in many modern information systems (like big science projects), in order to explain the lineage of the current data. This explanation often requires "flashing back" to the original schema and, thus, supporting database provenance under schema versioning could be an interesting issue. Although provenance has been studied under schema evolution (Gao & Zaniolo, 2012), to the best of our knowledge, currently there is no work on data provenance under schema versioning.

CONCLUSION

In this work, we propose a comprehensive approach for schema versioning in τXSchema-based multitemporal XML repositories. It allows designers to change the temporal schema, the conventional schema, and the logical and physical annotations. Versions of the conventional schema and those of the annotation document are subsequent in time; alternative versions are not allowed and each version has its own temporal interval during which it was in force. A new version of the conventional schema (of the annotation document, respectively) is created after applying a sequence of schema change operations to the current version of this schema (of this document, respectively). This corresponds to supporting transaction-time schema versioning (De Castro et al., 1997) of temporal data.

In particular, three sound and complete sets of schema change primitives have been introduced for the maintenance of temporal schema, conventional schema and logical and physical annotations; the syntax and operational semantics of each primitive have been defined. Notice that we are the first ones to fully address changes involving the W3C Part 0 recommendation (W3C, 2004), since our work considers all the features that were listed in such standard specification.

We have also proposed three sets of high-level operations for changing temporal schema, conventional schema, and annotations; semantics of all operations are described. These operations are user-friendly and help designers to express complex schema changes in a more compact way.

REFERENCES

Amavi, J., Chabin, J., Ferrari, M. H., & Réty, P. (2014). A ToolBox for Conservative XML Schema Evolution and Document Adaptation. *Proceedings of the 25th International Conference on Database and Expert Systems Applications (DEXA 2014)*, 299-307. 10.1007/978-3-319-10073-9_24

Baqasah, A., Pardede, E., & Rahayu, J. W. (2014a). A New Approach for Meaningful XML Schema Merging. *Proceedings of the 16th International Conference on Information Integration and Web-based Applications & Services (iiWAS 2014)*, 430-439. 10.1145/2684200.2684302

Baqasah, A., Pardede, E., & Rahayu, J. W. (2014b). XSM - A Tracking System for XML Schema Versions. *Proceedings of the 28th IEEE International Conference on Advanced Information Networking and Applications (AINA 2014)*, 1081-1088. 10.1109/AINA.2014.131

Baqasah, A., Pardede, E., & Rahayu, J. W. (2015b). Maintaining Schema Versions Compatibility in Cloud Applications Collaborative Framework. *World Wide Web (Bussum)*, *18*(6), 1541–1577. doi:10.100711280-014-0321-1

Baqasah, A., Pardede, E., Rahayu, J. W., & Holubová, I. (2015a). XS-Diff: XML schema change detection algorithm. *International Journal of Web and Grid Services*, *11*(2), 160–192. doi:10.1504/IJWGS.2015.068897

Bouchou, B., & Duarte, D. (2007). Assisting XML Schema Evolution that Preserves Validity. *Proceedings of the 22nd Brazilian Symposium on Databases (SBBD 2007)*, 270-284.

Brahmia, S., Brahmia, Z., Grandi, F., & Bouaziz, R. (2016a). τJSchema: A Framework for Managing Temporal JSON-Based NoSQL Databases. *Proceedings of the 27th International Conference on Database and Expert Systems Applications (DEXA'2016)*, 167-181. 10.1007/978-3-319-44406-2_13

Brahmia, S., Brahmia, Z., Grandi, F., & Bouaziz, R. (2017a). Temporal JSON Schema Versioning in the τJSchema Framework. *Journal of Digital Information Management*, *15*(4), 179–202.

Brahmia, Z., & Bouaziz, R. (2008). An approach for schema versioning in multi-temporal XML databases. *Proceedings of the 10th International Conference on Enterprise Information Systems (ICEIS 2008)*, 290-297.

Brahmia, Z., Bouaziz, R., Grandi, F., & Oliboni, B. (2010). *Schema Versioning in τXSchema-Based Multitemporal XML Repositories*. TimeCenter, Technical Report TR-93. Retrieved August 2, 2017, from <http://timecenter.cs.aau.dk/TimeCenterPublications/TR-93.pdf>

Brahmia, Z., Bouaziz, R., Grandi, F., & Oliboni, B. (2011). Schema Versioning in τXSchema-Based Multitemporal XML Repositories. *Proceedings of the 5th IEEE International Conference on Research Challenges in Information Science (RCIS 2011)*, 1-12.

Brahmia, Z., Bouaziz, R., Grandi, F., & Oliboni, B. (2012a). *A Study of Conventional Schema Versioning in the τXSchema Framework*. TimeCenter, Technical Report TR-94. Retrieved August 2, 2017, from <http://timecenter.cs.aau.dk/TimeCenterPublications/TR-94.pdf>

Brahmia, Z., Grandi, F., & Bouaziz, R. (2016b). Changes to XML Namespaces in XML Schemas and their Effects on Associated XML Documents under Schema Versioning. *Proceedings of the 11th International Conference on Digital Information Management (ICDIM'2016)*, 43-50. 10.1109/ICDIM.2016.7829765

Brahmia, Z., Grandi, F., & Bouaziz, R. (2016c). A Systematic Approach for Changing XML Namespaces in XML Schemas and Managing their Effects on Associated XML Documents under Schema Versioning. *Journal of Digital Information Management*, *14*(5), 275–289.

Brahmia, Z., Grandi, F., Oliboni, B., & Bouaziz, R. (2012b). Versioning of Conventional Schema in the τXSchema Framework. *Proceedings of the 8th International Conference on Signal Image Technology & Internet Systems (SITIS'2012)*, 510-518.

Brahmia, Z., Grandi, F., Oliboni, B., & Bouaziz, R. (2014a). *High-level Operations for Changing Temporal Schema, Conventional Schema, and Annotations, in the τXSchema Framework*. TimeCenter, Technical Report TR-96. Retrieved August 2, 2017, from http://timecenter.cs.aau.dk/TimeCenterPublications/TR-96.pdf

Brahmia, Z., Grandi, F., Oliboni, B., & Bouaziz, R. (2014b). High-level Operations for Creation and Maintenance of Temporal and Conventional Schema in the τXSchema Framework. *Proceedings of the 21st International Symposium on Temporal Representation and Reasoning (TIME'2014)*, 101-110. 10.1109/TIME.2014.14

Brahmia, Z., Grandi, F., Oliboni, B., & Bouaziz, R. (2014c). Schema Change Operations for Full Support of Schema Versioning in the τXSchema Framework. *International Journal of Information Technology and Web Engineering*, 9(2), 20–46. doi:10.4018/ijitwe.2014040102

Brahmia, Z., Grandi, F., Oliboni, B., & Bouaziz, R. (2015). Schema Versioning. In M. Khosrow-Pour (Ed.), *Encyclopedia of Information Science and Technology* (3rd ed.; pp. 7651–7661). Hershey, PA: IGI Global; doi:10.4018/978-1-4666-5888-2.ch754

Brahmia, Z., Grandi, F., Oliboni, B., & Bouaziz, R. (2017b). Schema Versioning in Conventional and Emerging Databases. In M. Khosrow-Pour (Ed.), *Encyclopedia of Information Science and Technology* (4th ed.; pp. 2054–2063). Hershey, PA: IGI Global. doi:10.4018/978-1-5225-2255-3.ch178

Brahmia, Z., Mkaouar, M., Chakhar, S., & Bouaziz, R. (2012c). Efficient Management of Schema Versioning in Multi-Temporal Databases. *The International Arab Journal of Information Technology*, 9(6), 544–552.

Cavalieri, F., Guerrini, G., & Mesiti, M. (2011a). Updating XML schemas and associated documents through exup. *Proceedings of the 27th International Conference on Data Engineering (ICDE 2011)*, 1320-1323. 10.1109/ICDE.2011.5767951

Cavalieri, F., Guerrini, G., Mesiti, M., & Oliboni, B. (2011b). On the reduction of sequences of XML document and schema update operations. *Proceedings of the 1st International ICDE Workshop on Managing Data Throughout its Lifecycle (DaLi 2011)*, 77-86. 10.1109/ICDEW.2011.5767649

Clifford, J., Croker, A., Grandi, F., & Tuzhilin, A. (1995). On Temporal Grouping. *Proceedings of the International Workshop on Temporal Databases*, 194–213.

Cobena, G., Abiteboul, S., & Marian, A. (2002). Detecting Changes in XML Documents. *Proceedings of the 18th International Conference on Data Engineering (ICDE 2002)*, 41-52. 10.1109/ICDE.2002.994696

Colazzo, D., Guerrini, G., Mesiti, M., Oliboni, B., & Waller, E. (2010). Document and Schema XML Updates. In C. Li & T. W. Ling (Eds.), *Advanced Applications and Structures in XML Processing: Label Stream, Semantics Utilization and Data Query Technologies* (pp. 361–384). Hershey, PA: IGI Global. doi:10.4018/978-1-61520-727-5.ch016

Cordeiro, R. L. F., Galante, R. M., Edelweiss, N., & dos Santos, C. S. (2007). A Deep Classification of Temporal Versioned Integrity Constraints for Designing Database Applications. *Proceedings of the 19th International Conference on Software Engineering & Knowledge Engineering (SEKE'2007)*, 416-421.

Currim, F., Currim, S., Dyreson, C. E., Joshi, S., Snodgrass, R. T., Thomas, S. W., & Roeder, E. (2009). *τXSchema: Support for Data- and Schema-Versioned XML Documents*. TimeCenter, Technical Report TR-91. Retrieved August 2, 2017, from <http://timecenter.cs.aau.dk/TimeCenterPublications/TR-91.pdf>

Currim, F., Currim, S., Dyreson, C. E., & Snodgrass, R. T. (2004). A Tale of Two Schemas: Creating a Temporal XML Schema from a Snapshot Schema with τXSchema. *Proceedings of the 9th International Conference on Extending Database Technology (EDBT 2004)*, 348-365. 10.1007/978-3-540-24741-8_21

De Castro, C., Grandi, F., & Scalas, M. R. (1997). Schema versioning for multitemporal relational databases. *Information Systems*, 22(5), 249–290. doi:10.1016/S0306-4379(97)00017-3

Dixon, M. B. (2013). A Graphical Based Approach to the Conceptual Modeling, Validation and Generation of XML Schema Definitions. *International Journal of Information Technology and Web Engineering*, 8(1), 1–22. doi:10.4018/jitwe.2013010101

Domínguez, E., Lloret, J., Pérez, B., Rodríguez, Á., Rubio, A. L., & Zapata, M. A. (2011). Evolution of XML Schemas and documents from stereotyped UML class models: A traceable approach. *Information and Software Technology*, 53(1), 34–50. doi:10.1016/j.infsof.2010.08.001

Dyreson, C. E. (2001). Observing Transaction-time Semantics with TTXPath. *Proceedings of the 2nd International Conference on Web Information Systems Engineering (WISE 2001)*, 193-202.

Dyreson, C. E., & Grandi, F. (2009). Temporal XML. In L. Liu & M. T. Özsu (Eds.), *Encyclopedia of Database Systems* (pp. 3032–3035). Heidelberg, Germany: Springer-Verlag.

Dyreson, C. E., Snodgrass, R. T., Currim, F., Currim, S., & Joshi, S. (2006). Validating Quicksand: Schema Versioning in τXSchema. *Proceedings of the 22nd International Conference on Data Engineering Workshops (ICDE Workshops 2006)*, 82. 10.1109/ICDEW.2006.161

Eisenberg, A., & Melton, J. (2004). Advancements in SQL/XML. *SIGMOD Record*, 33(3), 79–86. doi:10.1145/1031570.1031588

Faisal, S., & Sarwar, M. (2014). Temporal and multi-versioned XML documents: A survey. *Information Processing & Management*, 50(1), 113–131. doi:10.1016/j.ipm.2013.08.003

Galante, R. M., Dos Santos, C. S., Edelweiss, N., & Moreira, A. F. (2005). Temporal and versioning model for schema evolution in object-oriented databases. *Data & Knowledge Engineering*, 53(2), 99–128. doi:10.1016/j.datak.2004.07.001

Gao, D., & Snodgrass, R. T. (2003). Temporal slicing in the evaluation of XML documents. *Proceedings of the 29th International Conference on Very Large Data Bases (VLDB 2003)*, 632-643.

Gao, S., & Zaniolo, C. (2012). Supporting Database Provenance under Schema Evolution. *Proceedings of the 5th International ER Workshop on Evolution and Change in Data Management and on Non Conventional Data Access (ECDM – NoCoDa 2012)*, 67-77.

Genevès, P., Layaïda, N., & Quint, V. (2011). Impact of XML Schema Evolution. *ACM Transactions on Internet Technology*, 11(1), 4. doi:10.1145/1993083.1993087

Grandi, F. (2002). A relational multi-schema data model and query language for full support of schema versioning. *Proceedings of SEBD 2002 – National Conference on Advanced Database Systems*, 323-336.

Grandi, F. (2004). Introducing an Annotated Bibliography on Temporal and Evolution Aspects in the World Wide Web. *SIGMOD Record*, 33(2), 84–86. doi:10.1145/1024694.1024709

Grandi, F. (2015). Temporal Databases. In M. Khosrow-Pour (Ed.), *Encyclopedia of Information Science and Technology* (3rd ed.; pp. 1914–1922). Hershey, PA: IGI Global; doi:10.4018/978-1-4666-5888-2.ch184

Grandi, F., & Mandreoli, F. (2003). A formal model for temporal schema versioning in object-oriented databases. *Data & Knowledge Engineering, 46*(2), 123–167. doi:10.1016/S0169-023X(02)00207-0

Guerrini, G., & Mesiti, M. (2008). X-Evolution: A Comprehensive Approach for XML Schema Evolution. *Proceedings of the 19th International Workshop Database and Expert Systems Applications (DEXA 2008)*, 251-255. 10.1109/DEXA.2008.128

Guerrini, G., & Mesiti, M. (2009). XML Schema Evolution and Versioning: Current Approaches and Future Trends. In E. Pardede (Ed.), *Open and Novel Issues in XML Database Applications: Future Directions and Advanced Technologies* (pp. 66–87). Hershey, PA: Information Science Reference – IGI Global. doi:10.4018/978-1-60566-308-1.ch004

Guerrini, G., Mesiti, M., & Rossi, D. (2005). Impact of XML Schema Evolution on Valid Documents. *Proceedings of the 7th ACM International Workshop on Web Information and Data Management (WIDM 2005)*, 39-44. 10.1145/1097047.1097056

Hasegawa, K., Ikeda, K., & Suzuki, N. (2013). An Algorithm for Transforming XPath Expressions According to Schema Evolution. *Proceedings of the 1st International Workshop on Document Changes: Modeling, Detection, Storage and Visualization (DChanges 2013)*, paper 4.

Haubold, F., Schildgren, J., Scherzinger, S., & Deßloch, S. (2017). ControVol Flex: Flexible Schema Evolution for NoSQL Application Development. *Proceedings of the 17th Conference on Database Systems for Business, Technology, and Web (BTW'2017)*, 601-604.

Klettke, M., Störl, U., Shenavai, M., & Scherzinger, S. (2016). NoSQL Schema Evolution and Big Data Migration at Scale. *Proceedings of the 2016 IEEE International Conference on Big Data (BigData'2016)*, 2764-2774. 10.1109/BigData.2016.7840924

Klímek, J., Malý, J., Mlýnková, I., & Nečaský, M. (2012). eXolutio: Tool for XML Schema and Data Management. *Proceedings of the 12th Annual International Workshop on DAtabases, TExts, Specifications and Objects (DATESO 2012)*, 69-80.

Klímek, J., Malý, J., Nečaský, M., & Holubová, I. (2015). eXolutio: Methodology for Design and Evolution of XML Schemas using Conceptual Modeling. *Informatica, 26*(3), 453–472. doi:10.15388/Informatica.2015.58

Kulkarni, K. G., & Michels, J.-E. (2012). Temporal features in SQL:2011. *SIGMOD Record, 41*(3), 34–43. doi:10.1145/2380776.2380786

Kwietniewski, M., Gryz, J., Hazlewood, S., & Van Run, P. (2010). Transforming XML Documents as Schemas Evolve. *Proceedings of the VLDB Endowment International Conference on Very Large Data Bases, 3*(2), 1577–1580. doi:10.14778/1920841.1921043

Leonardi, E., Hoai, T. T., Bhowmick, S. S., & Madria, S. (2007). DTD-Diff: A change detection algorithm for DTDs. *Data & Knowledge Engineering, 61*(2), 384–402. doi:10.1016/j.datak.2006.06.003

Malý, J., Mlýnková, I., & Nečaský, M. (2011). XML Data Transformations as Schema Evolves. *Proceedings of the 15th International Conference on Advances in Databases and Information Systems (ADBIS 2011)*, 375-388. 10.1007/978-3-642-23737-9_27

Meurice, L., & Cleve, A. (2017). Supporting Schema Evolution in Schema-Less NoSQL Data Stores. *Proceedings of the 24th IEEE International Conference on Software ANalysis, Evolution and Reengineering (SANER'2017)*, 457-461. 10.1109/SANER.2017.7884653

Nečaský, M., Klímek, J., Malý, J., & Mlýnková, I. (2012). Evolution and change management of XML-based systems. *Journal of Systems and Software*, *85*(3), 683–707. doi:10.1016/j.jss.2011.09.038

Noh, S.-Y., & Gadia, S. K. (2006). A comparison of two approaches to utilizing XML in parametric databases for temporal data. *Information and Software Technology*, *48*(9), 807–819. doi:10.1016/j.infsof.2005.10.002

Prashant, B. V. N., & Kumar, P. S. (2006). Managing XML data with Evolving Schema. *Proceedings of the 13th International Conference on Management of Data (COMAD'2006)*, 174-177.

Rae, I., Rollins, E., Shute, J., Sodhi, S., & Vingralek, R. (2013). Online, Asynchronous Schema Change in F1. *Proceedings of the VLDB Endowment International Conference on Very Large Data Bases*, *6*(11), 1045–1056. doi:10.14778/2536222.2536230

Rizzolo, F., & Vaisman, A. A. (2008). Temporal XML: Modeling, Indexing, and Query Processing. *The VLDB Journal*, *17*(5), 1179–1212. doi:10.100700778-007-0058-x

Saur, K., Dumitras, T., & Hicks, M. W. (2016). Evolving NoSQL Databases Without Downtime. *Proceedings of the 32nd IEEE International Conference on Software Maintenance and Evolution (ICSME'2016)*, 166-176. 10.1109/ICSME.2016.47

Scherzinger, S., Sombach, S., Wiech, K., Klettke, M., & Störl, U. (2016). Datalution: a tool for continuous schema evolution in NoSQL-backed web applications. *Proceedings of the 2nd International Workshop on Quality-Aware DevOps (QUDOS@ISSTA'2016)*, 38-39. 10.1145/2945408.2945416

Shute, J., Vingralek, R., Samwel, B., Handy, B., Whipkey, C., Rollins, E., ... Apte, H. (2013). F1: A Distributed SQL Database That Scales. *Proceedings of the VLDB Endowment International Conference on Very Large Data Bases*, *6*(11), 1068–1079. doi:10.14778/2536222.2536232

Snodgrass, R. T., Böhlen, M. H., Jensen, C. S., & Steiner, A. (1998). Transitioning temporal support in TSQL2 to SQL3. In O. Etzion, S. Jajodia, & S. Sripada (Eds.), *Temporal Databases: Research and Practice* (pp. 150–194). Berlin, Germany: Springer. doi:10.1007/BFb0053702

Snodgrass, R. T., Dyreson, C. E., Currim, F., Currim, S., & Joshi, S. (2008). Validating Quicksand: Schema Versioning in τXSchema. *Data & Knowledge Engineering*, *65*(2), 223–242. doi:10.1016/j.datak.2007.09.003

Su, H., Kramer, D., Chen, L., Claypool, K. T., & Rundensteiner, E. A. (2001). XEM: Managing the evolution of XML Documents. *Proceedings of the 11th International Workshop on Research Issues in Data Engineering: Document Management for Data Intensive Business and Scientific Applications (RIDE 2001)*, 103-110.

W3C. (2004). *XML Schema Part 0: Primer Second Edition*. W3C Recommendation, October 28, 2004. Retrieved August 2, 2017, from http://www.w3.org/TR/2004/REC-xmlschema-0-20041028/

W3C. (2007). *XSL Transformations (XSLT) Version 2.0*. W3C Recommendation, January 23, 2007. Retrieved August 2, 2017, from http://www.w3.org/TR/2007/REC-xslt20-20070123/

W3C. (2008). *Extensible Markup Language (XML) 1.0 (Fifth Edition)*. W3C Recommendation, November 26, 2008. Retrieved August 2, 2017, from http://www.w3.org/TR/2008/REC-xml-20081126/

W3C. (2010). *XQuery 1.0: An XML Query Language (Second Edition)*. W3C Recommendation, December 14, 2010. Retrieved August 2, 2017, from http://www.w3.org/TR/2010/REC-xquery-20101214/

W3C. (2011). *XQuery Update Facility 1.0*. W3C Candidate Recommendation, March 17, 2011. Retrieved August 2, 2017, from http://www.w3.org/TR/2011/REC-xquery-update-10-20110317/

W3C. (2014). *XML Path Language (XPath) 3.0*. W3C Recommendation, April 8, 2014. Retrieved August 2, 2017, from http://www.w3.org/TR/2014/REC-xpath-30-20140408/

Wang, F., & Zaniolo, C. (2008). Temporal queries and version management in XML-based document archives. *Data & Knowledge Engineering*, *65*(2), 304–324. doi:10.1016/j.datak.2007.08.002

Wang, F., Zaniolo, C., & Zhou, X. (2008). ArchIS: An XML-based approach to transaction-time temporal database systems. *The VLDB Journal*, *17*(6), 1445–1463. doi:10.100700778-007-0086-6

Wang, Y., DeWitt, D. J., & Cai, J. (2003). X-Diff: An Effective Change Detection Algorithm for XML Documents. *Proceedings of the 19th International Conference on Data Engineering (ICDE 2003)*, 519-530. 10.1109/ICDE.2003.1260818

Wei, H.-C., & Elmasri, R. (2000). Schema versioning and database conversion techniques for bi-temporal databases. *Annals of Mathematics and Artificial Intelligence*, *30*(1-4), 23–52. doi:10.1023/A:1016622202755

Wu, Y., & Suzuki, N. (2016). An algorithm for correcting XSLT rules according to DTD updates. *Proceedings of the 4th International Workshop on Document Changes: Modeling, Detection, Storage and Visualization (DChanges 2016)*, Article no. 2. 10.1145/2993585.2993588

KEY TERMS AND DEFINITIONS

Database Schema: The formal structure of the database, described by means of a data definition language.

Schema Changes: Operations performed on a (populated) database schema, in order to adapt it to new application requirements.

Schema Change Propagation: The effects of a schema change at instance level, involving suitable conversions necessary to adapt extant data to the new schema.

Schema Change Semantics: The effects of a schema change at schema level.

Schema Version: A complete database schema as created by the initial design or by the application of schema changes to an existing schema.

Schema Versioning: A schema change modality that provides for the maintenance of previous schema versions, such that extant data are accessible through any of the supported schema versions.

Temporal Database: A database with built-in support for managing time-varying data.

Temporal Schema Versioning: A schema versioning technique in which different schema versions are indexed by timestamps.

Chapter 14
A Personalized Approach for Web Service Discovery in Distributed Environments

Nadia Ben Seghir
University of Biskra, Algeria

Okba Kazar
University of Biskra, Algeria

Khaled Rezeg
University of Biskra, Algeria

ABSTRACT

Web services are meaningful only if potential users may find and execute them. Universal description discovery and integration (UDDI) help businesses, organizations, and other web services providers to discover and reach to the service(s) by providing the URI of the WSDL file. However, it does not offer a mechanism to choose a web service based on its quality. The standard also lacks sufficient semantic description in the content of web services. This lack makes it difficult to find and compose suitable web services during analysis, search, and matching processes. In addition, a central UDDI suffers from one centralized point problem and the high cost of maintenance. To get around these problems, the authors propose in this chapter a novel framework based on mobile agent and metadata catalogue for web services discovery. Their approach is based on user profile in order to discover appropriate web services, meeting customer requirements in less time and taking into account the QoS properties.

INTRODUCTION

According to numerous studies in Internet technologies area, the number of different software systems, which use Web technologies, such as Web services is constantly growing. According to W3C definition, Web service is a software system designed to support interoperable machine to machine interaction over a network (Haas & Brown, 2004). In general, there are three main instances that interact with a Web ser-

DOI: 10.4018/978-1-5225-5384-7.ch014

vice: service requestor, service provider, service broker. As the service is developed, performer (service provider) registers it in the directory (service broker) where it can be found by the potential customers (service requestor). As the customer found the appropriate service in the directory, he can import the WSDL specification for further usage in the process of development his software. WSDL describes the format of requests and responses exchanged between the customer and performer in the process of work. These standards are used to ensure interoperability:

1. **XML (Extensible Markup Language):** Is used to store and transfer of structured data;
2. **SOAP (Simple Object Access Protocol):** A messaging protocol based on XML;
3. **WSDL (Web Service Description Language):** Language which describes the external Web service interface based on XML;
4. **UDDI (Universal Discovery, Description and Integration):** Is the directory of Web services and information about the companies that provide Web services into the public domain, or specific companies. By the moment, UDDI is not very common; it is mostly spread in small corporate networks.

In the 2010 it was offered a new concept of the Internet technologies development which was called Web 3.0 or also known as semantic Web. The technical part of the Semantic Web consists of a family of standards for description languages, including XML, XML Schema, RDF, RDF Schema, OWL, as well as some others. We consider only the last three of mentioned above:

1. RDF (Resource Description Framework) is a simple way to describe the instance data in the format of the subject-object relation, where any member of the trio uses only resource identifiers.
2. RDF Schema defines a set of attributes, such as rdfs:Class, to define new types of RDF-data. The language also supports an inheritance relationship type rdfs:subClassOf.
3. OWL (Web Ontology Language) expands the description of new types (in particular, the addition of transfers), and also allows us to describe new types of RDF Schema data in terms of the existing ones (for example, to determine the type, which is the intersection or the union of the two existing).

The important part of the semantic Web is the concept of the semantic Web services. In general, semantic Web services could be defined as finished program elements with uniquely described semantics, which could be accessed via the Internet and are suitable for automated search, composition and performance based on their semantics.

Current trends in service discovery are essentially based on centralized discovery methods, where Web services are described by service interface functions (WSDL) and they publish their capabilities and functionalities with a directory (such as UDDI, ebXML) (Fragopoulou, Mastroianni, Montero, Andrjezak, & Kondo, 2010), (Furno & Zimeo, 2013), (Huayou, Zhong, Yong, & Lian, 2013). These directories are restricted by the syntactic description of the functionality of service as they are known for their low accuracy and poor performance, and sometimes for their low availability. Centralized discovery methods cannot manage large and continuously growing spaces of Web services with reasonable resolution times. Moreover, the centralized methods of published services suffer from problems such as high operational and maintenance cost. The centralized methods do not ensure the required scalability to support the dynamic, flexible and evolutionary environment (Boukhadra, Benatchba, & Balla, 2014), (Klusch & Kapahnke, 2010).

Discovering of Web services in a distributed registry is becoming a real challenge and an important task due to availability of various Web services which provide similar functional requirements over the network. It makes an ability to locate capabilities and components in a distributed registry in a large scale, contributing to the resolution and simplification of a very complicated problem expressed by the user. It allows, in other words, fulfilling the users requirements evolving over time. It is not easy for the users to effectively discover and share these Web services which satisfies his specific requirements as the number of retrieved services is huge (Bianchini, De Antonellis, & Melchiori, 2010), (Furno & Zimeo, 2013).

In this chapter, we deal with two major problems that are encountered in the Web services discovery approaches. The first is linked to the central point of publication and discovery implemented generally by a UDDI registry. The second problem is related to the common descriptive languages such as WSDL, which lack semantic richness in order for machines to process them automatically. They require human intervention to interpret their meanings for discovery, composition, and invoking. Manual intervention is an error prone and time consuming task. W3C supports the use of software agents for automating the above tasks. An agent is defined as application software acting on behalf of a person, a system or an organization (Haas & Brown, 2004). Accordingly, an agent could discover, compose and invoce Web services. In order for agent to perform those tasks, it requires a reference specification that includes domain informational knowledge, and operational knowledge of how to perform domain tasks. Ontology is an effective way to provide such specification.

In this chapter, the researchers present a novel framework for Web services discovery based on metadata catalogue, agent mobile and user profile. This framework is based on a distributed architecture composed of three layers: service requester layer, middleware layer, service provider layer. The Web service discovery process became more efficient and more dynamic by exploiting the parallelism and the distribution given by agent technology.

Our work aims at simplifying and optimizing the Web services discovery using metadata, QoS information and user profile, in order to reduce the search space and increase the number of relevant services.

The remainder of this chapter is organized as follows. Next section presents preliminaries and the necessary concepts to elaborate our work. Then presented is the proposed framework indicating the general model architecture, and then we express the architectural and behavioral aspect of each component. Our implementation of the prototype is described and then we provide an illustrative example. Related works section shows some related works, and presents a comparative study of WS discovery approaches. Finally, future research directions and conclusion assess this approach and present the envisaged perspectives.

BACKGROUND AND CONTRIBUTION

In this section we present some useful definitions and formalisms that help us to clarify the proposed work.

Semantic Web Service

Web service technology allows computer applications to communicate information over the Internet (Martin D., Burstein, Mcdermott, Mcilraith, Paolucci, & Sycara, 2007). However, Web services have a number of limitations: (1) they provide syntactic interoperability which requires data be transferred in a specific format, (2) interfaces of a Web service must not change, otherwise, applications communicating with the service break, and (3) the content of a message exchanged with a Web service cannot be interpreted by computers; this prevents any workflow automation. To add semantics to the content of a Web service message, the content must be formally and explicitly conceptualized using ontologies. To extend the capabilities of Web services in the direction of dynamic interoperability, Semantic Web and Web service technologies are combined to create Semantic Web Services (Grasic & Podgorelec, 2010).

In general, semantic Web services can be defined as finished program elements with uniquely described semantics, which could be accessed via the Internet and are suitable for automated search, composition and performance based on their semantics. The major difference between semantic Web service and common Web service is that user can access not only Web interface description (normally WSDL description) in terms of data transmitted service, return values and generated errors, but also its semantic description, i.e. what this service does, its domain, destination and so on. There are a number of semantic Web services description languages: SAWSDL, OWL-S and WSMO. All of these languages are oriented to interact with the WSDL.

In our work, a Web service (WS) is defined by (Ben-Seghier, Kazar, & Rezeg, 2015):

$$WS = < IOPE; \ QOS; \ META >$$
$$Where:$$
$$IOPE = < input ; \ output ; \ precondition ; effect >$$
$$QOS = < Q_1; \ Q_2; \ ... ; \ Q_n >$$
$$Q_k = < Reliability; Availability; Execution\_price ; Response \ time ; \ ... >$$
$$META = < Type ; \ Spatial\_Data ; Access\_Constraints ; \ Goal ; \ ... >$$

Metadata Catalogue

Literally, metadata is data about data. NISO defines metadata as "structured information that describes, explains, locates, or otherwise makes it easier to retrieve, use, or manage an information resource" (NISO, 2005). Tannenbaum defines metadata as "detailed description of the instance data; the format and characteristics of populated instance data; instances and values dependent on the role of metadata recipient" with instance data is defined as the input for receiving tool, application, database, or simple processing engine (Tannenbaum, 2001). Three main types of metadata are (NISO, 2005):

1. **Descriptive Metadata:** Resources intended for the discovery and identification data.
2. **Structural Metadata:** Shows how some of the objects collected, for example: a collection of pages sorted by chapter.
3. **Administrative Metadata:** Provides information to help manage resources, such as when and how it is created, file type and other technical information, and who has access to this information.

Metadata is used as a term for describing formal schemes of resource description by:

- Providing resources retrieval by entering the keyword criteria (searching).
- Providing identification of the resources.
- Grouping the resources according to some characteristics.

- Distinguishing different resources.
- Providing information on the location of the resources.

Catalogue services support the ability to publish and search collections of descriptive metadata for data, services, and related information objects. Metadata in catalogues represent resource characteristics that can be queried and presented for evaluation and further processing by both humans and software. Organizations that establish metadata standards are very numerous such as:

- ISO (International Organization for Standardization)
- IEEE (Institute of Electrical and Electronics Engineers)
- OASIS(Organization for the Advancement of Structured Information Standards)
- OMG (Object Management Group)
- OGC (Open Geospatial Consortium)
- W3C (World Wide Web Consortium)

After studying examples of metadata cited above, we have collected 17 metadata elements that represent the most repeated and most important attributes from our point of view. The Table 1 shows the proposed metadata elements used to identify and discover Web services.

Table 1. Metadata elements used to describe Web services

N°	Element	Type	Description
01	MetadataIdentifier	Integer	Unique number to differentiate each metadata per participant in the catalog
02	MetadataLanguage	String	The language of the metadata set.
03	MetadataCreationDate	Date	Date on which the metadata was created or updated
04	MetadataContactPoint	String	Name of an organization (or a person) providing the function of contact for the metadata.
05	ServiceID	String	to differentiate each service per adherent within a directory
06	ServiceTitle	String	A name given to the service, normally used for display to a human
07	ServiceType	String	Describes the type of service and can manage groupings service.
08	ServiceTypeVersion	String	Version of this service type implemented by this server.
09	ServiceDescription	String	Brief narrative description of service, normally available for display to a human
10	ServiceKeywords	String	List of words used to describe a service.
11	Goal	String	The objective of this service
12	Popularity	String	Information about the number of WS using
13	SpatialData	String	The spatial or temporal topic of the service.
14	PublicationDate	Date	Information to date data available in the catalog
15	ServiceContact	String	Information for contacting service provider
16	AccessConstraints	String	Conditions applying to access and use of service
17	ServiceParameter	String	Contains at least the position of the first service in the UDDI registry.

Ontologies

Ontology can be defined as a common set of terms that are used to describe and represent a domain (Heflin, 2004). It defines terms used to describe and represent an area of knowledge. Ontology is created for a specific domain, such as science, education, and people, for example. It defines concepts or classes, establishes relationships between these classes and also defines properties, which describe various features and attributes of the classes. It can be said that an ontology encodes the knowledge of a given domain, so that this knowledge can be understood by machines, making the Semantic Web possible. By means of knowledge described by an ontology, the machine can perform inferences, reason and deduce new facts based on the relationships between terms described in ontologies. It is essential that there exist languages for building ontologies, the so-called meta-ontologies. Existing meta-ontologies are RDF-Schema (rdfs) (Brickley & Guha, 2014) and Web Ontology Language (OWL) (Mcguiness & Harmelen, 2004). Sparql Protocol and RDF Query Language (SPARQL) is the standard query language and access protocol for RDF data (Harris & Seaborne, 2013). RDF is an abstract data model. The use of concrete standard syntaxes for the representation of RDF triples is required before these graphs to be actually published on the Web. The most popular syntaxes are: RDF/XML (Gandon & Shreiber, 2014) and Turtle (Beckett & al., 2014).

For the implementation of our prototype we develop a general ontology which presents the different concepts of an application domain which is in our case the tourism field. Tourism is an area that is characterized by a multitude of distributed data sources. These data sources are often heterogeneous, distributed and autonomous. Figure 1 presents the proposed tourism ontology in the form of four arborescences: Hotel, Activity, Region, and Transport.

Figure 1. The proposed tourism ontology generated by the editor Protégé

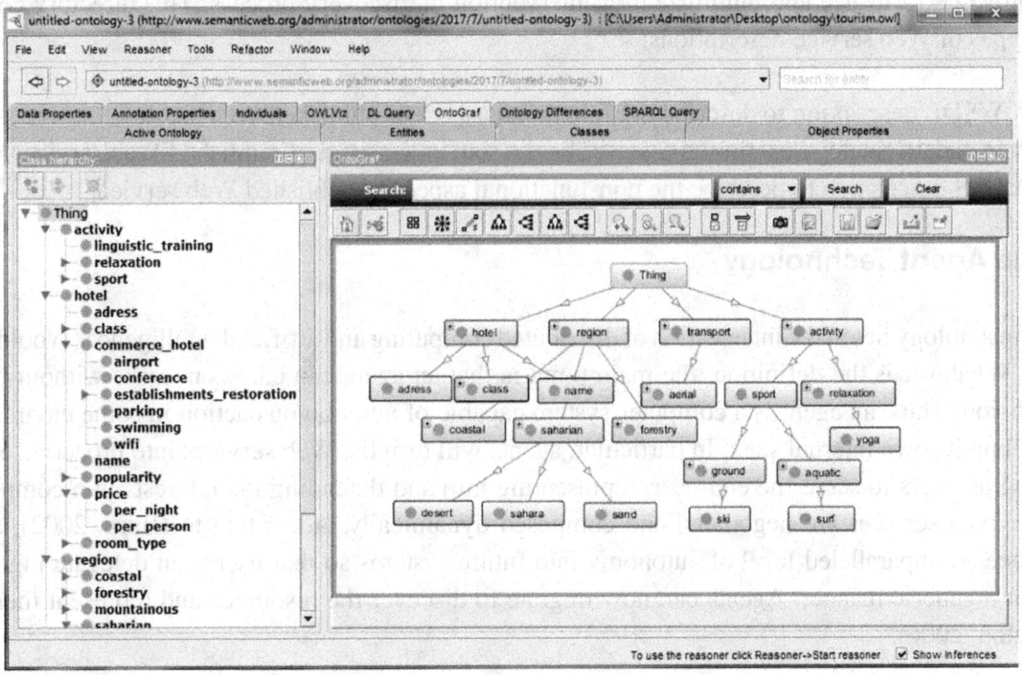

The UDDI Registry

The philosophy of UDDI is to centralize the entry points of Web services, meaning the creation of a central directory for Web services provided by different owners (enterprises or individuals). UDDI allows the enterprises to discover and share information with regard to the Web services and other electronic and non-electronic services that are registered in a registry. A UDDI registry service is a WS that manages information about service providers, service implementations, and service metadata. The UDDI specifications include: a) SOAP APIs that allow querying and publishing of information, b) XML representation for the registry data model and the SOAP message formats, c) WSDL interface definitions of the SOAP and d) APIs Definitions of various technical models that facilitate category systems for identification and categorization of UDDI registrations.

Despite its simplicity and ease of implementation, it has some disadvantages such as:

- Returns a large number of results or rather little.
- It suffers from one centralized point problem (point of failure) and the high cost of maintenance.
- The lack of security and reliability.
- No consideration of the quality of service (QoS) and dynamic composition of Web services.
- The UDDI provides poor search facilities (research on the ID, the name of the service, or on elements of the WSDL document).

In this chapter, we propose a distributed architecture for semantic Web services discovery to solve the limitations of centralized architectures. Our architecture is mainly built around the distribution of semantic directory. Using multiple directories in a discovery process offers the advantage to overcome the problem of "single point of failure" such as when using a single centralized directory.

The proposed semantic directory is based on the automation of the publication and discovery phases to improve performance and minimize user intervention in discovery process. This directory contains three types of Web service descriptions:

- A WSDL description to describe the functional aspect of published Web service;
- A metadata catalog description to describe the semantic aspect of published Web service;
- A QoS description to describe the non-functional aspect of published Web service;

Mobile Agent Technology

Agent technology lies in the intersection of distributed computing and artificial intelligence (Wooldridge, 2002). Whatever is the definition, the main point is that an agent can carry out tasks without human supervision. Thus, an agent is a computer system capable of autonomous action in some environment controlling its own internal state. In particular, agents will turn the Web services into proactive entities working as peers to serve the end-user, representing him and defending his interests in a competitive world where services are negotiated and composed dynamically. According to (Burg, 2002), agents introduce an unparalleled level of autonomy into future systems so that users can delegate high-level tasks in a generic manner. Agents can now migrate to discover the resources and represent their user (EL Falou, 2006).

In this chapter, the authors present one of possible applications of mobile agent technology to manage the process of Web services discovery. Our interest in mobile agents is due to several reasons:

- Agent mobility allows a client to interact locally with a server, so it reduces the network traffic by transmitting only the relevant services.
- Execution of specialized agent offers more flexibility advantage than execution of a standard procedure on servers' sites, and enables more robust transaction than remote transactions.
- Asynchrony and autonomy of agents allow them to perform a task while they are disconnected from the client, which is particularly useful in the case of physically mobile devices.
- Agents are able to communicate and cooperate with each other, which accelerates and facilitates the discovery process.

PROPOSED FRAMEWORK

The proposed architecture is an extension of service oriented architecture (SOA). In SOA, Web service is offered by a service provider that publishes the description of Web service in a registry built for this purpose. Generally, service providers use UDDI as a repertory. The description of the Web service is performed by the WSDL definition language. When a user introduces his query to search for a Web service, he uses the same UDDI registry. The user becomes aware of services available in UDDI registry through the WSDL definitions diffused by the service providers. Once a Web service is selected by the user, the link between these two entities is established via the SOAP language.

Our work takes into account the user preferences in the Web service discovery process. We aim to ensure that the user will obtain a list of Web services that meets his needs. The proposed architecture is distributed as shown in Figure 2, the use of multiple registers in a discovery process offers the advantage to overcome the problem of "single point of failure" and avoids bottlenecks such as when using a single centralized registry.

In our work, the discovery phase passes through three levels as shown in Figure 3: 1) Semantic match, 2) Functional match, 3) QoS score computing, each level uses the result of the previous level and aims to decrease the number of candidate Web services.

We briefly explain what happens in each level as follows:

1. In level 1, we apply the matching algorithm (Chabeb, Tata, & Ozanne, 2010) at the level metadata catalogue. It is used to find the mappings between Web service characteristics presented in the user request and those stored in Web services metadata catalogue.
2. In level 2, we use the matching algorithm based on the interrogation mechanism of UDDI registry. It searches by keyword, by tModel and therefore, by implication, a search specification (e.g., classification, service using WSDL...). It is based on the comparison of the information available to the user request to that provided by the UDDI registry using the white pages, yellow pages and green pages.
3. In level 3, we calculate the QoS score of each candidate Web service and eliminate Web service that does not meet the constraints or the preference of Web service requester.

Figure 2. Proposed architecture for semantic Web services discovery

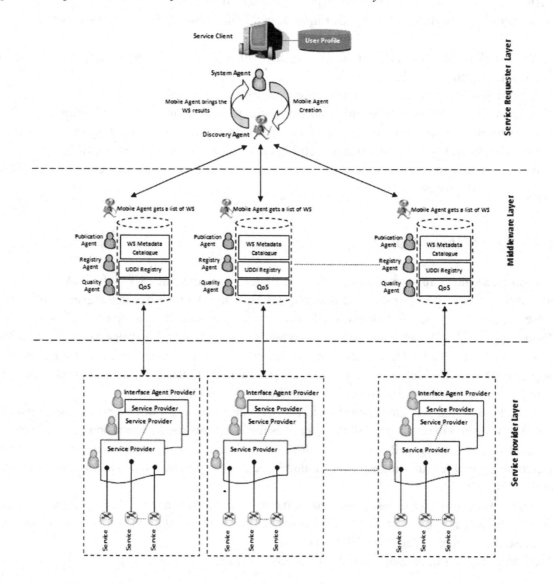

ARCHITECTURAL AND FUNCTIONAL ASPECT

The proposed framework is based on the interaction, semantically, between six different agents.

System Agent

System agent is in charge of all search activities in the proposed framework, it acts as an intermediary between the service requestor and our architecture. It performs the following functions:

- Ensure effective communication between the client and the system.
- Construction of user profile according to the information provided directly from the client.

Figure 3. Phases of Web services discovery

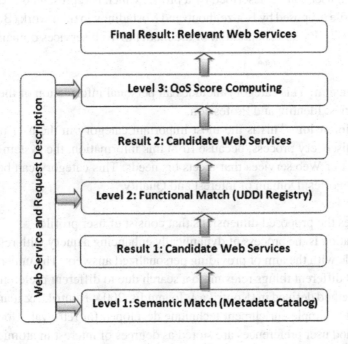

- Construction of user request.
- Enrichment of user request depending to the user profile.
- Generation of mobile agent for Web services discovery.
- Sending back the results (list of relevant services) to be exploited by the client.
- Update the user profile.

The internal architecture of system agent composes of four modules as shown in Figure 4.

Figure 4. Architecture of system agent

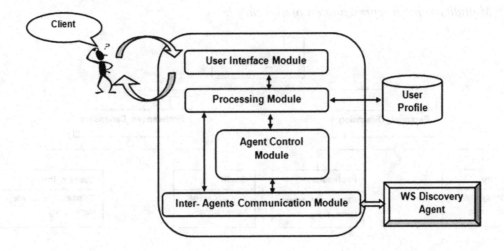

In our system, each user can be described by a profile which is represented according to the generic model of the user profile proposed by Bouzeghoub and Kostadinov in their work (Bouzeghoub & Peralta, 2004; Kostadinov, 2007). By an instantiation of the model in Web services domain, we are particularly interested to:

- **Personal Dimension:** This category includes all personal information of the user. It is divided in two sub categories: Identity and Profession.
- **Preferences Dimension:** This is the most important category in the user profile. It has a direct impact on the discovery process, because from this information, the system ensures that the user will obtain a list of Web services that meets his needs. This category can be decomposed in two distinct sub categories: Domain of interest and Quality.

Figure 5 elaborates the proposed dimensions that consist of user profile:

Query personalization is the process of dynamically enhancing a query with related user preferences stored in a user profile with the aim of providing personalized answers. The underlying idea is that different users may find different things relevant to a search due to different preferences.

We adapted the method defined in (Koutrika & Ioannidis, 2004; Koutrika & Ioannidis, 2005) for Web services discovery. It is simple enrichment technique developed for retrieval information and database systems. In this method user preferences are stored as degrees of interest in atomic query elements (selection and join conditions), which may be used to transform a query. The degree of interest expresses the interest of a person to include the associated condition into the qualification of a query. Specific logic is introduced for derivation of preferences combining stored atomic ones. This model combines expressivity and concision and provides a direct way to personalize queries.

Interface Agent Provider

Each interface agent provider implements a number of Web services described semantically with metadata catalogue enhanced with QoS attributes. Its internal architecture composes of three modules, as it is shown in Figure 6. It performs the following functions:

Figure 5. Multidimensional representation of user profile

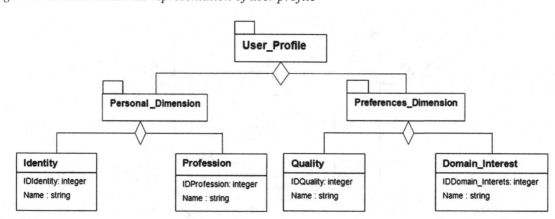

- Receives the description of Web services to be registered in metadata catalogue, UDDI registry and QoS file.
- Consistency control of WS description.
- Transfers the WS description to WS publication agent.
- Verifies changes in the quality or functionality of registered services during each period of time.

Web Service Publication Agent

The internal architecture of publication agent composes of two modules as shown in Figure 7. It performs the following functions:

- Insertion of WS metadata in the catalogue.
- Transfers the WS description (WSDL) to WS registry agent.
- Transfers the WS description (QoS) to WS quality agent.
- Returns the confirmation of publication of the service to interface agent provider.

Web Service Discovery Agent

It is a mobile agent, which represents the user in the network. It is capable of roaming, finding and executing services and delivering results to the user. This agent may also spawn clones that execute the selected WS in parallel to minimize the total processing time. Clones can migrate and invoke simultaneously the chosen WS and return to the service requestor with the results. The internal architecture of mobile agent composes of four modules as shown in Figure 8.

The Web service discovery agent applies the matching algorithm (Chabeb, Tata, & Ozanne, 2010) at the level metadata catalogue. It is used to find the mappings between WS characteristics presented in the user request and those stored in the metadata catalogue. The comparison is based on domain ontology.

A match between an advertisement and a request consists of the match of all the outputs of the request against the outputs of the advertisement; and all the inputs of the advertisement against the inputs of the

Figure 6. Architecture of interface agent provider

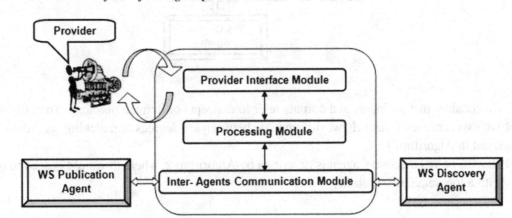

Figure 7. Architecture of Web service publication agent

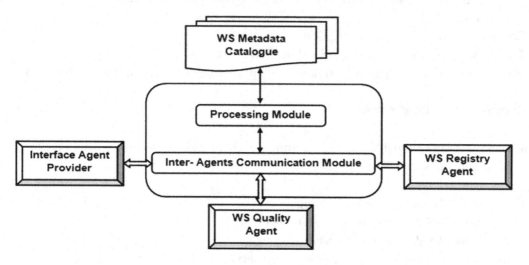

Figure 8. Architecture of Web service discovery agent

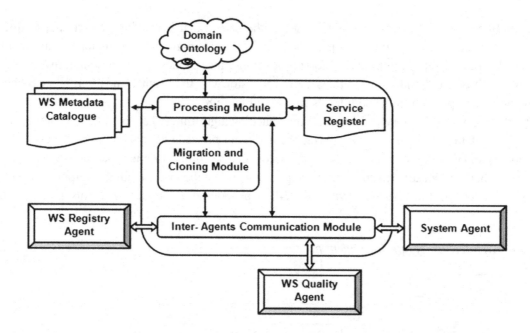

request. We consider that all inputs and outputs refer to concepts of domain ontology. To calculate the similarity of two concepts R and A, we differentiate between six degrees of matching according to the rule displayed in Algorithm 1.

The behavior of WS discovery agent is described by Algorithm 2, where threshold is used to ignore services with a low semantic similarity.

Algorithm 1. Get score of degree of match

```
Inputs: R - request, A - advertisement
Outputs: Score of matching
 Begin
  If A = R then Return 5
   Else if subsumes (R, A) then Return 4
    Else if subsumes (A, R) then Return 3
     Else if Has-same-class (A, R) then Return 2
      Else if Unclassified (A, R) then Return 1
       Else Return 0
       Endif
      Endif
     Endif
    Endif
   Endif
 End
```

Algorithm 2. Service discovery process

```
Inputs: service= {service₁, …, serviceₙ}, request
Outputs: resultat
Integer: resultat=ø;
Float: semantic_similarity;
Begin
Foreach (serviceⱼ) do
semantic_similarity=∑ᵢ₌₁ᵐ Getscore(degreeofMatch(InputsRᵢ,InputsAᵢ))+
                    ∑ᵢ₌₁ᵐ Getscore(degreeofMatch(outputsRᵢ,outputsAᵢ));
If (semantic_similarity > threshold) then
resultat= resultat ∪ {serviceⱼ};
Endif
Endfor
```

Web Service Registry Agent

It is a stationary agent that acts as a broker between the mobile agent and the UDDI registry. In the discovery case, it applies the matching algorithm based on the interrogation mechanism of UDDI registry, finding the mappings between the functionality of Web services and those of the query, the result of previous discovery phase will be operated in this level to restrict the search space. The pertinent services are stored in service register, this latter will be initialized at each request. WS registry agent communicates the results obtained (set of pertinent services) with WS quality agent. In the case of the publication, WS registry agent inserts the Web service in the UDDI, It communicates the results obtained (the confirmation of publication of the service and the necessary information for invoking the service) with WS publication agent. Figure 9 illustrates the internal architecture of WS registry agent.

Figure 9. Architecture of Web service registry agent

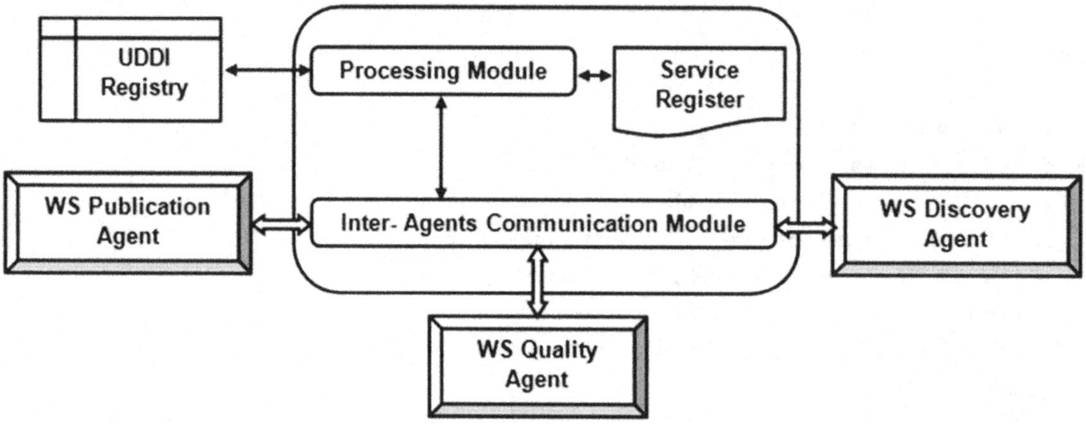

Web Service Quality Agent

In the discovery case, the behavior of quality agent is to calculate the QoS score of each candidate Web service and eliminate the Web service that does not meet the constraints or the preference of Web service requester. Its behavior is described by Algorithm 3. The set A is the set of QoS attributes requested by the user, such that for each attribute $Qos_i \left(1 \le i \le m\right)$ a weight (W_i) assigned to it. SWS is the set of m Web services results from the previous step. V_{ij} represents the value of QoS attribute.

We take into account that each QoS attribute is positive or negative criterion. A positive criterion means increases in the value reflects improvements in the quality (e.g. Reliability and Availability), while negative criterion means decreases in the value reflects improvements in the quality (e.g. Execution price and Response time) (Xu, Martin, Powley, & Zulkernine, 2007).

In the case of the publication, WS quality agent inserts the QoS information in the QoS file. Figure 10 illustrates the internal architecture of this agent.

IMPLEMENTATION

For the implementation of our architecture, we propose the tourism field as application domain; we use a prototype ontology which includes only the part of the terminology field of tourism. The architecture adopted here can be applied to other domains where a specific ontology can be specified.

To program and test our architecture, we have used: Editor Protégé 2000, JADE platform (Wooldridge, 2002; Jars, 2005), XML / XML Schemas, MySQL.

A set of interface is available to the user (Provider / Customer), the interface is made using JSP technology (Java Server Pages) that helps software developers create dynamically generated Web pages based on HTML, XML, or other document types. Figure 11 shows an example of Web service description interface, and Figure 12 represents Web service publication interface.

Figure 13 shows an example of a user preferences interface with weights of some domains of interest and some QoS attributes. We propose that service consumer does not have to give the value of each

Algorithm 3. Selection based on QoS

```
Inputs: A= {Qos₁, …, Qosₙ}, SWS={sws₁, …, swsₘ}, W={w₁, …, wₙ}, threshold.min,
threshold.max;
Outputs: resultat
Begin
Resultat=ø; j=1;
While (j ≠ m) do
f(swsj)= ∑Vᵢⱼ*Wᵢ;
If(swsⱼ.criterion="positive") and (f(swsⱼ)>threshold.min) then
        resultat=resultat ∪ {swsⱼ};
Else eliminate(swsⱼ);
Endif
If(swsⱼ.criterion="negative") and (f(swsⱼ)<threshold.max) then
        resultat=resultat ∪ {swsⱼ};
Else eliminate(swsⱼ);
Endif
j=j+1;
Endwhile
End.
```

Figure 10. Architecture of Web service quality agent

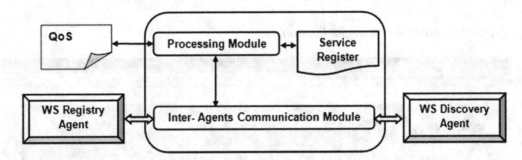

preference but he should get the means to specify that a preference is more important than another one. Degree of interest equal to 0 indicates lack of any interest in the condition, while degree equal to 1 indicates extreme ('must have') interest.

A request signifies a service demand. Request description includes functional and non-functional requirements. The former describes the functional characteristic of the service demand, such as name, brief description, inputs and outputs. Figure 14 shows an example of a user request interface.

ILLUSTRATIVE EXAMPLE

In this section, we give an illustrative example to clarify our work. For this, we assume that there are six Web services published on the Web. Table 2, 3 and 4 illustrate the description of Web services:

Figure 11. Interface for Web service description

Figure 12. Interface for Web service publication

Figure 13. User preferences interface

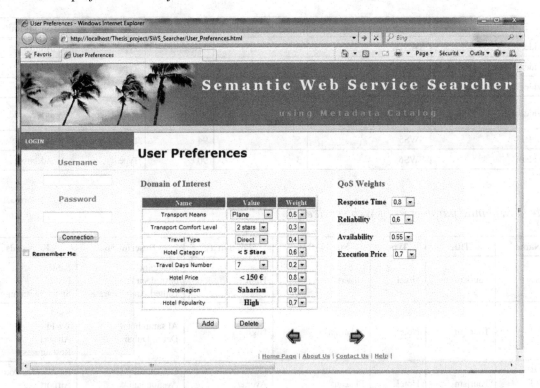

Figure 14. Interface for searching a Web service

Table 2. Functional parameters of Web services

ProviderName	ServiceName	Category	Price	Inputs	Outputs
Provider1	SWS1	5	318 €	Type	Address
Provider2	SWS2	3	51 €	Type	Address
Provider3	SWS3	4	138 €	Type	Address
Provider4	SWS4	4	91 €	Type, Date	Price, Address
Provider5	SWS5	5	94 €	Type, Region	Price
Provider6	SWS6	3	90 €	Type	Address

Table 3. Semantic parameters of Web services

Name	Title	Type	Spatial Data	Popularity	Description	Keywords
SWS1	Tourism	Hotel	Desert	High	Anantara qasr al sarab, United Arab Emirates	Sable Food Sport Swimming
SWS2	Tourism	Hotel	Saharian	High	Al sarab hotel Deira, Dubai	Sand Wi-Fi Airport Restaurants
SWS3	Tourism	Hotel	Plateaus	Average	Golden tulip sfax, Avenue habib bourguiba,	Restaurants Pool Airport Conference
SWS4	Tourism	Hotel	Mountainous	Low	Novotel Constantine, Algeria	Food Parking
SWS5	Tourism	Hotel	Coastal	High	Sofitel algiers hamma garden Algeria	Restaurant Swimming
SWS6	Tourism	Hotel	Oases	Average	Premier Inn Dubai silicon oasis	Restaurants Pool Sand Airport

Table 4. QoS attributes of Web services

ServiceName	ResponseTime	Reliability	Availability	ExecutionPrice
SWS1	0.2	0.6	0.5	0.3
SWS2	0.1	0.7	0.6	0.5
SWS3	0.5	0.6	0.4	0.4
SWS4	0.2	0.5	0.5	0.2
SWS5	0.1	0.5	0.8	0.6
SWS6	0.4	0.6	0.7	0.4

Example: For illustration, we take the preferences shown in Figure 13 which can be expressed with the following set of predicates:

Profile

```
TransportMeans= 'plane'            0.5
HotelPrice < 150 €                 0.8
TravelType = 'dir                  0.4
TransportComfortlevel= 2           0.3
TravelDaynumber = 7                0.2
HotelCategory < 5                  0.6
HotelRegion = 'saharian'           0.9
HotelPopularity='high'             0.7
ResponseTime = 0.8
Reliability = 0.6
Availability = 0.55
ExecutionPrice = 0.7
```

Step 1: Preference Selection

The first step of the query personalization process deals with for the extraction of the top K preferences related to a query. A basic question to be answered by a system is which preferences are considered related to a query. Our approach is to take into account that the desired degree of interest should be greater than 0.5

Step 2: Generation of Personalized Answer

The top K preferences derived from the user profile may be integrated into the initial query so that the resulting one should return results satisfying at least L from the top K preferences.

Take for example the request shown in Figure 14: a user, whose profile is illustrated in Figure 13, issues a query about hotels.

Initial Query

```
For $z in $doc // ("SWS_Description.xml")
Where $z/name= "tourism" and $z/type="hotel" and $z/keywords = "sand airport
restaurant" and $z/description = "gives information about hotel reservation
service" and $z/inputs="type" and $z/outputs="address"
Return $z/ServiceName
```

After preference selection step, the following preferences have been selected by the system for inclusion in the query:

```
HotelPrice < 150 €                    0.8
HotelCategory < 5                     0.6
HotelRegion = 'saharian'             0.9
HotelPopularity='high'                0.6
ResponseTime =                        0.8
Reliability =                         0.6
Availability =                        0.55
ExecutionPrice =                      0.7
```

A set of sub-queries is constructed, each one separately integrating one of these preferences into the original query. The final query is built as the union of these sub-queries:

Enriched Query

```
For $z in $doc // ("Metedata_File.xml")
Where $z/name="tourism" and $z/type="hotel" and $z/keywords = "sand airport
restaurant" and $z/description = "gives information about hotel reservation
service"; and $z/HotelRegion = "saharian" and $z/HotelPopularity="high"
Return $z/ServiceName
Union
For $w in $doc// ("WSDL_File.xml")
Where $w/name= "tourism" and $z/inputs="type" and $z/outputs="address" and $w/
HotelPrice <150 € and $w/HotelCategory < 5
Return $w/ServiceName
Union All
For $p in $doc// ("QoS_File.xml")
Where $p/Type= "hotel" and $p/ResponseTime= 0.8 and $p/Reliability= 0.6 and
$p/Availability = 0.55 and $p/ExecutionPrice = 0.7
Return $p/ServiceName
```

Step 3: Semantic Match

At this step, the WS discovery agent applies the matching algorithm at the level metadata catalogue using domain ontologies. Figures 15, 16, represent the relations graphs of Activity ontology and Region ontology generated by the editor Protégé.

Table 5 shows the result of semantic matching algorithm.

We assume that the threshold = 22, so the result of semantic match is SWS2, SWS6, SWS1 and SWS3.

Step 4: Functional Match

In this step, we calculate the syntactic similarity between functional properties of request and Web service. The result of functional match is SWS2, SWS3 and SWS6.

Figure 15. Relations graphs of activity ontology

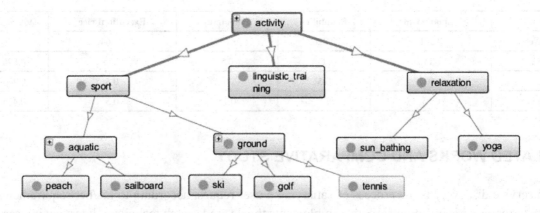

Figure 16. Relations graphs of region ontology

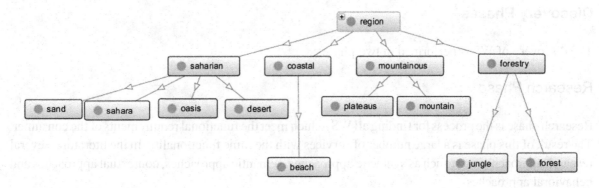

Table 5. Result of semantic similarity

Name	Title	Type	Spatial Data	Popularity	Keywords	Degree Semantic
SWS1	5	5	4	5	4	23
SWS2	5	5	5	5	15	35
SWS3	5	5	1	2	10	23
SWS4	5	5	1	2	3	16
SWS5	5	5	1	5	5	21
SWS6	5	5	4	2	15	31

Step 5: Selection According to QoS

Each QoS value needs to be normalized to have a value in the range of 0 to 1. To calculate the overall QoS score of services, each normalized QoS attribute is multiplied the corresponding weight as shown Table 6.

As a result, we can see that there is one semantic Web service (SWS2) satisfies the user request.

Table 6. Result of QoS score computing

	ResponseTime	Reliability	Availability	ExecutionPrice	QoS Score
Weight	0.301	0.226	0.207	0.264	
SWS2	1	1	0.5	0.25	0.696
SWS3	0	0.5	0	0.5	0.245
SWS6	0.25	0.5	0.75	0.5	0.475

RELATED WORKS AND COMPARATIVE STUDY

Web service discovery is the process of satisfying a user request according to his/her requirements. It refers to the process of finding WS that implements the desired search technique, interviewing service books, to know what Web service is available for binding.

Discovery Phases

The discovery of WS is performed in two phases:

Research Phase

Research phase is the process for finding all WS, which meet the functional requirements of the consumer. The result of this phase is a large number of services with the same functionality. In the literature, several research approaches exist such as syntactic approaches, semantic approaches, contextual approaches and behavioral approaches.

Syntactic Approaches

Syntactic approaches are generally based on the comparison between the query based on keywords and syntax descriptions of WS (WSDL), namely UDDI (Clement, Hately, Riegen, & al., 2004) and AASDU (Palathingal & Chandra, 2004)

- UDDI (Universal Description Discovery and Integration) allows searching by keyword, by tModel or by specification. It offers four main types of XML data structures:
  - **BusinessEntity:** Provides information about the company offering the service.
  - **BusinessService:** Gives information about the service offered.
  - **BindingTemplate:** Provides information for using a particular Web service.
  - TModel (technical model) represents any kind of information. This can be a service interface, a classification, semantics of an operation ...
- AASDU (Agent Approach for Service Discovery and Utilization) is a syntactic approach to discover WS. The consumer launches his request via the GUI interface. The request is then sent to the QAA (Query Analyzer Agent) that selects the agents of referential system of service agent expertise areas using the TFIDF (Term Frequency Inverse Document Frequency). Based on rel-

evant keywords extracted from the service consumer request, the QAA agent selects a set of expert agents that transmit thereafter the parameters of service with whom they are related to the composition agent. The composition agent invokes the service satisfying the consumer requirement.

Semantic Approaches

Semantic approaches are based mainly on semantic Web technologies (OWL-S, WS-Policy and WSDL-S). They are classified according to the concept of ontology. The ontology is a structured set of terms and concepts representing the direction of a domain of information, developed to facilitate knowledge sharing and reuse. Semantic approaches are generally designed in three categories; logical semantics discovery, non-logical semantic discovery and hybrid semantic discovery.

- Logical semantics: The logical approaches exploit the inferences to verify compatibility between the query and service annotation.
  - **PSD (P2P-Based Semantic Web service Discovery):** The approach (Vu, Hauswirth, & Aberer, 2005) is a logical approach based on the P2P network. The services are described according WSMO ontology (Web Service Modeling Ontology), research WS adopts QoS as non-functional property and the matchmaker handles the service selection and transmission to the consumer that in turn invokes the service suitable.
  - In (Lu, Wang, Zhang, & Li, 2012), authors propose a Web service discovery method based on the domain ontologies. The proposed method calculates semantic similarity based on ontology distance between concepts in both service request and service advertisement. The Web service discovery algorithm in this paper only calculates the semantic similarity of the functional description of the Web service, and jumps over the semantic similarity of the description of the input/output parameters.
- **Non Logical Semantics:** The non-logical approaches exploit implicit or informal semantic of services and uses other techniques such as data mining, matching of graphs, research information, similarity measures...
  - **iMatcher:** In the case of (Schumacher, Helin, & Schuldt, 2008), the authors use a syntactic matchmaker of service profiles, which are described in OWL-S. The idea is to calculate the similarity between syntactic consumer request and WS offered.
  - Folino et al. propose an efficient model for discovering data mining Web services. This model proposes a Chord DHT extension that takes into account taxonomy of data mining services (Folino, Pisani, & Trunfio, 2014).
- **Hybrid Semantics:** Hybrid approaches combine the logical and non-logical mechanisms. They implement the idea to identify the limitations of the two semantic approaches (logical and non-logical) and to overcome these limitations by combining the two approaches in one called hybrid that succeeds where each of these approaches fails.
  - **OWLS-iMatcher2:** As a solution, the authors of (Kiefer & Bernstein, 2008) cite OWLS-iMatcher2, which is a hybrid approach of WS discovery that takes syntactic matching to calculate the syntactic similarity between the consumer request and WS offered and the semantic matching to translate the service consumer inputs and outputs.

Contextual Approaches

Contextual approaches are based on context. The context is the set of all the information that can be used to characterize the situation of an entity, an entity is a person, place or object that may be relevant to the interaction between user and application including the user and the application themselves.

- **UDDI+:** In (Pokraev, Koolwaaij, & Wibbels, 2003), the authors proposed the UDDI approach; the idea is to make extensions at the UDDI server to consider the context of information during the discovery services.
- **CASD (Context Aware Service Discovery):** Other authors have defined architecture CASD (Doulkeridis, Loutas, & Vazirgiannis, 2005). It is a WS discovery system based on the context in which a semantic discovery module is designed to determine the categories of services, which have a semantic relationship with the consumer request based on domain ontologies.

Behavioral Approaches

In literature, the behavior of WS is described by sequences of messages, data types, constraints and data properties that specify the time within which the messages are exchanged (Kari, 2013). This aspect has also been described by sequences of messages, called conversations that support WS. The set of conversations is called a conversation protocol. It can be specified using BPEL (Business Process Execution Language), OWL-S (semantic markup for Web services) or WSCL (Web Services Conversation Language) (Albreshne & al., September 2009).

- **BBS (Behavior Based on Synchronization):** The WS behavioral modeling approach (Maamar & al., 2009) is based on two types of behavior: control (the business logic supports the functioning of WS) and operational (which regulates progression of behavioral control execution indicating the actions to be implemented, and constraints to put on this progress). The idea is to coordinate the two behaviors at runtime by the development of message conversation and transmit information between these two behaviors.
- **BVV (Behavioral Verification and Validation):** The approach in (Ramollari & al., 2008) is based on the formal modeling of WS behavioral aspects as SXM (stream X-machine). The principle is to improve the WSDL for each service by SXM, to check and validate the WS during the process of publication and discovery. The behavior aspect is particularly relevant in WS with state, where operations answers not only depend on the service consumer inputs, but also on the internal state of the WS.

Selection Phase

In cases where several WS meet the functional needs of the service consumer query, the discovery phase can be completed by a selection phase to choose the most appropriate service based on functional and non-functional requirements extracted from the query launched. The functional properties of WS describe what the service can do (functionality). The non-functional properties describe how the service works (quality). Considering the rapid growth of WS having the same functionality, the selection process becomes increasingly unavoidable. In the literature, various efforts have been spent to solve this problem based on the functional and nonfunctional properties of the WS (Boudjelaba, June 2012). Two types of selection are possible:

- **Service Selection Based on Functional Requirements:** After searching the WS that meet the service consumer requirements, it was necessary to select among them the most relevant WS, which admits the functional requirements mentioned by the consumer. Many works are based on the selection means of syntactic services; others have adapted the basic semantics which makes selection more effective.

- **Services Selection Based on Non-Functional Requirements:** Non-functional properties, also called QoS service quality, are used to evaluate the degree of which WS meets the quality requirements specified in a service request. It is a set of non-functional attributes that can influence the quality of service provided in terms of availability, performance, summoning cost, reliability, etc.

  ○ The approach proposed in (Çelik & Elçi, 2013) presents a semantic matching approach for discovering Semantic Web services through a broker-based semantic agent (BSA). The BSA includes knowledge-bases and several processing steps. The BSA's knowledge-bases are concept, task, and process ontologies built to describe both functional and non-functional parameters of services. The BSA executes semantic-based matching algorithms to discover similar services through the semantic matching step, process equivalence task, and matching of quality of service parameters. Relevant services are ranked by client preferences utilizing the semantic descriptions of available services.

  ○ In the paper (El Bouhissi, Malki, & Sidi Ali Cherif, 2014), the authors address the issue of the Web service discovery given nonexplicit service description semantics that match a specific service request. Their approach is based on a captured user goal from an HTML form and the traceability and involves semantic based service categorization, semantic discovery and selection of the best Web service. Furthermore, the authors' proposal employs ontology matching algorithms to match a specific goal to an existing Web service.

Comparative Study

This section presents a set of criteria that take into account issues related to the discovery and selection of WS. Through 13 works, existing solutions will be discussed in terms of a set of comparison criteria mentioned below. To compare the different approaches presented above, the following comparison criteria are identified:

- **Discovery Approach:** According to this study, the majority of discovery approaches are listed in four categories; syntactic, semantic, contextual and behavioral.
- **Approach Type:** For semantic approaches, as mentioned earlier they are distinguished into three types; logical approaches, non-logical approaches, and hybrid approaches.
- **Description Model:** The model description is used to describe the Web service. Several kinds of service descriptions are presented as: WSDL, WSMO …
- **Adopted Architecture:** Distributed or centralized architecture.
- **Matching Type:** The matching type evaluates the equivalence between the concepts used to describe the WS properties and properties described in the service consumer query. The matching

should not be limited to the syntactic level. It should cover the semantic aspect or cover the two levels if necessary.

- **Formalism:** Formalism criterion provides information about concepts used to represent approach. Each approach evokes its manner of representation (query representation and service search representation). It can be RDF (Resource Description Framework); storage of services in the form of RDF graphs in an RDF database, by means of an extension of iRDQL language (RDF Data Query Language). The formalism can also be designed as OWL-S, WSMO, OWL graph or simple terms.
- **Adopted Technologies:** Formalisms and concepts used to develop the proposed approach.
- **Ontology:** It is the fact of considering the ontology.
- **QoS:** It is the fact of considering the QoS properties in selection phase.
- **User Profile:** It is the fact of considering the user preferences in discovery process.

Table 7 presents a comparative study based on a number of criteria.

This chapter examines a range of issues concerning the WS discovery. The comparative study draws weaknesses and strengths of each approach in order to design a new semantic approach encompassing a set of concepts that overcomes the problems associated with other types of discovery.

In our proposed approach we deal with three purposes. The first is to take into account the user profile concept in the discovery process in order to focus and direct the search of services. The second is to enrich the Web services description by the semantic aspect using metadata catalogue, and QoS properties which aims to reduce the search space and increase the number of relevant services. The third is the use of mobile agents as a communication entity; this is to reduce the traffic on the network and to minimize the quantity of exchanged information.

FUTURE RESEARCH DIRECTIONS

In this section, the researchers highlight several key directions for future research into the design of semantic Web services discovery approaches.

- Enrichment of metadata to support other quality criteria of Web services to enhance the semantic discovery through experimentation in different areas;
- Compose the functionality of several Web services into one composite service to satisfy the requests when there is no single fit service;
- Another direction for future research is to integrate the Internet of Things (IoT) with Web Services and Cloud Computing. Cloud computing and the IoT both serve to increase efficiency in our everyday tasks, and the two have a complimentary relationship.

CONCLUSION

In this chapter, we provided a general overview of a framework for semantic Web services discovery. We showed the different kinds of agents composing the proposed architecture and how they are organized. The particularity of this work is summarized in the following points:

Table 7. Comparative study of Web service discovery approaches

	Discovery Approach	Approach Type	Description Model	Adopted Architecture	Matching Type	Adopted Technologies	Ontology	QoS	User Profile
(Palathingal & Chandra, 2004)	Syntactic	-	WSDL	Distributed	Syntactic	Textual description, TFIDF, Multi-Agents	Neglected	Neglected	Neglected
(Doulkeridis, Loutas, & Vazirgiannis, 2005)	Contextual	-	CASD	Distributed	Semantic	OWL graph	OWLS	Adopted	Adopted
(Ramollari & al., 2008)	Behavioral	-	WSDL	Centralized	Syntactic or semantic	SXM	Neglected	Neglected	Neglected
(Maamar & al., 2009)	Behavioral	-	CASD	Centralized	Semantic	Finite state machine	Neglected	Neglected	Neglected
(Lu, Wang, Zhang, & Li, 2012)	Semantic	Logic	Mapping between WSDL and domain ontology	Centralized	Semantic	SOAP	OWLS	Neglected	Neglected
(El Bouhissi, Malki, & Sidi Ali Cherif, 2014)	Semantic	Non Logic	WSMO Ontology	Centralized	Semantic	WordNet domain ontology	WSMO	Neglected	Neglected
(Elfirdoussi, Jarir, & Quafafou, 2014)	Semantic	Logic	WSDL	Centralized	Syntactic and semantic	WSPS	Neglected	Adopted	Adopted
(Guidara, Guermouche, Chaari, Jmaiel, & Tazi, 2015)	Syntactic	-	WSDL	Distributed	Syntactic	SOAP	Neglected	Adopted	Neglected
(Maabed, El-Fatatry, & El-Zogh, 2016)	Syntactic	-	WSDL	Distributed	Syntactic	SOAP	Neglected	Adopted	Neglected
(Fellah, Malki, & Elci, 2016)	Semantic	Non logic	multi ontology context	Distributed	Semantic	OWL graph	OWLS	Neglected	Neglected
(Ben Messaoud, Ghedira, & Ben Halima, 2016)	Behavioral	-	WSDL	Centralized	Semantic	WordNet domain ontology	OWLS	Adopted	Neglected
(Ben-Seghier, Kazar, Rezeg, & Bourakkache, 2017)	Semantic	Hybrid	Mapping between WSDL and Metadata catalogue	Centralized	Syntactic and semantic	Mobile agent technology	OWLS	Neglected	Adopted
Proposed Approach	Semantic	Hybrid	Mapping between WSDL and Metadata catalogue	Distributed	Syntactic and semantic and QoS score computing	Mobile agent technology	OWLS	Adopted	Adopted

- The richness of Web services description in metadata catalogue, and in UDDI registry.
- The semantic Web services discovery reduces the number of relevant services through the application of matching algorithm "semantic match". The result of this first matching restricts the search space at the level of UDDI registry, which allows users have good results for "functional match".
- Decentralization of Web services. Indeed, the use of distributed UDDI solves the limitations of centralized architectures. It offers the advantage to overcome the problem of "single point of failure" and avoids the bottleneck (performance point of view).
- Use of mobile agents as a communication entity. This is to reduce the traffic on the network and to reduce the quantity of exchanged information, thus minimizing customer wait time.
- Satisfying the QoS requirements for the selection of the best available Web service.
- Integration of user profile in the service discovery process facilitates the expression of user needs and makes intelligible the selected service.

REFERENCES

Albreshne, A. (2009). *Web Services. Orchestration and Composition Case Study of Web services Composition*. Working Paper.

Beckett, D. (2014). *RDF 1.1 Turtle: Terse RDF triple language*. W3C Recommendation. Retrieved from http:// www.w3.org/TR/turtle/

Ben Messaoud, W., Ghedira, K., & Ben Halima, Y. (2016). Towards behavioral web service discovery approach:State of the art. *Procedia Computer Science*, *96*, 1049–1058. doi:10.1016/j.procs.2016.08.126

Ben-Seghier, N., Kazar, O., & Rezeg, K. (2015). A Decentralized Framework for Semantic Web Services Discovery Using Mobile Agent. *International Journal of Information Technology and Web Engineering*, *10*(4), 20–43. doi:10.4018/IJITWE.2015100102

Ben-Seghier, N., Kazar, O., Rezeg, K., & Bourakkache, S. (2017). A semantic web services discovery approach based on a mobile agent using metadata. *International Journal of Intelligent Computing and Cybernetics*, *10*(1), 12–29. doi:10.1108/IJICC-02-2015-0006

Bianchini, D., De Antonellis, V., & Melchiori, M. (2010). P2P-SDSD: On-the-fly service-based collaboration in distributed systems. *International Journal of Metadata, Semantics and Ontologies*, *5*(3), 222–237. doi:10.1504/IJMSO.2010.034046

Boudjelaba, H. (2012). *Sélection des Web Services Sémantiques*. Ecole Doctorale Réseaux et Systèmes Distribués.

Boukhadra, A., Benatchba, K., & Balla, A. (2014). Ranked Matching of OWL-S Process Model for Distributed Discovery of SWs in P2P Systems. In *Network-Based Information Systems, (NBiS) 17th IEEE International Conference on 2014* (pp. 106-113). IEEE.

Bouzeghoub, M., & Peralta, V. (2004). A Framework for Analysis of Data Freshness. In *1st International Workshop on Information Quality in Information Systems (IQIS)* (pp. 59-67). Paris, France: Academic Press. 10.1145/1012453.1012464

Brickley, D., & Guha, R. V. (2014). *RDF Schema 1.1*. W3C Recommendation. Retrieved from http://www.w3.org/TR/rdfschema/

Burg, B. (2002). *Agents in the World of Active Web-services*. Hewlett-Packard Laboratories.

Celik, D., & Elçi, A. (2013). A broker-based semantic agent for discovering Semantic Web services through process similarity matching and equivalence considering quality of service. Science China Information Sciences (SCI), 56(1), 012102:1–012102:24.

Clement, L., Hately, A., & Riegen, C. V. (2004). *UDDI Version 3.0.2*. UDDI Spec Technical Committee Draft. Retrieved from http://uddi.org/pubs/uddi_v3.htm

Doulkeridis, C., Loutas, N., & Vazirgiannis, M. (2005). A system architecture for context-aware service discovery. *International Workshop on Context for Web Services CWS-05*.

El Bouhissi, H., Malki, M., & Sidi Ali Cherif, M. A. (2014). From user's goal to semantic Web services discovery: Approach based on traceability. *International Journal of Information Technology and Web Engineering*, 9(3), 15–39. doi:10.4018/ijitwe.2014070102

Elfirdoussi, S., Jarir, Z., & Quafafou, M. (2014). Ranking Web services using Web service popularity score. *International Journal of Information Technology and Web Engineering*, 9(2), 78–89. doi:10.4018/ijitwe.2014040105

Falou, E. L. S. (2006). Programmation répartie, optimisation par agent mobile. CEAN University.

Fellah, A., Malki, M., & Elci, A. (2016). A Similarity Measure across Ontologies for Web Services Discovery. *International Journal of Information Technology and Web Engineering*, 11(1), 22–43. doi:10.4018/IJITWE.2016010102

Folino, G., Pisani, F., & Trunfio, P. (2014). *Efficient Discovery of Data Mining Services over DHT-based Overlays*. High Performance Computing & Simulation (HPCS), International Conference.

Fragopoulou, P., Mastroianni, C., Montero, R., Andrjezak, A., & Kondo, D. (2010). Self and adaptive mechanisms for large scale distributed systems. In Grids, P2P and Services Computing (pp. 147-156). Springer. doi:10.1007/978-1-4419-6794-7_12

Furno, A., & Zimeo, E. (2013). Efficient cooperative discovery of service compositions in unstructured P2P networks. In *Parallel, Distributed and Network-Based Processing (PDP), 21st Euromicro International Conference on 2013* (pp. 58-67). IEEE.

Gandon, F., & Shreiber, G. (2014, Feb 25). *RDF 1.1: XML syntax*. W3C Recommendation. Retrieved from http://www. w3.org/TR/rdf-syntax-grammar/

Grasic, B., & Podgorelec, V. (2010). Automating ontology based information integration using service orientation. *WSEAS Transactions on Computers*, 9, 547–556.

Guidara, I., Guermouche, N., Chaari, T., Jmaiel, M., & Tazi, S. (2015). Time-dependent QoS Aware Best Service Combination Selection. *International Journal of Web Services Research*, 12(2), 1–25. doi:10.4018/IJWSR.2015040101

Haas, H., & Brown, A. (Eds.). (2004). *Web Services Glossary*. Retrieved from https://www.w3.org/TR/2004/NOTE-ws-gloss-20040211/

Harris, S., & Seaborne, A. (2013). *SPARQL 1.1: Query language*. W3C Recommendation. Retrieved from http://www. w3.org/TR/sparql11-query/

Heflin, J. (2004). *OWL web ontology language use cases and requirements*. W3C Recommendation. Retrieved from http:// www.w3.org/TR/webont-req/

Huayou, S., Zhong, C., & Yong, D. (2013). Semantic web services publication and OCT-based discovery in structured P2P network. *Service Oriented Computing and Applications*, *7*(3), 169–180. doi:10.100711761-011-0097-4

Jars, I. (2005). *Contribution des sciences sociales dans le domaine de l'intelligence artificielle distribuée ALONE, Un modèle hybride d'agent apprenant*. Claude Bernard Lyon I University.

Kari, J. (2013). *Automata and formal languages*. University of Turku.

Kiefer, C., & Bernstein, A. (2008). The Creation and Evaluation of iSPARQL Strategies for Matchmaking. *Proceedings of the 5th European Semantic Web Conference (ESWC)*, 463– 477. 10.1007/978-3-540-68234-9_35

Klusch, M., & Kapahnke, P. (2010). isem: Approximated reasoning for adaptive hybrid selection of semantic services. In The semantic web: Research and applications (pp. 30-44). Springer.

Kostadinov, D. (2007). *Personnalisation de l'information: une approche de gestion de profils et de reformulation de requêtes*. University of Versailles Saint-Quentin-En-Yvelines.

Koutrika, G., & Ioannidis, Y. (2004). Personalization of Queries in Database Systems. *Proceedings of the 20th International Conference on Data Engineering*, 597-608. 10.1109/ICDE.2004.1320030

Koutrika, G., & Ioannidis, Y. (2005). Personalized Queries under a Generalized Preference Model. *Proceedings of the 21st International Conference on Data Engineering*, 841-852. 10.1109/ICDE.2005.106

Lu, G., Wang, T., Zhang, G., & Li, S. (2012). Semantic Web Services Discovery Based on Domain Ontology. In *World Automation Congress (WAC)* (pp. 1-4). Puerto Vallarta, Mexico: IEEE.

Maabed, U. M., El-Fatatry, A., & El-Zogh, A. (2016). Enhancing Interface Understandability as a Means for Better Discovery of Web Services. *International Journal of Information Technology and Web Engineering*, *11*(4), 1–23. doi:10.4018/IJITWE.2016100101

Maamar, Z. (2009). A New Approach to Model Web Services Behaviors based on Synchronization. *International Conference on Advanced Information Networking and Applications Workshops*. 10.1109/WAINA.2009.65

Martin, D., Burstein, M., Mcdermott, D., Mcilraith, S., Paolucci, M., Sycara, K., ... Srinivasan, N. (2007). Bringing semantics to web services with OWL-S. *World Wide Web (Bussum)*, *10*(3), 243–277. doi:10.100711280-007-0033-x

Mcguiness, D. L., & Harmelen, F. V. (2004). *OWL Web Ontology Language: Overview*. W3C Recommendation. Retrieved from http://www.w3.org/TR/owl-features/

NISO. (2005). *Understanding Metadata*. Bethesda, MD: NISO Press.

Palathingal, P., & Chandra, S. (2004). Agent approach for service discovery and utilization. HICSS. doi:10.1109/HICSS.2004.1265292

Pokraev, S., Koolwaaij, J., & Wibbels, M. (2003). Extending UDDI with context-aware features based on semantic service descriptions. ICWS, 184–190.

Ramollari, E., Kourtesis, D., Dranidis, D., & Simon, A. J. H. (2008). Towards Reliable Web Service Discovery through Behavioral Verification and Validation. *Proceedings of the 3rd European Young Researchers Workshop on Service*.

Schumacher, M., Helin, H., & Schuldt, H. (2008). Chapter 4, CASCOM: Intelligent Service Coordination in the Semantic Web. Dans Semantic Web Service Coordination.

Tannenbaum, A. (2001). *Metadata Solutions*. Upper Saddle River, NJ: Addison-Wesley.

Vu, L.-H., Hauswirth, M., & Aberer, K. (2005). Towards P2P-based semantic Web service discovery with Qos support. Business Process Management Workshops, 18–31.

Wooldridge, M. (2002). *An Introduction to Multi-Agent systems*. Wiley Publication.

Xu, Z., Martin, P., Powley, W., & Zulkernine, F. (2007). Reputation-Enhanced QoS-based Web Service Discovery. In *Proceedings of the International Conference on Web Services* (pp. 249- 256). IEEE.

KEY TERMS AND DEFINITIONS

Agent: An autonomous entity that observes through sensors and acts upon an environment using actuators and directs its activity towards achieving goals.

Matching: The process of determining correspondences between concepts in ontologies, a set of correspondences is also called an alignment.

Metadata: A set of data that describes and gives information about other data.

Ontology: A set of concepts and categories in a subject area or domain that shows their properties and the relations between them.

Personalization: Sometimes known as customization, consists of tailoring a service to individual users' characteristics or preferences.

QoS: Description or measurement of the overall performance of a service, such as reliability, availability, execution price, and response time.

Selection: Choose the most appropriate service based on functional and non-functional requirements extracted from the query launched.

Service: Any piece of software that makes itself available over the internet and uses a standardized XML messaging system.

Chapter 15

Measurable and Behavioral Non-Functional Requirements in Web Service Composition

Ilyass El Kassmi
Cadi Ayyad University, Morocco

Zahi Jarir
Cadi Ayyad University, Morocco

ABSTRACT

Handling non-functional requirements (NFRs) in web service composition has gained increasing attention in the literature. However, this challenge is still open, despite the efforts of the scientific community, due to its complexity. This complexity starts from the fact that NFRs can represent structural constraints, QoS attributes, temporal constraints, or behavioral attributes. Therefore, this characterization makes the task of web service composition lifecycle (e.g., specification, verification, integration, etc.) increasingly complicated. Therefore, this chapter investigates this point of view and suggests a complete approach supporting specification, formalization, validation, and code generation of desired composite web service. This approach has the advantage to tackle with quantifiable (i.e., measurable) and behavioral NFRs, and provide a support for composing NFRs with FRs using seamless weaving.

INTRODUCTION

Web services technologies representing a more important instance of Service-Oriented Architecture (SOA) are gaining a considerable momentum as a computing paradigm to provide and support rapid development of complex and flexible services, applications and infrastructures in several domains such as Cloud computing, Machine-To-Machine paradigm (M2M), Internet of Things (IoT), etc. Web services (WSs) represent autonomous pieces of code developed in different programming languages by different providers. They offer specific functionality to fulfill a desired goal. In addition, they respect a strict separation of concerns, which is a core principle of SOA. They are also designed to facilitate interoperability among heterogeneous systems, and to be published, discovered, invoked, and integrated

DOI: 10.4018/978-1-5225-5384-7.ch015

into composition processes to fulfill complex tasks. This integration commonly named Web service composition or aggregation is built according to user's requirements or system's requirements as in M2M. These requirements are known in software engineering by attributes, properties or concerns. They are classified mainly into two main classes: Functional Requirement (FR) and Non-Functional Requirement (NFR). FRs are related to the conformance of Web service composition to the desired business goal on its functionality. Whereas NFRs are focusing on how the service should perform their goals that concern in general measurable QoS (Quality of Service) properties (e.g., availability, performance).

Authors in (Galster & Bucherer, 2008) worked on a taxonomy proposition to classify non-functional attributes according to their categories, i.e. process requirements, non-functional service requirements and non-functional external requirements. They also introduced the term of "quantifiability" to evaluate NFRs. Some of these non-functional attributes are classified as quantifiable using specific metrics while others can only get quantifiable by specifying whether they are met or not met. In our opinion, an NFR can be measurable, i.e., quantifiable when a specific metric exists to evaluate it. Otherwise, it represents a behavioral NFR, which requires a specific modeling.

The topic of WS composition including NFRs has gained a lot of attention from scientific and academic researchers. These attentions focused on different challenges related to complex Web services composition such as NFRs specification, formalization, validation, integration, enforcement, etc. In general, NFRs offer several advantages such as:

- Representing a crucial criterion for the selection of the appropriate service from discovered services offering similar functionalities (i.e., FRs): This track was raised by several contributions. Among the interesting contributions the work in (Çelik & Elçi, 2013) proposed Broker-based Semantic Agent (BSA) allowing to discover Web services, in accordance to needed functional requirements and quality of service parameters, using a semantic-based matching algorithm rather than syntactical techniques. This BSA executes semantic-based matching algorithm to verify the validity of the service in term of semantic and the matching of QoS parameters.
- Controlling the behavior of FRs in the composition processes: The work in (Sheng, Maamar, Yao, Szabo, & Bourne, 2014) raised this advantage and suggested an approach that includes a Web service model that separates service behaviors into operational and control. The coordination of operational and control behaviors at runtime is based on conversational messages.
- Enforcing required NFRs such as security policies in business processes: In (Schmeling, Charfi, Thome, & Mezini, 2011) the authors suggest an approach and a toolset for the specification and realization of the composition of multiple NFRs in Web services. This approach proposes a methodology supporting the NFR composition from requirements to enforcement, and putting a strong emphasis on separation of responsibilities between different roles involved in the composition process.

Before integrating NFRs with each concerned FR, there is a clear need to specify and formalize them correctly, which is really a fastidious task that several approaches focused on. To formalize NFR, some interesting surveys are proposed such as (Beek, Bucchiarome, & Gnesi, 2007a) and (Beek, Bucchiarome, & Gnesi, 2007b). They outlined the most used formalization methods including Automata, Process Algebra, and Petri Nets. Once NFRs are formalized, some algorithms and techniques are then required to combine them seamlessly with associated FRs to avoid any feature interaction.

Based on a review study, the authors conclude that at design time NFRs are often described differently and can be represented as: (1) a QoS attribute or property such as response time, availability, etc.; (2) a specific policy (e.g. WS Policy, WS Transaction, etc.) using a declarative approach as introduced in (Schmeling et al., 2011); and, (3) a behavioral feature (e.g. access control) considered as non-measurable NFR that needs to be modeled before integration into WS composition (El Kassmi & Jarir, 2016). Therefore, despite the active research in NFR specification and integration, Web service composition is still not mature yet, especially when considering defined NFR cases (QoS property, WS-* policy, and behavioral feature) in WS composition at design and deployment times. This remains an open challenge when considering a Web service composition model tackling shortcomings such as FR and NFR specifications, NFR formalization, NFR interdependencies, FR and NFR integration, composed FR and NFR behavior validation, code generation, etc.

To the best of the authors' knowledge, there is a lack of contribution in the literature that considered complete development process tackling in details NFRs attributes and behaviors integration process into WS composition starting from specification until code generation. A deeper discussion will be presented below in related work section. More specifically this paper contributes as follows:

- Handling measurable and behavioral NFRs,
- Providing a support for composing NFRs with FRs using seamless weaving,
- Introducing a complete approach supporting specification, formalization, validation and code generation of a desired composite WS.

The remainder of the paper is organized as follows. "Non-functional requirements background" Section gives an overview on the classifications schemes of NFRs proposed in the literature. "A proposed approach" Section suggests a novel approach handling both measurable and behavioral NFRs and their integration with functional requirements. "Case study" Section presents a case study to illustrate in more details this approach. "Verification using UPPAAL model checker" Section describes verification steps of proposed case study. "Related work" Section exposes works describing some interesting contributions tackling NFRs. "Future research directions" Section summarizes suggested further work. Then conclusions are offered.

NON-FUNCTIONAL REQUIREMENTS BACKGROUND

According to (Chung & do Prado Leite, 2009) NFRs can be presented as soft or hard constraints. These constraints refer respectively to the satisfaction of user's preferences and the desired composition system. Authors in (Galster & Bucherer, 2008) proposed a Web service oriented taxonomy for categorizing non-functional requirements by introducing quantifiable and measurable requirements. In addition, they suggested an interesting classification for non-functional requirements in service-oriented context, complete with a dedicated taxonomy. This classification is splitting NFRs into three main classes: "Process requirements" which consists of properties dealing with service design, discovery, composition and runtime. The second class is the "External requirements", which mainly consists of external economic or legal constraints on the development or deployment process. The third and main class is the "Service requirements", which unlike the other classes that require more domain and environmental analysis, are placed directly on the service-oriented system, and can be derived directly from user needs.

The international standard for the evaluation of software quality proposes a scheme based on four quality levels, namely, quality in use, internal, external, and process quality attributes (ISO/IEC9126, 2001). FURPS+, acronym of Functionality, Usability, Reliability, Performance, Supportability, is another classification for software quality attributes, which depicts a software quality tree, and aims to address concerns for key types of NFRs and importantly possible correlations among them. An important contribution (Hasan, Loucopoulos, & Nikolaidou, 2014) classified the NFR approaches according to different criteria and provided a qualitative analysis of their scopes and characteristics. This work focused on the three main classes of NFR approaches, which are Goal-oriented, Aspect-oriented, and Pattern-based approaches.

An important literature review studied by (Mairiza, Zowghi, & Nurmuliani, 2010) exposed that the most frequently used NFR in industrial specifications are performance, reliability, usability, security, and maintainability. Other similar review studies described the same result but differed between them in the order of importance of their uses. Among them, (Broy, 2015) and (Eckhardt, Vogelsang, & Méndez Fernandez, 2016) that qualified NFRs as usually defined vaguely, and not well defined, which render them not quantified, and as a result difficult to analyze. In addition, the NFRs analysis study presented by (Eckhardt et al., 2016) assigned NFRs to structured views according to Broy's views. These structured views correspond to representational NFRs that refer to the way a system is syntactically or technically represented, structured, coded, or executed, and behavioral NFRs that describe behavioral properties of a system.

In general, most of contributions addressed NFRs as QoS attributes or properties in order to meet the challenge of Web service selection according to user's functional requirements. These properties characterize quality aspects of published Web service such as response time and performance. Sometimes QoS attribute values may change during time and thus selecting an appropriate Web service is really a tedious task. So besides structural constraints, temporal constraints can also be specified to meet desired requirements (Guidara, Guermouche, Chaari, Jmaiel, & Tazi, 2015).

The work in (Glinz, 2007) argued that evaluating NFRs in service-oriented systems represents one of the most critical issues. For that reason, it introduced "Quantifiability" that refers to defining metrics to make NFR measurable, and therefore helping to select a more appropriate Web service in term of required and measurable QoS. However, in real world application NFRs could be non-quantifiable (e.g. security). In such case, these NFRs must be defined as behavioral aspects of a system, capturing the properties and constraints under which a system must operate such as access control or authentication. Therefore, this category of NFRs should be modeled and coded in particular programming language to integrate with the corresponding FRs thereafter. In this case, a more efficient programming environment used for handling NFRs is Aspect Oriented Programming (AOP). In addition, an appropriate modeling should be proposed with conformance to the corresponding FRs modeling. This conformance consists also in avoiding feature interaction between composed NFRs associated to the same FR. A model checker such as Promela Spin (Holzmann, 2007), Uppsala-Aalborg verification tool (UPPAAL) (Behrmann, David, & Larsen, 2004), etc. is mandatory to verify behavioral NFRs integration with FRs.

In SOA, three aspects play an important role: the specification, the validation and the realization of NFRs. However, focusing on all these aspects is still a challenging task. This open issue motivates the authors to address shortcomings of these aspects through an approach for composing the NFRs of Web services. The details of this approach represent the goal of the following section.

A PROPOSED APPROACH

The aim of this contribution is to propose an approach handling NFR analysis, and a distinction between the Quality of Service properties, and non-quantifiable NFRs such as security requirements. In (Firesmith, 2003), the author addressed many security attributes, most of which can only be set as satisfied or not satisfied at the execution time, and do not have any measurable metrics. In such cases, and in order to implement any of them, a prior knowledge of their behavior is required. Authentication or access control is a significant example represented as behavioral non-functional attribute dealing with how the current system process performs in term of security, without being part of its functional behavior that impacts the business process or user's primary requests. However, each of these NFR attributes can have different implementations, as various authentication methods, and access control models exist. This leads to conclude that integrating such non-functional requirements will affect the composite Web service, according to which authentication and access control model are used. These non-quantifiable NFR attributes, unlike measurable quality of service attributes, need a complete modeling at the design time to meet the existing functional process for the Web service composition. In order to satisfy both mentioned classes of NFRs, a common modeling approach should be proposed, combining both quality attributes and behavioral attributes with the functional process.

To address both NFR classes in Web service composition, this paper suggests a comprehensive approach where the designer has a multitude of options for modeling a reliable Web service composition, including both functional goals and non-functional requirements either measurable or not. As a first step, a user has to depict all functional goals and place them with respect to composition aspects like sequences, parallelism, choice, etc. This approach uses automata-based modeling to design concurrent needed Web services as different goals. Each goal defines the desired functional need, and is modeled as a state, which will be assigned later to Web services fulfilling this specific need. The goals interactions, which constitute the further Web service interactions, are modeled using transitions between states (cf. Figure 1).

In (Elfirdoussi, Jarir, & Quafafou, 2014b) the authors focused on measurable NFR attributes representing a more appropriate and decisive factor to distinguish similar Web services. The novelty of the proposed approach lies in its simplicity since it is based on Web Service Popularity Score (WSPS). This score is computed using an algorithm based on both user's requirements and quality measures of each discovered Web services including Availability, Usability, Pertinence, Age, Frequency, Notoriety and Matching quality. This approach allows to cover a large variety of measurable quality attributes, to help

Figure 1. Functional Automaton matching user's goals

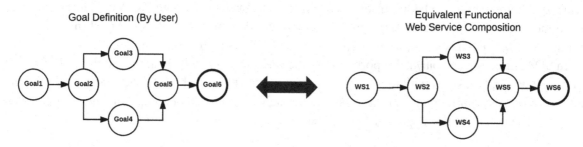

the user to automatically get the Web service composition matching the best quality requirements. The proposed formulas allowing to calculate the evoked QoS properties, in addition to their corresponding popularity score are defined below:

- **Availability:** It is calculated using the "HttpURLConnection" to get a connection to its URL. The value we get by the metric is either 0 or 1, 0 if the WS is not available and 1 if the WS is available. The metric represents the number of the WS availability divided by the number of Invoke or Discover.

$$Av(ws) = \frac{\sum Av(ws)}{NbUse(ws)} \tag{1}$$

- **Usability:** This metric represents a number of WS calls using its URL when invoking or discovering such service. In this case, each operation can be identified as a link. The formula will summarize the number of registration grouping by URL and the types of calls (invoke or discover).

$$Us(ws) = \frac{\sum NumberInvoque(ws)}{\sum NumberDiscover(ws)} \tag{2}$$

- **Pertinence:** It is related to the WS category considering the user's query, and defines the degree to which the content of the WS is focused on the topic.

$$Pe(ws) = \frac{\left(N*(N-1)/2\right) - \left(M*(M-1)/2\right) + Pij}{N*(N-1)/2} \tag{3}$$

- *N is the maximum number of top matching topics requested. The query user is classified in a different topic on the ontology and N presented as a Vector. The N is the vector Size.*
- *M is the number of matching topics returned, it's the number of the words presented in the WS, using file description, semantic description, and matching to each topic defined in the Vector presented in N.*
- P_{ij} *is the length of the shared path between topic i and topic j divided by the height of the ontology. It is presented as the dependence degree between topic i and topic j. Its related information can be extracted from the ontology using vector space classifier. The result is divided by the size of the vector presented in N.*
- **Age:** This metric is measured by using the number of days between the last dates of invoke or discover interaction and the current date. We estimate that the best WS is the one that is also recently used.

$$Age(ws) = now() - LastCallDate(ws) \tag{4}$$

- *LastCallDate refers to the last date concerning the WS invocation or WS discovering operation.*

- **Frequency:** This metric presents the number of using the WS by duration (day, week, month or year), and it's presented by the number of use and its duration. In our case, we choose to use month duration, and this information is defined as a parameter that users can modify.

$$Fr\left(ws\right) = \frac{\sum NbUse\left(ws\right)}{NbMonth\left(ws\right)} \tag{5}$$

- *"NbUse" is the total of WS call (discover or invoke operation) by each duration. And the "NbMonth" is the number of months where the WS was consumed.*
- **Notoriety**: The notoriety metric presents the relationship between each WS and the number of WSs used by or for this one. The Notoriety score presents the number of WS used (in composition or semantic description) in other WS. For example, a composite WS "cws" is automatically related to another "ws". The metric is calculated as a sum of WS used to compose or composite pointed to simple.

$$No\left(ws\right) = \frac{\sum Link\left(ws\right)}{\sum Nb\left(ws\right)} \tag{6}$$

- **Matching Quality:** The metric "Matching Quality" represents the degree of similarity by matching query and information that defines the WS. It is calculated as a number of words similar to the user's query by extracting information from WS description and using semantic search techniques, such as word sense disambiguation, stemming, etc. The idea is to summarize the number of words matching to query users and dividing this number by the number of operations proposed by the WS.

$$Mq\left(ws\right) = \frac{\sum Match\left(ws,\ query\right)}{\sum Number\left(ws, operation\right)} \tag{7}$$

- **Popularity Score:** All aforementioned metrics constitute a more fine-grained WS metrics taxonomy. The combination of these metrics will help surely to get eligibility (popularity) of WSs. In this score, each quality metric is associated to a coefficient represented by an integer having a value between 0 and 5. This coefficient reflects its importance among other proposed metrics when searching a user appropriate WS. The one which is more important has higher value.

$$WSPS\left(ws\right) = \frac{\sum \left(Metric\left(ws\right) * Coef\left(Metric\right)\right)}{\sum \left(Coef\left(Metric\right)\right)} \tag{8}$$

- *Metric in {"Availability", "Usability", "Pertinence", "Age", "Frequency", "Notoriety", "Matching Quality"}*

To evaluate the performance of popularity score, the authors in (Elfirdoussi, Jarir & Quafafou, 2014a) developed a framework called DIVISE (DIscovery and VIsual Search Engine). DIVISE is a Web service search engine that has the advantage to discover a required simple, composite or semantic Web service and to help user to select the more appropriate Web service regarding her/his needs from a generated returned list. This list contains in addition to classical Web service information a rate of its previous invocations, which is useful for deciding which one to select. Moreover, after selecting the appropriate Web service from a returned results list, a generated Web form input to invoke it is proposed. The proposed framework deals with automatic or semi-automatic Web service discovery taking in to consideration users preferences. It is based on Web services tracking approach by monitoring either discovery, invocation and publishing both users and service provider's requests. This approach is implemented by monitoring exchanged SOAP messages, parsing discovered or invoked Web service and storing captured pertinent information in to "trackingDB" database. DIVISE takes advantage of knowledge stored in this database to help users to select more appropriate Web service regarding their needs. This selection is based on WS availability, frequency of use, etc. A similar implementation is proposed in (Çelik & Elçi, 2008) that consists of a Semantic Search Agent (SSA) allowing to discover and return the best matching Web services according to user's query and QoS information provided.

In integrating non-functional requirements in the current modeling, the approach uses a specific notation as presented by Sun, Basu, Honavar, & Lutz (2010) to associate an atomic non-functional attribute to a specific component or subset of components. This notation is called a scope. Designers use it to delimit precisely the concerned elements. Figure 2 shows some examples of such scopes and the following paragraphs give more details.

In order to provide a more fine-grained Web service selection a coefficient is associated to each measurable attribute to ensure the respect of weight when there is more than one attribute required by the same Web service. The value attributed is also needed to restrict the Web service selection on only those honoring this condition. For example, in Figure 2-b, the Web service WS3 requires two measurable attributes which are the availability with coefficient 3 and a condition "availability > 90%", whereas the response-time attribute has coefficient 5 and a condition "response-time < 500ms". These NFRs are measurable and contribute to computing the popularity score according to metrics and specified coefficient for each attribute. In this current approach, the same concept is used to specify weight of quality attributes and evaluate the returned matching selection, and to attach measurable attribute to the measurable scope, which is modeled as dashed line surrounding the state or subset concerned by the measurable attribute.

In case of behavioral NFRs class, these requirements are generally too complex to measure; they can only be quantified by specifying whether met or not met, which might not be accurate in either design or execution time. To deal with this problem, a single behavioral model is necessary for each desired attribute. These attributes are modeled using a dotted line scope surrounding the affected subset of states (cf. Figure 2-a). Behavioral attributes do not need any coefficient specification, but instead have a temporal specification, allowing to define whether the integrated process well take effect right before or right after the specified subset. This is expressed by using a backward or forward edge in the dedicated scope.

Behavioral non-functional attributes are treated separately than measurable ones. Each scope concerns a single process that needs to be injected on the current functional automaton. In order to take effect in the composition process, by adding appropriate Web services to the current composition. To model the interactions between Web services and the appropriate non-functional requirement attributes, the authors use the automata-based modeling approach as applied to functional automaton in DIVISE framework described hereafter. Definition 1 below describes the used composition formalization.

Figure 2. Scoping of behavioral and measurable non-functional attributes

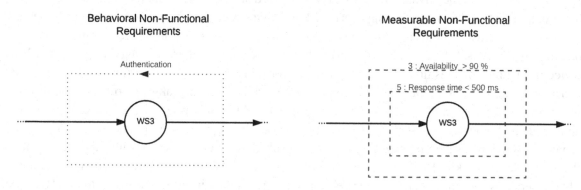

Whereas behavioral attributes are injected to current automaton process, the measurable attributes are modeled in a functional automaton using scopes, but do not affect the composition skeleton, as they don't require any behavioral change in the current functional automaton. They are rather used in discovery and selection process, in order to return the best matching Web services fulfilling the user's query.

Definition 1: Web Service Composition Automaton (WSCA) M is a septuplet $M = (A, S, s_0, S_f, T, \delta, N)$.

A is the signature of M, denoted as a triple $A = (I, F, O)$, where I, F, O are pair-wise disjoint and represent sets of inputs, internal functions, and outputs, respectively. Let $Msg = (I \cup F \cup O)$ be the set of actions according to the function's input parameters and the function's outputs.

S is a set of states

- $s_0 \in S$ is the initial state,
- $S_f \subseteq S$ is a set of final states.
- $T \subseteq (EX \cup \{\Omega\}) \times BX \times (\wp(AX \cup O) \cup \{\Omega\})$ is a set of transitions, where:
  - ○ EX is the set of expressions over input sets I.
  - ○ Let V be a countable infinite set of variables of M.
  - ○ AX is the set of assignments over V.
  - ○ BX is the set of Boolean expressions over V, linked by logical operators AND, OR, and NOT, denoted as $\wedge$, $\vee$, and $\neg$ respectively.
- For each transition $t = (ex, g, a) \in T$ (graphically denoted as ex[g]/a), $ex \in EX \cup \{\Omega\}$ is the input expression, $g \in BX$ is the guard predicate, and $a \subseteq \wp(AX \cup O) \cup \{\Omega\}$ is the action set composed of assignments and output events. Ω indicates the omission of an input expression or an output action. The components of transition t are denoted as t.ex = ex, t.g = g, t.a = a.
- $\delta \subseteq S \times T \times S$ is the transition relation (graphically denoted as $s_{src} \rightarrow t\ s_{tar}$). If $s_{src} \rightarrow t\ s_{tar}$ with $t = (ex, g, a)$, then if the composition is in the source state s_{src}, and the t.g is evaluated to true, then the composition system executes the set of instructions a, and change to the target state to star.
- $N = (B \cup Q)$ is the set of Non-functional properties over M, such that B is a subset of behavioral non-functional attributes, and Q a subset of measurable quality oriented attributes.

Figure 3. Web Service Composition Automaton

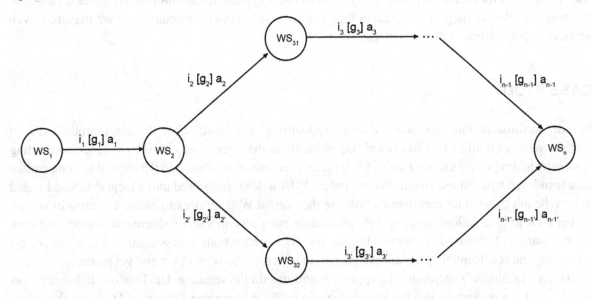

Then Figure 4 shows the proposed process. The input is the functional automaton, which meets the user's goals and non-functional requirements defined by the scopes. A verification is ensured to check whether the automaton requires behavioral or/and measurable non-functional attributes. In case the automaton contains behavioral attributes, an automata modelling for each of these attributes is required to be integrated to the composition automaton. Then a Linear Temporal Logic (LTL) validation is performed using UPPAAL model checker, to verify the validity of this composition automaton. The corresponding Web services are then returned by the discovery module in order to generate the appropriate BPEL

Figure 4. The proposed process for NFR aware Web service composition

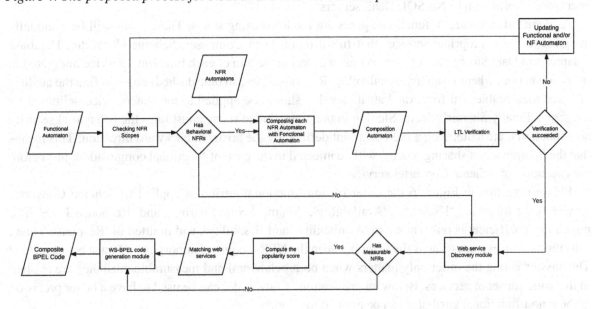

code (Business Process Execution Language). In the order in hand, if the automaton requires measurable attributes, a selection is performed according to discovered services to return the best matching Web services in accordance to their popularity score.

CASE STUDY

In order to illustrate this approach, a case study focusing on a Health Care domain is studied, due to various needs in term of non-functional requirements in that field. The aim is to enhance an existing system by adding various quality and behavioral non-functional attributes. In the current system, patient data is indexed by a Patient Health Record Index (PHR-index), and stored into a local database located in each health center. Our contribution will use the current Web services to create a composition with higher security level; allowing to encrypt patient data using Shamir's secret sharing algorithm, and store them in various Database-as-a-Service (DaaS) servers, with accurate access control policies to protect efficiently the confidentiality of data exchanged, in both directions, put/post and get requests.

Recall that Shamir's secret sharing approach aims to split the sensitive data D into n different pieces $D_1, D_2..., D_n$, in such a way that the knowledge of a predefined number t shares of D_i allows the reconstruction of the secret data D. This mechanism is called (t,n) threshold, where only t or more number of pieces are able to reconstruct the secret data D.

This case study considers both post and get cases, where the first case consists on storing patient data into databases, and the second case for getting these data back from the databases.

1. **Case Study 1:** Storing data using high-level privacy system

The proposed system is a simple composition allowing first to get the data that will be encrypted using Shamir's secret sharing algorithm, then to allow a schema converting from SQL to No-SQL in order to store encrypted data as documents instead of data rows. Therefore, a database adapter will dispatch encrypted information to No-SQL DaaS servers.

As depicted in Figure 5, functional goals are modeled using states. These goals will be eventually assigned to the appropriate services that fulfill them. Data Composer, Scheme Converter, Database Adapter and Data Storage are chosen names to describe the aim of each functional service integrated in the composition, where Usability, Availability, Response-Time in blue dashed scopes define the quality-oriented measurable non-functional attributes that should be applied to the state/service delimited by the scope. Finally Shamir's Secret Sharing in the green dotted scope constitutes the behavioral security non-functional attribute, with a pre-constraint defined by the arrow in backward direction. This means that the Shamir secret sharing process will be injected in the current functional composition, just before the execution of Scheme Converter service.

Please note that in Figure 6 the order of non-functional attributes applied to Scheme Converter service is the following 'Usability', 'Availability', 'Shamir Secret Sharing', and 'Response Time'. The popularity coefficient is only shown in 'Availability' and 'Usability', and omitted in 'Response Time'. This remark raises a question: is the order between the NFRs scopes is important and must be respected? The answer is that the order only matters when both behavioral and measurable attributes are applied to the same subset of services. Below an explication of how order can be used to have a better precision on how non-functional attributes can be applied to services:

Figure 5. Representation of Functional Requirements Automaton with associated NF attributes

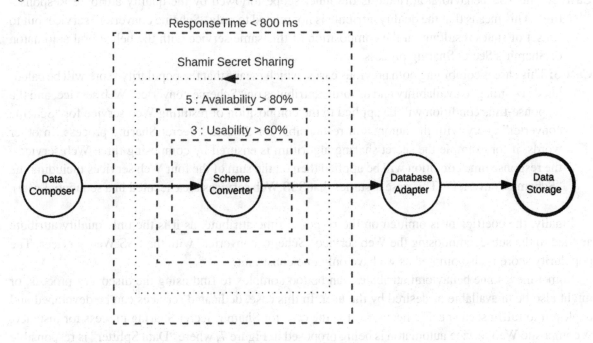

Figure 6. Non-functional attributes ordering possibilities

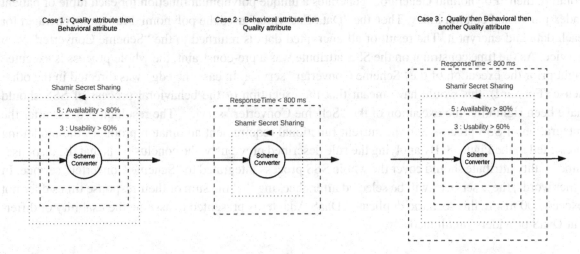

Case 1: The inner scopes correspond to quality attributes Usability and Availability, followed by the behavioral attribute Shamir's Secret Sharing (SSS). This means that the popularity score will be calculated according to the conditions and coefficients of quality attributes for the Web service satisfying the "Scheme Converter" request, allowing to return the best matching Web service for this request during the discovery and selection process. Where the SSS behavioral attribute will be integrated first in the modeling using the composition automaton, then in the runtime by performing the appropriate Web services.

Case 2: The SSS behavioral attribute is the inner scope followed by the quality attribute Response-time. This means that the quality attribute is not related to only "Scheme converter" service, but to subset of states resulting on the composition of this same service with the behavioral automaton of Shamir's Secret Sharing process.

Case 3: This case is combining both previous cases, which means that the popularity score will be calculated according to availability and usability attributes on "Scheme converter" Web service, and the response-time condition will be applied to the composition of resulting Web service for "Scheme converter" query with the automaton responsible for Shamir's Secret Sharing process. In other words, if for example the secret sharing algorithm is ensured by composing three Web services, the response time condition will be applied then on the sum of the four Web services including the "Scheme Converter" (This case assumes that SSS Web services are executed in a sequential way).

Finally, the coefficient is omitted on the response-time attribute, as it is the only quality attribute applied to the subset composing the Web service "Scheme converter" with the SSS Web services. The popularity score is also omitted as we have only one constraint.

Sometimes, some behavioral attributes can be too complex to find using the discovery process, or might also be unavailable as desired by the user. In this case, dedicated services can be developed and deployed to fulfill such specific needs, as it is the case for Shamir Secret Sharing process for instance. A composite Web service automaton is being proposed in Figure 7, where "Data Splitter" is responsible of decomposing specific data into distinct columns and returning a collection of separated data for each column, then "Polynomial Generator" generates a unique polynomial function for each tuple of patient index phr-id and column index. Then the "Data Encrypter" uses the polynomial function generated for each data and encrypt it. The result of all encrypted data is returned to the "Scheme Converter" Web service. As the time constraint on the SSS attribute was a pre-constraint, the whole process is executed right prior the execution of the "Scheme Converter" service. In case the edge was directed in the other sense (Forward), this would have meant that the execution of the behavioral process of SSS should have been right after the execution of the "Scheme Converter" service. The resultant process after the integration of SSS process into the current functional requirement automaton produces the modelling presented in the Figure 8. By applying the rule described previously, the conclusion is that the response-time quality attribute should cover the whole SSS process integrated to "Scheme Converter" service. In other words, these services will be selected after checking that the sum of their response times does not exceed 800 ms. In this scenario duplicated DaaS Adapter is presented to assume the usability of different DaaS providers simultaneously.

2. **Case Study 2:** Getting the secured data from Cloud DaaS:

To get the stored data as presented in the previous case study, the first step is to arrange how security policies should be applied to this system. In healthcare centers, please take note that the information

Figure 7. Automata representation of Shamir's Secret Sharing behavioral attribute

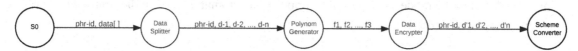

Figure 8. Automata representation of the integrated behavioral attribute

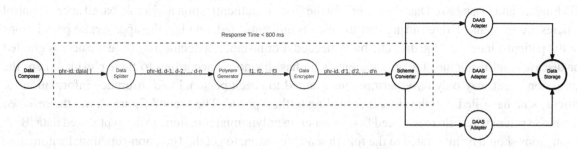

system is used by different actors, such as, admission agents, and doctors. Each of these actors has a particular role, and each role has its own permissions to access a specific portion of the patient's data and be prevented from reading the rest of the data. For instance, admission agents have only the privilege to verify personal information and insurance data, where doctors can modify or consult diseases, symptoms, etc. Thus, the aim of this second case study is to integrate such behavioral non-functional attributes in the current functional composition, in order to develop and deploy the Web services allowing to fulfill these needs. As the authors did for the first case study, they start by modeling the functional automaton with desired non-functional attributes as scopes.

The "Data Analyzer" Web service filters the user's query and returns the patient's information with the needed data. According to the previous service's response, the "ID Finder" returns all patient health record indexes (phr-id) for the requested patient. The "Database Adapter" service allows us to connect to database to get the needed data for the requested phr-id. As previously explained, the "Database Adapter" will be replaced by DaaS Adapters as Multi-Clouds access is used in this secret sharing process case study. In Figure 9, the quality attribute "Availability" wraps both the "Authentication" and "Access Control RBAC" behavioral attributes, which means that the availability condition should be applied to the entire potential composition attributed to the "ID Finder" Web service. The same operation is performed to the "Database Adapter" for which the "Response time" scope wraps the entire "Shamir Decrypter" process. The next step is then to model both behavioral processes to meet the existing functional automaton modeling.

Figure 9. Representation of Functional Requirements Automaton with associated NF attributes for the second scenario

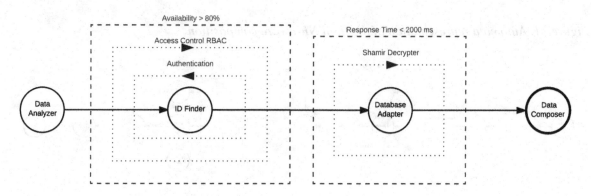

The Figures 10-a and 10-b above show respectively the behavioral automaton allocated to services "ID Finder" and "Database/DaaS Adapter". In the first, an authentication and a role based access control policies are implemented, ensuring that the user is authenticated, and has the appropriate permissions for the patient's index and the data attributes needed. For instance, a doctor may have the access granted for diseases and medicines for only patients s/he has diagnosed according to their phr-id. Where the admission agent may only have permissions granted to check personal and insurance information for patients s/he has filled into the system according to their phr-id. The second figure shows the reversed Shamir's system where there is a need first to generate polynomial functions to decrypt stored data. Both automatons should be integrated to the functional automaton, to get the final non-functional automaton, which is presented in Figure 11.

The non-functional automaton now shows the complete process of getting secured data from Multi-Clouds DaaS providers by introducing a double role based access control policy to verify first whether the user has the right to access to a patient's record using his/her index, and also if his/her role allows him to access to the desired data attributes. Most of the integrated Web services will be developed to

Figure 10. Automata representation for behavioral non-functional attributes

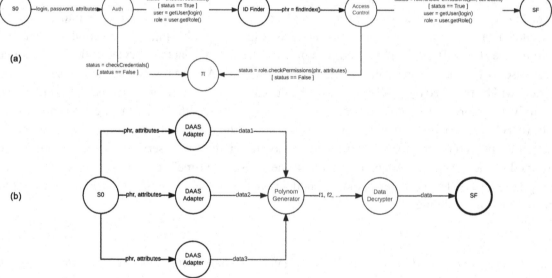

Figure 11. Automata representation of the final NF-aware composition

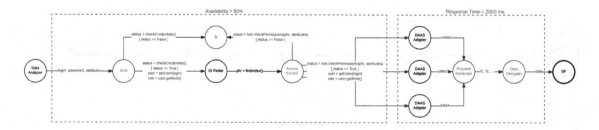

fulfill exactly these requirements. The automata based modelling allows the architect to analyze and validate the business process, after checking its validity using the model checking validation. To do so, we are using UPPAAL model checking (Uppsala-Aalborg Verification Tool), due to its completeness regarding the proposed automata based approach.

VERIFICATION USING UPPAAL MODEL CHECKER

To verify the conformity of NFRs automaton integration with associated FRs, the process uses Uppsala-Aalborg Verification Tool (UPPAAL) as a model checker. UPPAAL is a toolbox for verification of real-time systems jointly developed by Uppsala University and Aalborg University. It has been applied successfully in cases of studies ranging from communication protocols to multimedia applications (Behrmann et al., 2004). This tool allows modeling and verifying the correctness of NFRs aware composition using the model checking. To guarantee a realistic and efficient modeling, the proposed approach focuses to model first each atomic and composite service independently in separated templates, and thereafter the main composition automaton gathering all modeled templates with a respect to the composition activities such as choice, loop, synch, join, etc. Each service is modeled using states, directly connected to other services states in case of composite Web service, or only to its initial and final state otherwise.

Figure 12-a defines UPPAAL modeling for an atomic Web service, surrounded by the initial state S, and the final committed state F. Whereas Figure 12-b depicts a composite service for Shamir's Secret Sharing Algorithm, composed of three Web services, surrounded also by the initial and final states S and F. The transition from the final state back to start state is omitted, it aims to avoid deadlocks after performing the corresponding Web service. The blue labels on some transitions are the synchronization channels to communicate with the main composition automaton, where the green labels constitute the condition guards that should be satisfied to perform the transition, and dark blue are the updates occurring during the transition. Figure 12-c represents the main composition automaton, which is getting synchronized with all other atomic and composite services by using channels.

In this composition, synchronization channels ending by exclamation mark "!" define the outgoing channels, where the channels ending by interrogation point "?" define the incoming channels. For instance, the "DC!" label in the composition automaton performs a synchronization with the automaton in Figure 12-c, having the "DC?" which lead to the state "DataComposer" corresponding to the desired Web service. After performing this state, a new synchronization is opened by the DataComposer automaton denoted by EndDC! outgoing to the composition automaton as EndDC? to inform it that the Web service has been executed. The committed states denoted by "C" ensure the interfacing between all synchronization states, allowing to perform the next synchronization once the current one has been completed.

As defined in the first case study, a parallel execution of three DaaS Adapters is planned, corresponding to the three different DaaS providers. The corresponding automatons are presented in Figure 12-d.

The three automatons receive the same signal, allowing them to perform the "DAASAdapters" services in parallel. However, it is normal that their execution time will differ due to the diversity of target DaaS providers. To deal with this constraint, we added a junction control guards to verify whether all services have been performed or not. To do so, three variables are introduced in the UPPAAL global declarations, to be shared with all automaton templates. These variables are initialized by "0" before performing the parallel calls, then each variable's value is updated to "1" after performing its corre-

Figure 12. UPPAAL representation for the composition automaton and corresponding services

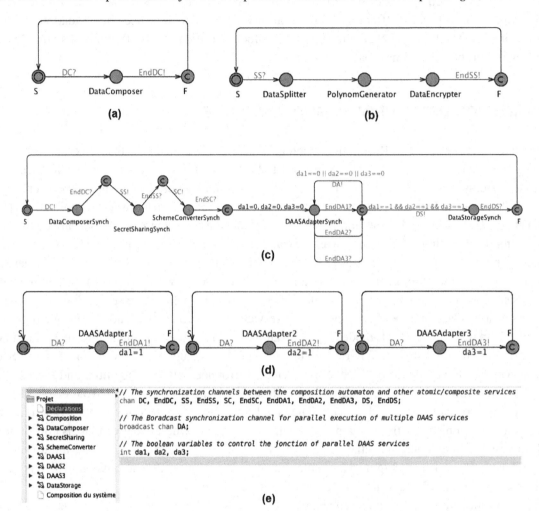

sponding Web service. To control the junction, there is only the need to verify whether all variables are updated to "1" which means that all DaaS automatons have been successfully performed. This junction control allows us to customize the desired automata behavior according to user's need. For instance, in the second case study, to get data from the remote DaaS servers, Shamir's threshold can allow us to reconstitute secret data by only having two responses out of the three servers. In such a specific case we can use the junction control and define the validity of the composite automaton by allowing two variables set to "1" out of the three variables.

UPPAAL model checking allows also to verify the conformance of native properties such deadlock freeness and reachability properties, or custom properties e.g. verifying whether at least two out of the three DaaS services are performed in the composition execution. Figure 12-d and Figure 13 show some examples of UPPAAL execution.

Reachability is a fundamental problem that appears in different contexts in finite state automata, these properties are used while modelling in order to perform sanity checks. These properties do not by themselves guarantee the correctness of the modeled process, but they validate the basic behavior

Figure 13. UPPAAL verification for the composition automaton

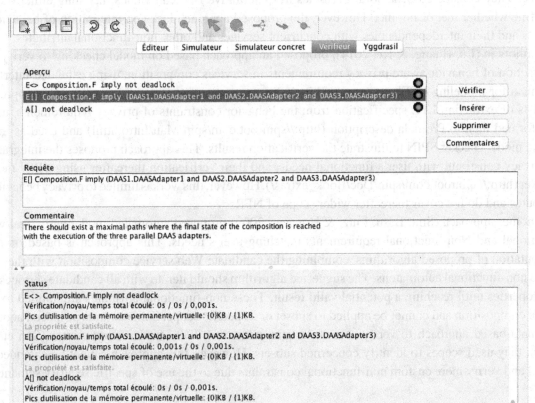

of the model. In UPPAAL the prefix E<> is used to verify the reachability for a specific formula. The prefixes in LTL language define the safety and liveness properties. They are used to check whether the requested formulae must be true for all reachable states, i.e. A[], or true for a maximal paths of states, i.e. E[], or that the formulae is eventually satisfied, i.e. A<>.

RELATED WORK

Over the last few years some interesting contributions proposed to tackle NFRs challenges in Web service composition.

Authors in (Eckhardt et al., 2016) published a report presenting the result of an investigation of NFRs in practice, in order to define whether these attributes may have a behavioral aspect allowing users to deal with them the same way as with functional requirements. This work also classified 530 NFRs extracted from 11 industrial requirement specification to be able to analyze to which extent these NFRs describe system behaviors.

In the literature most of contributions are limited to QoS oriented NFRs due to their measurability. Recently scientific researchers have assigned more attention to behavioral attributes. Authors in (Guidara et al., 2015) proposed an approach to integrate both qualitative and quantitative non-functional attributes to select the best matching services regarding the potential changes of QoS values for these attributes in time. They considered behavioral attributes as quantitative Boolean values matching either 0 or 1 to define whether met or not met. However, the proposed approach lacks on integration of behavioral aspects and their interdependencies with concurrent services and other non-functional attributes.

Authors in (Lu, Huang, & Ke, 2014), proposed an approach based on model checking to verify the satisfaction of behavior-aware privacy requirements in services composition, using extended interface automata for modeling BPEL process, and including a support for privacy semantics. This approach consists of extracting LTL specification from the behavior constraints of privacy requirements, to be transformed then to Promela description (http://spinroot.com/spin/Man/Intro.html) and used as input for the model checker SPIN to illustrate the verification results. This approach proposes the integration of privacy constraint with user's functional needs, and their verification thereafter using SPIN model checker (http://spinroot.com/spin/Doc/Book_extras/). However, this work is limited to privacy behavioral attributes and do not cover thereafter wider scope of NFRs.

Another approach (Sun, Basu, Lutz, & Honavar, 2009) proposed automated modeling to deal with Functional and Non-functional requirements matching user's needs. This approach is based on pre-computation of proposed algorithms, combining the candidate Web service composition with the proposed non-functional automatons. The suggested algorithm should iterate with all candidate services for all properties until reaching a potential valid result. These non-functional attributes are applied to the whole composition and cannot be applied to subset or a specific scope. Same authors proposed another automata-based approach to verify security requirements in a Web service composition (Sun et al., 2010); they used scopes to identify concerned subsets. However, this approach cannot be extended to model and verify more custom non-functional constraints due to the use of specific security semantics.

FUTURE RESEARCH DIRECTIONS

The current contribution concerns mainly the design and the deployment time. Verification stage requires to be dynamic rather than using manually UPPAAL model checking as adopted by the proposed approach. This shortcoming is actually under working in order to complete the WS composition process.

Another ultimate objective concerns awareness adaptation of generated composite Web service based on BPEL. To attain this objective exploring the flexibility of Aspect Oriented Programming remains a very promising solution.

Also the proposed approach deals only with WS using SOAP protocol, so using Restful WSs represents a promising research direction since actually several domains such as M2M, Internet-of-Things, etc. use them.

CONCLUSION

This contribution deals with Web service composition at design and deployment time using both Functional Requirements (FRs) and Non-Functional Requirements (NFRs). NFRs concern both measurable and behavioral attributes. The aim of this work is to suggest a complete approach consisting on modeling NFRs as scopes and defining their interdependencies, performing a composition with associated FRs and verifying the conformance of generated result according to users requirements.

To verify the conformance of compositions, UPPAAL model checker based on expressed LTL verification is used, which allows verifying, in addition to deadlock-free and reachability properties, the execution of prior actions for each non-functional interdependency, or in other case verifying the execution of all components of a composite system.

REFERENCES

Beek, M. H., Bucchiarome, A., & Gnesi, S. (2007a). A Survey on Service Composition Approaches: From Industrial Standards to Formal Methods. *Second International Conference on Internet and Web Applications and Services*. 10.1109/ICIW.2007.71

Beek, M. H., Bucchiarome, A., & Gnesi, S. (2007b). Formal Methods for Service Composition *Annals of Mathematics, Computing & Teleinformatics, 1*(5).

Behrmann, G., David, A., & Larsen, K. G. (2004). A Tutorial on Uppaal. In M. Bernardo & F. Corradini (Eds.), Lecture Notes in Computer Science: Vol. 3185. *Formal Methods for the Design of Real-Time Systems*. Berlin: Springer. doi:10.1007/978-3-540-30080-9_7

Broy, M., (2015). Rethinking Nonfunctional Software Requirements. *Computer, 48*(5).

Çelik, D., & Elçi, A. (2008). Ontology-based QoS Model for Appropriate Selection and Composition of Web Services. *International Review on Computers and Software, 3*(2).

Çelik, D., & Elçi, A. (2013). A broker-based semantic agent for discovering Semantic Web services through process similarity matching and equivalence considering quality of service. *Science China. Information Sciences, 56*(1), 1–24. doi:10.100711432-012-4697-1

Chung, L., & do Prado Leite, J. C. S. (2009). On Non-Functional Requirements in Software Engineering. In. Lecture Notes in Computer Science: Vol. 5600. *Conceptual Modeling: Foundations and Applications* (pp. 363–379). Berlin: Springer. doi:10.1007/978-3-642-02463-4_19

Eckhardt, J., Vogelsang, A., & Méndez Fernandez, D. (2016). Are "Non-functional" Requirements really Non-functional? An Investigation of Non-functional Requirements in Practice. *38th IEEE International Conference on Software Engineering*.

El Kassmi, I., & Jarir, Z. (2016). Security Requirements in Web Service Composition: Formalization, Integration, and Verification. *25th International Conference on Enabling Technologies: Infrastructure for Collaborative Enterprises (WETICE)*. 10.1109/WETICE.2016.47

Elfirdoussi, S., Jarir, Z., & Quafafou, M. (2014b). Ranking Web Services using Web Service Popularity Score. *International Journal of Information Technology and Web Engineering, 9*(2).

Elfirdoussi, S., Jarir, Z., & Quafafou, M. (2014a). Discovery and Visual Interactive WS Engine based on popularity: Architecture and Implementation. *International Journal of Software Engineering and Its Applications, 8*(2).

Firesmith, D. G. (2003). Engineering Security Requirements, *Journal of Object Technology*. doi:10.5381/jot.2003.2.1.c6

Galster, M., & Bucherer, E. (2008). A Taxonomy for Identifying and Specifying Non-functional Requirements in Service-oriented Developmen. *IEEE Congress on services.* 10.1109/SERVICES-1.2008.51

Glinz, M. (2007). On Non-Functional Requirements. *Requirements Engineering Conference.*

Guidara, I., Guermouche, N., Chaari, T., Jmaiel, M., & Tazi, S. (2015). Time-Dependent QoS Aware Best Service Combination Selection. *International Journal of Web Services Research, 12*(2).

Hasan, M. M., Loucopoulos, P., & Nikolaidou, M. (2014). Classification and Qualitative Analysis of Non-Functional Requirements Approaches. In *Enterprise, Business-Process and Information Systems Modeling* (pp 348-362). Springer. doi:10.1007/978-3-662-43745-2_24

Holzmann, G. J. (2007). The model checker SPIN. *IEEE Transactions on Software Engineering, 23*(5), 279–295. doi:10.1109/32.588521

ISO/IEC9126-1:2001(E). (2001). *Software Engineering-Product Quality-Part1: Quality Mod*el.

Lu, J., Huang, Z., & Ke, C. (2014). Verification of Behavioral-aware Privacy Requirements in Web Service Composition. *Journal of Software, 9*(4).

Mairiza, D., Zowghi, D., & Nurmuliani, N. (2010). An investigation into the notion of non-functional requirements. *ACM Symposium on Applied Computing*, 311-318. 10.1145/1774088.1774153

Schmeling, B., Charfi, A., Thome, R., & Mezini, M. (2011). Composing Non-Functional Concerns in Web Services. *IEEE International Conference on Web Services (ICWS).*

Sheng, Q. Z., Maamar, Z., Yao, L., Szabo, C., & Bourne, S. (2014). Behavior modeling and automated verification of Web services. In Information Sciences, Informatics and Computer Science Intelligent Systems Applications (pp 416-433). Elsevier. doi:10.1016/j.ins.2012.09.016

Sun, H., Basu, S., Honavar, V., & Lutz, R. (2010, November). Automata-Based Verification of Security Requirements of Composite Web Services. *21th International Symposium on Software Reliability Engineering*, 348-357. 10.1109/ISSRE.2010.20

Sun, H., Basu, S., Lutz, R., & Honavar, V. (2009). *Automata-Based Verification of Non-Functional Requirements in Web Service Composition.* Iowa State University.

KEY TERMS AND DEFINITIONS

DIVISE: Acronym of discovery and visual search engine is a web service search engine allowing an interactive discovery and selection of services according to users' queries and quality of service metrics.

Formalization: Also known as formal specification, describes mathematical oriented techniques used to specify a system or its behavior.

Functional Requirement: A requirement that describes a main functionality or behavior of a system.

Model Checking: Automatic checking that a model meets given specifications and the verification of the correctness of its given properties.

Non-Functional Requirement: Requirements that define constraints describing how a system should behave.

System Verification: Methods and procedures used to check whether a system meets its requirements and specifications.

UPPAAL: Model checking tool allowing real-time systems verification. This tool is developed with a collaboration between Uppsaala University and Aalborg University.

Web Service: An autonomous function designed to allow interoperability between heterogonous systems. It is deployed by the provider to be consumed by end users.

Web Service Composition: Represents a process aggregating web services in order to perform actions that cannot be fulfilled by a standalone service.

Chapter 16
Integrating Heterogeneous Services for Semantic Mashup Construction

Khayra Bencherif
Djilali Liabes University, Algeria

Djamel Amar Bensaber
High School of Computer Science of Sidi Bel Abbes, Algeria

Mimoun Malki
High School of Computer Science of Sidi Bel Abbes, Algeria

ABSTRACT

Semantic mashup applications allow automating the process of services and data integration to create a composite application with a new user interface. Nevertheless, existing mashup applications need to improve the matching methods for discovering semantic services. Moreover, they have to create or modify workflows in mashup applications without the assistance of the original developers. Automating the combination of user interfaces is another challenge in the context of semantic mashups construction. In this chapter, the authors propose an approach that allows automating the combination of data, services, and user interfaces to provide a composite application with an enhanced user interface. The construction of the semantic mashup application is based on the use of domain ontology, a matching tool, and a collection of patterns. In order to demonstrate the effectiveness of this proposal, the authors present a use case to construct a semantic mashup application for a travel agency.

INTRODUCTION

With the coming of the Web 2.0, the user can show his existence through use of many technologies like social networking, collaborative environments, mashups, etc. (Lytras, Damiani, & Pablos, 2008). A mashup application allows integrating user interfaces, data and services from various sources to build a single Web application (Khokhar, Benjamin, Farkhund, Alhadidi, & Bentahar, 2016). Generally, the

DOI: 10.4018/978-1-5225-5384-7.ch016

mashups take the form of a Webpage or a Website that manually combines heterogeneous information and services from multiple sources (Garriga, Mateos, Flores, Cechich, & Zunino, 2016). However, the development of mashup applications allows the developers to understand the structure and the semantics of APIs and data, which make the integration process more difficult. Thus, the semantic mashups are developed to facilitate automatic integration of data and services using a semantic layer. On the other hand, patterns are software architectures that help the designers to build solution blocks which have been shown to present useful information in the past and will provide more efficient solutions in the future (Liu, Liang, Xu, Staples, & Zhu, 2011).

Several approaches have dealt with automatic integration of data and APIs in mashup applications (Kopecký, Vitvar, Bournez, & Farrell, 2007; Lathem, Gomadam, & Sheth, 2007; Maleshkova, Pedrinaci, & Domingue, 2009; Ngu, Carlson, Sheng, & Paik, 2010; Liu, Li, Pedrinaci, Kopecký, Maleshkova, & Domingue, 2011; Meditskos & Bassiliades, 2011; Malki & Benslimane, 2012; Malki & Benslimane, 2013; Lee, 2014; Tjoa, Wetz, Kiesling, Trinh, & Do, 2015; Park, Yoo, Hur, Bae, & Lung, 2015; Lee, 2015; Trinh, Do, Wetz, Aryan, Kiesling, & Tjoa, 2017; Karakostas & Kalamboukis, 2017).

Key challenges of these approaches are the need to 1) create or modify workflows in mashup applications without enlisting the talents of the original developers or vendor, 2) compute semantic and syntactic similarities between data in different services, and 3) automate the combination of user interfaces to construct an enhanced composite application.

In order to address these challenges and enhance the quality of data and services integration in mashup applications, this chapter puts forward a novel approach which consists in building a patterns-based semantic mashup for the enterprise 2.0. This approach is based on the use of domain ontology and a matching tool to identify similar information and services in different sites. In addition, the authors use a set of patterns to facilitate construction and use of the semantic mashup application. First, the pattern 'Content Integration' is used to integrate data after the matching process. Then, the pattern 'Usability Enhancer' is used to present the application in a single interface instead of wasting time to switch between different applications. Finally, the pattern 'Workflow' is used to manage the chaining of the spots.

The authors evaluate the system prototype with a study use case to develop a mashup application for a travel agency. It provides a single widget that allows the user to specify starting location, destination and favorite transportation (flight or train). After submission of data, the system retrieves the availability of the flight or train as well as hotels and car rental options using domain ontology and a matching tool.

Consequently, the main contributions of this chapter are as follows:

1. A review of existing approaches and tools that are developed to build semantic mashup applications. The authors provide also a comparative study of these approaches to outline their limitations.
2. Development of domain ontology and a matching tool to resolve the problem of data heterogeneity.
3. Use of a collection of patterns to facilitate the construction of a composite application and provide an enhanced interface to the end user.
4. Presentation of a use case of a semantic mashup application for a travel agency.

Rest of this chapter is organized as follows. Definitions and detailed descriptions of Web 2.0, mashups, process of computing data mashups, semantic mashups and mashups patterns types will be introduced in the next section. Then an overview of existing semantic mashup approaches as well as a comparison of them is provided. The authors give an overview of their approach and illustrate a study use case to evaluate the prototype system. Some future research directions and conclusion are described in the final sections.

PRELIMINARIES

This section gives definitions and detailed descriptions of the mashups, process of computing data mashups, semantic mashups and mashup patterns types.

Web 2.0, Mashup, Semantic Mashup

In 2004, Web 2.0 was best defined by Tim O"Reilly as:"*The business revolution in the computer industry caused by the move to the Internet as platform, and an attempt to understand the rules for success on that new platform.*" (O"Reilly, 2005).

In contrast to Web 1.0 where the users were passive, Web 2.0 allows the users to cooperate and work together in a social media conversation. Moreover, the latter facilitates creating, searching, sharing, using and reusing of Web resources (O"Reilly, 2005). In this context, various technologies are developed based on the concepts of Web 2.0 (e.g. social networking sites, blogs, mashups, folksonomies and wikis) (Lee, Tang, Tsai, & Chen, 2009). Mashup is an approach that allows the user to combine multiple services and integrate heterogeneous data to create a composite application with a new user interface (Yu, Benatallah, Casati, & Daniel, 2008). Typically, the main components of a mashup application are data, Web services, RSS feeds, Linked Data, CSV, service platforms, so on.

Mashup applications allow reducing the development time and the cost of Web applications (Doan, Halevy, & Ives, 2012). Nevertheless, the manual approach for the development of mashup applications requires programming competences of the user, understand the structure and semantics of APIs, generate visualizations and create new functionalities.

The semi-automatic approach helps the user to construct an application using existing tools such as: IBM-CENTER, Convertigo, Dapper, Serena, Yahoo cleaners, Popfly, etc. (Hoyer & Fischer, 2008).

The automatic approach for the development of mashup applications (named Semantic Mashup) solves the problem of APIs combination and does not require intervention of developers. The semantic mashup approach gives an effective solution to create a composite application with less computer skills and guarantee automatic discovery, selection and combination of heterogeneous APIs (Anjomshoaa &Tjoa, 2014).

In fact, automatic generation of mashups requires not only semantization of APIs, but also a matching algorithm that can automatically discover the different APIs that can be combined with a given service (Wan, Chen, Yu, Liang, & Wu, 2016).

Building Semantic Mashup Applications

Current approaches apply workflows which consist of several steps to perform semantic mashup construction. The input of the workflows includes several types of data. Generally, input data may be provided in the form of XML files, Web applications, Web services, RSS feeds, portlets, CSV and JSON files, etc. The output of the workflows is a composite application that contains all components of the input data. Figure 1 depicts the workflow of semantic mashups construction.

The process of automatically building mashup applications is composed of three main phases: choosing the appropriate APIs from a registry, semantic matching of the selected APIs and automatic combination of the selected APIs (Lee, 2015).

The API discovery phase helps to automatically discover a set of APIs from the registry using a query q. Generally, a semantic relationship is established if the similarity scores between the query q and the APIs are higher than a threshold θ. Typically, a query matches an API if both the input and the output parameters of the query are equivalents to the input and the output parameters of the API. However, the match fails if an input parameter of the query is not mapped to any of APIs output parameters.

The APIs combination phase allows searching the set of APIs that can be aggregated based on the semantic matching step. Typically, the inputs of an API are the outputs generated by another API. In other words, the input parameters of an API at any stage of the combination are provided by the output parameters of the previous API. Generally, the outputs produced by the API in the last step of the combination should contain all the output parameters that the query needs.

The Graphical User Interface (GUI) provides the user the visualization of the composition results.

Mashup Patterns

Generally, the end user reuses physical assets in their applications such as code and libraries. The patterns complement these efforts by providing a format for converting good ideas into repeatable architectural designs. Then, a mashup pattern is a model or guide for solving various problems that are considered difficult or unsolvable. (Ogrinz, 2009) classify the mashup patterns into five classes: Harvest, Enhance, Assemble, Manage, and Test Patterns. In fact, some patterns are used to create or reduce the content,

Figure 1. The workflow of semantic mashups construction

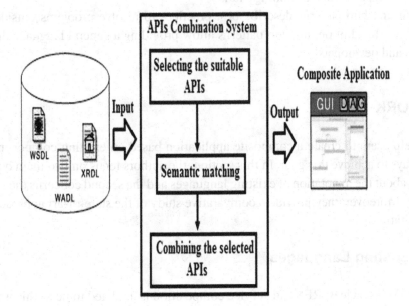

while others deal with consuming it. Moreover, there is a set of patterns that concentrate on the development of application functionalities.

Harvest Patterns are a collection of models that aim to reach traditional tools using data from external Web sources. They provide a way to navigate and retrieve important information by extracting and accessing data from sources. Data are retrieved from structured sources (e.g. databases, RSS feeds, XML, and tabular data streams) or unstructured sources (e.g. Web sites, binary files (e.g., Excel or PDF), or a text). In addition, the patterns of this class allow automating the development of the presentation layer of Web applications.

The main challenge of every organization is enhancing its existing systems to get the most value from its asset. *Enhance Patterns* are used to extend and improve existing systems. These improvements can be made without the assistance of the original developers. So, the access to the source code of applications is not needed and hence programming competences are not a necessity.

Many of the solutions rely on the mashup's ability to dynamically insert or remove presentation instructions from an existing user interface. *Assemble Patterns* are mainly used to combine a large number of data and presentations from different sources. If data are extracted from a large number of different sources, it will be difficult to mold them to a single format. Thus, this class of patterns presents new models and solutions to mix new streams of data in a logical way.

Managing new solutions is a main challenge that arises when combining a large number of stream data to build new solutions. *Manage Patterns* are used as new solutions to help organizations deal with their ability more efficiently. In contract to the previous classes of patterns that are open to the implementation of end users, most of the manage patterns are typically under the control of an Information Technology (IT) Department. In fact, end users use the tools provided by the IT departments to manipulate information.

The National Institute of Standards and Technology (NIST) estimated that the cost of software errors to the U.S. economy is approximately $60 billion. The impact of software errors is enormous because virtually every business in the United States now depends on software for the development, production, distribution, and after-sales support of services and products. Thus, users require performing some degree of test when they develop new solutions. Consequently, *Test Patterns* are used to test applications to avoid suffering damages when technology fails.

As conclusion, mashup patterns describe best practices to resolve problems outside the realm of traditional solutions. In addition, mashup patterns allow providing a general language that can be used by both business and developers.

RELATED WORK

Mashup tools help users to create a composite application based on existing components; these tools have different ways to achieve this goal. In this section, the authors focus on two main bodies of related work: the first is about the annotation of existing languages and the second concerns the semantic mashups construction. Moreover, they provide a comparative study of the state-of-art approaches in order to outline their limitations.

Annotating Existing Languages

In the context of Web services, RESTful service composition is a related topic to this work.

RESTful Web service is a lightweight service founded on REST (Representational State Transfer) architecture for connecting hypermedia applications, and usually it uses HTTP protocol (Fielding, 2000). RESTful services are usually used to build mashup applications because they are easier to compose and consume compared to SOAP services (Garriga et al. 2016).

SAWSDL (Kopecký et al., 2007) provides a mechanism for annotating semantically described services with associated WSDL and XML schema. In (Lathem et al., 2007), the authors used the microformat RDFa, which integrate RDF triples over HTML description to append semantics to the REST service and make it readable by the machine. SWEET (Maleshkova et al., 2009) proposed hREST to describe REST Web services, and then it is completed by MicroWSMO for the semantic annotation of REST Web services. SOOWL-S advertisements (Meditskos & Bassiliades, 2011) allow semanticizing different types of APIs (e.g. SOAP, JS, REST, RSS, etc.). SAWADL (Malki & Benslimane, 2012) is an extension of WADL language, which allows semantization of REST Web services; it uses a matching algorithm based on semantic similarity to automatically find the different mappings that can exist between APIs.

Table 1 shows a comparison among approaches to annotate existing languages. In fact, there are two main types of semantization: service ontology, such as SOOWL-S, allows developing a language to describe Web services and their semantics; semantic annotation allows annotating existing Web services with semantic information. For example, SAWSDL and SAWADL are used to annotate WSDL and WADL descriptions with elements of ontologies. Other approaches are developed to annotate several descriptions such as: HTML, HREST and the Inputs/Outputs of Web services. These approaches used different types of APIs, such as: SOAP, REST, RSS, etc.

Semantic Mashups Construction

In (Ngu et al., 2010), the authors developed a new approach that allows composing non-Web Services (Web applications, portlets, etc.) by end users from a list of components without a thorough information about the components in the list. In (Liu et al., 2011), the authors proposed an approach to develop dynamic mashups using Web services with lightweight semantics and unified interface instead of invoking those services directly. They used iServe for service selection and invocation. (Malki & Benslimane, 2013) extended their previous work (Malki & Benslimane, 2012) to improve the process of building mashup applications by deploying the APIs in a cloud environment. This approach allows providing less expensive, easily configurable, and powerful physical infrastructure. In (Lee, 2014), the author presented a new method to construct semantic ontologies; it is based on hierarchical clustering and pattern analysis. In addition, they propose an algorithm to compute the similarity in the matching process

Table 1. Comparing approaches to annotate existing languages

Approach	Semantization Type	Type of the Semantized API	Annotated Description	Type of the Used Ontology
SAWSDL (Kopecký et al., 2007)	Annotation	SOAP	WSDL, XML Schema	All
SA-REST (Lathem et al., 2007)	Annotation	REST	HTML	All
SWEET (Maleshkova et al., 2009)	Annotation	REST	HREST	All
SOOWL-S (Meditskos & Bassiliades, 2011)	Service ontology	REST, SOAP, RSS	Input/output of services	OWL
SAWADL (Malki & Benslimane, 2012)	Annotation	REST	WADL	All

and to compose the APIs. By this approach, the intervention of the programmers is not needed. (Tjoa et al. 2015) addressed the problem of integrating and leveraging the streaming data for non-technical users, for example: data on city's climate, contamination or passage conditions. For this purpose, the authors give a summary of a platform prototype to build a streaming data mashup for the dynamic integration of heterogeneous data sources. It is composed of data, processing and visualization gadgets. Another work (Park et al. 2015) proposed a semantic service mashup for the development of a smart TV application. To this end, they construct a semantic service discovery and a semantic service matching to automate the mashup process. The proposed services are based on the use of service ontology to give the synonyms, hyponyms and hypernyms of a given query. In (Lee, 2015), the author proposed new algorithms to automatically discover and compose Web APIs using the ontology learning method described in (Lee, 2014). The discovery algorithm filters out the APIs that do not match the query. The composition algorithm constructs CSG to search the composition candidates. In (Trinh et al, 2017), the authors introduced a mashup platform that combines mashup concepts and semantic Web to help non-expert users to integrate various data sources. They develop a Linked Widgets that consume and produce Linked Data. The connections between an output terminal of a widget and an input terminal of another widget help the users to integrate data without any programming skills. (Karakostas & Kalamboukis, 2017) built a travelling mashup application by analyzing and composing travel APIs. In order to improve the delivering travel information in mashups, the authors create an API annotation engine that uses the WordNet and the Concept Net ontologies.

Table 2 illustrates a comparison between the approaches that help building semantic mashups. Various criteria are used to compare these approaches, for example: input data format, matching algorithms

Table 2. Comparing approaches to build semantic mashup

Approach	Input Data Format	Semantization Type	Type of the Semantized API	Matching Algorithm	Automation Level
(Ngu et al., 2010)	Non- Web services (Webapplications, portlets, native widgets, Java Beans, legacy systems)	Annotation	REST, SOAP	Algorithm described by T. Syeda-Mahmood (Syeda-Mahmood, Shah, Akkiraju, Ivan, & Goodwin, 2005)	Automatic
(Malki & Benslimane, 2013)	XML (WADL files)	Annotation	REST	semantic similarity described in (Ngu et al., 2010)	Automatic
(Liu et al., 2011)	Linked data (RDF files)	Annotation	REST	iServe	Automatic
(Lee, 2014)	XML (WSDL, WADL, XRDL files)	Service ontology	REST, SOAP	Semantic matching algorithm based on the clustering (TF/IDF)	Automatic
(Tjoa et al. 2015)	Stream Data (xml, csv, json)	Service ontology	REST	*Not mentioned*	Automatic
(Park et al. 2015)	XML (WSDL and WADL files)	Service ontology	REST	Functional similarity, non-functional similarity, data similarity	Semi-automatic
(Trinh et al, 2017)	RAW DATA (CSV, XML, RDF, JSON)	Annotation	REST	Terminal matching module	Automatic
(Karakostas & Kalamboukis, 2017)	XSD, JSON *1.1*	*Annotation*	REST	Semantic simialrities of WordNet	Semi-automatic

used by each approach, type of semantization, level of automation, etc. These approaches received as input different formats of data, such as, Web applications, WML files, CSV, JSON, XSD, etc. Some approaches use the annotation as a type of semantization while others use the service ontology to add semantics to the input data. Typically, REST and SOAP are the main types of APIs that have been used to construct semantic mashup applications. Several algorithms of matching are proposed or used to automate the process of semantic mashup construction. The most of these approaches aim to automate the construction of a composite application, while other approaches give the upper hand to the user to check the accuracy of the matching process and correct the errors.

We remark that these approaches have three main challenges: 1) the need for other methods to compute semantic and syntactic similarity, 2) automating the combination of the user interfaces to build an enhanced composite application, and 3) the need to create or modify workflows in mashup applications without the assistance of the original developers or vendors.

Therefore, in order to resolve these challenges and enhance the quality of data and services integration in mashup applications, the authors use the WordNet (Miller, 1995) to compute semantic similarities and a set of metrics to compute syntactic similarities, such as Levenshtein (Levenshtein, 1966) and Jaro (Jaro, 1989) similarities. In addition, a set of patterns are used for enhancing the user interface, integrating heterogeneous data and managing the chaining of the spots.

Consequently, this approach is complementary to the state-of-art approaches. It provides a more generic architecture solution for constructing semantic mashups by means of architecture patterns. Thus, the following points make the proposed approach different and complementary to other approaches:

1. The use of both the WordNet to compute semantic similarity and two string similarity measures to compute syntactic similarity between Input/Output of Web services and ontological concept improves the precision of this approach and hence enhances the quality of data and service integration in the mashup applications.
2. The use of the workflow patterns allows creating and modifying the workflows in mashup applications without enlisting the talents of the original developers or vendor and hence managing the chaining of the spots to integrate the services.
3. The use of patterns helps the architects of mashup applications to identify solution building blocks that provide the basis for effective solutions in the future.

PROPOSED FRAMEWORK

In this section, the authors propose an approach to develop a semantic mashup application using patterns. Figure 2 depicts the architecture of the proposed approach.

The Architecture of the Proposed Approach

The main purpose of this approach is to achieve a semantic mashup based on a set of patterns, namely Content Integration, Usability Enhancer, and Workflow Patterns. The user can access the application using a single improved interface. Thus, the Usability Enhancer Pattern is used to create an enhanced

Figure 2. The architecture of the proposed approach

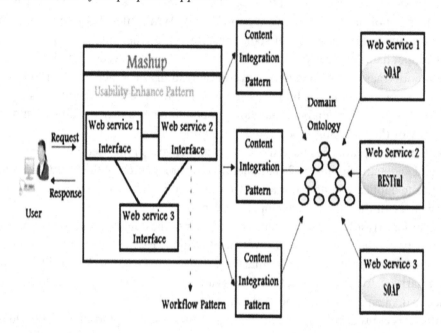

and updated interface for the mashup application that combines data from different Web services. After login, the user has to fill out a form to specify his needs. Once he clicks the Search button, an ontological query will be posed. Then, the query is rewritten as sub-queries using the results of mapping established a priori and representing the correspondence between the input/output of Web services and ontological concepts (the authors use domain ontology to solve semantic and syntactic conflict emanating from the diversity of the data sources of an exported data mashup as far as Web services). These requests are put on different data sources to retrieve their results after using the Content Integration Pattern to combine the query results and put them in an XML file to display the final result of the user query.

Domain Ontology

Ontologies allow semantic description as well as deductive reasoning of data. For example, in a travel system, they are used in the matching process to indicate two different entities that describe the same real-world object. In the domain ontology, the authors use concepts and relations related to the tourism from the real world such as: geographical terms, peoples, dates, locations, vehicles used in the travels, etc. It includes the popular terms specific to tourism and vacation as well as important for travelers, such as transport, accommodation, food services, room types in hotels, etc.

In the mashup application, domain ontology is used to solve semantic and syntactic conflicts of the inputs/outputs of Web services. The system matches description files of SOAP and RESTful Web services with ontological concepts. In the matching process, correspondences between inputs/outputs of Web services are established based on a semantic similarity (using the WordNet similarities) and a syntactic similarity (as Levenshtein and Jaro similarities). If the similarity score is higher than a given threshold, then two strings are considered similar.

The Matching Process

String matching consists of discovering strings that refer to the same real-world entity. For example, the input *nmrVol* in a Web service is similar to the input *numeroVol* in another Web service. String matching plays an important role in data integration in the mashup applications.

Let X be the set of inputs/outputs of the Web services to be integrated and Y be the set of the ontological concepts. We aim to find all pairs of strings (x, y), where x ∈ X and y ∈ Y, such as x and y refer to the same real-world entity.

In order to find similar strings, we have to compute a *similarity measure* that takes the two strings x and y as input and returns a score between 0 and 1. Therefore, the two strings are considered equivalents if the similarity measure of two strings is at least a given threshold: s(x, y) >= Θ where Θ ∈ [0, 1] (Koudas, Sarawagi, & Srivastava, 2006).

Several similarity measures are proposed in the literature, among them (for more information, see (Doan et al., 2012)):

Levenshtein measure is defined as follow

$$sim(x, y) = 1 - \frac{d(x, y)}{\max\left(length(x), length(y)\right)}$$

where: *d(x, y)* is the minimal cost to transform the string x to string y (substitute one character for another, insert a character or delete a character).

And Jaro measure is defined as follows

$$sim(x, y) = \frac{1}{3\left[\dfrac{c}{|x|} + \dfrac{c}{|y|} + \dfrac{(c-t)/2}{c}\right]}$$

where: c is the number of the common characters between the strings x and y, and t is the number of transpositions. Consequently, the matching algorithm of this approach would be as follow:

```
Inputs: ontological concepts and Web services inputs
Outputs: a list of matched pair M
    for each Web service input x do
        for each ontological concept y do
            if x and y are synonyms in the WordNet then M=M ∪ {(x, y)}
            else if sim (x, y)>= Θ  then  M=M ∪ {(x, y)}
        end for
    end for
return M
```

Initially, the algorithm checks if an input of a Web service is synonymous with an ontological concept, then it adds them to the list of matched pairs M without computing the string similarities. Else if they are not synonyms in the WordNet, then the algorithm computes the string similarities, and then it checks if their similarity is at least a threshold Θ, it adds the pair to the list of matched pairs M.

Thus, the runtime complexity of the matching process can be measured by the number of comparisons needed to complete this task (it needs O (|X||Y|) comparisons).

Content Integration Pattern

Just as the process of visiting several pages is overwhelming for a single user, the task of aggregating the collected material is equally herculean. Whenever data are extracted from a large number of different sources, the likelihood that it will adhere to a common format is low (Ogrinz, 2009). So, a data integration model allows integrating existing applications to create a homogeneous output.

In this context, the Content Integration Pattern provides a quick method for combining data flows from various sources into a composite stream. Several transformations can be applied on existing business processes and applications to provide an integrated application. Naturally, the patterns of the Harvest category extract data from multiple sources, and then they are mixed together or converted to new formats using the Content Integration Pattern. The main characteristic of this pattern is that it can be implemented by people who are not expected to have knowledge on data integration. Figure 3 shows the architecture of the Content Integration Pattern.

First, this pattern seamlessly combines the results of the user query from the input data sources. Then, it repackages the results to a new XML file to display the final result of the query using the Usability Enhancer Pattern. Typically, this pattern can serve as a stop-gap measure to create new composite data feeds across systems.

Figure 3. The architecture of the Content Integration Pattern

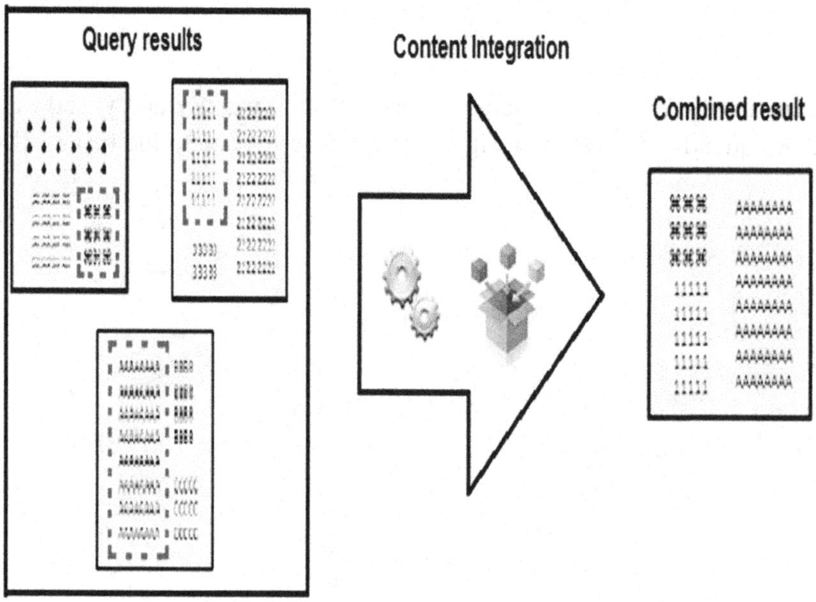

Usability Enhancer Pattern

The usability term was best defined by software developers as *"The measurement of how easy it is to use an application to complete a particular task"* (Ogrinz, 2009).

Mashups address usability issues to create a single widget from many application interfaces. Generally, mashup applications handle the communication between the new interface and the existing systems, and hence the remediation of the original application is not needed. Nevertheless, existing approaches fail to solve the usability issues for a complex interface that combines information from several interfaces, and therefore several problems of access for end users can be created. As consequence, the original developers have to alter the source codes of many applications to build a single interface. Therefore, if the source codes are not available, then additional time and effort are required to acquire and train the new talent.

The authors use the Usability Enhancer Pattern to present the mashup application in a single interface instead of wasting time to switch between different applications. Thus, this pattern increases the ease of use of mashup application and consequently customer satisfaction.

Figure 4 depicts the architecture of the Usability Enhancer Pattern. It shows how existing user interfaces are used to enrich the new user interface. This pattern receives as input a collection of existing applications, and then it provides an enhanced user interface using the following functionalities:

1. Generate new navigation paths based on the user interfaces of existing applications.
2. Automatically apply commonly used values and settings.
3. Add corporate branding, change screen colors, and employ other design-oriented measures to repackage a set of disparate applications as a unified suite.

Figure 4. The architecture of the Usability Enhancer Pattern

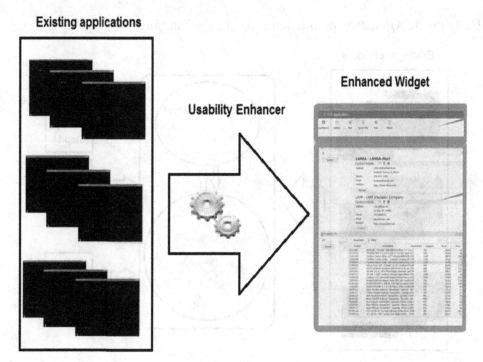

4. Accept additional input formats (e.g., Jan 15, 2008; 01/15/08; 15/01/08; 1/15/2008) and automatically translate them to a format the underlying application will recognize.
5. Break a text description into separate values using a custom code and pass the results to the user.

Thus, the Usability Enhancer Pattern allows the system to be enhanced and updated with considerably less effort and risk. Much of the work requires no more than basic familiarity with the application. Likewise, programming skills are not a requirement. The Usability Enhancer Pattern will be combined with the Workflow Pattern to extend the original system and enhance its appearance.

Workflow Pattern

(Ogrinz, 2009) defined the "Workflow" as "*A term that generally describes the organizational system of exchange of information between governor's people and business processes*".

The Workflow Pattern is not concerned with a particular discipline or product, but rather with how mashups can address the challenge of creating or modifying workflows without enlisting the talents of the original vendor or developers. So, mashups can also be used to add workflow capabilities to a system that does not natively support this functionality.

Figure 5 illustrates how the Workflow Pattern is used to generate a new user interface. The authors combine the Workflow Pattern with the Usability Enhancer Pattern to improve the user interface of the mashup application. First, this pattern determines the existing systems to be integrated. Then, it identifies the status of information to be displayed, and it applies on them the techniques described by the Usability Enhancer Pattern to build a collection of interfaces. Finally, the Workflow Pattern constructs a new user interface using the status information obtained from API Enabler implementations. Obviously, this pattern is used to manage the sequence of tasks for increasing the ease of use of the mashup application.

Figure 5. Using the Workflow Pattern to generate a new user interface

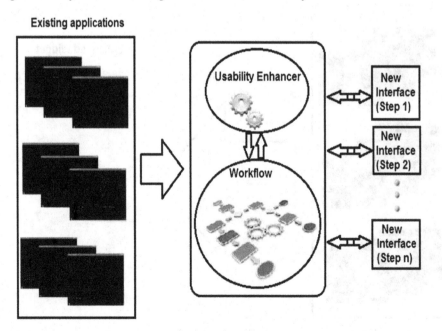

DETAIL OF RUNNING THE SEMANTIC MASHUP APPLICATION

Figure 6 illustrates all steps through which the mashup application passes. When the user wants to invoke a Web service, an ontological query will be posed, then, the query is rewritten as sub-queries using the results of the mapping established a priori, and which represents the correspondences between the inputs/outputs of Web services and the ontological concepts. In rewriting the query, the system establishes the correspondences between inputs/outputs of Web services and ontological concepts by combining semantic similarity (by using WordNet similarities) and syntactic similarity (by using Levenshtein and Jaro similarities). These requests are put on different data sources to retrieve their results after which the Content Integration Pattern is used integrating query results and putting them in an XML file to display the final result of the user's request under a single format using the Usability Enhancer Pattern.

EXPERIMENTATION

In this section, a scenario-based architecture evaluation will be presented. Moreover, the authors present an illustrative example to demonstrate the smooth running of the semantic mashup application. The scenario demonstrates the existence of:

1. An OWL DL ontology for a travel agency.
2. Three RESTful and SOAP Web services of three French airlines (Air France, AigleAzur and Air Caraïbes).
3. The use of Content Integration, Workflow and Usability Enhancer Patterns in this prototype.

Figure 6. All steps by which the mashup application passes

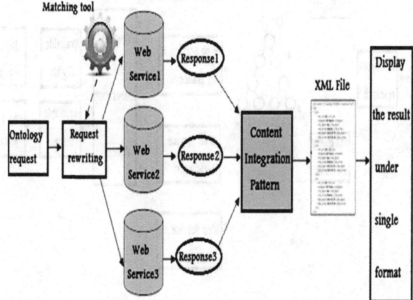

The purpose of the proposed approach is to develop a pattern-based semantic mashup for the enterprise 2.0. As a study use case, the authors develop a semantic mashup application for a travel agency; it provides a single interface that allows the user to specify the starting location, the destination and the favorite transportation (flight or train). After the submission of data, the system retrieves available flights or trains using domain ontology and a mapping tool. Then, it retrieves available hotels and car rental options.

The client-side data are obtained directly from the browser invoking the compounds services through the domain ontology to resolve the semantic conflicts of data. The recovered information is then used in combination with client-side scripting to provide a richer interface for calling of additional services and handling results.

Figure 7 represents all stages through which the application passes to book flights: First, the user has to log into the application as shown in Figure 8. After logging into the application, the user has to fill out a form to specify information about departure city, arrival city, departure date and arrival date. Once he clicks the Search button, an ontological query will be posed. Then, the query is rewritten as sub-queries using the results of the mapping established a priori that represents the correspondence between the input/output of Web services (Air France, AigleAzur and Air Caraïbes) and ontological concepts (see the travel ontology). These requests are put on different data sources (Air France, AigleAzur and Air Caraïbes) to retrieve their results after using the Content Integration Pattern to integrate the query results and put them in an XML file to display the final result of the search for available flights under a sorting criterion. The same process will be replicated for the selection of hotels and car rentals.

Figure 7. All stages through which the application passes to book flights

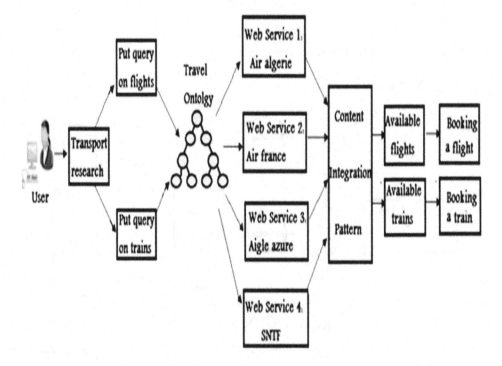

Figure 8. The home page of the application mashup

The Travel Ontology

In order to create a Semantic Mashup, we need to create an ontology that will be used to enrich data with different ontological concepts. Thus, the authors propose the creation of OWL DL ontology for a travel agency using the Protégé tool. In order to create the domain ontology, the system extracts the keywords from the input/output of the Web services as well as their names. Thus, the resulting ontology contains 40 classes and sub-classes, 46 relationships between classes, users, destinations...etc., and 100 instances. It was referred as the travel domain ontology. Figure 9 gives a picture of the travel ontology. For example the traveler class (in French: *Voyageur*) has several sub-classes such as *Id_Voyageur*, *Nom_Voyageur* and *Age*. It is used for the reformulation of the user query: when the user poses its query on the application, the query is analyzed and reformulated using the matching tool to detect the equivalent terms.

Usage of the Content Integration Pattern in the Prototype

As the process of combining data from a large number of sources is herculean for the end user, the Content Integration Pattern can extract data from several data sources and molds them to a common format.

In this mashup application, the authors use the Content Integration Pattern as follows: After querying different data sources and retrieving the result of the user query, the Content Integration Pattern extracts and combines all retrieved information and puts them in an XML file (as shown in Figure 6). Then, they will be displayed using the Usability Enhancer Pattern.

Figure 9. The travel ontology

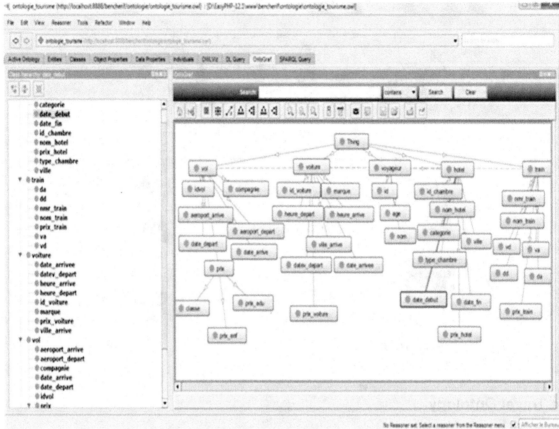

As mentioned before, the authors use the Content Integration Pattern to help the architects to combine all responses (by using this pattern, the accuracy of this system is 100%) of the user query from multiple Web services after the matching process and then put them in an XML file. Thus, the accuracy of the results does not depend on the Content Integration Pattern but on the matching process.

Usage of the Workflow Pattern in the Prototype

In this subsection, the authors show how this mashup application can address the challenge of creating or modifying workflows without the assistance of the original developers or vendors and how the Workflow Pattern is used to manage the sequence of tasks.

Figure 10 shows the BPMN model of this case study: when the service composition receives a travel search, trains or flights are retrieved depending on user choice and the corresponding event (flight or the train offers) is returned to the user interface that generated the trigger event. The authors note that Flight and Train activities are mutually exclusive as specified by the XOR Gateway. Then, the hotel and car rental services are performed, and their corresponding events (rental and hotel offers) are sent to the user interface.

Figure 10. The BPMN model of the case study

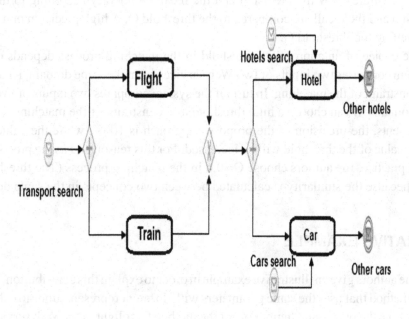

Usage of the Usability Enhancer Pattern in the Prototype

As this application has a complex interface (interface that combine information from three Web services), the authors use the Usability Enhancer Pattern to tackle usability issues. For the mashup application treats the connection between three Web services and the new interface, the original interfaces of the Web services are not needed because the process of visiting several Web pages is very cumbersome for a single user. So, this pattern is run on this application as follows:

1. Alter data-entry so it matches the Workflow Pattern.
2. Visualize data according to the ontological concepts.
3. Change visualization colors of the Web services and other design measures to enhance the new interface.
4. Accept further input formats, for example date formats, and automatically transform them to the format of the application.

In order to calculate the precision and the recall of this approach, the authors compare the set of non-matching and matching data for each input/output of the Web services given by an expert and by the system.

The precision is defined as: $P=\dfrac{tp}{tp+fp}$ and the recall as: $R=\dfrac{tp}{tp+fn}$, where:

- **True Positive** tp : In the case where both the approach and the expert select the matches.
- **False Positive** fp : In the case where the approach selects a match while the expert does not.
- **False Negative** fn : In the case where the expert selects a match while this approach does not.

Figure 11 demonstrates how the precision and the recall could vary according to the threshold Θ. Thus, the precision and the recall are compared to the threshold Θ. A high precision or a high recall can be obtained by setting the threshold Θ.

Typically, the choice of an appropriate threshold in the matching process depends on the domain. Thus, if the system compares two inputs of two Web services from the same domain, it can choose a low threshold as a constraint of the matching. In turn, if the system compares two inputs of two Web services from different domains, it can choose a high threshold as a constraint of the matching.

In all experiments, the precision of the proposed approach is 100%, while the values of the recall reduce when the value of the threshold will be increased. For this reason and as the precision is the most useful metric in practice, the authors choose Θ=0.6 in the matching process (The threshold was 0.6 in the experiment because the similarity is calculated between two concepts in the same domain).

AN ILLUSTRATIVE EXAMPLE

In this section, the authors give an illustrative example in order to explain this contribution. In the example, GetFlight() is a method that uses the same parameters with different representations to call different Web services (for example the parameter "numrVol" of the method GetFlight of the Web service of the airline "AigleAzur" is identical to the parameter "numVol" of the method GetFlight of the Web service of the airline "Air Caraïbes"). So, the system maps these parameters with the ontological concepts using the matching algorithm that combines the use of the semantic and syntactic similarities. Then, it retrieves

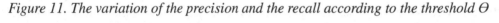

Figure 11. The variation of the precision and the recall according to the threshold Θ

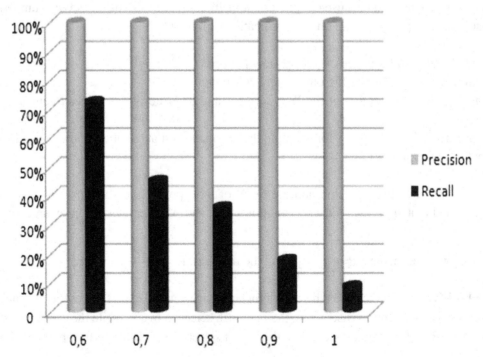

the response from the Web services using the common form of the parameters and it puts them in an XML file using the Content Integration Pattern.

For the Web service of the airline "Air France", the authors define the method GetFlight with the following inputs:

```
GetFlight(int nmrVol, String villeD, String villeA, Date dateD, Date dateA);
```

In a similar fashion, the authors define the method GetFlight for the Web service of the airline "Air Caraïbes" as follows:

```
GetFlight(int numVol, String villeDep, String villeArr, Date dateDep, Date dateArr);
```

And the method GetFlight for the Web service of the airline "AigleAzur" like this:

```
GetFlight(int numrVol, String ville_depart, String ville_arrivee, Date date_depart, Date date_arrivee);
```

In turn, the sub classes of the ontological concept "vol" are defined as follows: numeroVol, villeDepart, villeArrivee, dateDepart and dateArrivee which respectively mean: flight number, start city; end city, start date and end date.

Table 3 shows an example of the similarities between an ontological concept and the input of the Web services. After the matching process, the system can identify that nmrVol, numVol, idVol and numeroVolare similar using the Jaro similarity. Similarly, it can identify that villeD, villeDep, ville_depart and villeDepart are similar.

The next step entails rewriting the user query using the ontological concepts. Therefore, the method GetFlight is rewritten as follows:

```
GetFlight(int numeroVol, String villeDepart, String villeArrivee, Date dateDepart, Date dateArrivee);
```

Thus, we have to request all Web services with this query. After querying the Web services and getting the responses, the system uses the Content Integration Pattern to integrate heterogeneous data and

Table 3. The similarities between the ontological concepts and the input of the Web services

Concept	Input	Similarity
numeroVol	nmrVol	0.83
numeroVol	numVol	0.83
numeroVol	numrVol	0.86
villeDepart	villeD	0.84
villeDepart	villeDep	0.9
villeDepart	Ville_depart	0.91

repackage the results into a new XML file. An example of an XML file for the available flight is given as follows:

```
<?xml version="1.0" encoding="ISO-8859-1" standalone="true"?>
<vols>
        <vol>
                <numeroVol>100 </ numeroVol>
                <compagnie>Air France </compagnie>
                <villeDepart>lyon</villeDepart>
                <villeArrivee>paris</villeArrivee>
                <dateDepart>02/07/2016 </dateDepart>
                <dateArrivee>09/07/2016 </dateArrivee>
        </vol>
        <vol>
                <numeroVol>101 </ numeroVol>
                <compagnie>Aigle Azur</compagnie>
                <villeDepart>lyon</villeDepart>
                <villeArrivee>paris</villeArrivee>
                <dateDepart>02/07/2016 </dateDepart>
                <dateArrivee>09/07/2016 </dateArrivee>
        </vol>
        <vol>
                <nmr_vol>102 </nmr_vol>
                <compagnie> Air Caraïbes</compagnie>
                <villeDepart>lyon</villeDepart>
                <villeArrivee>paris</villeArrivee>
                <dateDepart>02/07/2016 </dateDepart>
                <dateArrivee>09/07/2016 </dateArrivee>
        </vol>
</vols>
```

The final step allows displaying the result of the generated XML file in a clear format for the end users using the pattern Usability Enhancer. Figure 12 depicts an example of the available flights of a mashup that combines 3 Web services.

FUTURE RESEARCH DIRECTIONS

In fact, the time complexity of the matching process is impractical when composing a large number of Web services. Thus, possible future directions will involve improving the time complexity to quickly find the list of matched pairs. In addition, the developers of semantic mashup applications can use several optimization techniques that can be applied on the matching algorithm. For example, automatic choice of similarity measures can increase the ease-of-use for the users of the matching framework.

Figure 12. An example of the available flights of a mashup that combines 3 Web services

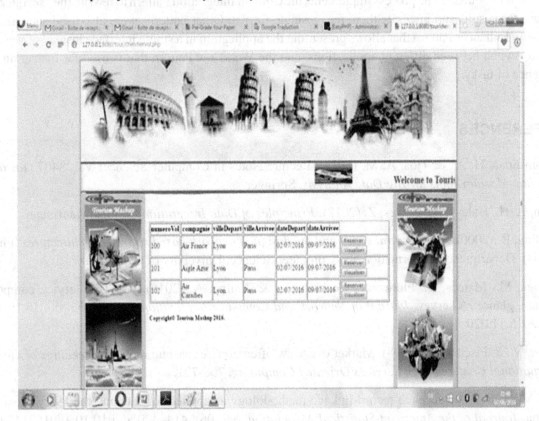

The efficiency of the data integration systems will be increased if the developers of semantic mashup applications use test patterns. This will avoid software errors and suffering damages. Other trends will also impact the way in which the Harvest pattern will be used to extract information from heterogeneous sources. This will help the user to obtain data of high quality.

CONCLUSION

Mashup consists of creating applications based on the combination and the aggregation of a set of content and features published and exhibited through specific APIs that use different techniques and protocols to disseminate various resources (REST, SOAP, RSS, etc.). The use of semantic matching allows the machine interpreting the processed data and APIs handled for the automatic construction of mashup applications.

The patterns help the designers to discover combinations of architecture and develop solution blocks that have been shown to present useful solutions in the past and provide efficient solutions in the future. In this chapter, the authors presented an approach that helps to create a pattern-based semantic mashup application that is based on the use of domain ontology and matching tool to make connections between different data sources. The process implements the Content Integration Pattern to rewrite the user queries, retrieve the results and integrate them into a single format. Other patterns were also used such as: the Usability Enhancer Pattern that allows presenting the application in a single interface instead of wasting time to switch between different applications, and the Workflow Pattern that is used for managing the sequence of tasks.

REFERENCES

Anjomshoaa, H. A., & Tjoa, A. M. (2014). Lecture Notes in Computer Science: Vol. 8407. *Towards Semantic Mashup Tools for Big Data Analysis*. Springer.

Doan, A. H., Halevy, A., & Ives, Z. (2012). *Principles of Data Integration*. Morgan Kaufmann.

Fielding, R. (2000). *Architectural styles and the design of network-based software architectures* (Ph.D. Thesis). Department of Information and Computer Science, University of California.

Garriga, M., Mateos, C., Flores, A., Cechich, A., & Zunino, A. (2016). RESTful service composition at a glance: A survey. *Journal of Network and Computer Applications*, *60*, 32–53. doi:10.1016/j.jnca.2015.11.020

Hoyer, V., & Fischer, M. (2008). Market overview of enterprise mashup tools. *Proceedings of the 6th International Conference on Services Oriented Computing*, 708-721.

Jaro, M. (1989). Advances in record-linkage methodology as applied to matching the 1985 census of Tampa. *Journal of the American Statistical Association*, *84*(406), 414–420. doi:10.1080/01621459.1989.10478785

Karakostas, B., & Kalamboukis, Z. (2017). API mashups: How well do they support the travellers' information needs? *Proceedings of the 8th International Conference on Ambient Systems, Networks and Technologies (ANT 2017)*, 204-209.

Khokhar, R. H., Benjamin, C. M. F., Farkhund, I., Alhadidi, D., & Bentahar, J. (2016). Privacy-preserving data mashup model for trading person-specific information. *Electronic Commerce Research and Applications*, *17*, 19–37. doi:10.1016/j.elerap.2016.02.004

Kopecký, J., Vitvar, T., Bournez, C., & Farrell, J. (2007). Sawsdl: Semantic annotations for wsdl and xml schema. *IEEE Internet Computing*, *11*(6), 60–67. doi:10.1109/MIC.2007.134

Koudas, N., Sarawagi, S., & Srivastava, D. (2006). Record linkage: Similarity measures and algorithms. *Tutorial, the ACM SIGMOD Conference*.

Lathem, J., Gomadam, K., & Sheth, A. P. (2007). Sa-rest and (s)mashups: Adding semantics to restful services. *Proceedings of the International Conference on Semantic Computing, ICSC'07*, 469-476. 10.1109/ICSC.2007.94

Lee, C. J., Tang, S. M., Tsai, C. C., & Chen, Y. C. (2009). Toward a New Paradigm: Mashup Patterns in Web 2.0. *WSEAS Transactions on Information Science and Applications*, *6*(10), 1675–1686.

Lee, Y. (2014). Semantic-based data mashups using hierarchical clustering and pattern analysis methods. *Journal of Information Science and Engineering, 30*(5), 1601–1618.

Lee, Y. (2015). Semantic-Based Web API Composition for Data Mashups. *Journal of Information Science and Engineering, 31*, 1233-1248.

Levenshtein, V. (1966). Binary codes capable of correcting deletions, insertions, and reversals. *Soviet Physics, Doklady, 10*, 707–710.

Liu, D., Li, N., Pedrinaci, C., Kopecký, J., Maleshkova, M., & Domingue, J. (2011). An approach to construct dynamic service mashups using lightweight semantics. *Current Trends in Web Engineering - Workshops, Doctoral Symposium, and Tutorials, Held at ICWE 2011.*

Liu, Y., Liang, X., Xu, L., Staples, M., & Zhu, L. (2011). Composing enterprise mashup components and services using architecture integration patterns. *Journal of Systems and Software Archive, 84*(9), 1436-1446.

Lytras, M. D., Damiani, E., & Pablos, P. O. (2008). *Web 2.0 The Business Model*. Springer Publishing Company, Incorporated.

Maleshkova, M., Pedrinaci, C., & Domingue, J. (2009). Supporting the creation of semantic restful service descriptions. *Proceedings of the 8th International Semantic Web Conference (ISWC 2009).*

Malki, A., & Benslimane, S. M. (2012). Building semantic mashup. *Proceedings of the 4th International conference on Web and Information Technologies, ICWIT 2012*, 40-49.

Malki, A., & Benslimane, S. M. (2013). Semantic Cloud: Building Dynamic Mashup in Cloud Environment. *International Journal of Information Technology and Web Engineering, 8*(4), 20–35. doi:10.4018/ijitwe.2013100102

Meditskos, G., & Bassiliades, N. (2011). A combinatory framework of Web 2.0 mashup tools, owl-s and uddi. *Expert Systems with Applications, 38*(6), 6657–6668. doi:10.1016/j.eswa.2010.11.072

Miller, G. (1995). Wordnet: A Lexical Database for English Language. *Communications of the ACM, 38*(11), 39–41. doi:10.1145/219717.219748

Ngu, A. H. H., Carlson, M. P., Sheng, Q. Z., & Paik, H. Y. (2010). Semantic-based mashup of composite applications. *IEEE Transactions on Services Computing, 3*(1), 2–15. doi:10.1109/TSC.2010.8

O'Reilly, T. (2005). *What Is Web 2.0? Design Patterns and Business Models for the Next Generation of Software*. Academic Press.

Ogrinz, M. (2009). *Mashup Patterns: Designs and Examples for the Modern Enterprise*. Addison-Wesley Professional.

Park, Y., Yoo, H., Hur, C., Bae, H., & Lung, Y. (2015). Semantic Service Discovery and Matching for Semi-automatic Service Mashup. *Proceedings of the 9th IEEE International Conference on Semantic Computing.*

Syeda-Mahmood, T., Shah, G., Akkiraju, R., Ivan, A., & Goodwin, R. (2005). Searching Service Repositories by Combining Semantic and Ontological Matching. *Proceedings of the Third Intl. Conf. on Web Services (ICWS'05).* 10.1109/ICWS.2005.102

Tjoa, A. M., Wetz, P., Kiesling, E., Trinh, T., & Do, B. (2015). Integrating Streaming Data into Semantic Mashups. *Proceedings of the Third Information Systems International Conference.*

Trinh, T., Do, B., Wetz, P., Aryan, P. R., Kiesling, E., & Tjoa, A. M. (2017). Linked Widgets Platform for Rapid Collaborative Semantic Mashup Development. *Proceedings of the Second International Rapid Mashup Challenge.*

Wan, Y., Chen, L., Yu, Q., Liang, T., & Wu, J. (2016). Incorporating Heterogeneous Information for Mashup Discovery with Consistent Regularization. *Springer International Publishing Switzerland, LNAI, 9651,* 436–448.

Yu, J., Benatallah, B., Casati, F., & Daniel, F. (2008). Understanding mashup development. *IEEE Internet Computing, 12*(5), 44–52. doi:10.1109/MIC.2008.114

KEY TERMS AND DEFINITIONS

Domain Ontology: Is an abstraction of a domain that identifies the relevant concepts in that domain.

Ontology: Is an explicit and formal specification of a conceptualization. It consists of hierarchical descriptions of concepts and a set of properties that describe each concept.

Query Rewriting: Is the process that translates a user query expressed via a mediated schema that does not contain any data into a query over the underlying data sources.

REST: Is a protocol that provides a lighter weight alternative to web services. Usually, the REST protocol relies on a simple URL to make a request on a set of web services.

SOAP: Is a standard communication protocol developed by Microsoft. It relies on the XML language to exchange messages between web services.

Web Service: Is a software component or application that can be described by XML artifacts. The web services use XML messages to interact with other software components or applications.

Web Services Composition: Refers to the process that combines a set of web services to offer a compound one.

Section 4
Analytics to the Rescue?

Using semantic technology to recover knowledge from semi-/unstructured data sources has always been a trying case. Sheer size of and multiply-sourced data, compounded with lack of pre-specified clear semantics required resorting to approaches statistical in nature, such as machine learning and analytics. Here sampled in this section are approaches to social network analysis; entity recognition in user content; data mining for effective management of telecom users; and, customer reviews rating.

Chapter 17
Social Network Analysis:
Basic Concepts, Tools, and Applications

Soufiana Mekouar
Mohammed V University Rabat, Morocco

ABSTRACT

The study of social network analysis has grown in popularity in the past decades and has been used in many areas. It is an interesting and useful field that gained an increasing popularity due to the explosion of social media that has emerged with advances in communication systems, which play a critical role in forming human activities and interactions in social systems. The authors present some techniques from a data mining perspective and statistical graph measure that can be used in various applications such as to perform community detection, clustering in a social network, identify spurious and anomalous users, predict links between vertices in a social network, model and improve the information diffusion, design trust models, and improve other applications. Then, the authors provide a recent literature review of such applications and thus outline challenges of social network applications.

INTRODUCTION

Networks are omnipresent everywhere and almost in every situation. Biological, social, computer and Web networks can be represented as a graph. Taking the social network as a primary example, they contain billions of individuals (vertices) interacting with each other by exchanging contents, photos, and videos (Hannema & Riddle, 2005). Another example is the Web network that consists of billions of pages as vertices and their hyperlinks to each other as edges (Broder et al., 2000). So, collecting and processing the input of Web users (queries, clicks), social interaction (posting contents, retweets, likes, comments) make the appearance of diverse forms of networks, such as the query graph (Zhao & Han, 2010) and social graph. The authors argue that social network constitutes a rich network to study and analyze since it contains wealthy sources of information about both users and links that represent relationships between these users.

DOI: 10.4018/978-1-5225-5384-7.ch017

A Social network includes a set of nodes that can be individuals, organizations or computers which are connected by different types of relationships, for instance, scientists in a discipline, employees in a firm, co-authors of a research paper, and computers in wireless networks. The relationship in the social network depends mainly on the studied network, it could be a friendship, scientific collaboration, business relationship, and so on.

Online social networks have become one of the most powerful and crucial sources of information that permit to its users to share, discuss and exchange ideas and opinions about a topic of interest. The main goal of social networks is to generate opportunities, to develop friendships by supporting a system that enables its users to organize and update their own profile, and sharing, exchanging contents of interest to users within the network. As well as, they improve learning for its users by sharing valuable contents on the subject of interest and permit making social connections within users preferences and find people of interest by sharing profiles for academic and business purposes.

Social network analysis (SNA) is an in-depth analysis of social networks, which tries to measure the flows between entities of social graph in the aim to extract insight and knowledge (Wasserman & Faust, 1994; Knoke & Yang, 2008). SNA enables performing both mathematical and visual analysis of interactions between social entities, which permits to understand the patterns that occur in social network and discovers complex communications, gets features and properties of the network and the change and evolution of the structure of the social graph.

The main goal of this chapter is to review progress and developments regarding interesting applications in social network analysis such as diffusion of information (Mekouar, El-Hammani, Ibrahimi, & Bouyakhf, 2015), community detection (Bedi & Sharma, 2016), link prediction (Al Hasan & Zaki, 2011), anomaly detection (Mekouar, Zrira, & Bouyakhf, in press), and trust models (Mekouar, Ibrahimi, & Bouyakhf, 2014). This is with the aim to provide a simplified view of the advancement of such applications in the field of social network analysis. In this sense, the authors point out strengths and weaknesses of existing approaches and provide some data mining techniques that may be applied to such listed applications of SNA. As well as, the authors provide measure metrics used in social network analysis for the purpose of analysis from graph theory perspective. Therefore the authors provide some tools to analyze, visualize and gain insight from the social graph.

Some surveys investigate relational and cultural structures with a few simple network concepts. Some other papers investigate the analysis of individuals and ties that bind them (Erçetin & Neyişci, 2016; Serrat, 2017). This chapter concentrates on discussing, analyzing and outline limitations that should further be explored of some major applications in social network analysis. The chapter provides readers with essential background to understand the basic concepts of data mining and graph theory applied to some potential applications of SNA.

This research chapter is designed to serve as guidelines for scientists and practitioners who intend to design new methods in this field of study and provide the readers with recent advancements in some of the most influential topics in the social network. This study will permit readers from different backgrounds to understand social network analysis easily and will be helpful to use and develop new approaches based on techniques from data mining and graph theory perspectives.

The rest of the chapter is organized as follows. Section 2 describes some data mining techniques used in social network analysis. Next, structures, properties, and graph models are provided in Section 3. Section 4 includes some tools used for visualization purpose of social network. Section 5, outlines some major applications of social network. Section 6, provides interesting challenges and future research directions. Finally, section 7, concludes the chapter.

DATA MINING TECHNIQUES FOR SOCIAL NETWORK ANALYSIS

Probabilistic Relational Models

Probabilistic relational models (PRMs) are a wealthy portrayal of relational language for structured statistical models to model relational data based on the relational language. It extends the Bayesian networks with the concept of objects, their properties, and relationships between them.

PRMs represent a joint probability distribution over the attributes of a relational data. They enable the properties of an object to dependent probabilistically both on other properties of that object and on properties of the related objects. For example, take a set of objects, a PRM identifies a probability distribution over a set of interpretations implying the participation of these objects and others objects. Performing a PRM analysis on a database containing objects and corresponding relations, permits specifying a probability distribution over the attributes of the objects (Koller, 1999). PRMs include two components which are the dependency structure and the parameters associated with the structure (Getoor, Friedman, Koller, & Taskar, 2001).

Dependency Structure for Probabilistic Relational Models

The dependency structure is constructed of a combination of attributes and their parents. The dependency structure is defined by associating each descriptive attribute with a set of formal parents, $P_p(X, A)$ where X represents class an A represents an attribute of class X which is denoted by $X.A$. The formal parent $P_p(X, A)$ are attributes that have a direct influence on $X.A$. The formal parents will be instantiated in different ways for different objects in X, and there are two distinct types of formal parents, namely, internal dependencies, and external dependencies. Internal dependency means attribute $X.A$ depends on another attribute $X.B$ of the same class. While external dependency refers to an attribute $X.A$ depending on attributes of the related object(s) (Getoor et al., 2001).

Parameters Associated With the Structure for Probabilistic Relational Models

Parameters form a local probability model for a descriptive attribute $X.A$. The local probability model is defined, specifying the parents' probability $P_p(X, A)$ by the conditional probability $P(X.A \mid P_p(X.A))$. Let $U_i = P_{p_i}(X.A)$ where each of these parents U_i have a set of values $V(U)$ or each value $u \in V(U)$ where $n = |P_{p_i}(X.A)|$ represents the number of parents, then, a distribution $P(X.A \mid u)$ over $V(X.A)$ is determined. This entire set of parameters comprises parameters Θ_s (Getoor et al., 2001).

Probabilistic relational models contain three graphs which are data graph, model graph, and the inference graph. The data graph presents the input network, where nodes are the objects in the data and edges represent the relationships among the objects. The model graph represents the dependencies among attributes at the level of item types. Attributes of an item (either node or edge) can depend probabilistically on other attributes of the same item, on attributes of other related objects or links in graph model. The inference graph depicts the probabilistic dependencies among all the variables in a single test set. It can be instantiated by a roll out process of data graph and graph model. Each item-attribute pair in graph data gets a separate, local copy of the corresponding conditional probability distribution from graph model. The relations in graph data determine the way that graph model is rolled out to form inference graph. Therefore the structure of inference graph is determined by both graph data and graph model (Neville & Jensen, 2007).

Support Vector Machine

Support Vector Machine (SVM) was introduced by (Boser, Guyon, & Vapnik, 1992), as supervised machine learning algorithm used for classification and regression purposes. The objective is to maximize predictive accuracy while avoiding the data over-fit.

SVM involves utilization of hypothesis space in a high dimensional feature space, to train training data with an optimization learning algorithm that performs a learning bias obtained from statistical learning theory. In other words, given labeled training data, the algorithm yields an optimal hyperplane which classifies new instances. SVM's technique tries to identify a hyperplane that classifies better the data set into two or more classes, in such way that the data points nearest to the hyperplane, which considered critical if removed, would change the position of the hyperplane that separates classes. So, from this the hyperplane is a line that linearly separates and classifies a set of data, as an ideal deal, the data points should be as far away from the hyperplane as possible, while still being on the correct side (Cortes & Vapnik, 1995).

It is being used for many applications and purpose, such as handwriting analysis (Bahlmann, Haasdonk, & Burkhardt, 2002), anomaly detection (Hu, Liao, & Vemuri, 2003), face analysis (Osuna, Freund, & Girosit, 1997), community detection (Van Laarhoven, & Marchiori, 2013), and others.

There is some advantage to the use of SVM, such as, it provides good accuracy, works well on small data, and it is efficient because of the use of a subset of training data points. However, it is not suited for big data and less effective on noisy data with overlapping classes.

Expectation Maximization (EM)

The expectation maximization (EM) algorithm allows the estimation of the parameter in probabilistic models such as Bayesian network and hidden Markov model with incomplete data. The purpose of EM is to find the maximum likelihood estimator of θ a probability distribution. It is an iterative method that aims to approximate the maximum likelihood function. The maximum likelihood estimation can find the "best fit" model for a set of data. The EM proceeds by the choice of random values for the missing dataset and then uses these hypotheses or drives to estimate the new data set. The new values are used to create a better hypothesis for the first data set then the process continues till the algorithm converges to a fixed point (Moon, 1996).

The EM algorithm has become a popular tool in statistical estimation problems employing incomplete data, or in problems which can be laid in a similar form, such as mixture estimation, estimation of Gaussian mixture models (Piater, 2002). It is also, used in biological data (Bailey, & Elkan, 1995), community detection (Ball, Karrer, & Newman, 2011), weather forecasting (Sloughter, Raftery, Gneiting, & Fraley, 2007) and others.

The maximum likelihood estimation (MLE) "is a method of estimating the parameters of a statistical model given observations, by finding the parameter values that maximize the likelihood of making the observations given the parameters" (Nam, 2017).

The EM algorithm is based on iterating the Q function in such a way that at each step obtaining an estimator that maximize the value Q function and therefore gives a larger value of log likelihood function $L()$ (Scholz,1985).

The authors describe in the following, the EM-algorithm in two steps.

The EM algorithm is a powerful iterative method to compute MLE in the presence of missing or hidden data. The purpose of MLE is to estimate the model parameter(s) for which the observed data occur.

Each iteration of EM algorithm consists of two procedures: The E-step, and the M-step.

In E-step, the missing data are estimated given the observed data and the current estimate of the model parameters. This is realized based on the conditional expectation.

In the M-step, the likelihood function is maximized under the supposition that the missing data are known. The estimate of the missing data from the E-step is used instead of the actual missing data.

EM algorithm works well when there is a small amount of missing data and the small dimensionality of the data. Indeed, EM algorithm can be extremely slow, even on the fastest computer. Convergence is insured since the algorithm tries to increase the likelihood at each iteration with a high guarantee.

K-MEANS

K-Means clustering is an unsupervised learning algorithm, which is mainly employed when there is unlabeled data. The method attempts to improve the intergroup similarity while keeping the groups as far as possible from each other. Basically, K-Means uses the Euclidean Distance to compute the distance between each two given points in the data.

The purpose of this technique is to find groups in the data, given the number of groups denoted by K. The algorithm works in an iterative manner to assign each data point to one of the K groups based on the features that are provided to the algorithm. The data points are grouped based on a similarity metric. It keeps iterating until it reaches the best solution (Hartigan & Wong, 1979; Kanungo et al., 2002).

The K-Means algorithm includes the following steps:

1. Each centroid determines one of the clusters in the data. Where each data point is attributed to its nearest centroid, based on the Euclidean distance.
2. Assign each data point to the group that has the closest centroid. When all data points have been assigned, re-compute the positions of the K centroids. This is performed by taking the mean of all data points attributed to the centroid in question.
3. The algorithm repeat steps 1 and 2 until a stopping criterion is met such as no data points change clusters, or the maximum number of iterations is reached.

Advantages of K-Means Algorithm:

- K-Means (for small K) is useful and fast when there is a large number of variables
- K-Means may produce tighter clusters than hierarchical clustering.

Disadvantages of K-Means Algorithm:

- Hardness to compare the quality of the clusters produced, since different K affects the outcome of partitions.
- It is difficult to guess the exact number of clusters K (Improved Outcomes Software Inc., 2004).

DECISION TREE

The decision tree is one of the best methods used for classification and regression purpose. It is a supervised machine learning algorithm used mainly for predictive modeling and it can be applied for categorical and continuous variables. Generally, the data is divided into two or more subset samples depending on the differentiation in the input variables. The type of decision tree is classified according to the type of output variables which could be categorical or continuous variables. The decision tree attempts to represent a problem. Each internal node in the tree corresponds to a variable in the data and each leaf node represents a class or target variable (output). The data is divided into training and test data. The decision tree proceeds as follows, at first assign the best variable of the data to the root of the tree. The training data is divided into subsets, in which each subset should include the same value of a variable. The process is repeated till a leaf node is found at each branch of each subset of the tree. There are some advantages of using decision tree such as it is one of the fastest supervised learning algorithms that can identify the relationship between two or more variables and determine the most important variable. As well as, it is not impacted a lot by outliers and missing values and does not require any assumptions about the classifier and space distribution (Safavian & Landgrebe, 1991). A decision tree is used in various applications such as the detection of anomaly and link prediction.

FUZZY BAYESIAN NETWORK

The Fuzzy Bayesian Network (FBN) is a model that permits the knowledge and reasoning representation under uncertainty based on probability and graph theory. It is a manner to represent a "probabilistic reasoning over different events with causality and probabilistic relativity which are expressed by network graphs" (Tang & Liu, 2007). FBN was applied to a various cases such as health care, financial investment, and social network analysis. "A fuzzy set is a class of objects with a continuum of grades of membership. Such a set is characterized by a membership (characteristic) function which assigns to each object a grade of membership ranging between zero and one" (Zadeh, 1965). FBN was introduced to overcome some drawbacks of the Bayesian Network. FBN permits to alleviate and determine the level of degradation within a given environment by using fuzzy membership values with a Bayesian network. This system uses fuzzy membership values in the network, and output a fuzzy membership value as a level of degradation within the system (Pan & Liu, 1999).

STRUCTURES, PROPERTIES, AND MODELS OF GRAPHS IN SOCIAL NETWORKS

Network Structures

- **Reciprocity:** In network science, reciprocity is a measure of the possibility of nodes in a directed network to be mutually linked to each other. In other words, it is the tendency of a user i that is linked to user j , to be reciprocated from user j to user i.This type of relationship can also be seen in friendship network of Facebook or co-authorship network of scientists. Analysis of reciprocity in directed networks is crucial in many scenarios such as the understanding of the degree of importance of any node (Jiang, Zhang, & Towsley, 2015).
- **Transitivity:** Transitivity is the tendency that a friend of your friend is also your friend. This suggests that if i is linked to j through ties, and j is bonded to k, then i is linked to k as well. This phenomenon is rarely to occur in real world networks since it implies that each pair of reachable nodes in the graph would be linked by ties (Snijders, 2012).
- **Preferential Attachment:** Preferential attachment is the tendency of nodes to be linked to nodes that have the high degree of connectivity. So, as consequence of this process the nodes that are highly connected become more highly connected. The preferential attachment is alluded to by the names of Yule process, "cumulative advantage", "the rich get richer", and, the "Matthew effect". This could be observed in citation network, the paper that gained more citations has a great probability to be referenced (Akbaş, Brust, Turgut, & Ribeiro, 2015).
- **Structural Equivalence:** Structural equivalence is the tendency that two nodes are connected to the same social environments. The nodes are structurally equivalent will be similar in attitudes, behaviors or performance. In other terms, the authors argue that two nodes are structurally equivalent if they share many neighbors. Various measures have been used to measure the structural equivalence, such as Cosine similarity, Pearson coefficient, and Euclidean distance (Sailer, 1978).

Network Properties

Centralization is defined as the change in the centrality scores of the nodes in the network since this variation indicates in which extent the node is central and which nodes are very central, and a periphery in which nodes have a very low centrality scores. The authors expose here major centrality metrics (Freeman, 1978; Wasserman & Faust, 1994; Newman, 2010):

- **Degree Centrality:** The degree centrality of a node is the number of links incident to a node. A node is important if it has many neighbors.
- **Betweenness Centrality:** It measures the involvement of a node that connects two nodes on all shortest paths within the network. The nodes with high betweenness centrality may have great influence within the network since they have authority over information exchange between other nodes. The betweenness centrality can be computed as follows:

$$C_B(v) = \sum_{s \neq v \neq d \in V} \frac{\sigma_{sd}(v)}{\sigma_{sd}}$$

σ_{sd} : Total number of shortest paths from node s to d .

$\sigma_{sd}(v)$: Total number of shortest paths that pass through v .

- **Closeness Centrality:** The closeness centrality of a node is the average length of the shortest path between the node and all other nodes in the graph. Thus it is the mean distance from a node to other nodes. The low values of this quantity for node means better access to information at other vertices or more direct influence on other vertices. Closeness is defined as:

$$C(v) = \frac{1}{\sum_{u} d(u,v)}$$

$d(u,v)$: The distance between nodes u and v .

- **Eigenvector Centrality:** It attributes scores to all nodes in the network based on the assumption that nodes that are connected to nodes with high degree contribute more to the score of the node in question. So, a node is important if it is bonded to other important nodes. This metric is considered as a ranking measure. The Eigenvector centrality of node v is given as follows:

$$eig(v) = \frac{1}{\lambda} \sum_{t \in M(v)} x_t$$

$M(v)$ is a set of the neighbors of v {\displaystyle v}. λ is an eigenvalue

- **Katz Centrality:** It measures influence by considering the total number of walks between a pair of nodes.

This metric allows computing the number of the immediate neighbors and all other nodes in the network that connect to the node in question through these immediate neighbors.

The relationships made with distant neighbors are penalized by an attenuation factor α . The Katz centrality of node v is:

$$C_{katz}(v) = \sum_{k=1}^{\infty} \sum_{u=1}^{n} \alpha^k (A^k)_{uv}$$

That is, the adjacency matrix A raised to the power k represents the total number of k degree connections between nodes u and v . And, α is a value for the attenuation factor.

- **PageRank:** PageRank is a way to measure the importance of a node. It is a variant of eigenvector centrality and takes into consideration the issue encountered in Katz centrality. The issue that occurs with Katz centrality in directed graphs is that, once a node becomes an authority, it provides its centrality to all its out-degree nodes. Which is not the case in the real problem situation, one who knows a well-known person (celebrity for example) do not necessarily become a known person.

PageRank centrality measure is used by the Google search engine as a measure for ranking web pages. PageRank is based on a node in degrees. In particular, the rank of page i is defined as follows:

$$rank(i) = \alpha \sum_{j} A_{ij} \frac{rank(j)}{k_j^{out}} + \beta$$

This equation is only defined when k_j^{out} is non-zero. Otherwise, the authors set up k_j^{out} equal to 1.

- **Clustering Coefficient:** It analyzes transitivity in an undirected graph. Since transitivity is observed when triangles are formed, this metric is the probability at which extent two nodes that are connected to an intermediary node, will be linked directly. The degree of clustering in a network allows to figure out which information can diffuse over the network.

The authors compute some measure metrics of the following graph (Figure 1), which are shown in Table 1.

Figure 2, illustrates measure metrics score for each node. The authors notice that the degree centrality and betweenness centrality have the highest score values. In order to investigate more the relationship between these metrics, the authors compute the correlation between score values of these metrics in Table 2.

Figure 1. Graph g with 10 vertices and 20 edges

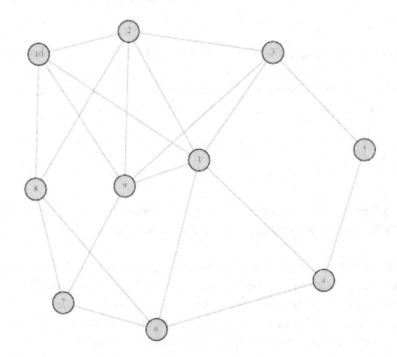

Table 1. Score values of metrics for each vertex in graph g displayed in the Figure 1

Vertex	Degree	Betweenness	Closeness	Eigenvector	Katz	PageRank	Clustering Coefficient
1	6	6.8333333	0.08333333	1.000000	1.096025	0.14247897	0.4000000
2	5	2.7500000	0.07692308	0.9314202	1.080540	0.11871280	0.6000000
3	4	4.2500000	0.07142857	0.7105355	1.064328	0.10109391	0.5000000
4	3	2.7500000	0.06666667	0.4243643	1.047873	0.08221050	0.3333333
5	2	0.5000000	0.05263158	0.2605816	1.031683	0.05977543	0.0000000
6	4	3.8333333	0.07142857	0.5876340	1.063838	0.10174788	0.3333333
7	3	0.8333333	0.06250000	0.4901967	1.048120	0.07808997	0.3333333
8	4	2.0000000	0.06666667	0.6447361	1.063860	0.09950537	0.3333333
9	5	3.5833333	0.07692308	0.9025627	1.080307	0.11955092	0.5000000
10	4	0.6666667	0.06666667	0.7987402	1.064811	0.09683424	0.6666667

Figure 2. Metrics measure score for each node

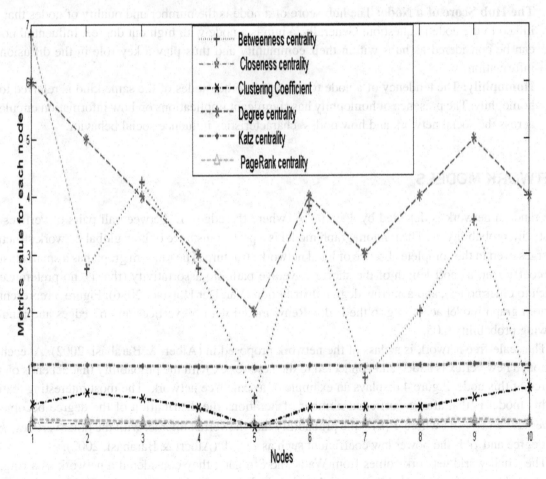

Table 2. Correlation score between metrics

Metric 1	Metric 2	Correlation Score
Degree centrality	Katz centrality	0.9998495
Betweenness centrality	Closeness centrality	0.8388774
Closeness centrality	PageRank centrality	0.9727139
Eigenvector centrality	Katz centrality	0.9672001
Katz centrality	Degree centrality	0.9998495
PageRank centrality	Degree centrality	0.9998495
Clustering coefficient	Eigenvector centrality	0.7838228

- **The Authority Score of a Node:** The authority of a node is expressed by the number of times gained links to it and the quality of the nodes that linked to it. Generally, an authority is a node with high in-degree (that is, the number of links pointing to a node). Authority node refers to a popular node.
- **The Hub Score of a Node:** The hub score of a node is the number and quality of nodes that are linked to the node in question. Generally, a hub is a node with high out degree. Influential nodes can be considered as hubs within their community and thus play a key role in the diffusion of information.
- **Homophily:** The tendency of a node to connect to other nodes of the same kind is referred to as homophily. The presence of homophily has significant implications on how information circulates across the social network and how nodes' characteristics influence social behavior.

NETWORK MODELS

The random network is depicted by $V = (G, E)$ where the edges E between all pairs of vertices V exist with probability p. The random graph model is a perfect instance of how global network structure emerges even in the complete absence of local network structure. The random graph has a small clustering coefficient, a short length of the shortest average path, no assortativity (that is, no preference to attach to other nodes), and a narrow degree distribution (Van Der Hofstad, 2016). Figure 3 represents a random graph model according to the Erdos-Renyi model with 50 vertices and 67 edges and random drawing probability 0.05.

The scale-free network is a class of the network proposed in (Albert & Barabási, 2002). At each iteration, a new vertex is added and connected to the new vertex with the probability that depends on the degree of this node. Figure 4 displays an example of a scale free network. The most interesting feature of this model is that after a sufficient number of iterations the distribution of the degree becomes a power law $P(k) = k^{\alpha}$ where $P(k)$ is the probability that the vertex interact with the other vertices, k is the degree and α is the power law coefficient such as $\alpha \succ 1$ (Albert & Barabási, 2002).

The small world network comes from Watts and Strogatz; they considered a network as a ring, in which each vertex is connected to the neighboring k. It has a high clustering coefficient, a long path

Figure 3. Random graph according to the Erdos-Renyi model with 50 vertices and 67 edges and random drawing probability 0.05

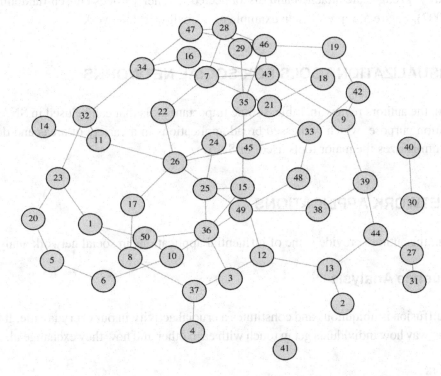

Figure 4. Scale-free graph according to the Barabasi-Albert model with 50 vertices and 49 edges

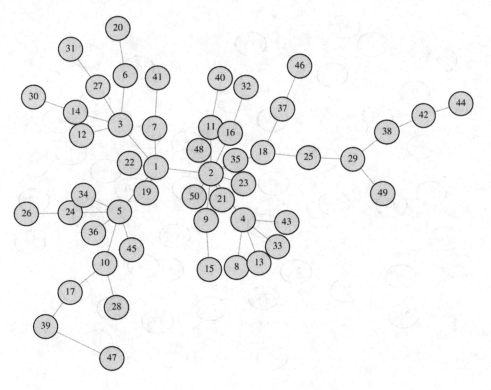

length of the shortest average path, no modularity or assortativity, and symmetric degree distribution. With probability p edges are attached and disconnected at other vertices chosen randomly (Easley & Kleinberg, 2007). Figure 5, represents an example of a small world network.

GRAPH VISUALIZATION TOOLS FOR SOCIAL NETWORKS

In this section, the authors review in Table 3 some important tools that can be used in SNA for analysis and visualization purpose, which witnessed broad applications in a variety of areas and domains. The table below summarizes the major tools used for SNA.

SOCIAL NETWORK APPLICATIONS

In this section, the authors provide some of influential applications in social network analysis.

Social Influence Analysis

Information diffusion is ubiquitous and constitutes a crucial activity in our everyday life. It has changed completely the way how individuals get in touch with each other and how they exchange ideas, opinions,

Figure 5. Small world network according to the Watts-Strogatz network model, with 50 vertices and 150 edges and rewiring probability 0.05

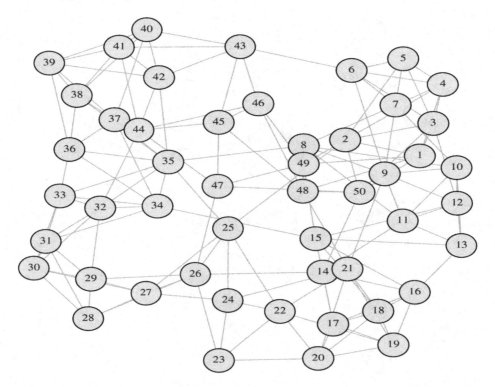

Table 3. Tools and their description for social network analysis

Tools	Description of Tools
Centrifuge	This tool provides to analysts and researcher a suitable manner that assists to understand, extract and gain insight from data. As well as, it permits to visualize, finding patterns by interacting with data, and permits to extract conclusions and findings (Centrifuge Analytics, 2017).
EgoNet	This tool is for collection and analysis of egocentric network data. The data collection proceeds by creating a questionnaire, collecting data, visualizing and offering network measures. The collected data can be used by other software for extensive analysis (EgoNet, 2017).
Gephi	Gephi is an interactive visualization and exploration tool for all types of networks including complex networks and dynamic graphs. It enables to explore, visualize, analyze and understand graphs (Bastian, Heymann, & Jacomy, 2009).
Network Workbench	This is for large-scale network analysis, modeling, and visualization purpose of various disciplines including biomedical and social sciences. This tool permits evaluation, conception and operation of a distinctive distributed resources environment for large-scale network analysis, modeling, and visualization (NWB Team, 2006).
Pajek	Pajek is widely used in academic research with the aim of observing many origins of big networks that were previously present only in the machine-readable form. Pajek provides tools for analysis and visualization of various networks including collaboration networks, organic molecule, protein receptor interaction networks, Internet networks, citation networks, and diffusion networks phenomena (Batagelj, & Mrvar, 2003).

and information. The information diffusion field studies how news, rumors disseminate, propagate and exchange among users within the network. Diffusion of information, ideas, opinions, behaviors, and diseases are ubiquitous in nature and modern life society.

Diffusion is a process by which information is communicated through certain channels over time between users of a social system. The tree major elements derived from this definition, which are users, reciprocal interactions, and communication channels, are considered as the basis for the future analytical system in such process (Rogers, 1976).

Information diffusion plays a critical role in a variety of applications, ranging from the dissemination of information to the adoption of political opinions and technologies, the spread of disease, and viral marketing.

The authors focus here on the particular case of information diffusion in online social networks, and they outline the major models proposed in the diffusion of information literacy (Kimura & Saito, 2006) which include: Deterministic Models, Independent Cascade Models, Linear Threshold Models, Evolutionary Graph Theory, and Logic Programming Models. Studying and giving an overview of such existing models will enable the research community to select the model that fits better to the tackled problem. As well as, this raises questions about the efficiency of each model to maximize, study or minimize the information diffusion and how to identify key (central) users that maximize or minimize the adoption of products. How pieces of information become viral and which one becomes popular? How and which paths information take to achieve the objective of the study either maximizing the product adoptions or minimizing the spread of misinformation? So, the authors give an overview of existing models of information diffusion.

- **Deterministic Models:** The deterministic model was introduced in (Granovetter & Soong, 1983) and is named sometimes as "opinion dynamics" models. These models rely on the fact that each individual in a social network adopts a certain new behavior once the number of influencing friends that adopted already such behavior surpasses a certain threshold. The authors refer the reader for further research works on this subject in (Kawachi, 2008; Sîrbu, Loreto, Servedio, & Tria, 2017; Das, Gollapudi & Munagala, 2014).

- **Independent Cascade Model:** The Independent Cascade model is a stochastic information diffusion model where the information circulates by means of cascade within the network. This model describes a diffusion process as active which means that the node already adopted or influenced by the information, and inactive which means that nodes are either unaware of the information or not yet influenced or touched by the information. The process takes place in discrete synchronized time steps. In each time step, each active node tries to activate each of its inactive neighbors. The activation of each inactive neighbor is determined by a probability of success. If an active node succeeds in achieving informing any of its neighbors, those neighbors become active in the next time step. The attempt of activation is independent of all previous attempts. This process stops when no further activation of nodes is possible (Shakarian, Bhatnagar, Aleali, Shaabani, & Guo, 2015).

- **Linear Threshold Models:** The users vary in the level in which they are affected by the behavior of others in their social system. The threshold model is also based on stochastic diffusion of information. The nodes are either active or inactive, and the model starts with an initial seed diffusing information. So, in the linear diffusion model, a node is influenced by each neighbor with a certain weight. Every node has a certain threshold value which presents its resilience to adopt a certain behavior or product. A node will adopt the behavior if and only if the sum of weights of influenced neighbors surpasses the threshold value. Then, the threshold model differs from Independent Cascade model on the way the spread of information occurs (Shakarian, Bhatnagar, Aleali, Shaabani, & Guo, 2015).

- **Evolutionary Graph Theory Models:** This kind of models is a class of stochastic diffusion models that has received much attention and is known as evolutionary graph theory (EGT). It models the spread of a mutant gene in a structured population. EGT investigates the capability of a mutant gene to overcome a finite structured population. The population's structure is represented as a directed graph and the diffusion process here is considered as the progression of the mutant gene across the population. The authors refer the reader to the following research papers for a deep understanding of this model and their extension (Lieberman, Hauert, & Nowak, 2005; Broom, Rychtář & Stadler, 2011).

Community Detection in Social Network

Community detection constitutes an effective way to analyze complex networks and smart manner to study large-scale network by studying structures of the underlying network that often holds structural and functional proprieties and then permits to gain useful insight from online users' activities.

Community detection is valuable in various domains, such as biology, social sciences, and computer networks. According to Yang, Liu, & Liu (2010) that defines a community as a group of nodes within which the links connecting nodes are dense but between communities, they are sparse. A community in a social network might indicate a circle of friends on Facebook, a group of pages on related topics on the Web.

Various surveys have investigated the study of community detection methods and classify these methods according to some criteria; here the authors try only to expose a survey on community detection methods.

The structures of communities and between communities are important for the demographic identification of network components and the function of dynamical processes that operate on networks such as the spread of opinion and disease. Fortunato provides an in-depth overview of several community detection methods based on graph representation (Fortunato, 2010). This survey gives a helpful summary of what is done in the field and describes in details the methodology of designing community detection techniques, based on a statistical physics perspective. So, the survey focuses on various techniques and classifies methods according to eight categories:

- Methods based on clustering, like k-means,
- Algorithms based on modularity,
- Statistical inference-based methods,
- Divisive algorithms based on hierarchical clustering,
- Spectral algorithms,
- Dynamic algorithms,
- Multi-resolution methods,
- Methods to find overlapping communities.

The survey carried by Papadopoulos, Kompatsiaris, Vakali, & Spyridonos (2012) classifies community detection methods into five categories:

- Cohesive subgraph discovery,
- Vertex clustering,
- Community quality optimization,
- Model-based divisive approach, and
- Model-based methods.

The survey conducted in (Porter, Onnela, & Mucha, 2009) includes only graph partitioning approaches. Various techniques are outlined; and then, application examples of these methods are also stated on some of the social networks graphs. They classified the techniques of community detection to following five categories:

- Centrality based techniques,
- Local methods around the k-Clique percolation method,
- Modularity optimization methods,
- Spectral partitioning methods, and
- Physics-based methods inspired by Potts law.

Anomaly Detection in Social Network

Outlier detection has received a great attention in recent time (Chakrabarti, 2004; Chandola, Banerjee, & Kumar, 2009) being a hard problem, despite its obvious simplicity. According to Chandola, Banerjee, & Kumar (2009) anomalies are called as outliers, abnormities, deviants, discordant, and exceptions. An anomaly refers to an individual data instance that is inconsistent with respect to the rest of the data. In other words, an anomaly is a set of activities that deviate from the normal and usual behavior of the user.

Anomaly detection on graphs of social or communication networks has significant security applications (Lane & Brodley, 1997). The definition of a graph anomaly specifically relies on the analyzed data and the domain of application and interest. Generally, an outlier or anomaly is any type of inconsistent and strange behavior of a user from the usual one in its neighborhood. Likewise, anomaly detection in social networks is the identification of such irregular and strange behavior which does not fit to the rest of the society.

Even the definition of an anomaly is very challenging since various factors should be considered and it varies following the domain of application. Hawkins (1980) defines an outlier as an observation that deviates so much from other observations as to arouse suspicion that it was generated by a different mechanism. Similarly, Barnett and Lewis (1994) assert that an outlier is one that appears to deviate markedly from the other members of the sample in which it occurs.

The anomaly detection can be categorized into two major types (Chandola, Banerjee, & Kumar, 2009):

- **Point Anomaly:** The abnormal behaviors of individual users
- **Group Anomaly:** The unusual patterns of groups of people

According to Chandola, Banerjee, & Kumar (2009), there is three types of anomaly detection used for social media which can be classified according to the following three criterion:

1. The first one depends on Anomaly Type, in this case, there are two types of research work, either a study deals with point anomaly detection or a group anomaly detection
2. The second concerns the data that the study used for anomaly detection; here there are two alternatives working with activity data or graph data for anomaly detection.
3. The last one is the temporal factor that takes into consideration the dynamic of social network to detect anomalous behaviors.

Link Prediction

Social networks are dynamic in nature since new nodes join the network by linking to existing users by creating new edges and some nodes leave the network which consequently removes all links to users within the network. Understanding the dynamics that drive the evolution of social network is a complex problem due to a large number of variable parameters. In the aim to alleviate this problem, one predicts or infers a link between two nodes. This could be studied in the dynamic social network or in a snapshot of social network that seeks to identify future interactions between users. This problem is referred as Link Prediction, and permits to predict the probability of a future link between two nodes, that are not previously linked in the social graph.

Of various research has been proposed, one of the interesting models of link prediction was proposed for the social network (Liben-Nowell & Kleinberg, 2007). They proposed a learning paradigm that extracts the similarity between a pair of nodes using various graph based similarity metrics and then computes the similarity scores between nodes and according to obtained scores, they predict a link between two nodes that are not previously connected.

Adamic and Adar (2003) computed the probability that uses similarity when two user pages are strongly related. They proceeded by calculating features that are shared between nodes and then specified the similarity implying these nodes.

Popescul and Ungar (2003) proposed a link prediction model based on statistical relational learning method to predict citations in scientific publications. The method requires carrying out a constrained search, in the space of database queries in order to generate selected features that will be used in a logistic regression to predict the presence or absence of a link between two entities. So, this method consists of two tasks which are a generation of features from relational data and their selection with statistical model selection criteria.

Various approaches have been proposed and carried out in the context of link prediction for social networks; the authors refer the reader to an in-depth literature review on this subject (Getoor, & Diehl, 2005; Wang, Xu, Wu, & Zhou, 2015).

Trust Computation in Social Network

Trust plays a crucial role in the relationship that links two users and in the intelligence and security domain in social networks. In general, it is a measure of belief that a user will act in an expected behavior.

It is a subjective concept that varies substantially between nation, situations, and social environment. Currently, trust in the majority of Online Social Networks (OSNs) is narrowed down to a simple personalized access control method for all users in a very simplified way.

On the one hand, trust in social networks cannot be expressed through the user activities; it should be always customized by the user. On the other hand, it is very difficult, to personalize and manage it manually, particularly with a great number of users. It is considered as the most important ingredient of valuable and successful communication, where users may connect and share their experiences and idea by using these OSNs. In summary, trust cannot be defined by a single consensus, it is a challenging concept to define exactly, what trust means or what its synonyms are.

In computer science, trust is an extensively used term whose definition varies among scientists and application areas. It is generally classified into two categories: user and system. The notion of user trust is defined as a subjective expectation an entity has about another's future behavior (Mui, 2002). In online systems, trust is based on the feedback on past interactions and behavior between members (Artz, & Gil, 2007; Resnick, Kuwabara, Zeckhauser, & Friedman, 2000).

A variety of trust models have been studied in the literature which are classified according to the tools used in the trust models. These techniques are based on statistical and machine learning approaches that provide a mathematical model for trust management, on heuristics approaches that concentrate on defining a model for implementing effective trust systems, and behavioral approaches which study and concentrate on user behavior within the network. Various techniques have been proposed in the literature (Klos, & La Poutré, 2005; Zhou, & Hwang, 2007; Xiong, & Liu, 2004; Mekouar, Ibrahimi, & Bouyakhf, 2014).

Most of these trust models, such as PowerTrust (Zhou & Hwang, 2007), PeerTrust (Xiong & Liu, 2004) and (Mekouar, Ibrahimi, & Bouyakhf, 2014), are based on feedback. The feedback is used to capture a user's experience when interacting with other users. Survey papers such as (Mui, Mohtashemi, & Halberstadt, 2002; Sabater & Sierra, 2005; Jøsang, Ismail, & Boyd, 2007), discuss trust models ranging from Bayesian networks to belief models that are all based on user experiences. Mekouar, Ibrahimi, &

Bouyakhf (2014), designed a computational model that compute trust between adjacent users based on direct interactions performed on exchanged contents by taking into account three type of relationship that can link users to the social network. Then, they compute trust between non-adjacent users based on Dempster-Shafer Theory.

Ruan and Durresi (2016) provided an interesting survey on trust modeling, inference, and attacks. They provided a review of previous trust management systems for online social communities. They also listed four attacks including naïve attack, in which attackers who have any knowledge about the system, provide misleading, dishonest recommendation to their neighbors; traitor attack, in which attackers provide at first honest recommendations to be trustworthy then they disseminate dishonest recommendation; Whitewashing attack in which attackers hide their identities and act like they are newcomers in the social media; and, collusion attack, in which attackers may use some or all previous kinds of attacks. Then they analyze the vulnerabilities of the existing system.

Jiang, Wang, Bhuiyan, and Wu (2016) concentrated on conducting a comparative review for two graph-based trust models including simplification by using some combination of trust path and analogy that relies on exploring the similarity to other graph-based models. Then, they discussed their individual challenges in which manifest on path length limitation, evidence availability, normalization and scalability. Then they outlined common challenges that manifest on trust decay, path dependence, opinion conflict and attack resistance.

FUTURE RESEARCH DIRECTIONS

Recently, social network analysis has witnessed unprecedented interest and popularity among scientists who tried to investigate in all of the aspects of the large social graph getting insight and knowledge from data. Many social networks exhibit large and rich data, which provides revolutionary opportunities, issues from data mining to analysis, processing and gaining insight, and extracting useful knowledge from phenomena inherent in social networks.

In this section, the authors try to provide readers from network science community with some useful research challenges that should be investigated and that are currently being considered by scientists as future research directions for further exploration. The authors try here to expose some research issues that face the research community to design a better, performant and secure social web graph.

Information Diffusion in Social Networks

Social networks can be used as a medium to promote new ideas, product or generally disseminate information. This permits the exchange of information and performs various interactions between users. However, the analysis of such behavior is challenging in a social network, since capturing and studying the dynamic of such interactions and exchange of contents are not easy to be completely known. As well as, the network over which diffusion takes place is, in fact, implicit or even unknown. For instance, the observed fact in the diffusion of information is only the node which gets infected, but the individual does not know who infected whom. Since users usually get new information without explicitly acknowledging the source who influence them (Chen, Lakshmanan, & Castillo, 2013; Guille, Hacid, Favre, & Zighed, 2013).

Community Detection and Analysis in Large Scale Social Networks

The problem of community detection is closely related to the problem of finding cohesive groups that have a lot of links (i.e., connections) with the members of the same group than members of other groups in the network. These structures are known and referred as 'communities'.

There are two types of research that deal with community detection which are non-overlapping communities that are investigated and discussed in various research papers (Goldberg, Kelley, Magdon-Ismail, Mertsalov, & Wallace, 2010). Methods for non-overlapping communities have been studied extensively (Xu, Xu, & Zhang, 2015).

The problem of community detection arises both in a static network in which the study concerned on a network snapshot, as well as in dynamic network in which network structure evolves over time. Another challenge is that there is a growing need to the design of scalable algorithms that deal with large-scale networks; researchers started to increasingly develop parallel and distributed algorithms for community detection in social networks. The multi-level algorithms that depend on graph coarsening and refinement provide good results (Abou-Rjeili & Karypis, 2006). As well as, the rise of the exploitation architecture algorithms based GPU and multi-cores give another orthogonal approach (Lacoste, Faverge, Bosilca, Ramet, & Thibault, 2014) and facilitate streaming algorithms (Saríyüce, Gedik, Jacques-Silva, Wu, & Çatalyürek, 2013). With the recent development of cloud computing, various algorithms have been designed for community detection based platforms such as Hadoop (Moon, Lee, & Kang, 2014) and Spark (Hung, Araujo, & Faloutsos, 2016).

Another challenge that arises in the context of community detection is community visualization, which constitutes an important task to visualize and identify structural and topological characteristic; displaying the behavior and membership of billion nodes is often running out of pixel space. In order to deal with that, one should display just the part of network that is of interest. A significant issue is to identify how dynamic information should be modeled and visualized effectively (Steinhaeuser & Chawla, 2008; Papadopoulos, Kompatsiaris, Vakali, & Spyridonos, 2012).

Link Prediction in Social Networks

Link prediction problem is of identifying important future linkages in the social network or identifying missing relationships in social graph data. Link prediction is useful in a variety of applications in the criminal network, for example in which one does not know the future bond of a terrorist in the terrorist network.

One of the major challenges of link prediction concerns the evolution of social networks like Facebook, MySpace, Twitter, and so on. These networks are huge in size and highly dynamic for which existing algorithms may not scale up and thus perform poorly on such large-scale graphs. This fact raises issues from data mining perspective, what should be done with such social graph data, what about the evaluation methodologies like the precision of the existing techniques (Al Hasan & Zaki, 2011).

Anomaly Detection in Social Networks

The main challenge faced is identifying outliers; one does not know what they are and even the definition of such concept is argued and not defined well. As well as, the existing algorithms suffer from scalability problems especially in streaming data and interpretation of statistical test fails to give us precise ideas and insight to detected anomalies. This is so especially when dealing with a large-scale data graph, which has a direct relationship with big data including its characteristics, namely volume, velocity, and a variety of massive, streaming datasets. Scale and dynamics of social graph data make it difficult to identify patterns and the majority of data are without any class labels, that is, why the ground truth of data instances are anomalous or non-anomalous is not known. Another issue is the rise of a novel anomaly, in which the more the fraudsters understand how the detection algorithms work, the more they change their techniques to hide their anomalous behaviors and try fit to the normal data (Savage, Zhang, Yu, Chou, & Wang, 2014).

Trust Computation in Social Networks

Trust is most essential and a crucial ingredient in all relationships between users in a social graph. There are various issues confronting trust in the social graphs: there are a vast number of users; easy to join & leave communities; individuals often interact with strangers who are not their friends or have encountered before. Another challenge is bootstrapping trust, that is, initial trust attribute value assigned to a new user. And, various properties of trust have received little attention in the literature, such as asymmetry, self-reinforcement, and event sensitivity.

The majority of approaches neglect the types, duration and intimacy of interactions, which constitute essential elements and provide a unique way of trust formation within the social graphs, and which need to be taken into account with the network structure. These aspects determine distinct types of trust relationships and trust levels within the community. These are important elements to include in trust model for social networks (Jøsang & Golbeck, 2009).

CONCLUSION

Social network analysis aims to measure qualitatively, quantitatively and analyze the intensity of the relationship between individuals and the influence on each other. As social networking becomes a powerful tool permitting users to interact, it alleviates performance of distinct kinds of activities every day. Outcomes of such interactions, both research investigation and practical applications on the social network, will continue to emerge and grow in use. Therefore, effective and efficient social network applications will be increasingly in high demand to satisfy the needs of users either ordinary users (internauts) or marketers, advertisers and so forth.

In this chapter, the authors focused on providing a brief overview of the field of social network analysis in a simple manner. The authors covered various aspects of social network analysis and described different techniques used in social network analysis from data mining paradigm. Then, they provided basic concepts of statistical measures of networks such as centralization, clustering coefficient, and exposes some network models studied in social network analysis. Thereafter, the authors provided an overview of some of the most influential applications studied in social network analysis and outlined issues and challenges that face each application for further research investigation.

This chapter provided a brief introduction to social network analysis and outlined advancement and limitation of some popular topics such as influence analysis, community detection, link prediction, and so on. This research area is still in development, and the authors anticipate that more techniques and methods will be developed in the future.

REFERENCES

Abou-Rjeili, A., & Karypis, G. (2006, April). Multilevel algorithms for partitioning power-law graphs. In *Parallel and Distributed Processing Symposium, 2006. IPDPS 2006. 20th International*. IEEE. 10.1109/IPDPS.2006.1639360

Adamic, L. A., & Adar, E. (2003). Friends and neighbors on the web. *Social Networks*, 25(3), 211–230. doi:10.1016/S0378-8733(03)00009-1

Adewole, K. S., Anuar, N. B., Kamsin, A., Varathan, K. D., & Razak, S. A. (2017). Malicious accounts: Dark of the social networks. *Journal of Network and Computer Applications*, 79, 41–67. doi:10.1016/j.jnca.2016.11.030

Akbaş, M. İ., Brust, M. R., Turgut, D., & Ribeiro, C. H. (2015). A preferential attachment model for primate social networks. *Computer Networks*, 76, 207–226. doi:10.1016/j.comnet.2014.11.009

Al Hasan, M., & Zaki, M. J. (2011). A survey of link prediction in social networks. In Social network data analytics (pp. 243-275). Springer US. doi:10.1007/978-1-4419-8462-3_9

Albert, R., & Barabási, A. L. (2002). Statistical mechanics of complex networks. *Reviews of Modern Physics*, 74(1), 47–97. doi:10.1103/RevModPhys.74.47

Artz, D., & Gil, Y. (2007). A survey of trust in computer science and the semantic web. *Journal of Web Semantics*, 5(2), 58–71. doi:10.1016/j.websem.2007.03.002

Bahlmann, C., Haasdonk, B., & Burkhardt, H. (2002). Online handwriting recognition with support vector machines-a kernel approach. In *Frontiers in handwriting recognition, 2002 proceedings, Eighth international workshop on* (pp. 49-54). IEEE. 10.1109/IWFHR.2002.1030883

Bailey, T. L., & Elkan, C. (1995). Unsupervised learning of multiple motifs in biopolymers using expectation maximization. *Machine Learning*, 21(1), 51–80. doi:10.1007/BF00993379

Ball, B., Karrer, B., & Newman, M. E. (2011). Efficient and principled method for detecting communities in networks. *Physical Review. E*, 84(3), 036103. doi:10.1103/PhysRevE.84.036103 PMID:22060452

Barnett, V., & Lewis, T. (1994). Outliers in statistical data: Vol. 3. *No. 1*. New York: Wiley.

Bastian, M., Heymann, S., & Jacomy, M. (2009). Gephi: an open source software for exploring and manipulating networks. *International AAAI Conference on Weblogs and Social Media*.

Batagelj, V., & Mrvar, A. (2003). Pajek - Analysis and Visualization of Large Networks. In *Graph Drawing Software*. Springer. Available from http://mrvar.fdv.uni-lj.si/pajek/default.htm

Bedi, P., & Sharma, C. (2016). Community detection in social networks. *Wiley Interdisciplinary Reviews. Data Mining and Knowledge Discovery*, 6(3), 115–135. doi:10.1002/widm.1178

Boser, B. E., Guyon, I. M., & Vapnik, V. N. (1992, July). A training algorithm for optimal margin classifiers. In *Proceedings of the fifth annual workshop on Computational learning theory* (pp. 144-152). ACM. 10.1145/130385.130401

Broder, A., Kumar, R., Maghoul, F., Raghavan, P., Rajagopalan, S., Stata, R., & Wiener, J. (2000). Graph structure in the web. *Computer Networks*, *33*(1), 309–320. doi:10.1016/S1389-1286(00)00083-9

Broom, M., Rychtář, J., & Stadler, B. T. (2011). Evolutionary dynamics on graphs-the effect of graph structure and initial placement on mutant spread. *Journal of Statistical Theory and Practice*, *5*(3), 369–381. doi:10.1080/15598608.2011.10412035

Centrifuge Analytics. (2017). Centrifuge Analytics v3(Version 3) [Software]. Available from http://centrifugesystems.com/

Chakrabarti, D. (2004, September). Autopart: Parameter-free graph partitioning and outlier detection. In *European Conference on Principles of Data Mining and Knowledge Discovery* (pp. 112-124). Springer. 10.1007/978-3-540-30116-5_13

Chandola, V., Banerjee, A., & Kumar, V. (2009). Anomaly detection: A survey. *ACM Computing Surveys (CSUR)*, *41*(3), 15.

Chen, W., Lakshmanan, L. V., & Castillo, C. (2013). Information and influence propagation in social networks. *Synthesis Lectures on Data Management*, *5*(4), 1–177. doi:10.2200/S00527ED1V01Y-201308DTM037

Cortes, C., & Vapnik, V. (1995). Support vector machine. *Machine Learning*, *20*(3), 273–297. doi:10.1007/BF00994018

Das, A., Gollapudi, S., & Munagala, K. (2014, February). Modeling opinion dynamics in social networks. In *Proceedings of the 7th ACM international conference on Web search and data mining* (pp. 403-412). ACM. 10.1145/2556195.2559896

Easley, D., & Kleinberg, J. (2007, Spring). The small-world phenomenon. *Networks*.

EgoNet. (2017). Egocentric Network Study Software [Software]. Available from https://omictools.com/egocentric-network-study-software-tool

Erçetin, Ş. Ş., & Neyişci, N. B. (2016). Social Network Analysis: A Brief Introduction to the Theory. In *Chaos, Complexity and Leadership 2014* (pp. 167–171). Cham: Springer. doi:10.1007/978-3-319-18693-1_16

Fortunato, S. (2010). Community detection in graphs. *Physics Reports*, *486*(3), 75–174. doi:10.1016/j.physrep.2009.11.002

Freeman, L. C. (1978). Centrality in social networks conceptual clarification. *Social Networks*, *1*(3), 215–239. doi:10.1016/0378-8733(78)90021-7

Getoor, L., & Diehl, C. P. (2005). Link mining: A survey. *ACM SIGKDD Explorations Newsletter*, *7*(2), 3–12. doi:10.1145/1117454.1117456

Getoor, L., Friedman, N., Koller, D., & Taskar, B. (2001, June). Learning probabilistic models of relational structure. In ICML (Vol. 1, pp. 170-177). Academic Press.

Goldberg, M., Kelley, S., Magdon-Ismail, M., Mertsalov, K., & Wallace, A. (2010, August). Finding overlapping communities in social networks. In *Social Computing (SocialCom), 2010 IEEE Second International Conference on* (pp. 104-113). IEEE. 10.1109/SocialCom.2010.24

Granovetter, M., & Soong, R. (1983). Threshold models of diffusion and collective behavior. *The Journal of Mathematical Sociology*, 9(3), 165–179. doi:10.1080/0022250X.1983.9989941

Guille, A., Hacid, H., Favre, C., & Zighed, D. A. (2013). Information diffusion in online social networks: A survey. *SIGMOD Record*, 42(2), 17–28. doi:10.1145/2503792.2503797

Hartigan, J. A., & Wong, M. A. (1979). Algorithm AS 136: A k-means clustering algorithm. *Journal of the Royal Statistical Society. Series C, Applied Statistics*, 28(1), 100–108.

Hawkins, D. M. (1980). *Identification of outliers* (Vol. 11). London: Chapman and Hall. doi:10.1007/978-94-015-3994-4

Hu, W., Liao, Y., & Vemuri, V. R. (2003, June). Robust Support Vector Machines for Anomaly Detection in Computer Security. In ICMLA (pp. 168-174). Academic Press.

Hung, S. C., Araujo, M., & Faloutsos, C. (2016). Distributed community detection on edge-labeled graphs using spark. In *12th International Workshop on Mining and Learning with Graphs (MLG)* (Vol. 113). Academic Press.

Improved Outcomes Software Inc. (2004, January). K-Means Clustering Overview [Web log comment]. Retrieved from http://www.improvedoutcomes.com/docs/WebSiteDocs/Clustering/K-Means_Clustering_Overview.htm. (2017, August 10).

Jiang, B., Zhang, Z. L., & Towsley, D. (2015, August). Reciprocity in social networks with capacity constraints. In *Proceedings of the 21th ACM SIGKDD International Conference on Knowledge Discovery and Data Mining* (pp. 457-466). ACM. 10.1145/2783258.2783410

Jiang, W., Wang, G., Bhuiyan, M. Z. A., & Wu, J. (2016). Understanding graph-based trust evaluation in online social networks: Methodologies and challenges. *ACM Computing Surveys*, 49(1), 10. doi:10.1145/2906151

Jøsang, A., & Golbeck, J. (2009, September). Challenges for robust trust and reputation systems. In *Proceedings of the 5th International Workshop on Security and Trust Management (SMT 2009)* (p. 52). Academic Press.

Jøsang, A., Ismail, R., & Boyd, C. (2007). A survey of trust and reputation systems for online service provision. *Decision Support Systems*, 43(2), 618–644. doi:10.1016/j.dss.2005.05.019

Kanungo, T., Mount, D. M., Netanyahu, N. S., Piatko, C. D., Silverman, R., & Wu, A. Y. (2002). An efficient k-means clustering algorithm: Analysis and implementation. *IEEE Transactions on Pattern Analysis and Machine Intelligence*, 24(7), 881–892. doi:10.1109/TPAMI.2002.1017616

Kawachi, K. (2008). Deterministic models for rumor transmission. *Nonlinear Analysis Real World Applications*, 9(5), 1989–2028. doi:10.1016/j.nonrwa.2007.06.004

Kimura, M., & Saito, K. (2006). Tractable models for information diffusion in social networks. *Knowledge Discovery in Databases: PKDD, 2006,* 259–271.

Klos, T. B., & La Poutré, H. (2005). Decentralized reputation-based trust for assessing agent reliability under aggregate feedback. *Lecture Notes in Computer Science, 3577,* 110–128. doi:10.1007/11532095_7

Knoke, D., & Yang, S. (2008). *Social network analysis* (Vol. 154). Sage. doi:10.4135/9781412985864

Koller, D. (1999, June). Probabilistic relational models. In *International Conference on Inductive Logic Programming* (pp. 3-13). Springer. 10.1007/3-540-48751-4_1

Lacoste, X., Faverge, M., Bosilca, G., Ramet, P., & Thibault, S. (2014, May). Taking advantage of hybrid systems for sparse direct solvers via task-based runtimes. In *Parallel & Distributed Processing Symposium Workshops (IPDPSW), 2014 IEEE International* (pp. 29-38). IEEE. 10.1109/IPDPSW.2014.9

Lane, T., & Brodley, C. E. (1997, July). Sequence matching and learning in anomaly detection for computer security. In *AAAI Workshop: AI Approaches to Fraud Detection and Risk Management* (pp. 43-49). AAAI.

Liben-Nowell, D., and Kleinberg, J. (2007). The link-prediction problem for social networks. *Journal of the Association for Information Science and Technology, 58*(7), 1019-1031.

Lieberman, E., Hauert, C., & Nowak, M. A. (2005). Evolutionary dynamics on graphs. *Nature, 433*(7023), 312–316. doi:10.1038/nature03204 PMID:15662424

Mekouar, S., El-Hammani, S., Ibrahimi, K., & Bouyakhf, E. H. (2015, May). Optimizing Diffusion Time of the Content Through the Social Networks: *Stochastic Learning Game. In International Conference on Networked Systems* (pp. 367-381). Springer International Publishing.

Mekouar, S., Ibrahimi, K., & Bouyakhf, E. H. (2014, August). Inferring trust relationships in the social network: Evidence theory approach. In *Wireless Communications and Mobile Computing Conference (IWCMC), 2014 International* (pp. 470-475). IEEE.

Mekouar, S., Zrira, N., & Bouyakhf, E. H. (in press). Community outlier detection in social networks based on graph matching. *International Journal of Autonomous and Adaptive Communications Systems.*

Moon, S., Lee, J. G., & Kang, M. (2014, January). Scalable community detection from networks by computing edge betweenness on mapreduce. In *Big Data and Smart Computing (BIGCOMP), 2014 International Conference on* (pp. 145-148). IEEE.

Moon, T. K. (1996). The expectation-maximization algorithm. *IEEE Signal Processing Magazine, 13*(6), 47–60. doi:10.1109/79.543975

Mui, L. (2002). *Computational models of trust and reputation: Agents, evolutionary games, and social networks* (Doctoral dissertation). Massachusetts Institute of Technology.

Mui, L., Mohtashemi, M., & Halberstadt, A. (2002, July). Notions of reputation in multi-agents systems: a review. In *Proceedings of the first international joint conference on Autonomous agents and multiagent systems: part 1* (pp. 280-287). ACM. 10.1145/544741.544807

Nam, D. H. (2017) Prediction of Concrete Compressive Strength Using Multivariate Feature Extraction with Neuro fuzzy Systems. In *Int'l Conf. Information and Knowledge Engineering IKE'17* (pp 46-51). Academic Press.

Neville, J., & Jensen, D. (2007). Relational dependency networks. *Journal of Machine Learning Research*, *8*(Mar), 653–692.

Newman, M. (2010). *Networks: an introduction*. Oxford University Press. doi:10.1093/acprof:oso/9780199206650.001.0001

Osuna, E., Freund, R., & Girosit, F. (1997, June). Training support vector machines: an application to face detection. In Computer vision and pattern recognition, 1997. Proceedings. 1997 IEEE computer society conference on (pp. 130-136). IEEE. doi:10.1109/CVPR.1997.609310

Pan, H., & Liu, L. (1999). Fuzzy bayesian networks-a general formalism for representation, inference and learning with hybrid bayesian networks. In *Neural Information Processing, 1999. Proceedings. ICONIP'99. 6th International Conference on* (Vol. 1, pp. 401-406). IEEE. 10.1109/ICONIP.1999.844022

Papadopoulos, S., Kompatsiaris, Y., Vakali, A., & Spyridonos, P. (2012). Community detection in social media. *Data Mining and Knowledge Discovery*, *24*(3), 515–554. doi:10.100710618-011-0224-z

Piater, J. H. (2002). *Mixture models and expectation-maximization*. Lecture at ENSIMAG.

Popescul, A., & Ungar, L. H. (2003, August). Statistical relational learning for link prediction. In IJCAI workshop on learning statistical models from relational data (Vol. 2003). Academic Press.

Porter, M. A., Onnela, J. P., & Mucha, P. J. (2009). Communities in networks. *Notices of the American Mathematical Society*, *56*(9), 1082–1097.

Resnick, P., Kuwabara, K., Zeckhauser, R., & Friedman, E. (2000). Reputation systems. *Communications of the ACM*, *43*(12), 45–48. doi:10.1145/355112.355122

Rogers, E. M. (1976). New product adoption and diffusion. *The Journal of Consumer Research*, *2*(4), 290–301. doi:10.1086/208642

Ruan, Y., & Durresi, A. (2016). A survey of trust management systems for online social communities–Trust modeling, trust inference and attacks. *Knowledge-Based Systems*, *106*, 150–163. doi:10.1016/j.knosys.2016.05.042

Sabater, J., & Sierra, C. (2005). Review on computational trust and reputation models. *Artificial Intelligence Review*, *24*(1), 33–60. doi:10.100710462-004-0041-5

Safavian, S. R., & Landgrebe, D. (1991). A survey of decision tree classifier methodology. *IEEE Transactions on Systems, Man, and Cybernetics*, *21*(3), 660–674. doi:10.1109/21.97458

Sailer, L. D. (1978). Structural equivalence: Meaning and definition, computation and application. *Social Networks*, *1*(1), 73–90. doi:10.1016/0378-8733(78)90014-X

Sarıyüce, A. E., Gedik, B., Jacques-Silva, G., Wu, K. L., & Çatalyürek, Ü. V. (2013). Streaming algorithms for k-core decomposition. *Proceedings of the VLDB Endowment International Conference on Very Large Data Bases*, *6*(6), 433–444. doi:10.14778/2536336.2536344

Savage, D., Zhang, X., Yu, X., Chou, P., & Wang, Q. (2014). Anomaly detection in online social networks. *Social Networks*, *39*, 62–70. doi:10.1016/j.socnet.2014.05.002

Scholz, F. W. (1985). Maximum likelihood estimation. Encyclopedia of statistical sciences.

Serrat, O. (2017). Social network analysis. In *Knowledge solutions* (pp. 39–43). Springer Singapore. doi:10.1007/978-981-10-0983-9_9

Shakarian, P., Bhatnagar, A., Aleali, A., Shaabani, E., & Guo, R. (2015). The Independent Cascade and Linear Threshold Models. In Diffusion in Social Networks (pp. 35-48). Springer International Publishing. doi:10.1007/978-3-319-23105-1_4

Sîrbu, A., Loreto, V., Servedio, V. D., & Tria, F. (2017). Opinion dynamics: models, extensions and external effects. In Participatory Sensing, Opinions and Collective Awareness (pp. 363-401). Springer International Publishing. doi:10.1007/978-3-319-25658-0_17

Sloughter, J. M. L., Raftery, A. E., Gneiting, T., & Fraley, C. (2007). Probabilistic quantitative precipitation forecasting using Bayesian model averaging. *Monthly Weather Review*, *135*(9), 3209–3220. doi:10.1175/MWR3441.1

Snijders, T. (2012). *Transitivity and triads*. University of Oxford. Retrieved from http://www.stats.ox.ac.uk/snijders/Trans_Triads_ha.pdf

Steinhaeuser, K., & Chawla, N. V. (2008). Community detection in a large real-world social network. *Social computing, behavioral modeling, and prediction*, 168-175.

Tang, H., & Liu, S. (2007, August). Basic theory of fuzzy Bayesian networks and its application in machinery fault diagnosis. In *Fuzzy Systems and Knowledge Discovery, 2007. FSKD 2007. Fourth International Conference on* (Vol. 4, pp. 132-137). IEEE. 10.1109/FSKD.2007.202

Team, N. W. B. (2006). Network Workbench Tool [Software]. Indiana University, Northeastern University, and University of Michigan. Available from http://nwb.slis.indiana.edu

Van Der Hofstad, R. (2016). Random graphs and complex networks. *Cambridge Series in Statistical and probabilistic Mathematics, 43*.

Van Laarhoven, T., & Marchiori, E. (2013). Network community detection with edge classifiers trained on LFR graphs. ESANN.

Wang, P., Xu, B., Wu, Y., & Zhou, X. (2015). Link prediction in social networks: The state-of-the-art. *Science China. Information Sciences*, *58*(1), 1–38.

Wasserman, S., & Faust, K. (1994). *Social network analysis: Methods and applications* (Vol. 8). Cambridge university press. doi:10.1017/CBO9780511815478

Xiong, L., & Liu, L. (2004). Peertrust: Supporting reputation-based trust for peer-to-peer electronic communities. *IEEE Transactions on Knowledge and Data Engineering*, *16*(7), 843–857. doi:10.1109/TKDE.2004.1318566

Xu, Y., Xu, H., & Zhang, D. (2015). A novel disjoint community detection algorithm for social networks based on backbone degree and expansion. *Expert Systems with Applications*, *42*(21), 8349–8360. doi:10.1016/j.eswa.2015.06.042

Yang, B., Liu, D., & Liu, J. (2010). Discovering communities from social networks: Methodologies and applications. In Handbook of social network technologies and applications (pp. 331-346). Springer US.

Zadeh, L. A. (1965). Fuzzy sets. *Information and Control*, *8*(3), 338–353. doi:10.1016/S0019-9958(65)90241-X

Zhao, P., & Han, J. (2010). On graph query optimization in large networks. *Proceedings of the VLDB Endowment International Conference on Very Large Data Bases*, *3*(1-2), 340–351. doi:10.14778/1920841.1920887

Zhou, R., & Hwang, K. (2007). Powertrust: A robust and scalable reputation system for trusted peer-to-peer computing. *IEEE Transactions on Parallel and Distributed Systems*, *18*(4), 460–473. doi:10.1109/TPDS.2007.1021

KEY TERMS AND DEFINITIONS

Anomaly Detection: Is the detection of the noise, misbehavior, incoherent data point in the data that deviate markedly from the rest of the data.

Centralization: In this chapter is a set of metrics such as degree centrality, closeness centrality, Katz centrality, and so forth that permit us to know in which extent a user within the network is central.

Community Detection: Is of methods that permit to identify a group of users that share the same interest and make them into the same group other than the users who do not share the same interest.

Data Mining: Is the process of analyzing for knowledge discovery in databases to identify patterns and gain knowledge from large data sets.

Influence Propagation: Is the process by which the information is exchanged and transmitted within a network.

Link Prediction: Is a method that estimates the probability that two nodes that are not currently connected will be connected in the future.

Network Models: Refer to the types of graph appearing in social network analysis, such as a random graph, scale free network, and small world network.

Network Structures: Refer to the process of network formation, characteristics and properties that governs the formation, such as transitivity, reciprocity, and others.

Trust Computation Models: A set of computational models that compute trust between adjacent and non-adjacent users within the network.

Chapter 18
Effective Entity Linking and Disambiguation Algorithms for User–Generated Content (UGC)

Senthil Kumar Narayanasamy
VIT University, India

Dinakaran Muruganantham
VIT University, India

ABSTRACT

The exponential growth of data emerging out of social media is causing challenges in decision-making systems and poses a critical hindrance in searching for the potential information. The major objective of this chapter is to convert the unstructured data in social media into the meaningful structure format, which in return brings the robustness to the information extraction process. Further, it has the inherent capability to prune for named entities from the unstructured data and store the entities into the knowledge base for important facts. In this chapter, the authors explain the methods to identify all the critical interpretations taken over to find the named entities from Twitter streams and the techniques to proportionally link it with appropriate knowledge sources such as DBpedia.

INTRODUCTION

The conventional methods followed for information extraction in text documents (as they are structured and well-formed) is totally different with information extraction in social media contents. The social media contents are mostly unstructured and especially ill-formed to extract the information from it. As stated by the authors Laere, Schockaert, Tanasescu, Dhoedt, & Jones (2014) and Giridhar, Abdelzaher, George, & Kaplan (2015, March), it was estimated that the accuracy rate of precision in structured documents is pointing to 89% whereas unstructured documents hold below 64%. To culminate this difference, several approaches have been discussed and techniques were proposed to boost the precision and recall rate of unstructured documents as given by Lee, Ganti, Srivatsa, & Li (2014, December) and Imran, Castillo, Diaz, & Vieweg (2015); but still, problems persist and pertaining in many situations. In

DOI: 10.4018/978-1-5225-5384-7.ch018

order to streamline the accuracy rate over precision and recall, we have here proposed some methods to augment the precision and use new strategies to overcome the impeding difficulties.

To start with the extraction process, the principal task is to find the potential named entities out from the unstructured text. In our case, we have taken Twitter social media content and identified the named entities from its streams. But the objectivity comes when we deal with real world entities which have been mapped with one-to-many cardinality over knowledge sources and pinches in for the major setbacks for further processes. Besides as the tweets are very short and most of the instances informal in nature, finding potential named entities out of tweet is a crucial task for any automated systems. This sort of ambiguity conundrum is very high in information retrieval context and yields huge difficulties to Named Entity Recognition (NER) systems. To conduct entity identification process, we have used the Markov Network (Lee et al., 2014, December), that was deployed for many conventional information extraction tasks and yielded high accuracy rate. In our cases as we have taken Twitter social media streams, the entities were represented with nodes and the edges will get connected between the conditional dependencies over selected named entities. If we dig deep closer to this whole network, it would almost resemble to Bayesian Network except the fact that edges were cyclic and undirected. For any document, the entity is appropriately mapped with its sheer interpretation of selected named entities suggested by the knowledge source. In some worst cases as we had witnessed in the empirical results, it has shown that few entities has no link to relate with the knowledge source and it has paved way for ambiguous connection and lead to bad search results. This was taken as one of the research gap identified in the extraction process and we had given the solution for the same in the following sections.

The Hidden Markov Model uses many language processing tasks such as POS tagging, Named Entity Detection, and Classification, etc. In this proposed approach, we have taken Twitter as a social media site and carry out the process of identifying the potential named entities from Twitter streams. As the tweets are very short and noisy, finding named entities is a challenging task and linking named entities to appropriate knowledge base mentions is yet another cumbersome process to deal with. Hence, in this proposed system, we have explained the mechanism to link entities to knowledge base, removing the ambiguity persisting over the extracted named entities and enhance the capabilities of searching much easier than before using semantic Web technologies like RDF/SPARQL.

Linking to Web Content

This part of the framework manages extraction of all the entities identified with the entered term from Web. This can comprehensively incorporate Wikipedia pages, news articles, blog entries, and so on. To catch a feeling of all the entities identified with the entered search term, the procedure is done in two levels. At the primary level there is an ordinary 'Google Search' through the programming interface. For example, R programming utilizes the 'getGoogleURL' and 'getGoogleLinks' calls to scan for the given subject. It impersonates an ordinary Web search however specifically posts the list items on the R interface. These outcomes frame the premise of the rundown. At the second level of handling a few connections are chosen from the Google list items and the entities on these site pages are scratched for synopsis. The RCurl bundle in R for writing computer programs is one of the effectively accessible bundles that permit content extraction upon providing it with a URL. Consequently, at this level of handling, we get all the Web content accessible on the World Wide Web relating to the point.

The essential partner of engineering is the potential users of the system. The user enters the query for acquiring search results and consequently is the essential hotspot for the information. The user is then returned the results of the particular rundown, top tweets, information from the cloud and so forth. Our proposed framework catches the setting of the subject by condensing pre-accessible Web content on the premise of highlights produced from user tweets. It subsequently carries out disambiguation to invalidate the unfitting (Bunescu & Pasca, 2006, April). The whole procedure involves three noteworthy advances: Extraction, Retrieval and Filtration as explained point by point below.

Identification and Extraction of Tweets

This is the initial step of the framework. The user enters the subject for synopsis on the interface which is then conveyed forward for extraction from Twitter. Openly accessible Twitter outsider applications are utilized for this extraction of tweets. OAuth is the official API utilized for extraction. The API is provided with the string variable that stores the expression; then the API plays out a consecutive look for tweets in view of the expression and subsequently 450 tweets containing the expression are returned in about 10 seconds. The tweets are at first put away in a .json record; they are then utilized by stacking into a content record for additionally handling.

Potential Retrieval of Web Content

The highlight of our proposed framework is the use of effectively accessible entities to shape the search results. The accessible entities are those on the Internet identified with that subject. The pages are put away as a content record and utilized later during the outline step.

Filtration

The tweets gathered after extraction is then handled further to remove non-English tweets, spams, rages, unessential information and different wellsprings of deception. The framework throws away all the non-English tweets, halting words, stems those tweets, relates a level of importance on the tweets, and produces a recurrence tally of the considerable number of words after filtration. Subsequently, an arrangement of the most frequent phrases, which have the greatest weight from the gathered tweets, is created.

RELATED WORKS

As indicated by authors (Derczynski et al., 2015), they have distinguished distinctive sorts of named entities, and grouped the entities into their separate class of spaces. Besides, locating appropriate relationships existing between the entities is also needed. A portion of the Named Entity Taggers have been utilized to discover the entities in various sorts of reports and ordered it. Further to that, with a specific goal to discover the classification of entities, the ideal approach depicted by (Bunescu & Pasca, 2006, April), that they have summed up the entity types as areas, people, associations, timestamp, and so forth. At the same time, most of the entity types fall under the classification as stated above. It has encouraged the way toward settling the proper spaces to the entities and connecting the entities to the right level of importance.

In the paper (Presutti et al, 2014, November), the authors recognized the potential entities from the tweets and utilized Wikipedia as helpful asset for distinguishing the potential candidate entities from the documents. As indicated by (Lee, et al., 2014, December), the named entities are extricated; ranking the entities is the essential assignment which requires scrutiny over the entity sets. Eventually, the authors did entity level ranking by utilizing INEX and TREC. A few methodologies had been endeavored from that point in ranking the named entities but marginally failed to satisfy the significant changes to be joined in this procedure. In addition, lexical comparability measures were employed to classify the entities into a single cluster when the entities are excessively vague. This significance relevance was utilized to shift through the mentions which didn't link to its appropriate Wikipedia content.

Mendes, Jakob, García-Silva, & Bizer (2011, September) created DBpedia Spotlight for clarifying the content with DBpedia URIs. The absolute capacity of the DBpedia Spotlight is that it initially recognizes the entities in the given sentences and matches with appropriate mention with the DBpedia entity. Disambiguating the entity against the arrangement of DBpedia mention is the testing assignment and for that it took Vector Space Model (VSM). The significant hindrance in this proposed approach is that it did not secure the out of the vocabulary sets (OOV) and NULL mention sets.

In the paper (Bansal, 2014), the author stated out the problems of dealing with the disambiguated entity sets in Twitter streams. The author proposed some way to deal with disambiguated entity sets utilizing three components: 1) Find the similarity between the entity in tweet and its relating element in Wikipedia URL; 2) Find the Jaccard Similarity amongst entities and content over different sites; and 3) Estimating the prominence of the mentions utilizing Twitter Trends. In spite of the fact that it appears to have tackled the blocking issues of disambiguation, effectiveness of the approach definitely addressed, and the time computation of this approach was drastically increased.

The significant commitment of the paper (Alahmari, Thom, & Magee, 2014) is that it depicted about the issue of entity description i.e., giving potential users the important certainties about the selected entity. They took three key parameters to appraise this errand, for example, mention detection, entity type and properties. For the user query ambiguity, they recognized two sorts of vagueness; one is semantic polysemy which entails when one mention is colliding with different true entities. Second, semantic synonymy which is different mentions are connecting with one appropriate entity. Despite the fact that they have proposed this approach, it has the deficiency of semantic introduction of entity linking and entity disambiguation.

ENTITY EXTRACTION AND CLASSIFICATION

Provided the tweet streams of the predefined occasion, the assignment is to extricate the potential named entities and identify the dependency connections between the named entities and other related mentions in the tweets. Considering this as a challenging task to perform, we have marginally adjusted the Standard POS Tagger calculation (Gattani et al., 2013) and proposed the new calculation as indicated by the prerequisite of our extraction study. In the Standard POS Tagger, the parser divides the sentences and gathers Noun Phrases, Verb Phrases and so forth and gives the suitable naming for all the isolated tokens. In any case, there is an issue in the technique that it considers the classification of each occurrence in the sentence. The goal of this exploration is to interface the distinguished entities to suitable learning bases and allow the machine to escalate the data stream of the extracted entities (see Figure 1). Henceforth, the reason for examining the entities prevalently occurred in the tweets fizzled in the event that we simply take after the standard POS tagger. In this way, we take a heuristic look at the sheer class of noted instances and expand its semantic closeness to its proximity.

Algorithm 1

Input: Load the tweet streams $\left(T_1, T_2, \ldots T_n\right)$ for the event (T_E)

Output: Detect the potential named entities $\left(N_1, N_2, \ldots N_i\right)$ without any ambiguity

Begin:

- **Step 1:** For each named entity (N_i) from the tweet (T_n), recognize a URI that totally delineate mention (m) in the information base (KB).
- **Step 2:** Suppose for the named entity (N_i), there would be more than one mention in the information base, the connection likelihood (Hellmann, Stadler, Lehmann, & Auer. 2009) for a mention m to the entity e would be figured as:

$$F_{(e,m)} = \frac{\text{Count}(m, e)}{Count(m)}$$

- ○ **Step 2.1:** Then the potential mention can be distinguished by utilizing the minimum edit distance method.
- ○ **Step 2.2:** Then utilize the suitable ontologies to disambiguate the mentions which have been positioned in minimum edit distance measure and select the entities that are fall in a similar class of decisions.
- ○ **Step 2.3:** Select the potential entity which have high rank and measure up to likeness in the information base.
- **Step 3:** Link that potential entity to the information base.

End

As stated in the above algorithm, it has given the particular way of selecting the candidate entity sets and its significant mention detection strategies. When we manage the procedure of entity - mention identification between the named entity from the tweets and the mention predominance in the knowledge base like DBpedia (Presutti, et al., 2014, November) and Milne & Witten (2008, October), the mention detection ought to be made simple and predominant. In such manner, the DBpedia (Hellmann et al., 2009) has proclaimed the Infobox which holds the points of interest of the entity and gives the fitting URL connecting to different pages for a portion of the entities. Consequently, to the setting of semantic relatedness between the named entities from the tweets and mention detection from the DBpedia Infobox, we have characterized it as follows:

$$S(e, m) = SR\left(e, \ C_{\text{Infobox}}(m)\right)$$

The advantage of using the Infobox is that it gives the supplementary facts about the given entity, for instance, the entity Barack Obama would give the relational attributes like Occupation and Spouse that links to other entities in the DBpedia. Hence, it gives the search context further facilitating and robust by transforming the entity object into Linked Data. But the Infobox has some inherent drawbacks such as birth places; some canonical names have no specific links found on the DBpedia.

Entity Linking and Disambiguation

Entity Linking (EL) is the significant procedure of recognizing named entity sets from Web-based social networking webpage (e.g. Twitter) and connecting them to the proper URI in the referenced knowledge base (e.g. DBpedia). Once in a while, amid the procedure of entity mapping, there would be the shot of distinguishing the named entities which are altogether pointing to different named entities in the knowledge base. In such cases, we have to cluster those comparable named entity sets and apply the Vector Space Model (VSM) to proportionately rank the entity sets as per the comparability measures ascertained. Through this, we identify the unique entry for the ambiguous named entity into the knowledge base. These equivocal issues were prevailing (Zwicklbauer, Seifert, & Granitzer, 2013, September) in Information Retrieval as far as Word Sense Disambiguation (WSD). Many investigations, such as Bunescu & Pasca (2006, April) and Kulkarni, Singh, Ramakrishnan, & Chakrabarti (2009, June), were completed in Word Sense Disambiguation to remove the difference in the data. Currently we are relating the WSD techniques to entity linking for yielding higher exactness and review for the mapping of appropriate entity set.

By and large, the disambiguation strategies are grouped into supervised techniques, unsupervised strategies and knowledge based strategies. The administered strategies are essentially machine learning methods which ordinarily gather the outcomes in view of the informational index. It is a Decision List containing some arrangement of proposed leads and orders the results through the If–then-else method. The unsupervised strategies are not deriving anything from the distracted datasets. Rather, it has completely dependent on associated words in the neighboring settings. The co-referenced words in the content would frame a cluster which focuses to a similar subject or referring to a similar sense. In less difficult terms, it clusters the words which are semantically comparative. Despite the above stated methods, the information based strategies have utilized the learning assets, (for example, Dictionaries, Collocations, Thesaurus, Ontologies) to adequately disambiguate the entities and yields better outcomes when contrasted with the other two supervised techniques. Subsequently we have taken this last technique to propose an answer for entity linking from the tweets to the connected knowledge base.

PROPOSED WORK

In this section, we propose the issue and computational strategies to tackle the obstructing challenges in the Web-based social networking content (e.g., Twitter) and make the posts more sensible and unambiguous. The major focus pinning here is to order the arrangement of tweets $T = \left(T_1, T_2, \ldots T_n \right)$ regardless of whether they are identified with the given particular event E. Initially, we guarantee that each tweet Ti is identified with the event E, $related\left(T_i, E \right)$ if and only if the tweet is connected or has a place with the classification of the predefined event.

The preparatory approach for the proposed work comprises of three stages: Entity Detection, Feature Extractor and Entity Ranking, and Category Similarity Score.

Figure 1. Proposed architecture for the system

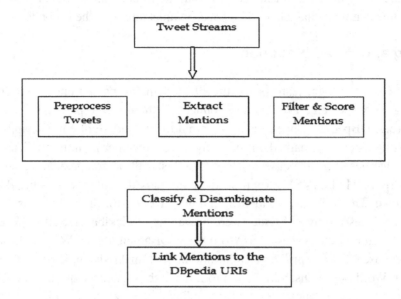

Entity Detection: Named Entity Identification Strategies

Given the tweet $T = \left(T_1, T_2, \ldots\ldots T_n \right)$ for the predefined event E, we have to preprocess the tweet such that it eliminates the whitespaces, separators, emoticons, client IDs, URLs, HTML labels and so on and complete the lightweight POS labeling to distinguish the formal people, places or things from the tweets. At that point, we have to group them as potential named entities and recognize the conceivable connections in the DBpedia knowledge base. For characterization, we have connected Naïve Bayes Classifier (Cano Basave, Varga, Rowe, Stankovic, & Dadzie, 2013) to channel the extracted noun phrases (tokens) from the tweets and connected them to the suitable named entities. The Naïve Bayes Classifier can separate the named entities by assuming the following facts:

1.   If the selected candidate entity from the tweets found on the WordNet;
2.   If the candidate entity shown its presence in DBpedia Knowledge Base;
3.   If the candidate entity has given the path to the valid link in any Web sites.

The entity recognition and disambiguation is the real work of the data recovery and we have given below (Table 1) the measurable execution of entity detection strategies.

Table 1. Performance of entity detection techniques

Entity Detection Technique	Accuracy
ARK POS TAGGER	77%
T-NER POS TAGGER	92%
ARK + T-NER (Merged)	98%

Given the measure of tweets T for the predetermined event E, the challenge is to recognize the events in the tweets T which fall in the class of given entity sets "e" on the given time interval. Subsequently to decide the capacity for the entity selection from the tweets, it needs to set as related or not related. For each tweet t, we have to recognize the entity sets e with the goal that it would relate that element to the predefined occasion.

$$f(t) = T \rightarrow \{related | not related\}$$

That is,

$$f(t) = \begin{cases} related & if\, t \in Te \\ Not\, related & Otherwise \end{cases}$$

The confusion matrix for evaluation the entity relatedness and filtering is as follows (Table 2).

Subsequently we have taken the ARK POS tagger combined with T-NER POS tagger for separating the named entities from the tweets given and split the tweets into potential tokens (i.e. Named Entities). In addition, there were some words not well framed occurred in the tweets and normalizing the poorly shaped words is the testing task (Gattani, et al., 2013). The standardization of badly framed words is taken and we picked the applicable word in view of the quantity of lexical proximity score.

Feature Extractor and Entity Linking

When we identified the potential named entities from the tweets, we have to interface them to the fitting knowledge base like DBpedia to increase its setting relatedness and get the vicinity of perception. Keeping in mind the goal to play out this undertaking, the entity occurrences ought to be checked against at DBpedia Infobox and data introduced in the Infobox ought to be mapped with named entity selection in the tweets. Thus, we characterize the task (Hogan, Zimmermann, Umbrich, Polleres, & Decker, 2012) of named entity (e_i) to delineate with the mention (m_j) in the Infobox as:

$$F(e, m) = \begin{cases} 1\, if\, e \in C_{info}(m) \\ 0\, Otherwise \end{cases}$$

Amid this mapping procedure, it had been noticed that there were many mentions connecting to the candidate named entities (i.e., one – to – many cardinality). As per the DBpedia pages (Bunescu &

Table 2. Confusion matrix for entity relatedness

	Related	Not Related
Related	True Positive	False Positive
Not Related	False Negative	True Negative

Pasca, 2006, April), the entities may have a few implications and connections to various DBpedia URIs. For example, "Bank" can be connected to 'Savings Bank' or 'Government Bank' or mapped with 'Bank shores'. In the event that we take the entity "Panther", it may be a creature or an automobile product yet it has diverse URI references in the DBpedia Spotlight. In such cases, we have to take the connection likelihood (Huang, 2008) for the mention (m) against the named entity (e) and characterized as:

$$F_{(e,m)} = \frac{Count(m, e)}{Count(m)}$$

The proximity score between the named entity and its related ideas of similar ontology would not be involved specifically into the DBpedia classification of connections and the subcategory in DBpedia has not produced any progressive system. By and large, the possibility of precursors, ancestors, subclassifications can be still followed up for the mapping of updated query refinement. Here, we utilized an outlined ontology to order the mentions (m_j) for the given named entity (e) and gauge the comparability difference between a named entity (e) and the list of mentions (m_j) recognized in the DBpedia knowledge base. Presently the fundamental rule to appraise the difference factor for the named entity is depended with the determination of fitting mentions from the recommended set of mentions.

The similarity difference between the named entity and relevant concepts is figured by the cosine proximity relevance. The cosine similarity measure will be taken for all the connection probabilities and noted down the comparability score separately. The cosine similarity (Huang, 2008) measure taken for the entity and mention can be characterized as:

$$CosSim(e, m) = \frac{Product(e, m)}{\|e\| * \|m\|}$$

Through these lines, we give a marker to delineate candidate entity into the DBpedia referenced mention with no uncertainty. For each mention 'm' recognized to be disambiguated, we gathered the conceivable rundown of candidate entities through the DBpedia Spotlight (Gillani, Naeem, Habibullah, & Qayyum, 2013) and set up the reasonable capacity to interface the appropriate entity utilizing the semantic comparability measures. In the method given underneath, we utilized the vectors of the entities and yielded the possible entity sets which have the most prominent similarity score. The semantic similarity for the calculation for mention disambiguation is given as follows:

Algorithm 2

Input: Fetch the candidate list of ambiguous mention from DBpedia
Output: Acquire the suitable entity which has the highest rank for the DBpedia URI

For each mention m Ɛ M

- Find the set of ambiguous entities ei of mention m

- High ← MaxSim (vector(e_i), vector(m))
- Assign High → mention m
- Return High

End for

Then, we used DBpedia Spotlight to fetch the URI reference for the entity which has attained the highest score in Algorithm 2 and collect the JSON structure of entity along with type and resources. It can be implemented as follows:

```
def filter(entity):
    return JSON (DBpediaSpotlight.annotate(entity));
```

Semantic Similarity Score

Once the preceding process of ambiguous problem gets solved, we create a binary relation for the named entity and DBpedia mention URI (See Table 3).

Generally, all the entities in DBpedia have relevant name, label, type etc. and to know the entity name given in the DBpedia for the specified URI, it can be queried through the SPAQRL query (Meij, Weerkamp, & De Rijke, 2012, February) as follows:

```
Select distinct *
where {
    ?URI rdf:label ?name
    ?URI dbpprop:iupacname ?name
    filter(str(?name) = "Donald Trump")
}
```

In order to get the category of the given entity from the DBpedia, we can issue the SPARQL query as follows:

```
Select *
where
{
<http://dbpedia.org/resource/Vehicle>
<http://purl.org/dc/terms/subject>
```

Table 3. Identifying the relation between named entity and candidate mention

Mention	NE Class	NE Link	DBpedia Ontology Class	Score
Donald Trump	Person	Dbpedia: Trump, USA	Dbpedia-owl: Person	2
New York	Location	Dbpedia: New York, USA	Dbpedia-owl: Place	3
Tennis	Sports	Dbpedia: Tennis	Dbpedia-owl: Sports	3

```
?categories.
}
```

Adaptive Entity Ranking

This section introduces the entity arrangements which divides into segments of 4-tuples (t, u, tw_i, tw_j) utilized as part of the characterized neural system engineering.

The description of the data arrival time, t, comprises of the day of the week and schedule vacancy. The information time part and the granularity of schedule opening too, are imperative to find regularities in the informational index about the minutes when the user associate on Twitter. We picked to consider four schedule openings segregating among morning, afternoon, evening and night. The description of the user, u, comprises of a vector of frequencies of themes speaking to the level of enthusiasm as for a settled arrangement of classes inferred by considering tweet content points of the user's past posts. The settled arrangement of classes is the same used to speak to the tweet content. At last, the portrayal of the elements of the tweets (i.e., tw_i or tw_j) comprise of the accompanying full scale parts:

- **Tweet Content Topics:** Trademark vector comparing to the settled arrangement of classes covering the general arrangement of the tweet stream;
- **Quality and Popularity:** An arrangement of entities accepted to speak to quality and prevalence of the tweet;
- **Publisher's Authority:** Highlights intending to measure specialist of the distributer as far as number of supporters and the recency of his movement on Twitter.
- **Social Relations:** Highlights that measure the social connection between the user and the tweet distributer.

Let us take note of the tweets and comparing highlights have been removed by methods for Twitter Streaming API, while the social entities about followers and companionship have been separated by the discoveries about social diagram shared from (Laere, Schockaert, Tanasescu, Dhoedt, & Jones, 2014). The accompanying subsections detail the organization of the previously mentioned highlights.

Tweet Content Topics

In this work, we utilized sentence Wikification (Imran et al., 2015) to semantically similar tweet description by connecting Wikipedia articles relating to the significance of the sentence. Sentence Wikification uncovered to be not traded off by the short idea of the tweet (Lee, et al., 2014, December). Given a tweet, tw_i, the sentence Wikification service recovers $wiki(tw_i)$ that is a rundown of sets ($topic_{ik}$, $rdtopic_{ik}$) where the principal part is the Wikipedia article identified with the tweet content and the second one is its particular importance degree.

Quality and Popularity

The quality of the tweet is deemed important for further classification and deep understanding. In this connection, we gather the following tweet properties to assert the tweet content.

- **Length:** Beginning from the way the length of the tweet may affect the client's advantage, this entity considers the aggregate number of words.
- **Hash-Tags:** The semantic nearness of hashtags makes the tweet pretty much useful and helpful. Along these lines, we consider the aggregate number of hashtags.
- **URLs:** Tweets are constrained as far as permitted characters (i.e., 140), and creators are accustomed to including at least one URL that, for instance, point to the augmentation of their data. Such property is considered as an extra quality measure, thus, this component considers whether the tweet contains no less than one URL.
- **Re-Tweets:** The quantity of the re-tweets that is a sign of the prominence and helpfulness of the tweet.
- **Likes:** The quantity of the circumstances somebody has communicated a positive feeling about the tweet is additionally viewed as a quality pointer.

Publishers Authority

These entities mean to quantify the authority of the tweet distributer. Regularly, users may want to peruse tweets distributed by a pretty much legitimate distributer and, in the meantime, the tweet quality is considered straightforwardly relative to the creator's power (i.e., a definitive creator is probably going to post an intriguing and helpful tweet). Along these lines, the distributer specialist is measured with the accompanying properties:

- **Followers:** The quantity of followers.
- **Status:** The aggregate number of user's tweets.

User's Relation

This arrangement of components models the connection between the user and the tweet distributer. The instinct is that users ought to be pretty much keen on perusing tweets posted by their companions, individuals they take after or sharing basic interests.

Topic Modeling

The next crucial aspect of operation after the successful classification of tweets into their respective predefined domain classes is to filter the topic of the tweet and thereby enhance the search operation semantically easier. It has been argued by Cano Basave et al. (2013) that topic modeling can be utilized to find the coherent meaning of the tweets and thus collectively improve the coherence of the given tweets. The most challenging task underlying in the topic modeling approaches is the automatic process by which the topic modeling can be identified and fixed. As this process is challenging and crucial, sustainable improvement has been made in the algorithms called LDA. LDA is the most popular and Bayesian probabilistic model which is identifying the hidden topics associated in documents in information retrieval. As we are proposing here the semantic based entity retrieval search operation, LDA is not most suited for the classification to topics underlining in the twitter streams. Hence, we have taken TLDA and PAM which is an extension of LDA for augmenting the topic modeling in twitter streams (Kulkarni et al., 2009).

The TLDA and PAM combination is hierarchical extensions of LDA where collected twitter streams can be represented as a multinomial distribution over the topics. This multinomial distribution helps to resolve the binary relation between the topics and subtopics. PAM is useful in generating the topics out of the tweets with higher degree of coherence and improving the most likelihood of topics to be present in the given collected tweets. But it has been observed that finding the topic out of the tweets is challenging with the simpler reason that most of the instances, the tweets covered almost single topic and in many cases, it is highly ambiguous. To counter this problem, TLDA has been proposed which implies the Bernoulli term distribution which effectively controls the relation between the real topic and the background terms associated in the formation of tweets. Hence, both the TLDA and PAM has effectively reported the topic modeling approaches in a good way and covered the aforementioned problems precisely.

Automatic Topic Coherence Metrics

In this section, we describe how a topic is generated from the stored tweets and metrics used to automatically extracting the topics from the tweets. There are two types of metrics followed here to find the topic coherence metrics of the tweets: 1) Semantic similarity based metric, and 2) Twitter background datasets.

Metrics based on Semantic Similarity

In this semantic similarity measure, a topic is alternatively identified with top 10 relevant candidate words ({w1,w2, ……..w10}) and ranked them accordingly to the term weight probabilities (p(w|z)) in the given term distribution φ. The coherence of the topic for the tweets is calculated on the average semantic similarity score measured against all the words pairs given in the top 10 candidate terms for the word (i.e. the word pair of a given topic is calculated by choosing any two words from the top 10 words). The semantic similarity of any given word pair is optionally calculated using any one of the external sources such as WordNet, DBpedia and Twitter Datasets. To calculate the semantic similarity for the word pair, we have the equation given below:

$$\text{Semantic Similarity of any word Pair } (W_i, W_j) = \log \frac{P\left(W_i, W_j\right)}{P\left(W_i\right)P\left(W_j\right)}$$

In order to facilitate the comparison task and render the manual comparison process smoother, we generate for each topic model a list of candidate topics where each topic is denoted as a vector using its overall term distribution as given in Milne & Witten (2008, October).

$$closest\left(Topic_j^{T1}\right) = argmin_{i<K}(1 - cosine(Vector_{Topic_j^{T1}}, Vector_{Topic_i^{T2}}))$$

In simpler terms, we have taken some of the topics from one topic model T1 and for each topic covered in the topic model T1, we have used the equation to choose the topic which is proximity to the topic model T2 using the cosine similarity score. For every comparison, we have taken some set of topic pairs that are relevant and used for final proximity score for topic modeling.

Twitter Background Dataset

In some cases, we cannot use the semantic similarity based measure to classify or identify the entities due to the tweets that contains mostly with abbreviations and acronyms. And also, most of the tweets are referring to tweets with hashtags which played crucial role on the day of events and many people have just retweeted what was given in the hashtags. In such critical cases, classifying or finding the appropriate topic for the tweets would end up in ambiguous results and implying any semantic similarity measure would assist the searching process easier. Hence we have taken the account of tweets stored in the database and referred the tweet that is likely reflecting the semantic similarity of the word that occurred in Twitter. Using the Twitter datasets for the event, we crawl back to the tweets and identify the meaning or semantic similarity of the word with possible co-occurrence of the tweet. By this way, we identify and recognize the proper form of the abbreviations or acronyms used in the tweets.

EVALUATION MEASURES

To prove the effectiveness of our approach, we have utilized just four sorts of tweets (Current Events, Sports, Politics and Celebrities). The purpose behind choosing these classes as experiments for the proposed approach is that immense numbers of tweets have been posted in these four classifications and we tried the same for the proposed approach. We used DBpedia Spotlight for referencing the entities from the tweets and connecting them to proper DBpedia URIs. That is, for each case, we are mapping the named entity (e) and the right DBpedia URI(/URL) where DBpedia URI offers substantial reference to this present reality element (e.g. http://dbpedia.org/asset/Donald_Trump). Sometimes, there were chances that there would be no DBpedia URI referencing to the selected mention; in such cases, we connect them to the non-DBpedia namespaces to keep away from disambiguation. For each element distinguished in the tweets, we build the transformed list that would bring the DBpedia URIs related with the entity. At that point we pick the best coordinating DBpedia URI for the element utilizing the SPARQL query. To rank the DBpedia literals related with the given entity, we used the previous mappings in DBpedia and developed the rational tree by <rdfs:subClassOf> connections and to take out the deceptions, utilized <rdfs:equivalentClass>. The positioning of the DBpedia URIs rundown can be performed on the given setting. Henceforth, we took after the setting considered ways to deal with discovering the co-events of the entity e with other related elements in a similar tweet setting. This would be accomplished by the proper SPARQL inquiry as foloows:

```
    select  ?x where { <e>  <dbpedia-prop:wikilink> ?x.  ?x <rdfs:type>  <t_
i>}
```

And, to find the entity types linked to the given entity, we utilized the entity graph from the knowledge base <owl:sameAs> to discriminate the differences as follows:

```
    select  ?x where {<e> <owl:sameAs> ?x . ?x <rdfs:type>  <t_i> }
```

In order to test the performance and accuracy of the proposed method, we took the following real time named entities from recent *Pathankot Attack* and found the exact match of the DBpedia URI references of every potential named entity identified (See Table 4).

The F-Score is defined as follows:

$$R = 2\,X\,\frac{Precision\;.Recall}{Precision + Recall}$$

The F-measure is the harmonic mean of the precision and recall. Given below (Table 5) are the candidate mentions of the entities and calculated F-Score of each against their ambiguity prevalence. We witnessed improvement of the accuracy rate of the precision and attained satisfactory results in the proposed work.

FUTURE RESEARCH DIRECTIONS

It is fundamental to find new entities for the enhancement of KBs. In any case, one of the vital lessons that we have learned is that, few out of every odd entity that has been found can be inserted into a KB. Its realness should be checked and in addition its connection and pertinence w.r.t different elements in this present reality must be contemplated to refresh ideas in KBs. Improvement of KBs, particularly advancing the dictionary of an entity in a KB utilizing data removed from Web-based social networking is a standout amongst the most imperative open issues in the Semantic Web people group.

Table 4. Find the exact match of DBpedia URI for collected named entities

Trending Events	Collected Tweets Related to Events	Named Entities Identified	Matched DBpedia Links
French Presidential Election	2,00,000	15000	43101
Demonetization in India	3,5,0000	17600	15539
Data Breach at Yahoo	2,20,000	12200	10890
Brexit	3,50,000	20000	16765
Climate Change	2,50,000	12810	11704

Table 5. Sample accuracy score of the test

Entity	Precision	Recall	F-Score
Donald Trump	0.87	0.42	0.82
Vladimir Putin	0.9	0.65	0.87
Narendra Modi	0.9	0.44	0.71
Xi Jinping	0.9	0.58	0.89

Starting now, we have directed an assortment of investigations for enhancing disambiguation. While we keep on improving it, the following stage in this examination work would be working towards enhancement of KBs in time and expanding them with quality data extracted from Social Media and the Web.

CONCLUSION

In this paper, we represented the working arrangement of the named entity disambiguation techniques and mapping the entities into the correct match of the information base like DBpedia. Dissimilar to different models of methodologies, we have portrayed the utilitarian work of the model and displayed the difficulties in the extracted named entity connecting procedure, for example, managing the varieties of the potential named entities, entity-mention uncertainty, non-appearance of entities in the DBpedia, entity clustering and so forth. We demonstrated the working standards of these difficulties and techniques to overcome all such specialized glitches. Moreover, we proposed the strategy that firmly suggests when ought not to interface the entities to the knowledge base despite the fact that it has high precision. This illustrated work will additionally be upgraded with entity linking mechanism and clear up the obstructing problems in different field of uses.

REFERENCES

Alahmari, F. A., Thom, J., & Magee, L. (2014). A model for ranking entity attributes using DBpedia. *Aslib Journal of Information Management, 66*(5), 473–493. doi:10.1108/AJIM-12-2013-0148

Bansal, R. (2014). Linking entities in #Micropost. In *#Microposts2014 Workshop Proceedings*. CEUR.

Bunescu, R. C., & Pasca, M. (2006, April). Using Encyclopedic Knowledge for Named entity Disambiguation. In EACL (Vol. 6, pp. 9-16). Academic Press.

Cano Basave, A. E., Varga, A., Rowe, M., Stankovic, M., & Dadzie, A. S. (2013). *Making sense of microposts (# msm2013) concept extraction challenge*. Academic Press.

Derczynski, L., Maynard, D., Rizzo, G., van Erp, M., Gorrell, G., Troncy, R., ... Bontcheva, K. (2015). Analysis of named entity recognition and linking for tweets. *Information Processing & Management, 51*(2), 32–49. doi:10.1016/j.ipm.2014.10.006

Gattani, A., Lamba, D. S., Garera, N., Tiwari, M., Chai, X., Das, S., ... Doan, A. (2013). Entity extraction, linking, classification, and tagging for social media: A wikipedia-based approach. *Proceedings of the VLDB Endowment International Conference on Very Large Data Bases, 6*(11), 1126–1137. doi:10.14778/2536222.2536237

Gillani, S., Naeem, M., Habibullah, R., & Qayyum, A. (2013). Semantic schema matching using DBpedia. *International Journal of Intelligent Systems and Applications, 5*(4), 72–80. doi:10.5815/ijisa.2013.04.07

Giridhar, P., Abdelzaher, T., George, J., & Kaplan, L. (2015, March). On quality of event localization from social network feeds. In *Pervasive Computing and Communication Workshops (PerCom Workshops), 2015 IEEE International Conference on* (pp. 75-80). IEEE. 10.1109/PERCOMW.2015.7133997

Hellmann, S., Stadler, C., Lehmann, J., & Auer, S. (2009). DBpedia live extraction. On the Move to Meaningful Internet Systems. *OTM, 2009*, 1209–1223.

Hogan, A., Zimmermann, A., Umbrich, J., Polleres, A., & Decker, S. (2012). Scalable and distributed methods for entity matching, consolidation and disambiguation over linked data corpora. *Journal of Web Semantics, 10*, 76–110. doi:10.1016/j.websem.2011.11.002

Holzmann, H., Tahmasebi, N., & Risse, T. (2013, September). BlogNEER: Applying Named Entity Evolution Recognition on the Blogosphere? In SDA (pp. 28-39). Academic Press.

Huang, A. (2008, April). Similarity measures for text document clustering. *Proceedings of the sixth new zealand computer science research student conference (NZCSRSC2008)*, 49-56.

Imran, M., Castillo, C., Diaz, F., & Vieweg, S. (2015). Processing social media messages in mass emergency: A survey. *ACM Computing Surveys, 47*(4), 67. doi:10.1145/2771588

Kulkarni, S., Singh, A., Ramakrishnan, G., & Chakrabarti, S. (2009, June). Collective annotation of Wikipedia entities in web text. In *Proceedings of the 15th ACM SIGKDD international conference on Knowledge discovery and data mining* (pp. 457-466). ACM. 10.1145/1557019.1557073

Laere, O. V., Schockaert, S., Tanasescu, V., Dhoedt, B., & Jones, C. B. (2014). Georeferencing Wikipedia documents using data from social media sources. *ACM Transactions on Information Systems, 32*(3), 12. doi:10.1145/2629685

Lee, K., Ganti, R. K., Srivatsa, M., & Liu, L. (2014, December). When twitter meets foursquare: tweet location prediction using foursquare. In *Proceedings of the 11th International Conference on Mobile and Ubiquitous Systems: Computing, Networking and Services* (pp. 198-207). ICST (Institute for Computer Sciences, Social-Informatics and Telecommunications Engineering). 10.4108/icst.mobiquitous.2014.258092

Meij, E., Weerkamp, W., & De Rijke, M. (2012, February). Adding semantics to microblog posts. In *Proceedings of the fifth ACM international conference on Web search and data mining* (pp. 563-572). ACM. 10.1145/2124295.2124364

Mendes, P. N., Jakob, M., García-Silva, A., & Bizer, C. (2011, September). DBpedia spotlight: shedding light on the web of documents. In *Proceedings of the 7th international conference on semantic systems* (pp. 1-8). ACM. 10.1145/2063518.2063519

Milne, D., & Witten, I. H. (2008, October). Learning to link with wikipedia. In *Proceedings of the 17th ACM conference on Information and knowledge management* (pp. 509-518). ACM.

Presutti, V., Consoli, S., Nuzzolese, A. G., Recupero, D. R., Gangemi, A., Bannour, I., & Zargayouna, H. (2014, November). Uncovering the semantics of Wikipedia pagelinks. In *International Conference on Knowledge Engineering and Knowledge Management* (pp. 413-428). Springer, Cham.

Zwicklbauer, S., Seifert, C., & Granitzer, M. (2013, September). Do we need entity-centric knowledge bases for entity disambiguation? In *Proceedings of the 13th International Conference on Knowledge Management and Knowledge Technologies* (p. 4). ACM. 10.1145/2494188.2494198

KEY TERMS AND DEFINITIONS

DBpedia: The DBpedia DataID vocabulary is a metadata system for detailed descriptions of datasets and their physical instances, as well as their relation to agents like persons or organizations in regard to their rights and responsibilities.

LDA: In natural language processing, latent dirichlet allocation is a generative statistical model that allows sets of observations to be explained by unobserved groups that explain why some parts of the data are similar.

NER: Named-entity recognition (NER; also known as entity identification, entity chunking, and entity extraction) is a subtask of information extraction that seeks to locate and classify named entities in text into predefined categories such as the names of persons, organizations, locations, expressions of times, quantities.

RDF: Resource description framework (RDF) is a family of world wide web consortium (W3C) specifications originally designed as a metadata data model.

SPARQL: SPARQL (pronounced "sparkle," a recursive acronym for SPARQL protocol and RDF query language) is an RDF query language, that is, a semantic query language for databases, able to retrieve and manipulate data stored in resource description framework (RDF) format.

URI: In information technology, a uniform resource identifier (URI) is a string of characters used to identify a resource. Such identification enables interaction with representations of the resource over a network, typically the world wide web, using specific protocols.

Word Sense Disambiguation: In computational linguistics, word-sense disambiguation (WSD) is an open problem of natural language processing and ontology. WSD is identifying which sense of a word (i.e., meaning) is used in a sentence, when the word has multiple meanings.

Chapter 19
Dynamic Quota Calculation System (DQCS):
Pricing and Quota Allocation of Telecom Customers via Data Mining Approaches

Ulaş Çelenk
Innova IT Solutions Inc., Turkey

Duygu Çelik Ertuğrul
Eastern Mediterranean University, North Cyprus

Metin Zontul
Istanbul Aydin University, Turkey

Atilla Elçi
Aksaray University, Turkey

Osman Nuri Uçan
Istanbul Kemerburgaz University, Turkey

ABSTRACT

One of the most important IT sectors that requires big data management is mobile data communication systems (MDCS) of GSM companies. In the charging mechanism of current MDCS, a subscriber "surfs" on the internet that creates data traffic and a counter subtracts the amount of data used by the user from the subscriber's quota. In other words, instant constant quota values are assigned to subscribers without concern for their previous amount of internet usage in current MDCS. Moreover, constant quota values cause constant charge calls in control traffic that are repeated for all new quota requests. Thus, performance degradation occurs because of the repetition of quota request calls and allocations. In this chapter, a dynamic quota calculation system (DQCS) is proposed for dynamic quota allocations and charging in MDCS using data mining approaches as two cascaded blocks. The first block is self-organizing map (SOM) clustering based on a sliding window (SW) methodology followed by the second block, which is the markov chain (MC); the overall system is denoted as "SOM/SW and MC."

DOI: 10.4018/978-1-5225-5384-7.ch019

INTRODUCTION

The advancement of Web and wireless technologies have allowed mobile users to demand various kinds of services through mobile devices at anytime and anyplace. Quota sizes of mobile users can highly benefit the enhancements on mobile communication system performance and quality of services. Mobile Data Communication System (MDCS) companies must satisfy a wide and varied customer base. There are two types of Internet quota sizes for mobile users, monthly and instant, where instant (750 KB) is given initially. When instant quota is depleted, a new request call is generated on MDCS to obtain a new instant quota. The charging system blocks 750 KB of data from a subscriber's monthly quota, which is resolved along with the quota system. The arrangement of instant quota size with respect to customers with low data use can cause various performance problems, such as heavy signalization in the cases of heavy users. On the other hand, the arrangement of quota size only with respect to customers with high data use clearly leads to unnecessary quota allocation.

This research aims at data mining the quota usage patterns such that suitable quota size can be predicted and assigned automatically for users. Hence, a dynamic quota allocation system is required to gain better performance using mobile user data and profile knowledge. However, to the best of our knowledge, there are few studies related to dynamic instant quota sizes in the literature. Most studies are based on Internet bandwidth and service quality employing mobile user profiles and Internet usage. Due to this reason, our study has a contribution to the literature in terms of user dependent dynamic quota calculation for telecommunication systems.

The rest of this paper is organized as follows: Section 2 gives the literature background originating our study. Section 3 describes the working mechanism for the proposed Dynamic Quota Calculation System (DQCS); then, Section 4 discusses the evaluation of simulation results and comparison of the statically-based charging and quota transfer in current MDCS with the proposed algorithm. Section 5 presents implementation of DQCS to the LTE communication systems; finally, Section 6 and Section 7 are dedicated to the future research directions and conclusions respectively.

LITERATURE BACKGROUND

Quota-based charging of mobile users was investigated in several studies. Abidogun & Omlin (2004) presented a Self-Organizing Map (SOM) model for outlier detection in call data from subscribers, over a period of time in a mobile telecommunication network so that suspicious call behavior could be isolated in order to identify abnormal call patterns from subscribers. The researchers applied the SOM model to the unsupervised classification of call data for prepaid service subscribers from a real mobile telecommunication network. They indicated that the ideas presented in their study might be used for clustering call patterns in order to label them as normal or abnormal.

Next similar study by Lehtimäki & Raivio (2005) presented an analysis process based on SOM to visualize MDCS network performance data. They applied SOM in the analysis of 3G network performance, including advanced network monitoring and cell grouping. After outlining the overall SOM based analysis process for MDCS performance data, they demonstrated the use of the analysis process in two problem scenarios in which the capacity problems in the signaling and traffic channels were analyzed.

In the study of Ozianyi & Ventura (2005), an approach was proposed for charging mobile Internet use based on subscriber profiles. The researchers attempted to determine the Internet use habits of subscribers by considering their economic and social status, and they established a model for charging subscribers temporarily by considering usable Internet bandwidth and service quality as parameters.

Multanen, Raivio, & Lehtimäki (2006) used a SOM-based model to develop a method for exploring the data of an entire MDCS network. They preferred SOM because it has the ability of reducing highly visual data. In their study, SOM was used both in clustering and in visualization.

Kiang, Hu, & Fisher (2006) applied an extended version of SOM networks to a consumer data set from American Telephone and Telegraph Company (AT&T) for market segmentation in which the first and primary component was the formation of groups. Their SOM model grouped the nodes on the output map into a subscriber specified number of clusters. Their study showed that SOM as a nonparametric approach with no assumptions about the underlying population distribution might be more appropriate than parametric models to describe this data set. They also indicated that the extended SOM network performed better than the two-step procedure that combined factor analysis and K-means cluster analysis in uncovering market segments.

Fessant, Lemaire, & Clérot (2008) reported again SOM-based approach to the discovery of broadband customers' usage patterns by directly mining network measurement data. They have focused on two aspects of customers' usages: usage of types of applications and customers' daily traffic. By developing a multi-level exploratory data analysis approach based on SOM, they defined accurate and easily interpretable profiles of the customers that exhibited very heterogeneous behaviors ranging from a large majority of customers with a low usage of the applications to a small minority with a very high usage.

Zaghloul, Bziuk, & Jukan (2008) studied the problems experienced during assigning bandwidths to subscribers because scaling the base station was not easy. In their study, differently from other studies, Markov processes were utilized. Thus, using the Markov processes of real-time usage of base stations, the super state values of those base stations could be obtained. It was aimed at allocating stations among subscribers in the most efficient way.

In the study of Li, Chen, & Soh (2009), dynamically changing the bandwidth assigned for subscribers based on desires of the subscribers was evaluated. Through calculating the connection bandwidth unit prices according to usage rate of actual capacity synchronously and providing it for preferences of subscribers, it was aimed at allowing subscribers to use internet environment more productively in accordance with their needs.

Tulankar & Wajgi (2012) demonstrated how SOM can be used efficiently for clustering mobile customers in order to design suitable marketing strategies for each group and thereby enhance business profitability. They collected sample mobile telecommunication data that contained information on mobile customer usage records where each record was characterized by approximately 16 attributes. They used Emergent Self Organizing Maps (ESOMs) to cluster customers based on their usage profile characterized by the chosen 16 attributes. According to their study, ESOM, along with U-Matrix representation, facilitated identification of clear cluster boundaries shown by mountains and valleys that depicted the clusters. They also stated that revenue for mobile telecom operators can be increased by formulating effective, strategic, and possibly different marketing policies for different clusters.

On the other hand, Rejeb, Nasser, & Tabbane (2014) used Markov model to evaluate mobile system performance in terms of probability of blocking and probability loss, throughput, and residence time. Their proposed mechanism employs adaptive modulation and coding that divide the geographical area into several concentric regions.

There are other research studies related to dynamic packet scheduling and bandwidth allocation (Yang, Chen, & Wu, 2014), call blocking and handover analysis (Vegni & Natalizio, 2014), spectrum cost analysis (Mölleryd & Markendahl, 2014), and mobile termination rate (Baigorri & Maldonado, 2014). The general idea prevailing in these studies is to find the optimal value for the involved parameter in order to enhance mobile communication.

However, determining mobile Internet instant quota sizes fairly in order to reach optimal signalization and bandwidth usage is also necessary. For this purpose, customers can be clustered with respect to particular properties, such as country, personal user characteristics, mobile Internet attribute perceptions/behavioral intentions and factual use conditions, etc. for a specific time interval (Gerpott & Thomas, 2014). Moreover, for subsequent time intervals, the quota sizes for a particular cluster can be estimated based on the cluster quota sizes.

There are recent studies (Huang, Su, Liang, & Tseng, 2015) related to dynamic quota allocation and customer segmentation in telecommunication sector. In the study of Huang et al. (2015), a new scheme was proposed for dynamically assigning Granted Units to User Equipments belonging to the same Family Shared Plan, based on their historical data usage and total monthly data allowance. This study showed that the proposed model can decrease the communication signaling by at least 22%, with respect to fixed scheme under unpredictable behaviors. Cheng et al. (2016) proposed a cluster algorithm based on K-means and Multivariable Quantum Shuffled Frog Leaping Algorithm for customer segmentation in telecom customers marketing with the advantage of convergence rate comparable to K-means. In another study, an improved K-means clustering algorithm was proposed for identifying internet user behavior by using Web log data. The efficiency of the algorithm was analyzed by considering certain parameters such as date, time, S_id, CS_method, C_IP, User_agent and time taken (Padmaja & Sheshasaayee, 2016).

In our study, we choose to cluster our data with the SOM-based data mining approach which is an excellent tool for data survey because it has prominent visualization properties. In addition, while the SOM model is used for customer behavior analysis or clustering mobile nodes (Fessant, François, & Clérot, 2007; Fessant et al., 2008), the Markov model is used for predicting future values of customers' data (Netzer, Lattin, & Srinivasan, 2008; Mark & Csaba, 2007) in literature. Thus, it is decided, as a contribution to the literature, to combine the SOM and Markov models in order to determine the optimal Internet instant quota size. Therefore, in the proposed DQCS, two cascaded blocks/steps are considered:

- Firstly, SOM is used to determine customer clusters and calculate their quota sizes with regard to customer age, gender, home city, customer profile (CRM segment), and tariff information. During system simulations, a bottleneck occurred in the determination of the weight values for each cluster. Therefore, in order to provide the SOM algorithm with the dynamic adaptivity property, a Sliding Window (SW) structure is included and denoted as (SOM/SW).
- Secondly, Markov Chain (MC) approach is applied to the future prediction of quota values based on the historical values of Internet usage of subscribers. The overall system is thus denoted as "(SOM/SW) & MC."

PROPOSED DQCS APPROACH

As it is mentioned, in current MDCS, constant instant quota value (750 KB) is assigned to each subscriber without concern for their previous amount of Internet usage. Moreover, the constant quota value causes constant charge calls that are repeated for all new quota requests for each subscriber. Thus, performance degradation occurs because of the repetition of quota request calls and allocations. Therefore, in the charging infrastructure of current MDCS, while a given subscriber "surfs" the Internet and creates data traffic, a counter subtracts the amount of data used from subscriber's quota. When the allotted quota is depleted, this is confirmed by communicating with the system's Home Location Register (HLR), the amount of fixed quota charged to subscriber, and then the Call Detail Record (CDR) ends. If the subscriber continues using the Internet, the steps are repeated, and a new quota is blocked.

The proposed DQCS is modeled dynamically for MDCS charging and quota transfers. To do so, SOM is executed with an SW approach during the clustering task depending on time as the first routine (Figure 1). Then, DQCS performs a prediction step to define the next quota value of each cluster based on the subscriber Internet usage habits in each cluster by the MC approach as the second routine (Figure 1). Therefore, the chain of these routines is denoted as (SOM/SW) & MC, and it is discussed in the rest of this section.

First Routine: SOM With Sliding Window (SOM/SW) Routine in DQCS

Extended Self-Organizing Map (SOM)

Statistical methods are commonly used in practical problems (Snell & Grinstead, 1997). For Self-Organizing Map (SOM) is a competitive one, Kohonen (1990; 2001) introduced it as an unsupervised method for use in the field of artificial neural networks. SOM, one of the most popular neural network models, belongs to the category of competitive learning networks that is based on unsupervised learning, which means that no human intervention is needed during learning phase and that little need be known about the characteristics of the input data. SOM performs quite intuitively, thus leading to its great popularity and numerous applications.

In this study, the classical SOM is extended with Sliding Window (SW) approach to determine dynamically number of subscriber clusters and calculate quota sizes of these clusters with regard to involved subscriber characteristics: *Age, Tariff, Gender, City,* and *CRM_SEGMENT*. The classical SOM alone is not able to produce dynamic results while specifying the average quota size for each cluster. For example, as shown in Figure 2, the long-term continuous arrival of incoming data leads to classical SOM clusters to lose their elasticity or dynamism (cluster weighting average value). Let the cluster shown in Figure 2 (a) and Figure 2 (b) be approximately 100 KB (Data 1) and 200 KB (Data 2), respectively. In

Figure 1. Proposed Dynamic Quota Calculation System (DQCS) performs dynamic quota allocations and charging in MDCS using two cascaded blocks

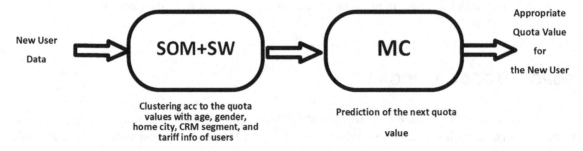

Figure 2. Data flow for SOM Clustering: (a) First data into typical SOM cluster (b) Second data into typical SOM cluster (c) After 10^6th data into typical SOM cluster

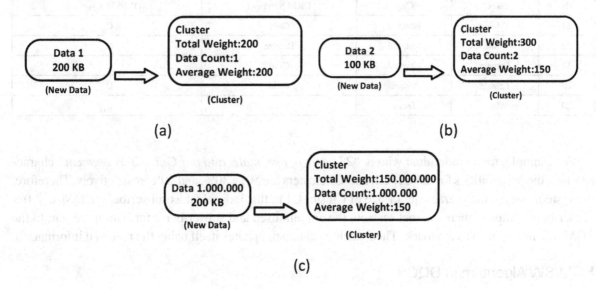

(a) (b)

(c)

Figure 2 (b), the second set of data of 100 KB (Data 2) arriving at the same cluster affects the cluster by 50% weight. However, as seen in Figure 2 (c), the effect on the cluster of 10^6 incoming data with a value of 200 KB (Data 1.000.000) is only 10^{-6}. The cluster loses its *dynamism*, but the cluster's mean weight value remains *fixed*. In order to solve this problem, SW logic is added to the classical SOM and denoted as (SOM/SW). According to SOM/SW logic, the new incoming data are added to the cluster in this situation. However, they are excluded from the cluster after 1 hour; therefore, only the data from the last hour can affect the cluster's weight, and the cluster's dynamism is protected.

Generating and Applying the Max Probability Table

The clusters where the subscribers are involved and the intensities of those clusters are found based on subscriber characteristics, which are: *Age, Tariff, Gender, City,* and *CRM_SEGMENT*.

The system creates clusters by using the SOM/SW algorithm according to the amount of Internet usage of subscribers. To do this, the system has enough information about which user is included in which cluster. With this information, the system can classify the involved number of subscribers of a particular characteristic (in terms of *Age, Tariff, Gender, City,* and *CRM_SEGMENT*) in any cluster. In the same way, the system can identify the number of subscribers involved in each cluster having the same characteristics. This information allows to create a Max Probability Table (Table 1). The Max Probability Table provides the system with the maximum probable clusters for $T_{(n+1)}$ moments. Therefore, using the Max Probability Table (simple statistical records with the largest probability values), the most appropriate quota is allocated to subscribers at the start of their Internet session. When a new subscriber enters the system, if most of the present subscribers are having similar parameters as the new subscriber, then the system sets the quota size of the subscriber according to the average quota size of that cluster by considering the Max Probability Table (see Table 1).

Table 1. Max probability table

Age	Sex	City	CRM Segment	SOM/SW Clusters
23	Male	Istanbul	Gold	C_{32}
22	Male	Istanbul	Bronze	C_{33}
32	Female	Istanbul	Gold	C_{16}
20	Female	Ankara	Gold	C_{11}
20	Male	Izmir	Silver	C_{10}

For example, for an individual who is *"23 years of age, male, and has Gold CRM segment"* characteristics, the probabilities for the C1, C2, and C3 clusters are 50%, 30%, and 20%, respectively. Therefore, the system assigns the average quota size of Cluster C1 to this individual as subscriber quota size. After subscribers complete their Internet session, the amount used and subscriber information are sent to the SOM/SW mechanism as feedback. Then, such mechanism updates itself using the received information.

SOM/SW Algorithm in DQCS

The developed SOM/SW mechanism is presented in the flow diagram shown in Figure 3 and its pseudocode is given in Algorithm 1.

- After subscribers complete their Internet session, the related amount of used data is entered into the system, and the flow starts (Total usage amount of session, depicted in Step 1 of Figure 3).
- The closeness of a subscriber's usage amount is defined with regard to the average weight values of the clusters created by the SOM/SW mechanism (depicted in Step 2 of Figure 3). Therefore, the cluster with the closest average weight value is found.
- If the distance 'd' (Eq. 1, C=) to the closest cluster's average weight value is lower than the *RANGE* value (i.e. 500 KB), new data is added into that cluster (depicted in Step 3 of Figure 3). Then the average weight value for the cluster is updated.

$$d = \sqrt{\begin{array}{c}\left(C_{Age} - U_{Age}\right)^2 + \left(C_{Tariff} - U_{Tariff}\right)^2 + \left(C_{Gender} - U_{Gender}\right)^2 \\ \ldots + \left(C_{City} - U_{City}\right)^2 + \left(C_{CRM} - U_{CRM}\right)^2\end{array}} < \left|RANGE\right|$$

$Any\, Cluster\, C = Cluster_i\, \&\, A\, New\, User\, U = User_x$ Step 3-4 of Figure 3 (1)

- If the distance (or diameter) 'd' to the closest cluster's average weight value is higher than the *RANGE* value (i.e. 500 KB), a new cluster is created using that usage data (In this way, the number of clusters is updated dynamically, Step 4 of Figure 3).
- As seen in Figure 3, the SOM/SW mechanism starts for the usage amount and cluster where it is involved. After 1 hour, this usage amount is excluded from the cluster where it was involved, and

Figure 3. SOM/SW mechanism

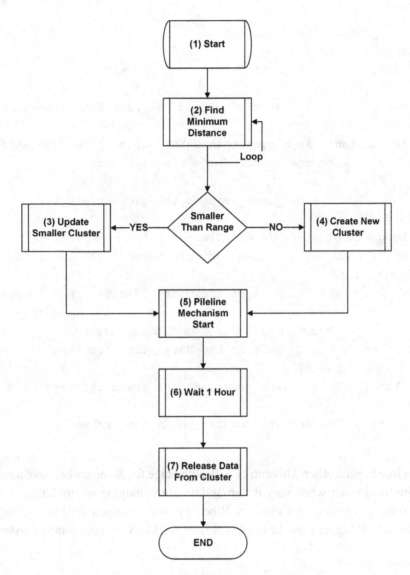

the cluster's average weight value is updated. In this way, the clusters stay always dynamic in data since the average weights of these clusters change according to the amounts of Internet usages within 1-hour time slots (depicted in Step 5, 6 and 7 of Figure 3).

There are several other algorithms similar to SOM. For example, k-means is a clustering algorithm which aims to cluster n-data points into k-clusters so that each data point belongs to the cluster with the nearest mean (MacQueen, 1967). In order to dynamically change the number of clusters, X-means clustering algorithm was developed (Pelleg & Moore, 2000). It is possible to use sliding window in X-means algorithm as in SOM in a way that any data at any cluster can be removed at the end of windows time period and the related cluster weight can be updated dynamically. Unlike SOM, in order to create a new cluster, an old cluster must be divided into two parts in X-means. In this case, the two newly cre-

Algorithm 1. SOM/SW working mechanism

```
1   Input new_user_data /*New User Data*/
2   Loop 1:  Loop all clusters
3                Find closest cluster
4   End Loop 1
5   Find distance between closest cluster and new_user_data according to
    distance formula /*Eq. 1*/
6        If the distance is bigger than RANGE value /*i.e. 500 KB*/
7                Create new cluster with new_user_data
8                    Else
9                Add the new_user_data to the closest cluster
10       End If
11  Loop 2:  Loop all clusters /* all Cluster İ */
12       Loop 3: Loop all data for each clusters /* all users' data in the
             Cluster İ */
13               If the data of the Userj is older than 1 hour /*
                 sessions data for the Userj (i.e. session_start_time,
                 session_end_time, used_quota) */
14                   Release the Userj data from the Cluster İ
15               End If
16       End Loop 2 /* All users' session data are considered in each Cluster
             İ */
17  End Loop 3 /*All clusters are considered in the system */
```

ated clusters are close to each other. This can be a disadvantage for X-means because new data may have little relation with this cluster when very different data not belonging to any cluster occurs. In SOM/SW, diameter is used for creating new clusters. When a new data which does not belong to any cluster arrives and its distance is bigger than the closest cluster, SOM/SW creates a new cluster.

SECOND ROUTINE: MARKOV CHAIN APPROACH IN DQCS

In principle, when we observe a sequence of stochastic experiments, all past outcomes can influence the predictions of the next sequence of experiments. In 1907, A. A. Markov began the study of an important new type of probabilistic process (Markov, 1971). In this process, the outcome of a given experiment can affect the outcome of the next experiment. This type of process is called "Markov Chain (MC)" and it is a random process usually characterized as "memoryless", that is, the next state depends only on the current state and not on the sequence of events that preceded it. This specific type of "memorylessness" is called the "Markov property." MCs have many applications, such as statistical models of real-world processes.

In this study, the MC is applied to the charging and quota algorithms of the MDCS sector by considering the history of subscriber Internet usage habits in order to estimate future Internet usage rates. The

Markov approach is used to calculate the next quota allocation value according to particular subscriber properties. In addition, the weight value of each cluster input from the SOM/SW routine is included in the calculation of the next quota allocation value at time $T_{(n+1)}$. In other words, analysis is performed based on subscribers, not clusters. In this case, the data such as "for 22 year-old male subscribers, there are 10,000 subscribers in C_1 cluster, 15,000 subscribers in C_2 cluster and 14,000 subscribers in C_3 cluster" is obtained. When a new male subscriber at the age of 22 arrives, it is estimated via possibility calculations in which cluster he should belong. At this point, Markov processes have been used for possibility calculations. The utilization of Markov Chain mechanism in DQCS system is presented in flow diagram in Figure 4. The algorithm used for the Markov approach of the proposed model is as follows:

- Subscriber clusters are calculated for $T_{(n-1)}$ and $T_{(n)}$ times, and subscriber numbers $C_{1(n-1)}$ for $T_{(n-1)}$ and $C_{1(n)}$ for $T_{(n)}$ are calculated in C_1 cluster. This way, $C_{2(n-1)}$, $C_{2(n)}$,......$C_{X(n-1)}$, $C_{X(n)}$ clusters and subscriber numbers are calculated (Step 1 of Figure 4).
- The three clusters with the most subscriber numbers are taken, and a 3×3 transition matrix is formed as in Eq.2. In the related matrix, the possibility of passing from C_1 to C_1, from C_1 to C_2, from C_1 to C_3, and other possibilities are available (Step 2 of Figure 4).

$$\begin{bmatrix} C_{1(n-1)} \rightarrow C_{1(n)} & C_{1(n-1)} \rightarrow C_{2(n)} & C_{1(n-1)} \rightarrow C_{3(n)} \\ C_{2(n-1)} \rightarrow C_{1(n)} & C_{2(n-1)} \rightarrow C_{2(n)} & C_{2(n-1)} \rightarrow C_{3(n)} \\ C_{3(n-1)} \rightarrow C_{1(n)} & C_{3(n-1)} \rightarrow C_{2(n)} & C_{3(n-1)} \rightarrow C_{3(n)} \end{bmatrix} \tag{2}$$

- The possibility of being found in the current cluster is multiplied by these passing possibilities; their possibility of being found in the next time slot is calculated; finally, the quota amount of the cluster with the highest possibility is assigned to the subscriber, as indicated in Eq.3 and mentioned in Step 3 of Figure 4.

$$\begin{bmatrix} C_{1(n)} & C_{2(n)} & C_{3(n)} \end{bmatrix} \times \begin{bmatrix} C_{1(n-1)} \rightarrow C_{1(n)} & C_{1(n-1)} \rightarrow C_{2(n)} & C_{1(n-1)} \rightarrow C_{3(n)} \\ C_{2(n-1)} \rightarrow C_{1(n)} & C_{2(n-1)} \rightarrow C_{2(n)} & C_{2(n-1)} \rightarrow C_{3(n)} \\ C_{3(n-1)} \rightarrow C_{1(n)} & C_{3(n-1)} \rightarrow C_{2(n)} & C_{3(n-1)} \rightarrow C_{3(n)} \end{bmatrix} = \begin{bmatrix} C_{1(n+1)} & C_{2(n+1)} & C_{3(n+1)} \end{bmatrix}$$

- The Max Probability Table is considered in MC step as well (Step 4 of Figure 4). An example of Max Probability Table is given in Table 1. Table 1 contains the SOM/SW clusters (C_{32}, C_{33}, C_{16}, C_{11}, and C_{10}) that show the maximum possibilities according to subscriber characteristics. As it is mentioned before, the Max Probability Table is rearranged (updated) hourly. For instance, the MC mechanism finds that C_{32} is a suitable cluster for a subscriber who is 23 years of age (first row of Table 1). As a result, the hourly rearrangement of the Max Probability Table gives the system the maximum probable clusters for the moment $T_{(n+1)}$. In Markov mechanism, number of clusters, the same characteristics of the subscribers in clusters are analyzed, and then max passing possibilities

Figure 4. Markov Chain mechanism

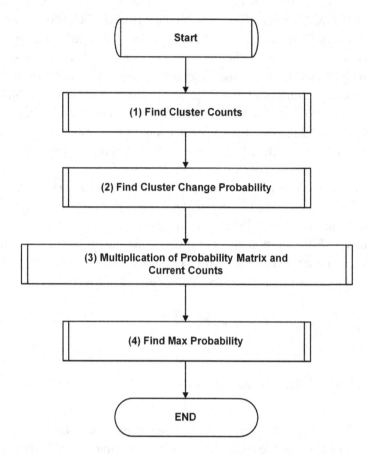

are calculated for $T_{(n+1)}$ moment. The Max Probability Table presents the maximum possibility clusters for the moment $T_{(n+1)}$ (as presented in sample Table 1). Th.is table is used in order to allocate the suitable quota size for a new subscriber

Combination of Two Cascaded (SOM/SW) and MC Routines

As presented in Figure 5, the DQCS system successively uses the SOM/SW & MC routines explained in detail in the previous sections (Algorithm 2). In Step 1 of Figure 5, the total data amount information is sent to DQCS after the subscriber completes his/her Internet session. This sending step is executed by the Content Service Gateway (CSG) unit via the Diameter protocol, whereas the quota request is triggered by the Gateway GPRS Support Node (GGSN) in current MDCS. The sent data triggers the SOM/SW mechanism, and is assigned to the most appropriate SOM/SW cluster (as depicted in Step 2 of Figure 5). Then, Markov mechanism calculations are performed hourly on SOM/SW clusters (as depicted in Step 3 of Figure 5).

In the Markov mechanism, all clusters and the subscriber characteristics in those clusters are analyzed, and the maximum possibilities are calculated for moment $T_{(n+1)}$. The Max Probability Table presents

Figure 5. Proposed DQCS routines

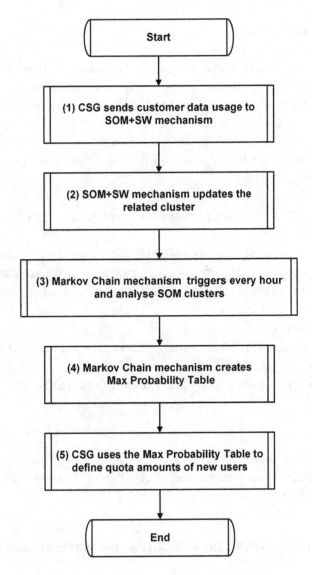

the maximum possibility clusters for moment $T_{(n+1)}$ (as presented in the sample demonstrated in Table 1 and depicted in Step 4 of Figure 5). This table is used to allocate the quota value for a new subscriber (as depicted in Step 5 of Figure 5).

SIMULATION RESULTS AND EVALUATION

In this section, the quota algorithms of the current MDCS and that of the proposed DQCS are driven into a simulation and the resulting values are compared. Data usage for the tests performed from 01/06/2012 to 30/06/2012 is transferred with samples from one of the MDCS companies in Turkey (AVEA GSM Company, 2004). Table 2 depicts a portion of the dataset as a case study that are used in simulations.

Algorithm 2. Pseudocode of the DQCS algorithm

```
1  Loop 1: Loop for each hour
2      Loop 2:  Loop all clusters
3          Loop 3: Loop all data in each clusters /* loop session data for
           each user (i.e. session_start_time, session_end_time, used_quota) */
4              Save the Age, Tariff, Gender, City, and CRM_SEGMENT values
               in data /* for the Userk */
5          End Loop 3
6      End Loop 2 /* All clusters are ready. Any Clusterj keeps the similar
       type of subscribers*/
7
8      Loop 4: Loop all Age, Tariff, Gender, City, and CRM_SEGMENT values for
       each user /*Useri */
9          Find the largest cluster whose data has same characteristics with
           Useri: Age, Tariff, Gender, City, and CRM_SEGMENT values
10          Find the largest cluster whose data has same characteristics with
            Useri for previous hour: Age, Tariff, Gender, City, and CRM_SEG
            MENT values
11          Find the largest cluster in which the probability of finding for
            the next one hour of Useri
12              Update ith row of the Max Probability Table
13      End Loop 4
14  End Loop 1
15
16  Input new data /*New User Data*/
17  Find proper cluster from Max Probability Table (using Age, Tariff, Gender,
    City, and CRM_SEGMENT)
```

Four different datasets from 01/06/2012 to 30/06/2012 are used for the simulation performed, as follows:

- Dataset 1 covers data from 01/06/12 to 07/06/12 (1st week, Table 3),
- Dataset 2 covers data from 08/06/12 to 14/06/12 (2nd week, Table 5 in Appendix A),
- Dataset 3 covers data from 15/06/12 to 21/06/12 (3rd week, Table 6 in Appendix B),
- Dataset 4 covers data from 22/06/12 to 30/06/12 (4th week, Table 7 in Appendix C).

Quota requests were observed by entering the datasets into the current static charging system simulation as input. The comparison of the results retrieved from the charging algorithm of the current MDCS and the proposed DQCS systems are presented as graphics in Figures 6 through 9.

The numbers of quota requests occurred during simulation are presented in Table 3. The numbers of requests are classified based on 6-hour periods. In the 1st column, the hour zones are presented where the grouping belonged. The format is YYYYMMDDHH for example 2012060100 means 01 June 2012, 00 AM.

Table 2. A part of the subscribers with their internet usage for the system's simulations

CALL_ID	CALL_END_DATE	Total Data Usage	Birth Date	Gender	City	Current CRM Segment	Tariff
825391939	10.06.2012 21:31	4869	28.10.1960	M	GIRESUN	Bronze	Plan Voucher
303468087	24.06.2012 13:05	156	28.10.1960	F	ISTANBUL	Gold	Plan Voucher
840674542	13.06.2012 04:57	3906	13.03.1969	M	ANKARA	Bronze	Free Voice Call
143299257	28.06.2012 23:57	11723	25.09.1990	M	ADANA	Bronze	Free Video Call
143300073	28.06.2012 23:59	3028	25.09.1990	F	SAMSUN	Silver	Student
143301516	29.06.2012 00:00	9008	12.08.1980	F	ORDU	Silver	Plan Voucher
143301516	29.06.2012 00:05	364	11.09.1985	F	IZMIR	Bronze	Plan Voucher
143308109	29.06.2012 00:09	4950	11.09.1985	M	KONYA	Silver	Plan Voucher
143311654	29.06.2012 00:14	1070	12.08.1980	F	ISTANBUL	Gold	Free Video Call
143400179	29.06.2012 06:51	3763	06.10.1975	F	ORDU	Bronze	Plan Voucher
128973574	06.06.2012 16:33	44	10.03.1972	M	ISTANBUL	Bronze	Student
128975654	06.06.2012 16:37	130	20.10.1962	M	ISTANBUL	Bronze	Plan Voucher
129403267	07.06.2012 09:38	4000	15.10.1972	M	ADANA	Bronze	Plan Voucher
129403292	07.06.2012 09:38	44	02.08.1983	F	ISTANBUL	Silver	Student
129790498	07.06.2012 21:19	2900	18.11.1967	M	ISTANBUL	Silver	Student
131378138	10.06.2012 11:58	44	18.05.1974	F	ANTALYA	Gold	Free Video Call
131560344	10.06.2012 17:16	304	20.03.1952	F	ISTANBUL	Bronze	Student

In the 2nd column, the number of quota requests is presented as a result of the available quota algorithm in current MDCS. The 3rd column displays the number of quota requests for DQCS algorithm. At the bottom of the table, the sums of quota requests are presented.

$$\left(\left(1 - DQCSTot / Current\ MDCSTot \right) \times 100 \right) \tag{4}$$

The quota requests decreased with the DQCS algorithm; 22% saving was obtained from 01/06/2012 to 07/06/2012. This percentage value is calculated using $((1 - 11023 / 14258) \times 100)$ formulated by Eq.4. The chart in Figure 6 is obtained from Dataset 1. As shown in Figure 6, the DQCS algorithm consistently provides better results than the current MDCS in charging. Although the X-axis in the chart refers to dates, the Y-axis corresponds to the total number of quota requests made during the involved dates. The other datasets were calculated similarly.

The chart in Figure 7 was obtained from Dataset 2. The quota requests decreased with the DQCS algorithm, and 17% savings was obtained from 08/06/2012 through 14/06/2012.

The chart in Figure 8 was obtained from Dataset 3. The quota requests decreased with the DQCS algorithm, and 24% savings was obtained from 15/06/2012 through 21/06/2012.

The chart in Figure 9 was obtained from Dataset 4. The quota requests decreased with the DQCS algorithm, and 18% savings was obtained from 22/06/2012 through 30/06/2012.

Table 3. The results retrieved from current MDCS and the proposed DQCS algorithm for first week duration of dataset. Time is between 01.06.2012 00:00 AM and 07.06.2012 23:59 PM

Time	Quota Requests According to Existing Quota Algorithm in the Current MDCS	Quota Requests of the Proposed DQCS
2012060100	460	366
2012060106	333	267
2012060112	535	440
2012060118	821	619
2012060200	425	392
2012060206	334	289
2012060212	407	380
2012060218	392	340
2012060300	252	224
2012060306	561	377
2012060312	703	527
2012060318	987	719
2012060400	471	364
2012060406	435	333
2012060412	439	379
2012060418	641	545
2012060500	511	338
2012060506	365	268
2012060512	498	402
2012060518	801	650
2012060600	467	331
2012060606	939	492
2012060612	490	331
2012060618	501	415
2012060700	278	254
2012060706	222	209
2012060712	380	318
2012060718	610	454
TOTAL	**14258**	**11023**

As indicated in Table 4, the quota requests are compared in terms of the four datasets with saved rates. As depicted in Table 4, *53618* quota requests were made by the algorithm of the current MDCS in total. Then, the proposed DQCS routines were performed on the same datasets in simulations. In total, *42442* quota requests were made by the algorithm of the proposed DQCS. The results depict the reduced quota requests according to the proposed dynamic quota DQCS algorithm in comparison with the current system's quota algorithms in current MDCS sector, and a total of *20%* savings was obtained in one month.

Figure 6. Graph depicts comparison between static quota allocation in current MDCS and proposed DQCS system from 01.06.2012 00:00 AM through 07.06.2012 23:59 PM

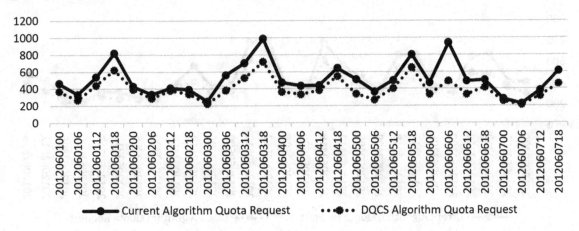

Figure 7. Graph depicts comparison between static quota allocation in current MDCS and proposed DQCS system from 08.06.2012 00:00 AM through 14.06.2012 23:59 PM

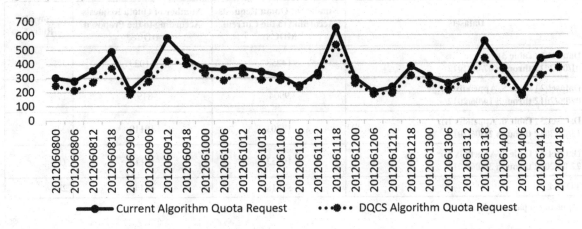

Figure 8. Graph depicts comparison between static quota allocation in current MDCS and proposed DQCS system from 15.06.2012 00:00 AM through 21.06.2012 23:59 PM

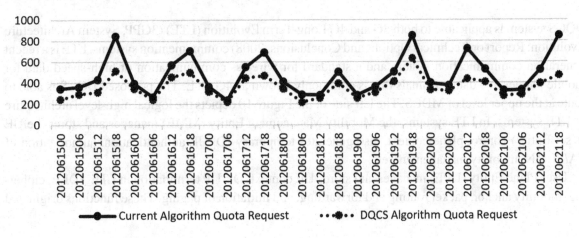

Figure 9. Graph depicts comparison between static quota allocation in current MDCS and proposed DQCS system from 22.06.2012 00:00 AM through 30.06.2012 23:59 PM

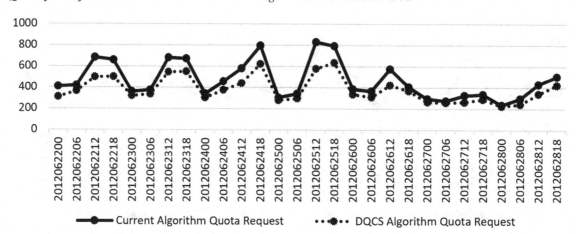

Table 4. Results from four different datasets

Datasets	Number of Quota Requests According to the Current MDCS*	Number of Quota Requests According to the Proposed DQCS*	Saved Rates*
Dataset 1 (Table 3): 01/06/2012 through 07/06/2012	14258	11023	22%
Dataset 2 (Table 5, Appendix A): 08/06/2012 through 14/06/2012	9904	8197	17%
Dataset 3 (Table 6, Appendix B): 15/06/2012 through 21/06/2012	13303	10110	24%
Dataset 4 (Table 7, Appendix C): 22/06/2012 through 30/06/2012	16153	13112	18%
TOTAL	53618	42442	20%

*Fractional parts are discarded.

IMPLEMENTATION OF THE PROPOSED DQCS TO THE CURRENT LONG-TERM EVOLUTION (LTE) COMMUNICATION SYSTEMS

DQCS system is applicable to both 3G and 4G Long-Term Evolution (LTE) (3GPP, System Architecture Evolution: Report on Technical Options and Conclusions, 2008) communication systems. LTE is a recent generation communication system and a standard for wireless communication of high-speed data for mobile phones and data terminals that is commonly known as 4G LTE. The proposed DQCS is able to route at the upper level of MDCS. The left side of the Figure 10 depicts the logical high-level architecture of LTE systems. In LTE systems, the Mobility Management Entity (MME) manages and stores the UE (User Entity) control plane context, also generates temporary ID, UE authentication, authorization of TA/PLMN, mobility management, etc.

User Plane Entity (UPE) manages and stores UE context, DL UP termination in LTE_IDLE, ciphering, mobility anchor, packet routing and forwarding, and initiation of paging. These functions originated recently with LTE. The charging mechanism of LTE systems is Policy and Charging Rules Function (PCRF) that has online and offline charging functionalities through the Packet Data Network (PDN) Gateway (P-GW). The connection between PCRF and PGW provides to transfer the QoS policy and charging rules from PCRF to Policy and Charging Enforcement Function (PCEF) in the PDN GW. DQCS system can be implemented in offline charging functionality of the PGW. The right side of the Figure 10 depicts a simple presentation for the implementation of the DQCS in LTE systems.

FUTURE RESEARCH DIRECTIONS

SOM clusters contain customer information as age, gender home city, customer profile (CRM Segment) and tariff. While in the Max probability table creation phase, only the number of users in the clusters is considered. It can be considered that there is a link between clusters with similar user characteristics. A relationship between clusters can be created using semantic-based matching approaches. Clusters can also be affected by the weight values of similar clusters. This can be used to create more successful Max probability table.

There are several clustering algorithms similar to SOM for example X-means and K-means. These latter algorithms have same problems on a time-stream data sets when clustering. They can lose their dynamism with time. In other words, an average weight of a cluster is not affected when one newer weighted data is added as an input to the cluster if where former inputs are stored in the same cluster forever. Sliding Window has brought a successful solution for this problem by using SOM. Therefore, it is expected to retrieve similar success by using Sliding Window along with other clustering algorithms as a future work.

Figure 10. Logical high-level architecture of LTE systems is shown on left. In addition, the implementation of DQCS to the LTE systems is depicted on right. (3GPP System Architecture Evolution: Report on Technical Options and Conclusions (Release 8)- 3GPP TR 23.882 V8.0.0 (2008-09), Page 16)

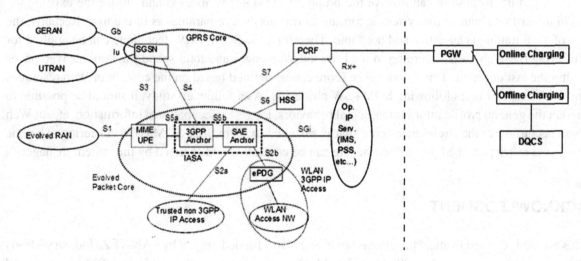

CONCLUSION

In this article, a Dynamic Quota Calculation System (DQCS) is proposed for dynamic quota allocations and charging in Mobile Data Communication Systems (MDCS) using two cascaded routines. The first routine is Self-Organizing Map (SOM) clustering based on a Sliding Window (SW) followed by the second routine, which is a Markov Chain (MC); the overall system is denoted as "(SOM/SW) & MC."

In DQCS, it is aimed to arrange charging and quota allocation algorithms for MDCS dynamically for the subscribers in different groups in order to decrease the signaling intensity on the charging mechanism of MDCS and eliminate unfair situations all over subscribers. As a first routine, an extended SOM approach (SOM/SW) is considered in the charging mechanism of the MDCS for the first time by this study. The SOM/SW algorithm is used in the charging mechanism of the MDCS for clustering all over subscribers according to their age, tariff, gender, city, and CRM_SEGMENT values in the last hour of the system.

According to the performed simulation results, it is observed that many subscribers who are similar in terms of age, tariff, gender, city, and CRM_SEGMENT values can be in different clusters at different possibilities. In addition, the possibility of their existence in SOM/SW clusters varies based on time. Therefore, Markov approach is used to calculate the next quota allocation value according to particular subscriber properties as a second routine. In addition, the weight value of each cluster input from the SOM/SW routine is included in the calculation of the next quota allocation value at time $T_{(n+1)}$. The new quota value for a particular subscriber depends on the average Internet use intensity of the cluster where the cluster is found to be the most appropriate. This way, the optimal quota arrangement in the current system and maximum efficiency in signalization could be obtained.

In simulations, the quota algorithms of the current MDCS and the proposed DQCS were driven and their resulting values were compared. Quota requests made from 01/06/2012 to 30/06/2012 were collected from one of the leading MDCS companies in Turkey (AVEA GSM Company, 2004). One-month's dataset was separated to the datasets of four weeks from 01/06/2012 to 30/06/2012. The results showed that the proposed DQCS algorithm reduced the number of quota request calls at a rate of 20% on average. To conclude, the proposed DQCS is considered as an intelligent software service for both 3G and 4G LTE technologies that is designed to run at the upper MDCS level.

As a result, any system can involve the proposed SOM + SW method and cluster the existing users in the last one hour in the system according to various data or parameters of the user. Recently, the use of Web mining is an active and hot topic. Therefore, the SOM + SW technique can be applied for clustering the Web users according to the browsed Web pages and total spend time on the Web pages within the last one hour. Thus, a relevance score can be defined based on the content of Web resources and Web usage of users following SOM+SW clustering. As a follow up study, it should be possible to predict the general profile information, social behaviors, interests, occupational information, etc. of Web users according to their relevance score that is assigned to them after SOM+SW clustering. The one hour time restriction of SOM+SW clustering can be controlled and changed by the system managers.

ACKNOWLEDGMENT

This article is derived from a Ph.D. thesis study and also a funded project by SAN-TEZ (Industry-Thesis Project with the grant number: 00874.STZ.2011-1) in cooperation with the AVEA GSM company and Istanbul Aydin University with the support of the Ministry of Science, Industry and Technology in Turkey.

REFERENCES

Abidogun, O. A., & Omlin, C. W. (2004, August). A self-organizing maps model for outlier detection in call data from mobile telecommunication networks. *Proc. of the 8th Southern Africa Telecommunication Networks and Applications Conference (SATNAC),* 4.

Avea GSM company. (n.d.). *Turkey, Foundation 2004.* Retrieved from http://www.avea.com.tr/web/en/

Baigorri, C. M., & Maldonado, W. F. (2014). Optimal mobile termination rate: The Brazilian mobile market case. *Telecommunications Policy, 38*(1), 86–95. doi:10.1016/j.telpol.2013.05.002

Cheng, C., Cheng, X., Yuan, M., Song, C., Xu, L., Ye, H., & Zhang, T. (2016, September). A novel cluster algorithm for telecom customer segmentation. In *Communications and Information Technologies (ISCIT), 2016 16th International Symposium on* (pp. 324-329). IEEE. 10.1109/ISCIT.2016.7751644

Fessant, F., François, J., & Clérot, F. (2007). Characterizing ADSL customer behaviours by network traffic data-mining. *Annales des Télécommunications, 62*(3), 350–368.

Fessant, F., Lemaire, V., & Clérot, F. (2008). Combining several SOM approaches in data mining: application to ADSL customer behaviours analysis. *Data Analysis, Machine Learning and Applications,* 343-354.

Gerpott, T. J., & Thomas, S. (2014). Empirical research on mobile Internet usage: A meta-analysis of the literature. *Telecommunications Policy, 38*(3), 291–310. doi:10.1016/j.telpol.2013.10.003

Huang, H. S., Su, T. C., Liang, J. M., & Tseng, Y. C. (2015, March). A dynamic reservation scheme in online charging system for family shared plan. In *Wireless Communications and Networking Conference (WCNC)* (pp. 2279-2284). IEEE.

Istanbul Aydin University. (n.d.). Retrieved from http://www.aydin.edu.tr/index_eng.asp

Kiang, M. Y., Hu, M. Y., & Fisher, D. M. (2006). An extended self-organizing map network for market segmentation—a telecommunication example. *Decision Support Systems, 42*(1), 36–47. doi:10.1016/j.dss.2004.09.012

Kohonen, T. (1990). The self-organizing map. *Proceedings of IEEE,* 1464-1480.

Kohonen, T. (2001). *Self-Organizing Maps* (3rd ed.). Springer. doi:10.1007/978-3-642-56927-2

Lehtimäki, P., & Raivio, K. (2005). Lecture Notes in Computer Science: Vol. 3533. *A SOM based approach for visualization of MDCS network performance data.* Berlin: Springer. doi:10.1007/11504894_82

Li, Z. G., Chen, C., & Soh, Y. C. (2009, May). Pricing based differentiated bandwidth and delay services with weighted Max-Min fairness. In *Industrial Electronics and Applications, 2009. ICIEA 2009. 4th IEEE Conference on* (pp. 773-779). IEEE. 10.1109/ICIEA.2009.5138309

Long-Term Evolution (LTE). (2008). 3rd Generation Partnership Project; Technical Specification Group Services and System Aspects. *3GPP System Architecture Evolution: Report on Technical Options and Conclusions (Release 8) – 3GPP TR 23.882 V8.0.0 (2008-09).* Retrieved from http://www.qtc.jp/3GPP/Specs/23882-800.pdf

MacQueen, J. (1967, June). Some methods for classification and analysis of multivariate observations. In *Proceedings of the fifth Berkeley symposium on mathematical statistics and probability* (*Vol. 1*, No. 14, pp. 281-297). Academic Press.

Mark, K., & Csaba, L. (2007, June). Analyzing customer behavior model graph (CBMG) using Markov chains. In *Intelligent Engineering Systems, 2007. INES 2007. 11th International Conference on* (pp. 71-76). IEEE.

Markov, A. A. (1971). Extension of the limit theorems of probability theory to a sum of variables connected in a chain. John Wiley and Sons.

Mölleryd, B. G., & Markendahl, J. (2014). Analysis of spectrum auctions in India—An application of the opportunity cost approach to explain large variations in spectrum prices. *Telecommunications Policy*, *38*(3), 236–247. doi:10.1016/j.telpol.2014.01.002

Multanen, M., Raivio, K., & Lehtimäki, P. (2006). Hierarchical analysis of MDCS network performance data. *14th European Symposium on Artificial Neural Networks ESANN 2006*, 449-454.

Netzer, O., Lattin, J. M., & Srinivasan, V. (2008). A hidden Markov model of customer relationship dynamics. *Marketing Science*, *27*(2), 185–204. doi:10.1287/mksc.1070.0294

Ozianyi, V. G., & Ventura, N. (2005, November). Dynamic pricing for 3G NETWORKS using admission control and traffic differentiation. In *Networks, 2005. Jointly held with the 2005 IEEE 7th Malaysia International Conference on Communication., 2005 13th IEEE International Conference on* (Vol. 2, pp. 838-843). IEEE.

Padmaja, S., & Sheshasaayee, A. (2016). Clustering of User Behaviour based on Web Log data using Improved K-Means Clustering Algorithm. *IACSIT International Journal of Engineering and Technology*, *8*(1), 305–310.

Pelleg, D., & Moore, A. W. (2000, June). X-means: Extending K-means with Efficient Estimation of the Number of Clusters. In ICML (Vol. 1, pp. 727-734). Academic Press.

Rejeb, S. B., Nasser, N., & Tabbane, S. (2014). A novel resource allocation scheme for LTE network in the presence of mobility. *Journal of Network and Computer Applications*, *46*, 352–361. doi:10.1016/j.jnca.2014.07.017

Snell, L., & Grinstead, C. M. (1997). Introduction to Probability (2nd ed.). Academic Press.

The Ministry of Science, Industry and Technology. (n.d.). Retrieved from http://www.sanayi.gov.tr/Default.aspx?lng=en

Tulankar, K., & Wajgi, R. (2012). Clustering Telecom Customers using Emergent Self Organizing Maps for Business Profitability 1. *Int J Comput Sci Technol*, *3*, 256–259.

Vegni, A. M., & Natalizio, E. (2014). A hybrid (N/M) CHO soft/hard vertical handover technique for heterogeneous wireless networks. *Ad Hoc Networks*, *14*, 51–70. doi:10.1016/j.adhoc.2013.11.005

Yang, F. M., Chen, W. M., & Wu, J. L. C. (2014). A dynamic strategy for packet scheduling and bandwidth allocation based on channel quality in IEEE 802.16 e OFDMA system. *Journal of Network and Computer Applications*, *39*, 52–60. doi:10.1016/j.jnca.2013.04.008

Zaghloul, S., Bziuk, W., & Jukan, A. (2008, May). A scalable billing architecture for future wireless mesh backhauls. In *Communications, 2008. ICC'08. IEEE International Conference on* (pp. 2974-2978). Beijing: IEEE. 10.1109/ICC.2008.560

KEY TERMS AND DEFINITIONS

CDR: A call detail record (CDR) in voice over IP (VoIP) is a file containing information about recent system usage such as the identities of sources (points of origin), the identities of destinations (endpoints), the duration of each call, the amount billed for each call, the total usage time in the billing period, the total free time remaining in the billing period, and the running total charged during the billing period. The format of the CDR varies among VoIP providers or programs. Some programs allow CDRs to be configured by the user.

Charging: A function whereby information related to a chargeable event is formatted and transferred in order to make it possible to determine usage for which the charged party may be subsequently billed.

Clustering: Clustering is a grouping of a particular set of objects based on their characteristic, that is, aggregating them according to their similarities. Regarding to data mining, this methodology partitions the data implementing a specific join algorithm, most suitable for the desired information analysis.

GSM: Global system for mobile communication is a digital mobile telephony system that is widely used in Europe and other parts of the world. GSM uses a variation of time division multiple access (TDMA) and is the most widely used of the three digital wireless telephony technologies (TDMA, GSM, and CDMA). GSM digitizes and compresses data, then sends it down a channel with two other streams of user data, each in its own time slot. It operates at either the 900 MHz or 1800 MHz frequency band.

LTE: Long term evolution (LTE) is a 4G wireless broadband technology developed by the third-generation partnership project (3GPP), an industry trade group.

Self-Organizing Map: The self-organizing map (SOM) is a well-known neural network and certainly one of the most popular unsupervised learning algorithm. Since its invention by Finnish Professor Teuvo Kohonen in the early 1980s, more than 4000 research articles have been published on the algorithm, its conception, and uses. The SOM mapping is preserving, namely the most similar two data samples are in the input space, and the closer they will appear together on the final displayed map. This allows the user to identify clusters such as large sets of a specific type of input pattern.

Session: Logical connection between parties involved in a packet-switched-based communication. This term is used for IP connections rather than the term "call" that is normally used for a connection over conventional (circuit switched) systems.

APPENDIX A

Dataset 2

See Table 5.

Table 5. The table presents second dataset that involves the data between 08.06.2012 00:00 AM and 14.06.2012 23:59 PM

Time	Quota Requests According to Existing Quota Algorithm in the Current MDCS	Quota Requests of the Proposed DQCS
2012060800	301	366
2012060806	278	267
2012060812	353	440
2012060818	483	619
2012060900	215	392
2012060906	334	289
2012060912	580	380
2012060918	443	340
2012061000	365	224
2012061006	358	377
2012061012	366	527
2012061018	343	719
2012061100	313	364
2012061106	240	333
2012061112	331	379
2012061118	653	545
2012061200	295	338
2012061206	199	268
2012061212	230	402
2012061218	377	650
2012061300	304	331
2012061306	256	492
2012061312	298	331
2012061318	555	415
2012061400	364	254
2012061406	184	209
2012061412	432	318
2012061418	454	454
TOTAL	**9904**	**8197**

APPENDIX B

Dataset 3

See Table 6.

Table 6. The table presents third dataset involves the data between 15.06.2012 00:00 AM and 21.06.2012 23:59 PM

Time	Quota Requests According to Existing Quota Algorithm in the Current MDCS	Quota Requests of the Proposed DQCS
2012061500	346	245
2012061506	362	294
2012061512	430	312
2012061518	846	515
2012061600	394	347
2012061606	266	241
2012061612	569	456
2012061618	706	500
2012061700	365	317
2012061706	236	222
2012061712	550	448
2012061718	691	468
2012061800	411	346
2012061806	290	218
2012061812	283	254
2012061818	506	395
2012061900	284	256
2012061906	363	308
2012061912	504	413
2012061918	849	631
2012062000	397	333
2012062006	373	321
2012062012	726	436
2012062018	530	409
2012062100	325	274
2012062106	329	288
2012062112	525	394
2012062118	847	469
TOTAL	**13303**	**10110**

APPENDIX C

Dataset 4

See Table 7.

Table 7. The table presents fourth dataset involves the data between 22.06.2012 00:00 AM and 30.06.2012 23:59 PM

Time	Quota Requests According to Existing Quota Algorithm in the Current MDCS	Quota Requests of the Proposed DQCS
2012062200	409	311
2012062206	418	365
2012062212	684	498
2012062218	660	500
2012062300	360	321
2012062306	375	335
2012062312	682	546
2012062318	671	550
2012062400	340	302
2012062406	455	375
2012062412	580	439
2012062418	794	621
2012062500	304	278
2012062506	340	296
2012062512	830	578
2012062518	792	633
2012062600	384	336
2012062606	365	308
2012062612	576	421
2012062618	404	366
2012062700	294	263
2012062706	274	256
2012062712	325	262
2012062718	335	288
2012062800	233	224
2012062806	296	240
2012062812	430	339

continued on following page

Table 7. Continued

Time	Quota Requests According to Existing Quota Algorithm in the Current MDCS	Quota Requests of the Proposed DQCS
2012062818	504	422
2012062900	334	292
2012062906	190	181
2012062912	453	341
2012062918	521	379
2012063000	400	297
2012063006	331	310
2012063012	413	335
2012063018	397	304
TOTAL	**16153**	**13112**

Chapter 20
A Novel Method for Calculating Customer Reviews Ratings

Ioannis S. Vourgidis
De Montfort University, UK

Jenny Carter
De Montfort University, UK

Leandros Maglaras
De Montfort University, UK

Helge Janicke
De Montfort University, UK

Zoe Folia
National Technical University of Athens, Greece

Pavlina Fragkou
Technical Educational Institute of Athens, Greece

ABSTRACT

The number of consumers consulting online reviews in order to purchase a product or service, keeps growing. In addition to that, consumers can add an online review in order to express their experience upon the services or products received. This iterative process makes reviews matter regarding consumer's purchase decision. Apart from reviews, consumers are welcomed to provide numerical ratings for the product or services they bought. If a hotel is exposed to an online hotel review site, then it very possible to improve the possibility of a consumer to consider booking a room in this hotel. According to this chapter, regardless of positive or negative reviews, hotel awareness is enhanced. Online reviews significantly improve hotel awareness for lesser-known hotels than for well-known hotels.

DOI: 10.4018/978-1-5225-5384-7.ch020

INTRODUCTION

Over the last years, almost a decade, more and more consumers consult online reviews before making any hotel arrangements (Wong & Law, 2005). On the other hand, consumers can make a post on an online review site as part of a retaliation response, when they feel betrayed by the organization or business (Grégoire & Fisher, 2008; Grégoire, Tripp, & Legoux, 2009). However, Hennig-Thurau, Gwinner, Walsh, & Gremler (2004) note the motivation to make a post can be attributed to a multitude of reasons, one of which is concern for other customers. Importantly, future consumers may rely on other consumer reviews as these are seen as relatively unbiased and independent from marketing. Chen (2008) found that recommendations of other consumers exerted more influence on their choice than did reviews from expert or firm related advisors. Apart from reviews consumers are welcomed to provide numerical ratings for the product or services they bought.

According to Vermeulen & Seegers (2009), and a study carried out, if a hotel is exposed to an online hotel review site, then it very possible to improve the possibility a consumer to consider book a room in this hotel. According to this research, regardless of positive or negative reviews, hotel awareness is enhanced. Online reviews significantly improve hotel awareness for less-known hotels than for well-known hotels. Another study had been carried out by Sparks & Browning (2011), investigating the impact of online reviews on hotel booking intentions and perception of trust. Trust is one of the most important factors in determining whether people will purchase online or not. Therefore, consumer/customer satisfaction has a two-way relation with consumer trust, if a consumer trusts the service provider that will be satisfied and simultaneously a satisfied customer will trust again the service provider.

Chen (2008) argues that potential consumers use online consumer reviews as one way to reduce risk and uncertainty in the purchase situation. The reviews and recommendations of other customers can assist in determining whether to trust the hotel under consideration. According to Papathanassis & Knolle (2011), there is a trend where positive reviews have less impact than negative reviews. According to Ye, Law, & Gu (2009), there is a significant relationship between the number of hotel/rooms bookings and hotel room rates as computed by customers' reviews. Moreover, this study proved that positive reviews contribute significantly in the number of bookings. Also, hotels with high star ratings received more online bookings, but room rate, price per night, had a negative impact on the number of online bookings.

Since, online reviews are one of the most important factors for customers to book a room or to plan a trip, this kind of information would provide valuable insights to hotel management, if this data, structured and unstructured, is efficiently and effectively analysed. In this chapter we present, a novel approach to answer the research question "Is the average rating of each hotel that has been rated by customers close to the average Sentiment Score extracted from each review?". In order to carry out this research, the TripAdvisor datasets were used (being available at http://archive.ics.uci.edu/ml/datasets/OpinRank+Review+Dataset; directly linking to the author of these datasets http://kavita-ganesan.com/entityranking-data). Two types of datasets were used for this work; a set of reviews datasets and a set of hotel dimensional information concerning the hotels for which reviews were recorded. In order to come up with solid results, significant data management, text mining and sentiment analysis were carried out.

Our work was motivated by the fact that previous methods were using only a limited number of features and did not give emphasis in exploiting the semantic/conceptual information hidden inside those selected features. Moreover, sentiment analysis techniques prove to provide valuable information influencing actual rating. This is the reason why, sentiment analysis was considered as an additional feature in our method. The methodology developed, the results and the conclusions are presented and discussed in this order, while the background or literature review, comes before them.

BACKGROUND

The rapid growth of Internet applications on hospitality and tourism leads to an enormous amount of consumer-generated online reviews on different travel-related facilities, while three-quarters of travellers considered online customer reviews as information source when planning their trips (Ye et al., 2009). In other disciplines, studies had shown that online user generated reviews could significantly influence sales of products like books and CDs. A study was carried out in 2008, to investigate the influence of customer online reviews on the number of hotel room bookings. Data was collected by a major travel website in China, where customers could add their reviews regarding the hotel they stayed. This study focused on consumer reviews posted during the period from February 2007 to January 2008. In total, 3625 reviews from 248 hotels were used (Ye et al., 2009). Results produced by this research justified that, there is a strong relationship between positive online reviews and significant increase in number of bookings.

In 2014 a study was conducted by Zhou, Ye, Pearce, & Wu (2014), in order to explore and demonstrate the utility of big data analytics within hotel guest experience and hotel customer satisfaction. These two aspects have been widely recognized contributing to customer loyalty, repeat purchases, and favourable word-of-mouth. This study employed one of the most important types of consumer-generated content, online customer reviews of hotel properties, to understand hotel guest experience and its relationships with guest satisfaction. Regression analysis indicated that, factors Hybrid and Deals were the most important factors associated with guest satisfaction. One of the most important insights revealed by this study was that 34 words explained nearly 63% of the total variance in customer satisfaction. This evidence shows that a customer tends to use words to describe his/her experience when he/she is happy or unhappy about a hotel (Xiang, Schwartz, Gerdes, & Uysal, 2015).

A Web-based opinion mining system for hotel reviews and user comments was developed by Kasper & Vela (2011) to support hotel management and monitor customer published user reviews. This system was capable to detect, retrieve, classify and analyse them. A custom word dictionary that was developed determined the polarity of each review i.e., whether a review was negative, neutral or positive. Sentiment analysis was performed in two steps. The first was to carry out a statistical polarity classification where each review was broken down in segments of 4-grams. This method classified these segments of reviews in two categories, positive or negative, while the second classification methodology classified these segments of reviews in three categories, positive, neutral, negative. The second method applied, was based on an information extraction tool using a dictionary of domain specific terms relevant to hotel domain and a sentiment dictionary used to associate basic polarity values with terms. Also, via these two dictionaries a specific hotel topic term to each text segment was assigned. Via this method, each text segment was assigned with a polarity rating. By combining results produced by these two methods, final polarity for each review was derived. Polarity values provided by the first methodology were used as the baseline value and ratings from the second method were used to correct or smooth that value.

Study performed by Hargreaves (2015) focused on analysing hotel guest satisfaction ratings reviews. For this study, TripAdvisor reviews concerning five hotels located in Singapore were analysed. The analysis was based on six main attributes: (i) location; (ii) sleep; (iii) quality; (iv) rooms; (v) service quality; and (vi) cleanliness. For these attributes, ratings were provided by customers as part of the review process. Moreover, text analysis, on customer text reviews, was performed in order to flag each review as negative or positive. The TripAdvisor's dataset contained 14.175 reviews from 09/2005 - 09/2014, including a text review and a rating from one to five for each of the above six attributes. Hence, by carrying out text analytics and combining them with ratings for these six attributes useful insights were provided, such as which attribute affected more negative reviews, which specific hotel amenities are the most important for a hotels customer, and which are the main keywords hotel managers should pay attention to.

Another study was carried out where a technique was developed in order to detect TripAdvisor's reviews sentences containing contextual information. To achieve this, a text mining tool and a rule based induction kit for text were used. The dataset used included 100 reviews from TripAdvisor. Two-thirds of the data was used for training and the rest for testing purposes. Hence, by adding new reviews from TripAdvisor this prototype could classify the review as "Contextual" or as "Preferences". The "Contextual" category group included those sentences that contain information about the context in which the review was expressed while "Preferences" category groups included those sentences that contain information about some features that consumer evaluated (Aciar, 2010).

As it can easily be seen from work presented above, most of the methods use datasets taken from TripAdvisor, which is considered the most reliable source of information in travel reservation business. The difference between them lies in the following factors: (a) the problem examined (such as parameters that influence reviews); (b) the features selected and examined of each review; (c) the method chosen to process data (such as regression analysis, sentiment analysis, other); (d) text processing depth, i.e., exploitation of conceptual information (using dictionaries or information extraction techniques). It must be stressed that, recent approaches reveal a trend towards use of sentiment analysis techniques in combination with semantic information as this is provided after applying information extraction techniques.

Our work differs from the ones presented in the following factors: (a) the problem examined, i.e. the fact that comparison takes under consideration the average sentiment analysis score of each review in other words it provided a more in-depth analysis of each review; (b) the number of parameters examined during the text mining process, as this is described in the methodology section; (c) use of publicly available dictionary and database, i.e. Wordnet 3.0. In other words, our method follows a holistic text processing approach.

RELATED METHODS

According to Berry & Linoff (1997), text mining is the process of finding and exploiting useful patterns in text data. Text mining may serve many purposes, such as to understand documents either summarizing them or clustering them into similar groups. According to Berry & Linoff (1997), one of the most challenging aspects of text mining is to manage the text itself. Even though there are several text information retrieval methods in the literature, Gaikwad, Chaugule, & Patil (2014) state that there are four main methods used in order to retrieve information from text. These are:

1. **Term Based Method (TBM):** In term based method, a document is analysed based on term. The method presents many advantages such as efficient computational performance as well as mature

theories for term weighting. Term based methods suffer from the problems of polysemy and synonymy. Polysemy means a word has multiple meanings and synonymy is multiple words having the same meaning.

2. **Phrase Based Method (PBM):** Phrase carries more semantics like information and is less ambiguous. In phrase based method, a document is analysed on phrase basis since phrases are less ambiguous and more discriminative than individual terms. However, the performance of this method could be daunting for several reasons, such as a significant number of redundant and noisy phrases are present while they have low frequency of occurrence.

3. **Concept Based Method (CBM):** In concept based method, terms are analysed on sentence and document level. Statistical analysis of term frequency captures the importance of a word within a document. Two terms can have the same frequency in the same document, but the meaning is that one term contributes which can be more appropriate than the meaning contributed by the other term. Terms that capture the semantics of a text should be given more importance so, a new concept-based mining is introduced.

This model includes three components. The first component analyses the semantic structure of sentences. The second component constructs a conceptual ontological graph to describe the semantic structures and the last component extracts top concepts based on the first two components, to build feature vectors using the standard vector space model. Concept-based model can effectively discriminate between non-important terms and meaningful terms which describe a sentence's meaning. The concept-based model usually relies upon natural language processing techniques. Feature selection is applied to query concepts to optimize representation and remove noise and ambiguity. The overall performance of this method could be considered as drawback, especially in case of large datasets.

4. **Pattern Taxonomy Method (PTM):** In pattern taxonomy method, documents are analysed on pattern basis. Patterns can be structured into taxonomy by using is-a relation. Pattern mining has been extensively studied in data mining communities for many years. Patterns can be discovered by data mining techniques like association rule mining, frequent item set mining, sequential pattern mining and closed pattern mining. Use of discovered knowledge in the field of text mining is difficult and ineffective, because some useful long patterns with high specificity lack in support. Not all frequent short patterns are useful, hence known as misinterpretations of patterns and this leads to the ineffective performance.

According to Jusoh & Alfawareh (2012), technically wise, text mining involves use of automated tools for exploiting the enormous amount of knowledge available in documents, while simultaneously represents a step forward from text retrieval. In research community, this is also known as Text Data Mining, TDM, and Knowledge Discovery in Textual Databases. Text mining is a scientific field combining information retrieval, data mining, machine learning and computational linguistics. A text mining process or a business intelligence text mining tool incorporates the following steps:

*   Pre-processing of text document collection including text categorization, information extraction, term extraction and tokenization.

- Analysing results produced by the above process with a technique such as clustering, association rules and trend analysis.
- Visualising results produced by the analysis process.

The same authors, (Jusoh & Alfawareh, 2012), expressed the opinion that despite the numerous efforts performed by the research community to apply some techniques or methods such as rule base, knowledge base and machine learning, the two essential text mining methods are Natural Language Processing (NLP), and Information Extraction (IE), which are briefly introduced below.

1. **Natural Language Processing:** It deals with Natural Language Generation (NLG) and Natural Language Understanding (NLU). NLG uses some level of underlying linguistic representation of text, to ensure that generated text is grammatically correct and fluent. Most NLG systems include a syntactic analyser to reassure that grammatical rules are obeyed, and text planner to decide how to effectively arrange sentences into paragraph. The most well-known NLG application is a machine translation system. The system analyses text from a source language into grammatical or conceptual representations and then generates corresponding text in the target language. NLU has to do with understanding and using languages since words are initially recognized. The scope of such a system is to adopt the way(s) humans carry out linguistic tasks such as reading, writing, speaking and hearing. Development of an NLU system requires detailed understanding of language structure and combinations of complex language idioms. By this manner, a NLU system would be able to understand sentences that may have mistakes.
2. **Information Extraction:** This scientific area is closely related with creating structured information from unstructured data such as text. Extracted structured information may include events, entities and relationships between them. Results are stored in a database in a structured manner in order to apply data mining techniques having as an objective to discover knowledge.

There are three main steps that consist Information Extraction: text pre-processing; rule selection, where rules are chosen in order to trigger text relationships; and rule application where rule conditions are applied so that to determine which rules are satisfied or not. Attention must be paid to the fact that, two knowledge types are necessary for extracting information from text; lexical knowledge and linguistic grammar.

Apart from mining text data in order to produce meaningful results and insights, sentiment analysis or sentiment text detection has been one of the most interesting research topics during recent years. Huge amount of reviews is available on the Web, that are related to produce reviews, services reviews, reviews that are available on websites (Longo, Land, Schramm, Fraas, Hoskins, & Howell, 1997) or reviews that are available on websites within a specific topic of interest (Jeacle & Carter, 2011). Reviews are also available on social networks, personal websites and blogs, which are then aggregated by websites (Ziegler, Lausen, & Schmidt-Thieme, 2004). Sentiment analysis or sentiment detection has been used for products comparison and opinion summarization where opinions from reviews are summarized, by providing sentiment polarities and correlated events. Another area that sentiment detection is very useful is opinion reason mining, where providing sentiment polarity, either binary or multiple, is not enough especially for cases where reasoning is required. This may apply to film reviews, hotel reviews and more general in services reviews.

According to Tang, Tan, & Cheng (2009), sentiment detection could be used in providing solutions to problems of subjectivity classification and sentiment classification. Subjectivity classification deals with trying to distinguish, within a document, those sentences that present personal opinions from those that objectively present a current state of fact. On the other hand, document sentiment classification includes two kinds of classification labels, binary sentiment classification (positive or negative) and multi-class sentiment classification (such as very negative, negative, neutral, positive, very positive). The majority of research carried out so far follows the binary classification approach.

According to Tang et al. (2009), subjectivity classification is a task to investigate whether a paragraph or sentence presents the opinion of its author/reviewer or reports facts. Most of research showed that there was very tight relation between subjectivity classification and document sentiment classification. Some major techniques that have been used so far are Similarity Approach and Multiple Naïve Bayes Classifier.

Similarity Approach classifies sentences under the hypothesis that, opinion sentences are more similar to other opinion sentences than factual sentences. There are three main steps that are involved with this approach. Firstly, Information Retrieval method is applied in order to acquire documents that are on the same topic as the sentence in question. Secondly, calculate similarity scores with each sentence in those documents and measure an average value. Thirdly, assign a sentence to the category, either opinion or fact, for which the average value is the highest one.

Naïve Bayes Classifier is one of the most widely used supervised machine learning algorithms. This method sets as initial rule i.e., that all sentences are either opinions or facts. According to Liu (2012), a work carried out by Wiebe, Bruce, & O'Hara (1999), performed subjectivity classification using Naïve Bayes Classifier with a set of binary features, e.g., the presence in the sentence of a pronoun, an adjective, a cardinal number, a modal other than 'will' and an adverb other than 'not'.

According to Tang et al. (2009), the task of document sentiment classification usually involved manual or semi-manual construction of semantic orientation word lexicons. Research showed that, most adjectives and adverbs, as well as a small group of nouns and verbs possess semantic orientation. Automatic methods of sentiment annotation at a word level can be grouped into two major categories: (1) corpus-based approaches and (2) dictionary-based approaches. The first group includes methods that rely on syntactic or co-occurrence patterns of words in large texts to determine their sentiment. The second group uses WordNet information (Pedersen, Patwardhan, & Michelizzi, 2004), in order to acquire sentiment-marked words or to measure the similarity between candidate words and sentiment-bearing words such as 'good' and 'bad'.

According to Mann & Kaur (2013a), clustering is a significant task in data analysis and data mining applications. It arranges a set of objects so that these objects in the identical group are more related to each other than to those in other groups or clusters. Clustering is an unsupervised learning data mining method, since hidden patterns are discovered from bulky datasets. In this case, there is no desired output already provided, in order to train a subset of a data set and evaluate results versus required or real figures; this is the main difference between supervised and unsupervised learning data mining methods. Supervised data mining models are Neural Networks, Decision Trees while unsupervised data mining models are Clustering and Self Organizing Maps. As far as Clustering algorithms, according to Mann & Kaur (2013a), these are categorized, into partition-based algorithms, hierarchical-based algorithms, density-based algorithms, and grid-based algorithms. These methods vary in the procedures used for measuring similarity within and between clusters, the use of thresholds in constructing clusters and the way of clustering, meaning, whether they allow objects to belong strictly to one cluster or can belong to more clusters in different degrees.

Partitioning algorithms split data points into k partitions, where each partition represents a cluster. Each cluster has a centre data point. According to Berry & Linoff (1997), the best assignment of cluster centres could be defined as the ones that minimize the sum of the distance from every data point to its nearest cluster centre. It is difficult to find the optimal solution therefore these kinds of algorithms are trying to improve their performance. The main disadvantage of these algorithms is whenever a point is close to centre of another cluster, poor results are produced due to data points overlapping, while one of its strong advantages is its time performance. The most well know partitioning algorithm is K-Means.

Hierarchical clustering is a technique that divides data by developing a hierarchy of clusters. According to Mann & Kaur (2013a), this method is based on the connectivity approach, while it uses distance matrix criteria for data clustering. There are two main categories of these algorithms; agglomerative and divisive algorithms.

Hence, according to Berry & Linoff (1997), agglomerative clustering method creates a tree-like structure of clusters, where clusters can be investigated. In the beginning of this process clusters are small and pure, since the members of each cluster are few and closely related. At the end of the process clusters are large and not well defined. On the other hand, divisive algorithms adopt a top down clustering approach. It starts by using k-means to split data into two clusters. The larger of these two clusters is split again until the process is stopped and the required number of clusters has been reached.

The advantage of hierarchical clustering is that it can handle any type of variable, such as, binomial, nominal, ordinal while also providing flexibility in handling granularity. On the other hand, according to Berry & Linoff (1997) its main disadvantage is that it can be computationally expensive, difficult to visualize the clusters while it may be sensitive to outliers. One of the most well-known divisive algorithms is the Expectation Maximization algorithm which may produce good results with the only drawback of slow convergence.

Density based algorithms find clusters according to data regions growing with high density. These kinds of algorithms can correctly identify outliers and noise. The most well-known algorithm is DBSCAN which stands for Density Based Spatial Clustering of Applications with Noise. It groups together points that are close to each other, these points have many nearby neighbours, while marking as outlier points these data points that are far away from their nearest neighbours. It is not required to determine specific clusters before execution, while it handles effectively the outliers. On the other hand, in some cases border data points may be accessible from more than one cluster. For that reason, DBSCAN has been implemented, as a variation of DBSCA, where border data points are handled as noise.

Grid Density Based Clustering Algorithm: According to Mann & Kaur (2013b), Grid Density based clustering method considers the value space that surrounds the data points. This method uses grid structure and dense grids to determine clusters. The steps of this method are the following:

- Divide the data space into a finite number of cells, in order to create the grid structure.
- Cell density calculation; according to Mann & Kaur (2013b), cell density can be defined as the number of data points into the cell.
- Sorting cells according to their densities.
- Cluster identification.

According to Mann & Kaur (2013b), the main advantage of this method is that it handles noise, whereas it can also effectively handle arbitrary shaped clusters. Also, processing time could be decreased.

However attention should be paid to the input parameters since inefficient results could be produced. The main advantage of this method is that the number of clusters could not be defined in advance.

In literature, there have been many researches where clustering methods are compared either in terms of performance or in terms of accuracy, to serve text mining and text mining analysis. Hence, an experimental research done by Jain, Bajpai, & Rohila (2012), in order to apply a methodology named as Description Comes First, DCF, on two text clustering methods; a clustering method using results returned by Web search engines, known as Lingo and a descriptive K-Means algorithm for clustering collections of large documents. Authors defined text clustering at the main process of organising pieces of textual information or documents, whose members are similar in some way, and groups or clusters are dissimilar to each other. The authors of this research provided a concise overview of several clustering techniques and eventually presented the two above clustering methods; Lingo and Descriptive K-Means. In the search results clustering process four phases were engaged: input pre-processing; frequent phase extraction; cluster label induction; and, content location. In the input pre-processing phase, input documents were tokenized and split into two terms. After this process, a term document matrix was created including terms that exceed a predefined term frequency threshold. Moreover, terms that were present in document titles had been assigned with a predefined constant, since it might contain important information. In the frequent phase extraction, cluster label candidates were identified, as either phrases or single terms. In the phase of cluster label induction, label candidates produced by the previous step are excluded, according to what better describes the input collection. In the phase of cluster content allocation, documents are grouped into clusters according to the similarity between the document and the cluster label. As far as the other clustering technique, descriptive K-Means algorithm's process was like the first one, with some changes. In the pre-processing phase, an index was assigned to each document while another index was assigned to cluster candidate labels. In the dominant topic detection phase K-Means clustering algorithm was executed against a sample of documents in order to identify dominant topics. In this phase, the authors used two methods for clustering label: the first is the extraction of frequent phases; and, shallow linguistic pre-processing resulting in extraction phases. It should be mentioned that shallow linguistic processing stands for a machine learning process where constituent sentence parts like verbs, nouns are identified and afterwards these are linked to groups that have a discrete grammatical meaning such as verb groups and noun groups. Afterwards, since dominant topics were identified, phrases or single terms that were irrelevant with the dominant topics were excluded in the pre-processing phase and afterwards K-Means clustering was applied to all the documents by using cosine distance in order to calculate similarity between documents. According to the authors, the choice of cosine distance was made upon the need for computation efficiency for handling large numbers of documents. Authors mapped the number of dominant topics to the number of desired clusters for K-Means algorithm. Overall, conclusions from these researches were that Lingo clustering in combination with Description Comes First methodology produced satisfactory, while Descriptive K-Means algorithm produced relatively pure clusters from processing thousands of documents, even in the case that sampling of the initial set of documents has to be executed due to lack of hardware resources; this indicates that Descriptive K-Means algorithm could be used for text clustering and to produce effective results.

A comparative study was carried out by Mugunthadevi, Punitha, & Punithavalli (2011) to identify which out of six clustering techniques is the most suitable for text/documents clustering. These techniques were, K-Means and a generalized version of it named K* Means, Expectation Maximization and its variants, and Text Categorization Feature Selection (TCFS) method. In short, TCFS is a method where in text pre-processing state, term weights are estimated using TF/IDF values, providing information about each term's number of times appearance in a document or whole set of documents. For documents clustering, K-Means Algorithm was used.

The dataset Reuters-21758 was used by the authors and all six different algorithms were applied. The results indicated that TCFS method provided purer clusters, while the same method provided the highest F-Measure, which is a measure of test accuracy and the highest score is 1 while the lowest score is 0.

Another study was carried out by Punitha, Thangaiah, & Punithavalli (2014), assessing the performance of Partitioning and Hierarchical clustering techniques for implementing text clustering. The techniques used were the K-Means, Expectation Maximization, TCFS and the Hierarchical Agglomerative. The authors used 20 newsgroups datasets, and according to the F-Measure, the Hierarchical Agglomerative technique scored the highest F-Measure, while the TCFS scored the second highest score. It has to be mentioned that the authors did not apply any feature selection; in that case the TCFS technique might produce better F-Measures, according to the aforementioned studies.

According to the literature as far text clustering, TCFS technique by applying K-Means in combination with significant feature selection (therefore implementing a descriptive K-Means) could produce satisfactory clustering results. Additionally, according to Berry & Linoff (1997), Expectation Maximization algorithm produces satisfactory results, but as discussed earlier in some cases it is time consuming. Finally K-Means is relatively scalable and efficient in processing large datasets whereas Expectation Maximization's complexity may affect computation time.

METHODOLOGY

In this chapter, we will tackle the following research questions:

- Is the average Sentiment Score extracted from each review close to the average rating that each hotel has been rated by customers, via TripAdvisor.com?
- Is it possible to define such kind of groups of reviews (clusters) and to identify which are the most important features that affect customers' satisfaction?

To efficiently answer this, two different kind of datasets were available. The first containing for each hotel the review date, review title and full review. In total 259,000 reviews were included for 2568 hotels, hence on average 100 reviews for each hotel are available. The total number of datasets including all these reviews, is 2568, one dataset for each hotel. Reviews cover the period 03/01/2001-31/01/2009. As mentioned in the introduction, the second type of dataset contains dimensional information for each hotel. Hence, there are ten datasets, one per city, including information per hotel per record.

This section discusses how these datasets are merged in order to produce one dataset, the data cleansing process applied and the type of data mining techniques used, so to retrieve insights and provide recommendations. To apply data mining techniques, significant data manipulation takes place to cleanse data. Also, after data cleansing, data must be in the appropriate format ready for further analysis. Firstly, the 2568 datasets were merged into one, by adding a column with the hotel's name. Moreover, since these datasets include review title and detail review, a new column created containing both review title and detail review, so that text mining and sentiment analysis techniques can be discussed in later sections, to use them as a full review sentence, and not to omit any of them. Afterwards, this dimensional information for each hotel was appended, by duplicating this information; the benefit from this data step was to have fully denormalized data, ready to use for analysis. Last but not least, each review was assigned an ID. For this project, reviews written in English were taken into consideration; hence, it was necessary to detect the language each single review was written; this was done by uploading the full dataset on Google Spreadsheets and by using the *DetectLanguage*function; reviews written in a language other than English were filtered out. It has to be mentioned that reviews containing only symbols or records with missing reviews were filtered out as well. Also, hotels with overall rating equal to 0 or -1 were omitted as well. Therefore, of almost 259,000 reviews 231,279 remained via this data manipulation process, and the existence of noise in the data was eliminated. Also, after the data manipulation 2443 hotels remained in the dataset, due to duplications in the datasets. It has to be mentioned that the column Hotel_Url was omitted, since in some cases it was creating duplication due to two or more URLs for one hotel. Figure 1 presents in a graphical manner these data manipulation steps.

To efficiently and effectively answer the first question, sentiment analysis has to be carried out with some minor text mining process, and to provide a sentiment score for each review. Moreover, to answer the second question significant text mining and clustering must be carried out in one process. The results of those two methods are stored in the same dataset, so that to have a coherent view of initial data and results, and therefore easier to provide insights. Figure 2 illustrates the data mining methodology. It must be stressed that different text mining processes have been applied for clustering and sentiment analysis, since these two methods serve different purposes. The Data Mining methodology is illustrated in Figure 2.

Regarding the Clustering Process, Descriptive K-Means and Expectation Maximization algorithms were executed and tested. It proved that Descriptive K-Means produced more coherent clusters, and these are the following:

Figure 1. Data Manipulation

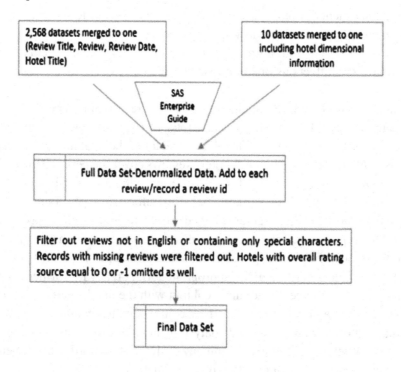

Figure 2. Data Mining Methodology

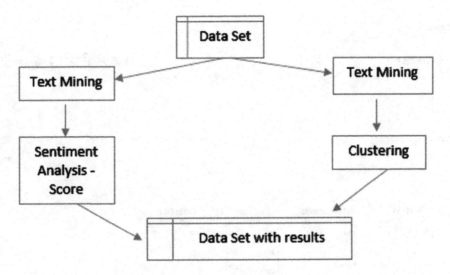

- Business purposes
- Family
- Couple
- Friends – Other

Customers who visit a hotel for business purposes mostly care for food quality, the desk services and service offered overall; and, they prefer suites for a room. Family customers care about the value paid for the services offered, cleanliness, and hotel's location, since they prefer some central points to be within walking distance while they prefer the hotel to be at a quiet place.

Couple customers, care about the bed quality, room's floor, shower, view, noise and reception services such as desk and lobby. Customers, whose reviews are grouped in Cluster 'Friends-Other', mostly pay attention to hotel's location, word 'place' indicates that; while they are concerned about the prices, yet they usually stay for a week.

Bregman Divergences was chosen for measure type and Squared Euclidean distance for divergence. According to Banerjee, Merugu, Dhillon, & Ghosh (2005), Bregman Divergences with Squared Euclidean distance produced satisfactory results for text clustering, and that's why it was chosen.

During the Sentiment Analysis process, it was investigated whether the average sentiment score, extracted by each single review, is close to hotel's average overall rating, provided by customers. Text processing was carried out to effectively calculate the sentiment score for each review. Figure 3 illustrates the whole process.

The details of the steps concerning this text mining process are the following:

- **Read CV:** Step during which the data set produced from the following process is retrieved.
- **Data to Documents:** Step during which each review record is transformed to document.
- **Process Documents:** Step during which significant documents processing takes place. The parameters of this step are the following:

Figure 3. Text processing for Sentiment Analysis

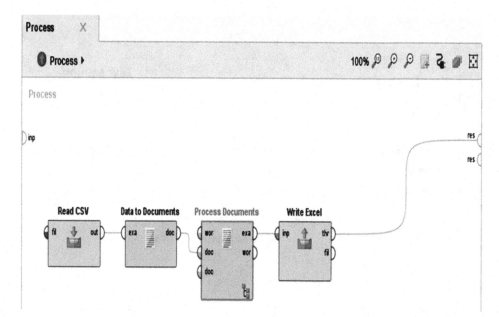

- ◦ **Create Word Vector:** No, because the aim of this sentiment analysis process is to produce an effective sentiment score, and not produce words or phrases.
- ◦ **Prune Method:** Perceptual was chosen as a prune method, because it is more understandable to prune words or not according to the percentage frequency.
- ◦ **Prune Below Percent:** After several tests, it was decided to set this value to 5, since it was preferable to prune words whose frequency is less than 5%, and in case they are useful for clustering, these words will be filtered out in the following steps.
- ◦ **Prune Above Percent:** After several tests, it was decided to set this value to 95, since it was essential to examine almost the whole sentence, and exclude words that their frequency was more than 95%, since due to their high frequency they will not affect the distribution of sentiment score.

The steps included in the Process Documents node, are the following:

- **Tokenize:** This operator splits document text into a sequence of tokens. By choosing non-letter, this results in tokens consisting of one single word and its frequency of occurrence.
- **Filter Stopwords (English):** This operator filters English stopwords from a document by removing every token which equals a stopword from RapidMiner's built-in stopword list. Some stopwords samples are the, is, at, which, on.
- **Filter Tokens (by Length):** At this node, tokens or words were filtered according to their length. Therefore, tokens with minimum three characters were kept. For instance, the word bed is very useful for this analysis and it contains three characters.
- **Open WordNet Dictionary:** At this node, WordNet dictionary is being used in order to load WordNet dictionary, from the PC's directory.

- **Extract Sentiment (English):** At this node, WordNet 3.0 database is used in order to calculate the sentiment value/score, within -1 and 1, where -1 means very negative and 1 means very positive. The sentiment value, calculated for each review, is added as a new column to the dataset. It has to be mentioned that nouns, verbs, adjectives and adverbs were used in order to calculate the sentiment value. Figure 4 illustrates these steps.

The sentiment value, per each comment, calculated by the above process is in the range of -1 to 1. Therefore, this value cannot be compared with hotel's overall rating score, being in the range of 1 to 5. Thus, the sentiment value had to be transformed using function $2(x) +3$ for the transformation, according to the following Table 1.

Therefore, by applying this function to all sentiment values, calculated for each review, values were transformed to the same range with hotel's overall rating range. Aggregated results, regarding the calculated sentiment value and hotel's overall rating, are provided in the following Table 2.

Figure 4. Sentiment Analysis Process

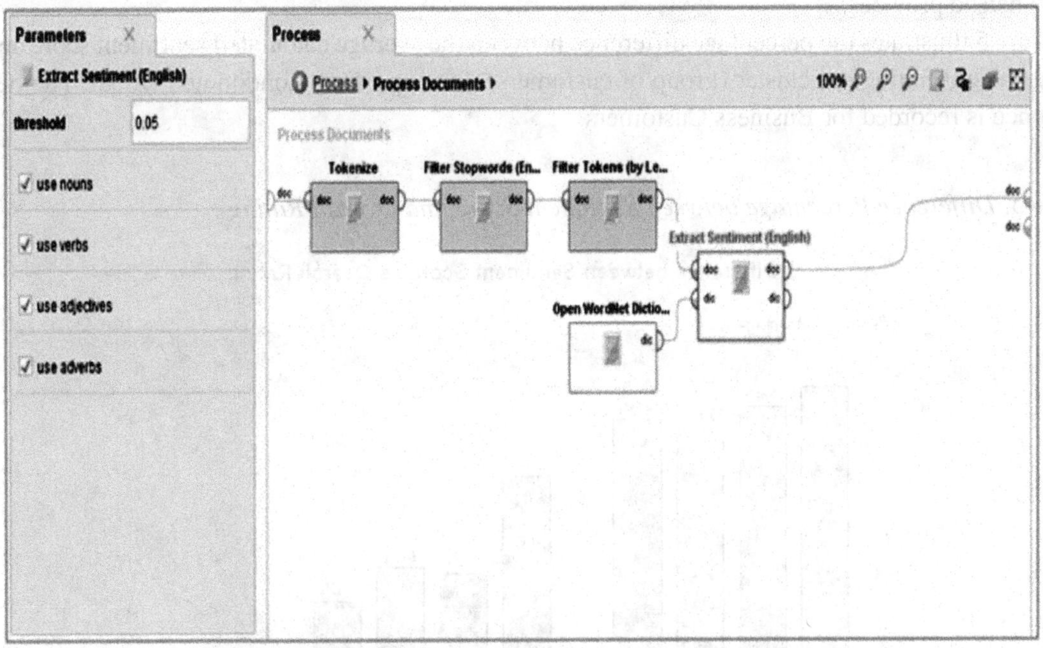

Table 1. Transformation of Sentiment Value

Sentiment Value (x)	Function's Result
-1	1
-0.5	2
0	3
0.5	4
1	5

Table 2. Sentiment Value vs Overall Rating per Country

Country	Num_Reviews	Avg_Overall_Rating	Avg_Sentiment_Value	Scores_Differences
ARE	11,154	4,19	3,26	0.94
CAN	8,854	4,01	3,25	0,75
CHINA	8,424	4,13	3,28	0,84
INDIA	4,636	3,66	3,25	0,41
UK	72,661	3,74	3,22	0,52
US	125,550	4,01	3,23	0,78
Total	231,279			0,71

The above results indicate that in overall, there is a difference of 0.7 between the average overall rating of all hotels per country and the average of the sentiment value calculated via our methodology. This means that, when a customer is asked to provide ratings from one to five concerning the service offered by a hotel, he tends to give in average a higher score, than the score that is calculated from the review he/she provides.

Figure 5 illustrates the percentage difference between the average calculated sentiment score and the average overall rating per cluster (group of customers), for two cities, London and Dubai. The biggest difference is recorded for Business Customers.

Figure 5. Difference Percentage between Sentiment Score and Overall Rating

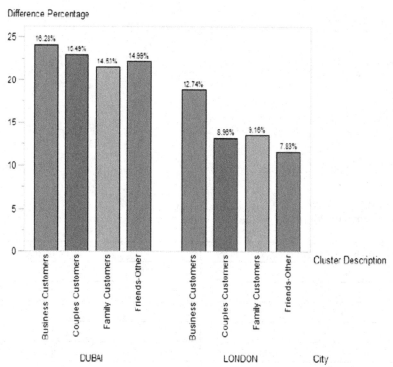

Therefore, we could say that the sentiment value provides a more 'subjective' and but close to reality results. In any case, both scores are important, since the overall rating is produced by the separate scores customer gives for 5 major services, cleanliness, room, service, location and value.

SOLUTIONS AND RECOMMENDATIONS

In this chapter, several academic and business aspects were investigated, analysed and presented. Significant research took place to find and assess those kinds of datasets that were suitable enough for carrying out tasks such as text processing, text mining and sentiment analysis, as well as to identify those variables that affect hotel customer satisfaction, as this is expressed via Web reviews. The main objective of this chapter was to suggest a method to derive ratings from one to five from customer reviews. The average of sentiment score calculated for each review, tends to be 0.70 less than the average hotel rating. This means that when a customer provides a review, then more subjective information is considered. Therefore, both sentiment score and overall rating, for each hotel, have to be taken into account.

The importance of our method lies in the fact that, it performs a holistic text processing approach which aims to reveal contextual information, taking into consideration a number of parameters/features. The most important of them is the average sentiment analysis score which proves to have a difference compared to the average hotel rating.

FUTURE RESEARCH DIRECTIONS

In order to better evaluate ratings calculated by our method, a good approach is to compare our rating and the rating provided by a customer, by predicting ratings from new customers. By that way, ratings will be evaluated for their integrity and how close to reality they are.

It must be stressed that, our approach can be applied in a number of other related fields requiring opinion mining process such as social networks (i.e., Facebook, Twitter, Instagram), public consultation Web pages and others.

CONCLUSION

Over the last years, several applications of text mining and sentiment analysis have been examined for academic and business purposes. Moreover, combinations of data mining techniques with those two fields can produce valuable insights. The main objective of this chapter was to investigate effective and efficient ways to carry out text mining and sentiment analysis against real datasets and a real business issue. Additionally, the chapter investigates unsupervised data mining technique i.e., clustering, that better describes data used. The outcome of this work is an innovative customer rating framework applying the methodologies discussed and by merging text clustering and sentiment scoring, produces interesting insights that could be used for further research and for many more businesses.

REFERENCES

Aciar, S. (2010, September). Mining context information from consumers reviews. In *Proceedings of Workshop on Context-Aware Recommender System*. ACM.

Banerjee, A., Merugu, S., Dhillon, I. S., & Ghosh, J. (2005, October). Clustering with Bregman divergences. *Journal of Machine Learning Research*, 6, 1705–1749.

Berry, M. J., & Linoff, G. (1997). *Data mining techniques: for marketing, sales, and customer support*. John Wiley & Sons, Inc.

Chen, Y. F. (2008). Herd behavior in purchasing books online. *Computers in Human Behavior*, 24(5), 1977–1992. doi:10.1016/j.chb.2007.08.004

Gaikwad, S. V., Chaugule, A., & Patil, P. (2014). Text mining methods and techniques. *International Journal of Computers and Applications*, 85(17).

Grégoire, Y., & Fisher, R. J. (2008). Customer betrayal and retaliation: When your best customers become your worst enemies. *Journal of the Academy of Marketing Science*, 36(2), 247–261. doi:10.100711747-007-0054-0

Grégoire, Y., Tripp, T. M., & Legoux, R. (2013, May). *When customer love turns into lasting hate: the effects of relationship strength and time on customer revenge and avoidance*. American Marketing Association.

Hargreaves, C. A. (2015). Analysis of hotel guest satisfaction ratings and reviews: An application in Singapore. *American Journal of Marketing Research*, 1(4), 208–214.

Hennig-Thurau, T., Gwinner, K. P., Walsh, G., & Gremler, D. D. (2004). Electronic word-of-mouth via consumer-opinion platforms: What motivates consumers to articulate themselves on the internet? *Journal of Interactive Marketing*, 18(1), 38–52. doi:10.1002/dir.10073

Jain, A., Bajpai, A., & Rohila, M. N. (2012, May). Efficient Clustering Technique for Information Retrieval in Data Mining. *International Journal of Emerging Technology and Advanced Engineering*, 2(5), 458–466.

Jeacle, I., & Carter, C. (2011). In TripAdvisor we trust: Rankings, calculative regimes and abstract systems. *Accounting, Organizations and Society*, 36(4), 293–309. doi:10.1016/j.aos.2011.04.002

Jusoh, S., & Alfawareh, H. M. (2012). Techniques, Applications and Challenging Issue in Text Mining. *IJCSI International Journal of Computer Science Issues*, 9(6), 431–436.

Kasper, W., & Vela, M. (2011, October). Sentiment analysis for hotel reviews. In Computational linguistics-applications conference (Vol. 231527, pp. 45-52). Academic Press.

Liu, B. (2012). Sentiment analysis and opinion mining. *Synthesis Lectures on Human Language Technologies*, 5(1), 1-167.

Longo, D. R., Land, G., Schramm, W., Fraas, J., Hoskins, B., & Howell, V. (1997). Consumer reports in health care: Do they make a difference in patient care? *Journal of the American Medical Association, 278*(19), 1579–1584. doi:10.1001/jama.1997.03550190043042 PMID:9370503

Mann, A., & Kaur, N. (2013b). Grid density based clustering algorithm. *International Journal of Advanced Research in Computer Engineering & Technology, 2*(6).

Mann, A. K., & Kaur, N. (2013a). Review paper on clustering techniques. *Global Journal of Computer Science and Technology, 13*(5).

Mugunthadevi, K., Punitha, S. C., & Punithavalli, M. (2011). Survey on feature selection in document clustering. *International Journal on Computer Science and Engineering, 3*(3), 1240–1244.

Papathanassis, A., & Knolle, F. (2011). Exploring the adoption and processing of online holiday reviews: A grounded theory approach. *Tourism Management, 32*(2), 215–224. doi:10.1016/j.tourman.2009.12.005

Pedersen, T., Patwardhan, S., & Michelizzi, J. (2004). WordNet: Similarity: measuring the relatedness of concepts. In Demonstration papers at HLT-NAACL 2004 (pp. 38-41). Association for Computational Linguistics.

Punitha, S. C., Thangaiah, P. R. J., & Punithavalli, M. (2014). Performance Analysis of Clustering using Partitioning and Hierarchical Clustering Techniques. *International Journal of Database Theory and Application, 7*(6), 233–240. doi:10.14257/ijdta.2014.7.6.21

Sparks, B. A., & Browning, V. (2011). The impact of online reviews on hotel booking intentions and perception of trust. *Tourism Management, 32*(6), 1310–1323. doi:10.1016/j.tourman.2010.12.011

Tang, H., Tan, S., & Cheng, X. (2009). A survey on sentiment detection of reviews. *Expert Systems with Applications, 36*(7), 10760–10773. doi:10.1016/j.eswa.2009.02.063

Vermeulen, I. E., & Seegers, D. (2009). Tried and tested: The impact of online hotel reviews on consumer consideration. *Tourism Management, 30*(1), 123–127. doi:10.1016/j.tourman.2008.04.008

Wiebe, J., Bruce, R., & O'Hara, T. (1999). Development and use of a gold standard data set for subjectivity classifications. *Proceedings of the 37th Annual Meeting of the Association for Computational Linguistics (ACL-99)*, 246–253. 10.3115/1034678.1034721

Wong, J., & Law, R. (2005). Analysing the intention to purchase on hotel websites: A study of travellers to Hong Kong. *International Journal of Hospitality Management, 24*(3), 311–329. doi:10.1016/j.ijhm.2004.08.002

Xiang, Z., Schwartz, Z., Gerdes, J. H. Jr, & Uysal, M. (2015). What can big data and text analytics tell us about hotel guest experience and satisfaction? *International Journal of Hospitality Management, 44*, 120–130. doi:10.1016/j.ijhm.2014.10.013

Ye, Q., Law, R., & Gu, B. (2009). The impact of online user reviews on hotel room sales. *International Journal of Hospitality Management, 28*(1), 180–182. doi:10.1016/j.ijhm.2008.06.011

Zhou, L., Ye, S., Pearce, P. L., & Wu, M. Y. (2014). (2014). Refreshing hotel satisfaction studies by reconfiguring customer review. *International Journal of Hospitality Management, 44*, 120–130.

Ziegler, C. N., Lausen, G., & Schmidt-Thieme, L. (2004, November). Taxonomy-driven computation of product recommendations. *Proceedings of the thirteenth ACM international conference on Information and knowledge management*, 406-415.

KEY TERMS AND DEFINITIONS

Clustering: It is the process of partitioning a set of data or objects into a set of meaningful subclasses, called clusters.

Customer Rating: Is a numerical rating provided by a customer, after he/she has purchased a product or a service, in order to express his/her satisfaction.

Customer Review: Is a review of a product or service made by a customer who has purchased it.

Customer Satisfaction: Is a marketing term that measures how products or services supplied by a company meet or surpass a customer's expectation.

Prediction: The action of predicting something, by applying statistical techniques.

Sentiment Analysis: The process of computationally identifying and categorizing opinions expressed in a piece of text.

Sentiment Score: Is a more precise numerical representation of the sentiment polarity.

Text Mining: The process of deriving high-quality information from text.

Compilation of References

2015 Cost of Data Breach Study: Global Analysis. (2015). Ponemon.

Abidogun, O. A., & Omlin, C. W. (2004, August). A self-organizing maps model for outlier detection in call data from mobile telecommunication networks. *Proc. of the 8th Southern Africa Telecommunication Networks and Applications Conference (SATNAC)*, 4.

Abou-Rjeili, A., & Karypis, G. (2006, April). Multilevel algorithms for partitioning power-law graphs. In *Parallel and Distributed Processing Symposium, 2006. IPDPS 2006. 20th International.* IEEE. 10.1109/IPDPS.2006.1639360

Abubakr, T. (2012). Cloud app vs. web app: Understanding the differences. *Techrepublic Cloud Newsletter.* Retrieved 17 November 2017 from https://www.techrepublic.com/blog/the-enterprise-cloud/cloud-app-vs-web-app-understanding-the-differences/

Aciar, S. (2010, September). Mining context information from consumers reviews. In *Proceedings of Workshop on Context-Aware Recommender System.* ACM.

Adamic, L. A., & Adar, E. (2003). Friends and neighbors on the web. *Social Networks, 25*(3), 211–230. doi:10.1016/S0378-8733(03)00009-1

Adewole, K. S., Anuar, N. B., Kamsin, A., Varathan, K. D., & Razak, S. A. (2017). Malicious accounts: Dark of the social networks. *Journal of Network and Computer Applications, 79*, 41–67. doi:10.1016/j.jnca.2016.11.030

Adiseshiah, E. (2016). *UX and prototyping - identifying problems and prototyping solutions for better UX design.* Retrieved July 14, 2017, from https://www.justinmind.com/blog/identifying-problems-and-prototyping-solutions-for-better-ux-design/

Agarwal, P., & Strötgen, J. (2017, April). Tiwiki: Searching Wikipedia with Temporal Constraints. In *Proceedings of the 26th International Conference on World Wide Web Companion* (pp. 1595-1600). International World Wide Web Conferences Steering Committee.

Agrawal, R., & Srikant, R. (1995, March). Mining sequential patterns. In *Data Engineering, 1995. Proceedings of the Eleventh International Conference on* (pp. 3-14). IEEE. 10.1109/ICDE.1995.380415

Ahmad, A., Khan, A., Javaid, N., Hussain, H. M., Abdul, W., Almogren, A., & Azim Niaz, I. (2017). An Optimized Home Energy Management System with Integrated Renewable Energy and Storage Resources. *Energies, 10*(4), 549. doi:10.3390/en10040549

Ahmed, M. S., Mohamed, A., Shareef, H., Homod, R. Z., & Ali, J. A. (2016, November). Artificial neural network based controller for home energy management considering demand response events. In *Advances in Electrical, Electronic and Systems Engineering (ICAEES), International Conference on* (pp. 506-509). IEEE. 10.1109/ICAEES.2016.7888097

Akbaş, M. İ., Brust, M. R., Turgut, D., & Ribeiro, C. H. (2015). A preferential attachment model for primate social networks. *Computer Networks*, *76*, 207–226. doi:10.1016/j.comnet.2014.11.009

Al Hasan, M., & Zaki, M. J. (2011). A survey of link prediction in social networks. In Social network data analytics (pp. 243-275). Springer US. doi:10.1007/978-1-4419-8462-3_9

Al Mamun, K. A., Bardhan, S., Ullah, M. A., Anagnostou, E., Brian, J., Akhter, S., & Rabbani, M. G. (2016, August). Smart autism—A mobile, interactive and integrated framework for screening and confirmation of autism. In *Engineering in Medicine and Biology Society (EMBC), 2016 IEEE 38th Annual International Conference of the* (pp. 5989-5992). IEEE.

Alahmari, F. A., Thom, J., & Magee, L. (2014). A model for ranking entity attributes using DBpedia. *Aslib Journal of Information Management*, *66*(5), 473–493. doi:10.1108/AJIM-12-2013-0148

Al-Ali, A. R., El-Hag, A., Bahadiri, M., Harbaji, M., & El Haj, Y. A. (2011). Smart home renewable energy management system. *Energy Procedia*, *12*, 120–126. doi:10.1016/j.egypro.2011.10.017

Albert, R., & Barabási, A. L. (2002). Statistical mechanics of complex networks. *Reviews of Modern Physics*, *74*(1), 47–97. doi:10.1103/RevModPhys.74.47

Albreshne, A. (2009). *Web Services. Orchestration and Composition Case Study of Web services Composition.* Working Paper.

Alchourrón, C. E., Gärdenfors, P., & Makinson, D. (1985). On the logic of theory change: Partial meet contraction and revision functions. *The Journal of Symbolic Logic*, *50*(02), 510–530. doi:10.2307/2274239

Alhazmi, E., Bajunaid, W., & Aziz, A. (2017). Important success aspects for total quality management in software development. *International Journal of Computers and Applications*, *157*(8), 8–11. doi:10.5120/ijca2017912783

Allen, A. A., & Shane, H. C. (2014). Autism spectrum disorders in the era of mobile technologies: Impact on caregivers. *Developmental Neurorehabilitation*, *17*(2), 110–114. doi:10.3109/17518423.2014.882425 PMID:24694311

Almeida, F., & Calistru, C. (2013). The main challenges and issues of big data management. *International Journal of Research Studies in Computing*, *2*(1), 11–20. doi:10.5861/ijrsc.2012.209

Almeida, F., & Monteiro, J. (2017). Approaches and Principles for UX Web Experiences. *International Journal of Information Technology and Web Engineering*, *12*(2), 49–65. doi:10.4018/IJITWE.2017040103

Alonso, O., Gertz, M., & Baeza-Yates, R. (2007). On the value of temporal information in information retrieval. In *ACM SIGIR Forum* (Vol. 41, No. 2, pp. 35-41). ACM. 10.1145/1328964.1328968

Alonso, O., Gertz, M., & Baeza-Yates, R. (2009). Clustering and exploring search results using timeline constructions. In *Proceedings of the 18th ACM conference on Information and knowledge management* (pp. 97-106). ACM. 10.1145/1645953.1645968

Alonso, O., Strötgen, J., Baeza-Yates, R. A., & Gertz, M. (2011). Temporal Information Retrieval: Challenges and Opportunities. *TWAW*, *11*, 1–8.

Al-Taee, M. A., Sungoor, A. H., Abood, S. N., & Philip, N. Y. (2013). Web-of-Things inspired e-Health platform for integrated diabetes care management. *2013 IEEE Jordan Conference on Applied Electrical Engineering and Computing Technologies (AEECT)*. 10.1109/AEECT.2013.6716427

Amavi, J., Chabin, J., Ferrari, M. H., & Réty, P. (2014). A ToolBox for Conservative XML Schema Evolution and Document Adaptation. *Proceedings of the 25th International Conference on Database and Expert Systems Applications (DEXA 2014)*, 299-307. 10.1007/978-3-319-10073-9_24

Amendola, S., Lodato, R., Manzari, S., Occhiuzzi, C., & Marrocco, G. (2014). RFID technology for IoT-based personal healthcare in smart spaces. *IEEE Internet of Things Journal, 1*(2), 144–152. doi:10.1109/JIOT.2014.2313981

American Heart Association - Building healthier lives, free of cardiovascular diseases and stroke. (n.d.). Retrieved from https://www.heart.org

Anjomshoaa, H. A., & Tjoa, A. M. (2014). Lecture Notes in Computer Science: Vol. 8407. *Towards Semantic Mashup Tools for Big Data Analysis*. Springer.

Arenas, M., Kantere, V., Kementsietsidis, A., Kiringa, I., Miller, R. J., & Mylopoulos, J. (2003). The Hyperion Project: From Data Integration to Data Coordination. *SIGMOD Record, 32*(3), 38–53. doi:10.1145/945721.945733

Aresti-Bartolome, N., & Garcia-Zapirain, B. (2014). Technologies as support tools for persons with autistic spectrum disorder: A systematic review. *International Journal of Environmental Research and Public Health, 11*(8), 7767–7802. doi:10.3390/ijerph110807767 PMID:25093654

Arıkan, I., Bedathur, S., & Berberich, K. (2009). Time will tell: Leveraging temporal expressions in ir. WSDM.

Arroqui, M., Mateos, C., Machado, C., & Zunino, A. (2012). Restful web services improve the efficiency of data transfer of a whole-farm simulator accessed by android smartphones. *Computers and Electronics in Agriculture, 87*, 14–18. doi:10.1016/j.compag.2012.05.016

Arsanjani, A. (2004). Service-Oriented Modeling and Architecture. *IBM Developer Works*. Retrieved from www.ibm.com/developerworks/library/ws-soa-design1

Artz, D., & Gil, Y. (2007). A survey of trust in computer science and the semantic web. *Journal of Web Semantics, 5*(2), 58–71. doi:10.1016/j.websem.2007.03.002

Atig, Y., Zahaf, A., & Bouchiha, D. (2016). Conservativity Principle Violations for Ontology Alignment: Survey and Trends. *International Journal of Information Technology and Computer Science, 8*(7), 61–71. doi:10.5815/ijitcs.2016.07.09

Aumueller, D., Do, H., Massmann, S., & Rahm, E. (2005). Schema and Ontology Matching with COMA++. *Proc. SIGMOD Conf.*, 906–908.

Avea GSM company. (n.d.). *Turkey, Foundation 2004*. Retrieved from http://www.avea.com.tr/web/en/

Aydın, A. (2008). *Adaptation of symbolic play test to Turkish and comparison of symbolic play behavior of children with normal, autistic, and mental disorder at pre-school period* (PhD thesis). Marmara University.

Ayres, J., Flannick, J., Gehrke, J., & Yiu, T. (2002, July). Sequential pattern mining using a bitmap representation. In *Proceedings of the eighth ACM SIGKDD international conference on Knowledge discovery and data mining* (pp. 429-435). ACM. 10.1145/775047.775109

Baader, F., Penaloza, R., & Suntisrivaraporn, B. (2007). Pinpointing in the Description Logic EL+. In *Annual Conference on Artificial Intelligence* (pp. 52-67). Springer Berlin Heidelberg.

Bachl, S., Tomitsch, M., Wimmer, C., & Grechening, T. (2010). Challenges for designing the user experience of multi-touch interfaces. *Proceedings of the ACM Symposium on Engineering Interactive Computing Systems*, 1-6.

Baeza-Yates, R., & Raghavan, P. (2010). Next Generation Web Search. In *Challenges and Directions*. Springer-Verlag Berlin.

Bahlmann, C., Haasdonk, B., & Burkhardt, H. (2002). Online handwriting recognition with support vector machines-a kernel approach. In *Frontiers in handwriting recognition, 2002 proceedings, Eighth international workshop on* (pp. 49-54). IEEE. 10.1109/IWFHR.2002.1030883

Baigorri, C. M., & Maldonado, W. F. (2014). Optimal mobile termination rate: The Brazilian mobile market case. *Telecommunications Policy*, *38*(1), 86–95. doi:10.1016/j.telpol.2013.05.002

Bailey, T. L., & Elkan, C. (1995). Unsupervised learning of multiple motifs in biopolymers using expectation maximization. *Machine Learning*, *21*(1), 51–80. doi:10.1007/BF00993379

Ball, B., Karrer, B., & Newman, M. E. (2011). Efficient and principled method for detecting communities in networks. *Physical Review. E*, *84*(3), 036103. doi:10.1103/PhysRevE.84.036103 PMID:22060452

Banerjee, A., Merugu, S., Dhillon, I. S., & Ghosh, J. (2005, October). Clustering with Bregman divergences. *Journal of Machine Learning Research*, *6*, 1705–1749.

Bansal, R. (2014). Linking entities in #Micropost. In *#Microposts2014 Workshop Proceedings*. CEUR.

Baqasah, A., Pardede, E., & Rahayu, J. W. (2014a). A New Approach for Meaningful XML Schema Merging. *Proceedings of the 16th International Conference on Information Integration and Web-based Applications & Services (iiWAS 2014)*, 430-439. 10.1145/2684200.2684302

Baqasah, A., Pardede, E., & Rahayu, J. W. (2014b). XSM - A Tracking System for XML Schema Versions. *Proceedings of the 28th IEEE International Conference on Advanced Information Networking and Applications (AINA 2014)*, 1081-1088. 10.1109/AINA.2014.131

Baqasah, A., Pardede, E., & Rahayu, J. W. (2015b). Maintaining Schema Versions Compatibility in Cloud Applications Collaborative Framework. *World Wide Web (Bussum)*, *18*(6), 1541–1577. doi:10.100711280-014-0321-1

Baqasah, A., Pardede, E., Rahayu, J. W., & Holubová, I. (2015a). XS-Diff: XML schema change detection algorithm. *International Journal of Web and Grid Services*, *11*(2), 160–192. doi:10.1504/IJWGS.2015.068897

Barnett, V., & Lewis, T. (1994). Outliers in statistical data: Vol. 3. *No. 1*. New York: Wiley.

Barret, L. (2015). *Web design and development in 2016: common challenges*. Retrieved July 7, 2017, from http://blog.debugme.eu/common-challenges-development/

Basile, P., Caputo, A., Semeraro, G., & Siciliani, L. (2016). Time Event Extraction to Boost an Information Retrieval System. In *Information Filtering and Retrieval* (pp. 1–12). Springer International Publishing.

Bastian, M., Heymann, S., & Jacomy, M. (2009). Gephi: an open source software for exploring and manipulating networks. *International AAAI Conference on Weblogs and Social Media*.

Batagelj, V., & Mrvar, A. (2003). Pajek - Analysis and Visualization of Large Networks. In *Graph Drawing Software*. Springer. Available from http://mrvar.fdv.uni-lj.si/pajek/default.htm

Baumgartner, R., Campi, A., Georg, G., & Herzog, M. (2010). Web Data Extraction for Service Creation. In *Challenges and Directions*. Springer-Verlag Berlin.

Bawaneh, A. K. A., Abdullah, A. G. K., Saleh, S., & Yin, K. Y. (2011a). The effect of Herrmann Whole Brain Teaching Method on Students' Understanding of Simple Electric Circuits. *European Journal of Physics Education*, *2*(2), 1–23.

Bawaneh, A. K. A., Abdullah, A. G. K., Saleh, S., & Yin, K. Y. (2011b). Jordanian student's thinking styles based on Hermann whole brain model. *International Journal of Humanities and Social Science*, *1*(9), 89–97.

Bawaneh, A. K. A., Zain, A. N. M., & Saleh, S. (2010). The Relationship between Tenth Grade Jordanian Students' Thinking Styles based on the Herrmann Whole Brain Model and Their Track Choice for the Secondary School Level. *European Journal of Soil Science*, *14*(4), 567–580.

Beaudin, M., & Zareipour, H. (2015). Home energy management systems: A review of modelling and complexity. *Renewable & Sustainable Energy Reviews, 45*, 318–335. doi:10.1016/j.rser.2015.01.046

Beckett, D. (2014). *RDF 1.1 Turtle: Terse RDF triple language.* W3C Recommendation. Retrieved from http:// www. w3.org/TR/turtle/

Bedi, P., & Sharma, C. (2016). Community detection in social networks. *Wiley Interdisciplinary Reviews. Data Mining and Knowledge Discovery, 6*(3), 115–135. doi:10.1002/widm.1178

Beek, M. H., Bucchiarome, A., & Gnesi, S. (2007b). Formal Methods for Service Composition *Annals of Mathematics, Computing & Teleinformatics, 1*(5).

Beek, M. H., Bucchiarome, A., & Gnesi, S. (2007a). A Survey on Service Composition Approaches: From Industrial Standards to Formal Methods. *Second International Conference on Internet and Web Applications and Services.* 10.1109/ ICIW.2007.71

Behrmann, G., David, A., & Larsen, K. G. (2004). A Tutorial on Uppaal. In M. Bernardo & F. Corradini (Eds.), Lecture Notes in Computer Science: Vol. 3185. *Formal Methods for the Design of Real-Time Systems.* Berlin: Springer. doi:10.1007/978-3-540-30080-9_7

Ben Messaoud, W., Ghedira, K., & Ben Halima, Y. (2016). Towards behavioral web service discovery approach:State of the art. *Procedia Computer Science, 96*, 1049–1058. doi:10.1016/j.procs.2016.08.126

Ben-Seghier, N., Kazar, O., & Rezeg, K. (2015). A Decentralized Framework for Semantic Web Services Discovery Using Mobile Agent. *International Journal of Information Technology and Web Engineering, 10*(4), 20–43. doi:10.4018/ IJITWE.2015100102

Ben-Seghier, N., Kazar, O., Rezeg, K., & Bourakkache, S. (2017). A semantic web services discovery approach based on a mobile agent using metadata. *International Journal of Intelligent Computing and Cybernetics, 10*(1), 12–29. doi:10.1108/IJICC-02-2015-0006

Bentley, J. (1984). Programming pearls: Algorithm design techniques. *Communications of the ACM, 27*(9), 865–873. doi:10.1145/358234.381162

Bernard, R. (2007). Information Lifecycle Security Risk Assessment: A tool for closing security gaps. *Computers & Security, 26*, 26-30.

Berners-Lee, T., Hendler, J., & Lassila, O. (2001). The semantic web. *Scientific American, 284*(5), 28–37. doi:10.1038 cientificamerican0501-34 PMID:11341160

Bernstein, P. A., Madhavan, J., & Rahm, E. (2011). Generic schema matching, ten years later. PVLDB, 4(11), 695-701.

Berry, M. J., & Linoff, G. (1997). *Data mining techniques: for marketing, sales, and customer support.* John Wiley & Sons, Inc.

Betts, G. (2016). *Security vs. UX: how to reconcile one of the biggest challenges in interface design.* Retrieved July 14, 2017, from https://www.fastcodesign.com/3059293/security-vs-ux-how-to-reconcile-one-of-the-biggest-challenges-in-interface-design

Bhatt, Y., & Bhatt, C. (2017). Internet of Things in HealthCare. In *Internet of Things and Big Data Technologies for Next Generation Healthcare* (pp. 13–33). Springer International Publishing. doi:10.1007/978-3-319-49736-5_2

Bianchini, D., De Antonellis, V., & Melchiori, M. (2010). P2P-SDSD: On-the-fly service-based collaboration in distributed systems. *International Journal of Metadata, Semantics and Ontologies, 5*(3), 222–237. doi:10.1504/IJMSO.2010.034046

Bi, Z., Da Xu, L., & Wang, C. (2014). Internet of things for enterprise systems of modern manufacturing. *IEEE Transactions on Industrial Informatics*, *10*(2), 1537–1546. doi:10.1109/TII.2014.2300338

Blackstock, M., & Lea, R. (2012, June). WoTKit: a lightweight toolkit for the web of things. In *Proceedings of the Third International Workshop on the Web of Things* (p. 3). ACM. 10.1145/2379756.2379759

Bonnot, O., Bonneau, D., Doudard, A., & Duverger, P. (2016). Rationale and protocol for using a smartphone application to study autism spectrum disorders: SMARTAUTISM. *BMJ Open*, *6*(11), e012135. doi:10.1136/bmjopen-2016-012135 PMID:27881525

Bono, Y. (1998). *The Cort Program for Teaching Thinking*. Publishing and Distribution Amman.

Boser, B. E., Guyon, I. M., & Vapnik, V. N. (1992, July). A training algorithm for optimal margin classifiers. In *Proceedings of the fifth annual workshop on Computational learning theory* (pp. 144-152). ACM. 10.1145/130385.130401

Bouchou, B., & Duarte, D. (2007). Assisting XML Schema Evolution that Preserves Validity. *Proceedings of the 22nd Brazilian Symposium on Databases (SBBD 2007)*, 270-284.

Boudjelaba, H. (2012). *Sélection des Web Services Sémantiques*. Ecole Doctorale Réseaux et Systèmes Distribués.

Boukhadra, A., Benatchba, K., & Balla, A. (2014). Ranked Matching of OWL-S Process Model for Distributed Discovery of SWs in P2P Systems. In *Network-Based Information Systems, (NBiS) 17th IEEE International Conference on 2014* (pp. 106-113). IEEE.

Bouquet, P., Giunchiglia, F., Van Harmelen, F., Serafini, L., & Stuckenschmidt, H. (2003, October). C-owl: Contextualizing ontologies. In *International Semantic Web Conference* (pp. 164-179). Springer Berlin Heidelberg.

Bouzeghoub, M., & Peralta, V. (2004). A Framework for Analysis of Data Freshness. In *1st International Workshop on Information Quality in Information Systems (IQIS)* (pp. 59-67). Paris, France: Academic Press. 10.1145/1012453.1012464

Bovet, G., & Hennebert, J. (2013). Offering web-of-things connectivity to building networks. *Proceedings of the 2013 ACM conference on Pervasive and ubiquitous computing adjunct publication - UbiComp '13 Adjunct*. 10.1145/2494091.2497590

Bozzon, A., Brambilla, M., Ceri, S., Corcoglioniti, F., Gatti, N., & Milano, P. (2010a). Building Search Computing Applications. In *Challenges and Directions*. Springer-Verlag Berlin.

Bozzon, A., Brambilla, M., Ceri, S., & Fraternali, P. (2010b). Liquid query: Multi-domain exploratory search on the web. In S. Ceri & M. Brambilla (Eds.), *Search Computing. Challenges and Directions. Springer-Verlag*. doi:10.1145/1772690.1772708

Bracamonte, T., & Poblete, B. (2011). Automatic image tagging through information propagation in a query log based graph structure. In K. S. Candan, S. Panchanathan, B. Prabhakaran, H. Sundaram, W.-c. Feng, & N. Sebe (Eds.), *Proceedings of the 19th ACM international conference on Multimedia* (pp. 1201-1204). Scottsdale, AZ: ACM. 10.1145/2072298.2071974

Bradley, S. (2006). *The Benefits Of Cascading Style Sheets*. Vanseo Design. Retrieved July 4, 2017, from http://vanseodesign.com/css/benefits-of-cascading-style-sheets/

Bragazzi, N. L. (2013). From P0 to P6 medicine, a model of highly participatory, narrative, interactive, and "augmented" medicine: Some considerations on Salvatore Iaconesi's clinical story. *Patient Preference and Adherence*, *7*, 353. doi:10.2147/PPA.S38578 PMID:23650443

Brahmia, Z., Bouaziz, R., Grandi, F., & Oliboni, B. (2010). *Schema Versioning in τXSchema-Based Multitemporal XML Repositories*. TimeCenter, Technical Report TR-93. Retrieved August 2, 2017, from <http://timecenter.cs.aau.dk/TimeCenterPublications/TR-93.pdf>

Brahmia, Z., Bouaziz, R., Grandi, F., & Oliboni, B. (2012a). *A Study of Conventional Schema Versioning in the τXSchema Framework*. TimeCenter, Technical Report TR-94. Retrieved August 2, 2017, from <http://timecenter.cs.aau.dk/TimeCenterPublications/TR-94.pdf>

Brahmia, Z., Grandi, F., Oliboni, B., & Bouaziz, R. (2014a). *High-level Operations for Changing Temporal Schema, Conventional Schema, and Annotations, in the τXSchema Framework*. TimeCenter, Technical Report TR-96. Retrieved August 2, 2017, from http://timecenter.cs.aau.dk/TimeCenterPublications/TR-96.pdf

Brahmia, S., Brahmia, Z., Grandi, F., & Bouaziz, R. (2016a). τJSchema: A Framework for Managing Temporal JSON-Based NoSQL Databases. *Proceedings of the 27th International Conference on Database and Expert Systems Applications (DEXA'2016)*, 167-181. 10.1007/978-3-319-44406-2_13

Brahmia, S., Brahmia, Z., Grandi, F., & Bouaziz, R. (2017a). Temporal JSON Schema Versioning in the τJSchema Framework. *Journal of Digital Information Management, 15*(4), 179–202.

Brahmia, Z., & Bouaziz, R. (2008). An approach for schema versioning in multi-temporal XML databases. *Proceedings of the 10th International Conference on Enterprise Information Systems (ICEIS 2008)*, 290-297.

Brahmia, Z., Bouaziz, R., Grandi, F., & Oliboni, B. (2011). Schema Versioning in τXSchema-Based Multitemporal XML Repositories. *Proceedings of the 5th IEEE International Conference on Research Challenges in Information Science (RCIS 2011)*, 1-12.

Brahmia, Z., Grandi, F., & Bouaziz, R. (2016b). Changes to XML Namespaces in XML Schemas and their Effects on Associated XML Documents under Schema Versioning. *Proceedings of the 11th International Conference on Digital Information Management (ICDIM'2016)*, 43-50. 10.1109/ICDIM.2016.7829765

Brahmia, Z., Grandi, F., & Bouaziz, R. (2016c). A Systematic Approach for Changing XML Namespaces in XML Schemas and Managing their Effects on Associated XML Documents under Schema Versioning. *Journal of Digital Information Management, 14*(5), 275–289.

Brahmia, Z., Grandi, F., Oliboni, B., & Bouaziz, R. (2012b). Versioning of Conventional Schema in the τXSchema Framework. *Proceedings of the 8th International Conference on Signal Image Technology & Internet Systems (SITIS'2012)*, 510-518.

Brahmia, Z., Grandi, F., Oliboni, B., & Bouaziz, R. (2014b). High-level Operations for Creation and Maintenance of Temporal and Conventional Schema in the τXSchema Framework. *Proceedings of the 21st International Symposium on Temporal Representation and Reasoning (TIME'2014)*, 101-110. 10.1109/TIME.2014.14

Brahmia, Z., Grandi, F., Oliboni, B., & Bouaziz, R. (2014c). Schema Change Operations for Full Support of Schema Versioning in the τXSchema Framework. *International Journal of Information Technology and Web Engineering, 9*(2), 20–46. doi:10.4018/ijitwe.2014040102

Brahmia, Z., Grandi, F., Oliboni, B., & Bouaziz, R. (2015). Schema Versioning. In M. Khosrow-Pour (Ed.), *Encyclopedia of Information Science and Technology* (3rd ed.; pp. 7651–7661). Hershey, PA: IGI Global; doi:10.4018/978-1-4666-5888-2.ch754

Brahmia, Z., Grandi, F., Oliboni, B., & Bouaziz, R. (2017b). Schema Versioning in Conventional and Emerging Databases. In M. Khosrow-Pour (Ed.), *Encyclopedia of Information Science and Technology* (4th ed.; pp. 2054–2063). Hershey, PA: IGI Global. doi:10.4018/978-1-5225-2255-3.ch178

Brahmia, Z., Mkaouar, M., Chakhar, S., & Bouaziz, R. (2012c). Efficient Management of Schema Versioning in Multi-Temporal Databases. *The International Arab Journal of Information Technology, 9*(6), 544–552.

Brickley, D., & Guha, R. V. (2014). *RDF Schema 1.1*. W3C Recommendation. Retrieved from http://www.w3.org/TR/rdfschema/

Broder, A., Kumar, R., Maghoul, F., Raghavan, P., Rajagopalan, S., Stata, R., & Wiener, J. (2000). Graph structure in the web. *Computer Networks*, *33*(1), 309–320. doi:10.1016/S1389-1286(00)00083-9

Brooke, J. (1996). SUS: A quick and dirty usability scale. In P. W. Jordan, B. Weerdmeester, A. Thomas, & I. L. McLelland (Eds.), *Usability evaluation in industry* (pp. 189–194). London: Taylor and Francis.

Broom, M., Rychtář, J., & Stadler, B. T. (2011). Evolutionary dynamics on graphs-the effect of graph structure and initial placement on mutant spread. *Journal of Statistical Theory and Practice*, *5*(3), 369–381. doi:10.1080/15598608.2011.10412035

Brown, E. (2016). *7 biggest challenges of Web design*. Retrieved July 7, 2017, from https://www.designmantic.com/blog/infographics/7-biggest-web-design-challenges/

Broy, M., (2015). Rethinking Nonfunctional Software Requirements. *Computer*, *48*(5).

Buch, K., & Sena, C. (2001). Accommodating diverse learning styles in the design and delivery of online learning experiences. *International Journal of Engineering Education*, *17*(1), 93–98.

Budiu, R. (2015). *Mobile user experience: limitations and strengths*. Nielsen Norman Group. Retrieved July 17, 2017, from https://www.nngroup.com/articles/mobile-ux/

Buitelaar, P., Eigner, T., & Declerck, T. (2004). OntoSelect: A dynamic ontology library with support for ontology selection. *Proceedings of the Demo Session at the International Semantic Web Conference*.

Buley, L. (2015). *How to modernize user experience?* Forrester Research. Retrieved July 6, 2017, from http://www.tandemseven.com/wp-content/uploads/2015/03/How_To_Modernize_User_Exp.pdf

Bunescu, R. C., & Pasca, M. (2006, April). Using Encyclopedic Knowledge for Named entity Disambiguation. In EACL (Vol. 6, pp. 9-16). Academic Press.

Burg, B. (2002). *Agents in the World of Active Web-services*. Hewlett-Packard Laboratories.

Cafarella, M. J., Halevy, A., & Madhavan, J. (2011). Structured data on the Web. *Communications*, *54*(2), 72–79.

Cai, H., Da Xu, L., Xu, B., Xie, C., Qin, S., & Jiang, L. (2014). IoT-based configurable information service platform for product lifecycle management. *IEEE Transactions on Industrial Informatics*, *10*(2), 1558–1567. doi:10.1109/TII.2014.2306391

Calver, C. A., Howard, R. A., & Lane, W. D. (1999). Enhacing Student Learning Through Hypermedia Courseware and Incorporation of Student Learning Style. *IEEE Transactions on Education*, *42*(1), 33–38. doi:10.1109/13.746332

Cameron, R. (2004). *CiteULike*. Retrieved August 15, 2017, from http://www.citeulike.org/

Campi, A., Ceri, S., Gottlob, G., Maesani, A., & Ronchi, S. (2010). Service Marts. In *Challenges and Directions*. Springer-Verlag Berlin.

Campos, R. (2011). *Google Insights for Search Query Classification dataset (GISQC_DS)*. Available from: http://www.ccc.ipt.pt/~ricardo/datasets/GISQC_DS.html

Campos, R., Dias, G., & Jorge, A. M. (2011). *What is the Temporal Value of Web Snippets?* TWAW.

Campos, R., Dias, G., Jorge, A. M., & Nunes, C. (2012). Enriching temporal query understanding through date identification: how to tag implicit temporal queries? In *Proceedings of the 2nd Temporal Web Analytics Workshop* (pp. 41-48). ACM. 10.1145/2169095.2169103

Cano Basave, A. E., Varga, A., Rowe, M., Stankovic, M., & Dadzie, A. S. (2013). *Making sense of microposts (#msm2013) concept extraction challenge*. Academic Press.

Cano-Garcia, F., & Hughes, E. H. (2000). Learning and Thinking Styles: An Analysis of their interrelationship and influence on academic achievement. *Educational Psychology, 20*(4), 413–430. doi:10.1080/713663755

Capretz, L. F. (2005). Y: A New Component-based software life cycle model. *Journal of Computer Science, 1*(1), 76-82.

Carbunar, B., Ramanathan, M. K., Koyutürk, M., Jagannathan, S., & Gram, A. (2009). Efficient tag detection in RFID systems. *Journal of Parallel and Distributed Computing, 69*(2), 180–196. doi:10.1016/j.jpdc.2008.06.013

Cardoso, S. D., Pruski, C., Da Silveira, M., Lin, Y. C., Groß, A., Rahm, E., & Reynaud-Delaître, C. (2016). Leveraging the Impact of Ontology Evolution on Semantic Annotations. In *Knowledge Engineering and Knowledge Management: 20th International Conference, EKAW 2016, Bologna, Italy, November 19-23, 2016 Proceedings, 20*, 68–82.

Castrounis, A. (2015). *Why software development time estimation doesn't work and alternative approaches*. Retrieved July 12, 2017, from https://www.innoarchitech.com/why-software-development-time-estimation-does-not-work-alternative-approaches/

Cavalieri, F., Guerrini, G., & Mesiti, M. (2011a). Updating XML schemas and associated documents through exup. *Proceedings of the 27th International Conference on Data Engineering (ICDE 2011)*, 1320-1323. 10.1109/ICDE.2011.5767951

Cavalieri, F., Guerrini, G., Mesiti, M., & Oliboni, B. (2011b). On the reduction of sequences of XML document and schema update operations. *Proceedings of the 1st International ICDE Workshop on Managing Data Throughout its Lifecycle (DaLi 2011)*, 77-86. 10.1109/ICDEW.2011.5767649

Çelik, D., & Elçi, A. (2008). Ontology-based QoS Model for Appropriate Selection and Composition of Web Services. *International Review on Computers and Software, 3*(2).

Çelik, D., & Elçi, A. (2008). Ontology-based QoS Model for Appropriate Selection and Composition of Web Services. *International Review on Computers and Software, Praise Worthy Prize S.r.l., 3*(2), 176-184. Retrieved from http://www.praiseworthyprize.com/IRECOS-latest/IRECOS_vol_3_n_2.html#Ontology-based

Celik, D., & Elçi, A. (2013). A broker-based semantic agent for discovering Semantic Web services through process similarity matching and equivalence considering quality of service. Science China Information Sciences (SCI), 56(1), 012102:1–012102:24.

Çelik, D., & Elçi, A. (2013). A broker-based semantic agent for discovering Semantic Web services through process similarity matching and equivalence considering quality of service. *Science China Information Sciences, 56*(1), 1–24. Retrieved from http://link.springer.com/article/10.1007/s11432-012-4697-1

Çelik, D., & Elçi, A. (2014). Semantic composition of business processes using Armstrong's Axioms. *The Knowledge Engineering Review, 29*(2), 248–264. Retrieved from http://journals.cambridge.org/repo_A92IA4Dd

Çelik, D., Elci, A., & Elverici, E. (2011, July). Finding suitable course material through a semantic search agent for Learning Management Systems of distance education. In Computer Software and Applications Conference Workshops (COMPSACW), 2011 IEEE 35th Annual (pp. 386-391). IEEE.

Çelik, D., & Elçi, A. (2011). Ontology-based matchmaking and composition of business processes. In *Semantic Agent Systems* (pp. 133–157). Springer Berlin Heidelberg. doi:10.1007/978-3-642-18308-9_7

Çelik, D., & Elçi, A. (2013). A broker-based semantic agent for discovering Semantic Web services through process similarity matching and equivalence considering quality of service. *Science China. Information Sciences*, *56*(1), 1–24. doi:10.100711432-012-4697-1

Centrifuge Analytics. (2017). Centrifuge Analytics v3(Version 3) [Software]. Available from http://centrifugesystems.com/

Ceri, S. (2010). Search Computing. In *Challenges and Directions*. Springer-Verlag Berlin.

CERN. (2013). *The birth of the Web*. Retrieved July 4, 2017, from https://home.cern/topics/birth-web

Cerqueus, T., Cazalens, S., & Lamarre, C. (2012). An Approach to Manage Semantic Heterogeneity in Unstructured *P2P Information Retrieval Systems*. *IEEE International Conference on Peer-to-Peer Computing*, Tarragona, Spain.

Chakrabarti, D. (2004, September). Autopart: Parameter-free graph partitioning and outlier detection. In *European Conference on Principles of Data Mining and Knowledge Discovery* (pp. 112-124). Springer. 10.1007/978-3-540-30116-5_13

Chandola, V., Banerjee, A., & Kumar, V. (2009). Anomaly detection: A survey. *ACM Computing Surveys (CSUR), 41*(3), 15.

Chavoshi, N., Hamooni, H., & Mueen, A. (2017, April). Temporal Patterns in Bot Activities. In *Proceedings of the 26th International Conference on World Wide Web Companion* (pp. 1601-1606). International World Wide Web Conferences Steering Committee.

Cheatham, M., Dragisic, Z., Euzenat, J., Faria, D., Ferrara, A., Flouris, G., ... Zamazal, O. (2015). Results of the Ontology Alignment Evaluation Initiative 2015. *Proc. 20th ISWC ontology matching workshop (OM)*, 60–115.

Chen, F., Deng, P., Wan, J., Zhang, D., Vasilakos, A. V., & Rong, X. (2015). Data mining for the internet of things: Literature review and challenges. *International Journal of Distributed Sensor Networks*, *11*(8), 431047. doi:10.1155/2015/431047

Cheng, B., Longo, S., Cirillo, F., Bauer, M., & Kovacs, E. (2015, June). Building a big data platform for smart cities: Experience and lessons from santander. In *Big Data (BigData Congress), 2015 IEEE International Congress on* (pp. 592-599). IEEE.

Cheng, C., Cheng, X., Yuan, M., Song, C., Xu, L., Ye, H., & Zhang, T. (2016, September). A novel cluster algorithm for telecom customer segmentation. In *Communications and Information Technologies (ISCIT), 2016 16th International Symposium on* (pp. 324-329). IEEE. 10.1109/ISCIT.2016.7751644

Chen, W., Lakshmanan, L. V., & Castillo, C. (2013). Information and influence propagation in social networks. *Synthesis Lectures on Data Management*, *5*(4), 1–177. doi:10.2200/S00527ED1V01Y201308DTM037

Chen, Y. (2014). The effect of using a Facebook group as a learning management system. *Computers in Education Journal*, *5*(4), 42–53.

Chen, Y. F. (2008). Herd behavior in purchasing books online. *Computers in Human Behavior*, *24*(5), 1977–1992. doi:10.1016/j.chb.2007.08.004

Chen, Y.-C., Chen, C.-C., Peng, W.-C., & Lee, W.-C. (2014). *Mining Correlation Patterns among Appliances in Smart Home Environment*. Advances in Knowledge Discovery and Data Mining.

Choi, J., Cho, Y., Shim, E., & Woo, H. (2016). Web-based infectious disease surveillance systems and public health perspectives: A systematic review. *BMC Public Health*, *16*(1), 1238. doi:10.118612889-016-3893-0 PMID:27931204

Choudhari, J., & Ugrasen, S. (2015). An Empirical Evaluation of Iterative Maintenance Life Cycle Using XP. *Software Engineering Notes*, *40*(2), 1–14. doi:10.1145/2735399.2735406

Choudhury, G. S. (2008). Case Study in Data Curation at Johns Hopkins University. *Library Trends*, *57*(2), 211–220. doi:10.1353/lib.0.0028

Chowdhury, G. G. (2003). Natural language processing. *Annual Review of Information Science & Technology*, *37*(1), 51–89. doi:10.1002/aris.1440370103

Chung, L., & do Prado Leite, J. C. S. (2009). On Non-Functional Requirements in Software Engineering. In. Lecture Notes in Computer Science: Vol. 5600. *Conceptual Modeling: Foundations and Applications* (pp. 363–379). Berlin: Springer. doi:10.1007/978-3-642-02463-4_19

Ciortea, A., Boissier, O., Zimmermann, A., & Florea, A. M. (2013). Reconsidering the social web of things. *Proceedings of the 2013 ACM conference on Pervasive and ubiquitous computing adjunct publication - UbiComp '13 Adjunct*. 10.1145/2494091.2497587

Clayton, R. (2014). *Software estimation is a losing game*. Retrieved July 12, 2017, from https://rclayton.silvrback.com/software-estimation-is-a-losing-game

Clement, L., Hately, A., & Riegen, C. V. (2004). *UDDI Version 3.0.2*. UDDI Spec Technical Committee Draft. Retrieved from http://uddi.org/pubs/uddi_v3.htm

Clifford, J., Croker, A., Grandi, F., & Tuzhilin, A. (1995). On Temporal Grouping. *Proceedings of the International Workshop on Temporal Databases*, 194–213.

Cobena, G., Abiteboul, S., & Marian, A. (2002). Detecting Changes in XML Documents. *Proceedings of the 18th International Conference on Data Engineering (ICDE 2002)*, 41-52. 10.1109/ICDE.2002.994696

Colazzo, D., Guerrini, G., Mesiti, M., Oliboni, B., & Waller, E. (2010). Document and Schema XML Updates. In C. Li & T. W. Ling (Eds.), *Advanced Applications and Structures in XML Processing: Label Stream, Semantics Utilization and Data Query Technologies* (pp. 361–384). Hershey, PA: IGI Global. doi:10.4018/978-1-61520-727-5.ch016

Collis, B., & Moonen, J. (2009). Collaborative Learning in a Contribution-Oriented Pedagogy. In P. L. Rogers, G. A. Berg, J. Boettcher, C. Howard, L. Justice, & K. D. Schenk (Eds.), *Encyclopedia of Distance Learning* (2nd ed.; pp. 327–333). IGI Global. doi:10.4018/978-1-60566-198-8.ch047

Connecting Health and Care for the Nation, A Shared Nationwide Interoperability Roadmap. (2015). Retrieved from The Office of the National Coordinator for Health Information Technology website: https://www.healthit.gov/sites/default/files/hie-interoperability/nationwide-interoperability-roadmap-final-version-1.0.pdf

Connolly, D., Keenan, F., & Ryder, B. (2008). Tag Oriented Agile Requirements Identification. In *Proceedings of the 15th Annual IEEE International Conference and Workshop on the Engineering of Computer Based Systems* (pp. 497-498). Belfast, UK: IEEE Computer Society.

Cooper, V., Lichtenstein, S., & Smith, R. (2009). Web-Based Self-Service Systems for Managed IT Support: Service Provider Perspectives of Stakeholder-Based Issues. In Self-Service in the Internet Age (pp. 231-255). Academic Press.

Cordeiro, R. L. F., Galante, R. M., Edelweiss, N., & dos Santos, C. S. (2007). A Deep Classification of Temporal Versioned Integrity Constraints for Designing Database Applications. *Proceedings of the 19th International Conference on Software Engineering & Knowledge Engineering (SEKE'2007)*, 416-421.

Corredor, I., Metola, E., Bernardos, A. M., Tarrío, P., & Casar, J. R. (2014). A Lightweight Web of Things Open Platform to Facilitate Context Data Management and Personalized Healthcare Services Creation. *International Journal of Environmental Research and Public Health*, *11*(5), 4676–4713. doi:10.3390/ijerph110504676 PMID:24785542

Correia, Z. P. (2005). Towards a stakeholder model for the co-production of the public-sector information system. *Information Research: An International Electronic Journal, 10*(3), n3.

Cortes, C., & Vapnik, V. (1995). Support vector machine. *Machine Learning, 20*(3), 273–297. doi:10.1007/BF00994018

Couturier, J., Sola, D., Borioli, G. S., & Raiciu, C. (2012). *How can the internet of things help to overcome current healthcare challenges.* Retrieved from https://papers.ssrn.com/sol3/papers.cfm?abstract_id=2304133

Crnkovic, I. (2005). Component-based software engineering for embedded systems. *ICSE '05. Proceedings of the 27th international conference on Software engineering.* 10.1145/1062455.1062631

Cronbach, L. J., & Snow, R. E. (1977). *Aptitudes and instructional methods.* New York, NY: Irvington.

Cruz, I., Xiao, H., & Hsu, F. (2004). *Peer-to-Peer Semantic Integration of XML and RDF Data Sources. Internal report.* Department of Computer Science, University of Illinois at Chicago.

Cumming, G., Fowlie, A., & McKendrick, D. (2010). H= P4+ C and Health Web Science: "A Hippocratic Revolution in Medicine." *Proceedings of the ACM WebSci, 11*, 14-17. Retrieved from http://www.websci11.org/fileadmin/websci/Papers/Health_WS_Workshop-A_Hippocratic_Revolution.pdf

Currim, F., Currim, S., Dyreson, C. E., Joshi, S., Snodgrass, R. T., Thomas, S. W., & Roeder, E. (2009). *τXSchema: Support for Data- and Schema-Versioned XML Documents.* TimeCenter, Technical Report TR-91. Retrieved August 2, 2017, from <http://timecenter.cs.aau.dk/TimeCenterPublications/TR-91.pdf>

Currim, F., Currim, S., Dyreson, C. E., & Snodgrass, R. T. (2004). A Tale of Two Schemas: Creating a Temporal XML Schema from a Snapshot Schema with τXSchema. *Proceedings of the 9th International Conference on Extending Database Technology (EDBT 2004),* 348-365. 10.1007/978-3-540-24741-8_21

Cutler, D. (2013). *Why Medicine Will Be More Like Walmart.* Retrieved from http://www.technologyreview.com/news/518906/why-medicine-will-be-more-like-walmart

D'Aquin, M., Gridinoc, L., Angeletou, S., Sabou, M., & Motta, E. (2007). *Watson: A gateway for next generation semantic Web applications.* Poster session at the International Semantic Web Conference (ISWC 2007), Busan, Korea.

Daniel, F., Casati, F., Silveira, P., Verga, M., & Nalin, M. (2011). Beyond Health Tracking: A Personal Health and Lifestyle Platform. *IEEE Internet Computing, 15*(4), 14–22. doi:10.1109/MIC.2011.53

Danielson, R. L., & DeLisi, P. S. (2002). Thinking Styles of North American IT Executives. *Proceedings of the Third Annual Global Information Technology Management World Conference.*

Darwish, A., & Lakhtaria, K. (2011). The impact of the new Web 2.0 technologies in communication, development, and revolutions of societies. *Journal of Advances in Information Technology, 2*(4), 204–216. doi:10.4304/jait.2.4.204-216

Das, A., Gollapudi, S., & Munagala, K. (2014, February). Modeling opinion dynamics in social networks. In *Proceedings of the 7th ACM international conference on Web search and data mining* (pp. 403-412). ACM. 10.1145/2556195.2559896

Dasgupta, S. (2010). *Social computing: concepts, methodologies, tools and applications.* IGI Global. doi:10.4018/978-1-60566-984-7

David, J., Guillet, F., & Briand, H. (2006). Matching directories and OWL ontologies with AROMA. *Proceedings of the 15th ACM international conference on Information and knowledge management,* 830– 831. 10.1145/1183614.1183752

De Bra, P., Aroyo, L., & Cristea, A. (2004). Adaptive web-based educational hypermedia. In Web dynamics, adaptive to change in content, size, topology and use. Springer. doi:10.1007/978-3-662-10874-1_16

De Castro, C., Grandi, F., & Scalas, M. R. (1997). Schema versioning for multitemporal relational databases. *Information Systems, 22*(5), 249–290. doi:10.1016/S0306-4379(97)00017-3

De Iongh, A., Fagan, P., Fenner, J., & Kidd, L. (2015). *A practical guide to self-management support. Key components for successful implementation.* Academic Press.

De Silva, D. (2011). *Evidence: helping people help themselves.* The Health Foundation.

Derczynski, L., Maynard, D., Rizzo, G., van Erp, M., Gorrell, G., Troncy, R., ... Bontcheva, K. (2015). Analysis of named entity recognition and linking for tweets. *Information Processing & Management, 51*(2), 32–49. doi:10.1016/j.ipm.2014.10.006

Dillon, S., Stahl, F., & Vossen, G. (2013a). Towards the Web in Your Pocket: Curated Data as a Service. In *Advanced Methods for Computational Intelligence.* Springer.

Dillon, S., Stahl, F., Vossen, G., & Rastrick, K. (2013b). A Contemporary Approach to Coping with Modern Information Overload. *Communications of the ICISA, 14*(1), 1–24.

Ding, L., Finin, T., Joshi, A., Pan, R., Cost, R. S., Peng, Y., & Sachs, J. (2004). Swoogle: a search and metadata engine for the semantic Web. In *Proceedings of the thirteenth ACM international conference on Information and knowledge management* (pp. 652-659). ACM. 10.1145/1031171.1031289

Directive (EU) 2016/1148 of the European Parliament and of the Council of 6 July 2016 concerning measures for a high common level of security of network and information systems across the Union. (2016). Retrieved from http://eur-lex.europa.eu/eli/dir/2016/1148/oj

Dixon, M. B. (2013). A Graphical Based Approach to the Conceptual Modeling, Validation and Generation of XML Schema Definitions. *International Journal of Information Technology and Web Engineering, 8*(1), 1–22. doi:10.4018/jitwe.2013010101

Do, H., & Rahm, E. (2002). COMA - a system for flexible combination of schema matching approaches. *28th International Conference on Very Large Data Bases,* 610–621.

Doan, A. H., Halevy, A., & Ives, Z. (2012). *Principles of Data Integration.* Morgan Kaufmann.

Domínguez, E., Lloret, J., Pérez, B., Rodríguez, Á., Rubio, A. L., & Zapata, M. A. (2011). Evolution of XML Schemas and documents from stereotyped UML class models: A traceable approach. *Information and Software Technology, 53*(1), 34–50. doi:10.1016/j.infsof.2010.08.001

Dopichaj, P. (2009). RankingVerfahren für Web-Suchmaschinen. In D. Lewandowski (Ed.), *Handbuch Internet-Suchmaschinen.* Heidelberg, Germany: Nutzerorientierung in Wissenschaft und Praxis. AKA, Akad. Verl.-Ges.

Dos Reis, J. C., Dinh, D., Pruski, C., Da Silveira, M., & Reynaud-Delaître, C. (2013). Mapping adaptation actions for the automatic reconciliation of dynamic ontologies. In *Proceedings of the 22nd ACM international conference on Information & Knowledge Management* (pp. 599-608). ACM. 10.1145/2505515.2505564

Dos Reis, J. C., Pruski, C., & Reynaud-Delaître, C. (2015). State-of-the-art on mapping maintenance and challenges towards a fully automatic approach. *Expert Systems with Applications, 42*(3), 1465–1478. doi:10.1016/j.eswa.2014.08.047

DotTag. (2007). *DotTag.* Retrieved August 12, 2017, from http://dottag.codeplex.com/

Doulkeridis, C., Loutas, N., & Vazirgiannis, M. (2005). A system architecture for context-aware service discovery. *International Workshop on Context for Web Services CWS-05.*

Du, Z., Fu, X., Zhao, C., Liu, Q., & Liu, T. (2012). Interactive and collaborative e-learning platform with integrated social software and learning management system. In *Proceedings of the 2012 International Conference on Information Technology and Software Engineering* (pp. 11-18). Springer Berlin Heidelberg.

Dunkels, A. (2003). Full TCP/IP for 8-bit architectures. *Proceedings of the 1st international conference on Mobile systems, applications and services - MobiSys '03*, 85-98. 10.1145/1066116.1066118

Dyreson, C. E. (2001). Observing Transaction-time Semantics with TTXPath. *Proceedings of the 2nd International Conference on Web Information Systems Engineering (WISE 2001)*, 193-202.

Dyreson, C. E., & Grandi, F. (2009). Temporal XML. In L. Liu & M. T. Özsu (Eds.), *Encyclopedia of Database Systems* (pp. 3032–3035). Heidelberg, Germany: Springer-Verlag.

Dyreson, C. E., Snodgrass, R. T., Currim, F., Currim, S., & Joshi, S. (2006). Validating Quicksand: Schema Versioning in τXSchema. *Proceedings of the 22nd International Conference on Data Engineering Workshops (ICDE Workshops 2006)*, 82. 10.1109/ICDEW.2006.161

Dzbor, M., Domingue, J., & Motta, E. (2003). Magpie–towards a semantic Web browser. In *International Semantic Web Conference* (pp. 690-705). Springer Berlin Heidelberg.

Easley, D., & Kleinberg, J. (2007, Spring). The small-world phenomenon. *Networks*.

Eckhardt, J., Vogelsang, A., & Méndez Fernandez, D. (2016). Are "Non-functional" Requirements really Non-functional? An Investigation of Non-functional Requirements in Practice. *38th IEEE International Conference on Software Engineering*.

EgoNet. (2017). Egocentric Network Study Software [Software]. Available from https://omictools.com/egocentric-network-study-software-tool

Eisenberg, A., & Melton, J. (2004). Advancements in SQL/XML. *SIGMOD Record*, *33*(3), 79–86. doi:10.1145/1031570.1031588

El Bouhissi, H., Malki, M., & Sidi Ali Cherif, M. A. (2014). From user's goal to semantic Web services discovery: Approach based on traceability. *International Journal of Information Technology and Web Engineering*, *9*(3), 15–39. doi:10.4018/ijitwe.2014070102

El Kassmi, I., & Jarir, Z. (2016). Security Requirements in Web Service Composition: Formalization, Integration, and Verification. *25th International Conference on Enabling Technologies: Infrastructure for Collaborative Enterprises (WETICE)*. 10.1109/WETICE.2016.47

Elçi, A. (2016). *Big Data and Analytics: What's Ahead.* Panel presentation, WEDA Symposium, @ 40th COMPSAC, Atlanta, GA. Available at https://www.linkedin.com/pulse/big-data-analytics-carve-nich-your-future-atilla-el%C3%A7i/

Elçi, A. (2017). *Issues and Innovation in Medical Informatics Panel Presentation* (in Turkish). Akademik Bilisim '17, 10 February, Aksaray, Turkey. Available at https://tinyurl.com/issues-e-health

Elçi, A., Elçi, A., & Çelik, D. (2016). Semantic Modelling for E-Learning Coordination. In B. Khan (Ed.), *Revolutionizing Modern Education through Meaningful Implementation*. IGI Global.

Elçi, A., Elçi, A., & Celik, D. (2016). Semantic Modelling for E-Learning Coordination. In B. Khan (Ed.), *Revolutionizing Modern Education through Meaningful Implementation*. IGI Global. Retrieved from http://www.igi-global.com/book/revolutionizing-modern-education-through-meaningful/146987

Elçi, A., Vural, M., & Elçi, A. (2017). Changing Role of Faculty Members in Technology Enhanced Learning Environments: Faculty Members 4.0. In *Proc. International Educational Technology Conference*. Harvard University.

Elfirdoussi, S., Jarir, Z., & Quafafou, M. (2014a). Discovery and Visual Interactive WS Engine based on popularity: Architecture and Implementation. *International Journal of Software Engineering and Its Applications, 8*(2).

Elfirdoussi, S., Jarir, Z., & Quafafou, M. (2014b). Ranking Web Services using Web Service Popularity Score. *International Journal of Information Technology and Web Engineering, 9*(2),.

Elfirdoussi, S., Jarir, Z., & Quafafou, M. (2014). Ranking Web services using Web service popularity score. *International Journal of Information Technology and Web Engineering, 9*(2), 78–89. doi:10.4018/ijitwe.2014040105

Emberton, O. (2011). *Why we gave up Web design after 10 successful years.* Retrieved July 7, 2017, from https://silktide.com/why-we-gave-up-web-design-after-10-successful-years/

Engineering the Internet of Things: Wearables and Medical Devices. (2016). Retrieved from ANSYS website: http://www.ansys.com/-/media/Ansys/corporate/resourcelibrary/brochure/ib-wearables-and-medical-devices.pdf

Erçetin, Ş. Ş., & Neyişci, N. B. (2016). Social Network Analysis: A Brief Introduction to the Theory. In *Chaos, Complexity and Leadership 2014* (pp. 167–171). Cham: Springer. doi:10.1007/978-3-319-18693-1_16

Erola, A., Castellà-Roca, J., Viejo, A., & Mateo-Sanz, J. M. (2011). Exploiting social networks to provide privacy in personalized web search. *Journal of Systems and Software, 84*(10), 1734–1745. doi:10.1016/j.jss.2011.05.009

European Chronic Disease Alliance Policy. (2010). Retrieved from http://www.alliancechronicdiseases.org/fileadmin/user_upload/policy_papers/ECDA_White_Paper_on_Chronic_Disease.pdf

Euzenat, J., & Shvaiko, P. (2016). *Ontology matching tutorial (v17).* The 13th International Conference on Concept Lattices and Their Applications (CLA-2016), Moscow, Russia.

Euzenat, J., Mocan, A., & Scharffe, F. (2008). Ontology alignment: an ontology management perspective. In M. Hepp, P. D. Leenheer, A. D. Moor, & Y. Sure (Eds.), Ontology management: semantic Web, semantic Web services, and business applications (pp. 177–206). New-York: Springer.

Euzenat, J. (2015). Revision in networks of ontologies. *Artificial Intelligence, 228,* 195–216.

Euzenat, J., Loup, D., Touzani, M., & Valtchev, P. (2004). Ontology alignment with OLA. *Proceedings of the 3rd EON Workshop at 3rd International Semantic Web Conference,* 59–68.

Euzenat, J., & Shvaiko, P. (2013). *Ontology matching* (Vol. 18). Heidelberg, Germany: Springer. doi:10.1007/978-3-642-38721-0

Faisal, S., & Sarwar, M. (2014). Temporal and multi-versioned XML documents: A survey. *Information Processing & Management, 50*(1), 113–131. doi:10.1016/j.ipm.2013.08.003

Falou, E. L. S. (2006). Programmation répartie, optimisation par agent mobile. CEAN University.

Fan, Y., Yin, Y., Da Xu, L., Zeng, Y., & Wu, F. (2014). IoT-Based Smart Rehabilitation System. *IEEE Transactions on Industrial Informatics, 10*(2), 1568–1577. doi:10.1109/TII.2014.2302583

Farinaccio, L., & Zmeureanu, R. (1999). Using a pattern recognition approach to disaggregate the total electricity consumption in a house into the major end-uses. *Energy and Building, 30*(3), 245–259. doi:10.1016/S0378-7788(99)00007-9

Fast, A., Jensen, D., & Levine, B. N. (2005, August). Creating social networks to improve peer-to-peer networking. In *Proceedings of the eleventh ACM SIGKDD international conference on Knowledge discovery in data mining* (p. 568-573). ACM. 10.1145/1081870.1081938

Faye, D. C. (2007). *Médiation de données sémantique dans SenPeer, un système pair-à-pair de gestion de données* (PhD thesis). Nantes University.

Felder, R. M. (1993). Reaching the Second Tier: Learning and Teaching Styles in Engineering Education. *Engineering Education, 78*(7), 674–681.

Fellah, A., Malki, M., & Elçi, A. (2016). Web Services Matchmaking Based on a Partial Ontology Alignment. *International Journal of Information Technology and Computer Science (IJITCS), 8*(6), 9-20. Retrieved from http://www.mecs-press.org/ijitcs/ijitcs-v8-n6/IJITCS-V8-N6-2.pdf

Fellah, A., Malki, M., & Elci, A. (2016). A similarity measure across ontologies for Web services discovery. *International Journal of Information Technology and Web Engineering, 11*(1), 22–43. doi:10.4018/IJITWE.2016010102

Fessant, F., Lemaire, V., & Clérot, F. (2008). Combining several SOM approaches in data mining: application to ADSL customer behaviours analysis. *Data Analysis, Machine Learning and Applications*, 343-354.

Fessant, F., François, J., & Clérot, F. (2007). Characterizing ADSL customer behaviours by network traffic data-mining. *Annales des Télécommunications, 62*(3), 350–368.

Fielding, R. (2000). *Architectural styles and the design of network-based software architectures* (Ph.D. Thesis). Department of Information and Computer Science, University of California.

Firesmith, D. G. (2003). Engineering Security Requirements, Journal of Object Technology. doi:10.5381/jot.2003.2.1.c6

Flickr. (2004). *Flickr*. Retrieved August 10, 2017, from http://www.flickr.com/

Folino, G., Pisani, F., & Trunfio, P. (2014). *Efficient Discovery of Data Mining Services over DHT-based Overlays*. High Performance Computing & Simulation (HPCS), International Conference.

Formo, J. (2012). *A Social Web of Things | Strategic Design Blog*. Retrieved from http://www.ericsson.com/uxblog/2012/04/a-social-web-of-things/

Formo, J., Laaksolahti, J., & Gårdman, M. (2011, August). Internet of things marries social media. In *Proceedings of the 13th International Conference on Human Computer Interaction with Mobile Devices and Services* (p. 753-755). ACM.

Fortunato, S. (2010). Community detection in graphs. *Physics Reports, 486*(3), 75–174. doi:10.1016/j.physrep.2009.11.002

Fourth Annual Benchmark Study on Patient Privacy & Data Security. (2014). Retrieved from Ponemon Institute website: http://www2.idexpertscorp.com/ponemon-report-on-patient-privacy-data-security-incidents/

Fragopoulou, P., Mastroianni, C., Montero, R., Andrjezak, A., & Kondo, D. (2010). Self and adaptive mechanisms for large scale distributed systems. In Grids, P2P and Services Computing (pp. 147-156). Springer. doi:10.1007/978-1-4419-6794-7_12

Freeman, L. C. (1978). Centrality in social networks conceptual clarification. *Social Networks, 1*(3), 215–239. doi:10.1016/0378-8733(78)90021-7

Furno, A., & Zimeo, E. (2013). Efficient cooperative discovery of service compositions in unstructured P2P networks. In *Parallel, Distributed and Network-Based Processing (PDP), 21st Euromicro International Conference on 2013* (pp. 58-67). IEEE.

Gabarre, S., Gabarre, C., Din, R., Shah, P. M., & Karim, A. A. (2013). Using mobile Facebook as an LMS: Exploring impeding factors. *GEMA Online Journal of Language Studies, 13*(3), 99–115.

Gaikwad, S. V., Chaugule, A., & Patil, P. (2014). Text mining methods and techniques. *International Journal of Computers and Applications*, *85*(17).

Gajowniczek, K., & Ząbkowski, T. (2017). Electricity forecasting on the individual household level enhanced based on activity patterns. *PLoS One*, *12*(4), e0174098. doi:10.1371/journal.pone.0174098 PMID:28423039

Galante, R. M., Dos Santos, C. S., Edelweiss, N., & Moreira, A. F. (2005). Temporal and versioning model for schema evolution in object-oriented databases. *Data & Knowledge Engineering*, *53*(2), 99–128. doi:10.1016/j.datak.2004.07.001

Galster, M., & Bucherer, E. (2008). A Taxonomy for Identifying and Specifying Non-functional Requirements in Service-oriented Developmen. *IEEE Congress on services*. 10.1109/SERVICES-1.2008.51

Gamila, O., Pavla, D., Jan, M., Katerina, S., & Václav, S. (2010). Using Spectral Clustering for Finding Students' Patterns of Behavior in Social Networks. DATESO 2010, 118-130.

Gandon, F., & Shreiber, G. (2014, Feb 25). *RDF 1.1: XML syntax*. W3C Recommendation. Retrieved from http://www.w3.org/TR/rdf-syntax-grammar/

Gao, D., & Snodgrass, R. T. (2003). Temporal slicing in the evaluation of XML documents. *Proceedings of the 29th International Conference on Very Large Data Bases (VLDB 2003)*, 632-643.

Gao, S., & Zaniolo, C. (2012). Supporting Database Provenance under Schema Evolution. *Proceedings of the 5th International ER Workshop on Evolution and Change in Data Management and on Non Conventional Data Access (ECDM – NoCoDa 2012)*, 67-77.

Garriga, M., Mateos, C., Flores, A., Cechich, A., & Zunino, A. (2016). RESTful service composition at a glance: A survey. *Journal of Network and Computer Applications*, *60*, 32–53. doi:10.1016/j.jnca.2015.11.020

Gartner. (2014). *Gartner says the Internet of Things will transform the data center*. Retrieved March 19, 2014, from http://www.gartner.com/newsroom/id/2684616

Gattani, A., Lamba, D. S., Garera, N., Tiwari, M., Chai, X., Das, S., ... Doan, A. (2013). Entity extraction, linking, classification, and tagging for social media: A wikipedia-based approach. *Proceedings of the VLDB Endowment International Conference on Very Large Data Bases*, *6*(11), 1126–1137. doi:10.14778/2536222.2536237

Genevès, P., Layaïda, N., & Quint, V. (2011). Impact of XML Schema Evolution. *ACM Transactions on Internet Technology*, *11*(1), 4. doi:10.1145/1993083.1993087

Gerpott, T. J., & Thomas, S. (2014). Empirical research on mobile Internet usage: A meta-analysis of the literature. *Telecommunications Policy*, *38*(3), 291–310. doi:10.1016/j.telpol.2013.10.003

Getoor, L., Friedman, N., Koller, D., & Taskar, B. (2001, June). Learning probabilistic models of relational structure. In ICML (Vol. 1, pp. 170-177). Academic Press.

Getoor, L., & Diehl, C. P. (2005). Link mining: A survey. *ACM SIGKDD Explorations Newsletter*, *7*(2), 3–12. doi:10.1145/1117454.1117456

Gillani, S., Naeem, M., Habibullah, R., & Qayyum, A. (2013). Semantic schema matching using DBpedia. *International Journal of Intelligent Systems and Applications*, *5*(4), 72–80. doi:10.5815/ijisa.2013.04.07

Gill, N. S., & Tomar, P. (2008). X Model: A New Component-Based Model. *IACSIT International Journal of Engineering and Technology*, *1*(1-2), 1–10.

Giridhar, P., Abdelzaher, T., George, J., & Kaplan, L. (2015, March). On quality of event localization from social network feeds. In *Pervasive Computing and Communication Workshops (PerCom Workshops), 2015 IEEE International Conference on* (pp. 75-80). IEEE. 10.1109/PERCOMW.2015.7133997

Giunchiglia, F., Autayeu, A., & Pane, J. (2012). S-Match: An Open Source Framework for Matching Lightweight Ontologies. Semantic Web Journal, 3(3), 307-317.

Giunchiglia, F., Yatskevich, M., & Shvaiko, P. (2007). Semantic matching: Algorithms and implementation. *Journal on Data Semantics, 9*, 1–38.

Glinz, M. (2007). On Non-Functional Requirements. *Requirements Engineering Conference.*

Goeller, K. E. (1998). Web-based collaborative learning: a perspective on the future. In *Proc. Seventh World Wide Web Conference.* Brisbane, Australia: Elsevier Science. 10.1016/S0169-7552(98)00129-9

Goldberg, M., Kelley, S., Magdon-Ismail, M., Mertsalov, K., & Wallace, A. (2010, August). Finding overlapping communities in social networks. In *Social Computing (SocialCom), 2010 IEEE Second International Conference on* (pp. 104-113). IEEE. 10.1109/SocialCom.2010.24

Golder, S. A., & Huberman, B. A. (2005). *The Structure of Collaborative Tagging Systems.* Computing Research Repository.

Gomes, J., Ricardo, B., Prudêncio, C., Meira, L., Azevedo Filho, A., ... Nascimento, O. H. (2013). Group Profiling for Understanding Educational Social Networking. *The 25th International Conference on Software Engineering and Knowledge Engineering,* 101-106.

Gorini, A., & Pravettoni, G. (2011). P5 medicine: A plus for a personalized approach to oncology. *Nature Reviews. Clinical Oncology, 8*(7), 444. doi:10.1038/nrclinonc.2010.227-c1 PMID:21629214

Grandi, F. (2002). A relational multi-schema data model and query language for full support of schema versioning. *Proceedings of SEBD 2002 – National Conference on Advanced Database Systems,* 323-336.

Grandi, F. (2004). Introducing an Annotated Bibliography on Temporal and Evolution Aspects in the World Wide Web. *SIGMOD Record, 33*(2), 84–86. doi:10.1145/1024694.1024709

Grandi, F. (2015). Temporal Databases. In M. Khosrow-Pour (Ed.), *Encyclopedia of Information Science and Technology* (3rd ed.; pp. 1914–1922). Hershey, PA: IGI Global; doi:10.4018/978-1-4666-5888-2.ch184

Grandi, F., & Mandreoli, F. (2003). A formal model for temporal schema versioning in object-oriented databases. *Data & Knowledge Engineering, 46*(2), 123–167. doi:10.1016/S0169-023X(02)00207-0

Granovetter, M., & Soong, R. (1983). Threshold models of diffusion and collective behavior. *The Journal of Mathematical Sociology, 9*(3), 165–179. doi:10.1080/0022250X.1983.9989941

Grasic, B., & Podgorelec, V. (2010). Automating ontology based information integration using service orientation. *WSEAS Transactions on Computers, 9*, 547–556.

Grégoire, Y., Tripp, T. M., & Legoux, R. (2013, May). *When customer love turns into lasting hate: the effects of relationship strength and time on customer revenge and avoidance.* American Marketing Association.

Grégoire, Y., & Fisher, R. J. (2008). Customer betrayal and retaliation: When your best customers become your worst enemies. *Journal of the Academy of Marketing Science, 36*(2), 247–261. doi:10.100711747-007-0054-0

Grimm, S., Abecker, A., Völker, J., & Studer, R. (2011). Ontologies and the semantic Web. In *Handbook of Semantic Web Technologies* (pp. 507–579). Springer Berlin Heidelberg. doi:10.1007/978-3-540-92913-0_13

Groß, A., Dos Reis, J. C., Hartung, M., Pruski, C., & Rahm, E. (2013). Semi-automatic adaptation of mappings between life science ontologies. In *International Conference on Data Integration in the Life Sciences* (pp. 90-104). Springer Berlin Heidelberg. 10.1007/978-3-642-39437-9_8

Groves, P., Kayyali, B., Knott, D., & Kuiken, S. V. (2016). *The 'big data' revolution in healthcare: Accelerating value and innovation.* Retrieved from http://repositorio.colciencias.gov.co:8081/jspui/bitstream/11146/465/1/1661-The_big_data_revolution_in_healthcare.pdf

Gruber, T. (2008). Ontology. *Encyclopedia of Database Systems (Springer-Verlag).* Retrieved from http://tomgruber.org/writing/ontology-definition-2007.htm

Gruber, T. R. (1993). A translation approach to portable ontology specifications. *Knowledge Acquisition, 5*(2), 199–220. doi:10.1006/knac.1993.1008

Grubert, J., Kranz, M., & Quigley, A. (2016). Challenges in mobile multi-device ecosystem. *The Journal of Mobile User Experience, 5*(5), 1–22.

Gruetze, T., Yao, G., & Krestel, R. (2015). Learning Temporal Tagging Behaviour. In *Proceedings of the 24th International Conference on World Wide Web (WWW '15 Companion).* ACM. 10.1145/2740908.2741701

Gruman, J., & Smith, C. W. (2009). Why the Journal of Participatory Medicine? *Journal of Participatory Medicine.* Retrieved from http://www.jopm.org/opinion/editorials/2009/10/21/why-the-journal-of-participatory-medicine/

Guarino, N., Oberle, D., & Staab, S. (2009). What is an Ontology? In *Handbook on ontologies* (pp. 1–17). Springer Berlin Heidelberg. doi:10.1007/978-3-540-92673-3_0

Guerrini, G., & Mesiti, M. (2008). X-Evolution: A Comprehensive Approach for XML Schema Evolution. *Proceedings of the 19th International Workshop Database and Expert Systems Applications (DEXA 2008),* 251-255. 10.1109/DEXA.2008.128

Guerrini, G., & Mesiti, M. (2009). XML Schema Evolution and Versioning: Current Approaches and Future Trends. In E. Pardede (Ed.), *Open and Novel Issues in XML Database Applications: Future Directions and Advanced Technologies* (pp. 66–87). Hershey, PA: Information Science Reference – IGI Global. doi:10.4018/978-1-60566-308-1.ch004

Guerrini, G., Mesiti, M., & Rossi, D. (2005). Impact of XML Schema Evolution on Valid Documents. *Proceedings of the 7th ACM International Workshop on Web Information and Data Management (WIDM 2005),* 39-44. 10.1145/1097047.1097056

Guidara, I., Guermouche, N., Chaari, T., Jmaiel, M., & Tazi, S. (2015). Time-Dependent QoS Aware Best Service Combination Selection. *International Journal of Web Services Research, 12*(2).

Guidara, I., Guermouche, N., Chaari, T., Jmaiel, M., & Tazi, S. (2015). Time-dependent QoS Aware Best Service Combination Selection. *International Journal of Web Services Research, 12*(2), 1–25. doi:10.4018/IJWSR.2015040101

Guille, A., Hacid, H., Favre, C., & Zighed, D. A. (2013). Information diffusion in online social networks: A survey. *SIGMOD Record, 42*(2), 17–28. doi:10.1145/2503792.2503797

Guinard, D., & Trifa, V. (2009, April). Towards the web of things: Web mashups for embedded devices. In *Workshop on Mashups, Enterprise Mashups and Lightweight Composition on the Web (MEM 2009), in proceedings of WWW (International World Wide Web Conferences), Madrid, Spain (Vol. 15).* Academic Press.

Guinard, D., Fischer, M., & Trifa, V. (2010, March). Sharing using social networks in a composable web of things. In *Pervasive Computing and Communications Workshops (PERCOM Workshops), 2010 8th IEEE International Conference on* (pp. 702-707). IEEE. 10.1109/PERCOMW.2010.5470524

Guinard, D., Trifa, V., & Wilde, E. (2010, November). A resource oriented architecture for the web of things. In Internet of Things (IOT), 2010 (p. 1-8). IEEE. doi:10.1109/IOT.2010.5678452

Guinard, D., Trifa, V., Mattern, F., & Wilde, E. (2011). From the Internet of Things to the Web of Things: Resource Oriented Architecture and Best Practices. In D. Uckelmann, M. Harrison & F. Michahelles (Eds.), Architecting the Internet of Things (pp. 97-129). Springer.

Guinard, D., & Trifa, V. (2016). *Building the web of things: with examples in node. js and raspberry pi.* Manning Publications Co.

Guo, J., Xu, L., Xiao, G., & Gong, Z. (2012). Improving multilingual semantic interoperation in cross-organizational enterprise systems through concept disambiguation. *IEEE Transactions on Industrial Informatics, 8*(3), 647–658. doi:10.1109/TII.2012.2188899

Gupta, K., & Goel, A. (2013). Software Engineering for Tagging Software. *International Journal of Software Engineering and its Application, 4*(4), 65-76. doi: 10.5121/ijsea.2013.4406

Gupta, K., & Goel, A. (2012). Tagging requirements for web application. In S. K. Aggarwal, T. V. Prabhakar, V. Varma, & S. Padmanabhuni (Eds.), *Proceedings of the 5th India Software Engineering Conference* (pp. 81-90). Kanpur, India: ACM. 10.1145/2134254.2134269

Gupta, K., & Goel, A. (2014). Requirement Estimation and Design of Tag software in Web Application. *International Journal of Information Technology and Web Engineering, 9*(2), 1–19. doi:10.4018/ijitwe.2014040101

Guralnik, V., & Karypis, G. (2004). Parallel tree-projection-based sequence mining algorithms. *Parallel Computing, 30*(4), 443–472. doi:10.1016/j.parco.2004.03.003

Haas, H., & Brown, A. (Eds.). (2004). *Web Services Glossary*. Retrieved from https://www.w3.org/TR/2004/NOTE-ws-gloss-20040211/

Hai-Jew, S. (2017). Flickering Emotions: Feeling-Based Associations from Related Tags Networks on Flickr. In S. Hai-Jew (Ed.), *Social Media Data Extraction and Content Analysis* (pp. 296–341). Hershey, PA: IGI Global; doi:10.4018/978-1-5225-0648-5.ch010

Haik, Y., & Moustafa, K. A. F. (2007). Thinking and learning preferences for a sample of engineering students at the United Arab Emirates university. *Emirates Journal for Engineering Research, 12*(1), 65–71.

Halevy, A., Ives, Z., Madhavan, J., Mork, P., Suciu, D., & Tatarinov, I. (2004). The piazza peer data management system. *IEEE Transactions on Knowledge and Data Engineering, 16*(7), 787–798. doi:10.1109/TKDE.2004.1318562

Han, J., Choi, C. S., Park, W. K., & Lee, I. (2011, June). Green home energy management system through comparison of energy usage between the same kinds of home appliances. In *Consumer Electronics (ISCE), 2011 IEEE 15th International Symposium on* (pp. 1-4). IEEE. 10.1109/ISCE.2011.5973168

Han, J., Pei, J., & Yan, X. (2005). Sequential pattern mining by pattern-growth: Principles and extensions. *Foundations and Advances in Data Mining*, 183-220.

Han, J., Pei, J., Mortazavi-Asl, B., Pinto, H., Chen, Q., Dayal, U., & Hsu, M. C. (2001, April). Prefixspan: Mining sequential patterns efficiently by prefix-projected pattern growth. *Proceedings of the 17th international conference on data engineering*, 215-224.

Han, J., Choi, C. S., & Lee, I. (2011). More efficient home energy management system based on ZigBee communication and infrared remote controls. *IEEE Transactions on Consumer Electronics, 57*(1).

Han, J., Pei, J., & Yin, Y. (2000, May). Mining frequent patterns without candidate generation. []. ACM.]. *SIGMOD Record*, *29*(2), 1–12. doi:10.1145/335191.335372

Hansson, S. O. (1994). Kernel contraction. *The Journal of Symbolic Logic*, *59*(03), 845–859. doi:10.2307/2275912

Hansson, S. O. (1999). *A Textbook of Belief Dynamics. Theory Change and Database Updating*. Dordrecht: Kluwer. doi:10.1007/978-94-007-0814-3

Hargreaves, C. A. (2015). Analysis of hotel guest satisfaction ratings and reviews: An application in Singapore. *American Journal of Marketing Research*, *1*(4), 208–214.

Harindranath, G., & Zupancic, J. (2002). *New Perspectives on Information Systems Development: Theory, Methods, and Practice*. Springer Science & Business Media. doi:10.1007/978-1-4615-0595-2

Harris, S., & Seaborne, A. (2013). *SPARQL 1.1: Query language*. W3C Recommendation. Retrieved from http://www.w3.org/TR/sparql11-query/

Harrison, A. F., & Bramson, R. M. (1984). *The Art of Thinking*. New York: Berkley Books.

Harrison, R., Lee, S. M., & West, A. A. (2004). Lifecycle engineering of modular automation machines. *Proceedings of the 2nd IEEE International Conference on Industrial Informatics (INDIN '04)*.

Hartigan, J. A., & Wong, M. A. (1979). Algorithm AS 136: A k-means clustering algorithm. *Journal of the Royal Statistical Society. Series C, Applied Statistics*, *28*(1), 100–108.

Hasan, M. M., Loucopoulos, P., & Nikolaidou, M. (2014). Classification and Qualitative Analysis of Non-Functional Requirements Approaches. In Enterprise, Business-Process and Information Systems Modeling (pp 348-362). Springer. doi:10.1007/978-3-662-43745-2_24

Hasegawa, K., Ikeda, K., & Suzuki, N. (2013). An Algorithm for Transforming XPath Expressions According to Schema Evolution. *Proceedings of the 1ˢᵗ International Workshop on Document Changes: Modeling, Detection, Storage and Visualization (DChanges 2013)*, paper 4.

Hassenzahl, M., Eckoldt, K., Diefenbach, S., Laschke, M., Lenz, E., & Kim, J. (2013). Designing moments of meaning and pleasure, experience design and happiness. *International Journal of Design*, *7*(3), 21–31.

Haubold, F., Schildgren, J., Scherzinger, S., & Deßloch, S. (2017). ControVol Flex: Flexible Schema Evolution for NoSQL Application Development. *Proceedings of the 17th Conference on Database Systems for Business, Technology, and Web (BTW'2017)*, 601-604.

Hauk, J., & Padberg, J. (2016). *The Customer in the Center of Digital Transformation*. Detecon Management Report. Retrieved July 10, 2017, from https://www.detecon.com/sites/default/files/dmr_crm_special_heft_e_01_2016_1.pdf

Hawkins, D. M. (1980). *Identification of outliers* (Vol. 11). London: Chapman and Hall. doi:10.1007/978-94-015-3994-4

Healthcare Financial Management Association (HFMA). (2017). Retrieved from http://www.hfma.org/DownloadAsset.aspx?id=46524

Healthcare Security: Improving Network Defenses While Serving Patients. (2016). CISCO.

He, C., Fan, X., & Li, Y. (2013). Toward Ubiquitous Healthcare Services With a Novel Efficient Cloud Platform. *IEEE Transactions on Biomedical Engineering*, *60*(1), 230–234. doi:10.1109/TBME.2012.2222404 PMID:23060318

He, D., & Zeadally, S. (2015). An Analysis of RFID Authentication Schemes for Internet of Things in Healthcare Environment Using Elliptic Curve Cryptography. *IEEE Internet Of Things Journal*, *2*(1), 72–83. doi:10.1109/JIOT.2014.2360121

Heflin, J. (2004). *OWL web ontology language use cases and requirements*. W3C Recommendation. Retrieved from http:// www.w3.org/TR/webont-req/

Heidorn, P., Tobbo, H., Choudhury, G., Greer, C., & Marciano, R. (2007). Identifying best practices and skills for workforce development in data curation. *Proceedings of the American Society for Information Science and Technology, 44*(1), 1–3. doi:10.1002/meet.1450440141

Helic, D., Strohmaier, M., Trattner, C., Muhr, M., & Lerman, K. (2011).Pragmatic evaluation of folksonomies. In S. Srinivasan, K. Ramamritham, A. Kumar, M. P. Ravindra, E. Bertino, & R. Kumar (Eds.), *Proceedings of the 20th international conference on World wide web*, (pp. 417-426). Hyderabad, India: ACM.

Hellmann, S., Stadler, C., Lehmann, J., & Auer, S. (2009). DBpedia live extraction. On the Move to Meaningful Internet Systems. *OTM, 2009*, 1209–1223.

Hellweger, S., Wang, X., & Abrahamsson, P. (2015). *The contemporary understanding of user experience in practice*. Retrieved July 12, 2017, from https://arxiv.org/ftp/arxiv/papers/1503/1503.01732.pdf

Hendler, J., Shadbolt, N., Hall, W., Berners-Lee, T., & Weitzner, D. (2008). Web Science: An Interdisciplinary Approach to Understanding the Web. *Communications of the ACM, 51*(7), 60–69. doi:10.1145/1364782.1364798

Hennig-Thurau, T., Gwinner, K. P., Walsh, G., & Gremler, D. D. (2004). Electronic word-of-mouth via consumer-opinion platforms: What motivates consumers to articulate themselves on the internet? *Journal of Interactive Marketing, 18*(1), 38–52. doi:10.1002/dir.10073

Henze, N., & Nejdl, W. (2004). A logical characterization of adaptive educational hypermedia. *New Review of Hypermedia and Multimedia, 10*(1), 77-113.

Hernandez, D. (2014, March 10). *Big data healthcare: The pros and cons of remote patient monitoring*. Retrieved from http://medcitynews.com/2014/03/big-data-healthcare-pros-cons-remote-patient-monitoring/

Hertling, S. (2012). *Hertuda Results for OEAI 2012. Seventh International Workshop on Ontology Matching*, Boston, MA.

Hey, I. (2016). *Google Analytics: these are the 10 most important KPIs for your website*. Retrieved July 12, 2017, from https://en.onpage.org/blog/google-analytics-these-are-the-10-most-important-kpis-for-your-website

Hibbard, J., & Greene, J. (2013). What The Evidence Shows About Patient Activation: Better Health Outcomes And Care Experiences; Fewer Data On Costs. *Health Affairs, 32*(2), 207–214. doi:10.1377/hlthaff.2012.1061 PMID:23381511

Hogan, A., Zimmermann, A., Umbrich, J., Polleres, A., & Decker, S. (2012). Scalable and distributed methods for entity matching, consolidation and disambiguation over linked data corpora. *Journal of Web Semantics, 10*, 76–110. doi:10.1016/j.websem.2011.11.002

Holmes, E., & Willoughby, T. (2005). Play behaviour of children with autism spectrum disorders. *Journal of Intellectual & Developmental Disability, 30*(3), 156–164. doi:10.1080/13668250500204034

Holzmann, H., Tahmasebi, N., & Risse, T. (2013, September). BlogNEER: Applying Named Entity Evolution Recognition on the Blogosphere? In SDA (pp. 28-39). Academic Press.

Holzmann, G. J. (2007). The model checker SPIN. *IEEE Transactions on Software Engineering, 23*(5), 279–295. doi:10.1109/32.588521

Honarvar, A. R., & Sami, A. (2016). Extracting Usage Patterns from Power Usage Data of Homes' Appliances in Smart Home using Big Data Platform. *International Journal of Information Technology and Web Engineering, 11*(2), 39–50. doi:10.4018/IJITWE.2016040103

Howell, F., & McNab, R. (1998). Simjava: a discrete event simulation library for java. In *First International Conference on Web-based Modelling and Simulation*. San Diego CA: Society for Computer Simulation.

Hoyer, V., & Fischer, M. (2008). Market overview of enterprise mashup tools. *Proceedings of the 6th International Conference on Services Oriented Computing*, 708-721.

Hu, W., Liao, Y., & Vemuri, V. R. (2003, June). Robust Support Vector Machines for Anomaly Detection in Computer Security. In ICMLA (pp. 168-174). Academic Press.

Huang, A. (2008, April). Similarity measures for text document clustering. *Proceedings of the sixth new zealand computer science research student conference (NZCSRSC2008)*, 49-56.

Huang, H. S., Su, T. C., Liang, J. M., & Tseng, Y. C. (2015, March). A dynamic reservation scheme in online charging system for family shared plan. In *Wireless Communications and Networking Conference (WCNC)* (pp. 2279-2284). IEEE.

Huayou, S., Zhong, C., & Yong, D. (2013). Semantic web services publication and OCT-based discovery in structured P2P network. *Service Oriented Computing and Applications*, 7(3), 169–180. doi:10.100711761-011-0097-4

Hung, S. C., Araujo, M., & Faloutsos, C. (2016). Distributed community detection on edge-labeled graphs using spark. In *12th International Workshop on Mining and Learning with Graphs (MLG)* (*Vol. 113*). Academic Press.

Hurley, C., & Chen, S. (2003). *Delicious*. Retrieved August 30, 2012, from https://del.icio.us/ http://www.delicious.com/

Hwang, A., Kessler, E. H., & Francesco, A. M. (2004). Student networking behaviour, culture, and grade performance: An empirical study and pedagogical recommendations. *Academy of Management Learning & Education*, 3(2), 139–150. doi:10.5465/AMLE.2004.13500532

Identity Theft Resource Center Breach Statistics. 2005-2015. (n.d.). Retrieved from http://www.idtheftcenter.org/images/breach/2005to2015multiyear.pdf

IEEE SA - 11073-20702-2016 - Standard for Medical Devices Communication Profile for Web Services. Health informatics--Point-of-care medical device communication Part 20702: Medical Devices Communication Profile for Web Services. (n.d.). Retrieved July 30, 2017, from http://standards.ieee.org/findstds/standard/11073-20702-2016.html

Improved Outcomes Software Inc. (2004, January). K-Means Clustering Overview [Web log comment]. Retrieved from http://www.improvedoutcomes.com/docs/WebSiteDocs/Clustering/K-Means_Clustering_Overview.htm. (2017, August 10).

Improving cyber security across the EU - Consilium. (2016). Retrieved from http://www.consilium.europa.eu/en/policies/cyber-security/

Imran, M., Castillo, C., Diaz, F., & Vieweg, S. (2015). Processing social media messages in mass emergency: A survey. *ACM Computing Surveys*, 47(4), 67. doi:10.1145/2771588

Inmon, W. H. (2005). *Building the Data Warehouse* (4th ed.). New York: John Wiley & Sons.

Introducing My Cardiac Coach. (n.d.). Retrieved from https://www.heart.org/HEARTORG/Conditions/HeartAttack/My-Cardiac-Coach_UCM_489280_SubHomePage.jsp

Inukollu, V., Keshamoni, D., Kang, T., & Inukollu, M. (2014). Factors influencing quality of mobile apps: Role of mobile app development life cycle. *International Journal of Software Engineering and Its Applications*, 5(5), 15–34. doi:10.5121/ijsea.2014.5502

IoT to Revolutionize Healthcare Industry: Survey. (2015). Retrieved from http://www.machinetomachinemagazine.com/2015/04/14/iot-to-revolutionize-healthcare-industry-zebra-survey/

ISO/IEC9126-1:2001(E). (2001). Software Engineering-Product Quality-Part1: Quality Model.

Istanbul Aydin University. (n.d.). Retrieved from http://www.aydin.edu.tr/index_eng.asp

Jabolokow, K. W. (2000). Thinking about Thinking: Problem Solving Style in the Engineering Classroom. *ASEE Annual Conference and Exposition: Engineering Education Beyond the Millennium.*

Jain, A., Bajpai, A., & Rohila, M. N. (2012, May). Efficient Clustering Technique for Information Retrieval in Data Mining. *International Journal of Emerging Technology and Advanced Engineering, 2*(5), 458–466.

Jamendo. (2005). *Jamendo - The #1 platform for free music.* Retrieved August 28, 2017, from http://www.jamendo.com/en

Jaro, M. (1989). Advances in record-linkage methodology as applied to matching the 1985 census of Tampa. *Journal of the American Statistical Association, 84*(406), 414–420. doi:10.1080/01621459.1989.10478785

Jars, I. (2005). *Contribution des sciences sociales dans le domaine de l'intelligence artificielle distribuée ALONE, Un modèle hybride d'agent apprenant.* Claude Bernard Lyon I University.

Jatowt, A., Antoine, É., Kawai, Y., & Akiyama, T. (2015, May). Mapping Temporal Horizons: Analysis of Collective Future and Past related Attention in Twitter. In *Proceedings of the 24th International Conference on World Wide Web* (pp. 484-494). International World Wide Web Conferences Steering Committee. 10.1145/2736277.2741632

Javaid, N., Naseem, M., Rasheed, M. B., Mahmood, D., Khan, S. A., Alrajeh, N., & Iqbal, Z. (2017). A new heuristically optimized Home Energy Management controller for smart grid. *Sustainable Cities and Society, 34*, 211–227. doi:10.1016/j.scs.2017.06.009

Jeacle, I., & Carter, C. (2011). In TripAdvisor we trust: Rankings, calculative regimes and abstract systems. *Accounting, Organizations and Society, 36*(4), 293–309. doi:10.1016/j.aos.2011.04.002

Jean-Mary, Y. R., Shironoshita, E. P., & Kabuka, M. R. (2009). Ontology matching with semantic verification. *Journal of Web Semantics, 7*(3), 235–251. doi:10.1016/j.websem.2009.04.001 PMID:20186256

Jean-Mary, Y., & Kabuka, M. R. (2007). *ASMOV: Ontology Alignment with Semantic Validation.* Vienna, Austria: SWDB-ODBIS Workshop.

Jena, R. D. F. API. The Apache Software Foundation (2011). Last accessed on January 30, 2015 from http://jena.apache.org/

Jeng, Y. L., Wu, T. T., Huang, Y. M., Tan, Q., & Yang, S. J. (2010). The add-on impact of mobile applications in learning strategies: A review study. *Journal of Educational Technology & Society, 13*(3), 3–11.

Jensen, K. (2016). *How Web design evolved in 2016: simplify or perish.* Retrieved July 13, 2017, from https://www.bopdesign.com/bop-blog/2016/10/web-design-evolved-2016-simplify-perish/

Jeong, J., & Moon, S. (2017, April). Interval Signature: Persistence and Distinctiveness of Inter-event Time Distributions in Online Human Behavior. In *Proceedings of the 26th International Conference on World Wide Web Companion* (pp. 1585-1593). International World Wide Web Conferences Steering Committee.

Jernej, R., Matevž, P., Andrej, K., Félix, B., & José, V. B. (2012). Integration of Learning Management Systems with Social Networking. *Platforms E-learning in a Facebook supported environment*, 100-105.

Jiang, B., Zhang, Z. L., & Towsley, D. (2015, August). Reciprocity in social networks with capacity constraints. In *Proceedings of the 21th ACM SIGKDD International Conference on Knowledge Discovery and Data Mining* (pp. 457-466). ACM. 10.1145/2783258.2783410

Jiang, W., Wang, G., Bhuiyan, M. Z. A., & Wu, J. (2016). Understanding graph-based trust evaluation in online social networks: Methodologies and challenges. *ACM Computing Surveys*, *49*(1), 10. doi:10.1145/2906151

Jimenez-Ruiz, E., & Cuenca Grau, B. (2011). Logmap: Logic-based and scalable on-ontology matching. The Semantic Web–ISWC 2011, 273–288.

Jokinen, J. (2015). Emotional user experience: Traits, events, and states. *International Journal of Human-Computer Studies*, *76*, 67–77. doi:10.1016/j.ijhcs.2014.12.006

Jones, R., & Diaz, F. (2007). Temporal profiles of queries. *ACM Transactions on Information Systems*, *25*(3), 14, es. doi:10.1145/1247715.1247720

Jordan, R. (2003). Social play and autistic spectrum disorders: A perspective on theory, implications and educational approaches. *Autism*, *7*(4), 347–360. doi:10.1177/1362361303007004002 PMID:14678675

Jøsang, A., & Golbeck, J. (2009, September). Challenges for robust trust and reputation systems. In *Proceedings of the 5th International Workshop on Security and Trust Management (SMT 2009)* (p. 52). Academic Press.

Jøsang, A., Ismail, R., & Boyd, C. (2007). A survey of trust and reputation systems for online service provision. *Decision Support Systems*, *43*(2), 618–644. doi:10.1016/j.dss.2005.05.019

Jscripters. (2017). *Developing a JavaScript based website with AJAX/JQUERY*. Retrieved July 4, 2017, from http://www.jscripters.com/javascript-advantages-and-disadvantages/

Juels, A., Rivest, R. L., & Szydlo, M. (2003). The blocker tag: selective blocking of RFID tags for consumer privacy. In S. Jajodia, V. Atluri, & T. Jaeger (Eds.), *Proceedings of the 10th ACM conference on Computer and communications security* (pp. 103-111). Washington, DC: ACM. 10.1145/948109.948126

Jusoh, S., & Alfawareh, H. M. (2012). Techniques, Applications and Challenging Issue in Text Mining. *IJCSI International Journal of Computer Science Issues*, *9*(6), 431–436.

Kalczynski, P. J., & Chou, A. (2005). Temporal document retrieval model for business news archives. *Information Processing & Management*, *41*(3), 635–650. doi:10.1016/j.ipm.2004.01.002

Kalfoglou, Y., & Schorlemmer, M. (2003). Ontology mapping: The state of the art. *The Knowledge Engineering Review*, *18*(01), 1–31. doi:10.1017/S0269888903000651

Kanungo, T., Mount, D. M., Netanyahu, N. S., Piatko, C. D., Silverman, R., & Wu, A. Y. (2002). An efficient k-means clustering algorithm: Analysis and implementation. *IEEE Transactions on Pattern Analysis and Machine Intelligence*, *24*(7), 881–892. doi:10.1109/TPAMI.2002.1017616

Karakostas, B., & Kalamboukis, Z. (2017). API mashups: How well do they support the travellers' information needs? *Proceedings of the 8th International Conference on Ambient Systems, Networks and Technologies (ANT 2017)*, 204-209.

Karande, A., Karande, M., & Meshram, M. (2011). Choreography and orchestration using business process execution language for SOA with web services. *International Journal of Computer Science Issues IJCSI*, *11*, 224–232.

Kari, J. (2013). *Automata and formal languages*. University of Turku.

Kasper, W., & Vela, M. (2011, October). Sentiment analysis for hotel reviews. In Computational linguistics-applications conference (Vol. 231527, pp. 45-52). Academic Press.

Katifori, A., Halatsis, C., Lepouras, G., Vassilakis, C., & Giannopoulou, E. (2007). Ontology visualization methods—a survey. *ACM Computing Surveys*, *39*(4), 10, es. doi:10.1145/1287620.1287621

Kaur, K., & Singh, H. (2010). Candidate process models for component based software development. *Journal of Software Engineering Academic Journal Inc, India, 4*(1), 16–29.

Kawachi, K. (2008). Deterministic models for rumor transmission. *Nonlinear Analysis Real World Applications, 9*(5), 1989–2028. doi:10.1016/j.nonrwa.2007.06.004

Kawai, H., Jatowt, A., Tanaka, K., Kunieda, K., & Yamada, K. (2010). ChronoSeeker: Search engine for future and past events. In *Proceedings of the 4th International Conference on Uniquitous Information Management and Communication* (p. 25). ACM. 10.1145/2108616.2108647

Kayed, M., & Shaalan, K. F. (2006). A Survey of Web Information Extraction Systems. *IEEE Transactions on Knowledge and Data Engineering, 18*(10), 1411–1428. doi:10.1109/TKDE.2006.152

Kaznacheev, V. I. (1969). Language of Regular Expressions. In *Synthesis of Digital Automata* (pp. 135–140). Springer.

Kelkar, K. (2017). *Predictions and trends for 2017*. Retrieved July 14, 2017, from https://www.userzoom.com/user-experience-research/predictions-ux-design-research-2017/

Khan, B. H. (2016). Revolutionizing Modern Education through Meaningful E-Learning Implementation. Hershey, PA: IGI Global. doi:10.4018/978-1-5225-0466-5

Khan, B. H. (1997). Web-based Instruction. *Educational Technology*.

Khan, B. H. (1997). Web-based instruction: What is it and why is it? In B. H. Khan (Ed.), *Web-Based Instruction* (pp. 5–18). Englewood Cliffs, NJ: Educational Technology Publications.

Khattak, A. M., Pervez, Z., Khan, W. A., Khan, A. M., Latif, K., & Lee, S. Y. (2015). Mapping evolution of dynamic Web ontologies. *Information Sciences, 303*, 101–119. doi:10.1016/j.ins.2014.12.040

Khokhar, R. H., Benjamin, C. M. F., Farkhund, I., Alhadidi, D., & Bentahar, J. (2016). Privacy-preserving data mashup model for trading person-specific information. *Electronic Commerce Research and Applications, 17*, 19–37. doi:10.1016/j.elerap.2016.02.004

Kiang, M. Y., Hu, M. Y., & Fisher, D. M. (2006). An extended self-organizing map network for market segmentation—a telecommunication example. *Decision Support Systems, 42*(1), 36–47. doi:10.1016/j.dss.2004.09.012

Kiefer, C., & Bernstein, A. (2008). The Creation and Evaluation of iSPARQL Strategies for Matchmaking. *Proceedings of the 5th European Semantic Web Conference (ESWC)*, 463– 477. 10.1007/978-3-540-68234-9_35

Kimura, M., & Saito, K. (2006). Tractable models for information diffusion in social networks. *Knowledge Discovery in Databases: PKDD, 2006*, 259–271.

Klein, M. (2004). *Change management for distributed ontologies* (PhD thesis). University of Vrije, Netherlands.

Kleinberg, J. (2008). The convergence of social and technological networks. *Communications of the ACM, 51*(11), 66–72. doi:10.1145/1400214.1400232

Klettke, M., Störl, U., Shenavai, M., & Scherzinger, S. (2016). NoSQL Schema Evolution and Big Data Migration at Scale. *Proceedings of the 2016 IEEE International Conference on Big Data (BigData'2016)*, 2764-2774. 10.1109/BigData.2016.7840924

Klímek, J., Malý, J., Mlýnková, I., & Nečaský, M. (2012). eXolutio: Tool for XML Schema and Data Management. *Proceedings of the 12th Annual International Workshop on DAtabases, TExts, Specifications and Objects (DATESO 2012)*, 69-80.

Klímek, J., Malý, J., Nečaský, M., & Holubová, I. (2015). eXolutio: Methodology for Design and Evolution of XML Schemas using Conceptual Modeling. *Informatica*, *26*(3), 453–472. doi:10.15388/Informatica.2015.58

Klos, T. B., & La Poutré, H. (2005). Decentralized reputation-based trust for assessing agent reliability under aggregate feedback. *Lecture Notes in Computer Science*, *3577*, 110–128. doi:10.1007/11532095_7

Klusch, M., & Kapahnke, P. (2010). isem: Approximated reasoning for adaptive hybrid selection of semantic services. In The semantic web: Research and applications (pp. 30-44). Springer.

Knoke, D., & Yang, S. (2008). *Social network analysis* (Vol. 154). Sage. doi:10.4135/9781412985864

Koçak, N. (2002). The importance of play and toys in the education of children with disorders. In *Proc. XI. National Special Education Congress*. Konya: Eğitim Kitapevi Yayınları.

Kohonen, T. (1990). The self-organizing map. *Proceedings of IEEE*, 1464-1480.

Kohonen, T. (2001). *Self-Organizing Maps* (3rd ed.). Springer. doi:10.1007/978-3-642-56927-2

Kolb, D. A. (1984). *Experiential Learning*. Englewood Cliffs, NJ: Prentice-Hall.

Koller, D. (1999, June). Probabilistic relational models. In *International Conference on Inductive Logic Programming* (pp. 3-13). Springer. 10.1007/3-540-48751-4_1

Kontogiannis, K., Smith, D., & O'Brian, L. (2003). On the Role of Services in Enterprise Application Integration. *Proc. 10th Int'l Workshop Software Technology and Engineering Practice (STEP)*, 103-113. 10.1109/STEP.2002.1267619

Kopecký, J., Vitvar, T., Bournez, C., & Farrell, J. (2007). Sawsdl: Semantic annotations for wsdl and xml schema. *IEEE Internet Computing*, *11*(6), 60–67. doi:10.1109/MIC.2007.134

Körner, C., Kern, R., Grahsl, H.-P., & Strohmaier, M. (2010). Of categorizers and describers: an evaluation of quantitative measures for tagging motivation. In M. H. Chignell, & E. Toms (Eds.), *Proceedings of the 21st ACM conference on Hypertext and hypermedia* (pp. 157-166). Toronto, Canada: ACM. 10.1145/1810617.1810645

Kostadinov, D. (2007). *Personnalisation de l'information: une approche de gestion de profils et de reformulation de requêtes*. University of Versailles Saint-Quentin-En-Yvelines.

Kotonya, G., Sommerville, I., & Hall, S. (2003). Towards A Classification Model for Component-Based Software Engineering. In *Proceedings of, Euro micro Conference, 29th*. Dept. of Computer., Lancaster Univ.

Koudas, N., Sarawagi, S., & Srivastava, D. (2006). Record linkage: Similarity measures and algorithms. *Tutorial, the ACM SIGMOD Conference*.

Koutrika, G., & Ioannidis, Y. (2004). Personalization of Queries in Database Systems. *Proceedings of the 20th International Conference on Data Engineering*, 597-608. 10.1109/ICDE.2004.1320030

Koutrika, G., & Ioannidis, Y. (2005). Personalized Queries under a Generalized Preference Model. *Proceedings of the 21st International Conference on Data Engineering*, 841-852. 10.1109/ICDE.2005.106

Kramer, J. (2014). *Responsive design frameworks: just because you can, should you?* Retrieved July 11, 2017, from https://www.smashingmagazine.com/2014/02/responsive-design-frameworks-just-because-you-can-should-you/

Kramer, S. (2017, January 16). *Overcoming Obstacles for IoT in the Healthcare Industry*. Retrieved from https://www.futurum.xyz/overcoming-obstacles-iot-healthcare-industry/

Kremen, P., Smid, M., & Kouba, Z. (2011). OWLDiff: A practical tool for comparison and merge of OWL ontologies. In *Database and Expert Systems Applications (DEXA), 2011 22nd International Workshop on* (pp. 229-233). IEEE. 10.1109/DEXA.2011.62

Kruchten, P. (1995). The 4+1 View Model of Architecture. *IEEE Software*, *12*(6), 42–50. doi:10.1109/52.469759

Kujala, S., Roto, V., Vainio-Mattila, K., Karapanos, E., & Sinnelä, A. (2011). UX curve: A method for evaluating long-term user experience. *Interacting with Computers*, *23*(5), 473–483. doi:10.1016/j.intcom.2011.06.005

Kulikova, T., Aldebert, P., & Althorpe, N. (2004). The EMBL Nucleotide Sequence Database. *Nucleic Acids Research*, *32*(90001), 27–30. doi:/gkh120 PMID:1468135110.1093/nar

Kulkarni, K. G., & Michels, J.-E. (2012). Temporal features in SQL:2011. *SIGMOD Record*, *41*(3), 34–43. doi:10.1145/2380776.2380786

Kulkarni, S., Singh, A., Ramakrishnan, G., & Chakrabarti, S. (2009, June). Collective annotation of Wikipedia entities in web text. In *Proceedings of the 15th ACM SIGKDD international conference on Knowledge discovery and data mining* (pp. 457-466). ACM. 10.1145/1557019.1557073

Kurtz, G. (2014). Integrating a Facebook group and a Course Website: The effect on Participation and Perceptions on Learning. *American Journal of Distance Education*, *28*(4), 253–263. doi:10.1080/08923647.2014.957952

Kwietniewski, M., Gryz, J., Hazlewood, S., & Van Run, P. (2010). Transforming XML Documents as Schemas Evolve. *Proceedings of the VLDB Endowment International Conference on Very Large Data Bases*, *3*(2), 1577–1580. doi:10.14778/1920841.1921043

Lacoste, X., Faverge, M., Bosilca, G., Ramet, P., & Thibault, S. (2014, May). Taking advantage of hybrid systems for sparse direct solvers via task-based runtimes. In *Parallel & Distributed Processing Symposium Workshops (IPDPSW), 2014 IEEE International* (pp. 29-38). IEEE. 10.1109/IPDPSW.2014.9

Laere, O. V., Schockaert, S., Tanasescu, V., Dhoedt, B., & Jones, C. B. (2014). Georeferencing Wikipedia documents using data from social media sources. *ACM Transactions on Information Systems*, *32*(3), 12. doi:10.1145/2629685

Lambrix, P., & Tan, H. (2006). SAMBO – a system for aligning and merging biomedical ontologies. *Journal of Web Semantics*, *4*(1), 196–206. doi:10.1016/j.websem.2006.05.003

Lane, T., & Brodley, C. E. (1997, July). Sequence matching and learning in anomaly detection for computer security. In *AAAI Workshop: AI Approaches to Fraud Detection and Risk Management* (pp. 43-49). AAAI.

Lassila, O., & Swick, R. R. (1999). Resource Description Framework (RDF). *Model and Syntax. W3C Recommendation*. Retrieved from https://www.w3.org/TR/WD-rdf-syntax-971002/

Lathem, J., Gomadam, K., & Sheth, A. P. (2007). Sa-rest and (s)mashups: Adding semantics to restful services. *Proceedings of the International Conference on Semantic Computing, ICSC'07*, 469-476. 10.1109/ICSC.2007.94

Law, E., Van Schaik, L., & Roto, V. (2014). Attitudes towards user experience (UX) measurement. *International Journal of Human-Computer Studies*, *72*(6), 526–541. doi:10.1016/j.ijhcs.2013.09.006

Lee, J. I., Choi, C. S., Park, W. K., Han, J. S., & Lee, I. W. (2011, September). A study on the use cases of the smart grid home energy management system. In *ICT Convergence (ICTC), 2011 International Conference on* (pp. 746-750). IEEE. 10.1109/ICTC.2011.6082716

Lee, J., Jie, L. S., & Wang, P. F. (2015). A Framework for Composing SOAP, Non-SOAP and Non-Web Services. IEEE Transactions on Services Computing, 8(2).

Lee, K., Ganti, R. K., Srivatsa, M., & Liu, L. (2014, December). When twitter meets foursquare: tweet location prediction using foursquare. In *Proceedings of the 11th International Conference on Mobile and Ubiquitous Systems: Computing, Networking and Services* (pp. 198-207). ICST (Institute for Computer Sciences, Social-Informatics and Telecommunications Engineering). 10.4108/icst.mobiquitous.2014.258092

Lee, Y. (2015). Semantic-Based Web API Composition for Data Mashups. *Journal of Information Science and Engineering, 31,* 1233-1248.

Lee, C. A., Marciano, R., Hou, C.-y., & Shah, C. (2009). From harvesting to cultivating. In *Proceedings of the 9th ACM/IEEE-CS joint Conference on Digital Libraries.* Austin, TX: ACM Press.

Lee, C. J., Tang, S. M., Tsai, C. C., & Chen, Y. C. (2009). Toward a New Paradigm: Mashup Patterns in Web 2.0. *WSEAS Transactions on Information Science and Applications, 6*(10), 1675–1686.

Lee, J., Lee, S.-J., Chen, H.-M., & Hsu, K.-H. (2013). Itinerary-Based Mobile Agent as a Basis for Distributed OSGi Services. *IEEE Transactions on Computers, 62*(10), 1988–2000. doi:10.1109/TC.2012.107

Lee, Y. (2014). Semantic-based data mashups using hierarchical clustering and pattern analysis methods. *Journal of Information Science and Engineering, 30*(5), 1601–1618.

Lehtimäki, P., & Raivio, K. (2005). Lecture Notes in Computer Science: Vol. 3533. *A SOM based approach for visualization of MDCS network performance data.* Berlin: Springer. doi:10.1007/11504894_82

Leonardi, E., Hoai, T. T., Bhowmick, S. S., & Madria, S. (2007). DTD-Diff: A change detection algorithm for DTDs. *Data & Knowledge Engineering, 61*(2), 384–402. doi:10.1016/j.datak.2006.06.003

Lestari, D., Hardianto, D., & Hidayanto, A. (2014). Analysis of user experience quality on responsive web design from its informative perspective. *International Journal of Software Engineering and Its Applications, 8*(5), 53–62.

Levenshtein, V. (1966). Binary codes capable of correcting deletions, insertions, and reversals. *Soviet Physics, Doklady, 10*(8), 707–710.

Li, S-H., Li-hong, T., & Dong, G. (2009). Research and implementation of related technology for a logistics information system based on SOA. Journal of University of Science and Technology Beijing, 31(1).

Li, X., Uricchio, T., Ballan, L., Bertini, M., Snoek, G. M., & Bimbo, A. (2016). Socializing the Semantic Gap: A Comparative Survey on Image Tag Assignment, Refinement, and Retrieval. *ACM Computing Survey, 49*(1). DOI: 10.1145/2906152

Li, Z. G., Chen, C., & Soh, Y. C. (2009, May). Pricing based differentiated bandwidth and delay services with weighted Max-Min fairness. In *Industrial Electronics and Applications, 2009. ICIEA 2009. 4th IEEE Conference on* (pp. 773-779). IEEE. 10.1109/ICIEA.2009.5138309

Liben-Nowell, D., and Kleinberg, J. (2007). The link-prediction problem for social networks. *Journal of the Association for Information Science and Technology, 58*(7), 1019-1031.

Lieberman, E., Hauert, C., & Nowak, M. A. (2005). Evolutionary dynamics on graphs. *Nature, 433*(7023), 312–316. doi:10.1038/nature03204 PMID:15662424

Li, J., Tang, J., Li, Y., & Luo, Q. (2009). Rimom: A dynamic multistrategy ontology alignment framework. *IEEE Transactions on Knowledge and Data Engineering, 21*(8), 1218–1232. doi:10.1109/TKDE.2008.202

Li, L., Ge, R., Zhou, S. M., & Valerdi, R. (2012). Guest editorial integrated healthcare information systems. *IEEE Transactions on Information Technology in Biomedicine, 16*(4), 515–517. doi:10.1109/TITB.2012.2198317

Li, L., Li, S., & Zhao, S. (2014). QoS-Aware Scheduling of Services-Oriented Internet of Things. *IEEE Transactions on Industrial Informatics*, *10*(2), 1497–1505. doi:10.1109/TII.2014.2306782

Lin, K. J., & Chang, S. H. (2010). A service accountability framework for QoS service management and engineering. Springer.

Liu, B. (2012). Sentiment analysis and opinion mining. *Synthesis Lectures on Human Language Technologies*, *5*(1), 1-167.

Liu, Y., Liang, X., Xu, L., Staples, M., & Zhu, L. (2011). Composing enterprise mashup components and services using architecture integration patterns. *Journal of Systems and Software Archive, 84*(9), 1436-1446.

Liu, D., Li, N., Pedrinaci, C., Kopecký, J., Maleshkova, M., & Domingue, J. (2011). An approach to construct dynamic service mashups using lightweight semantics. *Current Trends in Web Engineering - Workshops, Doctoral Symposium, and Tutorials, Held at ICWE 2011.*

Li, X., Lu, R., Liang, X., Shen, X., Chen, J., & Lin, X. (2011). Smart community: An internet of things application. *IEEE Communications Magazine*, *49*(11), 68–75. doi:10.1109/MCOM.2011.6069711

Li, Y. S., Chen, P. S., & Tsai, S. J. (2008). A comparison of the Learning Styles among Differenct Nursing Programs in Taiwan: Implications for Nursing Education. *Nurse Education Today*, *28*(1), 70–76. doi:10.1016/j.nedt.2007.02.007 PMID:17391813

Longo, D. R., Land, G., Schramm, W., Fraas, J., Hoskins, B., & Howell, V. (1997). Consumer reports in health care: Do they make a difference in patient care? *Journal of the American Medical Association*, *278*(19), 1579–1584. doi:10.1001/jama.1997.03550190043042 PMID:9370503

Long-Term Evolution (LTE). (2008). 3rd Generation Partnership Project; Technical Specification Group Services and System Aspects. *3GPP System Architecture Evolution: Report on Technical Options and Conclusions (Release 8) – 3GPP TR 23.882 V8.0.0 (2008-09).* Retrieved from http://www.qtc.jp/3GPP/Specs/23882-800.pdf

Lopez, V., Motta, E., & Uren, V. (2006). Poweraqua: Fishing the semantic Web. In *European Semantic Web Conference* (pp. 393-410). Springer Berlin Heidelberg.

Lopez, V., Pasin, M., & Motta, E. (2005). Aqualog: An ontology-portable question answering system for the semantic Web. In *European Semantic Web Conference* (pp. 546-562). Springer Berlin Heidelberg. 10.1007/11431053_37

Lu, J., Huang, Z., & Ke, C. (2014). Verification of Behavioral-aware Privacy Requirements in Web Service Composition. *Journal of Software*, *9*(4).

Lucero, S. (2016). *IoT platforms: Enabling the Internet of Things.* HIS Technology. Retrieved from https://cdn. ihs. com/www/pdf/enabling-IOT. pdf

Lu, G., Wang, T., Zhang, G., & Li, S. (2012). Semantic Web Services Discovery Based on Domain Ontology. In *World Automation Congress (WAC)* (pp. 1-4). Puerto Vallarta, Mexico: IEEE.

Lui, F. (2007). Personalized Learning Using Adapted Content Design for Science Students. *Proceedings of the ECCE 2007 Conference*, 293-296.

Luk, G. (2010). *GitHub.* Retrieved August 25, 2017, from https://github.com/freetag

Lytras, M. D., Damiani, E., Carroll, J. M., Tennyson, R. D., Avison, D., Naeve, A., . . . Vossen, G. (Eds.). (2009). *Visioning and Engineering the Knowledge Society - A Web Science Perspective: Second World Summit on the Knowledge Society, WSKS 2009, Chania, Crete, Greece, September 16-18, 2009. Proceedings.* Springer.

Lytras, M. D., Damiani, E., & Pablos, P. O. (2008). *Web 2.0 The Business Model*. Springer Publishing Company, Incorporated.

Maabed, U. M., El-Fatatry, A., & El-Zogh, A. (2016). Enhancing Interface Understandability as a Means for Better Discovery of Web Services. *International Journal of Information Technology and Web Engineering*, *11*(4), 1–23. doi:10.4018/IJITWE.2016100101

Maamar, Z. (2009). A New Approach to Model Web Services Behaviors based on Synchronization. *International Conference on Advanced Information Networking and Applications Workshops*. 10.1109/WAINA.2009.65

Mabroukeh, N. R., & Ezeife, C. I. (2010). A taxonomy of sequential pattern mining algorithms. *ACM Computing Surveys*, *43*(1), 3. doi:10.1145/1824795.1824798

MacQueen, J. (1967, June). Some methods for classification and analysis of multivariate observations. In *Proceedings of the fifth Berkeley symposium on mathematical statistics and probability* (Vol. *1*, No. 14, pp. 281-297). Academic Press.

Madhavan, J., Bernstein, P. A., & Rahm, E. (2001). Generic schema matching with cupid. *VLDB '01: Proceedings of the 27th International Conference on Very Large Data Bases*, 49–58.

Maedche, A., Motik, B., Silva, N., & Volz, R. (2002, October). MAFRA—a mapping framework for distributed ontologies. In *International Conference on Knowledge Engineering and Knowledge Management* (pp. 235-250). Springer.

Maedche, A., & Staab, S. (2002). Measuring similarity between ontologies. *EKAW '02: Proceedings of the 13th International Conference on Knowledge Engineering and Knowledge Management: Ontologies and the Semantic Web*, 251–263. 10.1007/3-540-45810-7_24

Mahdavinejad, M. S., Rezvan, M., Barekatain, M., Adibi, P., Barnaghi, P., & Sheth, A. P. (2017). Machine learning for Internet of Things data analysis: A survey. *Digital Communications and Networks*.

Maia, P., Batista, T., Cavalcante, E., Baffa, A., Delicato, F. C., Pires, P. F., & Zomaya, A. (2014). A web platform for interconnecting body sensors and improving health care. *Procedia Computer Science*, *40*, 135–142. doi:10.1016/j.procs.2014.10.041

Mairiza, D., Zowghi, D., & Nurmuliani, N. (2010). An investigation into the notion of non-functional requirements. *ACM Symposium on Applied Computing*, 311-318. 10.1145/1774088.1774153

Majava, J., Nuottila, J., Haapasalo, H., Kris, M., & Law, Y. (2014). Customer needs in market-driven product development: Product management and R&D standpoints. *Technology and Investment*, *5*(01), 16–25. doi:10.4236/ti.2014.51003

Maleshkova, M., Pedrinaci, C., & Domingue, J. (2009). Supporting the creation of semantic restful service descriptions. *Proceedings of the 8th International Semantic Web Conference (ISWC 2009)*.

Malki, A., & Benslimane, S. M. (2012). Building semantic mashup. *Proceedings of the 4th International conference on Web and Information Technologies, ICWIT 2012*, 40-49.

Malki, A., & Benslimane, S. M. (2013). Semantic Cloud: Building Dynamic Mashup in Cloud Environment. *International Journal of Information Technology and Web Engineering*, *8*(4), 20–35. doi:10.4018/ijitwe.2013100102

Malý, J., Mlýnková, I., & Nečaský, M. (2011). XML Data Transformations as Schema Evolves. *Proceedings of the 15th International Conference on Advances in Databases and Information Systems (ADBIS 2011)*, 375-388. 10.1007/978-3-642-23737-9_27

Mani, I., & Wilson, G. (2000). Robust temporal processing of news. In *Proceedings of the 38th Annual Meeting on Association for Computational Linguistics* (pp. 69-76). Association for Computational Linguistics.

Manimaran, P., & Duraiswamy, K. (2012). Identifying Overlying Group of People through Clustering. *International Journal of Information Technology and Web Engineering*, 7(4), 50–60. doi:10.4018/jitwe.2012100104

Mann, A. K., & Kaur, N. (2013a). Review paper on clustering techniques. *Global Journal of Computer Science and Technology, 13*(5).

Mann, A., & Kaur, N. (2013b). Grid density based clustering algorithm. *International Journal of Advanced Research in Computer Engineering & Technology, 2*(6).

Mark, K., & Csaba, L. (2007, June). Analyzing customer behavior model graph (CBMG) using Markov chains. In *Intelligent Engineering Systems, 2007. INES 2007. 11th International Conference on* (pp. 71-76). IEEE.

Markle Foundation & The Personal Health Working Group. (2013). *Final Report*. Available at http://www.markle.org/sites/default/files/final_phwg_report1.pdf

Markov, A. A. (1971). Extension of the limit theorems of probability theory to a sum of variables connected in a chain. John Wiley and Sons.

Martin, D., Burstein, M., Mcdermott, D., Mcilraith, S., Paolucci, M., Sycara, K., ... Srinivasan, N. (2007). Bringing semantics to web services with OWL-S. *World Wide Web (Bussum), 10*(3), 243–277. doi:10.100711280-007-0033-x

Martin, R. C. (2008). *Clean Code: A Handbook of Agile Software Craftsmanship*. Hoboken, NJ: Prentice-Hall.

Martins, H., & Silva, N. (2009). A User-driven and a Semantic-based Ontology Mapping Evolution Approach. ICEIS, (1), 214-221.

Mateos, C., Rodriguez, J. M., & Zunino, A. (2015). A tool to improve code-first web services discoverability through text mining techniques. *Software, Practice & Experience, 45*(7), 925–948. doi:10.1002pe.2268

Mayer, S., Guinard, D., & Trifa, V. (2012, October). Searching in a web-based infrastructure for smart things. In *Internet of Things (IOT), 2012 3rd International Conference on the* (p. 119-126). IEEE. 10.1109/IOT.2012.6402313

Mcguiness, D. L., & Harmelen, F. V. (2004). *OWL Web Ontology Language: Overview*. W3C Recommendation. Retrieved from http://www.w3.org/TR/owl-features/

McGuinness, D. L., & Van Harmelen, F. (2004). OWL web ontology language overview. *W3C recommendation, 10*(10), Retrieved from https://www.w3.org/TR/owl-features/

McKinsey, B. D. (2011). *Big data: The next frontier for innovation, competition, and productivity*. Retrieved from McKinsey Global Institute Report website: http://www.mckinsey.com/business-functions/digital-mckinsey/our-insights/big-data-the-next-frontier-for-innovation

McPartland, J., & Volkmar, F. R. (2012). Autism and Related Disorders. Handbook of Clinical Neurology, 106. doi:10.1016/B978–0–444–52002–9.00023–1

MEB. (n.d.). *Ministry of National Education of Turkey, Ankara*. Retrieved from http://www.meb.gov.tr/english/indexeng.htm

Meditskos, G., & Bassiliades, N. (2011). A combinatory framework of Web 2.0 mashup tools, owl-s and uddi. *Expert Systems with Applications, 38*(6), 6657–6668. doi:10.1016/j.eswa.2010.11.072

Meij, E., Weerkamp, W., & De Rijke, M. (2012, February). Adding semantics to microblog posts. In *Proceedings of the fifth ACM international conference on Web search and data mining* (pp. 563-572). ACM. 10.1145/2124295.2124364

Meilicke, C., & Stuckenschmidt, H. (2007). Applying logical constraints to ontology matching. In *Annual Conference on Artificial Intelligence* (pp. 99-113). Springer Berlin Heidelberg.

Meilicke, C., & Stuckenschmidt, H. (2009). An efficient method for computing alignment diagnoses. In *International Conference on Web Reasoning and Rule Systems* (pp. 182-196). Springer Berlin Heidelberg. 10.1007/978-3-642-05082-4_13

Meishar-Tal, H., Kurtz, G., & Pieterse, E. (2012). Facebook groups as LMS: A case study. *The International Review of Research in Open and Distributed Learning, 13*(4), 33–48. doi:10.19173/irrodl.v13i4.1294

Mekouar, S., Ibrahimi, K., & Bouyakhf, E. H. (2014, August). Inferring trust relationships in the social network: Evidence theory approach. In *Wireless Communications and Mobile Computing Conference (IWCMC), 2014 International* (pp. 470-475). IEEE.

Mekouar, S., El-Hammani, S., Ibrahimi, K., & Bouyakhf, E. H. (2015, May). Optimizing Diffusion Time of the Content Through the Social Networks: *Stochastic Learning Game. In International Conference on Networked Systems* (pp. 367-381). Springer International Publishing.

Mekouar, S., Zrira, N., & Bouyakhf, E. H. (in press). Community outlier detection in social networks based on graph matching. *International Journal of Autonomous and Adaptive Communications Systems.*

Mendes, P. N., Jakob, M., García-Silva, A., & Bizer, C. (2011, September). DBpedia spotlight: shedding light on the web of documents. In *Proceedings of the 7th international conference on semantic systems* (pp. 1-8). ACM. 10.1145/2063518.2063519

Meng, R., & He, C. (2013). A Comparison of Approaches to Web Service Evolution, International Conference on Computer Sciences and Applications. *Proc. ACM First Int'l Workshop Software Architectures and Mobility.*

Metzler, D., Jones, R., Peng, F., & Zhang, R. (2009). Improving search relevance for implicitly temporal queries. In *Proceedings of the 32nd international ACM SIGIR conference on Research and development in information retrieval* (pp. 700-701). ACM. 10.1145/1571941.1572085

Meurice, L., & Cleve, A. (2017). Supporting Schema Evolution in Schema-Less NoSQL Data Stores. *Proceedings of the 24th IEEE International Conference on Software ANalysis, Evolution and Reengineering (SANER'2017)*, 457-461. 10.1109/SANER.2017.7884653

Meyer, C. (2001). A Case in Case Study Methodology. *Field Methods, 13*(4), 329–352. doi:10.1177/1525822X0101300402

Milicevic, A. K., Nanopoulos, A., & Ivanovic, M. (2010). Social tagging in recommender systems: A survey of the state-of-the-art and possible extensions. *Artificial Intelligence Review, 33*(3), 187–209. doi:10.100710462-009-9153-2

Miller, G. (1995). Wordnet: A Lexical Database for English Language. *Communications of the ACM, 38*(11), 39–41. doi:10.1145/219717.219748

Milne, D., & Witten, I. H. (2008, October). Learning to link with wikipedia. In *Proceedings of the 17th ACM conference on Information and knowledge management* (pp. 509-518). ACM.

Minerva, R., Biru, A., & Rotondi, D. (2015). Towards a definition of the Internet of Things (IoT). *IEEE Internet Initiative*, (1).

Mislove, A., Gummadi, K. P., & Druschel, P. (2006, August). Exploiting social networks for internet search. In *5th Workshop on Hot Topics in Networks (HotNets06). Citeseer* (p. 79). Academic Press.

Mölleryd, B. G., & Markendahl, J. (2014). Analysis of spectrum auctions in India—An application of the opportunity cost approach to explain large variations in spectrum prices. *Telecommunications Policy, 38*(3), 236–247. doi:10.1016/j.telpol.2014.01.002

Moon, S., Lee, J. G., & Kang, M. (2014, January). Scalable community detection from networks by computing edge betweenness on mapreduce. In *Big Data and Smart Computing (BIGCOMP), 2014 International Conference on* (pp. 145-148). IEEE.

Moon, T. K. (1996). The expectation-maximization algorithm. *IEEE Signal Processing Magazine, 13*(6), 47–60. doi:10.1109/79.543975

Motlagh, O., Foliente, G., & Grozev, G. (2015). Knowledge-mining the Australian smart grid smart city data: A statistical-neural approach to demand-response analysis. In *Planning Support Systems and Smart Cities* (pp. 189–207). Springer International Publishing. doi:10.1007/978-3-319-18368-8_10

Motta, E., & Sabou, M. (2006). Next generation semantic Web applications. In *Asian Semantic Web Conference* (pp. 24-29). Springer Berlin Heidelberg.

Mugunthadevi, K., Punitha, S. C., & Punithavalli, M. (2011). Survey on feature selection in document clustering. *International Journal on Computer Science and Engineering, 3*(3), 1240–1244.

Mui, L. (2002). *Computational models of trust and reputation: Agents, evolutionary games, and social networks* (Doctoral dissertation). Massachusetts Institute of Technology.

Mui, L., Mohtashemi, M., & Halberstadt, A. (2002, July). Notions of reputation in multi-agents systems: a review. In *Proceedings of the first international joint conference on Autonomous agents and multiagent systems: part 1* (pp. 280-287). ACM. 10.1145/544741.544807

Mukherjee, S., & Shaw, R. (2016). Big data - concepts, applications, challenges and future scope. *International Journal of Advanced Research in Computer and Communication Engineering, 5*(2), 66–74.

Müller, B. (2016). *Designing native apps for Android and iOS: key differences and similarities*. Cheesecake Labs. Retrieved July 11, 2017, from https://cheesecakelabs.com/br/blog/designing-native-apps-for-android-and-ios-key-differences-and-similarities/

Multanen, M., Raivio, K., & Lehtimäki, P. (2006). Hierarchical analysis of MDCS network performance data. *14th European Symposium on Artificial Neural Networks ESANN 2006,* 449-454.

Murugesan, S., & Deshpande, Y. (2001). *Web Engineering: Managing Diversity and Complexity of Web Application Development*. Springer Science & Business Media. doi:10.1007/3-540-45144-7

Muschalle, A., Stahl, F., Löser, A., & Vossen, G. (2012). Pricing Approaches for Data Markets. *6th International VLDB Workshop on Business Intelligence for the Real Time Enterprise (BIRTE),* 129-144.

Nagar, Y., & Malone, T. W. (2011). Making Business Predictions by Combining Human and Machine Intelligence in Prediction Markets. *Proc. 32nd International Conference on Information Systems.*

Nam, D. H. (2017) Prediction of Concrete Compressive Strength Using Multivariate Feature Extraction with Neuro fuzzy Systems. In *Int'l Conf. Information and Knowledge Engineering IKE'17* (pp 46-51). Academic Press.

Nečaský, M., Klímek, J., Malý, J., & Mlýnková, I. (2012). Evolution and change management of XML-based systems. *Journal of Systems and Software, 85*(3), 683–707. doi:10.1016/j.jss.2011.09.038

Nejdl, W., Wolf, B., Qu, C., Decker, S., Sintek, M., Naeve, A., . . . Risch, T. (2002). EDUTELLA: A P2P Networking Infrastructure Based on RDF. *Proceedings of the 11th International World Wide Web Conference.*

Netzer, O., Lattin, J. M., & Srinivasan, V. (2008). A hidden Markov model of customer relationship dynamics. *Marketing Science, 27*(2), 185–204. doi:10.1287/mksc.1070.0294

Neville, J., & Jensen, D. (2007). Relational dependency networks. *Journal of Machine Learning Research, 8*(Mar), 653–692.

Newman, M. (2010). *Networks: an introduction.* Oxford University Press. doi:10.1093/acprof:oso/9780199206650.001.0001

Ng, W. S., Ooi, B. C., Tan, K., & Zhou, A. (2003). PeerDB: A P2P-based System for Distributed Data Sharing. *Proceedings of the 19th International Conference on Data Engineering (ICDE 2003),* 633–644.

Ngo, D. H., & Bellahsene, Z. (2012). YAM++:(not) Yet Another Matcher for Ontology Matching Task. BDA: Bases de Données Avancées.

Ngu, A. H. H., Carlson, M. P., Sheng, Q. Z., & Paik, H. Y. (2010). Semantic-based mashup of composite applications. *IEEE Transactions on Services Computing, 3*(1), 2–15. doi:10.1109/TSC.2010.8

NISO. (2005). *Understanding Metadata.* Bethesda, MD: NISO Press.

Njie, B., & Asimiran, S. (2014). Case study as a choice in qualitative methodology. *IOSR Journal of Research & Method in Education, 4*(3), 35–40.

Noh, S.-Y., & Gadia, S. K. (2006). A comparison of two approaches to utilizing XML in parametric databases for temporal data. *Information and Software Technology, 48*(9), 807–819. doi:10.1016/j.infsof.2005.10.002

Nordenhof, M. S., & Gammeltoft, L. (2007). *Autism, play and social interaction.* Jessica Kingsley Publishers.

Norris, S., Lau, J., Smith, S., Schmid, C., & Engelgau, M. (2002). Self-Management Education for Adults with Type 2 Diabetes: A meta-analysis of the effect on glycemic control. *Diabetes Care, 25*(7), 1159–1171. doi:10.2337/diacare.25.7.1159 PMID:12087014

Noy, N. F., Griffith, N., & Musen, M. A. (2008). Collecting community-based mappings in an ontology repository. In *International Semantic Web Conference* (pp. 371-386). Springer Berlin Heidelberg. 10.1007/978-3-540-88564-1_24

Noy, N., & Musen, M. (2001). Anchor- PROMPT: Using non-local context for semantic matching. Proceedings workshop on ontology and information sharing. *IJCAI,* 63–70.

Noy, N. F. (2009). Ontology mapping. In *Handbook on ontologies* (pp. 573–590). Springer Berlin Heidelberg. doi:10.1007/978-3-540-92673-3_26

Nunes, S., Ribeiro, C., & David, G. (2008). Use of temporal expressions in Web search. In *Advances in Information Retrieval* (pp. 580–584). Springer Berlin Heidelberg. doi:10.1007/978-3-540-78646-7_59

O'Reilly, T. (2005). *What Is Web 2.0? Design Patterns and Business Models for the Next Generation of Software.* Academic Press.

Ogrinz, M. (2009). *Mashup Patterns: Designs and Examples for the Modern Enterprise.* Addison-Wesley Professional.

Oliver, D., Livermore, C. R., & Sudweeks, F. (2009). *Self-Service in the Internet Age: Expectations and Experiences.* Springer Science & Business Media.

ORGM. (2008). *Special Education and Rehabilitation Centre Support Training Programme for Pervasive Developmental Disorders.* General Directorate of Special Education Institutions of Ministry of National Education. Retrieved from http://orgm.meb.gov.tr/meb_iys_dosyalar/2013_09/04010347_yaygngeliimselbozukluklardestekeitimprogram.pdf

Oshino, T., Asano, Y., & Yoshikawa, M. (2010). Time graph pattern mining for Web analysis and information retrieval. In *Web-Age Information Management* (pp. 40–46). Springer Berlin Heidelberg. doi:10.1007/978-3-642-14246-8_7

Ossher, H., Amid, D., Anaby-Tavor, A., Bellamy, R., Callery, M., Desmond, M., & ... . (2009).Using tagging to identify and organize concerns during pre-requirements analysis. In *Proceedings of the 2009 ICSE Workshop on Aspect-Oriented Requirements Engineering and Architecture Design* (pp. 25-30). IEEE Computer Society. 10.1109/EA.2009.5071580

Osuna, E., Freund, R., & Girosit, F. (1997, June). Training support vector machines: an application to face detection. In Computer vision and pattern recognition, 1997. Proceedings. 1997 IEEE computer society conference on (pp. 130-136). IEEE. doi:10.1109/CVPR.1997.609310

Ougouti, N. S., Belbachir, H., Amghar, Y., & Benharkat, N. (2011). Architecture Of MedPeer: A New P2P-based System for Integration of Heterogeneous Data Sources. *Proceedings of the International Conference on Knowledge Management and Information Sharing (KMIS)*, 351-354.

Ougouti, N. S., Belbachir, H., & Amghar, Y. (2015). A New OWL2 Based Approach for Relational Database Description. *International Journal of Information Technology and Computer Science*, 7(1), 48–53. doi:10.5815/ijitcs.2015.01.06

Ougouti, N. S., Belbachir, H., Amghar, Y., & Benharkat, N. (2010). Integration of Heterogeneous Data Sources. *Journal of Applied Sciences (Faisalabad)*, 10(22), 2923–2928. doi:10.3923/jas.2010.2923.2928

Ouni, A., Kessentini, M., Inoue, K., & Cinneide, M. O. (2017). Search-based web service antipatterns detection. IEEE Transactions on Services, 10(4).

Ouni, A., Gaikovina, R. K., Kessentini, M., & Inoue, K. (2015). Web service antipatterns detection using genetic programming. *Proc. Genetic Evol. Comput. Conf.*, 1351–1358. 10.1145/2739480.2754724

OWL 2.0. (n.d.). *OWL 2 Web Ontology Language Document Overview*. W3C Recommendation. Retrieved from http://www.w3.org/TR/owl2-overview/

Ozianyi, V. G., & Ventura, N. (2005, November). Dynamic pricing for 3G NETWORKS using admission control and traffic differentiation. In *Networks, 2005. Jointly held with the 2005 IEEE 7th Malaysia International Conference on Communication., 2005 13th IEEE International Conference on* (Vol. 2, pp. 838-843). IEEE.

Padmaja, S., & Sheshasaayee, A. (2016). Clustering of User Behaviour based on Web Log data using Improved K-Means Clustering Algorithm. *IACSIT International Journal of Engineering and Technology*, 8(1), 305–310.

Palathingal, P., & Chandra, S. (2004). Agent approach for service discovery and utilization. HICSS. doi:10.1109/HICSS.2004.1265292

Palma, R., Haase, P., Corcho, O., & Gómez-Pérez, A. (2009). Change representation for OWL 2 ontologies. In *Proceedings of the 6th International Conference on OWL: Experiences and Directions* (vol. 529, pp. 142-151). CEUR-WS.org.

Palmer, C. L., Allard, S., & Marlino, M. (2011). Data curation education in research centers. In *Proceedings of the 2011 iConference* (pp. 738–740). New York: ACM. 10.1145/1940761.1940891

Pan, H., & Liu, L. (1999). Fuzzy bayesian networks-a general formalism for representation, inference and learning with hybrid bayesian networks. In *Neural Information Processing, 1999. Proceedings. ICONIP'99. 6th International Conference on* (Vol. 1, pp. 401-406). IEEE. 10.1109/ICONIP.1999.844022

Paolucci, M., Kawamura, T., Payne, T. R., & Sycara, K. (2002, June). Semantic matching of web services capabilities. In *International Semantic Web Conference* (pp. 333-347). Springer Berlin Heidelberg.

Papadopoulos, S., Kompatsiaris, Y., Vakali, A., & Spyridonos, P. (2012). Community detection in social media. *Data Mining and Knowledge Discovery*, 24(3), 515–554. doi:10.100710618-011-0224-z

Papathanassis, A., & Knolle, F. (2011). Exploring the adoption and processing of online holiday reviews: A grounded theory approach. *Tourism Management*, *32*(2), 215–224. doi:10.1016/j.tourman.2009.12.005

Papazoglou, M., & Ribbers, P. (2006). *E-Business: Organizational and Technical Foundations*. New York: John Wiley & Sons.

Paraimpu - You are Web. (n.d.). Retrieved from http://www.paraimpu.com/

Park, Y., Yoo, H., Hur, C., Bae, H., & Lung, Y. (2015). Semantic Service Discovery and Matching for Semi-automatic Service Mashup. *Proceedings of the 9th IEEE International Conference on Semantic Computing*.

Park, H., Sung, T., & Kim, S. (2015). Strategic implications of technology life cycle on technology commercialization. *Proceedings of the International Association for Management of Technology (IAMOT 2015)*, 2736-2748.

Patel, P., & Cassou, D. (2015). Enabling High-Level Application Development for the Internet of Things. *Journal of Systems and Software*, *103*, 62–84. doi:10.1016/j.jss.2015.01.027

Pautasso, C., & Wilde, E. (2009). Why is the web loosely coupled? a multi-faceted metric for service design. In *Proceedings of the 18th international conference on World wide web* (pp. 911–920). ACM. 10.1145/1526709.1526832

Pedersen, T., Patwardhan, S., & Michelizzi, J. (2004). WordNet: Similarity: measuring the relatedness of concepts. In Demonstration papers at HLT-NAACL 2004 (pp. 38-41). Association for Computational Linguistics.

PeerEnergyCloud (PEC) Project. (2015). Retrieved 2016, from https://data.gov.au/dataset/smart-grid-smart-city-customer-trial-data

Pelleg, D., & Moore, A. W. (2000, June). X-means: Extending K-means with Efficient Estimation of the Number of Clusters. In ICML (Vol. 1, pp. 727-734). Academic Press.

Peppas, P. (2008). Belief revision. In Handbook of knowledge representation (pp. 317–359). Elsevier.

Petersen, K., & Wohlin, C. (2009). A comparison of issues and advantages in agile and incremental development between state of the art and an industrial case. *Journal of Systems and Software*, *82*(9), 1479–1490. doi:10.1016/j.jss.2009.03.036

Piater, J. H. (2002). *Mixture models and expectation-maximization*. Lecture at ENSIMAG.

Piette, F., Caval, C., Dinont, C., Seghrouchni, A., & Taillibert, P. (2017). *A Multi-Agent Approach for the Deployment of Distributed Applications in Smart Environments*. Academic Press. .10.1007/978-3-319-48829-5_4

Pimmer, C., Linxen, S., & Grohbiel, U. (2012). Facebook as a learning tool? A case study on the appropriation of social network sites from mobile phones in developing countries. *British Journal of Educational Technology*, *43*(5), 726–738. doi:10.1111/j.1467-8535.2012.01351.x

Pisano, G. (2015). You need an innovation strategy. *Harvard Business Review*. Retrieved July 13, 2017, from https://hbr.org/2015/06/you-need-an-innovation-strategy

Plessers, P. (2006). *An Approach to Web-based Ontology Evolution* (PhD thesis). University of Brussels, Belgium.

Pokraev, S., Koolwaaij, J., & Wibbels, M. (2003). Extending UDDI with context-aware features based on semantic service descriptions. ICWS, 184–190.

Popescul, A., & Ungar, L. H. (2003, August). Statistical relational learning for link prediction. In IJCAI workshop on learning statistical models from relational data (Vol. 2003). Academic Press.

Porter, M. A., Onnela, J. P., & Mucha, P. J. (2009). Communities in networks. *Notices of the American Mathematical Society*, *56*(9), 1082–1097.

Potti, P. K., Ahuja, S., Umapathy, K., & Prodanoff, Z. (2012). Comparing performance of web service interaction styles: Soap vs. rest. *Proceedings of the Conference on Information Systems Applied Research*, 2167, 1508.

Power, C., Freire, A., & Petrie, H. (2009). Integrating accessibility evaluation into web engineering processes. *International Journal of Information Technology and Web Engineering*, *4*(4), 54–77. doi:10.4018/jitwe.2009100104

Pradhan, R., & Sharma, D. K. (2014, August). Explicit Tense Classifier. In *Contemporary Computing (IC3), 2014 Seventh International Conference on* (pp. 443-448). IEEE. 10.1109/IC3.2014.6897214

Pradhan, R., & Sharma, D. K. (2015). TemporalClassifier: Classification of Implicit Query on Temporal Profiles. *International Journal of Information Technology and Web Engineering*, *10*(4), 44–66. doi:10.4018/IJITWE.2015100103

Prashant, B. V. N., & Kumar, P. S. (2006). Managing XML data with Evolving Schema. *Proceedings of the 13th International Conference on Management of Data (COMAD'2006)*, 174-177.

Presutti, V., Consoli, S., Nuzzolese, A. G., Recupero, D. R., Gangemi, A., Bannour, I., & Zargayouna, H. (2014, November). Uncovering the semantics of Wikipedia pagelinks. In *International Conference on Knowledge Engineering and Knowledge Management* (pp. 413-428). Springer, Cham.

Price, L. (2004). Cognitive control, cognitive style and learning style. *Educational Psychology*, *24*(5), 681–698. doi:10.1080/0144341042000262971

Protégé, O. W. L. (2014). *Ontology Editor, Protégé 4. 1 tool website, Stanford University*. Retrieved from http://protege.stanford.edu/

Punitha, S. C., Thangaiah, P. R. J., & Punithavalli, M. (2014). Performance Analysis of Clustering using Partitioning and Hierarchical Clustering Techniques. *International Journal of Database Theory and Application*, *7*(6), 233–240. doi:10.14257/ijdta.2014.7.6.21

Puri, C. P. (2009). *Agile Management: Feature Driven Development*. Global India Publications Pvt Ltd.

Purohit, M. (2016). A study on employee turnover in IT sector with special emphasis on Wipro and Infosys. *IOSR Journal of Business and Management*, *18*(4), 47-51.

Pustejovsky, J., Knippen, R., Littman, J., & Saurí, R. (2005). Temporal and event information in natural language text. *Language Resources and Evaluation*, *39*(2-3), 123–164. doi:10.100710579-005-7882-7

Qi, G., Ji, Q., & Haase, P. (2009). A conflict-based operator for mapping revision. In *International Semantic Web Conference* (pp. 521-536). Springer Berlin Heidelberg.

Queirós, A., Faria, D., & Almeida, F. (2017). Strengths and Limitations of Qualitative and Quantitative Research Methods. *European Journal of Education Studies*, *3*(9), 369–387.

Quikr. (2008). *Quikr Classifieds: Post Free Classifieds Ads, Search Free Classified Ads online*. Retrieved July 31, 2017, from http://www.quikr.com/

Rae, I., Rollins, E., Shute, J., Sodhi, S., & Vingralek, R. (2013). Online, Asynchronous Schema Change in F1. *Proceedings of the VLDB Endowment International Conference on Very Large Data Bases*, *6*(11), 1045–1056. doi:10.14778/2536222.2536230

Raggett, D. (2015a). Building the Web of Things. *Proceedings of the Conference on Open Web, Privacy, Security, Technology, Web of Devices, Web of Things*. Retrieved from https://www. w3. org/blog/2015/05/building-the-web-of-things

Raggett, D. (2015b). The Web of Things: Challenges and Opportunities. *Computer*, *48*(5), 26–32. doi:10.1109/MC.2015.149

Rahm, E. (2011). Towards large-scale schema and ontology matching. In *Schema Matching and Mapping* (pp. 3–27). New York: Springer Heidelberg. doi:10.1007/978-3-642-16518-4_1

Railean E., Walker, G., Elci, A., Liz, J. (2016). *Handbook of Applied Learning Theory and Design in Modern Education*. IGI Global.

Railean, E., Elçi, A., Çelik, D., & Elçi, A. (2015). Metasystems Learning Design Approach for STEM Teaching and Learning. In STEM Education: An Overview of Contemporary Research, Trends, and Perspectives. Cycloid Publications.

Railean, E., Elçi, A., & Elçi, A. (2017). *Metacognition and Successful Learning Strategies in Higher Education*. Hershey, PA: IGI Global; doi:10.4018/978-1-5225-2218-8

Rambe, P. (2013). Converged social media: Identity management and engagement on Facebook Mobile and blogs. *Australasian Journal of Educational Technology*, *29*(3), 315–336. doi:10.14742/ajet.117

Ramollari, E., Kourtesis, D., Dranidis, D., & Simon, A. J. H. (2008). Towards Reliable Web Service Discovery through Behavioral Verification and Validation. *Proceedings of the 3rd European Young Researchers Workshop on Service.*

Rappa, M. (2010). *Business Models on the Web*. Available online at http://digitalenterprise.org/models/models.html

Rastrick, K., Stahl, F., Vossen, G., & Dillon, S. (2015). WiPo for SAR: Taking the Web in Your Pocket when Doing Search and Rescue in New Zealand. *International Journal of Information Systems for Crisis Response and Management*, *7*(4), 46–66. doi:10.4018/IJISCRAM.2015100103

Rau, P. L. P., Huang, E., Mao, M., Gao, Q., Feng, C., & Zhang, Y. (2015). Exploring interactive style and user experience design for social web of things of Chinese users: A case study in Beijing. *International Journal of Human-Computer Studies*, *80*, 24–35. doi:10.1016/j.ijhcs.2015.02.007

Rawat, S. & Sah, A. (2013). An Approach to Integrate Heterogeneous Web Applications. *IJCA, 70*(23).

Rawat, S., & Sah, A. (2013). An Approach to Integrate Heterogeneous Web Applications. *IJCA, 70*(23).

Rawat, S., & Sah, A. (2012). An Approach to Enhance the Software and Services of Health Care Centre, Computer Eng. and Intelligent Systems. *IISTE, 3*(7), 2222–2863.

Rawat, S., & Sah, A. (2012). An Approach to Enhance the Software and Services of Health Care Centre.*Computer Eng. and Intelligent Systems. IISTE, 3*(7), 2222–2863.

Redmond, T., & Noy, N. (2011). Computing the changes between ontologies. *Joint Workshop on Knowledge Evolution and Ontology Dynamics*, 1-14.

Rehan, M., & Akyuz, G. A. (2010). Enterprise application integration (EAI) service oriented architectures (SOA) and their relevance to e-supply chain formation. *African Journal of Business Management*, *4*, 2604–2614.

Reiter, R. (1987). A theory of diagnosis from first principles. *Artificial Intelligence*, *32*(1), 57–95. doi:10.1016/0004-3702(87)90062-2

Rejeb, S. B., Nasser, N., & Tabbane, S. (2014). A novel resource allocation scheme for LTE network in the presence of mobility. *Journal of Network and Computer Applications*, *46*, 352–361. doi:10.1016/j.jnca.2014.07.017

Resnick, P., Kuwabara, K., Zeckhauser, R., & Friedman, E. (2000). Reputation systems. *Communications of the ACM*, *43*(12), 45–48. doi:10.1145/355112.355122

Rhatigan, C. (2016). *The 4 industries with the worst retention rates*. Retrieved July 12, 2017, from https://www.tinypulse.com/blog/industries-with-the-worst-retention-rates

Richardson, L., Ruby, S., Burgess, C. J., & Leey, M. (2008). RESTful web services Can genetic programming improve software effort estimation? a comparative evaluation. *Information and Software Technology*, *43*(14), 863–873.

Rising Stars, H. B. A. Healthcare Vision 2020 - PharmaVOICE: PharmaVOICE. (2016, May). Retrieved from http://www.pharmavoice.com/editors-choice-pdf/hba-rising-stars-healthcare-vision-2020/

Rizzolo, F., & Vaisman, A. A. (2008). Temporal XML: Modeling, Indexing, and Query Processing. *The VLDB Journal*, *17*(5), 1179–1212. doi:10.100700778-007-0058-x

Robert, J., & Lesage, A. (2011). Designing and evaluating user experience. In G. A. Boy (Ed.), *Handbook of Human-Computer Interaction: A Human-centered Design Approach* (pp. 321–338). Ashgate.

Roberts, M. J., & Erdos, G. (1993). Strategy selection and metacognition. *Educational Psychology*, *13*(3), 259–266. doi:10.1080/0144341930130304

Robu, V., Halpin, H., & Shepherd, H. (2009). Emergence of consensus and shared vocabularies in collaborative tagging systems. *ACM Transactions on the Web*, *3*(4), 1–34. doi:10.1145/1594173.1594176

Rogers, E. M. (1976). New product adoption and diffusion. *The Journal of Consumer Research*, *2*(4), 290–301. doi:10.1086/208642

Romer, K., Ostermaier, B., Mattern, F., Fahrmair, M., & Kellerer, W. (2010). Real-Time Search for Real-World Entities: A Survey. *Proceedings of the IEEE*, *98*(11), 1887–1902. doi:10.1109/JPROC.2010.2062470

Roth, G. A., Johnson, C., Abajobir, A., Abd-Allah, F., Abera, S. F., Abyu, G., ... Alla, F. (2017). Global, Regional, and National Burden of Cardiovascular Diseases for 10 Causes, 1990 to 2015. *Journal of the American College of Cardiology*.

Ruan, Y., & Durresi, A. (2016). A survey of trust management systems for online social communities–Trust modeling, trust inference and attacks. *Knowledge-Based Systems*, *106*, 150–163. doi:10.1016/j.knosys.2016.05.042

Ruiz, M. P. P., Díaz, M. J. F., Soler, F. O., & Pérez, J. R. P. (2008). Adaptation in current e-learning systems. *Computer Standards & Interfaces*, *30*(1-2), 62–70. doi:10.1016/j.csi.2007.07.006

Ruluks, S. (2014). *A brief history of Web design for designers*. FROONT. Retrieved July 4, 2017, from http://blog.froont.com/brief-history-of-web-design-for-designers/

Rymon, R. (1991). *A Final Determination of the Complexity of Current Formulations of Model-Based Diagnosis (Or Maybe Not Final?)*. Technical Report No. MS-CIS-91-13. University of Pennsylvania.

Sabater, J., & Sierra, C. (2005). Review on computational trust and reputation models. *Artificial Intelligence Review*, *24*(1), 33–60. doi:10.100710462-004-0041-5

Safavian, S. R., & Landgrebe, D. (1991). A survey of decision tree classifier methodology. *IEEE Transactions on Systems, Man, and Cybernetics*, *21*(3), 660–674. doi:10.1109/21.97458

Sah, A., Rawat, S., & Pundir, S. (2012). Design, Implementation and Integration of Heterogeneous Applications. *IJCA*, *54*(5).

Sailer, L. D. (1978). Structural equivalence: Meaning and definition, computation and application. *Social Networks*, *1*(1), 73–90. doi:10.1016/0378-8733(78)90014-X

Salah Eldeen, H. M., & Nelson, M. L. (2013). Carbon dating the Web: estimating the age of Web resources. In *Proceedings of the 22nd international conference on World Wide Web companion* (pp. 1075-1082). International World Wide Web Conferences Steering Committee. 10.1145/2487788.2488121

Salmiza, S. (2010). The effectiveness of brain based teaching approach in dealing with the problems of student's conceptual understanding and learning motivation towards physics. *Proceedings 2nd Paris International Conference on Education, Economy and Society*, 174–185

Sánchez, D. (2017). *UX best practices: home automation ecosystem design.* Retrieved July 14, 2017, from https://uiux. blog/ux-best-practices-home-automation-ecosystem-design-55b752b64bf5

Sanderson, R., Harrison, J., & Llewellyn, C. (2006). A curated harvesting approach to establishing a multiprotocol online subject portal: Opening information horizons. In *6th ACM/IEEE-CS Joint Conference on Digital Libraries 2006*. ACM.

Santos-Neto, E., Condon, D., Andrade, N., Iamnitchi, A., & Ripeanu, M. (2009).Individual and social behavior in tagging systems. In C. Cattuto, G. Ruffo, & F. Menczer (Eds.), *Proceedings of the 20th ACM conference on Hypertext and hypermedia* (pp. 183-192). Torino, Italy: ACM. 10.1145/1557914.1557947

Sarıyüce, A. E., Gedik, B., Jacques-Silva, G., Wu, K. L., & Çatalyürek, Ü. V. (2013). Streaming algorithms for k-core decomposition. *Proceedings of the VLDB Endowment International Conference on Very Large Data Bases*, *6*(6), 433–444. doi:10.14778/2536336.2536344

Sato, N., Uehara, M., & Sakai, Y. (2003). Temporal ranking for fresh information retrieval. In *Proceedings of the sixth international workshop on Information retrieval with Asian languages-Volume 11* (pp. 116-123). Association for Computational Linguistics. 10.3115/1118935.1118950

Saur, K., Dumitras, T., & Hicks, M. W. (2016). Evolving NoSQL Databases Without Downtime. *Proceedings of the 32nd IEEE International Conference on Software Maintenance and Evolution (ICSME'2016)*, 166-176. 10.1109/ICSME.2016.47

Sauro, J. (2016). The challenges and opportunities of measuring the user experience. *Journal of Usability Studies*, *12*(1), 1–7.

Savage, D., Zhang, X., Yu, X., Chou, P., & Wang, Q. (2014). Anomaly detection in online social networks. *Social Networks*, *39*, 62–70. doi:10.1016/j.socnet.2014.05.002

Saxena, V., Santosh, H., & Pradhan, C. (2017). *Processing ASP.Net Web Services Using Generic Delegation Approach.* Academic Press. .10.1007/978-981-10-2035-3_16

Scheer, A., & Habermann, F. (2000). Enterprise resource planning: Making ERP a success. *ACM*, *43*(4), 57-61.

Scherzinger, S., Sombach, S., Wiech, K., Klettke, M., & Störl, U. (2016). Datalution: a tool for continuous schema evolution in NoSQL-backed web applications. *Proceedings of the 2nd International Workshop on Quality-Aware DevOps (QUDOS@ISSTA'2016)*, 38-39. 10.1145/2945408.2945416

Schilder, F., & Habel, C. (2001). From temporal expressions to temporal information: Semantic tagging of news messages. In *Proceedings of the workshop on Temporal and spatial information processing-Volume 13* (p. 9). Association for Computational Linguistics. 10.3115/1118238.1118247

Schmeling, B., Charfi, A., Thome, R., & Mezini, M. (2011). Composing Non-Functional Concerns in Web Services. *IEEE International Conference on Web Services (ICWS)*.

Schockaert, S., De Cock, M., & Kerre, E. E. (2008). Acquiring vague temporal information from the Web. In *Proceedings of the 2008 IEEE/WIC/ACM International Conference on Web Intelligence and Intelligent Agent Technology-Volume 03* (pp. 265-268). IEEE Computer Society. 10.1109/WIIAT.2008.82

Schöfegger, K., Körner, C., Singer, P., & Granitzer, M. (2012).Learning user characteristics from social tagging behavior. In E. V. Munson, & M. Strohmaier (Eds.), *Proceedings of the 23rd ACM conference on Hypertext and social media* (pp. 207-212). Milwaukee, WI: ACM. 10.1145/2309996.2310031

Scholz, F. W. (1985). Maximum likelihood estimation. Encyclopedia of statistical sciences.

Schomm, F., Stahl, F., & Vossen, G. (2013). Marketplaces for Data: An Initial Survey. *SIGMOD Record, 42*(1), 15–26. doi:10.1145/2481528.2481532

Schumacher, M., Helin, H., & Schuldt, H. (2008). Chapter 4, CASCOM: Intelligent Service Coordination in the Semantic Web. Dans Semantic Web Service Coordination.

Schwarz, D. (2016). *What is adaptive design? (and is it different from responsive design?).* Retrieved July 11, 2017, from https://www.sitepoint.com/adaptive-design-different-responsive-design/

Sebestyen, G., Hangan, A., Oniga, S., & Gal, Z. (2014, May). eHealth solutions in the context of Internet of Things. In *Automation, Quality and Testing, Robotics, 2014 IEEE International Conference on* (p. 1-6). IEEE.

Self Care Reduces Costs And Improves Health: The Evidence. (2010). Expert Patients Programme.

Serrat, O. (2017). Social network analysis. In *Knowledge solutions* (pp. 39–43). Springer Singapore. doi:10.1007/978-981-10-0983-9_9

Sevinç, M. (2003). *Development in early childhood and new approaches in education.* İstanbul: Morpa Kultur Publicaitons.

Shahmarichatghieh, M., Härkönen, J., & Tolonen, A. (2016). Product development activities over technology life-cycles in different generations. *International Journal of Product Lifecycle Management, 9*(1), 19–44. doi:10.1504/IJPLM.2016.078861

Shakarian, P., Bhatnagar, A., Aleali, A., Shaabani, E., & Guo, R. (2015). The Independent Cascade and Linear Threshold Models. In Diffusion in Social Networks (pp. 35-48). Springer International Publishing. doi:10.1007/978-3-319-23105-1_4

Sharif, A. M., Elliman, T., Love, P. E., & Badi, A. (2004). Integrating the IS with the enterprise: Key EAI research challenges. *Journal of Enterprise Information Management, 17*(2), 164–170. doi:10.1108/17410390410518790

Sharma, D. K., & Sharma, A. K. (2012). Search Engine: A Backbone for Information. *ICT Influences on Human Development, Interaction, and Collaboration, 117.*

Sharma, D. K., & Sharma, A. K. (2017). Deep Web Information Retrieval Process. *The Dark Web: Breakthroughs in Research and Practice: Breakthroughs in Research and Practice, 114.*

Sharma, D. K., & Sharma, A. K. (2010). Deep Web Information Retrieval Process: A Technical Survey. *International Journal of Information Technology and Web Engineering, 5*(1), 1–22. doi:10.4018/jitwe.2010010101

Sharma, D. K., & Sharma, A. K. (2011). A Novel architecture for deep Web crawler. *International Journal of Information Technology and Web Engineering, 6*(1), 25–48. doi:10.4018/jitwe.2011010103

Shen, D., Pan, R., Sun, J. T., Pan, J. J., Wu, K., Yin, J., & Yang, Q. (2005). Q 2 C@ UST: Our winning solution to query classification in KDDCUP 2005. *ACM SIGKDD Explorations Newsletter, 7*(2), 100–110. doi:10.1145/1117454.1117467

Sheng, Q. Z., Maamar, Z., Yao, L., Szabo, C., & Bourne, S. (2014). Behavior modeling and automated verification of Web services. In Information Sciences, Informatics and Computer Science Intelligent Systems Applications (pp 416-433). Elsevier. doi:10.1016/j.ins.2012.09.016

Shin, D. (2014). A Socio-Technical Framework for Internet of Things Design: A Human-Centered Design for the Internet of Things. *Telematics and Informatics, 31*(4), 519–531. doi:10.1016/j.tele.2014.02.003

Shute, J., Vingralek, R., Samwel, B., Handy, B., Whipkey, C., Rollins, E., ... Apte, H. (2013). F1: A Distributed SQL Database That Scales. *Proceedings of the VLDB Endowment International Conference on Very Large Data Bases, 6*(11), 1068–1079. doi:10.14778/2536222.2536232

Shvaiko, P., & Euzenat, J. (2013). Ontology matching: State of the art and future challenges. *IEEE Transactions on Knowledge and Data Engineering, 25*(1), 158–176. doi:10.1109/TKDE.2011.253

Silva, L. M., & Schalock, M. (2012). Autism parenting stress index: Initial psychometric evidence. *Journal of Autism and Developmental Disorders, 42*(4), 566–574. doi:10.100710803-011-1274-1 PMID:21556967

Singh, R., & Sharma, D. K. (2013, April). Enhanced-RatioRank: Enhancing impact of inlinks and outlinks. In *Information & Communication Technologies (ICT), 2013 IEEE Conference on* (pp. 287-291). IEEE.

Singh, M. G., Mishra, A., Singh, H., & Upadhyay, P. (2015). Empirical Study of Agile Software Development Methodologies: A Comparative Analysis. *Software Engineering Notes, 40*(1), 1–6. doi:10.1145/2693208.2693237

Sîrbu, A., Loreto, V., Servedio, V. D., & Tria, F. (2017). Opinion dynamics: models, extensions and external effects. In Participatory Sensing, Opinions and Collective Awareness (pp. 363-401). Springer International Publishing. doi:10.1007/978-3-319-25658-0_17

Sloughter, J. M. L., Raftery, A. E., Gneiting, T., & Fraley, C. (2007). Probabilistic quantitative precipitation forecasting using Bayesian model averaging. *Monthly Weather Review, 135*(9), 3209–3220. doi:10.1175/MWR3441.1

Smartphone app directs first responders to cardiac arrest three minutes before ambulance. (2017, June). Retrieved from https://www.escardio.org/The-ESC/Press-Office/Press-releases/smartphone-app-directs-first-responders-to-cardiac-arrest-three-minutes-before-ambulance

Smith, D., O'Brian, L., Barbacci, M., & Coallier, F. (2003). A Roadmap for Enterprise Integration. *Proc 10th Int'l Workshop Software Technology and Engineering Practice (STEP)*, 94-102. 10.1109/STEP.2002.1267618

Smith, G. (2007). *Tagging: people-powered metadata for the social web*. New Riders Publishing.

Smith, P. L. II. (2008). Where IR you? Using "open access" to extend the reach and richness of faculty research within a university. *OCLC Systems & Services, 24*(3), 174–184. doi:10.1108/10650750810898219

Snell, L., & Grinstead, C. M. (1997). Introduction to Probability (2nd ed.). Academic Press.

Snijders, T. (2012). *Transitivity and triads*. University of Oxford. Retrieved from http://www.stats.ox.ac.uk/snijders/Trans_Triads_ha.pdf

Snodgrass, R. T., Böhlen, M. H., Jensen, C. S., & Steiner, A. (1998). Transitioning temporal support in TSQL2 to SQL3. In O. Etzion, S. Jajodia, & S. Sripada (Eds.), *Temporal Databases: Research and Practice* (pp. 150–194). Berlin, Germany: Springer. doi:10.1007/BFb0053702

Snodgrass, R. T., Dyreson, C. E., Currim, F., Currim, S., & Joshi, S. (2008). Validating Quicksand: Schema Versioning in τXSchema. *Data & Knowledge Engineering, 65*(2), 223–242. doi:10.1016/j.datak.2007.09.003

Soegaard, M. (2017). *Adaptive vs. responsive design*. Retrieved July 11, 2017, from https://www.interaction-design.org/literature/article/adaptive-vs-responsive-design

Sönmez, N., & Aykut, C. (2011). Teaching a child with pervasive developmental disorder how to use the bathroom independently by the mother via simultaneous clues. *International Journal of Human Science, 8*(2).

Son, Y.-S., Pulkkinen, T., Moon, K.-D., & Kim, C. (2010). Home energy management system based on power line communication. *IEEE Transactions on Consumer Electronics, 56*(3), 1380–1386. doi:10.1109/TCE.2010.5606273

Soomro, T. R., & Awan, A. H. (2012). Challenges and Future of Enterprise Application Integration. *International Journal of Computers and Applications*, *42*.

Sparks, B. A., & Browning, V. (2011). The impact of online reviews on hotel booking intentions and perception of trust. *Tourism Management*, *32*(6), 1310–1323. doi:10.1016/j.tourman.2010.12.011

Speaks, A. (2009). *ASD video glossary*. Retrieved from https://www.autismspeaks.org/what-autism/video-glossary/glossary-terms

Special report on managing information: Data, data everywhere. (2010). Retrieved from http://www.economist.com/node/15557443

Srini, J. (2011). *The Future of mHealth*. Retrieved from http://www.slideshare.net/HowardRosen129/the-future-of-mhealth-jay-srini-march-201.1

Srivastava, S., Pant, M., Abraham, A., & Agrawal, N. (2015). The technological growth in eHealth services. *Computational and Mathematical Methods in Medicine*. PMID:26146515

St. John, A., Davis, W. A., Price, C. P., & Davis, T. M. (2010). The value of self-monitoring of blood glucose: A review of recent evidence. *Journal of Diabetes and Its Complications*, *24*(2), 129–141. doi:10.1016/j.jdiacomp.2009.01.002 PMID:19230717

Stanton, G., & Ophoff, J. (2013). Towards a method for mobile learning design. *Issues in Informing Science and Information Technology*, *10*, 501–523. doi:10.28945/1825

State of the Market: The Internet of Things (IoT) 2015: Discover How IoT is Transforming Business Results. (2015). Retrieved from http://www.verizonenterprise.com/state-of-the-market-internet-of-things/

Steffen, D. (2013). *Parallelized Analysis of Opinions and their Diffusion in Online Sources* (Master thesis). University of Münster, Germany.

Steinhaeuser, K., & Chawla, N. V. (2008). Community detection in a large real-world social network. *Social computing, behavioral modeling, and prediction*, 168-175.

Stojanovic, L. (2004). *Methods and tools for ontology evolution* (PhD thesis). University of Karlsruhe.

Stokes, R. (2013). eMarketing: The essential guide to marketing in a digital world. Durham: Quirk Education Pty.

Strohbach, M., Ziekow, H., Gazis, V., & Akiva, N. (2015). Towards a big data analytics framework for IoT and smart city applications. In *Modeling and processing for next-generation big-data technologies* (pp. 257–282). Springer International Publishing. doi:10.1007/978-3-319-09177-8_11

Sucuoğlu, B. (2005). Autism and children with autistic disorders. In *Children with Special Needs and Introduction to Special Training* (pp. 359–34). Ankara: Gündüz Eğitim ve Yayıncılık.

Su, H., Kramer, D., Chen, L., Claypool, K. T., & Rundensteiner, E. A. (2001). XEM: Managing the evolution of XML Documents. *Proceedings of the 11th International Workshop on Research Issues in Data Engineering: Document Management for Data Intensive Business and Scientific Applications (RIDE 2001)*, 103-110.

Sun, H., Basu, S., Honavar, V., & Lutz, R. (2010, November). Automata-Based Verification of Security Requirements of Composite Web Services. *21th International Symposium on Software Reliability Engineering*, 348-357. 10.1109/ISSRE.2010.20

Sun, H., Basu, S., Lutz, R., & Honavar, V. (2009). *Automata-Based Verification of Non-Functional Requirements in Web Service Composition*. Iowa State University.

Sun, X., & May, A. (2014). Design of the user experience for personalized mobile services. *International Journal of Human-Computer Interaction*, 5(2), 21–39.

Sverrisdottir, H., Ingason, H., & Jonasson, H. (2014). The role of the product owner in scrum-comparison between theory and practices. *Procedia: Social and Behavioral Sciences*, 119, 257–267. doi:10.1016/j.sbspro.2014.03.030

SWoT: Semantic Web of Things. (n.d.). Retrieved from http://sensormeasurement.appspot.com/?p=m3api

Syeda-Mahmood, T., Shah, G., Akkiraju, R., Ivan, A., & Goodwin, R. (2005). Searching Service Repositories by Combining Semantic and Ontological Matching. *Proceedings of the Third Intl. Conf. on Web Services (ICWS'05)*. 10.1109/ICWS.2005.102

Tang, F., Yao, L., Sun, Y., & Qian, M. (2009, November). Visualizing semantic mapping based on view graph. In *Knowledge Acquisition and Modeling, 2009. KAM'09. Second International Symposium on* (Vol. 3, pp. 124-127). IEEE. 10.1109/KAM.2009.318

Tang, H., & Liu, S. (2007, August). Basic theory of fuzzy Bayesian networks and its application in machinery fault diagnosis. In *Fuzzy Systems and Knowledge Discovery, 2007. FSKD 2007. Fourth International Conference on* (Vol. 4, pp. 132-137). IEEE. 10.1109/FSKD.2007.202

Tang, H., Tan, S., & Cheng, X. (2009). A survey on sentiment detection of reviews. *Expert Systems with Applications*, 36(7), 10760–10773. doi:10.1016/j.eswa.2009.02.063

Tan, J., Rönkkö, K., & Gencel, C. (2013). A framework for software usability and user experience measurement in mobile industry. *Proceedings of Joint Conference of the 23rd International Workshop on Software Measurement and the 8th International Conference on Software Process and Product Measurement*, 156-164. 10.1109/IWSM-Mensura.2013.31

Tannenbaum, A. (2001). *Metadata Solutions*. Upper Saddle River, NJ: Addison-Wesley.

Taylor, A. (2014). A look at web-based instruction today: An interview with Badrul Khan, Part 1. *eLearn Magazine*. Retrieved from http://elearnmag.acm.org/archive.cfm?aid=2590180

Team, N. W. B. (2006). Network Workbench Tool [Software]. Indiana University, Northeastern University, and University of Michigan. Available from http://nwb.slis.indiana.edu

Text of the PM's Statement at the United Nations General Assembly. (2014, September 27). Retrieved from http://www.narendramodi.in/text-of-the-pms-statement-at-the-united-nations-general-assembly-2

The Business Case for People Powered Health. (2013). Retrieved from NESTA website: http://www.nesta.org.uk/sites/default/files/the_business_case_for_people_powered_health.pdf

The economic cost of cardiovascular disease from 2014-2020 in six European economies. (2014). Retrieved from Centre for Economics and Business Research website: https://www.cebr.com/wp-content/uploads/2015/08/Short-Report-18.08.14.pdf

The First Responder App Concept - firstresponderapps Webseite! (n.d.). Retrieved from https://www.firstresponderapp.com/

The International Statistical Classification of Diseases and Related Health Problems 10th Revision (ICF X). (n.d.). Retrieved from World Health Organization website: www.who.int/whosis/icd10/

The Ministry of Science, Industry and Technology. (n.d.). Retrieved from http://www.sanayi.gov.tr/Default.aspx?lng=en

The Value of Big Data and the Internet of Things to the UK Economy. (2016). Retrieved from Centre for Economics and Business Research website: https://www.sas.com/content/dam/SAS/en_gb/doc/analystreport/cebr-value-of-big-data.pdf

Themistocleous, M., & Irani, Z. A. (2002). *Evaluating and Adopting Application Integration: The Case of a Multinational Petroleum Company. In Proc 35th Ann. Hawaii Conf. System Sciences* (pp. 286–294). HICSS.

Tigrine, A., Bellahsene, Z., & Todorov, K. (2015). LYAM++ Results for OAEI 2015. *Proc. 20th ISWC ontology matching workshop (OM)*, 176-180.

Tjoa, A. M., Wetz, P., Kiesling, E., Trinh, T., & Do, B. (2015). Integrating Streaming Data into Semantic Mashups. *Proceedings of the Third Information Systems International Conference.*

Tomar, P., & Gill, N. S. (2010). Verification & Validation of Components with New X Component-Based Model. *Proceedings of, Software Technology and Engineering (ICSTE), 2nd International Conference.*

Topol, E. (2013). *The creative destruction of medicine: How the digital revolution will create better health care.* Basic Books.

Tournéa, N., & Godoy, D. (2012). Evaluating tag filtering techniques for web resource classification in folksonomies. *Expert Systems with Applications, 39*(10), 9723–9729. doi:10.1016/j.eswa.2012.02.088

Trifa, V., Wieland, S., Guinard, D., & Bohnert, T. M. (2009). *Design and implementation of a gateway for web-based interaction and management of embedded devices.* DCOSS.

Trinh, T., Do, B., Wetz, P., Aryan, P. R., Kiesling, E., & Tjoa, A. M. (2017). Linked Widgets Platform for Rapid Collaborative Semantic Mashup Development. *Proceedings of the Second International Rapid Mashup Challenge.*

Trisha, P. (n.d.). *Rethink.* Available: http://www.rethinkwords.com/

Troussas, C., Espnosa, J. K., & Virvou, M. (2016). Affect Recognition through Facebook for Effective Group Profiling Towards Personalized Instruction. *Informatics in Education, 15*(1), 147–161. doi:10.15388/infedu.2016.08

Tsai, C. W., Lai, C. F., Chiang, M. C., & Yang, L. T. (2014). Data mining for Internet of Things: A survey. *IEEE Communications Surveys and Tutorials, 16*(1), 77–97. doi:10.1109/SURV.2013.103013.00206

Tulankar, K., & Wajgi, R. (2012). Clustering Telecom Customers using Emergent Self Organizing Maps for Business Profitability 1. *Int J Comput Sci Technol, 3*, 256–259.

Turetken, O., Stojanov, I., & Trienekens, J. (2017). Assessing the adoption level of scaled agile development: A maturity model for scaled agile framework. *Journal of Software: Evolution and Process, 29*, 1–18.

Tversky, A. (1977). Features of similarity. *Psychological Review, 84*(4), 327–352. doi:10.1037/0033-295X.84.4.327

Uschold, M., & Gruninger, M. (2004). Ontologies and semantics for seamless connectivity. *SIGMOD Record, 33*(4), 58–64. doi:10.1145/1041410.1041420

Val, P. B., Garcia-Valls, M., & Estevez-Ayres, I. (2009). Simple asynchronous remote invocations for distributed real-time Java. *IEEE Transactions on Industrial Informatics, 5*(3), 289–298. doi:10.1109/TII.2009.2026271

Van Der Hofstad, R. (2016). Random graphs and complex networks. *Cambridge Series in Statistical and probabilistic Mathematics, 43.*

Van Laarhoven, T., & Marchiori, E. (2013). Network community detection with edge classifiers trained on LFR graphs. ESANN.

Van Rijsbergen, C. J. (1986). A non-classical logic for information retrieval. *The Computer Journal, 29*(6), 481–485. doi:10.1093/comjnl/29.6.481

Vanitha, K., Yasudha, K., Venkatesh, M., Ravindra, K., & Lakshmi, S. (2011). The development process of the semantic Web and Web ontology. *International Journal of Advanced Computer Science and Applications*, 2(7), 122–125. doi:10.14569/IJACSA.2011.020718

Veerbeek, M. A., Voshaar, R. C. O., & Pot, A. M. (2012). Clinicians' Perspectives on a Web-Based System for Routine Outcome Monitoring in Old-Age Psychiatry in the Netherlands. *Journal of Medical Internet Research*, 14(3), e76. doi:10.2196/jmir.1937 PMID:22647771

Vegni, A. M., & Natalizio, E. (2014). A hybrid (N/M) CHO soft/hard vertical handover technique for heterogeneous wireless networks. *Ad Hoc Networks*, 14, 51–70. doi:10.1016/j.adhoc.2013.11.005

Vermeeren, A., Law, E., Roto, V., Obrist, M., Hoonhout, J., & Mattila, K. (2010). User experience evaluation methods: current state and development needs. *Proceedings of the 6th Nordic Conference on Human-Computer Interaction: Extending Boundaries*, 521-530. 10.1145/1868914.1868973

Vermesan, O., & Friess, P. (Eds.). (2014). *Internet of things-from research and innovation to market deployment* (Vol. 29). Aalborg: River Publishers.

Vermeulen, I. E., & Seegers, D. (2009). Tried and tested: The impact of online hotel reviews on consumer consideration. *Tourism Management*, 30(1), 123–127. doi:10.1016/j.tourman.2008.04.008

Viriyasitavat, W., Xu, L., & Martin, A. (2012). SWSpec: The requirements specification language in service workflow environments. *IEEE Transactions on Industrial Informatics*, 8(3), 631–638. doi:10.1109/TII.2011.2182519

Vissak, T. (2010). Recommendations for Using the Case Study Method in International Business Research. *Qualitative Report*, 15(2), 370–388.

Volz, V. (2013). *Searching for Crowdfunding Projects using Mahout* (Bachelor Thesis). University of Münster, Germany.

Vossen, G., Schönthaler, F., & Dillon, S. (2017). *The Web at Graduation and Beyond – Business*. Springer Nature, Switzerland: Impacts and Developments. doi:10.1007/978-3-319-60161-8

Vu, L.-H., Hauswirth, M., & Aberer, K. (2005). Towards P2P-based semantic Web service discovery with Qos support. Business Process Management Workshops, 18–31.

W3C. (2004). *XML Schema Part 0: Primer Second Edition*. W3C Recommendation, October 28, 2004. Retrieved August 2, 2017, from http://www.w3.org/TR/2004/REC-xmlschema-0-20041028/

W3C. (2007). *XSL Transformations (XSLT) Version 2.0*. W3C Recommendation, January 23, 2007. Retrieved August 2, 2017, from http://www.w3.org/TR/2007/REC-xslt20-20070123/

W3C. (2008). *Extensible Markup Language (XML) 1.0 (Fifth Edition)*. W3C Recommendation, November 26, 2008. Retrieved August 2, 2017, from http://www.w3.org/TR/2008/REC-xml-20081126/

W3C. (2010). *XQuery 1.0: An XML Query Language (Second Edition)*. W3C Recommendation, December 14, 2010. Retrieved August 2, 2017, from http://www.w3.org/TR/2010/REC-xquery-20101214/

W3C. (2011). *XQuery Update Facility 1.0*. W3C Candidate Recommendation, March 17, 2011. Retrieved August 2, 2017, from http://www.w3.org/TR/2011/REC-xquery-update-10-20110317/

W3C. (2014). *XML Path Language (XPath) 3.0*. W3C Recommendation, April 8, 2014. Retrieved August 2, 2017, from http://www.w3.org/TR/2014/REC-xpath-30-20140408/

Wade, V., Ashman, H., & Smyth, B. (2006). *Adaptive Hypermedia and Adaptive Web-Based Systems: 4th International Conference, Dublin, Ireland, June 21-23, 2006, Proceedings*. Springer.

Wang, X., & Huang, J. Z. (2015). *Uncertainty in learning from big data*. Academic Press.

Wang, C., Bi, Z., & Da Xu, L. (2014). IoT and Cloud Computing in Automation of Assembly Modeling Systems. *IEEE Transactions on Industrial Informatics, 10*(2), 1426–1434. doi:10.1109/TII.2014.2300346

Wang, F., & Zaniolo, C. (2008). Temporal queries and version management in XML-based document archives. *Data & Knowledge Engineering, 65*(2), 304–324. doi:10.1016/j.datak.2007.08.002

Wang, F., Zaniolo, C., & Zhou, X. (2008). ArchIS: An XML-based approach to transaction-time temporal database systems. *The VLDB Journal, 17*(6), 1445–1463. doi:10.100700778-007-0086-6

Wang, P., & Xu, B. (2008). Debugging ontology mappings: A static approach. *Computer Information, 27*(1), 21–36.

Wang, P., Xu, B., Wu, Y., & Zhou, X. (2015). Link prediction in social networks: The state-of-the-art. *Science China. Information Sciences, 58*(1), 1–38.

Wang, T., & Dolezel, D. (2016). *Usability of Web-based Personal Health Records: An Analysis of Consumers* Perspectives. *AHIMA Perspectives in Health Information Management*.

Wang, Y., DeWitt, D. J., & Cai, J. (2003). X-Diff: An Effective Change Detection Algorithm for XML Documents. *Proceedings of the 19th International Conference on Data Engineering (ICDE 2003)*, 519-530. 10.1109/ICDE.2003.1260818

Wan, Y., Chen, L., Yu, Q., Liang, T., & Wu, J. (2016). Incorporating Heterogeneous Information for Mashup Discovery with Consistent Regularization. *Springer International Publishing Switzerland, LNAI, 9651*, 436–448.

Wasserman, A. (2010). Software engineering issues for mobile application development. *Proceedings of the FSE/SDP Workshop on Future Software Engineering Research*, 397-400. 10.1145/1882362.1882443

Wasserman, S., & Faust, K. (1994). *Social network analysis: Methods and applications* (Vol. 8). Cambridge university press. doi:10.1017/CBO9780511815478

Web of Things – Architecting the Web of Things, for techies and thinkers! (n.d.). Retrieved from https://webofthings.org

Web of Things (WoT) Architecture. (n.d.). Retrieved October 25, 2017, from https://www.w3.org/TR/wot-architecture/

Web Thing Model. (2017, April 25). Retrieved from http://model.webofthings.io/

Wei, H.-C., & Elmasri, R. (2000). Schema versioning and database conversion techniques for bi-temporal databases. *Annals of Mathematics and Artificial Intelligence, 30*(1-4), 23–52. doi:10.1023/A:1016622202755

WeIO. (n.d.). Retrieved from http://we-io.net/

Weiser, P., & Ellis, A. (2015). *The Information Revolution Meets Health: The Transformative Power and Implementation Challenges of Health Analytics*. SSRN Electronic Journal. doi:10.2139srn.2593879

Wesley, A., & Brebner, P. (2009). Service-oriented performance modeling the mule enterprise service bus (esb) loan broker application. In *Software Engineering and Advanced Applications, SEAA'09. 35th Euromicro Conference on* (pp. 404–411). IEEE.

Wheeler, J. R. (2003). Can a disease self-management program reduce health care costs? The case of older women with heart disease. *Medical Care, 41*(6), 706–715. doi:10.1097/01.MLR.0000065128.72148.D7 PMID:12773836

Wiebe, J., Bruce, R., & O'Hara, T. (1999). Development and use of a gold standard data set for subjectivity classifications. *Proceedings of the 37th Annual Meeting of the Association for Computational Linguistics (ACL-99)*, 246–253. 10.3115/1034678.1034721

Williams, J. (2016). *18 Web design trends for 2017*. Retrieved July 13, 2017, from https://webflow.com/blog/18-web-design-trends-for-2017

Winkler, W. E. (1999). *The state of record linkage and current research problems*. Statistical Research Division, US Census Bureau. Available from http://www.census.gov/srd/www/byname.html

Withagen, Y. (2014). *Determining Usability Factors of Tablet Applications for High Functioning Children with Autism Compared to Children Without Autism*. Academic Press.

Wong, J., & Law, R. (2005). Analysing the intention to purchase on hotel websites: A study of travellers to Hong Kong. *International Journal of Hospitality Management, 24*(3), 311–329. doi:10.1016/j.ijhm.2004.08.002

Wooldridge, M. (2002). *An Introduction to Multi-Agent systems*. Wiley Publication.

Work, S. (2011). *The Evolution of Web Design*. Kissmetrics. Retrieved July 4, 2017, from https://blog.kissmetrics.com/evolution-of-web-design/

WoTKit – a fully featured IoT platform. (n.d.). Retrieved from http://sensetecnic.com/products-and-services/wotkit-a-fully-featured-iot-platform/

Wu, Y., & Suzuki, N. (2016). An algorithm for correcting XSLT rules according to DTD updates. *Proceedings of the 4th International Workshop on Document Changes: Modeling, Detection, Storage and Visualization (DChanges 2016)*, Article no. 2. 10.1145/2993585.2993588

Wu, Z., Itälä, T., Tang, T., Zhang, C., Ji, Y., Hämäläinen, M., & Liu, Y. (2012, April). Gateway as a service: A cloud computing framework for web of things. In *Telecommunications (ICT), 2012 19th International Conference on* (p. 1-6). IEEE.

Wu, S., Xu, L., & He, W. (2009). Industry-oriented enterprise resource planning. *Enterprise Information Systems, 3*(4), 409–424. doi:10.1080/17517570903100511

Wu, Y., Yao, Y., Xu, F., Tong, H., & Lu, J. (2016). Tag2Word: Using Tags to Generate Words for Content Based Tag Recommendation. In *Proceedings of the 25th ACM International on Conference on Information and Knowledge Management (CIKM '16)*. ACM. 10.1145/2983323.2983682

Xiang, Z., Schwartz, Z., Gerdes, J. H. Jr, & Uysal, M. (2015). What can big data and text analytics tell us about hotel guest experience and satisfaction? *International Journal of Hospitality Management, 44*, 120–130. doi:10.1016/j.ijhm.2014.10.013

Xiong, L., & Liu, L. (2004). Peertrust: Supporting reputation-based trust for peer-to-peer electronic communities. *IEEE Transactions on Knowledge and Data Engineering, 16*(7), 843–857. doi:10.1109/TKDE.2004.1318566

Xu, B., Da Xu, L., Cai, H., Xie, C., Hu, J., & Bu, F. (2014). Ubiquitous Data Accessing Method in IoT-Based Information System for Emergency Medical Services. *IEEE Transactions on Industrial Informatics, 10*(2), 1578–1586. doi:10.1109/TII.2014.2306382

Xu, Y., Xu, H., & Zhang, D. (2015). A novel disjoint community detection algorithm for social networks based on backbone degree and expansion. *Expert Systems with Applications, 42*(21), 8349–8360. doi:10.1016/j.eswa.2015.06.042

Xu, Z., Martin, P., Powley, W., & Zulkernine, F. (2007). Reputation-Enhanced QoS-based Web Service Discovery. In *Proceedings of the International Conference on Web Services* (pp. 249- 256). IEEE.

Yadav, A., Sharma, D. K., & Pradhan, R. (2015, September). Implicit queries based Temporal Information Retrieval using temporal taggers. In *Reliability, Infocom Technologies and Optimization (ICRITO) (Trends and Future Directions), 2015 4th International Conference on* (pp. 1-6). IEEE. 10.1109/ICRITO.2015.7359271

Yadav, P., & Barwal, P. (2014). Designing responsive websites using HTML and CSS. *International Journal of Scientific & Technology Research*, *3*(11), 152–155.

Yang, B., Liu, D., & Liu, J. (2010). Discovering communities from social networks: Methodologies and applications. In Handbook of social network technologies and applications (pp. 331-346). Springer US.

Yan, G., Peng, Y., Chen, S., & You, P. (2015). QoS Evaluation of End-to-End Services in Virtualized Computing Environments: A Stochastic Model Approach. *International Journal of Web Services Research*, *12*(1), 27–44. doi:10.4018/IJWSR.2015010103

Yang, F. M., Chen, W. M., & Wu, J. L. C. (2014). A dynamic strategy for packet scheduling and bandwidth allocation based on channel quality in IEEE 802.16 e OFDMA system. *Journal of Network and Computer Applications*, *39*, 52–60. doi:10.1016/j.jnca.2013.04.008

Yang, G., Xie, L., Mantysalo, M., Zhou, X., Pang, Z., Xu, L., ... Zheng, L.-R. (2014). A Health-IoT Platform Based on the Integration of Intelligent Packaging, Unobtrusive Bio-Sensor, and Intelligent Medicine Box. *IEEE Transactions on Industrial Informatics*, *10*(4), 2180–2191. doi:10.1109/TII.2014.2307795

Yang, P., & Wu, W. (2014). Efficient Particle Filter Localization Algorithm in Dense Passive RFID Tag Environment. *IEEE Transactions on Industrial Electronics*, *61*(10), 5641–5651. doi:10.1109/TIE.2014.2301737

Yazar, D., & Dunkels, A. (2009). Efficient application integration in IP-based sensor networks. *Proceedings of the First ACM Workshop on Embedded Sensing Systems for Energy-Efficiency in Buildings - BuildSys '09*, 43-48. 10.1145/1810279.1810289

Ye, Q., Law, R., & Gu, B. (2009). The impact of online user reviews on hotel room sales. *International Journal of Hospitality Management*, *28*(1), 180–182. doi:10.1016/j.ijhm.2008.06.011

Yin, R. K. (2009). *Case study research: Design and methods* (4th ed.). Sage Publications.

YouTube. (2005). *YouTube*. Retrieved August 21, 2017, from http://www.youtube.com/

Yu, H., & Malnight, T. (2016). *The best companies aren't afraid to replace their most profitable products*. Retrieved July 7, 2017, from https://hbr.org/2016/07/the-best-companies-arent-afraid-to-replace-their-most-profitable-products

Yu, A. Y., Tian, S. W., Vogel, D., & Kwok, R. C. (2010). Can learning be virtually boosted? An investigation of online social networking impacts. *Computers & Education*, *55*(4), 1494–1. doi:10.1016/j.compedu.2010.06.015

Yu, J., Benatallah, B., Casati, F., & Daniel, F. (2008). Understanding mashup development. *IEEE Internet Computing*, *12*(5), 44–52. doi:10.1109/MIC.2008.114

Zadeh, L. A. (1965). Fuzzy sets. *Information and Control*, *8*(3), 338–353. doi:10.1016/S0019-9958(65)90241-X

Zaghloul, S., Bziuk, W., & Jukan, A. (2008, May). A scalable billing architecture for future wireless mesh backhauls. In *Communications, 2008. ICC'08. IEEE International Conference on* (pp. 2974-2978). Beijing: IEEE. 10.1109/ICC.2008.560

Zahaf, A. (2012). Alignment Between Versions of the Same Ontology. In ICWIT (pp. 318-323). Academic Press.

Zahaf, A., Fellah, A., Bouchiha, D., & Malki, M. (2016, July). Partial meet contraction and consolidation of ontology alignment. In *2016 7th International Conference on Computer Science and Information Technology (CSIT)* (pp. 1-6). IEEE.

Zahaf, A., & Malki, M. (2016a). Kernel Contraction and Consolidation of Alignment under Ontology Change. *Journal of Information Technology and Computer Science*, *8*(8), 31–42. doi:10.5815/ijitcs.2016.08.04

Zahaf, A., & Malki, M. (2016b). Alignment Evolution under Ontology Change. *International Journal of Information Technology and Web Engineering, 11*(2), 14–38. doi:10.4018/IJITWE.2016040102

Zainal, Z. (2007). Case study as a research method. *Journal Kemanusiaan, 9*, 1–6.

Zaki, M. J. (1998, November). Efficient enumeration of frequent sequences. In *Proceedings of the seventh international conference on Information and knowledge management* (pp. 68-75). ACM.

Zeng, D., Guo, S., & Cheng, Z. (2011). The Web of Things: A Survey (Invited Paper). *Journal of Communication, 6*(6). doi:10.4304/jcm.6.6.424-438

Zhang, J., Zhang, X., Chang, Y., & Lin, K. (2012). The Implementation of a Dependency Matrix-based QoS Diagnosis Support in SOA Middleware. *ICST Transactions on eBusiness, 12*, 7-9.

Zhang, Y., & Chu, S. K. W. (2016). New New Ideas on the Design of Web-Based Learning System Oriented to Problem Solving From the Perspective of Question Chain and Learning Community. *International Review of Research in Open and Distributed Learning, 17*(3).

Zhang, L., Tang, J., & Zhang, M. (2012).Integrating temporal usage pattern into personalized tag prediction. In Q. Z. Sheng, G. Wang, C. S. Jensen, & G. Xu (Eds.), *Proceedings of the 14th Asia-Pacific international conference on Web Technologies and Applications* (pp. 354-365). Kunming, China: Springer-Verlag. 10.1007/978-3-642-29253-8_30

Zhao, P., & Han, J. (2010). On graph query optimization in large networks. *Proceedings of the VLDB Endowment International Conference on Very Large Data Bases, 3*(1-2), 340–351. doi:10.14778/1920841.1920887

Zheng, X., Martin, P., & Brohman, K. (2014). CLOUDQUAL: A Quality Model for Cloud Services. *IEEE Transactions on Industrial Informatics, 10*(2), 1527–1536. doi:10.1109/TII.2014.2306329

Zhou, B., Yin, K., Jiang, H., & Zhang, S. (2011). QoS-based Selection of Multi-Granularity Web Services for the Composition. *Journal of Software, VOL., 6*(3), 366–373.

Zhou, K., Yang, S., & Shao, Z. (2017). Household monthly electricity consumption pattern mining: A fuzzy clustering-based model and a case study. *Journal of Cleaner Production, 141*, 900–908. doi:10.1016/j.jclepro.2016.09.165

Zhou, L., Ye, S., Pearce, P. L., & Wu, M. Y. (2014). (2014). Refreshing hotel satisfaction studies by reconfiguring customer review. *International Journal of Hospitality Management, 44*, 120–130.

Zhou, R., & Hwang, K. (2007). Powertrust: A robust and scalable reputation system for trusted peer-to-peer computing. *IEEE Transactions on Parallel and Distributed Systems, 18*(4), 460–473. doi:10.1109/TPDS.2007.1021

Zhuhadar, L., Thrasher, E., Marklin, S., & de Pablos, P. O. (2017). The next wave of innovation—Review of smart cities intelligent operation systems. *Computers in Human Behavior, 66*, 273–281. doi:10.1016/j.chb.2016.09.030

Ziegler, C. N., Lausen, G., & Schmidt-Thieme, L. (2004, November). Taxonomy-driven computation of product recommendations. *Proceedings of the thirteenth ACM international conference on Information and knowledge management*, 406-415.

Zwicklbauer, S., Seifert, C., & Granitzer, M. (2013, September). Do we need entity-centric knowledge bases for entity disambiguation? In *Proceedings of the 13th International Conference on Knowledge Management and Knowledge Technologies* (p. 4). ACM. 10.1145/2494188.2494198

About the Contributors

Atilla Elçi, emeritus full professor, chairman of Dept Electrical-Electronics and Computer Engineering, Faculty of Engineering at Aksaray University since August 2012. His Professional practice includes the Intl Telecom Union, Switzerland, as chief technical advisor for computerization field projects (1985-97) and Info Tech & Telecoms Pvt Ltd as founder/managing director, Turkey (1997-2003). He has organized/ served for committees of numerous international conferences. He has organized IEEE COMPSAC & ESAS since 2006, SinConfs since 2007; and, IJRCS Symposiums 2008-9. He has published over a hundred journal and conference papers, edited the Semantic Agent Systems (Springer, 2011), Theory and Practice of Cryptography Solutions for Secure Information Systems (IGI Global, 2013), The Handbook of Applied Learning Theory and Design in Modern Education (IGI Global, 2016), Metacognition and Successful Learning Strategies in Higher Education (IGI Global, 2017) and the proceedings of SIN Conferences by ACM, ESAS 2006-14 by IEEE CS. He was the program chair for the 36th IEEE COMPSAC (2012), track chair for 2008-2013, Standing Committee Member 2014 onwards. He is an associate editor of Expert Systems: The Journal of Knowledge Engineering and editorial board member of several other journals. BSEE METU, Ankara (1970), M.Sc. & Ph.D. in Computer Sciences, Purdue Univ, USA (1973, 1975).

* * *

Fernando Luís Almeida obtained in 2010 a degree as Doctor of Philosophy in Electrical and Computer Engineering at Faculty of Engineering of University of Porto (FEUP). He has also Master of Science in Innovation and Entrepreneurship and a Bachelors degree of 5 years in Engineering Computer Science and Computation. He has worked for 12 years in several positions as software engineer and project manager for large organization and researcher centers like Critical Software, CICA/SEF, INESC TEC and ISR Porto. During that time he had the possibility to work in partnership with big international organizations and universities in several European projects, namely with Morpho, Deutsche Telecom, PTC Consulting, Airbus, University of Klagenfurt, University of Karlsruhe and Lancaster University. He is currently a professor at ISPGaya and researcher at FEUP and INESC TEC in the Centre of Innovation, Technology and Entrepreneurship.

Hafida Belbachir was born in 1955. She is Professor of Computer Sciences at the University of Sciences and Technology of Oran–Mohamed Boudiaf (USTO-MB) in Algeria. She received her PHD in Computer Science at University of Oran in 1990. She heads the Database System Group in the LSSD Laboratory. Her field of teaching concerns Semantic Web, Information Systems, Databases, Artificial

Intelligence and Advanced Databases. Her research interests include Data Mining and Data Grid. She is author of more than 80 papers in reviews and proceedings and is responsible of research team working on the domain of Semantic Web and its applications.

Nadia Ben Seghier obtained her Engineering Diploma in 2005 from the Biskra University (Algeria) and obtained her Master's Degree in Computer Science Studying Artificial Intelligence and Distributed Systems in 2009 and her PhD Degree from the Biskra University in 2017. She is a Teacher in the Computer Science Department of the Biskra University. Dr Ben Seghier is interested in multiagent systems and their applications, web services and the semantic web.

Khayra Bencherif received the Master's degree in Computer Science from the University of Sidi Bel Abbes (Algeria) in 2013. She is currently a PhD student at the University of Sidi Bel Abbes. Her current research interests lie in the area of Linked Data integration, information heterogeneity, Semantic Mashup and Linked Data enrichment.

Djamel Amar Bensaber is an Assistant Professor at the High school of Computer Science of Sidi Bel Abbes, Algeria. He received the PhD degree in Computer Science from Sidi Bel Abbes University in 2008. He is currently Head of Research Team 'Data and Software Engineering' at the LabRI Laboratory. His research interests include data integration in big data, analysis and modelling in Big data, software engineering, model-driven engineering, semantic web technology, semantic social computing and ontology engineering.

Shuchi Bhadula is an Assistant Professor in Department of Computer Sciences and Engineering at Graphic Era University. She is meticulous and self motivated IT professional having an experience of 8 years in the field of teaching. She has done her Masters of Computer Application from Uttarakhand Technical University and subsequently received an M. Tech. degree in Computer Science and Engineering from Graphic Era University. Presently she is pursuing her Ph.D. in Computer Science and Engineering. Her research interest span in both software engineering and data mining. She has several research papers and conference proceedings in reputed journals.

Rafik Bouaziz, full professor on computer science, was the president of Sfax University, Tunisia, from August 1, 2014 to December 15, 2017. He was also the director of the economy, management and computer science doctoral school, in the same university. His PhD has dealt with temporal data management and historical record of data in Information Systems. The subject of his accreditation to supervise research was "A contribution for the control of versioning of data and schema in advanced information systems". Currently, his main research topics of interest are temporal databases, real-time databases, information systems engineering, ontologies, data warehousing and workflows. Between 1979 and 1986, he was a consulting Engineer in the organization and computer science and a head of the department of computer science at CEGOS-Tunisia.

Zouhaier Brahmia is currently an Associate Professor in the Department of Computer Science at the Faculty of Economics and Management of the University of Sfax, Tunisia. He is a member of the Multimedia, InfoRmation systems, and Advanced Computing Laboratory (MIRACL). His scientific interests include temporal databases, schema versioning, and temporal, evolution, and versioning aspects in emerging databases (XML, NoSQL) and ontologies. He received his MSc degree in Computer Science, in July 2005, and a PhD in Computer Science, in December 2011, from the Faculty of Economics and Management of the University of Sfax.

Duygu Çelik Ertuğrul is an Associate Professor in the Computer Engineering Department at the Eastern Mediterranean University, North Cyprus. Her research topics are related to the Web and Semantics; Composition and Discovery of Semantic Web Services, Semantic Search Agents, Rule-Based Expert Systems, m-Health and Healthcare Knowledgebase Systems. She is one of the organizers of two international workshops and one international symposium: "IEEE International Workshop on ESAS: E-Health Systems and Semantic Web", "Security of Information and Networks" and "IEEE COMPSAC Symposium on Web Technologies & Data Analytics (WEDA)". She also supervises a number of research and development projects supported by the university, government, and industrial companies. She has published numerous articles in several international/national journals and conferences on the topic of Web Semantics, Discovery and Composition of Web Services, Mobile Medical Healthcare Services and Expert Systems. She is also the author of various books or book chapters about 'Composition or Discovery of Semantic Web Services' and 'Semantic Web based e-Health Services'.

Stuart Dillon is an Associate Professor and Head of the School of Management and Marketing at the University of Waikato. He has published his research in academic journals such as MIS Quarterly, International Journal of Public Sector Management, and Journal of Global Information Management.

Ankur Dumka is working as Assistant Professor in University of Petroleum and Energy Studies, Dehradun. He is author of book on MPLS with LAP publication, Germany. He is also author of a chapter on Big Data Analytics with Taylor and Francis publication. He also published many papers in international journal and conferences. He is also associated with many conferences as chairperson and TPC member. He is Guest editor for Scopus indexed journals.

Zoe Folia received B.Sc. in Survey and Transportation Engineering and M.Sc. degree in Geoinformatics both from National Technical University of Athens in 2001 and 2004 respectively. She is currently working in the Technical Department of Municipality of Dionysos. From 2010 to 2017 she was working in the Technical Department of Municipality of Mykonos. She has extensive experience as Survey and Transportation engineer working in ANKA consulting engineers and IRIS G.P. companies from 2001 to 2010. From 2004 to 2009 she was Member of Road Safety Observatory of Technical Chamber of Greece.

Anita Goel is an Associate Professor in Computer Science, Dyal Singh College, University of Delhi, India. She has an experience of more than 28 years. She was Fellow in Computer Science, at Institute of Life Long Learning (ILLL) in University of Delhi. Dr. Goel has guided several students for their doctoral studies in the area of web applications, cloud computing and education management. She has several publications in reputed International journals and conferences. She has authored several books in Computer Science with a leading International publisher.

Fabio Grandi is currently an Associate Professor in the School of Engineering and Architecture of the University of Bologna, Italy. Since 1989 he has worked at the CSITE center of the Italian National Research Council (CNR) in Bologna in the field of neural networks and temporal databases, initially supported by a CNR fellowship. In 1993 and 1994 he was an Adjunct Professor at the Universities of Ferrara, Italy, and Bologna. In the University of Bologna, he was with the Dept. of Electronics, Computers and Systems from 1994 to 1998 as a Research Associate and as Associate Professor from 1998 to 2012, when he joined the Dept. of Computer Science and Engineering. His scientific interests include temporal, evolution and versioning aspects in data management, WWW and Semantic Web, knowledge representation, storage structures and access cost models. He received a Laurea degree cum Laude in Electronics Engineering and a PhD in Electronics Engineering and Computer Science from the University of Bologna.

Karan Gupta is an alumnus of University of Delhi. He did his Doctoral (Ph. D.) from Department of Computer Science, University of Delhi. He completed his Post-Graduation (M. Sc. Comp. Sc.) and Graduation (B. Sc. (H) Comp. Sc.) from University of Delhi as well. His areas of interest are Web Applications, Web 2.0 & Networking but he is not limited to these only. He has published research papers on these topics. He has been teaching in University of Delhi for around 3 years.

Mohamed Hafidi received his Ph.D. in computer science from the University of Badji Mokhtar Annaba (Algeria, 2014). He is currently working as an Associate Professor at the Computer Science Department of Annaba University, Algeria. He has several published papers in various books and international conferences. His current research interests are e-Learning, Intelligent tutoring system and adaptive hypermedia.

Ali Reza Honarvar is a lecturer and researcher in the Department of Computer Engineering at Shiraz University and Islamic Azad University since September 2010. His current research mainly focuses IOT, Big Data, Smart City and data analytics.

Zahi Jarir received his postgraduate degree in computer science in 1997 on Natural Language Processing at Faculty of Sciences in Rabat, Morocco. From 1997 to 2006, he was assistant professor at Faculty of sciences, Cadi Ayyad University in Marrakech, Morocco. In 2006, he received academic accreditation from Cadi Ayyad University in the field of Personalization of Telecommunication Services and Web applications. Currently, he is a full professor of Computer Science at Faculty of Sciences of Cadi Ayyad University. He has participated actively in several research projects (RNTL, Volubilis, CSPT, PMARS, etc.). His research interests include distributed systems, adaptive and reflective middleware, service-oriented computing, web and mobile technologies, cloud computing, Information Security and M2M and IoT coordination. He is a member of the editorial boards and member for several international journals, and a program committee member for multiple international conferences. He has published several publications in international conferences and journals, and chaired and organized several international scientific events.

Okba Kazar obtained his Magister's Degree in 1997 working in the Artificial Intelligence field and his Doctorate state degree in 2005 both from the Constantine University (Algeria). He is a Member of the Editorial Boards of several journals. He is an author of several publications in international journals and a session chair at international conferences. He is interested in the multi-agent systems and their applications, advanced information systems, web services, the semantic web, big data, the internet of things and cloud computing. Okba Kazar is a Full Professor in the Computer Science Department of the Biskra University and the Director of Intelligent Computer Science Laboratory.

Mahnane Lamia received her H.D.R in computer science from the University of Annaba (Algeria) in 2017. She is currently working as an Associate Professor at the Computer Science Department of Annaba University, Algeria. She has several published papers in various books and international conferences. Her current research interests are e-Learning, learning style and adaptive hypermedia, Mobile learning, social network, Data Mining, Ontology.

Leandros Maglaras received the B.Sc. degree from Aristotle University of Thessaloniki, Greece in 1998, M.Sc. in Industrial Production and Management from University of Thessaly in 2004 and M.Sc. and PhD degrees in Electrical & Computer Engineering from University of Volos, in 2008 and 2014 respectively. He is currently a Lecturer in the School of Computer Science and Informatics at the De Montfort University, U.K. He has participated in various research programs investigating vehicular and ICT technologies (C4C-project.eu, reduction-project.eu), sustainable development (islepact.eu, Smile-gov), cyber security (cockpitci.eu, fastpass-project.eu) and optimization and prediction of the dielectric behavior of air gaps (optithesi.webs.com). He is general (co-)Chair of INISCOM 2016, a new, annual, EAI and Springer sponsored conference on industrial networks and intelligent systems. He is an author of more than 65 papers in scientific magazines and conferences and is a senior member of IEEE.

Mimoun Malki is graduated with Engineer Degree in Computer Science from National Institute of Computer Science, Algiers, in 1983. He received the MS degree and the PhD degree in Computer Science from the University of Sidi Bel-Abbes, Algeria, in 1992 and 2002, respectively. He was an Associate professor in the Department of Computer Science at the University of Sidi Bel-Abbes from 2003-2010. Since 2011, he is a full Professor at Djillali Liabes University of Sidi Bel-Abbes. Currently, he is a full professor at the Ecole Supérieure en Informatique of Sidi Bel-Abbes. He is the head of the Evolutionary Engineering and Distributed Information Sytems Laboratory. His research interests include Databases, Information Systems Interoperability, Ontology Engineering, Web-based Information Systems, Semantic Web Services, Linked Data Services, Web Reengineering, Enterprise Mashup and Cloud Computing.

Soufiana Mekouar received her Ph.D. in Computer Science and Telecom from Faculty of Science of Mohammed V Rabat University. She is interested in Modelling and Analysis of users behavior and how users react with online resources in Online Social Network. Her current research focuses on modeling and simulating diffusion process in the social network. As well as she worked on the anomaly detection, computation of trust, reputation and popularity prediction in the social network. She is interested in designing and applying machine learning algorithms to real-world phenomena.

José Augusto Monteiro has MSc on Information Management from 'FEUP - Faculdade de Engenharia da Universidade do Porto' (2009). He is MCP - Microsoft Certified Professional, and has 'CAP - Certificado de Aptidão Pedagógica' from 'IEFP - Instituto de Emprego e Formação Profissional'. He has started his professional career on mechatronics and industrial equipment at Cimertex SA, has served in Portuguese Air Force as an operational in Radar Maintenance area, and it has been working in IT Systems area and office automation at 'Beltrão Coelho (Porto)' over 10 years. Since 2004, he teaches and researches at 'ISPGaya - Instituto Superior Politécnico Gaya'.

Dinakaran Muruganantham received his Doctorate in Computer Science from Anna University, Chennai and Master Degree in M.Tech IT from VIT University, Vellore. He is currently working as Associate Professor in VIT University, Vellore, India. He has good teaching experience of more than 8 years. His area of research includes Information Retrieval, Networking and Web Service Management.

Senthil Kumar N. received his Master Degree in M.Tech – IT from VIT University, Vellore and currently working as Assistant Professor in VIT University, Vellore, India. He has pocketed 10 years of teaching experience and his research areas includes Semantic Web, Information Retrieval and Web Services. He is currently holding a project on semantic understanding of named entities in the web and building a project on it.

Barbara Oliboni received the Master Degree in Computer Science by the University of Verona. In 2003 she received the Ph.D. degree in Computer Engineering by the Politecnico of Milan. Since March 2006 she has been an assistant professor at the Department of Computer Science of the University of Verona. Her main research interests are related to the database field, with an emphasis on XML, semistructured data and temporal information. She is part of the Program Committee of international conferences, and reviewer for international journals on databases.

Naïma Souâd Ougouti is born in 1971. She Holds an Engineer degree in the field of computer science in 1994 at Es-senia university of Oran (Algeria), then a Magister degree in 2004 at the university of sciences and technology of Oran –Mohamed Boudiaf (USTO-MB). She worked as Engineer of computer science in a big Algerian petroleum company from 1996 to 2005 then since 2006, she is an Assistant Professor at (USTO-MB) university. Her field of teaching concerns operating systems, networks and databases. She is also a Member of LSSD laboratory and an active participant in some research projects. Her current research interests include semantic web, information retrieval and interoperability.

Rahul Pradhan is Assistant Professor at GLA University, Mathura. He also pursuing PhD in Computer Science and Engineering. His area of research are Information Retrieval, Natural Language Processing and Big Data Analytics. He is certified in this field from Infosys. He also holds certificates in R Programming and Statistical Analysis. He had written papers and articles in various journals.

Karyn Rastrick is a Lecturer in Digital Business at the University of Waikato, New Zealand. Her research focuses on business technology adoption, technologies for emergency management, and digital health.

Saurabh Rawat is conscientious and self-motivated individual with great enthusiasm and determination to succeed through his pupils. The author is highly experienced professional with more than 15 years of experience in the field of Mathematics and computer science. An author specializes in Vedic mathematics, believes in concept based learning along with innovative techniques. Every year author is guiding many students on and off campus recruitment in various multinational companies like Infosys, Accenture, TCS, Wipro and many more. He has several books, research papers, conference proceedings in reputed journals.

Khaled Rezeg obtained an Engineering Diploma in 1992 from the Annaba University (Algeria), obtained his Master's Degree in Computer Science in Artificial Intelligence and images in 2003 and his PhD Degree from the Biskra University (Algeria) in 2011. He is a Teacher in the Computer Sciences Department of the Biskra University. He is currently working on geospatial web services and ontologies. He is interested in web services, geographical information systems, the engineering of human-machine interfaces and the automatic treatment of the natural language.

Anushree Sah is highly experienced IT professional having an experience of more than 11 years in the field of IT industry and education. The author has worked with the renowned companies like Oracle Financial Services & Software Ltd., Western Union, Dencare Ltd., DIT University, UPES etc. The author has completed her bachelor's in Computer Science and Engineering and has Master's degree from University of Greenwich, London, U.K. She holds various academic and administrative responsibilities in her current working place. The author specializes in Programming Languages, Web Technologies, Building Enterprise Application, Service Oriented Computing and Cloud Computing. She has several research papers, conference proceedings, Book Chapters and Project.

Dilip Sharma is Professor of Computer Science at GLA University, Mathura. He is Secretary of IEEE Uttar Pradesh Section.

Florian Stahl holds a BA in Business Administration (Giessen University, Germany), an MSc in E-Business and Information System (Newcastle University, UK), and a PhD in Information Systems (The University of Muenster, Germany). He is a former research assistant at Prof. Vossen's DBIS Group. His research focused on data provisioning, data marketplaces and data pricing.

Corneliu Octavian Turcu received the B.Sc. and Ph.D. degrees in automatic systems, from the University of Iasi, Romania, in 1991, and 1999, respectively. He also holds a degree in Informatics (M.Sc.) from the University of Suceava, Romania. Since 1991, he has been with the Faculty of Electrical Engineering and Computer Science, University of Suceava, where he is a full professor of System Theory and Intelligent Systems and also holds a joint appointment as head of Programmes Management Department. At University of Suceava he is also a supervisor for Ph.D. and M.S. theses. He has published over 90 research papers and 4 books. His research interests include intelligent systems, RFID, IoT and automatic control system design.

Cristina Elena Turcu is a Professor and currently vice-dean at the Faculty of Electrical Engineering and Computer Science, Stefan cel Mare University of Suceava, Romania. During the period 2004-2011, she was Head of Computer Department. Her research interests include software engineering, intelligent systems and Internet/Web of Things. She was an Editor for 6 books. She has served on various program committees of conferences in computing and Internet of Things. She also has served as a reviewer for numerous referred journals and conferences. She is an Associate Editor of the International Journal of Engineering Business Management. She has published over 80 publications in books or book chapters, refereed journals, technical reports, and refereed conference/workshop/seminar proceedings.

Osman Nuri Uçan was born in Kars, Turkey, on January 1960. He received his BS, MS and PhD degrees in Electronics and Communication Engineering from Istanbul Technical University in 1985, 1988 and 1995, respectively. He worked as a supervisor at TUBITAK Marmara Research Center in 1998. He is working as the Dean of the Engineering Faculty at Istanbul Aydin University. His current research areas include information theory, jitter analysis of modulated signals, channel modelling, cellular neural network systems, turbocoding and Markov random field applications on real geophysics data, satellite-based 2D data and underwater image processing.

Gottfried Vossen is a Professor of Computer Science in the Department of Information Systems at the University of Muenster in Germany. He is a Fellow of the German Computer Science Society and an Honorary Professor at the University of Waikato Management School in Hamilton, New Zealand. He received his master's and Ph.D. degrees as well as the German Habilitation from the Technical University of Aachen in Germany, and is the European Editor-in-Chief of Elsevier's Information Systems - An International Journal. His current research interests include conceptual as well as application-oriented challenges concerning databases, information systems, business process modeling, and Web 2.0 applications, cloud computing, and big data.

Ioannis Vourgidis is a seasoned business intelligence engineer having 13 years overall experience, within diverse business lines, such as retail, banking, insurance, gambling, marketing and health analytics. Currently, he is the Head of Business Intelligence for one of the biggest European Online Travel Agencies. Apart from that, he is a part time PhD student in the field of Intelligent Transport Systems within De Montfort University. During a project with Nottingham Trent University, introduced a novel method for ranking text mining results, as part of a project for NHS. Ioannis, on 2016 received his MSc in Business Intelligence Systems and Data Mining with Distinction from De Montfort University, while he holds an MSc in IT Systems from Heriot-Watt University, and MBA from the University of Wales and a BSc 2.1 Hons in Business Information Systems from the University of Wales.

Amghar Youssef was born in 1956. He is Professor of management information systems at the Scientific and Technical University of Lyon where he is the head of Computer Science Department. He holds a PhD in Computer Science from the same university in 1989 following by an HDR in 1997. His field of teaching concern project management, databases and development processes. His is an active member of laboratory of information system of INSA de Lyon. His current research interests include information retrieval, interoperability of applications and legal documents. He is author of more than 100 papers related to these research activities and managed some projects about decisions support. Actually, he is responsible of research team working on the domain of service oriented computing.

Ahmed Zahaf received his Engineer degree in computer science from Oran University, Algeria, in 1994, and Doctorat en Sciences in computer science from Sidi Bel Abbes University, Algeria. Currently, he is a lecturer at Dr Tahar Moulay, University of Saida, Algeria. His research interests include semantic web, Linked data, ontology engineering, knowledge management and information systems.

Metin Zontul was born in Darende, Turkey in 1971. He received his BS Degree in Computer Engineering from METU, Faculty of Engineering in 1993, received his MSC Degree from Erciyes University in 1996 and finally received his PHD Degree from Cumhuriyet University in 2004. He is now head of Software Engineering Department of Engineering Faculty at Istanbul Aydin University. His research interests are Software Architectures, Information Systems, Soft Computing and Data Mining.

Index

Stay Current on the Latest Emerging Research Developments

Become an IGI Global Reviewer for Authored Book Projects

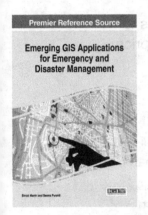
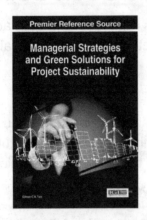

The overall success of an authored book project is dependent on quality and timely reviews.

In this competitive age of scholarly publishing, constructive and timely feedback significantly decreases the turnaround time of manuscripts from submission to acceptance, allowing the publication and discovery of progressive research at a much more expeditious rate. Several IGI Global authored book projects are currently seeking highly qualified experts in the field to fill vacancies on their respective editorial review boards:

Applications may be sent to:
development@igi-global.com

Applicants must have a doctorate (or an equivalent degree) as well as publishing and reviewing experience. Reviewers are asked to write reviews in a timely, collegial, and constructive manner. All reviewers will begin their role on an ad-hoc basis for a period of one year, and upon successful completion of this term can be considered for full editorial review board status, with the potential for a subsequent promotion to Associate Editor.

If you have a colleague that may be interested in this opportunity, we encourage you to share this information with them.

Printed in the United States
By Bookmasters